MW00438699

FARM JOURNAL'S COOKING AND ENTERTAINING IN AMERICA

FARM JOURNAL'S COOKING AND ENTERTAINING IN AMERICA

Two Volumes in One

Edited by

The Food Editors of *FARM JOURNAL*

Greenwich House
Distributed by Crown Publishers, Inc.
New York

This book was originally published as *Great Home Cooking in America* and *Informal Entertaining Country Style*

This 1983 edition is published by Greenwich House,
a division of Arlington House, Inc.
distributed by Crown Publishers, Inc., by arrangement with
Doubleday & Company, Inc.

Manufactured in the United States of America

Library of Congress Cataloging in Publication Data
Main entry under title:
Farm journal's cooking & entertaining in America.
    Previously published as separate titles: Great home
cooking in America and Informal entertaining, country
style.
    Includes index.
    1. Cookery, American.   2. Entertaining.   3. Menus.
I. Farm journal (Philadelphia, Pa. : 1956)   II. Great
home cooking in America. 1983.   III. Informal
entertaining, country style. 1983.   IV. Title:
Farm journal's cooking and entertaining in America.
TX715.F2239   1983   641.5   83-5640

ISBN: 0-517-414651

h g f e d c b a

Contents

See Index under Menus for individual meal plans

FARM JOURNAL'S COOKING AND ENTERTAINING IN AMERICA

Part I

OUR 200-YEAR HERITAGE OF AMERICAN COOKING

INTRODUCTION

Our native home cooking originated mainly on the farms of the New World, since most of the population lived on the land. Our cuisine is truly a melting pot of flavors, ingredients and customs, a potpourri of native produce and foreign heirlooms. New England's baked beans, boiled dinners . . . sauerkraut, the sweets and sours of the Pennsylvania Dutch . . . grits, biscuits, fried chicken from the South . . . Swedish rye bread . . . German stollens . . . Bohemian kolaches . . . Russian borscht . . . enchiladas and tortillas from the Southwest.

Immigrants brought with them on the long voyage across the Atlantic precious recipes, a few heirloom dishes or utensils, even seasonings—all these to nourish their spirits as well as their bodies. Favorite family dishes were reproduced as well as possible with new ingredients; some, in fact, improved tremendously with new plenty.

For especially as the settlers moved westward, regional recipes sprang up as new produce was discovered and as immigrants from Europe began pouring into the new land to seek a new life, their ethnic dishes took on the influence of their new homeland.

The Indians had a great influence on our cooking, teaching us to use the bounty of our new land. Early pioneer women learned from the Indians and adapted these new foods to interesting combinations of their own. Even before colonists came to the Atlantic coast, however, Spanish conquerors and colonists brought new foods with them from natives in South America and Mexico. Many of the early food patterns that were established have lasted through the generations.

For almost 100 years country women of many ethnic origins have shared their family recipes and food customs with Farm Journal editors for testing and publication. We proudly bring you 200 years of great home cooking in America from the past to the present.

Chapter 1

AMERICAN
FOOD
ORIGINALS

When you eat a piece of spicy pumpkin pie, baked beans or corn bread, you are enjoying foods that originated in early America. The recipes that follow are for traditionals created during colonial years and for new favorites developed during the 200 years of our Republic, adapting to newly available foods, cooking equipment and to changing life-styles.

Since the first settlers were predominantly English, their early cooking reflected to a degree the foods in homes left behind, but necessity forced changes. Many foods previously used were not available in the new country. Their new neighbors, the Indians, were growing and eating several varieties of maize (corn), beans of many sizes and colors and different kinds of squashes, including pumpkins. Indians also were hunters and fishers dependent on the bounty of the forests, streams and ocean for their protein foods. They introduced wild turkeys to the colonists.

The Indians taught colonists how to grind corn into meal and how to make hominy. They demonstrated baking beans in a small hole in the ground on heated stones. They shared their secret of slashing sugar maple trees early in the year when the sap was running to obtain a sweetener, and of gathering cranberries in the marshes. They hung foods in the summer sunshine to dry and eat during winter. Perhaps the most valuable lesson of all was advising colonists which native foods were edible.

Most of the first cookbooks used and compiled on this side of the Atlantic Ocean were more English than American. The first real American cookbook was compiled by Amelia Simmons, who called herself "an American Orphan." Her *American Cookery* was published in Hartford, Connecticut, in 1796. Reprinted and revised many times during the next 35 years, it was designed for fireplace cooking, which was universal.

Miss Simmons presented the first printed recipes listing corn-meal as an ingredient—five of them. She gave a recipe for American-style gingerbread (see our Index for Honeyed Ginger-bread) rather than the kind then baked in Europe.

Other firsts in her cookbook were Hartford Election Cake, the first printed recipe for pumpkin pie, cranberry sauce and "purified potash," a leavening that was the forerunner of baking powder.

Several cookbooks of the 1820s reflected the steady and mar-velous expansion of American dishes. Among them was the first regional cookbook, *The Virginia Housewife*. The "receipts," as recipes were called, left much to the imagination and judgment of the cook. They must have defied the beginner. For example, a typical recipe from an 1858 cookbook:

CHERRY PUDDING

"Place 3 or 4 layers of cherries in the bottom of a baking dish, sprinkle with 1 cup of sugar and add a few bits of butter. Take 2 cups sour cream, 2 eggs, 1 teaspoon saleratus, a little salt and flour to make a thin batter. Turn over cherries and bake half an hour. Serve with sauce."

Like most recipes of the 19th century, no mention is made of the size of the baking dish, the number of servings are not given, the cherries are not described as sweet or tart, the accompanying sauce is not identified, the measurements are not definite and no oven temperature is given.

That no baking temperature is specified is hardly surprising, for the first wood- and coal-burning cookstoves of the 1840s had no oven heat indicators. After 1850 cookbooks were designed for cookstoves instead of for fireplace cooking.

Women worked out ways to judge oven heat. The feel of the heat on the hand was one test. Another common practice was to place a little flour in a small pan, put it in the oven and count the minutes required to brown it.

Gas ranges followed wood- and coal-burning cookstoves in about 50 years. Their acceptance was rather slow at first. Some people believed they would "blow up" the house. The first so-called electric kitchen drew curious crowds in 1893 at the World's Fair in Chicago. It was one of the wonders on exhibit, but dependable electric ranges did not reach the market until 20 years later. And now microwave cooking is our newest form.

Problems with leavenings other than yeast plagued early American women. Most cookbooks emphasized that the "purified potash" for which *American Cookery* gave a recipe, could be used when saleratus was not available, but warned that if too much was added the food had an unpleasant taste. Saleratus, or baking soda, worked fine with buttermilk or sour milk. When baking powder was invented the middle of the 19th century, sweet milk came into use.

Changes in cooking followed. One of the striking developments was the creation of beautiful American cakes. They differed from those common in Europe in their lightness and delicacy. These cakes often were baked in layers—chocolate, white, spice, banana, burnt sugar, lemon, orange and coconut—frosted and sometimes filled. The angel food cake was invented and was followed in the 1930s by another American original, the chiffon cake. Then excellent packaged cake mixes came to food stores, making it possible for any woman to bake fine cakes quickly and with a minimum of time and effort, thanks also to the electric mixer.

Busy women switched at least partially to making these "mix cakes." The number of pages in cookbooks devoted to cake recipes dwindled. Pie recipes also decreased proportionately from earlier days when other desserts were scarcer. Women now frequently add their own creative touches to "mix cakes" (see Index for Pumpkin Spice Cake).

Equipment changes contributed to the rise of the American cake. Millers stabilized the quality of their flours. And in the early 20th century, under the leadership of Fannie Farmer, cups and spoons to make level measurements of ingredients were popularized. Electric refrigerators, invented in 1916, gradually came down in cost enough to allow installment on a wide scale. Next in demand, especially in country homes, was the electric freezer.

These changes affected the preparation of many foods. Cake baking is just one example. Hostesses delighted in serving the lovely refrigerator desserts (see Index for Lemon Angel Refrigerator Cake) and ice cream cakes and pies, all of which could be made at least a few days ahead.

Americans have come a long way in cooking during these 200 years. Efficient kitchen equipment, new and improved foods, the knowledge of nutrition and the increase in costs of some products all have had an influence.

What does the future hold? Changes will continue to come: adaptions of the old, but also exciting new dishes. Some women rebel at first at surrendering familiar ways—as they always have—but eventually will join the majority who accept the challenges. As they develop better balanced meals and wonderful but different dishes, more American originals will join the earlier favorites to continue to make good eating one of life's greatest pleasures.

AMERICAN SWISS STEAK

Swiss steak is American with no connection to Switzerland. Originally, round steak cut 1½ to 2″ thick, was the beef cut used, but in our recipe for American Swiss Steak, chuck steak is suggested as an alternative. It costs less and the gentle cooking tenderizes the flavorful meat so that you can cut it with a fork.

AMERICAN SWISS STEAK

Expert seasoning and slow cooking create a great steak

¼ c. flour
1 tsp. salt
½ tsp. dry mustard
¼ tsp. pepper
1½ to 2 lbs. round steak or
bone chuck steak, cut
1½" thick
2 tblsp. cooking oil
2 onions, sliced

1 (lb.) can tomatoes, cut up
1 clove garlic, minced
1 tsp. Worcestershire sauce
Water
¼ c. flour
½ tsp. salt
⅛ tsp. pepper
½ c. water

Combine ¼ c. flour, 1 tsp. salt, dry mustard and ¼ tsp. pepper. Spread half of mixture over one side of steak. Pound in with side of saucer or meat mallet. Repeat with other side of steak. Brown steak on both sides in hot oil in skillet. Add onions, tomatoes, garlic and Worcestershire sauce. Cover and simmer 1½ to 2 hours or until meat is tender. Place meat on warm platter and top with onions and tomatoes.

Add enough water to pan juices to make 1½ c. Return juices to skillet. Combine ¼ c. flour, ½ tsp. salt, ⅛ tsp. pepper and ½ c. water in jar. Cover and shake until well blended. Add to meat juices. Bring to a boil, stirring constantly, until mixture is thickened. Makes 6 servings.

YANKEE POT ROAST

This classic New England platter dinner has stood the test of time. Our recipe is practically the same as the one women knew by heart two centuries ago and used at least once a week. They browned the floured meat in fat rendered from salt pork or in beef suet. Sometimes a single bay leaf was added to the water in which the meat and vegetables cooked.

In looking through old, handwritten "receipt" books, it

becomes apparent that the gravy was of prime importance. It had to be rich and brown.

For a perfect Yankee Pot Roast follow the basic rules established long ago: Brown the floured meat slowly so it will be deeply browned. Add a small quantity of water, no more than a cupful. Replenish as needed. Let the meat stick to the utensil at least once during the cooking to insure brown gravy. Simmer slowly in a heavy, tightly covered utensil until pot roast is tender.

YANKEE POT ROAST

While the sliced turnip is traditional, it may be omitted

¼ c. flour
2 tsp. salt
¼ tsp. pepper
1 (3 to 4 lb.) chuck pot roast
3 tblsp. cooking oil
½ c. water
6 medium potatoes, pared and halved
6 medium carrots, pared and halved crosswise
6 small whole onions, or 1 large onion, sliced

1 small turnip, pared and sliced
Salt
Pepper
Water
¼ c. flour
½ tsp. salt
⅛ tsp. pepper
½ c. water

Combine ¼ c. flour, 2 tsp. salt and ¼ tsp. pepper. Pat into both sides of pot roast. Brown meat well on both sides in hot oil in heavy Dutch oven or large skillet 15 to 20 minutes. Add ½ c. water; cover tightly and simmer 1 hour 30 minutes. Add potatoes, carrots, onions and turnip; sprinkle vegetables with salt and pepper. Add more water if needed to prevent sticking. Continue cooking 1 hour or until meat and vegetables are tender. Remove meat and vegetables to platter to keep hot.

Skim part of fat from pan juices. Add enough water to pan juices to make 1½ c. Return to Dutch oven. Combine ¼ c. flour, ½ tsp. salt, ⅛ tsp. pepper and ½ c. water in jar. Cover and shake until well blended. Add to meat juices. Bring to a boil, stirring constantly, until mixture is thickened. Serve pot roast with gravy. Makes 6 servings.

CHICKEN-FRIED STEAK

Some ranchers insist that the West could not have been won without platters of Chicken-fried Steak and the bowls of brown gravy that came to the table with it. This steak was to its era what hamburger patties are to today.

Fried chicken inspired the specialty. Pieces of thin, round steak pounded to one-fourth inch in thickness, were dredged in flour, and cooked brown and tender in a skillet containing a little melted suet. The gravy gave this dish its special appeal.

CHICKEN-FRIED STEAK

Another name for this beef dish is country-fried steak

1¾ lbs. round steak, cut ½" thick	⅓ c. cooking oil
½ c. flour	3 tblsp. flour
1 tsp. salt	½ tsp. salt
¼ tsp. pepper	⅛ tsp. pepper
	1½ c. light cream

Cut meat in 6 serving pieces. Pound each piece ¼" thick. Coat meat with mixture of ½ c. flour, 1 tsp. salt and ¼ tsp. pepper. Brown meat slowly on both sides in hot oil in large skillet. Cover with tight-fitting lid; cook over low heat 45 to 60 minutes or until tender. Remove meat to platter and keep warm. Skim off fat from pan juices.

Add 3 tblsp. flour, ½ tsp. salt and ⅛ tsp. pepper to drippings in skillet, stirring to loosen browned bits on bottom. Add 1½ c. light cream or milk and cook over low heat, stirring constantly, until mixture comes to a boil and is thickened. Serve steak with gravy. Makes 6 servings.

OVEN-BARBECUED RIBS

Barbecues are a form of American cooking men enjoy. The method is borrowed from Indians who hundreds of years ago cooked game and fish over embers in a pit or a hole in the ground. Fish were split lengthwise in half, fastened to sticks and leaned against stones near the embers. Pit barbecues still are used to some extent in ranch country.

Today's back-yard barbecues are a simplified form of the old-style gatherings. Men often continue as the chefs. They marinate the meat, poultry or fish in highly seasoned sauces and brush the sauce on the food as it grills. The flavor of the smoke is one of the best tastes of barbecued foods.

In many areas where weather prohibits outdoor cook-outs, meat is "barbecued" in ovens. The sauce provides pleasing flavors, even though different from food cooked over live coals.

Our recipe for Oven-barbecued Ribs is lots less work than outdoor barbecuing. It eliminates the tedious brushing of meat with the sauce. Oven heat is easily controlled. Precooking the ribs reduces the amount of fat, a virtue calorie counters appreciate. And they're delicious!

OVEN-BARBECUED RIBS

For a feast, serve these ribs with baked beans and a green salad

4 lbs. pork back ribs	1 tsp. salt
1 c. chopped onion	¼ tsp. pepper
1 clove garlic, minced	2 tblsp. vinegar
1 c. ketchup	1 tblsp. Worcestershire
¼ c. brown sugar, firmly	sauce
packed	1 tblsp. prepared mustard

Cut ribs in serving-size portions. Place in large saucepan with enough salted water to cover ribs. Cover and simmer about 1 hour or until ribs are nearly tender.

Meanwhile, combine onion, garlic, ketchup, brown sugar, salt,

pepper, vinegar, Worcestershire sauce and mustard in sm
saucepan. Cover and simmer 10 minutes.

Arrange ribs with meaty side up one layer deep in large,
shallow roasting pans. Spoon sauce over ribs.

Bake in 350° oven 25 minutes or until meat is tender. Makes
6 to 8 servings.

DRIED-BEEF CASSEROLE

Lack of refrigeration forced early Americans to cure meats
and fish for safekeeping. The top round of beef, cured in a brine
and air-dried or smoked, was a great favorite. Women usually
simmered the beef, sliced thin and torn in pieces, briefly in water
to remove the surplus salt. They drained it and then cooked it
briefly in butter before stirring in flour and adding milk to make
what they called dried-beef gravy. This was spooned over hot
biscuits or baked potatoes.

In our recipe for Dried-beef Casserole we add cooked potatoes
to the sauce made with milk. Cheese and hard-cooked eggs boost
the protein in this main dish. Chopped onion and green pepper
step up flavors. The result is a tasty casserole that is quick and
that takes care of itself in the oven and will hold if the meal is
delayed.

DRIED-BEEF CASSEROLE

If dried beef is not available, substitute smoked, pressed beef

1 (5 oz.) jar dried beef,
or 2 (3 oz.) pkgs.
smoked, pressed beef,
torn
⅓ c. chopped onion
⅓ c. chopped green pepper
6 tblsp. butter or regular
margarine
6 tblsp. flour
⅛ tsp. pepper

2½ c. milk
2 c. shredded process,
sharp American cheese
(8 oz.)
4 c. cubed, cooked potatoes
(4 medium)
4 hard-cooked eggs, sliced
½ c. dry bread crumbs
2 tblsp. melted butter or
regular margarine

Cook dried beef, onion and green pepper in 6 tblsp. butter in 10″ skillet until beef edges are frizzled. Stir in flour and pepper. Add milk and cook, stirring constantly, until mixture thickens and bubbles. Add cheese and stir until melted. Stir in potatoes and eggs. Turn into greased 2-qt. casserole.

Toss bread crumbs with 2 tblsp. melted butter. Sprinkle over top of casserole.

Bake in 350° oven 30 minutes. Makes 6 servings.

NEW ENGLAND BOILED DINNER

Many enthusiastic gardeners are reviving the old-time New England Boiled Dinner to show off their succulent vegetable crops. They especially like to feature this meal-on-a-platter during autumn when vegetables are at their bountiful best. This is another of those one-pot meals developed by colonial women who had to cook over wood fires.

To serve this early American meal buffet style, give the platter the spotlight. Follow the traditional arrangement: Slices of hot, fork-tender meat in the center bordered with vegetables. With a pot of horseradish, hot yellow corn bread and plenty of butter, you have the makings of a good, old-fashioned dinner. Nothing is more appropriate for dessert than apple pie.

NEW ENGLAND BOILED DINNER

You can cook meat one day and refrigerate it—next day reheat, add vegetables and cook until they're tender

1 (5 lb.) corned beef
   brisket
Water
6 medium potatoes, pared
6 medium carrots, pared
6 medium onions or 12
   small onions
1 turnip, pared and sliced
1 medium head cabbage,
   cut in 6 wedges
12 small beets

Place corned beef in large kettle or Dutch oven. Add enough water to cover corned beef by 1"; bring to a boil. Reduce heat; cover and simmer 3 hours 30 minutes or until meat is tender.

Add potatoes, carrots, onions and turnip. Continue simmering 20 minutes. Remove meat and keep warm. Add cabbage; simmer 15 minutes or until all vegetables are tender.

Meanwhile, cook beets separately until tender. Remove skins.

To serve, slice meat, and arrange on large platter with cooked vegetables. Makes 6 servings with extra meat to make Red Flannel Hash (see Index) or use in other ways.

RED FLANNEL HASH

Red Flannel Hash is a classic example of an early American dish made with leftovers that has held its own in country meals through the years. Some people insist that the New England Boiled Dinner endures from one generation to another because it yields dividends the next day—savory hash, tinted pink-red by beets.

The traditional way to cook the hash is to pan-fry it slowly in a heavy skillet. Or as an old Vermont cookbook directs: "When the underside is brown and the hash is heated thoroughly, make a deep crease across the top with a spatula at right angles to the handle. Tip the skillet and fold the top over the bottom like an omelet. Slip onto a warm platter. Or, when the hash is cooked, invert a platter over the skillet and turn out the hash."

These old methods require patience and most women today prefer to bake the hash in a casserole, as in the recipe that follows. Notice that sour cream substitutes for the traditional sweet cream, giving the hash a marvelous flavor. With this old-fashioned New England country dish, serve mustard pickles and your favorite cabbage or apple salad. Keep hot biscuits coming from the oven, butter and honey or strawberry preserves on the table.

RED FLANNEL HASH

"Waste not, want not" was the maxim heeded in colonial homes where leftovers often evolved into noble dishes like this

¾ c. chopped onion
2 tblsp. melted butter or
    regular margarine
3 c. chopped, cooked
    potatoes
2 c. finely chopped
    corned beef

1½ c. chopped, cooked
    beets or 1 (1 lb.) can
    chopped beets,
    drained
½ c. dairy sour cream
1 tsp. salt
¼ tsp. pepper

Sauté onion in melted butter in small skillet until soft. Combine with potatoes, corned beef, beets, sour cream, salt and pepper. Spoon into greased 2-qt. casserole. Smooth out top.

Bake in 350° oven 35 minutes. Or fry mixture slowly in 3 tblsp. butter or bacon drippings in 12" skillet until bottom is crusty. Invert platter over skillet and turn out, crusty side up. Makes 6 servings.

SCALLOPED POTATOES WITH PORK CHOPS

Few American foods have experienced a history to equal that of potatoes, a native of Peru. The Spanish took them back to Spain in 1520, where they then were grown. They spread to other European countries, but were not accepted because people believed they caused fevers and other ailments. A Frenchman in 1773 published a pamphlet urging his countrymen to plant and eat potatoes, a healthful, nourishing food. Louis XVI wore potato blossoms in his buttonhole to publicize the tuber and ordered that potatoes be served on the royal tables.

Eventually, the prejudices were overcome and potatoes became an important crop in many European countries. The Irish accepted them long before the English who called them Irish potatoes because they were eaten extensively in Ireland. The name stuck.

Scalloped potatoes, plain or baked with pork chops or ham,

have long been farmhouse specials since many American men are meat and potato fans. This hearty dish is also popular for family reunions, church suppers, picnics and all kinds of co-operative suppers. They carry successfully and can be held without deteriorating.

The sauce for our Scalloped Potatoes with Pork Chops is made with chicken broth instead of milk. It gives the dish an interesting flavor and eliminates the concern many women have about the possible curdling as the potatoes bake.

SCALLOPED POTATOES WITH PORK CHOPS

For a hearty, country dinner serve this dish with broccoli, cranberry salad and pumpkin or banana cream pie

6 pork chops, cut ½" thick	1½ tsp. salt
2 tblsp. cooking oil	¼ tsp. pepper
Salt	2 c. chicken broth
Pepper	6 c. sliced pared potatoes
3 tblsp. butter or regular	1 medium onion, sliced and
margarine	separated into rings
3 tblsp. flour	

Brown pork chops on both sides in hot oil in 12" skillet. Sprinkle with salt and pepper to taste.

Meanwhile, melt butter in saucepan. Stir in flour, 1½ tsp. salt and ¼ tsp. pepper. Add chicken broth, and cook, stirring constantly, until mixture comes to a boil.

Place potatoes in bottom of 11×7×1½" baking dish. Top with onion rings. Pour chicken broth mixture evenly over top. Top with pork chops. Cover with foil.

Bake in 350° oven 1 hour. Remove cover and continue baking 30 minutes or until meat is tender. Makes 6 servings.

BAKED HAM SLICE

Pork was the most plentiful meat in early America and baked, home-cured hams were prestigious. Almost every colony boasted about its hams; Virginians and Georgians attributed the superiority of theirs to hogs fattened on peanuts. Families prized their special cures and choices of wood for smoking the meat. Some Pennsylvanians preferred sassafras, but hickory, oak and apple had the most supporters. Sometimes different kinds were mixed to produce fires that gave the desired smoky taste.

These were country hams that required, as they do today, slow precooking in water with seasonings before baking. Sometimes they simmered in cider instead of water.

Most hams in supermarkets today differ from country hams, which no longer are plentiful and are frequently unavailable. These commercial hams are precooked and need not be baked further unless warm meat with special seasoning and glazes is desired. Baked Ham Slice maintains a link to the past. With spices sprinkled on and cider and maple-flavored syrup poured over, Baked Ham Slice is fine for company dinners.

BAKED HAM SLICE

Serve with sweet potatoes, buttered limas and cabbage salad

1 (3 lb.) ham steak, cut 2″ thick	**Dash of ground cloves**
¼ tsp. ground nutmeg	**½ c. apple cider or juice**
¼ tsp. dry mustard	**¼ c. maple-flavored syrup**

Place ham in 11×7×1½″ baking dish. Sprinkle nutmeg, mustard and cloves over top. Pour cider and syrup over ham.

Bake in 325° oven 1 hour, basting 2 or 3 times. Makes 8 to 10 servings.

HAM HOCKS WITH COLLARD GREENS

Soul food is Afro-American and it is as southern as greens with pork and sweet potato pie, which bear this identity. Creators of this type of home cooking were brought from Africa to a strange land with strange foods. They took what they could find and used it skillfully in their humble kitchens. At first their dishes were food for the poor, but they tasted so good that other Southerners, including the affluent, adopted them.

Greens were an important ingredient in this cookery. They were cooked just right, which means for a comparatively short time. Pork was a favored teammate.

Collards, one of the great southern greens, are available in supermarkets across the country, a testimony to their wide acceptance. Ham Hocks with Collard Greens is one of the most revered of soul foods. Some women add more seasonings to the greens than our recipe lists, especially one or two little pods of dried red pepper and one or two very thin lemon slices. Add them to our recipe if you like. Serve the main dish steaming hot, with corn sticks.

HAM HOCKS WITH COLLARD GREENS

Do save the pot liquor to use in soups, but first ladle some of it over the greens and ham. Much of the credit for the fame of southern home cooking belongs to the early Afro-Americans

1 lb. crosscut smoked ham hocks	1½ lbs. collard greens
	⅛ tsp. pepper
6 c. water	Salt (optional)
1 c. chopped onion	

Combine ham hocks, water and onion in Dutch oven or large kettle. Cover and simmer about 2 hours or until ham hocks are tender.

Meanwhile, wash greens. Remove hard center vein and chop greens coarsely.

Remove ham hocks from liquid. Chop, discarding skin and bones. Add ham, greens and pepper to liquid. Cover and simmer 30 to 45 minutes or until greens are tender. Season with salt, if necessary. Makes 6 servings.

JAMBALAYA

Jambalaya is a hash often of leftovers with a rice base. Originating in New Orleans late in the 18th century, it is a dish popular in every state south of the Maxon-Dixon line between the Mississippi River and the Atlantic Ocean. In coastal regions shrimp, oysters and/or other fish are combined with the rice while inland, scraps of leftover cooked pork, ham or chicken are the common additions. Seasonings have much to do with the success of the dish.

In our Jambalaya ham and shrimp, as well as bacon and chicken broth, contribute to flavor.

JAMBALAYA

Cook rice tender, fluffy and dry, never moist or gummy. For company dish serve Jambalaya with green salad and lemon sherbet

6 slices bacon, chopped	1 tsp. salt
1 c. chopped onion	½ tsp. dried thyme leaves
2 medium green peppers, cut in strips	¼ tsp. ground red pepper
2 c. uncooked regular rice	1 lb. cooked, smoked ham, cut in strips
2 cloves garlic, minced	½ lb. cleaned, frozen
1 (1 lb. 12 oz.) can tomatoes, cut up	shrimp, thawed
2 c. chicken broth	2 tblsp. chopped fresh parsley (optional)

Cook bacon in Dutch oven until crisp. Drain on paper towels. Add onion to bacon drippings and cook over low heat, stirring occasionally, 5 minutes. Add green pepper; continue cooking 3 minutes. Add rice; cook over moderately hot heat, stirring frequently, until rice becomes somewhat opaque. Add bacon, garlic, tomatoes, chicken broth, salt, thyme, red pepper and ham. Bring to a boil.

Cover and bake in 350° oven 15 minutes. Stir in shrimp; continue baking 20 to 25 minutes or until rice is tender and liquid absorbed. Serve garnished with parsley, if desired. Makes 6 servings.

SAUSAGE/BEAN SUPPER

Indians were cultivating and eating lima beans, the most popular broad beans, when Europeans arrived in the New World. Champlain, the French explorer, reported that he planted Brazil beans, another name for them, in colonial days. Eventually, "Lima" won over "Brazil" in recognition of the capital city of Peru, the country in which the beans originated. But neither of these names is as poetic as the one the Incas used—"little doves" —because the blossoms of the bean vines resemble little birds.

Pork sausage was a staple item many months of the year in early American and later in pioneer homes. Sausage cakes were served for breakfast, but women also included sausage as an ingredient in many dishes. Sausage/Bean Supper is a contemporary casserole in which sausage and dried lima beans pair off in a hearty dish for cold-weather meals, suggestive of those served long ago in country homes.

SAUSAGE/BEAN SUPPER

A big recipe—freeze the surplus. It will come in handy

2 c. large, dry lima beans	1 tblsp. salt
1½ qts. water	½ tsp. pepper
2 lbs. bulk pork sausage	1 (1 lb. 12 oz.) can
1 c. chopped onion	tomatoes, cut up
1 c. chopped celery	1 (8 oz.) can tomato sauce
½ c. chopped green pepper	

Wash beans. Combine beans and water in Dutch oven. Bring to a boil; boil 2 minutes. Remove from heat, cover and let stand 1 hour. (Or soak beans overnight.) Drain.

Meanwhile, cook sausage, onion, celery and green pepper in large skillet until sausage is browned and vegetables are tender. Drain off fat.

Combine beans, sausage mixture, salt, pepper, tomatoes and tomato sauce. Turn into 3-qt. casserole.

Bake in 350° oven 1 hour or until beans are tender. Makes 12 servings.

BAKED SAUSAGE STUFFING

Roasting the turkey and the stuffing separately is an increasingly popular custom. The big bird cooks in a little less time when not stuffed and it is easier and quicker to get the turkey in the oven because it can be cooking while the stuffing is being made.

Cooked turkey and chicken, covered with broth, will keep up to six months when frozen, one month without the broth. The stuffing is best refrigerated for no longer than a day or two.

Baked Sausage Stuffing, a casserole, is the adaptation of a similar mixture baked in turkey. Serve it as a side accompaniment, or later to extend the leftover meat. It bakes at the same oven temperature as turkey.

BAKED SAUSAGE STUFFING

This stuffing is on the moist side, highly seasoned and tasty

1 lb. bulk pork sausage	1 tsp. rubbed sage
1 c. chopped onion	½ tsp. dried thyme leaves
1 c. chopped celery	¼ tsp. pepper
Butter or regular margarine	2 eggs, beaten
10 c. soft bread cubes	1 (13¾ oz.) can chicken
1 tsp. salt	broth

Cook sausage, onion and celery in skillet until meat is browned and vegetables tender. Pour off drippings, reserving ¼ c. Add melted butter or regular margarine if necessary to make ¼ c.

Combine bread cubes, sausage mixture, reserved drippings, salt, sage, thyme and pepper in large bowl.

Blend together eggs and chicken broth. Stir into bread mixture. Turn into greased 2-qt. casserole. Cover and bake in 325° oven 40 minutes. Uncover and continue baking 15 minutes. Makes 8 servings.

PERFECT ROAST TURKEY

Prepare the Turkey:
Thaw bird if frozen. Let it thaw unwrapped in refrigerator 2 to 4 days, depending on size. Or if package is watertight, place it under running cold water until bird is pliable, 2 to 6 hours. Rinse inside and out with cold water, drain and pat dry with paper towel. Stuff if you wish. Shake bird to settle stuffing, but do not pack it. Truss turkey; brush with fat.

To Roast Turkey:
Place breast side up on rack in shallow pan. Do not cover pan or add water. Cover turkey loosely with foil; then press the foil tightly at ends of drumsticks and neck; do not let foil touch top or sides of bird. Cook in 325° oven; lift foil to baste occasionally with fat (optional). This way of cooking gives the most attractive roast turkey for carving at the table.

When turkey is two-thirds done (see Roasting Guide), cut band of skin or cord that holds drumsticks against turkey. This shortens cooking time by letting heat penetrate to inside of thighs. If you use a meat thermometer, insert it now and continue roasting.

Roasting Guide for Turkey

Ready-to-Cook Weight	Approximate Cooking Time	Internal Temperature
6– 8 lbs.	3–3½	185°
8–12 lbs.	3½–4½	185°
12–16 lbs.	4½–5½	185°
16–20 lbs.	5½–6½	185°
20–24 lbs.	6½–7	185°

If you do not use a thermometer, test for doneness at least 30 minutes before approximate timetable indicates turkey will be done. If you do not stuff turkey, it cooks a little more quickly. Allow cooked turkey to stand at room temperature about 20 minutes. This makes carving easier.

AMERICAN-FRIED CHICKEN

Fried chicken in early days was a seasonal treat, since a new crop of chickens was started in the spring. When the baby chicks grew into birds weighing about two pounds, the big event—the year's first fried chicken dinner—occurred.

The "spring chickens," as they were called, were killed and dressed for each meal since there was no refrigeration. Chicken pieces were rolled in seasoned flour and cooked in a heavy skillet on the kitchen hearth in sizzling lard, or sometimes in a mixture of lard and butter. Bowls of milk gravy, made in the same skillet, accompanied the chicken. In this respect, American chicken differed from that of most nationalities in which the chicken was partially cooked or served in a sauce. In some American colonies, especially in Maryland, the cream gravy sometimes was poured over the fried chicken on the platter.

What the colonists called fried chicken in the winter was actually precooked not fried. The bird was mature and less tender, usually a hen. Here is a recipe from an 1873 handwritten "receipt" book of an up-state New York woman, which shows how incomplete old-time recipes could be:

"Thompkins Country Fryed Chicken: Boil in water until tender. Take and roll in flour and fry in hot butter. Season highly with salt and pepper."

Later with home refrigeration the chicken pieces were chilled in buttermilk or sweet milk to cover, then drained, rolled in flour and fried. The dipping milk was saved for the gravy. Sometimes herbs or a bit of garlic were added.

The menu for the season's first fried chicken varied with the area. In New York State new potatoes and peas were served, with strawberry shortcake for dessert, while the South preferred fluffy rice and corn pudding. On the frontier, there was no substitute for mashed potatoes, except for potato salad for the rare picnic.

AMERICAN-FRIED CHICKEN

Today's tender broiler-fryer makes frying chicken easy work

⅓ c. flour	Cooking oil
1 tsp. salt	3 tblsp. flour
¼ tsp. pepper	¼ tsp. salt
1 (2½ to 3 lb.) broiler-	Dash of pepper
fryer, cut up	1½ c. milk or light cream

Combine ⅓ c. flour, 1 tsp. salt and ¼ tsp. pepper in paper or plastic bag. Shake several pieces of chicken at a time in bag to coat with flour mixture. Heat ¼″ oil in large heavy skillet. Lightly brown chicken on all sides, 15 to 20 minutes. Cover tightly and cook over low heat 20 to 30 minutes or until chicken is tender. Uncover and continue cooking 10 minutes.

Pour off all but 3 tblsp. pan drippings from skillet, keeping crusty bits in the pan. Stir in 3 tblsp. flour, ¼ tsp. salt and dash of pepper. Add 1½ c. milk or light cream, and cook over low heat, stirring constantly or until mixture comes to a boil. Makes 4 servings.

CHICKEN FRICASSEE WITH SAGE DUMPLINGS

Chicken with dumplings suggests big farmhouses in up-state New York and company arriving after church for Sunday dinner. Many people in rural neighborhoods during the 19th century traditionally served a platter of chicken (usually an older hen), bordered by plump, light-as-a-feather dumplings, moist with broth. Traditional accompaniments were fluffy mashed potatoes, gravy made with the chicken broth, peas when available, home-made relishes and cherry pie. Green tomato and cucumber pickles came off the shelves of the fruit closet. Delicate, quivering grape jelly or sparkling crab apple jelly that had been poured hot into glasses containing a sage leaf were the choices to accompany chicken.

Times have changed. The recipe for Chicken Fricassee with

Sage Dumplings calls for a large broiler-fryer, much more available in supermarkets than stewing hens, a better buy and quick-cooking.

CHICKEN FRICASSEE WITH SAGE DUMPLINGS

This old-time chicken treat will provide a hearty and pleasing dinner that will uphold country cooking's fine reputation

1 (3 to 4 lb.) broiler-fryer, cut up	½ tsp. salt
	⅛ tsp. pepper
¾ c. flour	Milk
2 tsp. salt	1½ c. sifted flour
¼ tsp. pepper	2 tsp. baking powder
½ c. cooking oil	¾ tsp. salt
1 c. water	½ tsp. rubbed sage
¼ c. chopped onion	3 tblsp. shortening
1 tsp. parsley flakes	¾ c. milk
3 tblsp. flour	

Shake chicken pieces in mixture of ¾ c. flour, 2 tsp. salt and ¼ tsp. pepper. Brown on all sides in hot oil in large skillet, removing pieces as they brown. Drain off fat, reserving 3 tblsp.; set aside.

Return chicken to skillet; add water, onion and parsley. Cover and simmer about 45 minutes or until chicken is tender. Remove chicken from skillet. Pour off cooking liquid and reserve.

Add reserved 3 tblsp. fat to skillet. Blend in 3 tblsp. flour, ½ tsp. salt and ⅛ tsp. pepper. Add enough milk to reserved cooking liquid to make 3 c. Add to flour mixture in skillet and cook, stirring constantly, until mixture comes to a boil. Return chicken to skillet. Sift together 1½ c. flour, baking powder, ¾ tsp. salt and rubbed sage. Cut in shortening until mixture resembles meal. Stir in ¾ c. milk.

Drop dumplings by spoonfuls onto hot chicken. Cook uncovered 10 minutes. Cover and continue cooking 20 minutes. Makes 8 to 10 servings.

Note: If you use a stewing hen, simmer it 3 hours or until chicken is tender. Add more water if necessary.

TURKEY STUFFING CASSEROLE

Some people enjoy the stuffing and gravy as much or more than the roast turkey; so often the leftovers are sparse. Our Turkey Stuffing Casserole recipe tells how to make an excellent bread stuffing and a gravy or sauce with chicken broth to combine with cubes of leftover turkey. Aside from being a quick and thrifty dish, it is truly delicious.

TURKEY STUFFING CASSEROLE

Mildly seasoned, but you can add more seasoning if you like

1 c. chopped onion	3 c. cubed, cooked turkey
1 c. chopped celery	3 tblsp. butter or regular
½ c. butter or regular	margarine
margarine	3 tblsp. flour
2 qts. soft bread cubes	½ tsp. salt
(½")	1 (13¾ oz.) can chicken
1 tsp. salt	broth
½ tsp. rubbed sage	¾ c. water
½ tsp. poultry seasoning	2 eggs, well beaten
¼ tsp. pepper	2 tblsp. chopped parsley

Sauté onion and celery in ½ c. melted butter until soft.

Combine bread cubes, 1 tsp. salt, sage, poultry seasoning and pepper in greased 3-qt. casserole. Add onion mixture and toss gently. Top with turkey.

Melt 3 tblsp. butter in saucepan, blend in flour and ½ tsp. salt. Add chicken broth and water; cook, stirring constantly, until mixture comes to a boil. Stir hot broth slowly into eggs; add parsley. Pour over turkey in casserole.

Cover and bake in 350° oven 30 minutes. Uncover and continue baking 15 minutes. Makes 8 servings.

TENNESSEE TURKEY HASH

For good turkey hash the cooked meat is cut in cubes, not ground. Leftover gravy is added if available, a little sweet or sour cream if it is not. Potatoes are included only when necessary to stretch the meat. The hash is moist, but never runny, and it's crisp-crusted on the outside.

Tennessee Turkey Hash is the modern adaptation of an old-time dish with dry hashed browns added to increase the number of servings. A sauce of canned cream of mushroom soup and sour cream accompanies the hash.

TENNESSEE TURKEY HASH

For company, garnish this dish with pimiento and egg slices

1 (13¾ oz.) can chicken broth	½ c. butter or regular margarine
¾ c. water	3 c. chopped, cooked turkey
1 tsp. salt	¼ c. dairy sour cream
⅛ tsp. pepper	1 (10¾ oz.) can condensed cream of mushroom soup
1 (5½ oz.) pkg. dry hashed brown potatoes	¼ c. dairy sour cream
½ c. finely chopped onion	
½ c. finely chopped green pepper	

Combine chicken broth, water, salt and pepper in saucepan; bring to a boil. Remove from heat. Add potatoes and let stand 10 minutes.

Meanwhile, sauté onion and green pepper in butter in large, heavy skillet until soft.

Combine potato mixture, turkey and ¼ c. sour cream. Add to onion mixture in skillet. Fry until golden brown and crusty. Turn with wide spatula.

Meanwhile, combine soup and ¼ c. sour cream. Heat thoroughly, but do not boil. Serve with hash. Makes 6 servings.

CREAMED EGGS SUPREME

The egg-bacon team has had the approval of Americans from early days until now. And, when it comes to ways to combine the two foods, country women are clever.

Creamed Eggs Supreme make a superior supper dish, especially if served on toasted English muffins or on hot biscuits.

CREAMED EGGS SUPREME

New bacon and egg dish with cheese—appetite satisfying

3 tblsp. butter or regular
   margarine
3 tblsp. flour
¾ tsp. salt
⅛ tsp. pepper
1½ c. milk
1½ c. shredded process
   sharp American cheese
   (6 oz.)

6 hard-cooked eggs,
   chopped
4 slices crisp-cooked bacon,
   crumbled
Toast, toasted English
   muffins or hot biscuits

Melt butter in saucepan; blend in flour, salt and pepper. Add milk, and cook, stirring constantly, until mixture comes to a boil. Add cheese and stir until melted. Stir in eggs and bacon; heat thoroughly. Serve over toast. Makes 6 servings.

CURRIED SCRAMBLED EGGS WITH CORN

Along the Atlantic watershed from New England through Georgia, nine out of every ten people in the 17th and 18th centuries lived on family farms. Almost every household eventually had poultry flocks that furnished eggs for kitchen use. No wonder early Americans developed many excellent egg dishes.

The skill of Indians in combining corn with different foods was observed by early Americans. Then when trade developed with faraway places, captains of clipper ships returned home with exotic spices, including curry powder. Used sparingly, it enhanced many chicken and egg dishes. Curried Scrambled Eggs with Corn became a summer favorite.

CURRIED SCRAMBLED EGGS WITH CORN

With frozen corn this is an around-the-year special

1 c. frozen corn	⅓ c. milk
2 tblsp. butter or regular	1 tsp. salt
margarine	¼ tsp. curry powder
8 eggs	⅛ tsp. pepper

Cook corn in melted butter in 10″ skillet until hot.

Beat together eggs, milk, salt, curry powder and pepper; pour into skillet. Cook slowly, scraping bottom and sides of skillet with spatula until eggs are set. Makes 6 servings.

CATFISH GUMBO

A muddle in Carolina Low Country is a fish stew, but when it contains okra, it is called gumbo in some parts of the South. Gumbo is the African name for okra, which was imported from Africa. Gumbos are soul food, created by Afro-Americans, but all Southerners like them. The classic fish stew contains, in addition to fish, tomatoes, onions, pork in some form, salt, pepper, thyme and either bottled hot pepper or Worcestershire sauce.

Some of the favorite fish stews are made with catfish, which is popular not only in the South but also in many parts of the Midwest, where pan-frying is the common method of cooking.

Tributaries of the Mississippi River furnished fresh catfish for many years. Catfish "farming" now provides superior catfish for home and restaurant tables. The fingerlings—very small fish—are brought to man-made, fresh-water lakes or ponds and fed a high-protein diet.

CATFISH GUMBO

The classic accompaniment for catfish stew is corn bread; in the South it's usually hush puppies, a corn bread cooked in deep fat

2 beef bouillon cubes	1 (1 lb.) can tomatoes, cut
2 c. boiling water	up
1½ lbs. fresh, skinned	1 (10 oz.) pkg. frozen okra,
catfish, or frozen and	thawed
thawed	2 tsp. salt
1 c. chopped onion	¼ tsp. pepper
½ c. chopped green pepper	¼ tsp. dried thyme leaves
½ c. chopped celery	¼ tsp. bottled hot pepper
1 clove garlic, minced	sauce
3 tblsp. cooking oil or	1 bay leaf
bacon drippings	1 c. uncooked rice

Dissolve bouillon cubes in boiling water in large saucepan.

Cut catfish in serving pieces; add to bouillon. Cover and simmer 15 minutes or until fish flakes easily. Remove fish to paper toweling; reserve liquid.

Meanwhile, sauté onion, green pepper, celery and garlic in hot oil in Dutch oven until tender. Add reserved cooking liquid and tomatoes. Cut okra in crosswise slices and add to tomato mixture. Add salt, pepper, thyme, hot pepper sauce and bay leaf. Cover and simmer 30 minutes.

When fish is cool enough to handle, debone and break it in bite-size pieces with your fingers. Add to tomato mixture and simmer 5 minutes. Remove bay leaf.

Cook rice according to package directions. Place ½ c. cooked rice in each of 6 bowls. Fill with gumbo. Makes 6 servings.

OVEN-FRIED FISH

The favorite way to cook fish in midwestern country kitchens is to roll it in cornmeal, biscuit mix or flour and pan-fry it in butter, cooking oil or bacon drippings. Pan-frying takes only about 20 minutes, 10 minutes for each side. Two skillets are required to handle two pounds of fish fillets (enough to make 6 to 8 servings) however, and both need almost constant attention. The fish takes on a crisp, golden crust, but sometimes becomes dry. When close watching is inconvenient, try oven-frying. The fish can be forgotten for 20 to 25 minutes while the rest of the meal is prepared. It is not as crisp as pan-fried but is moist. Cooking fish this way on busy days is a real help.

OVEN-FRIED FISH

Serve with lemon wedges or tartar sauce, and finely shredded coleslaw

½ c. butter or regular margarine	1 egg, beaten
	1 c. cracker crumbs
2 lbs. fish fillets, fresh or frozen and thawed	1 tsp. seasoned salt
	¼ tsp. pepper

Melt butter in 15½ ×10½ ×1″ jelly roll pan in 375° oven.

Meanwhile, dip fish fillets in egg, then in mixture of cracker crumbs, seasoned salt and pepper. Place each fillet in pan, turning to coat with butter.

Bake in 375° oven 20 to 25 minutes or until a light golden brown. Makes 6 to 8 servings.

MAINE CORN CHOWDER

"Many people say hamburgers and apple pie are the typical American foods," an Oneida Indian woman recently confided to a Farm Journal food editor. "They are not what we true Americans call native foods," she added. "We think of corn soup, wild rice, milkweed, cowslip, ferns and other greens, and venison."

Corn has the Indians' enduring affection—it is the grain their ancestors believed was the food of gods. They knew from experience how important it was in sustaining life.

A variety of corn soups copied from Indians became standard

fare in colonial homes. When cattle and hog production made headway in the eastern colonies, milk and salt pork joined corn in soup kettles, and chowders were the result. Many women also added potatoes, which thickened the chowders slightly and contributed flavor. Maine Corn Chowder included potatoes, famous product of the region, especially in Aroostook County. Our recipe differs little from those that welcomed families to the supper table long ago, but because bacon and canned corn always are available, we use those ingredients instead of salt pork and fresh or dried corn.

MAINE CORN CHOWDER

Use salt pork instead of bacon, if you have it; fresh or dried corn instead of canned

5 slices bacon, chopped	⅛ tsp. pepper
2 medium onions, sliced	1 (1 lb. 1 oz.) can cream-
3 c. diced pared potatoes	style corn
2 c. water	2 c. milk
1 tsp. salt	

Cook bacon in Dutch oven until crisp. Remove and drain on paper towels. Set aside.

Sauté onion in bacon drippings until soft. Add potatoes, water, salt and pepper. Bring to a boil. Reduce heat; cover and simmer 12 to 15 minutes or until potatoes are tender.

Add corn and milk; heat thoroughly. Garnish with bacon. Makes about 9 cups.

WINTER CORN CHOWDER

Early colonists enjoyed steaming bowls of corn chowder made with dried corn. Many people still believe it tastes best that way (see Index for Oven-dried Corn).

An interesting difference between Winter Corn Chowder and others made with dried corn is that the liquid is chicken broth instead of milk. This produces a chowder in which the flavors of dried corn, bacon, chicken and onion mingle.

WINTER CORN CHOWDER

Serve with pickled beets and eggs, grilled cheese sandwiches and oven-warm gingerbread topped with thick applesauce for dessert

1½ c. Oven-dried Corn (see Index)	2 c. chopped onion
2 (13¾ oz.) cans chicken broth	4 c. milk
6 slices bacon, diced	2 tsp. sugar
	½ tsp. salt
	⅛ tsp. pepper

Rinse dried corn. Combine corn and chicken broth in large saucepan; bring to a boil. Remove from heat and let stand 2 hours. Heat to simmering; cover and cook 45 minutes.

Meanwhile, cook bacon in small skillet until crisp. Drain on paper towels. Sauté onion in bacon drippings until soft. Add to corn mixture and simmer 5 minutes. Add milk, sugar, salt and pepper, and heat thoroughly. Serve garnished with bacon. Makes 2½ quarts.

CHICKEN/CORN SOUP WITH RIVELS

While iron kettles of corn chowder bubbled in New England fireplaces, Pennsylvania Dutch women were dropping rivels into some of their soups. These remarkable cooks rubbed a mixture of flour, salt and egg through their fingers so that it flaked into boiling soup. The rivels held their shape while cooking and had a texture similar to that of boiled rice.

Perhaps the most famous Pennsylvania Dutch soups were those made with chicken and succulent corn cut from the cob. There are many recipes for them but they vary little. Chicken/ Corn Soup with Rivels is almost identical to soups made 200 years ago, except that the more available broiler-fryer substitutes for the stewing hen once culled from the farm flock because she was a lazy egg layer. Frozen corn substitutes for the seasonal fresh kernels today.

CHICKEN/CORN SOUP WITH RIVELS

Chopped parsley and hard-cooked egg are traditional garnishes. Add them to soup bowls just before serving

1 (3 to 3½ lb.) broiler-
    fryer, cut up
	1 (10 oz.) pkg. frozen corn,
	    thawed

2 qts. water	¼ c. chopped fresh parsley
1 c. chopped onion	1 c. sifted flour
½ c. chopped celery	¼ tsp. salt
3 tsp. salt	1 egg, beaten
¼ tsp. pepper	

Combine chicken, water, onion, celery, 3 tsp. salt and pepper in Dutch oven. Bring to a boil. Reduce heat; cover and simmer 1 hour. Remove chicken pieces. Cut chicken into bite-size pieces, discarding skin and bones. Return chicken to broth along with corn and parsley.

Combine flour, ¼ tsp. salt and egg to make a crumbly mixture the size of small peas. If necessary, add 1 to 2 tsp. milk. Drop into soup. Cover and simmer 15 minutes. Makes 11 cups.

GREEN BEAN SOUP

This hearty soup, thick with potatoes, chunks of ham and green beans has been a three-generation favorite in a Kansas home. It has been served since the early pioneer days as all the foods were plentiful on Mennonite farms.

GREEN BEAN SOUP

This heirloom recipe has been a favorite for generations

1 meaty ham bone (about 2 lbs.)	¼ c. chopped fresh parsley
2 qts. water	4 sprigs summer savory, chopped, or 1 tsp. dried
4 c. cut-up green beans (1" pieces)	savory
3 c. cubed pared potatoes	1 tsp. salt
2 medium onions, sliced	¼ tsp. pepper
	1 c. light cream

Cook ham bone in water in 6-qt. saucepan until tender, for about 1½ hours. Remove meat from bone and cut in chunks. Put back in soup base.

Add green beans, potatoes, onions, parsley, savory, salt and pepper. Bring to a boil; reduce heat and simmer, covered, for 20 minutes or until vegetables are tender. Skim off excess fat.

Just before serving, stir in light cream. Makes about 3½ quarts.

AMERICAN PEA SOUP PLUS

Meals that cooked in one pot were a joy to busy colonial women. It was easier to get a dinner of vegetables and meat in the heavy iron pot, hung over the fire with strong chains or a crane, than to prepare food over hearth coals. One-kettle meals did not disappear with kitchen fireplaces, because they require little watching.

American Pea Soup Plus resembles some old-fashioned dishes that cooked in one pot. The soup and smoked pork simmer together with occasional stirring.

AMERICAN PEA SOUP PLUS

Serve the soup in bowls, the meat on a platter with mustard; add rye bread and apple-cabbage salad to the menu

2 c. dry, split green peas	2 qts. water
3 lbs. smoked pork shoulder roll	½ tsp. whole peppercorns
1 c. chopped onion	¼ tsp. whole allspice
1 c. chopped celery	1 bay leaf
1 c. sliced peeled carrots	Salt

Wash peas. Combine peas, pork, onion, celery, carrots and water in Dutch oven. Bring to a boil.

Meanwhile, tie peppercorns, allspice and bay leaf in cloth; add to Dutch oven. Reduce heat; cover and simmer about 1 hour 45 minutes or until meat is tender. Stir occasionally. Remove spice bag and discard. Add salt to taste.

Remove pork from soup; let stand 10 minutes. Slice to serve with soup. Makes about 3 quarts.

DOWN-EAST BEAN SOUP

The Pilgrims made bean porridge, a thick soup, with the red, white, yellow-eyed and speckled beans of all sizes that the Indians grew and cooked. Before the 17th century ended, they were cooking meat with beans in soups as we do in Down-East Bean Soup. Notice that the recipe calls for New England-style beans, the traditional Boston baked beans processed in cans. This saves cooking fuel and speeds up meal preparation. Team with crackers or toast, lettuce salad, mustard pickles, baked apples or other fruit, and cookies and milk to drink for a pleasant meal.

DOWN-EAST BEAN SOUP

You can make this substantial soup in less than 20 minutes

1 c. finely chopped ham	1 tblsp. brown sugar
¼ c. chopped onion	1 tblsp. vinegar
¼ c. chopped green pepper	½ tsp. salt
2 tblsp. bacon drippings	1 (1 lb. 6 oz.) jar New
1 (1 lb.) can tomatoes, cut	England-style baked
up	beans
½ c. water	

Cook ham, onion and green pepper in bacon drippings in large saucepan until meat is browned and vegetables are soft. Add tomatoes, water, brown sugar, vinegar and salt; cover and simmer 10 minutes.

Reserve 1 c. beans from jar. Mash the remainder. Add reserved and mashed beans to soup. Heat thoroughly, stirring occasionally. Makes about 5 cups.

PLANTATION BEAN SOUP

An Englishman visiting Virginia's Roanoke Colony reported on his return that the Indians cooked beans until they fell apart in the broth. This was one of the earliest, if not the first description of American bean soup. It has become an American institution. Every region has favorites. Plantation Bean Soup is an up-to-date southern special.

PLANTATION BEAN SOUP

Turnip greens add subtle flavor, which, when combined with ham, beans and smoked sausage, produces soup that delights everybody

1½ c. dry Great Northern beans	1 tblsp. salt
3½ qts. water	¼ tsp. pepper
1 lb. ham hocks or meaty ham bone	2 c. cubed pared potatoes
1 c. chopped onion	1 (10 oz.) pkg. frozen chopped turnip greens
1 c. chopped celery	¾ lb. smoked garlic sausage

Wash beans. Combine beans and water in 8-qt. kettle. Bring to a boil and boil 2 minutes. Remove from heat; cover and let stand 1 hour. (Or soak beans overnight.)

Add ham hocks, onion, celery, salt and pepper to beans. Cover and simmer 1½ hours. Add potatoes, turnip greens and whole sausage; simmer 20 minutes or until vegetables are tender. Remove ham and sausage from soup. Chop ham and cut sausage in ¾″ slices. Return to soup and heat thoroughly. Add more salt if needed. Makes 4½ quarts.

COMPANY BEAN SOUP

Midwesterners like the taste of ham in their bowls of bean soup, and they frequently add tomatoes. Company Bean Soup, as its name suggests, can be the center of interest at a supper party. Serve buffet style: Ladle the soup from a tureen or big bowl into individual bowls and let guests help themselves to relishes and slices of homemade rye and white bread, which can be baked ahead and frozen. For dessert, set a bowl of mixed fruits and a plate of brownies on the buffet and invite guests to "come and get it" while you fill coffee cups.

COMPANY BEAN SOUP

Use condensed chicken broth to add flavor to this soup

2 c. dry navy beans	1 (1 lb.) can tomatoes, cut
2 qts. water	up
1½ lbs. ham hocks	2 tsp. salt
2 c. chopped onion	¼ tsp. pepper
1 c. chopped celery	1 bay leaf
2 cloves garlic, minced	2 c. shredded Cheddar
3 (10¾ oz.) cans condensed	cheese (8 oz.)
chicken broth	¼ c. chopped parsley
1 qt. water	

Wash beans. Combine beans and 2 qts. water in 8-qt. kettle. Bring to a boil; boil 2 minutes. Remove from heat; cover and let stand 1 hour. (Or soak beans overnight.)

Add ham hocks, onion, celery, garlic, chicken broth, water, tomatoes, salt, pepper and bay leaf. Bring to a boil; reduce heat, cover and simmer 2 hours or until ham and beans are tender.

Remove ham hocks; cut off meat and return it to kettle. Discard bones and bay leaf. Add cheese; cook, stirring, just until cheese is melted. Serve sprinkled with parsley. Makes about 5 quarts.

TUNA CLUB SANDWICHES

Chicken club sandwiches, an American concoction, now are served in many countries. In the beginning they consisted of two slices of bread, toasted and buttered, with a lettuce leaf spread with mayonnaise on the bottom slice of toast. On it were arranged in layers, cooked chicken, tomato and bacon slices. The second piece of toast, buttered side down, made the top. Somewhere and sometime a third slice of toast was inserted in the sandwich, possibly for a heartier version and the idea caught on.

These club sandwiches inspired the development of Tuna Club Sandwiches. Tuna salad assumes the role of chicken, cucumber slices replace the tomatoes and sliced hard-cooked eggs substitute for bacon. You can insert a lettuce leaf on the bottom slice of toast, if you like.

TUNA CLUB SANDWICHES

The availability of canned tuna certainly is a convenience in making this sandwich

2 cucumbers, pared and thinly sliced
2 tblsp. salt
2 tblsp. vinegar
2 tblsp. salad oil
⅛ tsp. pepper
⅛ tsp. dried dillweed
2 (7 oz.) cans tuna, drained and flaked
1 c. chopped celery
½ c. chopped parsley
½ c. mayonnaise or salad dressing
18 slices toast
Butter or regular margarine
6 hard-cooked eggs, sliced

Combine cucumbers and salt. Set aside in strainer to drain 1 hour; rinse with cold water. Place drained cucumbers in bowl. Stir in vinegar, oil, pepper and dillweed. Marinate at least 30 minutes.

Combine tuna, celery, parsley and mayonnaise.

Spread 6 slices toast with butter. Spread each with ½ c. tuna mixture. Top each with a toast slice, then with egg and drained cucumber slices.

Butter remaining 6 toast slices; place over cucumber slices, buttered side down. Cut sandwiches diagonally in halves. Hold layers together with wood pick. Makes 6 servings.

MIDWESTERN TURKEY/CHEESE SANDWICHES

The first Thanksgiving feast gave turkey a place of honor forever after in the American holiday. The birds served on that historic occasion were North American wild turkeys, for the delicate-fleshed bronze or Mexican turkeys domesticated by the Aztecs were unknown to New England Indians. The Pilgrims borrowed the idea of a thanks-giving celebration from their Indian neighbors, who every autumn feasted and gave thanks to their spirits and gods for crops of corn, beans and pumpkins and for an abundance of game.

Roast turkey on American holiday tables guarantees leftovers. Midwestern Turkey/Cheese Sandwiches, a combination main dish and salad, is a favorite in the Midwest. It is an adaptation of a Chicago restaurant's "specialty of the house." First cover rye bread slices with sliced, cooked turkey, then with thin Swiss cheese slices. Arrange mounds of finely shredded lettuce on the cheese and spoon on Easy Thousand Island Dressing. Cross bacon strips over the top. Garnish with tomato quarters.

MIDWESTERN TURKEY/CHEESE SANDWICHES

Build each open-face sandwich on serving plate and take to table

12 slices bacon	**6 c. shredded lettuce**
12 slices buttered rye bread	**3 c. Easy Thousand Island**
Sliced, cooked turkey	**Dressing (recipe follows)**
Salt	**12 tomato wedges (optional)**
8 oz. Swiss cheese, thinly	
sliced	

Cut bacon in half crosswise; pan-fry until crisp. Drain on paper towels; set aside.

On each of 6 plates place 2 slices buttered bread, side by side. Make open-face sandwiches as follows: Cover bread slices with turkey. Sprinkle with salt; cover with cheese slices. Mound 1 c. lettuce over cheese; spoon ½ c. Easy Thousand Island Dressing over. Top each with 4 half slices cooked bacon. Garnish with tomato wedges, if desired. Makes 6 servings.

Easy Thousand Island Dressing: Combine 3 c. mayonnaise or salad dressing, 3 hard-cooked eggs, chopped, ⅓ c. chili sauce, 3 tblsp. chopped dill pickle and 2 tsp. grated onion. Refrigerate several hours to blend flavors. Makes 5 cups.

STUFFED SUGAR PUMPKIN

Herds of deer troubled early colonists and western pioneers. When the pumpkins were ripe, the fleet animals moved in and hollowed them out leaving only the shells. That was a serious loss because pumpkins and winter squash were extremely important in the diet, as expressed by this ditty written in New England in 1638:

> We had pumpkins in the morning
> And pumpkins at noon
> If it were not for pumpkins
> We'd be undone soon.

One of the earliest ways to cook the vegetable was to slice off the top of a small, very ripe pumpkin, scoop out the seeds and stringy substance, fill with milk, put the top on for a lid and bake in the tin or brick fireplace oven 6 to 7 hours. Then milk was added again and the pumpkin was eaten from the shell.

In our recipe for stuffed pumpkin, the natural shell is stuffed with a nourishing meat and rice filling. This makes a spectacular dish to serve to guests.

STUFFED SUGAR PUMPKIN

A moist, flavorful, ground beef filling baked in a pumpkin shell

1 (3 to 4 lb.) sugar pumpkin	1 c. cooked regular rice
1 tsp. salt	¾ tsp. pepper
½ tsp. dry mustard	2 tsp. salt
1 medium onion, chopped	½ tsp. dry mustard
1 lb. ground beef	½ c. water
3 eggs, slightly beaten	

Cut lid out of pumpkin; remove seeds. Prick inside cavity with fork. Rub inside with 1 tsp. salt and ½ tsp. mustard.

Cook onion and ground beef in skillet until lightly browned. Remove from heat. Add eggs, rice, pepper, 2 tsp. salt and ½ tsp. mustard. Stuff pumpkin with mixture (size of cavity will vary with pumpkins—you may need more filling if pumpkin meat is very thick). Replace pumpkin lid.

Place stuffed pumpkin in shallow pan with ½ c. water. Bake in 350° oven 1 hour 30 minutes or until pumpkin is tender. Add more water if necessary. Makes 6 servings.

BOSTON BAKED BEANS

Indians, according to tradition, baked beans in small holes in the ground which they lined with stones. They built fires in the holes and heated the stones. Then they put beans in covered pots in the holes and covered the openings with sod or flat stones to retain the heat. The slow cooking continued for hours.

"Bean-hole Beans," as early colonists explained, tasted different from baked beans containing molasses or brown sugar and salt pork. Ten years after the Pilgrims disembarked from the *Mayflower,* the Puritans from England landed at Boston and Salem less than 50 miles up the coast. They came with more provisions than the Pilgrims—with some utensils, silver, pewter and linens. They installed fireplaces with brick ovens in most houses, which influenced the cooking and originated Boston Baked Beans.

The Puritan Sabbath started at sundown on Saturday and lasted until sundown on Sunday. Their religion forbade cooking but not serving of food during the 24 hours. On Saturday morning they put big pots of beans in their ovens to bake all day. These supplied hot beans for Saturday's evening meal, some still warm for Sunday breakfast, and for another meal, sometimes cold, after church on Sunday.

Although the strict observance of the Sabbath died out in the 19th century, the custom of having Boston Baked Beans for Saturday's evening meal and the leftovers for breakfast on Sunday was so firmly established that it continued and still does in some New England homes.

Recipes for Boston Baked Beans vary from one family to another, but they must contain salt pork and molasses, or a combination of molasses and brown sugar, or maple sugar. And they must cook a long time to develop flavor and a rich brown sauce. There are New Englanders who insist that the supremacy of their baked beans is due to the use of a bean pot—an earthen cooking utensil with a narrow throat and big, bulging sides.

Boston Brown Bread, a steamed bread, was the traditional and still is the favored accompaniment to Saturday night's baked beans. Most families now buy the bread from bakeries.

BOSTON BAKED BEANS

Stick two or three whole cloves in onion for subtle spicy taste, and give beans time to bake gently to perfection

2 c. dry navy beans	2 tsp. dry mustard
6 c. cold water	1/3 c. brown sugar, firmly
1 tsp. salt	packed
1/4 lb. salt pork	1/4 c. molasses
1 medium onion (optional)	

Wash beans. Combine beans and cold water in large kettle. Bring to a boil; boil 2 minutes. Remove from heat and let stand 1 hour. (Or soak beans overnight.)

Add salt; simmer about 1 hour or until beans are tender. Drain, reserving 1¾ c. bean liquid. Add water if necessary; set aside.

Cut a slice from salt pork and put it in bottom of bean pot or Dutch oven. Add beans. Place onion in center of beans.

Mix mustard, sugar and molasses into reserved bean liquid; pour over beans.

Cut 3 gashes in remaining salt pork; place on beans, rind side up.

Cover and bake in 300° oven 5 to 7 hours, adding more

water as needed. Remove cover from bean pot the last 30 minutes of baking so pork rind will brown and become crisp. Makes 6 servings.

NEW YORK BAKED BEANS

Boston Baked Beans are famous, but there are Americans who prefer the dried vegetable cooked in the old-time, up-state New York way. Great Northern beans, which do not hold their shape as well as the pea or navy beans cooked in New England, were used and brown sugar took the place of molasses. And the beans baked in a shallow dish, often a crock, instead of a bean pot with a small opening. Sometimes the beans were served cold, cut in squares.

Here are directions as given in an original up-state recipe: "Soak beans in water overnight. Slowly cook them next morning in the water in which they soaked until partly tender, about 2 hours. Add salt pork and sliced onions; simmer until beans are tender, about 1 hour. Add more hot water as needed. Drain, reserving liquid and place beans in a shallow, greased baking dish, covering the salt pork with them. Sprinkle with brown sugar mixed with a little pepper and add bean liquid almost to cover. Bake uncovered in a low oven until a soft, brown crust forms on top and along the sides, or about 2½ hours. As the beans dry out in baking, add more of the reserved liquid or hot water."

NEW YORK BAKED BEANS

A cruet of cider vinegar traditionally accompanies these beans

2 c. dry Great Northern
  beans
6 c. water
2 medium onions, sliced
¼ lb. salt pork

¼ c. brown sugar, firmly
  packed
2 tblsp. sugar
1 tsp. salt

Wash beans. Combine beans and water in Dutch oven. Bring to a boil; boil 2 minutes. Remove from heat and let stand 1 hour. (Or soak beans overnight.)

Add onions, salt pork, sugars and salt. Cover and simmer 2 to 2 hours 30 minutes. Add more water if necessary. Taste beans and add more salt if needed.

Bake in 350° oven 1 hour; uncover and continue baking 1 to 1 hour 30 minutes or until top edges are browned. Makes 6 to 8 servings.

MIDWESTERN BAKED BEANS

In the Midwest, tomatoes and dried beans were cooked together in pioneer kitchens. And since many desired a more pronounced tomato taste, they often topped their servings with ketchup or chili sauce, homemade or commercial, a definite conversion from Boston and New York baked beans. Baked beans are examples of regional food preferences time has not erased.

MIDWESTERN BAKED BEANS

Hot gingerbread or feathery rolls are good with these beans

2 c. dry navy beans	1 medium onion, sliced and
6 c. water	separated into rings
1 (1 lb. 12 oz.) can	⅓ c. brown sugar, firmly
tomatoes, cut up	packed
1 tsp. salt	¼ c. molasses
¼ lb. salt pork, sliced	1½ tsp. dry mustard

Wash beans. Combine beans and water in Dutch oven. Bring to a boil; boil 2 minutes. Remove from heat and let stand 1 hour. (Or soak beans overnight.)

Add tomatoes and salt; bring to a boil. Reduce heat; cover and simmer 1 to 1 hour 30 minutes or until beans are tender and skins burst.

Stir in salt pork, onion, brown sugar, molasses and mustard. Turn into 3-qt. casserole or bean pot. Cover and bake in 325° oven 3 hours. Remove cover and continue baking 1 hour or until top edges are browned. Makes 8 to 10 servings.

WINTER CORN PUDDING

Visions of the cruel cold and storms of winter kept early colonists busy during summers storing food to use in the months ahead. Drying vegetables and fruits was a chore not to be neglected. Corn was so important in the diet that practically every household tried to lay by a supply, and the Indians set a good example as they dried food in the sunshine. The habit of drying corn was so firmly established by the end of the first hundred years that it continued long after that. To this day even some country families who freeze corn every year try to dry at least a little because they like the taste.

It is a tradition in some rural households to serve dried corn in Thanksgiving holiday meals. As American as cranberries and turkey! Winter Corn Pudding is one of the best-loved dishes made with dried corn.

WINTER CORN PUDDING

The kernels are soaked in dairy half-and-half instead of in water, for a more flavorful dish

¾ c. Oven-dried Corn
   (recipe follows)
2 c. dairy half-and-half,
   scalded
2 eggs, slightly beaten
2 tblsp. chopped green
   onions

2 tblsp. melted butter or
   regular margarine
1 tblsp. sugar
1 tsp. salt
⅛ tsp. pepper

Rinse dried corn. Add to hot dairy half-and-half and let soak about 4 hours.

Combine corn mixture with eggs, green onions, butter, sugar, salt and pepper. Pour into greased 1-qt. casserole.

Bake in 325° oven 35 to 40 minutes or until knife inserted in center comes out clean. Makes 6 servings.

Oven-dried Corn: Cook large ears corn in large kettle of boiling water 5 minutes, or just until milk in kernels is set when pricked with fork. Cool. Cut kernels from cob (5 large ears yield about 3 c. kernels; 3 to 4 large ears, about 2 c.). Spread kernels in a single layer in large shallow pan (15½ × 10½ × 1" jelly roll pan will hold 5 c. kernels). Place in oven set at lowest temperature, 150 or 175°. Heat 6 to 7 hours, until kernels are thoroughly dry to touch. Stir several times during drying. Store in covered jars at room temperature (3 c. fresh kernels make ¾ c. dried corn; 2 c. fresh kernels make ½ c. dried corn).

CORN CUSTARD PUDDING

People in all the American colonies ate corn pudding. Like all vegetable dishes, it was seasonal. Southerners had a longer growing season for corn and so enjoyed it more days of a year than Northerners. Most of the corn eaten in America until around 1850 was hard and flinty, although a British army officer visiting western New York State in 1779, discovered the Iroquois Indians were growing sweet corn and obtained some seed.

Corn Custard Pudding is a rich, velvety custard flavored with corn. Although delicate, the custard holds its shape when served —especially congenial with fried chicken.

CORN CUSTARD PUDDING

Frozen corn now makes this pudding a year-round favorite

2 c. frozen corn, thawed, or fresh kernels, cut from cob	¼ c. flour
	1 tblsp. sugar
	1 tsp. salt
1 egg	⅛ tsp. pepper
1½ c. dairy half-and-half	

Combine all ingredients in electric blender container. Blend at high speed 30 seconds. Pour into ungreased 1½-qt. casserole. Place in pan of hot water.

Bake in 350° oven 1 hour 10 minutes or until knife inserted in center comes out clean. Serve at once. Makes 6 servings.

RED BEANS AND RICE

Red beans and rice have been served in New Orleans since its Spanish and French beginnings. They are to the Crescent City and to many homes in the South what baked beans are to Boston.

Cooking red beans with a ham bone or hocks and serving them over boiled rice was first a dish for low-income families. When hard times came to the South during and immediately after the War Between the States, Red Beans and Rice won acceptance in all social circles. And just as Boston Baked Beans were a Saturday-night special in New England, the bean-rice combination was the main dish in the noon meal on Monday in the South.

RED BEANS AND RICE

This is a nutritious, thrifty, hunger-satisfying and tasty dish, expertly seasoned with red pepper, a New Orleans trademark

2 c. dry red kidney beans	**¼ tsp. pepper**
2 qts. water	**2 cloves garlic, minced**
2 c. chopped onion	**1 bay leaf**
1 tsp. salt	**2 lbs. smoked ham hocks**
½ tsp. crushed, dried red	**2 c. uncooked rice**
pepper	

Wash beans. Combine beans and water in Dutch oven. Cover and bring to a boil; boil 2 minutes. Remove from heat and let stand 1 hour. (Or soak beans overnight.)

Add onion, salt, red pepper, pepper, garlic, bay leaf and ham hocks. Bring to a boil. Reduce heat; cover and simmer about 2 hours 30 minutes or until beans are very tender. Remove bay leaf.

Cut ham hocks into small pieces; discard skin and bones. Slightly mash beans. Return meat to beans; heat.

Meanwhile, cook rice according to package directions. Serve beans over rice. Makes 8 servings.

HOPPING JOHN

To start the year right, people in South Carolina and neighboring states say you must eat Hopping John on New Year's Day. According to a belief that has endured for many generations, the simple dish of black-eye peas and long-grain rice, when eaten on January 1, brings good luck in the year ahead.

Hopping John may be made successfully with fresh, frozen or dry beans (peas). South Carolinians like to cook bacon with them; many Texans prefer hog jowls; Virginians like to serve them with tomatoes.

How Hopping John acquired its name no one knows. One theory is that it derived from an old custom that the children hopped once around the table before the dish was served "to give them something to do and help them work off excess steam."

HOPPING JOHN

As traditional in the South as baked beans are in New England; cook the peas and rice with ham hocks for superior flavor

1 c. dry black-eye peas	Water
4 c. water	1 c. uncooked rice
½ lb. crosscut ham hocks	Salt
½ c. chopped onion	Pepper
½ tsp. salt	
⅛ tsp. crushed, dried red pepper	

Wash peas. Combine with 4 c. water in Dutch oven. Bring to a boil; boil 2 minutes. Remove from heat; cover and let stand 1 hour. (Or soak peas overnight.)

Add ham hocks, onion, ½ tsp. salt and red pepper. Bring to a boil. Reduce heat and simmer about 1½ hours or until ham and peas are tender. Remove ham hocks. Cut meat in small pieces, discarding rind and bone. Drain peas, reserving liquid. Add enough water to reserved liquid to make 2 c.

Return peas, liquid and ham to Dutch oven. Bring to a boil. Stir in rice. Reduce heat; cover and simmer 20 minutes or until rice is tender and liquid is absorbed. Add salt and pepper to taste. Makes 6 servings as a main dish, 10 as a side dish.

COMPANY MASHED POTATOES

Although potatoes were developed by Indians from wild plants that grew in the highlands of Peru, they came to North America by way of Europe. Records reveal that they arrived in New Hampshire in 1719. They were baked on the hearth in ashes or Dutch ovens in early American homes and were one of the vegetables in the New England Boiled Dinner (see Index). Not until the 19th century were they commonly and extensively used. Even then the South did not favor them but clung to sweet potatoes and rice.

Potatoes came into their own on the western frontier. As soon as pioneers arrived at their destination, they cut blocks of sod to build homes and planted corn and potatoes. Hot mashed potatoes heaped in warmed serving dishes became standard dinner fare.

Company Mashed Potatoes require no gravy. You can make them ahead and refrigerate until baking time, or if they are baked and ready a few minutes before serving time, you can hold them in a low oven. Cheese, onion and sour cream season them delightfully.

COMPANY MASHED POTATOES

You can use fresh or instant potatoes with equal success

4 c. hot, seasoned mashed   4 oz. sharp Cheddar cheese,
  potatoes   cut in ¼" cubes
1 c. dairy sour cream   ½ tsp. seasoned salt
⅓ c. chopped, green onions
  and tops

Combine potatoes, sour cream, green onions and cheese. Turn into greased 1½-qt. casserole. Sprinkle with seasoned salt.

Bake in 350° oven 25 minutes. Makes 6 servings.

ORANGE-CANDIED SWEET POTATOES

Most Southerners prefer sweet to white potatoes. Old southern cookbooks devote many more pages to them than to Irish potatoes. On the other hand, New England cookbooks devote pages to white potato recipes, but little space to sweets. New Englanders usually combine sweet potatoes with apples or maple syrup; Southerners use sweet potatoes in breads, pies and candied dishes.

Early colonists cooked sweet potatoes in their jackets on the hearth, smothered in ashes and hot coals. Candied sweets emerged before the Revolutionary War, enhanced by the flavor of such ingredients as lemon, orange, coconut, pineapple, apple, raisin, different spices, brown sugar, marshmallow, sherry, rum or bourbon.

ORANGE-CANDIED SWEET POTATOES

Juicy slices of orange and grated peel enhance the sweets

6 medium sweet potatoes, cooked and peeled	1 tsp. salt
1 small orange, peeled and cut in thin slices	1 tblsp. grated orange peel
⅔ c. brown sugar, firmly packed	¼ c. butter or regular margarine

Cut sweet potatoes in ½" slices. Place half the slices in greased 2-qt. casserole. Top with orange slices, then half the brown sugar, salt and orange peel. Dot with half the butter. Add remaining sweet potatoes. Top with remaining brown sugar, salt, orange peel and butter.

Bake uncovered in 375° oven 30 minutes or until glazed. Makes 6 servings.

WINTER SQUASH BAKE

Experts know that many more varieties of squash once flourished in Peru and other places in the Americas. Hairy or woolly squash seeds that no longer exist anywhere have been uncovered in ancient Peruvian graves. Since only the most highly prized foods were placed in Indian graves to feed the spirits after life on this planet ended, squash must have been special.

The number of superior varieties growing widely in the Americas when Europeans arrived was, and is still, great. The Indians, of course, were eating the seeds as well as the flesh of the squash. Among the highly valued types today are the long-necked butternuts and the buttercups that have been bred small enough to serve today's smaller families. Hubbard squash is especially favored in New England. Winter Squash Bake is an excellent dish made with any of these.

WINTER SQUASH BAKE

Onion and sour cream convert the squash flavor into something miraculous

3 lbs. butternut, buttercup or Hubbard squash	1 c. dairy sour cream
	⅓ c. finely chopped onion
2 tblsp. butter or regular margarine	1 tsp. salt
	¼ tsp. pepper

Cut squash in pieces. Pare and remove seeds. Cook in boiling salted water 15 to 20 minutes or until tender. Mash squash. Stir in butter, sour cream, onion, salt and pepper. Turn into greased 1½-qt. casserole.

Bake uncovered in 350° oven 30 minutes. Makes 8 servings.

BAKED SQUASH SUPPER

An acorn squash cut in half serves a family of two without waste, and more can be baked to fit the number of people to be served. Gardeners find them easy to grow and they usually are the first winter squash ready to use in autumn.

Baked Squash Supper pleases menu planners because individual servings come to the table as half a squash, stuffed with seasoned meat combined with a variety of vegetables and topped with cheese.

BAKED SQUASH SUPPER

Meal-in-a-squash-half; just add an apple salad, a beverage and have homemade spicy molasses cookies for dessert

3 large acorn squash	**2 tblsp. melted butter or**
1 lb. bulk pork sausage	**regular margarine**
1 (10 oz.) pkg. frozen mixed	**1 c. shredded process sharp**
vegetables, thawed	**American cheese (4 oz.)**
½ tsp. salt	

Cut squash in halves; remove seeds. Place cut side down in 15½ × 10½ × 1″ jelly roll pan. Bake in 350° oven 45 minutes.

Meanwhile, brown sausage, breaking it apart with a fork. Drain off excess fat. Stir in vegetables and salt.

Turn squash cut side up. Brush cavities with butter. Fill with sausage mixture. Continue baking 20 minutes. Sprinkle cheese over tops. Return to oven 2 to 3 minutes or just until cheese is melted. Makes 6 servings.

GREEN BEANS COMPANY STYLE

This vegetable casserole rates high for company dinners and buffet suppers. It is a good selection to take to co-operative meals. The canned bean sprouts and water chestnuts reflect Chinese influence, but the casserole topping is an American favorite, French-fried onions from a can. Flavor and texture contrasts are delightful. The ingredients may be combined in the morning and chilled to bake later in the day when getting the meal—a big advantage for the hostess.

GREEN BEANS COMPANY STYLE

Excellent companion for roast pork, chicken or turkey

2 (9 oz.) pkgs. frozen
French-style green beans
1 (8 oz.) can water
chestnuts, drained and
sliced
1 (1 lb.) can bean sprouts,
drained
2 (10¾ oz.) cans condensed
cream of celery soup

1 (4 oz.) can mushroom
stems and pieces
½ c. sliced green onions
1 tsp. salt
1 (3 oz.) can French-fried
onions

Cook beans as directed on package; drain. Combine with water chestnuts and bean sprouts.

Stir together soup, undrained mushrooms, green onions and salt. Stir into bean mixture. Turn into greased 2½-qt. casserole.

Bake in 350° oven 40 minutes. Cover with French-fried onions, and continue baking 5 minutes. Makes 8 to 10 servings.

SWEET-SOUR GREEN BEANS

Few vegetable dishes American women have cooked through the years surpass green beans seasoned with bacon. Originating with the Pennsylvania Dutch, they later won great acclaim at the old-time dinners for threshers in the Midwest. Green beans were then called snap or string beans to indicate they were so fresh they snapped when broken into pieces for cooking, or that there were strings to remove from every pod. The stringless beans available today were unknown.

SWEET-SOUR GREEN BEANS

This dish, attributed to the Pennsylvania Dutch, continues as a summer favorite when the bean vines are bearing generously

1 lb. green beans, cut up
3 slices bacon, cut up
1 c. chopped onion
2 tblsp. vinegar

1 tblsp. sugar
½ tsp. salt
⅛ tsp. pepper

Cook green beans in boiling salted water in large saucepan until tender. Drain.

Meanwhile, cook bacon in small skillet until crisp. Drain on paper towels.

Sauté onion in bacon drippings until tender. Add vinegar, sugar, salt and pepper; heat to boiling. Stir into hot green beans. Spoon into serving dish and sprinkle with bacon. Makes 6 servings.

SQUAW CORN

Squaw Corn may have originated in the East, but lumberjacks in Wisconsin and Minnesota claimed it as their own. Made with other ingredients they had in their camp kitchens, it cheered hungry, hard-working men for many years. The dish also became a favorite with campers. Canned corn eventually replaced the dried kernels. Our Squaw Corn recipe calls for one new ingredient.

SQUAW CORN

Sour cream adds a lot of flavor to this traditional dish

4 slices bacon, diced	1 tsp. sugar
¼ c. chopped onion	½ tsp. salt
2 (12 oz.) cans whole	⅛ tsp. pepper
kernel corn, drained	½ c. dairy sour cream

Cook bacon in saucepan until crisp. Drain on paper towels.

Sauté onion in bacon drippings until soft; pour off bacon drippings. Add corn, sugar, salt, pepper and sour cream. Heat thoroughly, but do not boil. Stir in reserved bacon. Makes 6 servings.

EASY CORN RELISH

First-time visitors in Iowa are astonished at the ever-present corn relish wherever they dine. Sometimes the relish served in homes is made during the sweet corn season and canned along with pickles, but more frequently these days it starts with a can of corn from the supermarket.

EASY CORN RELISH

This relish is as popular in Iowa as pickled beets were in Pennsylvania Dutch country during early days

1 (1 lb. 1 oz.) can whole kernel corn, drained	2 tblsp. chopped onion
	2 tblsp. chopped pimiento
1 c. chopped celery	½ c. French dressing
½ c. sweet pickle relish	½ tsp. salt
¼ c. chopped green pepper	⅛ tsp. pepper

Combine all ingredients. Chill several hours in refrigerator. Stir occasionally. Makes about 3½ cups.

SCALLOPED TOMATOES

Scalloped tomatoes, country style, originated in friendly kitchens where thrifty women stretched the all-American fruit (called a vegetable) with cubes of dry bread. Not until after 1850 did people in the United States lose their fear that tomatoes were poisonous. This is about the time love apples, as tomatoes were called, started to disappear from among flowers where they grew as ornamental plants. Gardeners began to set out the plants alongside rows of vegetables to produce food for the table.

How did the Indians find out which fruits and plants growing wild were edible and worthy of development and cultivation? Was it by the taste-test method? When they showed new European arrivals on these shores which ones were safe and good to eat, they extended the truly helpful hand of friendship.

SCALLOPED TOMATOES

For the most attractive dish, put scallop under the broiler two or three minutes to brown the top

½ c. chopped onion	1 tblsp. sugar
3 tblsp. melted butter or regular margarine	1 tsp. salt
3 slices bread, cubed	⅛ tsp. pepper
1 (1 lb. 12 oz.) can tomatoes, cut up	

Sauté onion in butter until soft. Add bread cubes, and toss together.

Combine tomatoes, sugar, salt and pepper. Place half the tomato mixture in greased 1½-qt. casserole. Top with half the bread mixture. Repeat layers.

Bake in 350° oven 50 minutes. Makes 6 servings.

HARVARD BEETS

This dish originated in New England, date unknown, but supposedly after the founding of Harvard University in 1636. Does the color of the vegetable stand for "the red of Harvard," as many people believe?

Beets were important in colonial times and later. They grew successfully in home gardens and stored well during winter months. Without them New England Boiled Dinner would have lacked the cheer of red on the platter, no one would have written eulogies to Red Flannel Hash, and hard-cooked eggs would not have turned red as they did in Pennsylvania Dutch Pickled Red Beets and Eggs (see Index for recipes).

HARVARD BEETS

For Yale beets, substitute orange juice for the vinegar!

⅓ c. sugar
1 tblsp. cornstarch
½ tsp. salt
½ c. vinegar
2 tblsp. butter or regular
   margarine

2 (1 lb.) cans sliced or diced
beets, drained, or 3 c.
sliced or diced, cooked
beets

Combine sugar, cornstarch and salt in saucepan. Stir in vinegar. Cook over medium heat, stirring constantly, until mixture boils and is thickened. Add butter; stir until it melts. Stir in beets.

Cook over low heat until thoroughly hot, stirring occasionally. Makes 6 servings.

PICKLED BEETS AND EGGS

For a summer picnic or a buffet supper during any season, treat your guests with old-fashioned Pickled Beets and Eggs, a creation of Pennsylvania Dutch kitchens. Serve the beautiful, pink eggs, sometimes called red beet eggs, in the center of a pottery, wooden or crystal bowl or on a plate, and surround them with a wreath of pickled beets cut in quarters or slices. Or cut the eggs lengthwise in quarters and nestle them in crisp celery hearts on the relish tray.

The egg slices—red borders around yellow centers—decorate lettuce salads and contribute nutrition as well as charm. And serve the colorful eggs during the Easter season, an appropriate thing to do since the Pennsylvania Dutch introduced Easter eggs and the Easter bunny to the neighboring colonies.

PICKLED BEETS AND EGGS

The longer the eggs marinate the deeper red their color

10 medium beets	2" stick cinnamon
1½ c. vinegar	6 whole cloves
½ c. water	½ c. vinegar
⅓ c. sugar	8 hard-cooked eggs
2 tsp. salt	

Boil unpeeled beets until just tender. Remove skins and place beets in bowl.

Combine 1½ c. vinegar, water, sugar and salt. Tie cinnamon and cloves in cloth. Add to vinegar mixture. Bring to a boil; boil 3 minutes. Remove spice bag. Pour mixture over beets; cover and refrigerate at least overnight.

Add ½ c. vinegar. Add eggs and refrigerate at least 24 hours. Makes 8 servings.

PERFECTION SALAD

Interest in new foods was high at the time of the St. Louis exposition. Iced tea, ice cream cones and meat patties in buns were first introduced there. And Perfection Salad entered the American cuisine at about the same time as powdered gelatin became commercially available. Earlier, extracting gelatin in home kitchens, usually by boiling calves' feet in water, was a tedious process.

A Pennsylvania homemaker submitted the recipe for Perfection Salad in a cookery contest conducted by Knox Gelatine Inc. and it was one of the winners. The original recipe has changed little, but the method has been simplified. Adding ice water hastens the setting. And instead of letting the gelatin soak in cold water until softened, today we heat the gelatin in water to dissolve it quickly. Here is the recipe for Perfection Salad, a favorite in America for 70 years.

PERFECTION SALAD

Too attractive and refreshing to lose its place in food history

2 envelopes unflavored
   gelatin
1 c. cold water
½ c. sugar
1 tsp. salt
1½ c. ice water
½ c. vinegar
2 tblsp. lemon juice

1½ c. finely shredded
   cabbage
1½ c. chopped celery
¼ c. chopped green pepper
2 pimientos, cut in small
   pieces
Salad greens

Sprinkle gelatin over 1 c. cold water in saucepan. Place over low heat; stir constantly until gelatin dissolves, about 3 minutes. Remove from heat. Stir in sugar and salt.

Add 1½ c. ice water, vinegar and lemon juice. Chill until slightly thicker than consistency of unbeaten egg white. Fold in cabbage, celery, green pepper and pimientos; turn into 1-qt. mold or individual molds. Chill until firm. To serve, unmold and garnish with salad greens. Makes 6 servings.

BRIDE'S PERFECTION SALAD

When any food becomes a great favorite, variations evolve in kitchens across the country. Some women like to put their own touch on the dishes they serve, satisfying their creative urge. This is what happened with Perfection Salad.

Bride's Perfection Salad is a third-generation development of the first Perfection Salad (see preceding recipe). The recipe is shared by a home economist who lives in the Midwest.

BRIDE'S PERFECTION SALAD

Great mixed-vegetable salad to serve with chicken and meats

1 c. boiling water
1 (3 oz.) pkg. lemon-flavor
  gelatin
1 tsp. salt
2 tblsp. lemon juice or
  vinegar
1 c. cold water

1 c. finely shredded
  cabbage
1 c. finely chopped celery
⅓ c. finely chopped green
  pepper
2 tblsp. finely chopped
  pimiento

Stir boiling water into gelatin and salt; stir until gelatin is dissolved. Add lemon juice and cold water. Chill until slightly thickened.

Fold in cabbage, celery, green pepper and pimiento. Pour into 6 individual molds or 8″ square pan. Chill until firm. Makes 6 servings.

CRANBERRY RELISH SALAD

Cranberries may have accompanied turkey at the first Thanksgiving feast after the harvest in 1621. At that season cranberry vines that grew along Cape Cod's shores must have been invitingly red with beautiful, bittersweet berries. Undoubtedly, friendly Indians, who ate cranberries both raw and cooked, had demonstrated they were a native fruit worth consideration. Since sugar was either unavailable or in scant supply to the Pilgrims during the first years in their new homes, cranberry sauce, if they made it, was really sour. This may not have mattered much for in that era Americans, due to heavy diets, relished more tart and less sweet foods than they do today.

When trade between New England and the West Indies had prospered enough that salt fish could be exchanged for sugar, cranberries came into their own. They are popular today not only in Massachusetts, New Jersey, Wisconsin, Washington and Oregon, where they are grown commercially, but also in all states and in all forms—fresh, canned sauce, bottled juice and frozen relishes. Most families consider them essential for Thanksgiving Day. And many household freezers hold a supply for us on the Fourth of July and other special occasions.

Cranberry Relish Salad is a good candidate for holiday and other meals where color and flavor mean so much. It is an ideal choice for carrying to co-operative suppers during the cold weather and family reunions.

CRANBERRY RELISH SALAD

Orange, cranberry and pineapple flavors blend temptingly

1 (3 oz.) pkg. lemon-flavor gelatin

1 (3 oz.) pkg. raspberry-flavor gelatin

½ c. sugar

3 c. boiling water

1 tblsp. lemon juice

1 (8¾ oz.) can crushed pineapple

2 c. fresh cranberries

1 small unpeeled orange, quartered and seeded

1 c. chopped celery

½ c. chopped pecans

Dissolve gelatins and sugar in boiling water. Stir in lemon juice and undrained pineapple. Chill until partially set.

Put cranberries and orange quarters through food chopper. Add to gelatin mixture along with celery and pecans. Turn into 2½-qt. mold or 9″ square pan. Chill until set. Makes 9 servings.

TOMATO ASPIC WITH VEGETABLES

Among the favorite make-ahead salads in country homes is tomato aspic. The universal liking for tomatoes and their cheerful color gives it a high rating. Seasonings give our Tomato Aspic with Vegetables a lively taste, including the olives that sharpen flavors. Finely shredded raw cabbage and carrots and chopped celery, green pepper and onion contribute interest and crispness.

TOMATO ASPIC WITH VEGETABLES

This garden-patch salad boosts good nutrition in meals—a great way to get the family to eat vegetables

2 c. tomato juice
½ c. finely chopped onion
¼ c. finely chopped celery
2 tblsp. brown sugar, firmly packed
1 tsp. salt
2 bay leaves
4 whole cloves
2 envelopes unflavored gelatin
1 c. tomato juice

3 tblsp. lemon juice
1 c. tomato juice
1 c. finely shredded cabbage
½ c. finely chopped celery
½ c. finely chopped green pepper
⅓ c. sliced pimiento-stuffed olives
Lettuce
Salad dressing (optional)

Combine 2 c. tomato juice, onion, ¼ c. celery, brown sugar, salt, bay leaves and cloves in saucepan. Simmer uncovered 5 minutes; strain.

Soften gelatin in 1 c. tomato juice; add to hot mixture and stir to dissolve. Add lemon juice and 1 c. tomato juice. Chill until partially thickened.

Fold in cabbage, ½ c. celery, green pepper and olives. Turn into 1½-qt. ring mold or 11×7×1½" baking dish. Chill until firm. Cut in serving pieces and arrange on lettuce leaves. Serve with salad dressing, if desired. Makes 8 servings.

PARTY WALDORF SALAD

When that famous New York chef, Oscar of the Waldorf, tossed chunks of apples and sliced celery with mayonnaise, he created a salad that spread across the continent. Even in country kitchens where apples are to this day the mainstay of many winter fruit salads, women depend on new ingredients for interest.

In Party Waldorf Salad—a southern special—dates, walnuts

and marshmallows are the extras. Grapes, bananas and pears frequently are included also. A Waldorf Salad that people in the Ozarks especially like has chopped black walnuts scattered over the top, while in New England a spoonful of cranberry sauce often garnishes individual servings.

PARTY WALDORF SALAD

It's at the peak of perfection made with new-crop apples and celery in autumn. Add your own choice of extra ingredients

2 c. diced unpared apples
2 tblsp. lemon juice
1 c. chopped celery
½ c. coarsely chopped
walnuts
½ c. chopped dates

½ c. miniature
marshmallows
⅓ c. mayonnaise or salad
dressing
1 tblsp. light cream or
milk

Toss apples with lemon juice to keep color bright. Combine with celery, walnuts, dates and marshmallows. (For an everyday salad, omit dates and marshmallows and increase apples and celery.)

Blend together mayonnaise and light cream. Stir into fruit mixture. Makes 6 to 8 servings.

24-HOUR FRUIT SALAD

Overnight fruit salads were a forerunner of frozen fruit salads, served in important meals, most frequently in holiday and family reunion dinners. Made with canned fruits, they were the first make-ahead salads containing no gelatin.

The syrup, drained from the fruits, cooked with egg and seasoned with a little sugar, vinegar and salt, makes a custard dressing. (Commercial salad dressings were not universally available when overnight salads originated.) The fruits and marshmallows are added to the homemade dressing and whipped cream folded in. Chilled overnight, the salad is spooned into crisp lettuce cups just before serving.

24-HOUR FRUIT SALAD

We add fresh grapes and oranges to canned fruits for flavor

1 (1 lb. 4 oz.) can pineapple
chunks

1 egg

2 tblsp. sugar

2 tblsp. vinegar

Dash of salt

1 tblsp. butter or regular
margarine

1 (1 lb.) can pitted light
sweet cherries, drained

2 oranges, peeled and cut up

1 c. green seedless grapes
or winter grapes, halved
and seeded

2 c. miniature
marshmallows

1 c. heavy cream, whipped

Drain pineapple, reserving 2 tblsp. juice. Beat egg slightly in heavy saucepan. Stir in reserved pineapple juice, sugar, vinegar, salt and butter. Cook over low heat, stirring constantly, until mixture thickens slightly and coats spoon. Turn into small bowl and cool to room temperature.

Combine well-drained pineapple, cherries, oranges, grapes and marshmallows. Pour custard dressing over and mix lightly. Fold in whipped cream. Cover and chill 24 hours. Makes 8 to 10 servings.

4-FRUIT FROZEN SALAD

Just as the first iceboxes revolutionized cooking and eating, mechanical refrigerators introduced new dishes. Hostesses of the 1930s frequently featured frozen fruit salads for club and other guest luncheons. Busy women welcomed these make-ahead specials and liked the idea that fruit salads could serve as dessert as well as salad.

This 4-Fruit Frozen Salad is a rich, special-occasion choice. Sour cream substitutes for the whipped cream incorporated in the first frozen salads. Canned dark cherries and golden apricots brighten the salad and blend their flavors with those of bananas and pineapple. When sliced or cut in individual servings and placed on lettuce-lined plates, 4-Fruit Frozen Salad is a thing of beauty.

4-FRUIT FROZEN SALAD

For a luncheon, serve with hot cheese biscuits and tea or coffee

1 (8 oz.) pkg. cream cheese,
  softened
1 c. dairy sour cream
¼ c. sugar
¼ tsp. salt
1 (8¾ oz.) can crushed
  pineapple
1 banana, diced

1 (1 lb. 1 oz.) can apricot
  halves, drained and cut
  in fourths
1 (1 lb.) can pitted dark
  sweet cherries, drained
1 c. miniature
  marshmallows

Beat cheese in large mixer bowl until fluffy. Beat in sour cream, sugar and salt.

Drain pineapple, reserving juice. Place diced banana in pineapple juice; drain.

Add pineapple, banana, apricots, cherries and marshmallows to cream cheese mixture. Turn into 5-c. mold or 8″ square pan. Freeze at least 8 hours.

Remove salad from mold and let stand at room temperature 10 minutes before cutting. Makes 8 servings.

SOUR CREAM COLESLAW

No one can leaf through a Pennsylvania Dutch cookbook without being impressed and tempted by the many recipes for cabbage salads. Many of them originated late in the 18th century. The Pennsylvanians borrowed the name, coleslaw, from their Dutch neighbors to the north in New York, but they developed their own salads. These frugal people were of German descent and the "Dutch" was a misnomer for "Deutsch," or German, and had no connection with Holland.

In our recipe for Sour Cream Coleslaw, a simple country dressing converts finely shredded cabbage into a superior salad.

The modern touch is the spoonful of mayonnaise which contributes a pleasing, although subtle, flavor.

SOUR CREAM COLESLAW

Excellent accompaniment for fried fish, meat and chicken

1 c. dairy sour cream	1 tblsp. mayonnaise or salad
2 tblsp. sugar	dressing
½ tsp. salt	6 c. finely shredded
¼ tsp. pepper	cabbage
2 tblsp. vinegar	

Blend together sour cream, sugar, salt, pepper, vinegar and mayonnaise. Stir into cabbage. Makes 6 servings.

WILTED SPINACH SALAD

As early as the Revolutionary War, greens tossed with a hot vinegar-bacon dressing were served at Pennsylvania Dutch tables. Salad content followed the seasons. Thrifty hands gathered tender, young dandelion leaves in spring. Garden lettuce, spinach and endive followed, then cabbage. Despite the name of these salads, they wilt little if correctly made. The hot dressing, doused on crackly leaves, takes away only part of the crispness and adds a lot of flavor.

In our recipe for Wilted Spinach Salad, chopped hard-cooked eggs are an important ingredient as they always have been in Pennsylvania Dutch kitchens.

WILTED SPINACH SALAD

For top success, drain the tender, crisp young spinach well and toss with hot dressing just before serving

6 c. spinach, torn in bite-size pieces	¼ c. vinegar
¼ c. sliced green onions	2 tblsp. water
3 hard-cooked eggs, coarsely chopped	2 tblsp. sugar
5 slices bacon, chopped	½ tsp. salt
	¼ tsp. pepper

Combine spinach, onions and eggs in salad bowl.

Cook bacon in skillet until crisp. Remove bacon and drain on paper towels. Pour off all but 3 tblsp. bacon drippings.

Add vinegar, water, sugar, salt and pepper to bacon drippings. Heat to boiling, stirring to blend. Pour over spinach mixture; toss gently. Sprinkle with bacon. Makes 6 servings.

CINNAMON SWIRL BREAD

A recipe that has been copied and passed on many times throughout a Kansas neighborhood. Everyone who samples it requests the recipe. A favorite at church suppers and fair entries . . . looks handsome too with the sweet glaze dripping over top and sides of the bread.

CINNAMON SWIRL BREAD

A Kansas homemaker makes lots of these to serve the field crew

1 c. milk	2 eggs
¼ c. butter or regular margarine	5 to 5½ c. sifted flour Melted butter or regular margarine
¼ c. sugar	
1 tsp. salt	⅓ c. sugar
1 pkg. active dry yeast	1 tblsp. ground cinnamon
¼ c. lukewarm water	Glaze (recipe follows)

Scald milk. Stir in butter, ¼ c. sugar and salt. Cool to lukewarm.

Sprinkle yeast on lukewarm water; stir to dissolve. Add yeast, eggs and 2 c. flour to milk mixture. Beat with electric mixer at medium speed until smooth, for about 2 minutes, scraping bowl occasionally. Or beat with spoon until batter is smooth.

Gradually add enough remaining flour, a little at a time, to make a soft dough that leaves the sides of the bowl. Turn onto lightly floured surface and knead until smooth and satiny, about 8 to 10 minutes.

Place in lightly greased bowl; turn dough over to grease top.

Cover and let rise in warm place until doubled, about 1 to 1½ hours.

Divide dough in half. Roll each half into a 10×8″ rectangle. Brush lightly with melted butter. Sprinkle with half of combined ⅓ c. sugar and cinnamon. Roll up like jelly roll, starting at narrow end. Seal long edge. Place seam side down in greased 9×5×3″ loaf pan. Repeat with remaining dough. Let rise until doubled.

Bake in 350° oven 30 minutes or until bread tests done. Remove from pans. Cool on racks. Drizzle with Glaze. Makes 2 loaves.

Glaze: Combine 1 c. sifted confectioners sugar, 4 tsp. milk and ½ tsp. vanilla; blend well.

PIPING HOT BISCUITS

First-time European visitors to America in the 19th century were amazed at the way little pieces of hot bread were hurried from oven to table and the number of times the bread basket was replenished during a meal. That was the golden age for biscuits. While they varied little from one region to another or from mansion to cottage, sod house or log cabin, biscuits in the North were larger and thicker than the biscuits of the South, which often were somewhat richer.

Cowboy biscuits of the Old West were the largest and thickest of all and they were somewhat more "bready." Packaged mixes today make excellent biscuits and they are a convenience. Cowboys invented the first mixes. When a lone cowboy was to be gone from ranch headquarters a few days, he mixed flour, salt and baking powder in a muslin sack and tied it along with his skillet, coffee pot, bacon and coffee to his saddle. When time to eat, he built a campfire, cooked bacon and used the drippings to shorten his biscuits, which he usually mixed with water in the flour sack. He shaped the dough in a roll, pinched off bits of it and baked them in the skillet. He called them pinch-offs.

Our Piping Hot Biscuits are a little richer than many of the hot breads, and touches of sugar and cream of tartar do good things to them.

PIPING HOT BISCUITS

Roll dough half as thick as you like your baked biscuits

2 c. sifted flour	½ tsp. cream of tartar
4 tsp. baking powder	½ c. shortening
2 tsp. sugar	⅔ c. milk
½ tsp. salt	

Sift together flour, baking powder, sugar, salt and cream of tartar. Cut in shortening until mixture resembles coarse crumbs. Add milk all at once. Stir with a fork just until moistened. Knead gently 10 times on lightly floured surface. Roll or pat dough ½″ thick. Cut with floured biscuit cutter. Place on ungreased baking sheet.

Bake in 450° oven 10 to 12 minutes or until golden brown. Makes 16.

CINNAMON FLOP COFFEE CAKE

Fertile land and farming skill met in Pennsylvania Dutch country in early America. One of the most remarkable cuisines of the thirteen original states developed there in country kitchens. The abundance of wheat flour started Pennsylvania Dutch women on a gigantic baking spree that lasted many years. Some of America's best breads, cakes, cookies and pies came from their ovens, commonly located outdoors near the kitchen door.

Cinnamon Flop Coffee Cake, a quick bread, tastes as good today as it did a hundred years ago. People in Lebanon County, Pennsylvania, sometimes call it Moravian Coffee Cake, a quick version of Moravian Sugar Cake, which is made with a yeast dough containing mashed potatoes.

CINNAMON FLOP COFFEE CAKE

During baking some of the crumb topping "flops" or permeates the coffee cake, giving it a marbleized look and a great flavor

1 c. brown sugar, firmly
    packed
½ tsp. ground cinnamon
¼ c. butter or regular
    margarine
2 c. sifted flour
2 tsp. baking powder

¼ tsp. salt
2 tblsp. shortening
1½ c. sugar
1 egg
1 tsp. vanilla
1 c. milk

Combine brown sugar and cinnamon; cut in butter until crumbly and well mixed. Set aside.

Sift together flour, baking powder and salt.

Cream shortening in mixer bowl. Gradually beat in sugar. Add egg and vanilla; beat well. Stir in flour mixture by hand alternately with milk, starting and ending with flour mixture. Pour into greased 8" square pan. Sprinkle with brown sugar mixture.

Bake in 425° oven 30 to 35 minutes or until golden brown. Serve warm. Makes 8 servings.

SPIDER CORN BREAD

We can imagine the problems the first colonial women had when they attempted to bake bread with their homemade yeast and cornmeal. Accustomed to using wheat flour, they probably did not know that cornmeal lacks gluten, a wheat protein that enables a loaf of bread to hold its increased height when baked. Had the Indians along the Eastern Seaboard known of tortillas, the paper-thin cornmeal cakes their Mexican and South American counterparts baked, they could have borrowed the techniques. By experimenting, the new Americans developed their own thin pancake, of which Rhode Island johnnycake became the most famous.

The next step was to leaven with eggs and saleratus and bake the corn bread in spiders, or three-legged iron skillets. The black utensil resembled a spider to imaginative women.

Our Spider Corn Bread is a descendant of the old-time favorites. It is moist and super-delicious. You can bake it in a heavy skillet or a 9″ square baking pan. Serve it with a fork.

SPIDER CORN BREAD

Another name for this is custard corn bread . . . really good

2 tblsp. butter or regular margarine	1 tsp. salt
	1 c. milk
1⅓ c. white cornmeal	2 eggs
⅓ c. sifted flour	1 c. buttermilk
2 tblsp. sugar	1 c. milk
1 tsp. baking soda	Butter, jelly or syrup

Place 2 tblsp. butter in a 9″ iron skillet or 9″ square baking pan. Place in oven and start heating oven to 400°.

Meanwhile, sift together cornmeal, flour, sugar, baking soda and salt into bowl. Beat in 1 c. milk and eggs. Stir in buttermilk. Pour over melted butter in skillet. Pour remaining 1 c. milk over top of batter; do not stir.

Bake in 400° oven 35 minutes or until golden brown. Serve hot from skillet with butter and tart jelly or syrup. Eat with a fork. Corn bread will have a layer of custard. Makes 6 to 9 servings.

SOUTHERN SPOON BREAD

The corn porridge friendly Indians showed early colonists how to make was the forerunner of the southern delicacy, spoon bread. Eggs became available and, incorporated in the porridge, they leavened it, resulting in a fluffy, soft and delicious bread. When baking soda became available early in the 19th century it was added to the cornmeal batter made with buttermilk or sour milk. The spoon bread was still fluffy and light but it had greater stability. Baking powder evolved later and it was also used for leavening spoon breads made with sweet milk. So soft they cannot be sliced, spoon breads are served with a spoon from the dish in which they bake. They are the aristocrats of corn breads.

There are two kinds of spoon breads, those made with cornmeal and with hominy grits. This cookbook contains recipes for both of them. Our recipe for Southern Spoon Bread calls for both baking powder and soda.

SOUTHERN SPOON BREAD

Southerners prefer white cornmeal for making corn breads

1½ c. boiling water	1 tsp. salt
1 c. white cornmeal	1 tsp. baking powder
1 tblsp. butter or regular	¼ tsp. baking soda
margarine	3 egg whites
1 c. buttermilk	Butter
3 egg yolks	

Pour boiling water into cornmeal in large bowl, stirring constantly. Add 1 tblsp. butter and continue stirring until mixture is lukewarm. Stir in buttermilk, then beat in egg yolks. Stir in salt, baking powder and soda.

Beat egg whites just until soft peaks form. Fold into batter. Pour into greased 2-qt. casserole.

Bake in 375° oven 45 to 50 minutes or until golden brown. Serve hot with butter. Makes 6 to 8 servings.

HOMINY SPOON BREAD

Southerners divide on preference for spoon bread of cornmeal or of hominy. In Charleston, South Carolina, a great colonial seaport, and in adjacent communities, hominy spoon bread was —and still is—the favorite.

In Virginia and to a lesser extent in other states, spoon breads are called batter breads. This explains the reference sometimes made to the "batter-bread express" that existed in wealthy plantation homes during the late colonial era. It consisted of the cook's helpers, frequently youngsters, who ran from the kitchen house to the dining room in the big house, carrying baking dishes, wrapped with linen napkins and filled with spoon bread just out of the oven.

HOMINY SPOON BREAD

This tastes best when hot enough to melt butter instantly

½ c. hominy grits	3 eggs, separated
2½ c. water	½ c. white cornmeal
½ tsp. salt	2 tsp. baking powder
1 tblsp. butter or regular	½ tsp. salt
margarine	Butter

Cook grits with water and ½ tsp. salt as directed on package. Stir in butter until melted. Cool slightly. Blend in egg yolks.

Sift together cornmeal, baking powder and ½ tsp. salt. Stir into grits mixture.

Beat egg whites until soft peaks form. Fold into grits mixture. Turn into greased 1½-qt. casserole.

Bake in 350° oven 1 hour or until golden brown. Serve immediately with butter. Makes 4 to 6 servings.

SOURDOUGH BREAD

Homemade sourdough bread's last stand is in Alaska where some people in the more remote areas still bake the tangy loaves, biscuits and pancakes. Sourdough was the bread of the 1849 California gold-rush days and 50 years later in the Klondike. Earthen crocks of sourdough starter went West with pioneers in covered wagons; they baked biscuits and pancakes over campfires along the way. Ranchers of the Mountain West also were expert with these breads in their cow and sheep camps.

The arrival of packaged yeast in grocery stores began the decline of sourdough bread. It was so much easier to reach in the cupboard for a dependable leavening than to pamper a temperamental starter. The success of a starter depends primarily on a blend of yeast and bacterial fermentation, which is determined by the flour and the types of bacteria in the air. It cannot be 100 per cent predictable.

Anyone who has tasted good sourdough biscuits or hotcakes laments their disappearance. So many requests for sourdough recipes came to the FARM JOURNAL COUNTRYSIDE TEST KITCHENS over the years that the following recipes for Sourdough Starter, Sourdough Biscuits and Silver Dollar Hotcakes were developed.

SOURDOUGH STARTER

Using your starter often is best for success with sourdoughs. Pioneers and prospectors used theirs every day

½ pkg. active dry yeast   2 tblsp. sugar
   (1¼ tsp.)   2½ c. warm water (110 to
2 c. unsifted flour   115°)

Combine all ingredients in a stone crock or glass or pottery bowl. Beat well with whisk or electric mixer until smooth. Cover with cheesecloth and let stand two days in a warm place free from drafts, such as in an unheated oven.

After using starter, add an equal amount of warm water and flour to the portion not used. Pour into a glass jar or crock with a tightly fitting lid. Cover and store in refrigerator.

SOURDOUGH BISCUITS

Serve these light biscuits hot with plenty of butter. Be sure to replenish starter so the next batch of biscuits will be good

1½ c. sifted flour   ¼ c. butter or regular
2 tsp. baking powder   margarine
¼ tsp. baking soda (½ tsp.   1 c. Sourdough Starter
   if Starter is quite sour)   Melted butter
½ tsp. salt

Sift together flour, baking powder, soda and salt. Cut in ¼ c. butter with pastry blender until crumbly. Add Sourdough Starter, and mix.

Turn dough out on lightly floured board. Knead lightly until satiny.

Roll dough ½" thick. Cut with floured 2½" cutter. Place biscuits in well-greased 9" square pan. Brush with melted butter. Let rise about 1 hour in a warm place. (Replenish Starter by stirring in 2 c. warm water and 2 c. flour. Cover tightly and store in refrigerator.)

Bake in 425° oven 20 minutes. Makes 12 biscuits.

SILVER DOLLAR HOTCAKES

These tiny pancakes were named when silver dollars were common. The size is traditional, but you can enlarge the "dollars"

1 c. Sourdough Starter	2 tsp. baking soda
2 c. unsifted flour	2 eggs
2 c. milk	3 tblsp. melted shortening
1 tsp. salt	2 tblsp. sugar

About 12 hours before mealtime, mix Sourdough Starter, flour, milk and salt; let stand in a bowl covered with cheesecloth. Set in a warm place.

Just before baking, remove 1 c. batter to replenish Starter in crock. To the remaining batter in bowl, add baking soda, eggs, shortening and sugar. Mix well.

Bake cakes the size of silver dollars on lightly greased, hot griddle. For thinner hotcakes, add more milk to the batter. Makes about 30 cakes.

BASIC PANCAKES

Call them griddlecakes, flapjacks, or flannel cakes—they are all American names for pancakes. The first cookbook published in the colonies that included recipes using native foods referred to them as slapjacks. (This modest 1796 Connecticut book presented the first printed recipe using maize, the Indian name for corn.) Regardless of what you call the cakes browned on a griddle, they are served hot and usually with butter and maple or other table syrup, which the cowboys called lick.

The American way is to serve pancakes in stacks of two or more. Some Vermont people like to butter seven or eight large pancakes, sprinkle them with maple sugar and stack them. These "shortcakes" are cut in wedges for serving.

Europeans brought their pancake recipes to America, many of which have been widely adapted. The thin crêpes of France, large, thin Swedish pancakes, frequently rolled, and German potato pancakes are different from the American type. Most pancakes today are made from packaged mixes, and with good results.

Some households cling to old-time recipes, which they think are unsurpassable. Basic Pancakes with five variations is a family treasure. Take your choice of apple, bacon, blueberry, buttermilk or corn pancakes.

BASIC PANCAKES

Five variations—good recipe for men's service club, money-raising suppers

2 c. sifted flour	**1 egg**
2½ tsp. baking powder	**1½ c. milk**
½ tsp. salt	**2 tblsp. cooking oil**

Sift together flour, baking powder and salt into mixing bowl. Add egg, milk and oil. Beat with rotary beater just until smooth. Pour ¼ c. batter onto hot, lightly greased griddle for each pancake. Bake until bubbles appear; turn over. Makes 1 dozen 5″ pancakes.

Variations

Bacon Pancakes: Add 5 slices crisp-cooked bacon, crumbled, to batter. Bake as directed. Makes about 13.

Blueberry Pancakes: Stir 1 c. fresh or frozen (thawed and drained) or drained canned blueberries into batter. Bake as directed. Makes about 16.

Corn Pancakes: Stir 1 c. drained, canned whole-kernel corn, or cooked fresh corn cut from cob into batter. Bake as directed. Makes about 16.

Apple Pancakes: Add 1½ c. finely chopped, pared, apples to batter. Bake as directed. Makes about 18.

Buttermilk Pancakes: Substitute buttermilk for milk in recipe for Basic Pancakes. Reduce amount of baking powder to 1 tsp. and add ½ tsp. baking soda. Mix and bake as directed. Makes 1 dozen.

CORNMEAL PANCAKES

The first griddlecakes the colonists baked were of meal, ground the Indian way between stones, with salt and water added. These hot cakes baked over coals were known in New England as journey cakes—by taking meal and salt, early travelers in the wilderness could heat water from streams over campfires to make the batter.

The water was poured over the meal and the mixture was allowed to stand until it was absorbed. (Traditional Rhode Island johnnycakes, still made today, contain white cornmeal preferably stone-ground.) The pancakes were crisp on the outside, soft within, and when served hot, spread with butter and doused with maple or other table syrup, they were delicious.

Our Cornmeal Pancakes are an adapted version. Buttermilk replaces the water, and baking soda leavens the batter; a mixture of flour and cornmeal, eggs and a dash of salt complete the list of ingredients.

CORNMEAL PANCAKES

Hot off the griddle and served with sizzling pork sausage, these are farmhouse favorites

½ c. sifted flour	2 c. yellow cornmeal
1½ tsp. salt	2 eggs, beaten
1 tsp. baking soda	2½ c. buttermilk

Sift together flour, salt and baking soda. Stir in cornmeal. Add eggs and buttermilk and beat just until smooth.

Pour ¼ c. batter for each cake onto lightly greased, hot griddle. Bake until golden brown on both sides. Serve hot. Makes about 20.

OLD-FASHIONED APPLE CIDER PIE

Cider presses worked overtime in youthful America. People were thrifty and they made every effort to keep apples from going to waste. Besides, they liked cider. It was a daily drink in many homes, much as orange juice is today. Good cooks also used it as an ingredient in pies, cakes and many other dishes. And from cider they made the year's supply of vinegar in wooden molasses barrels. Molasses was sold by the pint or quart from the big barrel.

Teamed with sliced apples, cider gives piquancy to Old-fashioned Apple Cider Pie, a dessert treat. If you do not have cider, you can use apple juice.

OLD-FASHIONED APPLE CIDER PIE

Good recipe to use when apples have lost their best flavor

1 c. apple cider or juice	2 tblsp. water
⅔ c. sugar	½ tsp. ground cinnamon
6 c. sliced pared apples (6 to 8)	1 tblsp. butter or regular margarine
2 tblsp. cornstarch	Pastry for 2-crust 9″ pie

Combine cider and sugar in large saucepan; bring to a boil. Add apples; cook uncovered about 8 minutes or until apples are tender. Drain, reserving syrup. Add enough additional cider to syrup to make 1⅓ c. Return syrup to saucepan.

Blend together cornstarch and water. Add to apple mixture along with cinnamon. Cook, stirring constantly, until mixture comes to a boil. Remove from heat and stir in butter.

Spoon into pastry-lined piepan. Cover with top pastry; flute edges and cut vents. Bake in 400° oven 40 to 45 minutes or until apples are tender. Cool. Makes 6 to 8 servings.

UPSIDE-DOWN APPLE PIE

The fragrance of apples cooking with spices frequently permeated colonial kitchens. The fruit, prepared in a variety of ways, appeared almost daily in meals. New settlers to America soon discovered that no fruit crop was so easy to grow and none was so versatile as apples. Stored in bins and barrels or as strings of dried fruit hanging from attic rafters, they provided the winter supply.

Women baked apple pies by the dozen in cold weather and stored them in cold rooms or sheds where they froze. They thawed and warmed them slowly in brick fireplace ovens and frequently served the pies more than once a day—often for breakfast as well as dinner.

Clever colonial pie bakers created many seasoning tricks to make up for the loss of flavor in apples stored a long time. After Christmas women used a heavier hand with spices and sometimes they added another food to the apples in pies, such as bits of salt pork, maple sugar and cider.

Upside-down Apple Pie is new to this generation, simple to make and delicious. It is a good basic apple pie which bakes on a mixture of brown sugar, butter and pecans. This forms a glaze on the pie when it is inverted.

UPSIDE-DOWN APPLE PIE

An out-of-ordinary apple pie, heritage from colonial days

¼ c. butter or regular margarine, softened	6 c. sliced pared apples
½ c. pecan halves	½ c. sugar
½ c. brown sugar, firmly packed	2 tblsp. flour
	½ tsp. ground cinnamon
Pastry for 2-crust 9″ pie	Dash of ground nutmeg

Spread butter over bottom and sides of 9″ pie pan. Press pecan halves, rounded side down, into butter. Sprinkle evenly with brown sugar; pat in gently.

Roll out enough pastry for bottom crust; place over brown sugar.

Combine apples, sugar, flour, cinnamon and nutmeg. Spoon into pie pan.

Roll out remaining pastry; place over apples. Trim to fit. Seal edges. Flute edges, and prick top with fork.

Bake in 400° oven 50 minutes or until apples are tender. Cool on rack 5 minutes. Place serving plate over pie; invert. Carefully remove pie pan. Serve warm or cool. Makes 8 servings.

GLAZED PEACH PIE

Peaches, originally a Chinese fruit, were plentiful in the South, and southern kitchens specialized in peach desserts. Glazed Peach Pie is an adaptation of an old-time Georgia open-face pie.

GLAZED PEACH PIE

Summer has few table treats to equal this—a peach-orange glaze lines the pastry and covers red and yellow peach slices

6 c. sliced pared peaches (6 large)	½ c. orange juice
1 c. sugar	1 baked 9″ pie shell
3 tblsp. cornstarch	Whipped cream or whipped dessert topping
¼ tsp. ground cinnamon	

Mash enough sliced peaches to measure 1 c. Reserve remaining sliced peaches.

Combine sugar, cornstarch and cinnamon in saucepan. Stir in orange juice and mashed peaches. Cook over medium heat, stirring constantly, until mixture comes to a boil. Boil, stirring, 1 minute. Spread half the glaze over bottom and sides of baked pie shell. Fill with reserved sliced peaches. Pour remaining glaze over fruit; spread to completely cover peaches. Chill at least 3 hours. Serve topped with whipped cream. Makes 8 servings.

STREUSEL PEAR PIE

Some of the world's best pear pie recipes originate in Oregon, where excellent pears are grown. Try this one when pears are available. The brown sugar, butter and delicate spicing do something good to the fruit filling.

STREUSEL PEAR PIE

For an elegant dessert, top servings of this pie with ice cream

½ c. sugar	½ c. butter or regular
1½ tblsp. quick-cooking	margarine
tapioca	1 c. sifted flour
½ tsp. ground cinnamon	1 c. brown sugar, firmly
⅛ tsp. ground mace	packed
2 tblsp. lemon juice	1 unbaked 9″ pie shell
6 c. sliced pared pears	

Combine sugar, tapioca, cinnamon and mace. Stir in lemon juice and pears. Let stand 15 minutes.

Meanwhile, cut butter into mixture of flour and brown sugar until crumbly.

Turn pear mixture into pie shell. Sprinkle crumb mixture evenly over top. Bake in 375° oven 45 to 50 minutes or until golden brown. Makes 6 to 8 servings.

DEEP-DISH PLUM PIE

Purple Italian prune plums come in late summer when many fruits have disappeared. Their superb flavor and their rather firm meat enables them to ship well so they are widely available. Due to their firmness, plums bake successfully. They may be slit and pitted, or left whole with skins and sprinkled with brown sugar and cinnamon. Add a little water and bake until tender or about 25 minutes in a 350° oven. A good supper dessert to serve warm or chilled with homemade cookies. Top the baked plums at serving time with sour cream.

The recipe for Deep-dish Plum Pie is shared by an Idaho woman, who calls the dessert September Plum Pie.

DEEP-DISH PLUM PIE

Add scoops of vanilla ice cream for a scrumptious dessert

1 c. sugar	2 tblsp. butter or regular
¼ c. flour	margarine
¼ tsp. ground cinnamon	Pastry for 1-crust 9″ pie
2½ lbs. prune plums, halved	Milk
and pitted	1 tsp. sugar

Combine 1 c. sugar, flour and cinnamon. Stir into plums. Turn into 8″ square pan. Dot with butter.

Roll pastry into a 9″ square. Place over plums. Turn edges under and seal to edge of pan. Cut steam vents. Brush top with milk.

Bake in 425° oven 45 to 50 minutes or until golden brown. Sprinkle top with 1 tsp. sugar. Serve warm or cold. Makes 6 servings.

CONCORD GRAPE PIE

The most important all-American grape is the blue Concord from which we get the flavorful grape juice. Pies made with Concords are a classic country dessert. Concord grapes are descendants of eastern wild grapes, which the colonists called "fox grapes."

In no area are juicy Concord grape pies more ardently praised than in the Finger Lakes region and in northwestern sections of New York, where the grapes have been grown extensively for years. Our Concord Grape Pie has two crusts with a tart-sweet filling in which the true grape flavor dominates.

CONCORD GRAPE PIE

One of the joys of early autumn, this is a dessert to remember. Some work to make but more than worth the effort

5 c. Concord grapes	**1 tsp. lemon juice**
1⅓ c. sugar	**Pastry for 2-crust 9″ pie**
¼ c. flour	**2 tblsp. butter or regular**
Dash of salt	**margarine**

Wash grapes. Remove skins by pinching grapes at end opposite stem. Save skins.

Heat grape pulp in saucepan without water until grapes come to a full rolling boil. Press through sieve to remove seeds. Combine pulp and skins.

Stir together sugar, flour and salt. Stir into grape mixture along with lemon juice. Pour grape filling into pastry-lined pie pan. Dot with butter. Cover with top pastry; flute edges and cut vents.

Bake in 425° oven 35 to 45 minutes or until crust is browned and juice begins to bubble through slits in top. Cool. Makes 6 to 8 servings.

RHUBARB/RUM PIE

Rhubarb brought the first taste of spring to the favorite dessert, pie—in fact, early Americans called it pie plant. Sloops and schooners sailed from our eastern seaports with salt fish, barrel staves and hoops of wood and other items of trade to the Caribbean Islands. They returned home with comparatively inexpensive molasses and more costly sugar and rum, all sugar cane products. A little rum was used in cooking to flavor otherwise common desserts. Rhubarb/Rum Pie is a good example.

The Connecticut woman who shares an old family recipe for it, says she thinks the dessert was an outgrowth of chess and other custard pies extensively served in the early days. Regardless of where and when the recipe for the pie originated, the dessert tastes wonderful and the bits of pink rhubarb give it appetite and eye appeal.

RHUBARB/RUM PIE

Extra-delicious when topped with whipped cream

1 unbaked 9" pie shell	1 c. milk
2 tblsp. butter or regular margarine	2 tblsp. dark rum
	¼ tsp. salt
1 c. sugar	¼ tsp. ground nutmeg
¼ c. flour	¼ tsp. ground cinnamon
2 eggs, separated	Whipped cream or whipped
2 c. cut-up rhubarb	dessert topping (optional)

Bake pastry shell in 350° oven 5 minutes. Remove from oven.

Meanwhile, cream together butter and sugar. Beat in flour, then egg yolks. Stir in rhubarb, milk, rum, salt, nutmeg and cinnamon.

Beat egg whites until soft peaks form. Fold into rhubarb mixture. Turn into pie shell.

Bake in 350° oven 45 to 50 minutes or until rhubarb is tender. Serve topped with whipped cream, if desired. Makes 6 to 8 servings.

SOUR CREAM/RAISIN PIE

When this recipe was invented in early America, fresh fruit was available only for a short season but raisins, like other dried fruits, could be kept on hand in the cupboard. And without refrigeration, sour cream frequently accumulated in kitchens. So this dessert became a favorite and is popular for its great taste today.

Supposedly the pie originated in New England, but raisin pies of many descriptions were served in all the colonies. The Funeral Pie of the Pennsylvania Dutch was the most famous. It was a two-crust pie, often with a lattice pastry top. The pie was served in the big meals that followed funerals, when relatives of the bereaved family gathered, bringing most of the food. Two-crust raisin pies carried more successfully than those topped with meringue.

So well established in Pennsylvania Dutch country was the pie that a dismal saying, still heard in reference to a serious illness, developed: "There will be a raisin pie soon." But our Sour Cream/Raisin Pie is special and sure to bring cheer.

SOUR CREAM/RAISIN PIE

There are many recipes for pie—this is one of the best

1 c. sugar	1½ c. raisins
1½ tblsp. cornstarch	1½ tblsp. lemon juice
½ tsp. ground cinnamon	1 baked 9″ pie shell
¼ tsp. ground nutmeg	¼ tsp. cream of tartar
¼ tsp. salt	6 tblsp. sugar
1½ c. dairy sour cream	½ tsp. vanilla
3 eggs, separated	

Stir together 1 c. sugar, cornstarch, cinnamon, nutmeg and salt in saucepan. Blend in sour cream.

Beat egg yolks slightly. Stir into mixture in saucepan along with raisins and lemon juice. Cook over medium heat, stirring constantly, until mixture thickens and boils. Boil 1 minute. Pour into baked pie shell.

Beat egg whites with cream of tartar until frothy. Beat in the 6 tblsp. sugar, 1 tblsp. at a time, until mixture is glossy and stiff peaks form. Beat in vanilla. Spread meringue over hot filling, sealing well to edge of crust to prevent shrinking.

Bake in 400° oven about 10 minutes or until lightly browned. Cool away from drafts. Makes 6 to 8 servings.

ORANGE/LEMON CHIFFON PIE

Gelatinized refrigerator pies, called chiffon pies because of their tall, light fillings, first came to tables around 40 years ago in an Iowa family restaurant located in the shadow of a railroad trestle. They won nationwide recognition quickly and menu planners still include them in many meals.

Orange/Lemon Chiffon Pie wins first for its beauty.

ORANGE/LEMON CHIFFON PIE

This dessert deserves its reputation. Perfect light finale for an otherwise substantial meal

1 envelope unflavored gelatin	¼ c. water
½ c. sugar	½ tsp. grated orange peel
Dash of salt	½ tsp. grated lemon peel
4 eggs, separated	⅓ c. sugar
½ c. orange juice	1 baked 9″ pie shell
⅓ c. lemon juice	Whipped cream or whipped dessert topping

Stir together gelatin, ½ c. sugar and salt in saucepan.

Beat together egg yolks, orange juice, lemon juice and water. Blend into gelatin mixture. Cook over medium heat, stirring constantly, until mixture comes to a boil and gelatin is dissolved. Remove from heat; stir in orange and lemon peels. Chill, stirring occasionally, until mixture is partially set.

Beat egg whites until soft peaks form. Gradually add ⅓ c. sugar, beating until stiff peaks form. Fold into gelatin mixture. Spoon lightly into pie shell; chill until set. Serve garnished with whipped cream. Makes 6 to 8 servings.

AMISH VANILLA PIE

This is a rich dark pie with brown sugar topping that melts on your tongue. A farm woman in Kansas makes this dessert often for her family. The recipe was handed down through several generations of great Amish cooks.

AMISH VANILLA PIE

A real old-fashioned pie that is certain to be a hit with coffee

½ c. brown sugar, firmly packed	½ c. brown sugar, firmly packed
1 tblsp. flour	½ tsp. cream of tartar
¼ c. dark corn syrup	½ tsp. baking soda
1½ tsp. vanilla	⅛ tsp. salt
1 egg, beaten	¼ c. butter or regular margarine
1 c. water	1 unbaked 9″ pie shell
1 c. unsifted flour	

Combine ½ c. brown sugar, 1 tblsp. flour, corn syrup, vanilla and egg in 2-qt. saucepan. Slowly stir in water. Cook over medium heat, stirring constantly, until mixture comes to a boil. Let cool.

Combine 1 c. flour, ½ c. brown sugar, cream of tartar, baking soda, salt and butter; mix until crumbly. Pour cooled mixture into pie shell; top with crumbs.

Bake in 350° oven 40 minutes or until golden brown. Makes 6 to 8 servings.

BLACK BOTTOM PIE

At the start of the 20th century Black Bottom Pie, with creamy chocolate- and rum-flavored fillings layered in a pie shell, was the pride of Gulf Coast hostesses. The chocolate filling, spread on the bottom of the pastry shell, gave its name. Hollywood, during the fabulous movie days, adopted Black Bottom

Pie as the dessert of desserts and it reached "big-time." Our recipe produces a pie that wins praises equal to those it received when it was a new dessert star.

BLACK BOTTOM PIE

Enchanting in flavor and intriguing in looks, this pie is a champion among refrigerator pies featuring a vanilla wafer crust

½ c. sugar	1 square unsweetened
2 tblsp. cornstarch	chocolate, melted
¼ tsp. salt	¼ tsp. vanilla
2 eggs, separated	Vanilla Wafer Crumb
2 c. milk	Crust (recipe follows)
1 envelope unflavored	¼ tsp. cream of tartar
gelatin	⅓ c. sugar
3 tblsp. cold water	1 c. heavy cream, whipped
3 tblsp. rum or 2 tsp. rum	Grated chocolate
flavoring	

Prepare Vanilla Wafer Crumb Crust.

Stir together ½ c. sugar, cornstarch and salt in saucepan.

Beat egg yolks slightly; blend in milk. Add to sugar mixture and cook over medium heat, stirring constantly, until mixture comes to a boil. Remove 1 c. custard mixture and set aside.

Soften gelatin in cold water; add to hot mixture in saucepan. Stir to dissolve. Stir in rum. Chill until mixture mounds slightly when dropped from a spoon.

Combine melted chocolate, vanilla and reserved custard mixture. Spread over bottom of Vanilla Wafer Crumb Crust.

Beat egg whites with cream of tartar until foamy. Add ⅓ c. sugar, 1 tblsp. at a time, beating until very stiff peaks form. Fold chilled custard mixture into meringue. Spread over chocolate mixture in pie shell. Chill at least 3 hours or until set.

Within 30 minutes of serving time spread whipped cream evenly over pie. Garnish with grated chocolate. Makes 6 to 8 servings.

Vanilla Wafer Crumb Crust: Combine 1½ c. fine vanilla wafer crumbs and 6 tblsp. melted butter or regular margarine. Press into 9″ pie pan. Chill about 45 minutes or until set. Or bake in 350° oven 10 minutes; cool and chill.

CHOCOLATE/PEANUT PIE

Peanuts are believed to have originated in Brazil, but the pre-Inca Peruvians called them, "ground seeds," as appear on the most ancient Peruvian pottery. And almost every Inca mummy has an accompanying supply of peanuts to help the spirit on its way.

Chocolate/Peanut Pie is rich and delicious. The dessert is at its best when served in small portions, eight to a 9-inch pie, and at the end of a light meal.

CHOCOLATE/PEANUT PIE

Filling bakes into layers with crunchy peanuts forming the top. Peanut and chocolate flavors are unusually harmonious

2 squares unsweetened chocolate	½ c. milk
¼ c. butter or regular margarine	¼ c. light corn syrup
¾ c. sugar	1½ tsp. vanilla
½ c. brown sugar, firmly packed	3 eggs
	1 c. coarsely chopped salted peanuts
	1 unbaked 9″ pie shell

Heat together chocolate and butter in heavy saucepan over low heat just until melted, stirring occasionally. Remove from heat and cool slightly.

Combine sugars, milk, corn syrup, vanilla and eggs in medium bowl. Beat with rotary beater until blended. Beat in chocolate mixture. Stir in peanuts. Pour into pie shell.

Bake in 350° oven 45 to 50 minutes or until knife inserted in center comes out clean. Cool thoroughly. Makes 8 servings.

SAVANNAH PECAN PIE

Early colonists in the South found the tall pecan trees, related to the hickory, growing wild. Indians were pounding the nuts into meal for little cakes and other dishes. They called the nuts pegans, which means bone (hard) shells. They bore little resemblance to today's big, thin-shelled pecans (most of the bitter tannin has been eliminated by breeding) now cultivated in Georgia and Florida west through Texas.

Who baked the first pecan pie no one knows, but the English chess pies apparently were adapted to accommodate the new nuts. Cane syrup and light molasses were sweeteners for the filling. Today corn syrup is generally used. Women throughout American history have substituted ingredients at hand in familiar dishes and thus often create new taste delights.

Our Savannah Pecan Pie is so rich and satisfying that one pie serves eight adequately.

SAVANNAH PECAN PIE

Crisp pastry holds jelly-like filling topped with crisp nuts

3 eggs	6 tblsp. melted butter or
⅔ c. sugar	regular margarine
⅛ tsp. salt	1 c. pecan halves or pieces
1 c. dark corn syrup	1 unbaked 9" pie shell

Beat eggs. Beat in sugar, salt, corn syrup and butter. Add pecans. Pour into unbaked pie shell.

Bake in 350° oven 50 minutes or until knife inserted halfway between center and edge comes out clean. Cool. Makes 8 servings.

FESTIVE PUMPKIN PIE

Even though American Indians never tasted pumpkin pie or saw a jack-o'-lantern before European colonists arrived, practically every tribe grew and ate large quantities of pumpkins and squash. New England Indians considered them almost as important for food as corn and beans. They grew the vegetables around hills of corn.

Different varieties of pumpkins had been enjoyed throughout the Americas for many centuries. On the ceramic ware in graves of Peru's pre-Inca people, much of which is thousands of years old, just about every known variety of squash, including pumpkins, is depicted.

Pumpkin pies were baked in reflector ovens on the kitchen hearth and in fireplace ovens in colonial days. New England women often substituted winter squash for the pumpkin, while in the South sweet potatoes sometimes took the pumpkin role.

Most pumpkin pies today are made with convenient canned pumpkin, although some enthusiastic gardeners grow, cook, and purée the vegetable for their pies. Our Festive Pumpkin Pie is a version of the old-fashioned pie. It is topped with sour cream, sweetened slightly and briefly baked on the pie.

FESTIVE PUMPKIN PIE

Cream cheese is the new note in this all-American treat

1 (8 oz.) pkg. cream cheese, softened	3 eggs
¾ c. brown sugar, firmly packed	1 c. canned pumpkin
	1 c. milk
1 tsp. ground cinnamon	1 tsp. vanilla
½ tsp. ground ginger	1 unbaked 9″ pie shell, edges crimped high
½ tsp. salt	
¼ tsp. ground cloves	1 c. dairy sour cream
	2 tblsp. sugar

Cream together cream cheese, brown sugar, cinnamon, ginger, salt and cloves. Add eggs, one at a time, beating thoroughly after each addition. Blend in pumpkin, milk and vanilla. Pour into pie shell.

Bake in 375° oven 45 to 50 minutes or until knife inserted halfway between center and edge comes out clean.

Blend together sour cream and sugar. Spread over top of pie.

Return pie to oven 3 to 5 minutes or just until topping is set. Chill before serving. Makes 6 to 8 servings.

HARTFORD ELECTION CAKE

Election cakes were sold by New England stores on town meeting days and women vied with one another to bake the best yeast-leavened and fruited cake. The first printed recipe for an election cake appeared in the 1800 second edition of Amelia Simmons' *American Cookery*. Practically all cakes baked in colonial homes and for another half century were yeast-leavened. The bread doughs baked successfully in brick fireplace ovens; besides other leavenings had not been developed.

About 1830, people started to refer to the Hartford Election Cake because politicians there served it to men who voted a straight party ticket. About the only connection it has with politics now is that it and coffee are traditional American refreshments for informal parties on election days.

HARTFORD ELECTION CAKE

This cake is rich, spicy, full of raisins and nuts, and frosted—a big recipe that makes as many as 16 servings

2 pkgs. active dry yeast	1½ tsp. ground cinnamon
1½ c. warm water (110 to 115°)	¼ tsp. ground cloves
2 tsp. sugar	¼ tsp. ground mace
1½ c. sifted flour	½ tsp. ground nutmeg
¾ c. butter or regular margarine	2 eggs
1 c. sugar	1½ c. raisins
3 c. sifted flour	½ c. chopped citron
1 tsp. salt	¾ c. chopped nuts
	Confectioners Sugar Frosting (recipe follows)

Sprinkle yeast on warm water; stir to dissolve. Add 2 tsp. sugar and 1½ c. flour; beat well by hand or 2 minutes with electric mixer at medium speed. Cover and let rise in warm place until bubbly, about 30 minutes.

Meanwhile, cream butter and 1 c. sugar until light and fluffy.

Sift 3 c. flour with salt, cinnamon, cloves, mace and nutmeg.

When yeast mixture is bubbly, add eggs to creamed mixture and beat well. Combine with yeast mixture. Add sifted dry ingredients, a little at a time, beating with spoon after each addition. Beat until smooth.

Stir in raisins, citron and nuts. Pour into well-greased and floured 10″ tube pan. Cover and let rise in warm place until doubled, about 1½ hours.

Bake in 375° oven 1 hour or until done. Cool in pan 5 minutes; turn out on rack to complete cooling. While faintly warm, spread with Confectioners Sugar Frosting. Makes 12 to 16 servings.

Confectioners Sugar Frosting: To 1 c. sifted confectioners sugar add enough milk or light cream to make mixture of spreading consistency. Add ½ tsp. vanilla and dash of salt (or flavor with ½ tsp. lemon juice and ¼ tsp. grated lemon peel). Stir until smooth.

LADY BALTIMORE CAKE

With the arrival of baking powder in 1856, American women had a new incentive for cake baking. That they reached such delicious heights with their productions was an achievement, for their ovens were without reliable heat controls.

The last part of the Victorian era and the first half of the 20th century was the golden age for homemade butter cakes, now known as "from-scratch" cakes to distinguish them from packaged mix cakes. During this period, the oven control regulator was perfected.

Lady Baltimore Cake had its greatest fame during the early 1900s. It had been enjoyed earlier in homes on Maryland's Eastern Shore and Tidewater Virginia but it was in Charleston, South Carolina, that it won wide recognition. At Christmastime hundreds of white boxes carrying tall, round, fragile gift cakes were sent from there to all parts of the country. It was a business in many home kitchens as well as of the Women's Exchange.

Thousands of homes across country prized their own recipes for this special-occasion cake. In some respects the cakes were alike. They were delicate white layer cakes with sides and tops covered with a cooked white frosting. Fillings varied, but most mixed some of the white frosting with such goodies as nuts, chopped raisins and soft dried figs. Sometimes there were two layers, often three. Our Lady Baltimore Cake meets all the criteria of this immortal cake.

LADY BALTIMORE CAKE

Delicate cake layers with fluffy, fruited frosting

2¼ c. sifted cake flour	1½ c. sugar
3½ tsp. baking powder	2 tsp. light corn syrup
1 tsp. salt	⅓ c. cold water
1½ c. sugar	Dash of salt
½ c. shortening	1 tsp. vanilla
1 c. milk	½ c. finely chopped nuts
1½ tsp. vanilla	½ c. raisins, cut up
4 egg whites	½ c. dried figs, cut in strips
2 egg whites	1 c. frosting

Sift together cake flour, baking powder and salt into large mixer bowl. Add 1½ c. sugar, shortening, ⅔ c. milk and 1½ tsp. vanilla. Blend 30 seconds at low speed, scraping bowl constantly. Beat at high speed 2 minutes, scraping bowl occasionally. Add remaining milk and 4 egg whites. Continue beating at high speed 2 minutes. Spread into 2 greased and floured 8 or 9" round layer cake pans.

Bake in 350° oven 30 to 35 minutes or until done. Cool in pans on racks 5 minutes. Cover another rack with a towel; place towel side down over one cake pan; invert and remove pan. Place original rack on bottom of layer and turn again. Repeat with other cake layer. Cool completely with top side of cake up.

To make frosting combine 2 egg whites, 1½ c. sugar, corn syrup, water and dash of salt in top of double boiler. Blend 30 seconds at low speed with electric mixer. Place over boiling water, making sure bottom of pan does not touch water. Cook, beating constantly at high speed, about 7 minutes or until stiff peaks form. Remove from heat and add 1 tsp. vanilla. If desired, for easier beating, turn into mixing bowl. Continue beating until of spreading consistency. Set aside 1 c. frosting for filling.

To make filling, combine nuts, raisins and figs. Stir in 1 c. frosting.

Spread filling between cooled cake layers. Cover sides and top of cake with frosting. Makes 12 servings.

DELUXE POUND CAKE

This rich, buttery cake was originally English but it is now truly a traditional southern specialty. At Christmastime, there is always a sugar-dusted pound cake on the buffet table along with a bowl of thick, creamy eggnog.

DELUXE POUND CAKE

Excellent, fine-textured pound cake with a buttery flavor

2 c. butter (1 lb.)	**4 c. sifted cake flour**
3 c. sugar	**⅔ c. milk**
6 eggs	**Confectioners sugar**
1½ tsp. vanilla	

Cream together butter and sugar until light and fluffy. Add eggs, one at a time, beating well after each addition. Add vanilla. (Total beating time: 10 minutes.)

Add cake flour alternately with milk, beating well after each addition. Pour batter into well-greased 10″ fluted tube pan.

Bake in 350° oven 1 hour 30 minutes or until cake tests done. (If you use a dark-colored fluted tube pan, reduce temperature to 325°.)

Cool in pan on rack 15 minutes. Remove from pan; cool on rack. Dust with confectioners sugar. Makes 12 servings.

Note: Cake is best if covered and allowed to stand for 24 hours before serving.

LEMON ANGEL REFRIGERATOR CAKE

Original American cakes appeared for the most part after the middle of the 19th century. During the late 17th and 18th centuries large fruitcakes were mixed in the kitchens of the more affluent families and taken to the bake shop for baking. Later settlers from Europe brought their cake recipes, usually for sponge and pound cakes. Then the first angel food cakes were made—this American, soufflé-like cake has had great popularity ever since.

Today this favorite cake usually is made with a packaged mix. Not only does the mix reduce the work and time required to bake a tall and handsome angel food cake, but it does away with the problem of all those leftover egg yolks.

When baking angel food cakes became easier, women began to make other desserts with the cake as a base. Lemon Angel Refrigerator Cake is an example. Lemon Angel consists of angel food cake with lemon custard, combined, molded and chilled in a tube pan. Before serving, you frost it with whipped cream.

LEMON ANGEL REFRIGERATOR CAKE

Hostesses like this yellow and white cake dessert because they can prepare it a day ahead, except for frosting

1 envelope unflavored gelatin	¾ c. lemon juice
¼ c. water	1 (10″) angel food cake
6 eggs, separated	¾ c. sugar
¾ c. sugar	1 c. heavy cream
2 tsp. grated lemon peel	1 tblsp. confectioners sugar

Soften gelatin in cold water.

Beat 6 egg yolks slightly in heavy saucepan. Add ¾ c. sugar, lemon peel and juice. Cook over low heat, stirring constantly, until mixture coats spoon and is slightly thickened. Remove from heat. Add gelatin; stir until dissolved. Cool to room temperature.

Meanwhile, rub surface of cake with hands to remove brown crumbs. Tear cake into bite-size pieces.

Beat egg whites until soft peaks form. Gradually add ¾ c. sugar, beating until stiff peaks form. Fold cooled custard into egg whites. Pour ½" layer of custard into buttered 10" tube pan. Add a layer of angel food pieces, then custard. Continue alternating layers, ending with custard. Chill at least 6 hours, or overnight, until firm. Unmold on round platter.

Whip cream with confectioners sugar. Spread over sides and top of cake. Makes 12 to 16 servings.

BOSTON CHOCOLATE CREAM PIE

When is a pie a cake? When it is Boston cream pie. It consists of two layers of a two-egg cake put together with a delicate custard filling and topped with chocolate frosting. Omit the frosting and sprinkle the top layer with confectioners sugar and you have another version. Some women gave the top a fancy design by sprinkling the confectioners sugar through a paper lace doily placed on top.

Keep Boston Chocolate Cream Pie with its custard filling in the refrigerator until serving time. Or make the cake part ahead (freezes too) and add the custard shortly before serving.

BOSTON CHOCOLATE CREAM PIE

This dessert is old enough to be new to many young families

1¼ c. sifted flour	Dash of salt
2 tsp. baking powder	1 egg, slightly beaten
¼ tsp. salt	½ tsp. vanilla
⅓ c. butter or regular margarine	2 tblsp. butter or regular margarine
¾ c. sugar	1 square unsweetened chocolate
2 eggs	
1 tsp. vanilla	2 tblsp. light cream or milk
½ c. milk	1¼ c. sifted confectioners sugar
1 c. light cream	
¼ c. sugar	½ tsp. vanilla
3 tblsp. flour	

Sift together 1¼ c. flour, baking powder and ¼ tsp. salt.

Cream ⅓ c. butter in small mixer bowl; gradually beat in ¾ c. sugar. Beat in 2 eggs, one at a time, beating well after each addition. Beat until mixture is light and fluffy. Beat in 1 tsp. vanilla. Stir in dry ingredients by hand alternately with milk. Spread in 2 greased and paper-lined 8″ layer cake pans.

Bake in 375° oven 20 to 25 minutes. Cool on racks 5 minutes; remove from pans. Cool thoroughly.

Meanwhile, scald 1 c. light cream. Combine ¼ c. sugar, 3 tblsp. flour and dash of salt in double boiler top. Gradually stir in scalded cream. Slowly stir hot mixture into 1 beaten egg. Cook over boiling water, stirring constantly, until mixture thickens. Remove from heat and stir in ½ tsp. vanilla. Cool custard thoroughly.

To make frosting, combine 2 tblsp. butter, chocolate and 2 tblsp. cream in small saucepan. Cook over medium heat until butter and chocolate are melted. Remove from heat. Add sugar and vanilla; beat until smooth and of spreading consistency.

To assemble Boston Chocolate Cream Pie, spread cooled filling between cooled cake layers. Spread chocolate frosting over top of pie. Refrigerate until serving time. Makes 12 servings.

PUMPKIN SPICE CAKE

American Indians made many dishes with pumpkins which they grew on tribal lands. While pumpkin pies took first place with early European settlers, pumpkin cakes also became popular a century and a half ago. The best compliment a woman received for her cake was: "It tastes like pumpkin pie."

Our Pumpkin Spice Cake is a recent recipe made with a packaged spice cake mix and canned pumpkin. The ease and speed with which you can bake this excellent cake would make a colonial woman marvel. She not only grew, cooked and strained the pumpkin, but she added it to a spice cake she made from scratch. No pumpkin cake ever tasted better than our short-cut version.

PUMPKIN SPICE CAKE

A rich, cheese frosting enhances the good pumpkin-pie taste

1 (18½ oz.) pkg. spice cake mix	2 eggs
	⅓ c. water
1 (1 lb.) can pumpkin	Cream Cheese Frosting
2 tsp. baking soda	(recipe follows)

Combine cake mix, pumpkin, baking soda, eggs and water in large mixer bowl. Beat as directed on cake-mix package. Spread in 2 greased and floured 9″ round layer cake pans.

Bake in 350° oven 25 to 30 minutes. Let cool 10 minutes, then turn out of pans. Cool.

Spread Cream Cheese Frosting between layers, then frost sides and top of cake. Makes 12 servings.

Cream Cheese Frosting: Cream together ½ c. butter or regular margarine, 1 (8 oz.) pkg. cream cheese and 1 tsp. vanilla until light and fluffy. Gradually add 1 lb. box sifted confectioners sugar, beating well after each addition. If mixture is too thick to spread, add a small amount of milk.

HONEYED GINGERBREAD

Honey, molasses and maple syrup were the most used sweetenings in colonial days. Early Americans watched the flights of wild bees and tried to chart them hoping they would lead to hollow "bee trees," where bees stored honey. Soon they began to domesticate bees into hives.

Plantations in the West Indies used manufacturing methods that could not extract all the sucrose from sugar cane juices. What was left they sold as molasses. It was inexpensive in comparison to costly white and brown sugars. American traders brought home barrels of molasses and the taste lingers especially in New England.

Molasses and honey are both ingredients in Honeyed Gingerbread. Lighter in color than many gingerbreads and mildly spiced, it is a soft gingerbread created in early America. European gingerbreads then were hard. For more than a century people considered gingerbread a hot bread to serve with butter, but today it often is a dessert with a variety of toppings, such as frosting, sweet sauce, whipped cream, ice cream and whipped dessert topping.

HONEYED GINGERBREAD

Easy-to-make, one-bowl gingerbread—heavenly taste

2¼ c. sifted flour	½ c. light molasses
⅓ c. sugar	½ c. honey
1 tsp. baking soda	¾ c. hot water
1 tsp. ground ginger	½ c. shortening
1 tsp. ground cinnamon	1 egg
¼ tsp. salt	

Sift together flour, sugar, baking soda, ginger, cinnamon and salt into large mixer bowl. Add molasses, honey, hot water, shortening and egg. Beat at low speed 30 seconds, scraping bowl constantly. Beat at medium speed 3 minutes, scraping bowl occasionally. Turn into greased 9" square pan.

Bake in 325° oven 50 to 55 minutes or until cake tests done. Serve warm. Makes 9 servings.

BLACK WALNUT BARS

Native black walnuts, once plentiful in the woods, contribute unique flavor to many foods. Since there are not enough black walnut trees now to meet the demands of the increased population, they are high-priced. Cracking and picking out the meat is a time-consuming job, but well worth it as evidenced by the many recipes from different parts of the country.

Some of the black walnut favorites are: On the Missouri-Kansas line, luscious black walnut pie, in the Ozarks, black walnut muffins; in Tennessee, sweet potato balls with black walnuts, rolled in crushed cornflakes and baked; Hoosier sweet sauces (butterscotch, caramel and chocolate) on ice cream and sprinkled with chopped black walnuts; in Pennsylvania Dutch country, loaf cakes, cookies, gingerbread and baked meringues all containing black walnuts; and in Iowa, fudge and brownies with black walnuts.

This recipe for Black Walnut Bars is from Iowa.

BLACK WALNUT BARS

The crisp bottom of the cookies is buttery and caramel flavored

2 c. sifted flour	2 tsp. vanilla
1 c. brown sugar, firmly packed	2 tblsp. flour
	½ tsp. baking powder
1 c. butter or regular margarine	½ tsp. salt
	2 c. chopped black walnuts
4 eggs	
2 c. brown sugar, firmly packed	

Mix together 2 c. flour and 1 c. brown sugar in large bowl. Cut in butter until crumbs form. Press into well-greased 15½ ×10½ ×1″ jelly roll pan. Bake in 350° oven 10 minutes. Remove from oven and cool slightly, about 10 minutes. Turn oven temperature to 375°.

Beat eggs until light. Gradually beat in 2 c. brown sugar, then vanilla.

Stir together 2 tblsp. flour, baking powder and salt. Add to egg mixture along with nuts. Spread over baked crust in pan.

Bake in 375° oven about 20 minutes or until light brown. Cool in pan on rack. Cut in 2×1″ bars. Makes 5 dozen.

SNICKERDOODLES

Inventors of old-time recipes used imagination in naming them that present-day food writers and editors sometimes envy. Who could think up a more unforgettable name for cookies than Snickerdoodles? Our recipe is similar to one used in New

England and Pennsylvania Dutch kitchens before baking powder was discovered—baking soda and cream of tartar are the leavening. Originally, hickory nuts frequently were added to the dough.

Balls of the cookie dough, rolled in cinnamon mixed with sugar, puff up in the oven, but settle down to crisp cookies with crinkly tops. When made into small balls these are light and dainty enough to serve at tea parties, or with ice cream.

SNICKERDOODLES

A splendid example of economical cookies that taste wonderful

½ c. butter or regular margarine, softened	2¾ c. sifted flour
	2 tsp. cream of tartar
½ c. shortening	1 tsp. baking soda
1½ c. sugar	¼ tsp. salt
2 eggs	3 tblsp. sugar
1 tsp. vanilla	3 tblsp. ground cinnamon

Mix together butter and shortening. Beat in 1½ c. sugar, eggs and vanilla.

Sift together flour, cream of tartar, baking soda and salt. Blend into creamed mixture. Shape rounded teaspoons of dough into balls.

Combine 3 tblsp. sugar and cinnamon; roll balls in mixture. Place 2″ apart on ungreased baking sheets.

Bake in 400° oven 8 to 10 minutes or until golden brown. Remove from baking sheets; cool on racks. Makes about 6 dozen.

CHOCOLATE CHIP/PEANUT COOKIES

Drop cookies dotted with chocolate were the talk of women's groups in the 1930s. The goodies were called Toll House Chocolate Chip Cookies, which indicates where they first were baked. When the Massachusetts home economist who operated the Toll House Restaurant found she was out of raisins to add to her cookie dough, she reached in desperation for a bar of chocolate, cut bits from it, stirred them into the dough and baked the cookies. When guests exclaimed over their tastiness and asked for more, she knew her improvisation was a winner. Enterprising food processors soon introduced packages of chocolate pieces to grocery stores.

Peanuts, grown extensively in the southeastern states for years, assume the role of nuts in our recipe. These beans (peanuts are not nuts, but legumes) are less expensive than nuts. They add the crunchiness that nuts, such as pecans and walnuts, provided in the first chocolate chip cookies.

CHOCOLATE CHIP/PEANUT COOKIES

The Americas gave the world chocolate and peanuts. Their flavors blend beautifully in these favorite cookies

½ c. butter or regular margarine
½ c. sugar
¼ c. brown sugar, firmly packed
1 egg
1 tsp. vanilla

1 c. sifted flour
½ tsp. salt
½ tsp. baking soda
1 (6 oz.) pkg. semisweet chocolate pieces
½ c. coarsely chopped, toasted, salted peanuts

Cream together butter, sugars, egg and vanilla until light and fluffy.

Sift together flour, salt and soda. Add to creamed mixture, blending well. Stir in chocolate and peanuts. Drop by teaspoonfuls about 2″ apart on greased baking sheets.

Bake in 375° oven 10 to 12 minutes or until golden brown. Remove from baking sheets; cool on racks. Makes about 3 dozen.

FROSTED DIAMONDS

Although cookie baking flourishes throughout the year in the Bethlehem, Pennsylvania region, the campaign swings into full tilt as Christmas approaches. To ancestors of the Moravians, who founded the city on Christmas Eve 1741, the holiday always has had special importance. And Christmas cookie baking became a custom that thrives today.

Many Bethlehem households have a collection of cookie cutters, some of them antiques, that produce cookies of different sizes and shapes. They represent dolls, houses, eagles, sitting cats, dogs, fish, horses, men on horseback, birds, chickens, bells, stars, angels, camels, sheep, shepherds, Santa Claus and Christmas trees.

Frosted Diamonds sometimes are called Moravian Scotch cookies. The dough traditionally is cut in diamond shapes either with a cutter or knife. If you like the taste of caraway seeds, these cookies are for you.

FROSTED DIAMONDS

Pink sugar decorates tops of these thin cookies frosted white

¼ c. butter or regular
  margarine
¼ c. shortening
½ c. sugar
2 eggs
1 tsp. vanilla
3 c. sifted flour

⅛ tsp. salt
1 tsp. caraway seeds
White Mountain Frosting
  (recipe follows)
¼ c. coarse pink decorating
  sugar

Beat butter and shortening until light; gradually add sugar, and beat until mixture is fluffy. Beat in eggs and vanilla, blending thoroughly.

Sift together flour and salt; add to creamed mixture. Stir in caraway seeds.

Roll dough thin, not more than ⅛", and cut in 2" diamonds with sharp knife or cookie cutter. Place ½" apart on lightly greased baking sheet.

Bake in 325° oven 10 to 12 minutes. Remove from baking sheets and cool on racks. Spread cookies with White Mountain Frosting; sprinkle with pink sugar. Makes about 6½ dozen.

White Mountain Frosting: Combine 1 c. sugar, ⅛ tsp. cream of tartar and ¼ c. water in small saucepan. Place over heat and stir until sugar dissolves. Continue cooking to soft ball stage (236°) on candy thermometer.

Meanwhile, add ⅛ tsp. salt to 1 egg white; beat until stiff. Pour hot syrup in a fine stream into egg white, beating constantly until frosting is of spreading consistency.

SPICED CHRISTMAS COOKIES

In Bethlehem, Pennsylvania, families on Christmas Eve visit from one home to another to exchange greetings and see the "putz" or Nativity scene. People there call the custom "putzing." Hostesses on these occasions pass a variety of homemade cookies to their callers. Two kinds of cookies usually are a tempting tradition—brown cookies and white cookies. Spiced Christmas Cookies are the brown special.

SPICED CHRISTMAS COOKIES

Big recipe—you can cut it in half and still have a lot of cookies to share with family and friends

½ c. butter or regular margarine	2 tblsp. light cream or dairy half-and-half
½ c. shortening	5 c. sifted flour
1½ c. brown sugar, firmly packed	1 tblsp. ground cinnamon
2 c. molasses	1½ tsp. ground ginger
	½ tsp. ground cloves

Cream together butter and shortening; gradually add sugar, beating until light and fluffy. Beat in molasses; blend in cream.

Sift together flour, cinnamon, ginger and cloves; stir into creamed mixture. Store in covered bowl in refrigerator overnight.

Roll dough thin, using floured pastry cloth on board and rolling pin. Cut in animal shapes. Place 1 to 1½" apart on greased baking sheets.

Bake in 350° oven 10 to 12 minutes. Remove from baking sheets and cool on racks. Makes 19 dozen.

WHITE CHRISTMAS COOKIES

Tradition in Bethlehem, Pennsylvania, decrees that White Christmas Cookies be thin and cut in fancy shapes, with the star most frequently used. Instead of rolling the soft dough, some women today find it easier to shape the dough in rolls, chill it overnight, slice and bake. Sliced or rolled, the cookies are best paper-thin.

WHITE CHRISTMAS COOKIES

These crisp, spicy cookies are straw-colored despite their name; cut the recipe in half for a smaller batch

½ c. butter or regular margarine	4 eggs, beaten
½ c. shortening	4 c. sifted flour
2 c. sugar	⅛ tsp. ground nutmeg
	⅛ tsp. ground cinnamon

Cream together butter and shortening; gradually add sugar, beating until light and fluffy. Beat in eggs.

Sift together flour, nutmeg and cinnamon; stir into creamed mixture (dough should be stiff). Store in covered bowl in refrigerator overnight.

Roll dough very thin, using floured pastry cloth on board and rolling pin. Cut in star shapes. Place 1 to 1½" apart on greased baking sheets.

Bake in 350° oven 10 to 12 minutes or until crisp and straw-colored. Remove from baking sheets and cool on racks. Makes 16 dozen.

OZARK APPLE PUDDING

Apples are important in Ozark country. Many of the recipes featuring them came from people of Anglo-Saxon stock who settled in the region before the War Between the States. Ozark Apple Pudding attracted much attention when the recipe for it was circulating across country during the 1940s. Our recipe is a big one—it makes 8 servings.

OZARK APPLE PUDDING

A distinctive feature of this pudding is that it contains no shortening. At its best served warm, topped with vanilla ice cream

1 c. sugar	3 c. chopped pared apples
2 eggs	½ c. chopped pecans
1½ tsp. vanilla	Whipped cream, whipped
⅓ c. flour	dessert topping or ice
1 tblsp. baking powder	cream
⅛ tsp. salt	

Combine sugar, eggs and vanilla; beat until thick. Stir in flour, baking powder, salt, apples and pecans. Spread in greased and floured 9" square pan.

Bake in 325° oven 30 to 35 minutes. Serve warm with whipped cream. Makes 8 servings.

RHUBARB BREAD PUDDING

Scraps of leftover homemade bread, honestly called stale, were a treasured ingredient in many early American dishes. Exquisite bread puddings of many flavors and descriptions were among them.

Rhubarb Bread Pudding is a classic example of a favorite country meal ending. The recipe went West in covered wagons for pioneer women to use with the first pink rhubarb stalks in their new gardens. It was the kind of food mothers made for their children to signal the long winter had ended.

RHUBARB BREAD PUDDING

Make this with firm bread more nearly like the old-time home-made. Some of today's breads in supermarkets contain chemicals that make the loaves softer, with less body

4 c. diced rhubarb	¼ c. chopped nuts (optional)
3½ c. bread cubes	¼ c. melted butter or
1⅓ c. sugar	regular margarine
½ tsp. ground nutmeg	Cream, whipped cream or
½ tsp. ground cinnamon	vanilla ice cream

Toss together rhubarb, bread cubes, sugar, nutmeg, cinnamon, nuts and melted butter in mixing bowl. Turn into greased 2-qt. casserole.

Cover and bake in 375° oven 45 minutes. Remove cover; continue baking 10 minutes. Serve warm or cold with cream. Makes 6 servings.

SNOW CUSTARDS

While snow custards had their beginning in colonial years, they are new to many people today. Many distinguished guests feasted on this simple, luscious dessert at candlelighted tables in Mount Vernon and Monticello, the elegant plantation homes of George Washington and Thomas Jefferson.

Victorian hostesses called the custards Floating Islands. Almost every farm produced ample milk and eggs for such desserts.

Old, handwritten recipes call for the meringues to be cooked in scalding milk, which then was used to make the custard. A better and easier way, now that ovens are heat-controlled, is to spoon the fluffy egg whites into custard cups and bake them.

SNOW CUSTARDS

Baked meringues are inverted on custards; float like fairy islands

4 eggs, separated	3 c. milk
¼ tsp. cream of tartar	2 eggs
Dash of salt	½ c. sugar
½ c. sugar	Dash of salt
½ tsp. vanilla	1½ tsp. vanilla

Combine egg whites, cream of tartar and dash of salt in large mixer bowl. Beat at high speed until soft peaks form. Gradually add ½ c. sugar, beating until stiff peaks form. Add ½ tsp. vanilla. Spoon meringue into six 5-oz. custard cups which have been buttered and coated with sugar. With a knife, press mixture gently into cups to remove air pockets. Place in shallow pan containing 1″ hot water.

Bake in 350° oven about 15 minutes or until lightly browned. Place on wire rack. Unmold meringues at once, browned side down, into individual serving dishes or 13×9×2″ pan sprinkled with sugar. Cool and chill.

Place milk in top of double boiler; heat over direct heat until bubbles form around edge.

Meanwhile, beat together egg yolks, eggs, ½ c. sugar and dash of salt. Gradually pour hot milk into egg mixture, beating constantly (a wire whisk is useful). Return mixture to top of double boiler. Cook over hot, not boiling, water. Stir constantly until custard coats a metal spoon. Place top of double boiler in cold water at once and stir to cool custard. Stir in 1½ tsp. vanilla. Chill.

To serve, spoon ½ c. custard around meringue "islands" in individual dishes. Or chill custard in large serving bowl, and just before serving top with meringues that were chilled in pan. Makes 6 servings.

CHERRY CRISP

Oh to be in Michigan when May is here! The concentration of cherry trees around Traverse City is a sight to behold. Pie made with tart cherries probably has been a great American dessert since the days of the Virginia boy's "truth" legend. There are other cherry specials, such as puddings, fritters, cakes, muffins, preserves, salads, sauces, cider, tarts, upside-down cakes, cobblers and the easiest of all, cherry crisps. Cherry Crisp takes about 10 minutes to get ready for the oven, 30 minutes for baking. It is equally good served warm or cold.

CHERRY CRISP

Keep a can of cherry pie filling for this short-notice dessert

1 (1 lb. 5 oz.) can cherry
  pie filling
¾ c. quick-cooking rolled
  oats
⅔ c. brown sugar, firmly
  packed
½ c. flour

¾ tsp. ground cinnamon
½ c. butter or regular
  margarine
Whipped cream, whipped
  dessert topping or vanilla
  ice cream

Place cherry pie filling in greased 8″ square pan.

Combine oats, brown sugar, flour and cinnamon. Cut in butter. Sprinkle mixture evenly over cherries.

Bake in 375° oven about 30 minutes or until topping is golden. Serve warm with whipped cream. Makes 6 servings.

BLUEBERRY CRISP

These little, native, dark berries dusted with soft blue color were—and are—great favorites. The long season encourages their wide use. They grow from the Virginia mountains, where they ripen first, through Pennsylvania and New England in summer and then to northern Maine and Canada. Blueberry country also includes northern Michigan, Wisconsin and Minnesota, as families who combine fishing trips with blueberry picking know so well. They also know how good blueberry pancakes cooked on a camp stove taste in the cool, early morning.

Blueberry Crisp is a simple, easy dessert. Most people today make it with cultivated berries available across country in supermarkets. The berries are juicy, and in this dessert a small amount of tapioca thickens the juice.

BLUEBERRY CRISP

Use fresh or frozen blueberries, wild or cultivated, and serve the dessert hot or cold with vanilla ice cream

4 c. fresh or frozen
  unsweetened blueberries
2 tblsp. tapioca
⅓ c. sugar
1 tblsp. lemon juice
½ tsp. grated lemon peel
⅔ c. brown sugar, firmly
  packed
¾ c. quick-cooking rolled
  oats

½ c. flour
½ tsp. ground cinnamon
⅛ tsp. salt
6 tblsp. butter or regular
  margarine
Cream, whipped cream or
  vanilla ice cream
  (optional)

Stir together blueberries, tapioca, sugar, lemon juice and peel. Place in greased 8″ square pan.

Combine brown sugar, rolled oats, flour, cinnamon and salt. Cut in butter. Sprinkle over blueberries.

Bake in 375° oven 40 minutes. Serve with cream, if desired. Makes 6 servings.

CHRISTMAS AMBROSIA

Among the Christmas delights in the Old South was a simple dessert of peeled and sectioned or sliced oranges, layered in a bowl with freshly grated coconut. It was properly named ambrosia.

Trading ships more than 200 years ago delivered coconuts from the Caribbean Islands to such cities as Savannah and Charleston. Combined with oranges introduced from Spain, the dessert's fame spread to all parts of the South. It became popular in other areas after packaged, shredded coconut became available.

Every old cookbook of the South contains at least one recipe for ambrosia. Here is a typical one from a Savannah cookbook: "Bowls of ambrosia are a sign of the holidays and company. A layer of sliced oranges, a light sprinkling of sugar and a layer of grated coconut and so on, ad infinitum, depending on the size of the bowl and the company. If a little wine is poured over all, it is even better."

Traditional ambrosia is a holiday special today outside the South as well. Through the years other fruits such as fresh or canned pineapple, sliced bananas, dates, grapefruit sections and frozen strawberries have been added. Most Southerners consider such additions rank intruders.

CHRISTMAS AMBROSIA

This recipe for Christmas Ambrosia calls for bananas and convenient canned, flaked coconut, garnished with maraschino cherries

6 oranges
3 bananas, sliced
1 (3½ oz.) can flaked
    coconut

Maraschino cherries
    (optional)

Peel oranges; cut crosswise in thin slices. Place half of orange slices in serving bowl. Top with banana slices and half of coconut. Top with remaining orange slices, then remaining coconut. Garnish with maraschino cherries, if desired. Refrigerate several hours. Makes 8 servings.

VIRGINIA PEANUT BRITTLE

In Virginia, the Carolinas, Georgia, northern Florida and other places where peanuts grow, little boys in summertime once hawked boiled peanuts along the streets. "Dee-licious boiled peanuts," they cried. These regional treats were green peanuts, shells and all, cooked in salted water.

The peanut snack that people across country can enjoy today is peanut brittle. Virginia Peanut Brittle is the choice of many wives of peanut growers in the Old Dominion. They claim raw peanuts make the best candy, but you can use roasted ones.

VIRGINIA PEANUT BRITTLE

Crushed and sprinkled over vanilla ice cream, this brittle adds a crisp, sweet, nutty taste

2 c. sugar	¼ tsp. salt
1 c. light corn syrup	1 tsp. butter or regular
1 c. water	margarine
2 c. unroasted peanuts, cut in pieces	¼ tsp. baking soda

Combine sugar, corn syrup and water in 12″ heavy skillet. Cook slowly over medium heat, stirring constantly, until sugar is dissolved. Continue cooking until mixture reaches soft ball stage (236°) on candy thermometer.

Add peanuts and salt; cook to just beyond the soft crack stage (290 to 300°). Add butter and baking soda, stirring to blend (mixture will foam).

Pour onto 2 large, buttered baking sheets or 2 large, inverted, buttered pans. Lift candy around edges with spatula and run spatula under candy to cool it partially and keep it from sticking. While candy is still warm, but firm, turn it over and pull edges to make the brittle thinner in the center. When cold, break into pieces with knife handle. Makes about 2¼ pounds.

CARAMEL CORN WITH NUTS

Watching Indians pop corn for the first time must have filled the colonists with wonder. Practically all Indian tribes grew several varieties of corn, including one or two that popped over embers. The Cherokees and Senecas, who were good farmers, cultivated as many as a dozen kinds. Early Americans first ate popped corn plain, but soon they served it as a cereal with milk. The Pennsylvania Dutch created a popcorn soup. And popped corn and cranberries were strung to decorate Christmas trees.

Later a hot syrup made with molasses and sugar was poured over popped corn, which was shaped into balls—a holiday treat children adored. As sugar became more plentiful and less expensive, other ingredients were added to the fluffy kernels. Caramel Corn with Nuts is an outgrowth of the early popcorn balls—a company-best version.

CARAMEL CORN WITH NUTS

Substitute toasted pecans for almonds in this American snack

1 c. blanched, whole almonds
2½ qts. popped corn
2½ c. brown sugar, firmly packed
½ c. dark corn syrup
½ c. water
½ tsp. salt
¼ c. butter or regular margarine
2 tsp. vanilla

Lightly toast almonds in shallow pan in 325° oven 12 to 15 minutes, stirring occasionally. Combine with popcorn in large ovenproof bowl and keep warm in 200° oven.

Combine brown sugar, corn syrup, water and salt in heavy 3-qt. saucepan. Bring to a full, rolling boil. Add butter; cook over medium heat to very hard ball stage (266°). Remove from heat; stir in vanilla. Immediately pour in steady stream over popcorn and nuts, stirring to coat evenly. Turn out on large piece of oiled aluminum foil. Pull apart with two forks to make 3" clusters. Makes about 3½ dozen.

CRANBERRY/GINGER SHERBET

Although the Indians prepared cranberries in many ways, women in colonial days were so pleased with the ruby sauce made from the ripe fruit that they did not branch out much farther. About 50 years ago exploration of uses for cranberries in home kitchens became popular. Among the new dishes was cranberry sherbet.

Hostesses sometimes garnished fruit salads and fruit plates with it for party luncheons. The color and refreshing flavor of the sherbet earned it a place in the main course of many special-occasion meals, especially turkey and chicken dinners.

Cranberry/Ginger Sherbet pampers the flavors of meats and poultry so successfully that the custom of serving such sherbets with them deserves revival, especially since electric beaters and freezers make easy work of preparing them at home.

CRANBERRY/GINGER SHERBET

Makes a colorful dessert especially good with coconut cake

4 c. cranberries	**1 tsp. unflavored gelatin**
2 c. water	**2 c. ginger ale**
2 c. sugar	

Combine cranberries and water; cook uncovered until skins burst. Press mixture through a sieve or food mill.

Meanwhile, combine sugar and gelatin; add to hot cranberry mixture. Stir until sugar and gelatin are dissolved. Cool to room temperature. Add ginger ale. Pour into 9″ square pan. Place in freezer until almost frozen.

Break mixture into chunks and place in chilled mixer bowl. Beat smooth. Return to pan or paper cups. Freeze firm. Serve as dessert or with main dish. Makes 5 cups.

HOT FUDGE SUNDAE SAUCE

Boston is the undisputed home of the bean and the cod, but ice cream devotees there are exceptionally proud also that the first hot fudge sundae originated in Boston—about 1900. The dessert quickly won favor in many states and countries. The woman who created the sundae, a proper Bostonian, insisted that the hot, thick chocolate sauce should cover the top of the vanilla ice cream and spill a little bit over the silver-footed dessert dish in which she served it.

Hot Fudge Sundae Sauce is easy to make. In our recipe evaporated milk helps insure a glossy, satiny smooth sauce. Ladled over scoops of vanilla ice cream, the thick sauce tastes so good that people forget calorie counting.

HOT FUDGE SUNDAE SAUCE

Keep a jar of the sauce in the refrigerator ready to reheat over hot water or very low heat

1 (14½ oz.) can evaporated milk	¼ c. butter or regular margarine
2 c. sugar	1½ tsp. vanilla
4 squares unsweetened chocolate	¼ tsp. salt

Combine milk and sugar in saucepan. Bring to a full, rolling boil, stirring constantly. Boil, stirring, 1 minute. Add chocolate; stir until melted. Beat over heat until smooth. Remove from heat and stir in butter, vanilla and salt. Serve hot or cold over ice cream or other desserts. Store in refrigerator. Makes about 3 cups.

Chapter 2

SOUTHWESTERN SPECIALTIES

Tomato salad, chocolate cake, avocado or chili-bean dip with corn chips—these are all treats that depend on foods grown and enjoyed in Mexico for centuries.

People in the Southwest eat the same foods as do Americans living in other parts of the country, but they particularly like many dishes inspired by south-of-the-border neighbors, and Indians who still live in the area. The recipes in this section of our cookbook are for these specialties, which are gaining acceptance in all parts of our country.

New Mexico and Arizona are the heart of the Southwest, flanked on one side by Texas, on the other by California with the southern third of Colorado also included. Once this area of lofty mountains, fertile green valleys, big ranches and deserts bathed in sunshine was all a part of Mexico. Europeans—Spaniards— explored the region years before the *Mayflower* reached our shores.

Some of the Indians in the Southwest are descendants of the tribes who lived in pueblos and farmed surrounding acres. They have modernized their dishes to fit life today. Recipes for some of their favorites appear on the following pages. Other people in this region, some of whom are ranchers, proudly trace their ancestry to early Spanish settlers, while other Southwesterners crossed over the border to become citizens of the United States. All have helped popularize dishes from Spanish and Mexican kitchens. Many of these have become popular in the West and Middle West. And there are those who predict that Mexican influence will increase in American cooking in the future.

Mexico has one of the most distinguished cuisines in the world and one of the oldest and largest—an estimated 2000 dishes. The rich variety of native foods, many of which now are grown and enjoyed around the world, has contributed to its continuing success.

Indians in Mexico, Central America and northern South America built remarkable civilizations before the Spanish conquistadors arrived early in the 16th century. Many foods, such as corn, beans and squash, were developed from wild plants by the Incas, Mayans, Aztecs and other Indian tribes before Columbus was born.

Other native foods from this early period include tomatoes, potatoes, sweet potatoes, chilies, peanuts, chocolate, avocados and vanilla. Turkeys also were domesticated in Mexico and our Thanksgiving birds are descendants of them. The American wild turkey has never been domesticated successfully. Americans have added their own touches to these foods of Mexican origin.

During the Spanish colonial era in Mexico, which started in the first half of the 16th century, cattle, hogs, sheep and wheat were introduced. The Spaniards also brought cuttings of olives, oranges, peaches, apricots, figs and almonds and planted them. They took back with them what they considered strange foods and introduced them to the Old World.

Southwesterners like the taste of chilies, which they call chili peppers. The sharpness of their flavor reminded the Spaniards of pepper, then obtained in Europe from the Orient. It was one of the spices that lured Columbus and other explorers to attempt to find a short route to the Indies. This explains why they called the vegetable chili peppers. Use of chilies for seasoning is one reason southwestern cooking is different.

Americans commonly use chili powder, made from the dried

pods, for seasoning. And perhaps the most famous dish that it seasons is chili con carne (see Index for American Chili). The hotness of the recipe varies to some extent with the place where it is served, and also from family to family. Practically everyone agrees that chili powder is used more generously in Texas than elsewhere in the Southwest and that the farther from its area of origin the recipe is prepared, the less highly seasoned it becomes.

Canned green chilies are being introduced into more supermarkets every year. As a result, recipes so seasoned are more widely used. One splendid example of the green chili recipes is Alamosa Corn Muffins (see Index).

Among other highly prized imports from Mexico are corn tortillas, those thin, pancake-like breads made with cornmeal. The meal is made by grinding hominy. Tortillas have been eaten for many centuries. In Mexican homes they are served like a hot bread. Americans prefer using them as an ingredient or base.

Tacos, or "Mexican sandwiches," are a favorite for instance (see Index for Easy Tacos). The tortilla, cooked briefly in hot oil until speckled with brown, is folded in half while hot, to make a pocket open at the top. The open top permits filling with shredded lettuce, chopped tomato, green onions, avocado, seasoned with a taco (chili) sauce. This sauce, used also for seasoning other foods in Mexico, usually is made in home kitchens. Our recipe gives an American version of a homemade sauce, but bottled taco sauce may be used as well. The recipe deserves to be called Easy Tacos because packaged taco shells ready for filling can be purchased—today an increasing number of supermarkets are stocking this convenience food. Markets carrying frozen tortillas also are increasing. Tortillas used for making tacos and other dishes in which they are rolled or folded, should be fresh or they will crack.

Wheat tortillas also have a following in Mexico and the Southwest; they are easily made at home. They are especially popular in northern Mexico. Burritos (see Index) are made with wheat tortillas folded around a beef and bean (or only bean) filling. Most burritos in Mexico are fried or baked before serving. Burritos always are served warm.

Beans of many kinds were a staple food in Mexico before anyone dreamed there ever would be a Boston famous for the contents of its bean pots. To this day they are eaten daily south of the border, often in every meal. The bean dish most popular in Mexico and the Southwest is Refried Beans (see Index). It usually is made with pinto or pink beans. Refried Beans improve in flavor when reheated.

Main dishes featuring beans with Mexican seasonings are an old-time favorite in western ranch homes. Excellent examples are Ranch-hand Beans, Ranchero Chili Corn and Chili Chip Bake, a perfect choice for a meal on the lighter side (see Index).

Mexican avocados grow in a variety of sizes. The Indians used them in many ways in pre-Columbian days, as they still do. Avocados now are grown commercially in the United States and are a favorite ingredient for dips and salads (see Index for Mexican Salad Bowl with Avocado Salad Dressing and Guacamole Burgers).

A festive Mexican fruit-vegetable salad served on Christmas Eve south of the border (see Index for Christmas Eve Salad) appears on southwestern tables and buffets during the holidays. Crisp, roasted peanuts are a traditional garnish.

Desserts of Mexico have entered American meals only to an extent. Some of them are tedious and time-consuming to make—sometimes ingredients are not available. The Mexican custom of ending a substantial meal with a bite or two of a sweet, such as a piece of candy, has American followers, however (see Index for Mexican Prune Candy and Buttermilk Pralines).

Caramel-flavored custards are a Mexican favorite and variations are made for special occasions in the Southwest. One example is Caramel Pumpkin Ring (see Index). Notice the lovely custard sauce served over Mexican Flag Dessert (see Index), a make-ahead, gala gelatin dessert that displays the colors of the Mexican flag.

Southwesterners like the Mexican cinnamon-chocolate desserts and hot chocolate (see Index for Mexican Chocolate Cake and Mexican Chocolate). An accompaniment to hot chocolate are the dainty, fiesta-gay Mexican Cookie Rings (see Index).

EASY TACOS

Tacos, as made north of the border, are a variation of those commonly served in Mexico. This is especially true now that packaged taco shells are an American convenience food. The shells are tortillas folded in half, making pockets ready to be filled. Mexican tacos generally consist of a strip of meat, chicken, beans or other filling, placed in the center of a warm tortilla, which is rolled around the filling and eaten as is or baked or fried until crisp. Accompaniments, some of which may be part of the filling, are shredded lettuce, cheese, taco sauce, radishes and chopped tomato and onion.

For a teen-age gathering, set out platters of tacos with only the meat filling added. Put bowls of chopped tomatoes and onions, shredded cheese and lettuce and guacamole on the table and let the youngsters add the fillings they prefer.

EASY TACOS

Great served with refried beans, either homemade or canned

1 (15 oz.) can tomato sauce
½ c. chopped onion
1 clove garlic, minced
4 tsp. chili powder
½ tsp. ground cumin
½ tsp. salt
¼ tsp. dried oregano leaves
1 lb. ground beef
1 c. chopped onion
½ tsp. salt
18 taco shells
2 c. shredded lettuce
1½ c. shredded sharp
   Cheddar cheese (6 oz.)
Chopped tomato, cubed
   avocado, chopped onion,
   refried beans

Combine tomato sauce, ½ c. onion, garlic, chili powder, cumin, ½ tsp. salt and oregano in saucepan. Cover and simmer 20 minutes. Remove ¾ c. cooked sauce; set aside.

Cook ground beef with 1 c. onion in skillet until meat is brown. Add reserved sauce and ½ tsp. salt. Cover and simmer 10 minutes. Stir occasionally.

Fill taco shells with meat filling, lettuce and cheese. Pass bowls of tomato, avocado, onion, refried beans and remaining cooked sauce to spoon into tacos. Makes 18 tacos or 6 servings.

CHILI CHIP BAKE

Not all Mexican-type dishes are hot with chilies or chili powder. An excellent example of a superior main dish on the mild side is Chili Chip Bake. The recipe is shared by a Colorado mountain woman who serves the casserole to her family, and to guests at informal company suppers. She also takes it to church suppers and other potluck meals.

The dish reflects three Mexican influences. There is a gentle taste of chilies provided by the sauce, the corn chips provide the crispness and cornmeal flavor of tortillas and the casserole is topped with sour cream.

CHILI CHIP BAKE

Quick main dish bakes in about 35 minutes . . . so easy to fix

1 lb. ground beef
1 (15 oz.) can pinto beans, drained and rinsed
1 (10 oz.) can hot enchilada sauce
1 (8 oz.) can tomato sauce
1 c. shredded process sharp American cheese (4 oz.)
1 tblsp. instant minced onion
1 (6 oz.) pkg. corn chips
1 c. dairy sour cream

Brown ground beef in skillet; drain off excess fat. Remove from heat. Add beans, enchilada sauce, tomato sauce, ½ c. cheese and onion.

Set aside 1 c. corn chips. Crush remaining corn chips and stir into meat mixture. Turn into greased 2-qt. casserole.

Cover and bake in 375° oven 30 minutes. Top with sour cream and sprinkle with remaining cheese. Arrange reserved corn chips around edge. Continue baking 3 to 4 minutes or until cheese melts. Makes 6 servings.

TAMALE SUPPER

The Aztecs called bundles of seasoned food, wrapped and cooked in cornhusks lined with cornmeal mush, *tamalli*. Early families north of the Rio Grande adapted the Mexican special to their taste. They eliminated the raisins, almonds and sweetenings that sometimes are included in Mexican tamales. Wrappers for tamales today usually are of cooking paper instead of cornhusks, although some people lament the loss of flavor they believe corn leaves imparted. The American fillings usually contain beef or chicken. Southwesterners also buy tamales from frozen food cases or in cans.

Our Tamale Supper is a good example of the kind of main dish Americans make with this old-time Indian creation. It is easy to combine the ingredients and they cook quickly—a good dish for busy days.

TAMALE SUPPER

California's contribution to tamales is ripe olives

1 c. chopped onion	½ c. sliced, pitted ripe olives
2 tblsp. butter or regular margarine	(optional)
	2 tsp. chili powder
1 (1 lb. 1 oz.) can whole kernel corn, drained	2 (15 oz.) cans of beef tamales, drained
1 (15 oz.) can tomato sauce	1½ c. shredded Cheddar cheese (6 oz.)
1 (15 oz.) can kidney beans, drained	

Sauté onion in butter in 10" skillet until soft. Add corn, tomato sauce, kidney beans, olives and chili powder. Bring to a boil; simmer uncovered 5 minutes. Turn into 11×7×1½" baking pan. Top with tamales.

Bake in 350° oven 15 minutes. Sprinkle with cheese. Continue baking 2 minutes or until cheese is melted. Makes 6 servings.

BEEF TAMALE PIE ARIZONA

Americans took the appetizing tamale ingredients Mexicans wrapped in cornhusks and baked the mixture in casseroles instead. They called it tamale pie.

Chili con carne frequently is the filling for the casseroles, lined and topped with cornmeal mush. Beef Tamale Pie Arizona has a filling of corn and cheese blended with ground beef.

BEEF TAMALE PIE ARIZONA

Make lattice design or drop dabs of mush on pie for fancy top

1 lb. ground beef	1 tsp. ground cumin
1 c. chopped onion	1 tsp. salt
1 c. chopped green pepper	1½ c. grated process sharp
1 (15 oz.) can tomato sauce	American cheese (6 oz.)
1 (12 oz.) can whole kernel	¾ c. yellow cornmeal
corn, drained	½ tsp. salt
1 c. sliced, pitted ripe olives	2 c. cold water
1 clove garlic, minced	1 tblsp. butter or regular
2 tsp. chili powder	margarine

Cook ground beef, onion and green pepper in skillet until beef is browned. Pour off excess fat. Add tomato sauce, corn, olives, garlic, chili powder, cumin and 1 tsp. salt. Cover and simmer 20 minutes. Add cheese; stir until it melts.

Meanwhile, stir cornmeal and ½ tsp. salt into cold water in saucepan. Cook, stirring constantly, until mixture thickens and bubbles. Remove from heat and stir in butter.

Turn meat mixture into greased 2-qt. casserole. Top with cornmeal mush. Bake in 375° oven 40 minutes or until hot and bubbly. Makes 6 servings.

AMERICAN CHILI

Who originated chili no one knows. Some people along the Rio Grande River Valley say it is a "Tex-Mex" creation; others insist it was invented in the Lone-Star State. It is a popular topic of debate along the border.

Chili peppers—the *aji* of the Incas and *chili* of the Aztecs— are the important seasonings in chili con carne. Usually chili powder, made by drying and pulverizing the hot peppers, is used. Sometimes it is supported by cumin and dried oregano. Recipes for this hot beef dish vary from state to state and from home to home in the Southwest. Texas chili, for instance, is more fiery than New Mexican.

Beans are added to chili in many places, while in others, mainly in the Southwest, they are served as Refried Beans in a side dish (see Index). Another point of difference in chili concerns tomatoes—Southwesterners generally do not add them to chili, while elsewhere they are included.

Our recipe for American Chili is the kind most people across the country prefer. Both tomatoes and pinto beans are listed as ingredients, with kidney beans suggested as an alternate if the speckled pinto beans are unavailable. And while ground beef frequently is the meat chosen to make chili, our selection is stew meat cut in small cubes, a gesture to the good judgment of southwestern chili experts who prefer it. Absence of grease is the hallmark of all good chili.

AMERICAN CHILI

Team bowls of hot chili with crackers and a tray of crisp relishes

2 lbs. stewing beef, cut in ½" cubes	1 beef bouillon cube
2 tblsp. cooking oil	2 tblsp. chili powder
2 c. chopped onion	1½ tsp. salt
2 cloves garlic, minced	1 tsp. dried oregano leaves
1 (1 lb.) can tomatoes, cut up	1 tsp. ground cumin
	2 (15 oz.) cans pinto or kidney beans

Brown meat in hot oil in Dutch oven. Add onion, garlic, tomatoes, bouillon cube, chili powder, salt, oregano and cumin. Cover and simmer 1¾ hours.

Add undrained beans; simmer 15 minutes. Makes 8 servings.

CHILI CON CARNE PIE

Southwestern cooks have a great wealth of recipes using chili con carne as a base ingredient. This recipe is a perfect example of how imagination and creativity can produce a hearty and handsome main dish.

CHILI CON CARNE PIE

Chili con carne casserole topped with corn bread dumplings

½ c. chopped onion
1 clove garlic, minced
1½ lbs. ground beef
1 (8 oz.) can tomato sauce
1 (1 lb.) can tomatoes, cut up
1 (20 oz.) can kidney beans, drained
1 tblsp. chili powder
1 tsp. salt

¾ c. cornmeal
¼ c. sifted flour
½ tsp. salt
1½ tsp. baking powder
1 egg
½ c. milk
¼ c. soft shortening
1 tblsp. chopped fresh parsley
¼ c. Parmesan cheese

Cook onion, garlic and beef until beef is well browned. Stir in tomato sauce, tomatoes, kidney beans, chili powder and 1 tsp. salt. Simmer 10 minutes, stirring occasionally.

Meanwhile, sift together cornmeal, flour, ½ tsp. salt and baking powder. Add egg, milk and shortening. Beat with rotary beater until smooth, about 1 minute. Do not overbeat. Stir in parsley.

Place hot filling in shallow 2-qt. baking dish; sprinkle with Parmesan cheese. Spoon corn bread topping around edge of dish.

Bake in 425° oven 15 to 18 minutes or until golden. Makes 6 servings.

BURRITOS

Burritos (pronounced boo-ree-tos) translated into English means "little burros." They are a form of tacos made with wheat tortillas. Wheat tortillas can easily and successfully be made in your own kitchen.

For a lunch or supper serve Burritos with a tomato or green salad, with baked custard or pineapple rings for dessert. Or omit dessert and have a cabbage-pineapple salad.

BURRITOS

Our filling is on the mild side; for a more aggressive taste add a few drops of hot pepper sauce

1½ lbs. stewing beef, cut in
   ½" cubes
2 tblsp. cooking oil
1 c. chopped onion
1 clove garlic, minced
1½ tsp. salt
1½ c. water
1 (4 oz.) can green chilies,
   drained and chopped

4 c. flour
2 tsp. salt
½ c. shortening or lard
1 c. warm water
1 (15½ oz.) can refried
   beans
1 tblsp. cooking oil
¼ c. shredded Cheddar
   cheese (1 oz.)

Brown meat in 2 hot oil in 10" skillet. Add onion, garlic, 1½ tsp. salt and 1½ c. water. Cover and simmer 2 hours until meat is fork tender and begins to fall apart. Gently flake meat with spoon. Add chilies; simmer uncovered until liquid evaporates.

Combine flour and 2 tsp. salt in mixing bowl. Cut in shortening until crumbly. Add 1 c. warm water, mixing until dough holds together. Turn out on lightly floured surface. Knead until smooth and elastic, about 3 minutes. Add more flour if necessary to keep dough from sticking to surface. Divide dough in 12 equal parts and form each into a ball. Cover with plastic wrap.

Roll each ball of dough into an 8" circle on lightly floured surface. Cook each circle of dough in ungreased heavy skillet over moderately high heat 1 minute or until golden brown spots cover it. Turn and cook 30 seconds. Stack in 9" round layer cake pan. Cover with foil. Keep hot in 300° oven.

Meanwhile, add beans to 1 tblsp. hot oil in saucepan. Sprinkle with cheese. Cook over medium heat, stirring occasionally, until cheese is melted and mixture hot.

To serve, place a heaping tblsp. of meat mixture and of bean mixture in center of each tortilla. Fold opposite sides of tortilla over filling. Roll up, starting at unfolded side, to make a package. Makes 12 burritos, or 6 servings.

SOUTHWESTERN BEEF ENCHILADAS

Cattle and hogs brought by Spanish colonizers revolutionized Mexican cooking. Combined techniques of Europeans and native Indians resulted in delicious dishes featuring tortillas or Indian corn bread.

Beef enchiladas are a classic example. To make them, tortillas are dipped in hot oil just until limp and then are filled with a ground beef mixture. They are rolled up and covered with tomato sauce and baked long enough to heat thoroughly.

Small tortilla factories dot the landscape in the Southwest. People buy tortillas uncooked or cooked, the choice depending on how they plan to use them. Freezer cases in supermarkets in many parts of the country now supply this corn bread.

Tortillas made from hominy meal and mixed with water to a dough, called masa, have delighted Americans for thousands of years. This is still the bread of Mexico; southwestern Americans eat it frequently. Indians divided the masa into pieces about the size of an egg and patted them with their hands into cakes about 8″ in diameter and ⅛″ thick. That took patience, practice and skill.

The first stoves on which they baked the corn bread consisted of three stones in the center of which burned a hearth fire. They placed a large clay griddle over the fire, resting it on the stones. They baked the tortillas on it without fat, until speckled brown on both sides.

SOUTHWESTERN BEEF ENCHILADAS

Seasonings are less "fiery" than in many southwestern dishes

1 c. chopped onion	1 c. chopped onion
2 tblsp. cooking oil	1 tsp. salt
3 (8 oz.) cans tomato sauce	Cooking oil
2 cloves garlic, minced	18 corn tortillas, canned or
1 tblsp. chili powder	frozen and thawed
½ tsp. ground cumin	Chopped onion
½ tsp. salt	1½ c. shredded sharp
¼ tsp. dried oregano leaves	Cheddar cheese (6 oz.)
1 lb. ground beef	

Sauté 1 c. onion in 2 tblsp. oil in saucepan until soft. Add tomato sauce, garlic, chili powder, cumin, ½ tsp. salt and oregano. Bring to a boil. Reduce heat; cover and simmer 30 minutes. Reserve ½ c. cooked sauce; set aside.

Cook ground beef and 1 c. onion in 10" skillet until beef is browned. Add reserved sauce and 1 tsp. salt. Cover and simmer 10 minutes.

Pour about ½" oil into small skillet; heat. Dip each tortilla in hot oil a few seconds until it becomes limp. Remove with tongs. Drain on paper towels.

Place 2 tblsp. meat filling in center of each tortilla; sprinkle with about 2 tsp. chopped onion. Top with heaping teaspoon of sauce. Fold sides over filling and place seam side down in 13×9×2" pan. Repeat with remaining tortillas. Pour remaining sauce over enchiladas. Sprinkle with cheese.

Bake in 350° oven 15 to 20 minutes or until thoroughly hot. Makes 6 servings.

AMERICAN-STYLE ENCHILADAS

This is truly an American adaptation of a Mexican-based dish. Paper-thin pancakes replace the tortillas and the generous amounts of fiery chili powder used in the Mexican version have been reduced considerably. This is a wonderful do-ahead main dish for company.

AMERICAN-STYLE ENCHILADAS

A great make-ahead company main dish with Mexican influence

6 eggs, well beaten	1 (10 oz.) pkg. frozen
3 c. milk	spinach, cooked, drained
2 c. sifted flour	and chopped
¾ tsp. salt	1 (29 oz.) jar or 2 (15 oz.)
1 lb. ground beef	cans meatless spaghetti
1 lb. bulk pork sausage	sauce
1 c. chopped onion	1 (8 oz.) can tomato sauce
½ c. chopped green pepper	1 c. water
2 cloves garlic, minced	1 tblsp. chili powder
1⅔ tblsp. chili powder	2 c. shredded Cheddar
1 tsp. salt	cheese

Combine eggs and milk. Add flour and ¾ tsp. salt; beat until smooth. Pour about ¼ c. batter into hot greased 6 to 7" skillet, tilting skillet so batter covers surface. Batter can also be spread into 6" rounds on greased griddle. Turn pancakes when the surface looks dry. Pancakes can be stacked while remaining pancakes are baked. Makes 30.

Brown ground beef and pork sausage in large skillet. Pour off all but 1 tblsp. fat. Add onion, green pepper, garlic, 1⅔ tblsp. chili powder and 1 tsp. salt. Simmer for 10 minutes. Add spinach; mix well. Let cool.

Combine spaghetti sauce, tomato sauce, water and 1 tblsp. chili powder; set aside.

Spoon scant ¼ c. meat mixture across center of each pancake. Fold sides over about ½". Starting at end closest to you, roll up each pancake. Place in two 13×9×2" baking dishes. Pour half of the sauce over the rolled pancakes in each baking dish. Top each with half of shredded cheese.

Bake in 325° oven 30 minutes or until hot and bubbly. Makes 15 servings.

Note: Prepared enchiladas can be frozen. To reheat: Bake in 375° oven 45 minutes or until hot and bubbly.

GUACAMOLE BURGERS

Mexico and California favorites combine in Guacamole Burgers. The yellow-green mashed avocado with a touch of peppery "fire" originated from Mexico, the beef patties in buns north of the border. Serving cooked beef patties in buns supposedly was introduced at the World's Fair in St. Louis in 1904, but it was in the 1920s that "hamburgers" skyrocketed to popularity, especially in California where hamburger stands mushroomed.

GUACAMOLE BURGERS

Beef patties topped with tomato slices, avocado and lettuce

1 medium avocado	1½ lbs. ground beef
1 tblsp. lemon juice	Salt
1 tblsp. finely chopped onion	Pepper
½ tsp. salt	6 hamburger buns, split and toasted
¼ tsp. bottled hot pepper sauce	6 slices tomato
	1 c. shredded lettuce

Mash avocado in small bowl. Stir in lemon juice, onion, ½ tsp. salt and hot pepper sauce.

Form ground beef into 6 patties. Pan-broil on both sides or broil in oven. Sprinkle with salt and pepper to taste. Place each patty on bun half. Top with tomato slice, avocado mixture, lettuce and bun top. Makes 6 servings.

CHICKEN TOSTADAS

If you are looking for something different to serve for supper or a snack, consider Chicken Tostadas, an old-time Mexican favorite. Although Southwesterners have naturalized it somewhat, it quite closely resembles the tostadas sold at school festivals and outside the church at semireligious fiestas in Mexico.

Our Chicken Tostadas start with tortillas quickly fried in shallow fat until crisp, then layered with food. Refried Beans (see Index) sprinkled with shredded cheese form the first layer. This is topped with cubes of cooked chicken, then with chopped tomatoes and shredded lettuce. Strips of avocado or mashed and seasoned avocado (guacamole), preferred in Mexico, garnish the top.

We suggest passing bottled taco sauce to drizzle over Chicken Tostadas, if desired. Mexicans often use a combination of vinegar and oil instead of the sauce.

CHICKEN TOSTADAS

Leftover turkey can also be used in this tasty recipe

12 corn tortillas, canned or frozen and thawed

Cooking oil

4 c. Refried Beans (see Index) or 2 (15½ oz.) cans refried beans

2 c. shredded Monterey Jack cheese (8 oz.)

2 c. cubed, cooked chicken

3 c. shredded lettuce

2 medium tomatoes, chopped

1 avocado, cut in 12 slices

Bottled or canned taco sauce

Fry tortillas in ½″ hot oil in 8″ skillet until crisp and golden brown, about 3 seconds. Hold top side of tortilla under fat with spatula during cooking. Drain on paper towels. (Tortillas can be fried in advance, stored airtight and heated in oven just before using.)

Heat beans. Spread ⅓ c. beans over each fried tortilla. Sprinkle with cheese, chicken, lettuce and tomatoes. Garnish each with strip of avocado. Pass taco sauce. Makes 6 servings.

PAELLA VALENCIANA

In Spain there are hundreds of "authentic" recipes for paella. It can be made with seafood only or meat or chicken. The green vegetable may be peas, beans, lima beans or artichoke hearts. There are basic rules for true Spanish paella however. It must always be made with olive oil and saffron must always be added to the rice to give it golden color. All ingredients are cooked together in a large shallow paella pan. We present our adaptation of Paella Valenciana. If you do not have a paella pan, cook the ingredients together in a skillet and transfer to a large casserole and finish baking in the oven.

PAELLA VALENCIANA

Accent this flavorful Spanish main dish with a crisp, green salad

4 chicken breasts, halved
Salt
Pepper
¼ c. butter or regular
    margarine, melted
Paprika
⅓ c. sherry (optional)
2 cloves garlic, minced
1 medium onion, chopped
1½ c. regular rice
⅓ c. olive oil
1 green pepper, chopped

2 c. clam broth plus 1 c.
    chicken broth (or 3 c.
    chicken broth)
1 (1 lb.) can tomatoes
1 tsp. salt
1 tsp. sugar
1 lb. frozen or fresh raw
    shrimp, shelled and
    deveined
⅛ tsp. red pepper
¾ c. pimiento-stuffed green
    olives, halved

Place chicken breasts, skin side up in greased 13×9×2″ baking pan. Season with salt and pepper; brush with melted butter. Sprinkle with paprika.

Cover with aluminum foil. Bake in 350° oven for 40 minutes. Uncover; pour sherry over chicken. Continue baking 20 minutes or until tender and nicely browned. Baste chicken occasionally with drippings from pan.

Cook garlic, onion and rice in hot oil in large skillet until golden, stirring constantly. Add green pepper, broth, tomatoes, 1 tsp. salt and sugar. Cover; boil gently for 20 minutes or until rice is tender. Stir occasionally.

Stir in shrimp, red pepper and olives. Cover and continue cooking for about 5 minutes or until shrimp is cooked and liquid is absorbed.

Spoon rice onto large platter or pan. Arrange chicken on rice. Makes 8 servings.

REFRIED BEANS

In the Old World, before Columbus discovered America, only soy and fava beans were known. Spanish conquistadors and early English colonists alike found Indians growing, cooking and eating many kinds of beans throughout the New World—from Cape Cod to the Andean heights thousands of miles apart.

The pre-Incas of Peru cultivated and developed most of the New World beans. Later the Mayas, Aztecs and other Indians in Central America and Mexico grew them. Refried Beans developed after the Spanish introduced hogs to Mexico and lard became available; heating the cooked vegetable in lard was a logical development.

Potato mashers are used more on beans than potatoes in the southwestern homes where Refried Beans are standard fare. (In Mexico "re" does not mean "again," but "thoroughly"—the beans are not "fried" a second time, but they are mashed thoroughly.) Frequently they accompany chili con carne; sometimes they are an ingredient in other Spanish-American dishes, such as Chicken Tostadas (see Index).

REFRIED BEANS

For a special treat, fold a little shredded Monterey Jack or Muenster cheese into beans 3 minutes before removing from heat

1 lb. dry pinto or red beans	½ c. bacon fat or lard
6 c. water	Salt
1 c. chopped onion	

Wash beans. Combine with water in Dutch oven. Bring to a boil; boil 2 minutes. Remove from heat; cover and let stand 1 hour. (Or soak beans overnight.) Add onion. Bring to a boil. Reduce heat and simmer 2½ to 3 hours or until beans are very tender. Stir occasionally the last 30 minutes so beans do not stick.

Mash beans with a potato masher. Add bacon fat. Continue cooking over low heat, stirring frequently, until beans are thickened and fat is absorbed. Add salt to taste. Makes 8 servings.

RANCH-HAND BEANS

Dry beans cooked with ham hocks are country food as American as the Fourth of July. This combination of farm favorites traveled West with pioneers. In the Southwest, they added seasonings reflecting the influence of Mexican kitchens.

Ranch-hand Beans are seasoned with garlic, tomatoes, onions, chili powder, cumin and marjoram.

Substantial bean and ham dishes rated high in the Old West around campfires and chuck wagons where cowboys gathered at mealtime. Today these dishes score equal success at picnics, community gatherings and family meals.

RANCH-HAND BEANS

Serve with corn sticks, Sour Cream Coleslaw or Wilted Spinach Salad (see Index)

1 lb. dry pinto or red beans
6 c. water
1 tsp. salt
2 c. chopped onion
1 large clove garlic, minced
1 lb. ham hocks
1 (1 lb. 12 oz.) can tomatoes, cut up

1 tblsp. chili powder
1 tsp. salt
½ tsp. ground cumin
½ tsp. dried marjoram leaves

Wash beans. Combine beans and water in Dutch oven. Bring to a boil; boil 2 minutes. Remove from heat; cover and let stand 1 hour. (Or soak beans overnight.)

Add 1 tsp. salt, onion, garlic and ham hocks. Bring to a boil. Reduce heat; cover and simmer about 2 hours or until beans are tender. Remove ham hocks. Cut in small pieces, discarding bones and skin. Drain beans, reserving 1 c. liquid.

Return beans and ham to Dutch oven. Add tomatoes, chili powder, 1 tsp. salt, cumin and marjoram. Stir in reserved bean liquid. Bring to a boil. Reduce heat; simmer uncovered 30 minutes, stirring occasionally. Makes 6 to 8 servings.

TEXAS BEANS AND HOMINY

Four native Mexican foods savored for centuries combine in Texas Beans and Hominy, a great side dish to serve with hamburgers, hot dogs, steaks or other meat grilled over coals. To the basic four—kidney beans, hominy, tomatoes (in sauce) and green chili peppers—Texans add vinegar, mustard and Worcestershire sauce.

For a summer evening meal bring Texas Beans and Hominy from the oven just as the sizzling steaks come off the grill. Set out a big bowl of tossed green salad. Pass crusty bread. Serve melon or sherbet for dessert.

TEXAS BEANS AND HOMINY

The earthy character and flavor especially delight most men

3 slices bacon, diced	1 (8 oz.) can tomato sauce
¾ c. chopped onion	1 to 2 tblsp. chopped,
1 (1 lb.) can hominy,	canned green chilies
drained	1 tblsp. vinegar
1 (15 oz.) can kidney beans,	1 tsp. prepared mustard
drained	1 tsp. Worcestershire sauce

Cook bacon in skillet until crisp. Remove from skillet and drain on paper towels. Drain off all but 1 tblsp. drippings.

Sauté onion in 1 tblsp. bacon drippings until soft. Add hominy, kidney beans, tomato sauce, chilies, vinegar, mustard and Worcestershire sauce. Turn into greased 1½-qt. casserole. Sprinkle bacon over top.

Cover and bake in 350° oven 1 hour or until hot and bubbly. Makes 6 servings.

PUEBLO GREENS AND BEANS

Although Pueblo Indians now have electricity, modern ranges and other conveniences, they continue to prepare many of the foods of their ancestors. Some of the dishes were influenced by the Spanish colonists, who settled in New Mexico in the 16th century, years before the *Mayflower* crossed the Atlantic Ocean.

Pueblo dishes also found their way into southwest kitchens. In Montezuma County, Colorado, where more than 6000 ruins of pueblos have been recorded, you still see fields of pinto beans as you drive through the area in summer.

In Pueblo Greens and Beans, frozen spinach substitutes for the spring greens Indians gathered and the beans come from cans. This makes it an easy all-American dish, but the seasonings have much to do with the success of the vegetable combination.

PUEBLO GREENS AND BEANS

A tasty New Mexican dish patterned after an old Indian favorite

6 slices bacon, chopped	½ tsp. salt
2 (10 oz.) pkgs. frozen chopped spinach	¼ tsp. pepper
	⅛ tsp. dried oregano leaves
¼ c. chopped onion	1 (15 oz.) can pinto or red beans, drained
1 clove garlic, minced	
¼ c. water	

Cook bacon in large saucepan until crisp. Drain on paper towels. Pour off all but 2 tblsp. bacon drippings. Add spinach, onion, garlic, water, salt, pepper and oregano to saucepan. Cover and simmer until spinach is cooked, stirring occasionally to break up spinach blocks. Add beans and bacon, and heat thoroughly. Makes 8 servings.

RANCHERO CHILI CORN

Chili, corn and cheese dishes are among the tasty Mexican favorites. Many of them also contain slightly sour cream, which is made in home kitchens by adding a little buttermilk to cream. Americans usually omit the cream and make their dish with canned chilies and corn; they use Monterey Jack cheese, a California original that went national in 1960. Some people consider it the American mozzarella.

RANCHERO CHILI CORN

The combination of flavors is rewarding and easy to make

½ c. chopped onion
1 clove garlic, minced
2 tblsp. melted butter or
   regular margarine
2 (12 oz.) cans whole kernel
   corn, drained

2 tblsp. chopped, canned
   green chilies
½ tsp. salt
½ c. shredded Monterey
   Jack cheese (2 oz.)

Sauté onion and garlic in melted butter in 2-qt. saucepan until tender. Add corn, chilies and salt; heat thoroughly, stirring occasionally. Sprinkle with cheese. Makes 6 servings.

FOUR-SEASON SUCCOTASH

American Indians, the people who first put corn and lima beans in a cooking pot together, used corn cut from cobs and fresh-shelled lima beans in summer, dried corn and dried beans the remainder of the year. Early colonists gratefully adopted and liked both kinds. This adapted Four-season Succotash uses frozen corn and dry beans, both available throughout the year.

All Indian tribes made succotash, but the dish varied from one region, as well as from one season, to another. For instance, bear fat, when available, often enriched it. In Four-season Succotash dairy half-and-half is used but you can substitute light cream if you prefer. And instead of dry red beans, you may wish to choose dry cranberry, pinto or kidney beans.

FOUR-SEASON SUCCOTASH

For a good, old-fashioned dinner, serve with roast pork or ham

1 c. dry pinto or red beans	½ c. dairy half-and-half
4 c. water	2 tblsp. butter or regular
1 tsp. salt	margarine
1 c. chopped onion	¼ tsp. pepper
2 c. frozen corn, thawed	

Wash beans. Combine beans and water in large saucepan. Bring to a boil; boil 2 minutes. Remove from heat; cover and let stand 1 hour. (Or soak beans overnight.)

Add salt and onion; simmer 1½ to 2 hours or until beans are tender. Pour off liquid.

Add corn and dairy half-and-half. Bring to a boil. Reduce heat and simmer about 3 minutes or until corn is tender. Add butter and pepper. Simmer, stirring, until butter is melted. Makes 8 servings.

PUEBLO SUCCOTASH

This corn-bean dish is somewhat different from that served in the Thirteen Original States (see Index for Winter Succotash and Ham Succotash Supper). Ground beef, tomato sauce and chili powder combine with green beans, but the surprise ingredient is sunflower seeds, toasted and salted, and added just before serving to keep them crisp. Early Pueblo Indians ate the native sunflower seeds raw or roasted; they also pounded them into meal, shaped into cakes and cooked them or served them as cereal. Many supermarkets and almost all health food stores carry sunflower seeds.

PUEBLO SUCCOTASH

The sunflower seeds make this a southwestern special

1 lb. ground beef	¼ tsp. pepper
1 c. chopped onion	1 (10 oz.) pkg. frozen green
1 (8 oz.) can tomato sauce	beans
2 tblsp. water	1 (10 oz.) pkg. frozen corn
1 tsp. salt	½ c. toasted salted sunflower
½ tsp. chili powder	seeds

Cook ground beef and onion in skillet until beef is browned. Add tomato sauce, water, salt, chili powder and pepper. Cover and simmer 5 minutes.

Add beans and corn. Cover and continue simmering about 10 minutes or until vegetables are tender. Add sunflower seeds. Heat thoroughly. Makes 6 servings.

INDIAN VEGETABLE SCALLOP

Indian Vegetable Scallop is a modern New Mexican dish that makes it easy for children to eat their share of vegetables at a meal. It is akin to dishes Indians put together over many years with sweet corn, yellow or green squash and juicy, red tomatoes.

INDIAN VEGETABLE SCALLOP

Good with cold cuts, hamburgers, fried chicken, meat loaves

¼ c. butter or regular	3 tomatoes, peeled and
margarine	chopped
4 small summer squash	½ c. chopped onion
(zucchini or yellow),	1 tsp. salt
sliced	¼ tsp. pepper
4 ears corn	

Melt butter in 3-qt. saucepan. Add squash, corn, cut from cob, tomatoes, onion, salt and pepper. Cover and cook over low heat, stirring occasionally, about 30 minutes or until tender. Makes 6 servings.

CALIFORNIA BAKED TOMATOES

Red, ripe, white-capped tomato halves add a decorative note to meals and it takes little work and time to prepare them. Top the cut surface of the tomatoes with a fluffy dressing made by combining mayonnaise and sour cream seasoned with basil, and put them in the oven to heat thoroughly, or for about 15 minutes. They are a great companion for grilled meats, such as steaks, beef patties and liver; they are equally at home with baked beans.

CALIFORNIA BAKED TOMATOES

Speedy special guaranteed to give both flavor and eye appeal

6 medium tomatoes	**¼ c. mayonnaise or salad**
¾ tsp. seasoned salt	**dressing**
½ c. dairy sour cream	**¼ tsp. dried basil leaves**

Remove stems from tomatoes. Cut in crosswise halves; place in 15½ ×10½ ×1″ jelly roll pan. Sprinkle with seasoned salt.

Stir together sour cream, mayonnaise and basil. Spread over cut surface of tomatoes.

Bake in 375° oven about 15 minutes or until tender. Makes 6 servings.

ZUNI VEGETABLE RELISH

Chili powder and dried oregano, a wild marjoram, are used to turn a commonplace dish into something special in the Southwest. These favorite seasonings, sparingly used, give Zuni Vegetable Relish its distinctive taste.

Chili powder, made from dried chili peppers with spices added, did not appear on the market until around 1900. Before then families made their own. Chili peppers are difficult to grow unless the climate is just right. The pods grow points down—the cup around the stems catches rain and excess moisture ruins peppers. They thrive successfully on some California coastal plains and in the arid, mountainous regions of interior Mexico.

ZUNI VEGETABLE RELISH

Make this a day ahead and chill to blend flavors—great served with fried fish or chicken

2 c. finely shredded cabbage	2 tblsp. sugar
½ c. grated peeled carrot	2 tsp. salt
½ c. chopped onion	⅛ tsp. dried oregano leaves
½ c. chopped green pepper	¼ tsp. chili powder
1 medium tomato, diced	¼ c. vinegar

Combine all ingredients. Cover and refrigerate at least 4 hours, or overnight. Stir occasionally. Makes 6 servings.

MEXICAN RICE

Mexican Rice, like many a southwestern dish, has a base of tomatoes, onion and green peppers. It takes the place of potatoes when served with hamburgers, pork chops or chicken.

Our recipe calls for bacon drippings, which have a way of accumulating in country kitchens. Chili powder, tomatoes, onion and green pepper and the drippings season the rice so successfully that people who usually do not care for rice enjoy this version adapted from Mexico.

MEXICAN RICE

Garnish the top of this rice dish with chopped green pepper

1 c. chopped onion	1 c. water
1 c. chopped green pepper	1½ c. uncooked rice
¼ c. bacon drippings	2 tsp. salt
1 (1 lb.) can tomatoes, cut up	1 tsp. chili powder

Sauté onion and chopped green pepper in bacon drippings in 3-qt. saucepan until soft. Add tomatoes, water, rice, salt and chili powder. Bring to a boil. Reduce heat; cover and simmer 20 minutes. Serve garnished with chopped fresh tomato and green pepper, if desired. Makes 6 to 8 servings.

BEEF/VEGETABLE STEW SAN JUAN

This meal-in-a-dish is strictly for the season when gardens supply vegetables at their succulent best. Select tiny squash—zucchini, pattypan or yellow crookneck or straightneck. All you have to do to prepare them for cooking is to remove stem ends, wash and slice. Use tender green beans.

Make this dish with sweet corn at its flavor peak. Husk, remove silks and instead of cutting the kernels from the cobs, do as many Mexicans do: Cut through the ears to divide them in 2-inch lengths. The corn, seasoned in the stew, can be eaten like corn on the cob.

While early Europeans in the eastern colonies did not praise the primitive stews the Indians there made with corn, beans and squash, people south of the border developed the dish so that it now is a favorite in the Southwest. Beef, ripe tomatoes and green onions touched with chili powder turn this stew into something very tasty.

BEEF/VEGETABLE STEW SAN JUAN

Serve for supper with crusty bread and chilled watermelon

2 lbs. stewing beef	2 tomatoes, peeled and
2 tblsp. cooking oil	chopped
4 c. water	¼ c. sliced green onions and
1 tblsp. salt	tops
½ tsp. chili powder	4 small zucchini, sliced
¼ tsp. pepper	3 ears corn, cut in 2″ pieces
½ lb. green beans, cut in	¼ c. sliced green onions and
pieces	tops

Brown meat in oil in Dutch oven. Add water, salt, chili powder and pepper. Cover and simmer 1½ to 2 hours or until tender. Skim off excess fat.

Add beans, tomatoes and ¼ c. green onions. Cover and simmer 20 minutes.

Add zucchini and corn; continue to simmer about 20 minutes or until all vegetables are tender. Sprinkle with ¼ c. green onions. Makes 6 servings.

TOMATO/CORN SOUP

For a quick and easy soup, try this southwestern favorite on a chilly day. Serve it with cheese sandwiches or hamburgers for a lunch or supper that usually satisfies even the hungriest men and boys. Round out the meal with crisp relishes and a chocolate dessert. For a lighter dessert, serve pink grapefruit for which the American side of the Rio Grande is now famous.

TOMATO/CORN SOUP

You can make this vegetable soup in less than 20 minutes

2 (13¾ oz.) cans chicken
  broth
1 (1 lb.) can tomatoes, cut
  up
1 (12 oz.) can whole kernel
  corn

¼ tsp. dried oregano leaves
¼ tsp. salt
⅛ tsp. pepper

Combine all ingredients in large saucepan. Bring to a boil. Reduce heat; cover and simmer 10 minutes. Makes about 2 quarts.

ESPAÑOLA VALLEY SOUP

Kitchens of families living in the green Española Valley between Taos and Santa Fe, New Mexico, turn out wonderful food that reflects three cultures—Indian, Spanish and American. Some of the dishes, adapted to changing times, have been enjoyed in this oasis since 1598 when a Spaniard at San Juan de Los Canalleros established the capital of New Spain. Social life has quickened in the valley since the Los Alamos project has brought many new residents. Buffet suppers now frequently take the place of sit-down dinners.

Española Valley Soup, a popular dish served from a tureen or bowl on the buffet, is worthy of duplication anywhere. Flanked by smaller bowls of soup toppings, such as shredded carrots, chopped lettuce, sliced radishes, avocado cubes and shredded Monterey Jack or Muenster cheese, the service is colorful and inviting. The taste of the soup lives up to its good looks.

ESPAÑOLA VALLEY SOUP

Serve with hot corn sticks or muffins or with crusty rolls

3 lbs. fresh pork hocks
3 qts. water
1 (1 lb.) can tomatoes, cut up
2 c. chopped onion
1 clove garlic, minced
5 tsp. salt
1 tblsp. chili powder
2 (1 lb.) cans whole kernel corn or hominy
1 (10 oz.) pkg. frozen lima beans
Chopped fresh parsley
Assorted toppings: shredded carrots, chopped lettuce, sliced radishes, sliced green onions, avocado cubes and shredded Monterey Jack or Muenster cheese

Combine pork hocks, water, tomatoes, onion, garlic, salt and chili powder in 8-qt. kettle. Cover and bring mixture to a boil. Reduce heat and simmer 1½ hours or until pork is tender. Remove pork. Cut up meat and return to broth; discard fat and bones. Cool broth. Refrigerate.

Skim off fat from broth. Add corn and lima beans to broth in kettle. Bring to a boil. Reduce heat and simmer 15 minutes or until beans are tender.

Garnish bowls of soup with parsley. Pass several bowls of the assorted toppings to spoon on soup. Makes about 4 quarts or 12 servings.

POTATO SALAD FRANCISCAN

For a distinctive potato salad to serve on special occasions, try Potato Salad Franciscan. Unusual ingredients are tiny cheese cubes and mashed, seasoned avocado, which contrast with the darker greens of chopped parsley and peppers.

POTATO SALAD FRANCISCAN

A delicious salad that contributes eye appeal to a buffet

4 c. hot, diced, cooked potatoes	**⅓ c. mayonnaise or salad dressing**
1 tsp. salt	**1 tsp. prepared mustard**
⅛ tsp. pepper	**1 large avocado**
2 tblsp. salad oil	**½ c. dairy sour cream**
2 tblsp. vinegar	**1 tblsp. chopped fresh parsley**
½ c. chopped celery	**1 tblsp. chopped green pepper**
½ c. small cubes Monterey Jack cheese	**2 tsp. lemon juice**
2 tblsp. finely chopped green pepper	**¼ tsp. salt**
2 tblsp. finely chopped onion	

Sprinkle hot potatoes with 1 tsp. salt and pepper. Add oil and vinegar and toss gently. Cool. Add celery, cheese, 2 tblsp. chopped green pepper and onion.

Blend together mayonnaise and mustard. Fold into salad mixture. Chill in shallow serving bowl.

Shortly before serving, mash avocado. Stir in sour cream, parsley, 1 tblsp. chopped green pepper, lemon juice and ¼ tsp. salt. Spread mixture completely over potato salad. Makes 6 servings.

SANTA CLARA TWO-BEAN SALAD

Pueblo Indian women, years before Europeans built homes in America, earned an enviable reputation for the clever ways they prepared vegetables. These were the women who created the basic cookery of the Southwest. Many foods served daily on our tables were first enjoyed in Pueblo country.

Santa Clara Two-bean Salad is a classic example. Canned red or pinto and cut green beans are the mainstays, with bits of green pepper and mild, not fiery, seasoning of chili powder.

Many menu planners rely on salads made with two or more kinds of canned beans to introduce variety, tastiness and protein to meals. Most everyone likes them, and busy women know such salads may be kept in the refrigerator a few days, ready to serve on short notice.

SANTA CLARA TWO-BEAN SALAD

Excellent for barbecues, good with grilled cheese sandwiches

1 (15 oz.) can pinto or red
    beans, drained and rinsed
1 (1 lb.) can cut green beans,
    drained
¼ c. chopped onion
¼ c. chopped green pepper

1 tblsp. sugar
½ tsp. chili powder
¼ tsp. salt
¼ c. vinegar
¼ c. salad oil

Combine all ingredients. Cover and refrigerate overnight. Drain before serving. Makes 6 servings.

OFF-THE-SHELF RANCHO SALAD

In this salad, pinto or kidney beans team with chick-peas, one of the oldest vegetables in the world. This legume has been cultivated in the Mideast from earliest biblical times. Spaniards brought it to Mexico more than 300 years ago and from there they came to the American Southwest where they are often called by their Spanish name, *garbanzos*. They now are available in supermarkets from coast to coast.

A mixture of lemon juice, vinegar and salad oil and seasoning make a delicious dressing for this Off-the-Shelf Rancho Salad. To develop the flavors, cover and chill the salad several hours or overnight, stirring occasionally.

OFF-THE-SHELF RANCHO SALAD

Proof that not all southwestern salads with chili powder are hot

1 (15 oz.) can kidney beans, drained and rinsed
1 (15 oz.) can garbanzos (chick-peas), drained and rinsed
1 c. chopped celery
¼ c. chopped onion

¼ c. chopped green pepper
⅓ c. salad oil
¼ c. lemon juice
2 tblsp. wine vinegar
1 tsp. garlic salt
¼ tsp. pepper

Combine all ingredients. Cover and refrigerate at least 4 hours. Stir occasionally. Makes 6 servings.

CHRISTMAS EVE SALAD

Americans who have sat in a sidewalk restaurant in Oaxaca, Mexico, on Christmas Eve, were as enchanted by the traditional Christmas Eve Salad served for supper as by the fireworks that lighted the skies. Many hostesses in the Southwest serve their version of the beautiful vegetable-fruit salad sometime during the holiday season. In our recipe apples substitute for *jacamas,* the bulbous roots of a plant native to Mexico. The vegetable is now appearing in some markets across the United States, however. To use jacamas, peel off the thin, light brown skin with a potato peeler and cut into thin slices—as crisp as spring radishes.

The traditional dressing for the salad is made with lime juice and oil; it provides delightful flavor to the vegetables and fruits, but you may use vinegar. Pomegranate seeds contribute color, and scattering peanuts over the salad is authentic.

The salad is a fine selection for a menu in which a Mexican-type main dish is chosen. This might be American Chili, Southwestern Beef Enchiladas or Beef Tamale Pie Arizona and Refried Beans (see Index) in the meal.

CHRISTMAS EVE SALAD

Color, texture and flavor contrasts make this salad memorable

1 head romaine, torn in
  bite-size pieces (about
  6 c.)
1 (13¼ oz.) can pineapple
  chunks, chilled
2 unpared apples, cored and
  sliced
2 bananas, sliced
2 oranges, peeled and sliced
1 (8 oz.) can whole beets,
  chilled, drained and
  sliced

¾ c. coarsely chopped
  peanuts
Seeds from 1 pomegranate
½ c. salad oil
3 tblsp. lime juice or
  vinegar
½ tsp. sugar
¼ tsp. salt

Place romaine in salad bowl.

Drain pineapple, reserving juice. Dip apple and banana slices in pineapple juice to prevent darkening. Arrange pineapple chunks, apple, banana, orange and beet slices on top of romaine. Sprinkle with peanuts and pomegranate seeds.

Shake together oil, lime juice, sugar and salt. Pour over salad and toss gently. Makes 8 servings.

MEXICAN SALAD BOWL

The avocado is at home in Mexican meals, for the trees that produce it have been cultivated there for centuries. The fruit is depicted on the ancient pottery and sculptures of such countries as Peru, Guatemala and Mexico (especially Yucatan). While avocados have many uses in Mexican meals, in the United States we use them mainly in salads and dips.

Avocado dressing is a California offshoot of guacamole. It is the perfect touch for Mexican Salad Bowl, which combines such foods as mixed greens, onion, green pepper, tomatoes, cheese and ripe olives. Crisp corn chips are a pleasing addition.

MEXICAN SALAD BOWL

Mexican-American variation of familiar tossed salads

2 qts. mixed greens	¼ c. shredded Cheddar
¼ c. chopped green onion	cheese
¼ c. chopped green pepper	1 c. coarsely crushed corn
¼ c. sliced, pitted ripe	chips
olives	Avocado Salad Dressing
2 tomatoes, cut in wedges	(recipe follows)

Combine greens, onion, green pepper, olives and tomatoes in salad bowl. Sprinkle with cheese, then corn chips. Top with Avocado Salad Dressing and toss lightly. Makes 6 to 8 servings.

Avocado Salad Dressing: Mash 1 avocado with 2 tblsp. lemon juice. Combine with ½ c. dairy sour cream, ¼ c. salad oil, 1 tsp. seasoned salt and ¼ tsp. chili powder. Cover and refrigerate several hours.

QUICK-AND-EASY BARBECUE SAUCE

In some sections of the Southwest the season for outdoor cooking over coals is longer than in other places in America. Barbecue sauces for basting the meat, fish and chicken are a year-round staple in these areas.

All the makings for Quick-and-Easy Barbecue Sauce may be kept on the shelf ready to use. Especially good with fish and chicken, but also on ground beef patties and other meats. And there is no law against adding more seasonings to meet personal tastes.

QUICK-AND-EASY BARBECUE SAUCE

Add a few extra drops of hot pepper sauce for more flavor

1 (8 oz.) can tomato sauce
¼ c. wine vinegar
2 tblsp. brown sugar, firmly
  packed
1 tblsp. Worcestershire
  sauce

2 tsp. instant minced onion
¼ tsp. bottled hot pepper
  sauce

Combine all ingredients in small saucepan. Bring to a boil. Reduce heat and simmer uncovered 5 minutes. Makes 1¼ cups.

INDIAN SUN BREAD

Anyone who has eaten Indian bread baked in adobe ovens, shaped like beehives, knows how wonderful it tastes. People in Santa Fe, New Mexico, frequently buy more than one loaf of the crusty bread sold by Indians on the sidewalk by the Governor's Palace. They like to have an extra loaf or two to store in their freezers for special occasions. Tourists in the fascinating old city buy a loaf to snack on in their motel rooms.

Indian Sun Bread has a distinctive shape, which honors the sun god. After the dough has risen and is light, it is rolled into a circle and one half is folded on top of the other half. Then it is cut in several places from the circular edge about two thirds of the way inward to the folded edge. The strips of dough are separated so they do not touch in baking and when the loaf comes from the oven, they resemble the rays of the sun. The texture and crust are not quite the same as loaves baked in beehive ovens, but no one will complain.

INDIAN SUN BREAD

This loaf of homemade bread will be the talk of any party

2 pkgs. active dry yeast
6 to 6½ c. sifted flour
2 c. water

3 tblsp. shortening
1 tblsp. sugar
1 tblsp. salt

Combine yeast and 2¼ c. flour in large mixer bowl.

Heat water, shortening, sugar and salt just until warm, stirring occasionally, to melt shortening. Add to flour mixture. Beat at low speed 30 seconds, scraping sides of bowl constantly. Beat 3 minutes at high speed, scraping bowl occasionally. By hand, add enough remaining flour to make a soft dough. Turn out on lightly floured board and knead until smooth and elastic, about 5 minutes. Place in large, greased bowl; turn dough over to grease top. Cover and let rise in warm place until double, about 1 hour.

Punch dough down. Divide in thirds. Shape each third into a ball. Cover and let rest 10 minutes. On lightly floured surface roll each ball into a 9″ circle. Fold each circle almost in half so that top circular edge is about ½″ from bottom circular edge. Place on greased baking sheets. Make 6 gashes in dough with kitchen scissors, cutting circular edges about two thirds of the way inward to the folded edges. Spread the strips of dough apart so they will not touch during baking. Let rise in warm place until double, about 45 minutes.

Bake in 350° oven 45 to 50 minutes or until loaves sound hollow when tapped. Remove from baking sheet. Cool on racks. Makes 3 loaves.

ALAMOSA CORN MUFFINS

Canned green chili peppers enhance dishes containing corn in some form. They are appearing more frequently on supermarket shelves elsewhere than in the Southwest.

This recipe was developed by an Iowa home economist after tasting a similar hot bread while visiting in southwestern Colorado. The small muffins have the texture and consistency of corn bread made without the addition of flour. They are tender, but not light.

ALAMOSA CORN MUFFINS

Delicious when served hot from the oven

1½ c. yellow cornmeal	1 c. dairy sour cream
3 tsp. baking powder	1 (8¾ oz.) can cream-style
½ tsp. salt	corn
½ c. shortening	⅓ c. chopped, canned
2 eggs	green chilies

Sift together cornmeal, baking powder and salt in a large mixing bowl. Cut in shortening until crumbly. Beat in eggs and sour cream until well blended. Stir in corn and chilies. Spoon into greased 2½" muffin-pan cups, filling two-thirds full.

Bake in 450° oven 12 to 15 minutes or until golden brown. Makes 18 muffins.

MEXICAN FLAG DESSERT

Southwesterners commonly call this the Mexican Flag Dessert, even though one layer of the gelatin mixture is tinted pink, rather than the red of the Mexican flag. One advantage of this dessert is that it is made ahead and chilled. Only the whipped cream needs to be folded into the velvety custard sauce at serving time.

MEXICAN FLAG DESSERT

An ideal light dessert in meals featuring Mexican-type foods

1 c. sugar	1 c. chopped, blanched
1 envelope unflavored	almonds
gelatin	Red food color
1¼ c. water	Green food color
5 eggs whites	Custard Sauce (recipe
¼ tsp. cream of tartar	follows)
¼ tsp. almond extract	

Stir together sugar and gelatin in medium saucepan; blend in water. Cook, stirring constantly, until gelatin dissolves. Chill until partially set.

Beat egg whites with cream of tartar and almond extract until stiff peaks form.

Beat gelatin mixture until frothy. Fold egg whites into gelatin mixture. Gently fold in almonds. Divide mixture equally in three bowls. Tint one pink and another pale green with food color; leave one mixture plain. Turn pink mixture into 1½-qt. mold or 9×5×3" loaf pan. Top with plain mixture, then green mixture. Chill until firm. Serve with Custard Sauce. Makes 8 servings.

Custard Sauce: Beat 3 egg yolks slightly. Combine with 2 tblsp. sugar and dash of salt in heavy saucepan. Gradually stir in 1 c. milk. Cook over low heat, stirring constantly, until mixture thickens and coats a metal spoon. Remove from heat and pour into bowl. Stir in ½ tsp. vanilla; chill. Fold in ½ c. heavy cream, whipped. Makes about 2 cups.

MEXICAN COOKIE RINGS

No matter how many other cookies are on the tray at the tea or coffee party or packed in the gift Christmas box, Mexican Cookie Rings will win compliments. And they don't take hours to make.

MEXICAN COOKIE RINGS

Twice as easy to shape as cookies made with a cookie press

1½ c. sifted flour	3 egg yolks
½ tsp. baking powder	1 tsp. vanilla
½ tsp. salt	5 tblsp. tiny multicolored
½ c. butter	decorating candies
⅔ c. sugar	

Sift together flour, baking powder and salt.

Cream together butter and sugar. Add egg yolks and vanilla; beat until light and fluffy. Mix in sifted dry ingredients. Shape into 1″ balls. Push your thumb through center of each ball and shape dough into a ring. Dip top of each ring in decorating candies. Place on lightly greased baking sheets.

Bake in 375° oven 10 to 12 minutes or until golden brown. Remove from baking sheets and cool on racks. Makes 2 dozen.

BUTTERMILK PRALINES

When in doubt about what to serve for dessert to end a Mexican-type meal, borrow an old custom of theirs and serve candy. The dividing line between desserts and candies in Mexico is indistinct. Some Texans pass a plate of pralines to top off such dinners. One advantage of candy is that everyone can take one or more pieces, depending on his appetite.

Buttermilk Pralines differ from both the sugary, brittle pecan candy originated in New Orleans during the French and Spanish colonial period, and also from the chewy Texan pralines that resemble soft caramels. They are the first choice of a rancher's wife, a sixth-generation American of Mexican descent, who lives in Colorado's San Luis Valley.

BUTTERMILK PRALINES

The unusual ingredient is buttermilk; candy discs are delicious

2 c. sugar	2 tblsp. butter or regular
1 tsp. baking soda	margarine
⅛ tsp. salt	1½ c. pecan halves
1 c. buttermilk	

Combine sugar, baking soda, salt and buttermilk in heavy 5-qt. Dutch oven. Cook over high heat to 210° on candy thermometer, about 5 minutes. Stir frequently, scraping sides and bottom of pan. Add butter and pecans. Cook, stirring constantly, to very soft ball stage, 230° on candy thermometer. Remove from heat; cool 2 minutes. Beat until thickened and creamy. Drop by tablespoonfuls onto waxed paper. Makes 15 (2½″) pralines.

MEXICAN CHOCOLATE

When conquering the Aztecs, Cortez and his soldiers were amazed at the quantities of a strange hot beverage, *cacaoquahitl,* the Emperor Montezuma drank—legend says as many as fifty cups a day. Indians made the beverage by boiling dried and cured cacao seeds in water. They also enjoyed a thicker chocolate drink, sweetened with honey and flavored with vanilla and spices. They called it *chocolatl*—this the Spaniards liked from the start. They called the beverages cacao and chocolate.

Pizarro found Incas in South America drinking a chocolate beverage which they called *cacahua.* Many years later in Peruvian archaeological excavations a ceramic chocolate cup was found. The design on it was of a man holding cacao seed pods.

Mexicans drink lots of hot chocolate, sweetened and flavored with cinnamon and vanilla. Southwesterners also make this beverage using commercial cocoa and the Mexican seasonings. Mexicans use a lovely, carved tool, *molinillos,* to whirl in the hot drink to make a frothy top. In this country, a rotary beater is used to make the chocolate foamy.

MEXICAN CHOCOLATE

If you have an antique chocolate set, use it to serve this drink

½ c. sugar
¼ c. baking cocoa
2 tsp. instant coffee
¾ tsp. ground cinnamon

Dash of salt
4 c. milk
1 tsp. vanilla

Combine sugar, cocoa, instant coffee, cinnamon and salt in heavy saucepan. Gradually add 1 c. milk, beating with wire whisk or rotary beater until smooth. Bring to a boil over low heat, stirring constantly. Add remaining milk; bring to a boil, stirring frequently. Add vanilla. Beat with rotary beater until frothy before serving. Makes 6 servings.

MEXICAN CHOCOLATE CAKE

Seeing cacao trees in bloom for the first time is a sight never forgotten. The tiny, pale pink flowers sprout directly from the bark of tree trunks and limbs. Large, rough pods develop—they are filled with a sticky mixture enclosing big, soft seeds called cacao beans, the source of chocolate. Indians crushed the seeds with grinding stones; efficient machinery does the work today.

Cacao trees now grow around the world, especially in Africa, but they originated in the Americas. Like many foods, they reached Europe through Spain. Chocolate cake is almost a universal favorite.

Mexican Chocolate Cake has an enthusiastic following in the Southwest. It combines cinnamon and vanilla with chocolate.

MEXICAN CHOCOLATE CAKE

Originally made in ranch kitchens with sour milk, but buttermilk is now more available

2 c. sifted flour	½ c. shortening
2 c. sugar	2 eggs
1 tsp. baking soda	4 squares unsweetened
1 tsp. salt	chocolate, melted
1½ tsp. ground cinnamon	1 tsp. vanilla
½ tsp. baking powder	Chocolate Frosting (recipe
¾ c. water	follows)
¾ c. buttermilk	

Sift together flour, sugar, soda, salt, cinnamon and baking powder into large mixer bowl. Add water, buttermilk, shortening, eggs, melted chocolate and vanilla. Blend 30 seconds at low speed, scraping sides and bottom of bowl constantly. Beat at high speed 3 minutes, scraping bowl occasionally. Spread batter evenly in greased and floured 13×9×2" pan or two 9" round layer cake pans.

Bake in 350° oven 40 to 45 minutes for large pan, 30 to 35

minutes for layer pans. Cool on rack. Spread cooled cake with Chocolate frosting. Makes 12 servings.

Chocolate Frosting: Combine ½ c. butter or regular margarine, 2 squares unsweetened chocolate and ¼ c. milk in saucepan. Heat until bubbles form around edge of pan, stirring occasionally. Remove from heat. Add 1 lb. box confectioners sugar, sifted (about 4¾ c.), 1 tsp. vanilla and ½ c. chopped pecans. Beat until of spreading consistency. If necessary, add 1 to 2 tblsp. milk.

CARAMEL/PUMPKIN RING

Suggesting a pumpkin dessert other than pie for the Thanksgiving and Christmas seasons receives at best a lukewarm reception. Pumpkin pie is traditional, it tastes wonderful and almost everyone likes it. So why change? Caramel/Pumpkin Ring is a good reason. Caramel and pumpkin combinations long have been favorites in Mexico.

Caramel/Pumpkin Ring is an adaptation which consists of caramel custard with pumpkin added and baked in a ring mold. Since thorough chilling is desirable, it is a good idea to make the dessert a day ahead, cover the mold with foil and store it in the refrigerator. When ready to serve turn out on a plate and fill the opening in the center with whipped cream or whipped dessert topping.

CARAMEL/PUMPKIN RING

Spicy pumpkin taste with rich caramel overtones—delicious

½ c. sugar
1 c. canned pumpkin
¾ c. sugar
½ tsp. salt
½ tsp. ground cinnamon
¼ tsp. ground ginger
¼ tsp. ground nutmeg

5 eggs, slightly beaten
1 (14½ oz.) can evaporated milk
1 tsp. vanilla
Whipped cream or whipped dessert topping (optional)

Melt ½ c. sugar in skillet over low heat until a golden syrup is formed, stirring constantly to prevent burning. Immediately pour into a 5-c. ring mold, turning and rolling from side to side to coat with sugar syrup. Set aside.

Stir together pumpkin, ¾ c. sugar, salt and spices. Blend in eggs. Stir in evaporated milk and vanilla. Pour into mold. Place in pan of hot water and bake in 350° oven about 1 hour or until knife inserted halfway between center and outer edge comes out clean. Cool, then chill thoroughly. To serve, run knife around sides of pan. Invert on serving plate. Serve with whipped cream, if desired. Makes 8 servings.

MEXICAN PRUNE CANDY

Many women in Mexico treasure candy recipes that have been handed down from one generation to another. One characteristic of many of their sweets is caramel flavor. In Mexican Prune Candy caramel and orange flavors blend delightfully with the prunes and nuts. Mexican Prune Candy is popular in our Southwest, especially in California, an important prune and walnut growing area.

MEXICAN PRUNE CANDY

Exceptionally easy to make but stuffing the prunes will take time

½ c. butter or regular margarine	2 tsp. grated orange peel
1 c. brown sugar, firmly packed	1 tsp. vanilla
½ c. orange juice	1 c. chopped walnuts
2 c. sifted confectioners sugar	2 (12 oz.) pkgs. pitted prunes

Melt butter in heavy saucepan. Add brown sugar and cook, stirring constantly, until mixture is bubbly. Stir in orange juice. Cook over low heat without stirring to the soft ball stage, 234°

on candy thermometer. Remove from heat and cool to lukewarm (110°) without stirring.

Add confectioners sugar and beat until mixture loses its gloss. Beat in orange peel and vanilla. Stir in nuts.

Meanwhile, prepare prunes. If necessary to soften, pour boiling water over them and let stand 5 to 10 minutes. Cut opening in prunes. Stuff with candy. Makes about 6½ dozen small stuffed prunes.

Part II

FROM THE OLD COUNTRY TO THE NEW LAND

INTRODUCTION

Immigrants came to America in waves from all over the European continent. A large migration to this country began in 1830 and continued through 1860. These were mostly people from Germany, Ireland, Scotland and Wales. Norwegian-Americans observed their Sesquicentennial in 1975—the 150th anniversary of their first migration.

But the largest group of Scandinavians immigrated from 1860 to 1890 along with Bohemians and Germans. Over 17 million came to find a new life within a 25-year period.

Packed into ships these brave people endured rough, stormy crossings and they were homesick for the relatives they had left behind. But they were sustained by the promise of this rich new land with its opportunities for those willing to work hard.

Our great-great-grandmothers labored in primitive surroundings from dawn until long after the sun had set. They worked as hard if not harder than the men. They corned beef, salted pork, grew and killed chickens, boiled calves feet to extract the gelatin, preserved and dried fruits and vegetables in readiness for the long winters ahead.

The family garden supplied the family with vegetables. Root vegetables were stored in the cellar or sometimes in a separate cellar dug nearby the house. Ham and bacon hung from rafters. Staples such as flour, sugar and salt were obtained in exchange for chicken and eggs.

Our pioneer women brought recipes from their home countries; often carried in their heads or written down hastily. They made do with what they had and turned out comforting and nourishing fare for the family. It might be a simple pudding of buttered bread and sour cherries stewed in a bit of sugar and water. After the mixture was cooked the deep stoneware was set out in the snow until the mixture half-froze into thick jelly, then served with custard sauce made from eggs and milk. This was the end of a hearty meal of smoked ham and tangy sauerkraut.

These women cooked as their mothers had done—by the feel and the look of the recipe. In those early days flour often was not listed as an ingredient—you simply remembered that it was added until the batter or dough felt right. Cookies were made by the tubful, with just enough flour so that the dough rolled easily. Baking day was Saturday in most households and the kitchen was a beehive of activity, producing cakes, tubs of cookies, batches of doughnuts and homemade, crusty bread.

At first the ethnic groups clung together and formed a tightly knit family. They cooked their recipes from the "old country" to help ease the pangs of homesickness. Then neighborhood and community husking bees and church suppers sprang up and brought the different nationalities together. And as women have done for generations, they compared, swapped and shared recipes. Soon a Yankee housewife, who had left her New England life to homestead in the Middle West, was serving her family her neighbor's Swedish meatballs while a German family was eating corn bread along with their own sauerbraten.

Our ancestors not only had the expertise to turn out a perfect meal, they had the ingenuity and skill of using what they had on hand to make their family's treasured dishes. The inspiration for many of our recipes arrived with the immigrants from Europe. Many survive in their original form while others have taken on the stamp of the American kitchen.

Chapter 1

THE HERITAGE
OF ENGLISH
COOKING

Our English ancestors combined their simple foods with a flourish of creativity and these dishes were brought with them when they came to this country and have lasted through the generations.

Our American favorites, apple crisp and baked apples filled with raisins and nuts then sweetened with sugar and dashed with cinnamon, are heirlooms from our English relatives.

The English were proud of their puddings. Every home had their special recipe for plum pudding. Even when times were hard and the larder was almost depleted, the English homemaker would combine flour, syrup, a few raisins and mix it with water and a bit of baking soda until a heavy dough was formed. Then she wrapped the dough in a floured cloth and boiled the mixture for hours. Served with a trickle of treacle, this makeshift sweet did wonders to cheer the family's spirits. These puddings were brought to America and through the years became our steamed puddings.

The early English farmers slaughtered their own pigs and cured their bacon. Every family had a pig—each farmer had his own formula for curing. Some used the simplest method, that of rubbing the hams thoroughly with salt and then covering them completely with salt for several days. Others were a little more inventive and devised their own pickling brew. The recipes also varied from area to area. In some regions saltpeter, coarse brown sugar, black treacle and vinegar were added to the salt. The hams were soaked in the pickling brine for several weeks, hung up to dry, and then smoked. Most of the English hams were delicately flavored and the recipes for proper curing were handed down through many generations. These techniques were brought to this country by the early settlers.

The hot mince pies, rich dark fruitcakes and flaming plum puddings that we prepare and are a part of our Christmas holidays are all of English origin. In northern England the fruitcakes were decorated with almonds and holly and in the south of England they were frosted with a thick white icing that had been swirled into many little peaks to simulate a mountain of snow. Today in our test kitchens we have many recipes from our farm women for fruitcakes and some are iced and others are simply decorated with cherries and nuts.

English farm cooks have always had a reputation for thrift. They invented some clever ways to use up Sunday's roast beef. The names were imaginative, too. Bubble and Squeak is one leftover that youngsters loved. The original recipe was simply a layer of cold meat covered with a layer of cabbage and onion. This was all stirred together until crusty and browned. As it cooked, it bubbled and squeaked. To this day every English household has their version of this easy leftover dish. Essentially though, it is chopped, leftover roast, potatoes and Sunday's leftover vegetables. When the immigrants brought it to this country, it became American hash. Two other leftover recipes are shepherd's pie and Toad-in-the-Hole. The shepherd's pie is a tasty combination of minced, cooked meat, onions, potatoes and gravy turned into a casserole, blanketed with fluffy mashed potatoes and baked. Toad-in-the-Hole (see Index) is simply sausages covered with a batter and baked until high and golden. Both these recipes have been passed down through English descendants in our country.

ENGLISH FISH AND CHIPS

Fish and chips run a close second to roast beef in popularity in England. Potatoes and fish are abundant in England so it's a natural combination.

Fish is coated with a batter of flour, eggs and milk and plunged into the sputtering hot fat. Then it emerges in a crisp golden jacket. The fried potatoes (chips) and fish are wrapped in a cornucopia of newspaper. A generous shake of salt and several dashes of vinegar and they're ready to eat. We give you a traditional fish and chips recipe but omit the newspaper!

ENGLISH FISH AND CHIPS

A very special treat . . . golden fries and batter-fried fish

3 lbs. potatoes, pared	6 tblsp. milk
Cooking oil	6 tblsp. water
2 c. sifted flour	2 lbs. white fish fillets, such
2 eggs, separated	as haddock, sole or
¼ c. beer	flounder
½ tsp. salt	Salt

Several hours before serving, cut potatoes in ⅜″ slices and then in lengthwise strips ⅜″ wide. Wash in very cold water; dry well between paper towels. Fry in deep, hot oil (370°) until tender but not brown, about 5 minutes. Drain on paper towels in baking pan. Cover with waxed paper; set aside until just before mealtime.

Combine flour, egg yolks, beer and ½ tsp. salt; mix well. Gradually add milk and water; stir until batter is smooth. Let stand 30 minutes.

Beat egg whites until stiff peaks form. Fold into batter.

Cut fish fillets into 5×3″ pieces. Coat fish with batter. Fry several pieces at a time in deep, hot oil (375°) until golden brown and tender, about 5 minutes. Turn fillets frequently to keep them from sticking. Drain on paper towels. Keep warm in 300° oven.

Brown precooked potatoes in deep, hot oil (390°) until crisp and brown. Drain on paper towels; sprinkle with salt. Keep warm in 300° oven. Makes 6 servings.

STEAK AND ONION PIE

A basic stew with a pleasant snap of spices and onion baked under a blanket of flaky pastry. An English recipe that originally had beef kidneys as an ingredient. But as it passed down through the families in America, round steak was substituted for kidneys.

A substantial meal to serve a hungry family and field crew. Toss a green salad, and end the meal with hot gingerbread topped with warm applesauce.

STEAK AND ONION PIE

Every "meat and potatoes" man will like this hearty main dish

3 tblsp. flour	4 c. beef broth
1 tsp. salt	2 c. sliced pared potatoes
½ tsp. paprika	(⅛″ thick)
⅛ tsp. pepper	2 tblsp. flour
⅛ tsp. ground ginger	3 tblsp. water
⅛ tsp. ground allspice	1 c. sifted flour
1 lb. round steak, cut in	¼ tsp. salt
½″ cubes	⅓ c. shortening
⅓ c. cooking oil	1 egg
2 c. chopped onion	

Combine 3 tblsp. flour, 1 tsp. salt, paprika, pepper, ginger and allspice. Coat beef cubes with flour mixture.

Cook beef cubes in hot oil in Dutch oven, stirring frequently. When beef begins to change color; add onion and sauté until mixture is well browned. Add beef broth. Cover. Bring to a boil; reduce heat and simmer 1 hour or until meat is tender. Add potatoes and cook 20 more minutes or until tender.

Combine 2 tblsp. flour and water. Gradually stir into meat mixture. Cook, stirring constantly, until mixture thickens.

Meanwhile, prepare pastry dough. Combine 1 c. flour and ¼ tsp. salt in bowl. Cut in shortening with pastry blender or two knives until mixture resembles coarse meal. Add egg; toss lightly to mix. Knead lightly until mixture holds together.

Roll dough on floured surface to 10″ circle.

Pour hot meat mixture into 2-qt. casserole. Top with dough. Seal edges and cut vents for steam.

Bake in 425° oven 25 minutes or until golden brown. Makes 6 servings.

WELSH RAREBIT

Creamy, tangy Leicester is a favorite English cheese for Welsh rarebit. Depending on how sharp you prefer your rarebit any of our cheeses will do. The original name, "rabbit," it is said comes from a Welsh joke. Cheese was often plentiful when rabbits were not so they called it rabbit. In the 18th century it becomes rarebit, but rabbit is the original name.

This nippy rarebit is a protein-rich nourishing supper. It's a great dish to make when unexpected guests arrive. Serve with frosty cold glasses of milk or a pitcher of chilled cider. A dish of fruit completes the meal.

WELSH RAREBIT

Also good served over toasted English muffins with tomato slices

1 lb. shredded, sharp Cheddar cheese	**2 tsp. Worcestershire sauce**
2 tblsp. flour	**1 tsp. dry mustard**
1 c. beer	**¼ tsp. cayenne pepper**
2 tblsp. butter or regular margarine	**12 slices bread, toasted and cut in triangles**

Combine cheese with flour in heavy 2-qt. saucepan. Add beer, butter, Worcestershire sauce, mustard and cayenne pepper; mix well. Cook over medium heat, stirring constantly, until cheese is completely melted and mixture is smooth (about 15 minutes).

Pour cheese sauce over hot toast, allowing 2 slices of toast per serving. If you wish, you can place Welsh rarebit under the broiler before serving. Place 2 slices toast in each ovenproof shallow baking dish or 8″ pie plate. Pour cheese sauce over all. Place under broiler, 4″ from source of heat, and broil 1½ minutes or until top is lightly browned and cheese is bubbly. Makes 6 servings.

CORNISH PASTIES

A Michigan farm woman shares her English recipe for meat and vegetable pasties. The miners in England carried them in their lunch pails wrapped in layers of newspaper. They kept warm for hours.

When the family heads for a football game, she has a triple batch of pasties ready for them. They are popular at picnics and family reunions, too.

CORNISH PASTIES

These flaky, individual meat pies are also good served cold

1 lb. stewing beef, minced	⅛ tsp. pepper
2 c. diced pared potatoes	3 c. sifted flour
1½ c. chopped onion	1½ tsp. salt
1 tblsp. Worcestershire sauce	1 c. lard
	4 to 5 tblsp. cold water
2 tsp. salt	1 egg, beaten

Combine beef, potatoes, onion, Worcestershire sauce, 2 tsp. salt and pepper; mix lightly. Set aside.

Sift together flour and 1½ tsp. salt into bowl. Cut in lard with pastry blender or two knives until mixture is like coarse cornmeal. Sprinkle with cold water, 1 tblsp. at a time, tossing lightly. (Mixture should be moist enough to hold together.)

Divide dough into 6 parts. Roll each part into a 7″ round. Place ⅙ of meat mixture on half of round. Fold other half over meat mixture; press edges together to seal. Cut slits in top of pastry. Place on ungreased baking sheet. Brush with beaten egg. Repeat with remaining dough.

Bake in 350° oven 45 minutes or until golden brown and meat mixture is tender. Makes 6 servings.

YORKSHIRE PUDDING

In an English family Yorkshire pudding is a must with a roast beef. Egg and milk batter is poured over the meat drippings and rises to a high, puffy crust. One of the secrets for a perfect Yorkshire pudding is a hot oven.

This recipe comes from a Nebraska homemaker; it is her husband's favorite and dates back to his great-grandmother. Every successive daughter-in-law was taught to make this crispy accompaniment to the roast. Half the family prefers the pudding slathered with softened butter, and the other half pour on a generous ladling of rich brown gravy.

YORKSHIRE PUDDING

Tastes like a huge popover . . . crusty brown with a moist center

¼ c. cooking oil or pan
   drippings from roast
   beef
2 eggs

1 c. milk
1 c. sifted flour
2 tsp. baking powder
½ tsp. salt

Pour oil into 9″ square baking pan. Heat in 425° oven 5 minutes.

Beat eggs until frothy with rotary beater. Add milk; blend well. Add flour, baking powder and salt. Beat until smooth. Pour batter into hot 9″ square baking pan.

Bake in 425° oven 35 to 40 minutes or until pudding is golden brown and puffy. Edges should be crusty. Serve hot with roast beef. (Pudding will fall in the middle as it cools.) Makes 6 servings.

TOAD-IN-THE-HOLE

Tastes like a popover. Crusty and golden brown on the outside and moist inside. Youngsters love to peer through the glass door of the oven and watch the batter climb against the sides of the pan while the sausages nestle in pockets of dough.

This is an economical, nourishing supper. Serve with fresh green beans and thick slices of tomato. A quick and easy meal.

TOAD-IN-THE-HOLE

Delight your family with this nourishing English supper dish

1 lb. small, fresh pork sausage links	1 c. milk
2 tblsp. water	1 c. sifted flour
2 eggs	½ tsp. salt
	⅛ tsp. pepper

Place sausages and water in 10″ skillet. Cover and cook over low heat 3 minutes. Remove cover; increase heat to medium. Continue cooking sausages, turning them frequently until the water evaporates and sausages begin to brown.

Meanwhile, prepare batter. Beat eggs with rotary beater. Add milk; blend well. Add flour, salt and pepper, beating until batter is smooth.

Pour ¼ c. sausage drippings in bottom of 11×7×1½″ baking dish. Arrange sausage links in bottom of dish. Pour batter over all.

Bake in 425° oven 30 minutes. Makes 6 servings.

ST. JAMES COFFEE CAKE

An Indiana woman sent us her recipe for St. James Coffee Cake that came from England. She has found this is a versatile coffee cake, inexpensive to make and a good keeper. When there is a church supper she makes several. She always greets a new neighbor with a warm hello and her special coffee cake. Everyone that tastes it asks for the recipe.

ST. JAMES COFFEE CAKE

An old-fashioned coffee cake that is great for Sunday breakfast

3 c. sifted flour	**2 c. sour milk**
2 c. sugar	**1 tsp. baking soda**
½ tsp. ground cinnamon	**1 egg, beaten**
½ tsp. ground cloves	**1 c. raisins**
½ tsp. ground nutmeg	**1 c. chopped walnuts**
¾ c. butter or regular margarine	**1 tblsp. flour**

Sift together 3 c. flour, sugar, cinnamon, cloves and nutmeg into bowl. Cut in butter until mixture resembles coarse meal. Reserve ½ c. crumbs; set aside.

Combine sour milk and baking soda. Add egg and milk mixture to remaining crumb mixture, beating well.

Combine raisins, walnuts and 1 tblsp. flour. Stir into batter. Spread batter in greased and floured 13×9×2″ cake pan. Sprinkle with reserved ½ c. crumbs.

Bake in 350° oven 55 minutes or until done. Serve warm or cold. Makes 16 servings.

ENGLISH SHORTBREAD

Perfect with a cup of scalding hot tea. The English and Scots are famous for their shortbreads. Some are richer than others— this one is not as rich as some, but flaky with a subtle flavor.

ENGLISH SHORTBREAD

The perfect choice for those who prefer a plain butter cookie

1 c. butter or regular margarine	**1 egg**
½ c. sugar	**3 c. sifted flour**
	1 tsp. baking powder

Cream together butter and sugar until light and fluffy. Beat in egg.

Sift together flour and baking powder. Add dry ingredients to creamed mixture, stirring well to blend. Knead dough lightly until it holds together.

Roll dough on floured surface to 14″ square. Cut into 49 (2″) squares. Place squares about 2″ apart on ungreased baking sheet. Prick each with fork.

Bake in 325° oven 12 minutes or until lightly browned. Remove from baking sheets; cool on racks. Makes 49 squares.

UNCLE JIM'S OATMEAL COOKIES

This old Welsh recipe written in a thin and spidery hand on yellowed paper has lasted through several generations. A Wisconsin farm woman makes a batch a week of these crisp-edged cookies that were a favorite of her great-great uncle. No temperature or baking time was given—after trial and error she perfected the recipe.

UNCLE JIM'S OATMEAL COOKIES

Good, basic oatmeal cookie to pack in children's lunch boxes

¾ c. butter or regular margarine	¾ tsp. baking soda
	½ tsp. baking powder
1 c. sugar	½ tsp salt
2 eggs, beaten	3 tblsp. sour milk
2 tblsp. molasses	3 c. rolled oats
1½ c. sifted flour	½ c. raisins
1 tsp. ground cinnamon	

Cream together butter and sugar until light and fluffy. Add eggs, one at a time, beating well after each addition. Beat in molasses.

Sift together flour, cinnamon, baking soda, baking powder and salt. Add dry ingredients alternately with sour milk to creamed mixture, mixing well after each addition. Stir in oats and raisins. Drop mixture by teaspoonfuls about 2″ apart on greased baking sheet.

Bake in 350° oven 10 to 12 minutes or until golden brown. Remove from baking sheets; cool on racks. Makes 6 dozen.

ENGLISH SCONES

Whenever she visited her grandmother, a South Carolina farm woman knew she would have a special treat awaiting . . . scones with lots of butter and three kinds of jam. They were rich and crumbly, not too sweet and not too hearty.

As she sipped her tea that was half-tea half-milk, her grandmother would tell her that her great-grandmother had brought the recipe from England.

ENGLISH SCONES

Like our American baking powder biscuits but not as flaky

2 c. sifted flour	¼ c. currants or chopped
3 tblsp. sugar	raisins
3 tsp. baking powder	2 eggs, beaten
1 tsp. salt	½ c. light cream
¼ c. butter or regular	1 egg white
margarine	

Sift together flour, sugar, baking powder and salt into bowl. Cut in butter until mixture is crumbly. Add currants.

Combine eggs and cream. Add to crumb mixture all at once, stirring just enough with fork to mix.

Roll dough on floured surface to ½" thickness. Cut with floured 2" cutter and place about 1" apart on greased baking sheet.

Beat egg white until frothy and brush tops of scones.

Bake in 375° oven 15 minutes or until golden. Makes 24.

CHEESE STRAWS

This English recipe that is popular at teatime makes a buttery-crisp pastry stick with a good cheese flavor. We suggest serving with chilled tomato juice spiked with lemon as an appetizer for a company meal. These would make a delightful Christmas gift, packed carefully in a pretty tin box.

CHEESE STRAWS

Make ahead to serve drop-in guests with an icy cold soft drink

¾ c. sifted flour
¼ tsp. salt
⅛ tsp. cayenne pepper
¼ c. finely shredded, sharp
  Cheddar cheese

¼ c. butter or regular
  margarine
1 egg yolk, beaten
2 tblsp. ice water

Sift together flour, salt and cayenne pepper into bowl. Mix in cheese. Cut in butter with pastry blender or two knives until mixture resembles coarse meal. Combine egg yolk and ice water. Sprinkle over mixture. Toss lightly until mixed. Shape into ball. Dust lightly with flour. Cover with plastic wrap. Chill in refrigerator at least 1 hour.

Roll dough on floured surface to 14×4" rectangle. Cut into 28 strips, 4" long and ½" wide. Place strips about 1" apart on ungreased baking sheet.

Bake in 400° oven 10 minutes or until straws are firm and light-colored. Remove from baking sheet; cool on racks. Cheese straws will keep up to two weeks in a tightly covered container. Makes 28 straws.

DUNDEE CAKE

Bring this out on your prettiest cake plate during the holidays. Studded with raisins, currants, candied peel, cherries—the batter is rich in eggs. Blanched, whole almonds form a pattern on top of the cake. This cake needs no glaze—it's handsome as it is. Make several and freeze ahead for the holidays.

DUNDEE CAKE

Serve wedges of this with coffee during the Christmas holidays

1 c. butter or regular
  margarine
1 c. sugar
5 eggs
1 tsp. baking soda
1 tsp. milk
2½ c. sifted flour
⅛ tsp. salt
¾ c. currants

¾ c. raisins
¾ c. chopped, mixed
  candied fruit
8 red candied cherries, cut
  in half
½ c. ground almonds
2 tblsp. grated orange peel
⅓ c. whole, blanched
  almonds

Cream together butter and sugar until light and fluffy. Add eggs, one at a time, beating well after each addition.

Dissolve baking soda in milk; add to creamed mixture.

Sift together flour and salt; reserve 1 tblsp. Gradually add dry ingredients to creamed mixture, blending well after each addition.

Combine currants, raisins, candied fruit, candied cherries, ground almonds, orange peel and reserved 1 tblsp. flour; mix well. Stir into batter. Spread batter in greased and floured 8" springform pan. Arrange whole almonds in concentric circles on top of batter.

Bake in 300° oven 1 hour 30 minutes or until cake tests done. Cool in pan on rack 5 minutes. Remove outer rim and cool completely. Makes 12 servings.

ENGLISH TRIFLE

English trifle can be made with leftover stale cake, the last of the jam and smidgens of leftover fruit. Combined with a creamy custard it tastes elegant.

You can also start with fresh cake and a lovely jar of homemade jam, lots of heavy cream and turn out a sublime dessert. A sweet finale that will bring accolades from guests.

ENGLISH TRIFLE

You can substitute a purchased spongecake for the jelly roll

5 eggs	1 egg
¾ c. sugar	2 eggs, separated
½ tsp. almond extract	1 tblsp. sugar
¾ c. sifted cake flour	2 c. milk, scalded
¾ tsp. baking powder	1 c. heavy cream
¼ tsp. salt	1 tblsp. sugar
1 c. red raspberry jam	½ c. toasted, sliced almonds
½ c. cream sherry	

Beat 5 eggs, ¾ c. sugar and almond extract until thick and lemon-colored, about 5 minutes.

Sift together cake flour, baking powder and salt. Fold dry ingredients into egg mixture. Spread batter in greased and waxed-paper-lined 15½ ×10½ ×1″ jelly roll pan.

Bake in 350° oven 20 minutes or until cake tests done. Loosen cake around edges. Turn out on rack to cool.

Divide cooled spongecake into fourths. Spread each quarter with ¼ c. jam. Cut each into 8 pieces. Place 8 pieces in bottom of 3-qt. serving bowl. Sprinkle with ¼ of sherry. Repeat layers. Cover with plastic wrap and let stand 1 hour at room temperature.

Combine 1 egg, 2 egg yolks and 1 tblsp. sugar in double boiler top. Beat well with rotary beater. Slowly beat in scalded milk. Cook over simmering water, stirring occasionally, until it begins to thicken (about 15 minutes). Remove from heat; cool 5 minutes. Pour warm custard over cake. Chill in refrigerator 1 hour.

Beat 2 egg whites until soft peaks form. Whip heavy cream until it begins to thicken. Slowly beat in 1 tblsp. sugar. Beat until soft peaks form. Fold egg whites into beaten cream. Spoon over top of trifle. Decorate with sliced almonds. Chill until serving time. Makes 8 servings.

BLACKBERRY JAM CAKE

Solid and moist with blackberry jam, this is a truly English cake and special company cake for an Ohio family. It can be made several days before eating as it improves with aging. Cut in small wedges as it is a rich cake—has a subtle, spicy flavor.

BLACKBERRY JAM CAKE

Also luscious if made with strawberry or raspberry jam

1 c. butter or regular margarine	1 tsp. baking powder
1 c. sugar	1 tsp. ground cinnamon
4 eggs	1 tsp. ground nutmeg
1 c. blackberry jam	1 tsp. ground allspice
3¼ c. sifted flour	¾ tsp. salt
1 tsp. baking soda	1 c. buttermilk
	1⅓ c. chopped walnuts

Cream together butter and sugar until light and fluffy. Add eggs, one at a time, beating well after each addition. Beat in jam.

Sift together flour, baking soda, baking powder, cinnamon, nutmeg, allspice and salt. Add dry ingredients alternately with buttermilk, beating well after each addition. Stir in walnuts. Spread batter in greased and waxed-paper-lined 9″ tube pan.

Bake in 325° oven 1 hour 30 minutes or until cake tests done. Makes 10 servings.

LEMON CAKE ROLL

This dessert looks and tastes like spring—a superb dessert to end an Easter dinner. The light, tender spongecake filled with a zingy lemon curd came to the United States from England and is a truly elegant English dessert.

LEMON CAKE ROLL

This delicate sponge roll makes a lovely last-minute dessert

3 eggs	Confectioners sugar
1 c. sugar	¼ c. butter or regular
¼ c. water	margarine
1 tblsp. lemon juice	⅔ c. sugar
1 tsp. grated lemon peel	3 tblsp. lemon juice
1 c. sifted cake flour	3 tblsp. water
1 tsp. baking powder	3 egg yolks, slightly beaten
¼ tsp. salt	1 tsp. grated lemon peel

Beat eggs at high speed until thick and lemon-colored, about 3 minutes. Gradually beat in 1 c. sugar. Continue beating until very thick. Blend in ¼ c. water, 1 tblsp. lemon juice and 1 tsp. lemon peel.

Sift together cake flour, baking powder and salt. Gently fold dry ingredients into egg mixture. Spread batter in greased and waxed-paper-lined 15½ × 10½ × 1″ jelly roll pan.

Bake in 375° oven 14 minutes or until cake tests done. Loosen edges of cake; turn out on towel dusted with confectioners sugar. Peel off paper carefully. Cut off browned edges of cake. Roll cake up in towel, starting from narrow side. Cool on rack.

Combine butter, ⅔ c. sugar, 3 tblsp. lemon juice, 3 tblsp. water and egg yolks in double boiler top; mix well. Cook over simmering water, stirring constantly, until mixture coats a spoon. Remove from heat. Pour into bowl. Stir in 1 tsp. lemon peel. Cover with plastic wrap and cool completely.

Unroll cake roll. Spread with cooled lemon curd. Refrigerate until serving time. Makes 8 servings.

OLD-FASHIONED SUET PUDDING

The English love their puddings as much now as they did generations ago. The recipes for suet pudding number in the hundreds, some plain and some fancier. This third-generation suet pudding is a hearty one that's served on cold winter days in a Wisconsin farm home. Everyone looks forward to Great-grandma's pudding.

The Wisconsin farm wife told us that when, for a change, she made a fancy custard sauce instead of the usual Nutmeg Sauce, everyone was disappointed. They all said that the Nutmeg Sauce belonged with the pudding—it just wasn't the same.

OLD-FASHIONED SUET PUDDING

A simple, hearty pudding with a sauce flavored with nutmeg

1 c. ground beef suet	¼ tsp. salt
1 c. sugar	1¼ c. milk
2 eggs	1 c. raisins
3 c. sifted flour	Nutmeg Sauce (recipe
3 tsp. baking powder	follows)

Mix together suet and sugar until well blended. Add eggs, one at a time, mixing well after each addition with spoon.

Sift together flour, baking powder and salt. Add dry ingredients alternately with milk to suet mixture, stirring well after each addition. Stir in raisins. Turn into greased 2-qt. ring mold. Cover with aluminum foil.

Place cooling rack or trivet in bottom of large kettle. Add 2" boiling water. Place mold in kettle. Cover and steam 1½ hours or until pudding tests done. Add more boiling water if necessary.

Remove mold from kettle. Let stand 2 minutes. Turn pudding out of mold onto serving plate. Serve pudding hot with Nutmeg Sauce. Makes 10 servings.

Nutmeg Sauce: Combine ½ c. sugar, 2 tblsp. cornstarch and ⅛ tsp. salt in 2-qt. saucepan. Gradually stir in 2 c. boiling water. Add 3 tblsp. butter or regular margarine. Cook over medium heat, stirring constantly, until thick and clear. Remove from heat. Stir in ¼ tsp. ground nutmeg and 1 tsp. vanilla.

SPICY SUET PUDDING

A treasured recipe that has been handed down through the family.

A Nebraska farm woman remembers her Christmas holiday as a child. Her mother would be up before dawn on Christmas morning to prepare suet pudding. Now all children fix the same pudding on Christmas day.

A solid pudding, rich in spices served with a warm Vanilla Sauce.

SPICY SUET PUDDING

A 2-qt. ring mold can also be used . . . just cover with foil

1 c. ground beef suet	**⅛ tsp. salt**
1 c. sugar	**1 c. sour milk**
2¼ c. sifted flour	**1 c. raisins**
½ tsp. ground cinnamon	**Vanilla Sauce (recipe**
½ tsp. ground cloves	**follows)**
½ tsp. baking soda	

Mix together suet and sugar until well blended.

Sift together flour, cinnamon, cloves, baking soda and salt. Add dry ingredients alternately with sour milk to suet mixture, stirring well after each addition. Stir in raisins. Turn into greased 2-qt. pudding mold. Cover.

Place cooling rack or trivet in bottom of large kettle. Add 2" boiling water. Place mold in kettle. Cover and steam 3 hours or until pudding tests done. Add more boiling water if necessary.

Remove mold from kettle. Let stand 2 minutes. Turn pudding out of mold onto serving plate. Serve pudding hot with Vanilla Sauce. Makes 10 servings.

Vanilla Sauce: Combine ½ c. sugar, 2 tblsp. cornstarch and ¼ tsp. salt in 2-qt. saucepan. Gradually stir in 2 c. boiling water. Cook over medium heat, stirring constantly, until it comes to a boil. Boil 5 minutes. Remove from heat. Stir in

¼ c. butter or regular margarine, 2 tsp. vanilla and ⅛ tsp. ground nutmeg; mix well.

STEAMED CHRISTMAS PUDDING

Rich in molasses, nuts, spices and raisins, this pudding stands 4 inches tall. The recipe is now in the files of a Nebraska farm woman descended from early English colonists. Always served during the holidays, this pudding is a favorite company dessert in the cold weather months. We suggest a cold Custard Sauce or a buttery hard sauce to go along with the pudding.

STEAMED CHRISTMAS PUDDING

Gently spiced and served with a pour of velvety sauce

1 c. ground beef suet	1 c. milk
½ c. sugar	½ c. chopped, mixed
1 egg	candied fruit
½ c. molasses	½ c. chopped walnuts
2 c. sifted flour	½ c. raisins
1 tsp. baking soda	1 tblsp. flour
½ tsp. ground cinnamon	Custard Sauce (recipe
½ tsp. ground cloves	follows)
½ tsp. ground nutmeg	

Cream together suet and sugar until well blended. Add egg and molasses, beating well.

Sift together 2 c. flour, baking soda, cinnamon, cloves and nutmeg. Add dry ingredients alternately with milk to suet mixture, beating well after each addition.

Combine candied fruit, walnuts, raisins and 1 tblsp. flour; mix well. Stir into mixture. Turn into greased 2-qt. pudding mold. Cover.

Place cooling rack or trivet in bottom of large kettle. Add 2" boiling water. Place mold in kettle. Cover and steam 3 hours or until pudding tests done. Add more boiling water if necessary.

Remove mold from kettle. Let stand 2 minutes. Turn pudding out of mold onto serving plate. Serve pudding hot with Custard Sauce. Makes 10 servings.

Custard Sauce: Combine 1 (3¼ oz.) pkg. vanilla pudding and pie filling and 2¾ c. milk in medium saucepan. Bring mixture to a boil, stirring constantly. Remove from heat. Stir in ½ tsp. vanilla. Cool slightly.

STEAMED CARROT PUDDING

English cooks were famous for their steamed puddings. When they came to this country, they brought their recipes with them. Carrots and potatoes were plentiful in their new land. Before long, steamed puddings were made using these two vegetables.

Grated potatoes and carrots, mixed with spices, raisins and nuts, steam to moist perfection. A Utah homemaker makes this heirloom recipe in 3-pound shortening cans and gives them to neighbors during the holidays. She often adds a small crock of Hard Sauce, too. Flecked with bits of bright orange carrots, this golden brown pudding makes a great homemade gift.

STEAMED CARROT PUDDING

So tender and moist, a lovely choice for a holiday dessert

¾ c. butter or regular margarine	½ tsp. ground nutmeg
1 c. sugar	¾ c. sour milk
2 eggs	1 c. grated carrots
2 c. sifted flour	1 c. grated pared potatoes
2 tsp. ground cinnamon	1 c. currants
1 tsp. baking powder	½ c. chopped walnuts
½ tsp. baking soda	1 tblsp. flour
½ tsp. ground allspice	Hard Sauce (recipe follows)

Cream together butter and sugar until light and fluffy. Add eggs, one at a time, beating well after each addition.

Sift together 2 c. flour, cinnamon, baking powder, baking soda, allspice and nutmeg. Add dry ingredients alternately with sour milk to creamed mixture, stirring well after each addition.

Combine carrots, potatoes, currants, walnuts and 1 tblsp. flour; mix well. Stir into batter. Turn into greased 2-qt. pudding mold. Cover. Place cooling rack or trivet in bottom of large kettle. Add 2″ boiling water. Place mold in kettle. Cover and steam 2 hours or until pudding tests done. Add more boiling water if necessary.

Remove mold from kettle. Let stand 2 minutes. Turn pudding out of mold onto serving plate. Serve pudding hot with Hard Sauce. Makes 10 servings.

Hard Sauce: Beat ½ c. butter or regular margarine and 1 c. sifted confectioners sugar until light and fluffy. Beat in ½ tsp. vanilla. Spoon into serving dish. Top with grated orange peel, if you wish. Refrigerate until firm.

STEAMED CHERRY PUDDING

Light, fine-textured cakes form the base for this heirloom pudding, a versatile dessert that can be served year round. While the pudding steams, make the bright red sauce to trickle over each individual cherry-studded pudding.

A favorite menu with an Iowa family is baked pork chops and scalloped potato, buttered carrots and their treasured Cherry Pudding. The children call them Cherry Puffs.

STEAMED CHERRY PUDDING

Light, airy pudding is steamed in individual custard cups

2 eggs
1 c. milk
⅓ c. melted butter or
    regular margarine
2 c. sifted flour
¼ c. sugar
2 tsp. baking powder
1 tsp. salt
2 tsp. vanilla

2 (1 lb.) cans pitted red
    sour cherries
½ c. sugar
2 tblsp. cornstarch
¾ c. water
1 tblsp. butter or regular
    margarine
10 drops red food color

Beat eggs until frothy with rotary beater. Beat in milk and ⅓ c. melted butter; blend well.

Sift together flour, ¼ c. sugar, baking powder and salt. Stir dry ingredients into milk mixture; mixing well. Add vanilla.

Drain cherries, reserving ¾ c. juice. Set aside.

Spoon batter into 8 greased 5-oz. custard cups, filling one-third full. Place 4 to 5 cherries in each cup. Top with remaining batter.

Place cooling rack or trivet in kettle or electric skillet. Add 2" boiling water. Place custard cups on rack. Cover and steam 30 minutes or until puddings test done. Add more boiling water if necessary.

Meanwhile, prepare Cherry Sauce. Combine ½ c. sugar and cornstarch in 2-qt. saucepan. Gradually stir in reserved ¾ c. cherry juice, ¾ c. water, 1 tblsp. butter and red food color. Cook over medium heat, stirring constantly, until mixture comes to a boil. Stir in remaining cherries. Remove from heat.

Remove individual puddings from custard cups and place on serving dishes. Spoon over Cherry Sauce. Makes 8 servings.

Chapter 2

THE HERITAGE OF GERMAN COOKING

German cooking has great variety and scope. It is more compatible with American tastes than some European cooking. The Germans are meat and potato fanciers as we are. They like thick, robust soups made from potatoes and dried peas and beans, and they also prefer creamed soups to clear.

Meat is the mainstay of German cooking; they prepare their meats in much the same manner as we, except that their famed sauerkraut goes with every meat served in some regions of Germany. Our American roasts and pot roasts are similar to theirs. They have cooked stews for centuries and are famous for one-pot meals where meat and vegetables are browned in fat, lightly seasoned with herbs and spices and then simmered in broth until tender. They are fond of dried fruits and began adding them to their meats years ago to provide a welcome break from the winter cabbages and turnips.

Sauerkraut is a star in German cuisine. Our pioneers brought the method of preserving cabbage by pickling from the old country, and in many yards there would be a barrel or two of sauerkraut.

Dumplings play an important role in German cooking, too.

They float in soups and stews and are served as a side dish to accompany meat. They vary in size, shape and texture. Some are even poached in a fruit sauce and served for dessert. Some cooks like to add a pinch of baking powder for lightness. There is a knack to making dumplings, German cooks explain. It takes an experienced hand to turn out perfect dumplings for the humidity in the air affects the amount of flour to be used.

Braised meats are favorites with German cooks. With the less tender, inexpensive cuts of meat, they make wonderful thick gravy that complements their famous dumplings.

Pot roast recipes vary with every region. In the Rhineland white raisins are stirred into a light brown cream gravy, while in other sections the tangy sweet-sour is prevalent and sometimes crusts of rye bread or crumbled gingersnaps are used as thickening.

In fact all German cuisine varies with the location, picking up the flavors of the bordering countries. Food in East Germany favors their Polish and Czech neighbors; there they use caraway seeds, paprika and sour cream often in the preparation of foods. There, too, you will find huge snowy dumplings, sauerkraut and pork. The Rhineland picks up the delicacy of French cooking, fewer sweets-and-sours, but generous amounts of butter, cream and eggs are incorporated into their cooking.

Cabbage, beets and potatoes appear often, especially in the winter months. Noodles are an important part of their diet. Often they are served plain with butter or dressed up with sautéed onions, crumbled bacon or buttered bread crumbs.

Sausages come in all sizes, shapes and degrees of spiciness. There are short stubby knockwurst, bratwurst, liverwurst and summer sausage that keeps for months if hung in a cool spot.

Some of the best bakers in the world are German cooks. Their desserts are rich and irresistible. Apples, cherries and macaroons are buried in clouds of whipped cream. Currant-studded yeast breads, fat, puffy stollens, tissue-thin strudels, spicy cookies and cakes are just a few of the baked goods that make German cooks famous.

German cooking is honest, down-to-earth and simple. We

present recipes that have been part of the American heritage for years; some have not changed while others have been altered to suit family tastes.

SAUERBRATEN WITH GINGERSNAP GRAVY

Every German kitchen boasts at least one recipe for sauerbraten, one of the most renowned of German beef recipes. And every cook has her special marinade. Some are marinated in wine and no vinegar. And in some sections of northern Germany the pot roast is marinated in buttermilk, imparting a distinctive flavor and very tender juicy meat. And instead of gingersnaps, lebkuchen may be broken into the gravy. Our recipe features a two-day steeping in vinegar and spices. The gravy is smooth, mellow and nippy with gingersnaps.

SAUERBRATEN WITH GINGERSNAP GRAVY

Let roast stand 15 minutes before cutting into thin slices

1 medium onion, sliced	1 c. chopped onion
1 c. cider vinegar	1 c. chopped carrots
2 c. water	½ c. chopped celery
2½ tsp. salt	1 c. water
12 whole peppercorns	1 beef bouillon cube
6 whole cloves	1 c. water
3 bay leaves	¼ c. flour
1 (5 lb.) boneless bottom	½ c. water
round, rolled and tied	½ c. crushed gingersnaps
¼ c. cooking oil	

Combine sliced onion, vinegar, 2 c. water, salt, peppercorns, cloves and bay leaves. Pour over roast in large glass dish, turning roast to coat all sides. Cover and refrigerate 2 days, turning meat twice daily.

Remove meat from marinade; dry with paper towels. Reserve 2 c. marinade. Brown meat on all sides in hot oil in Dutch oven, about 15 minutes. Remove meat. Add 1 c. onion, carrots and celery. Sauté until tender (do not brown).

Return meat to Dutch oven. Add reserved marinade and 1 c. water. Bring mixture to a boil. Reduce heat; cover and simmer 3 hours or until meat is tender.

Remove meat to hot platter. Add bouillon cube and 1 c. water to Dutch oven. Bring mixture to a boil.

Combine flour and ½ c. water; stir to blend. Gradually add to hot liquid, stirring constantly. Stir in gingersnaps. Bring mixture to a boil, stirring constantly. Boil 3 minutes. Serve gravy with sauerbraten. Makes 12 servings.

SOUR BEEF AND POTATO DUMPLINGS

Another version of the famous German sauerbraten; this one served with homemade Potato Dumplings. There's a surprise in the center—buttered, browned bread cubes, plus a thick, rich dark gravy to pour over the dumplings.

SOUR BEEF AND POTATO DUMPLINGS

Spicy gingersnaps thicken the gravy in this tangy main dish

4 lbs. stewing beef, cut in 1″ cubes	¼ c. sugar
1½ c. cider vinegar	¼ c. brown sugar, firmly packed
½ c. water	½ c. crushed gingersnaps
½ c. chopped onion	⅓ c. crushed gingersnaps
½ c. raisins	Potato Dumplings (see Index)
1 tblsp. salt	
1½ tsp. pickling spices	

Combine stewing beef, vinegar, water, onion, raisins and salt in 6-qt. kettle. Bring mixture to a boil.

Tie pickling spices in cheesecloth bag. Add to meat mixture. Cover. Reduce heat and simmer 2 hours.

Add both sugars and ½ c. gingersnaps. Simmer 45 more minutes or until meat is tender.

Stir in ⅓ c. gingersnaps and cook 2 minutes or until mixture thickens slightly. Remove spice bag. Serve with Potato Dumplings. Makes 10 servings.

MEATBALLS IN JACKETS

A rich noodle dough rolled paper-thin, filled with a flavorful ground beef mixture, then sealed tightly and popped into hot oil. The meatballs emerge with a crackling crisp crust. Often stewed Tomato Sauce and Creamy Mushroom Sauce are served to give a choice. We sampled a little of both on a pastry—pleasing combination.

MEATBALLS IN JACKETS

These crunchy, meat-filled squares would make great appetizers

1 lb. ground beef	1 tblsp. shortening
½ c. finely chopped onion	3 eggs, beaten
1 clove garlic, minced	2 tblsp. milk
½ tsp. salt	Cooking oil
⅛ tsp. pepper	Stewed Tomato Sauce
6 tblsp. beef broth	(recipe follows)
2½ c. sifted flour	Creamy Mushroom Sauce
1 tsp. baking powder	(recipe follows)
¾ tsp. salt	

Combine ground beef, onion, garlic, ½ tsp. salt, pepper and beef broth; mix lightly, but well. Set aside.

Sift together flour, baking powder and ¾ tsp. salt into bowl. Cut in shortening. Add eggs and milk; mix until moistened.

Divide dough in half. Roll each half to 13″ square. Trim to 12″ square; cut into 9 (4″) squares; reserve scraps of dough. Place 1 heaping tblsp. meat filling in center of each square. Bring corners of squares to center; pinch edges together. Repeat with remaining dough. Roll out scraps to 9″ square. Trim to 8″ square; cut in 4 (4″) squares.

Fry in deep, hot oil (350°) 2 minutes on each side. Drain on paper towels. Serve hot with either Stewed Tomato Sauce or Creamy Mushroom Sauce. Makes 22.

Stewed Tomato Sauce: Sauté 1 tblsp. minced onion and 1 tblsp. minced celery in 1 tblsp. melted butter or regular margarine until tender (do not brown). Add 1 (1 lb.) can stewed tomatoes and ¼ tsp. thyme leaves; simmer 20 minutes. Combine 1 tsp. cornstarch and 1 tblsp. water; stir into tomato mixture. Bring to a boil. Serve over meat pies. Makes 2 cups.

Creamy Mushroom Sauce: Combine 1 (10¾ oz.) can condensed cream of mushroom soup, 1 (3 oz.) can sliced mushrooms (undrained) and ⅓ c. of milk. Stir until smooth. Heat and serve over meat pies. Makes 1½ cups.

PORK CHOP SKILLET DINNER

The Germans are famous for their hearty and nourishing fare. This rib-sticking, down-to-earth dish is perfect to serve on a frosty winter night. When you serve this third-generation German favorite, the men in your family will say, "Let's have this again!"

PORK CHOP SKILLET DINNER

A complete meal-in-a-dish that is ready in one hour

6 lean pork chops	6 carrots, cut in 1″ pieces
½ tsp. salt	(2 c.)
¼ tsp. pepper	1½ c. coarsely chopped
1 tblsp. cooking oil	onion
½ tsp. dried savory leaves	3 medium potatoes, pared
½ bay leaf	and quartered
2 c. tomato juice	¼ tsp. salt
½ c. water	
1 small cabbage, cut in 6 wedges	

Season pork chops with ½ tsp. salt and pepper. Brown chops in hot oil in a large skillet. Add savory, bay leaf, tomato juice and water. Cover and simmer 30 minutes.

Add cabbage, carrots, onion, potatoes and ¼ tsp. salt. Cover. Cook for 35 minutes or until vegetables are tender. Makes 6 servings.

LIVER DUMPLINGS

These German dumplings can be served either in the broth or removed and served as the main course on a bed of tangy sauerkraut. Dip tablespoon in hot broth before dipping into dumpling batter—batter will slide right off the spoon into the hot soup. Dumplings are done when they bob to the surface. Sprinkle with chopped green parsley.

LIVER DUMPLINGS

Parsley-topped, liver dumpling soup makes a tasty first course

4 strips bacon	1 tsp. salt
1½ lbs. beef liver	¼ tsp. pepper
2 tblsp. dry bread crumbs	1 c. flour
½ c. minced onion	3 qts. beef broth
2 eggs, beaten	Chopped fresh parsley

Fry bacon until brown and crisp. Remove and drain on paper towels. Crumble; set aside.

Put liver through coarse blade of food grinder. Combine ground liver, reserved bacon, bread crumbs, onion, eggs, salt, pepper and flour; mix well.

Bring beef broth to a boil in a large kettle. Dip teaspoon into hot broth and then into dumpling mixture, filling ½ full. Drop half of this mixture into boiling broth. Cook in boiling broth 15 minutes or until dumplings rise to surface. Remove dumplings and keep hot. Repeat with remaining mixture, adding more broth if needed. Serve dumplings with broth as a soup and garnish with parsley. Dumplings can also be drained and served with sauerkraut. Makes 6 to 8 servings.

CHICKEN AND PRUNE FRICASSEE

Germans are partial to dried fruits cooked along with meat or poultry. And they always add a bit of spice—a dash of cinnamon or a touch of clove or ginger.

This heirloom from Germany tastes even better the second day, according to the farm wife who sent us this recipe. It is a "must" at their Thanksgiving and Christmas dinners. The family agrees that no one can make it quite like Mom, even though they follow her recipe.

Sometimes dried apricots are substituted for the prunes and it is served with jumbo dumplings.

CHICKEN AND PRUNE FRICASSEE

Succulent, moist chicken pieces served with a gently spiced sauce

½ c. flour	2 sticks cinnamon
2 tsp. salt	2 strips fresh ginger root
2 (3 lb.) broiler-fryers,	(2" long)
cut-up	1 tblsp. brown sugar, firmly
⅓ c. cooking oil	packed
1½ c. pitted prunes	3 tblsp. water
2 c. chicken broth	

Combine flour and salt. Coat chicken pieces with flour mixture. (Reserve remaining flour mixture to thicken sauce.)

Brown chicken on all sides in hot oil in Dutch oven. Remove chicken as it browns. Put chicken back into Dutch oven. Add prunes, chicken broth, cinnamon, ginger root and brown sugar. Bring to a boil. Reduce heat and cover. Simmer 40 minutes or until chicken is tender.

Combine reserved flour mixture with water. Remove chicken and prunes to serving platter and keep warm. Bring sauce to a boil. Slowly stir in flour and water mixture. Boil 2 minutes, stirring constantly. Spoon some of the sauce over the chicken. Pour remaining sauce into serving bowl. Delicious served with rice. Makes 8 servings.

GERMAN BREAD DRESSING

A great-great-grandmother brought this recipe from Germany, but each generation changed it a trifle. The latest revision was the addition of toasted, slivered almonds for crunch and flavor in this marvelous, moist dressing that complements roast goose, duck or turkey. On a cold winter day this Illinois homemaker often makes a pan of the stuffing and browns some sausages for a hearty supper. Fresh, buttered spinach and applesauce complete the meal.

GERMAN BREAD DRESSING

Do try stuffing your next turkey with this popular bread dressing

1 c. chopped celery and celery leaves	3 c. diced unpared apples
½ c. chopped onion	1 c. raisins
1 c. butter or regular margarine	1 c. toasted, slivered almonds
1 (10¾ oz.) can condensed chicken broth	3 eggs, beaten
4 qts. soft bread cubes (½″)	½ tsp. salt
	⅛ tsp. ground cinnamon
	⅛ tsp. pepper

Sauté celery and onion in melted butter in skillet until tender (do not brown).

Add enough water to chicken broth to make 2½ cups.

Combine sautéed vegetables, bread cubes, apples, raisins, almonds, eggs, salt, cinnamon, pepper and chicken broth mixture. Toss gently to mix. Place dressing in greased 13×9×2″ baking dish. Cover with aluminum foil.

Bake in 325° oven 1 hour 15 minutes. Uncover and bake 15 more minutes or until top is golden brown. Makes 8 servings.

EMILIE'S ONION/SAGE DRESSING

A three-generation heirloom, this dressing has been part of a family's holiday meal since the early 1800s. A big pan of dressing is baked the day before the holiday; the flavor improves when it's reheated. But this is also a year-round dressing in this Iowa farm home. It's perfect with pork chops, baked chicken, and the crew especially likes it layered with hamburger and baked—a hearty substantial after a long day in the fields.

EMILIE'S ONION/SAGE DRESSING

To reheat, place in a skillet with a little water and cover

1½ lb. loaf day-old, whole wheat bread, broken in pieces
1 qt. milk
1 lb. bulk pork sausage
4 c. chopped onion

2 c. chopped celery and celery leaves
2 eggs, beaten
2 tblsp. rubbed sage
1 tsp. salt
⅛ tsp. pepper

Soak bread in milk.

Sauté sausage in 10″ skillet. When meat begins to turn color, add onion and celery. Cook until mixture is well browned.

Add sausage mixture, eggs, sage, salt and pepper to bread mixture; mix lightly. Place dressing in greased 13×9×2″ baking dish.

Bake in 350° oven 45 minutes or until dressing is golden brown. Makes 8 servings.

HOMEMADE GERMAN NOODLES

Homemade noodles often replace potatoes as a meat accompaniment in a German meal. Usually they are boiled, drained and tossed with melted butter. The seasoning depends upon the family's taste. Some like just salt and pepper, while others like crumbled bacon or toasted bread crumbs mingled through the noodles. Thin noodles are preferred for soups, while wider ribbons are popular in hearty stews.

HOMEMADE GERMAN NOODLES

Tender egg-rich noodles are perfect with pot roast and brown gravy

2 c. sifted flour
½ tsp. salt

3 egg yolks, beaten
½ c. lukewarm water

Combine flour and salt. Stir in egg yolks and water; mix well. Knead on floured surface until smooth and elastic, about 5 minutes. Let dough rest 30 minutes.

Roll out to 18″ square. Let dry 1 hour.

Roll up loosely like jelly roll. Cut dough into ¼″ strips. Unroll strips. Cut in 4″ lengths. Lay out to dry again 1 hour.

Cook in 3 qts. boiling, salted water 18 minutes or until noodles are tender.

Drain in colander. Rinse with hot water. Drain well. Noodles can be served buttered with crumbs or as you would serve packaged noodles. Makes 6 servings.

GERMAN MILK SOUP

There is a quart of milk in this soup, which gives this dish its name. An American farm woman's ancestors brought this soup from Germany in 1810. Several generations ago it was no doubt the mainstay of their diet, as dried beef and vegetables were plentiful. This generation consumes generous portions after a day of skiing and it's a success on their camping trips, too. All the sons have taken the recipe to college and fixed it for their roommates —it makes a big hit every time.

GERMAN MILK SOUP

Serve soup piping hot with lots of homemade biscuits

2 c. chopped onion	3 c. diced carrots (¼" cubes)
1 c. sliced celery	2 tsp. salt
¼ c. butter or regular margarine	⅛ tsp. pepper
	3 c. water
4½ c. diced pared potatoes (¼" cubes)	4 oz. dried beef, cut up
	1 qt. milk
4 c. coarsely chopped cabbage	1 c. light cream

Sauté onion and celery in melted butter in 6-qt. kettle until tender (do not brown).

Add potatoes, cabbage, carrots, salt, pepper and water. Cover. Bring to a boil; reduce heat and simmer until vegetables are tender, about 30 minutes.

Add dried beef, milk and cream. Heat well over low heat (do not boil). Makes about 3 quarts or 9 servings.

CREAM OF TOMATO SOUP

Grated potato makes this a delightfully different tomato soup. Delicately flavored with savory, this soup can be made with fresh tomatoes as well as canned. According to a Michigan farm woman, this zesty soup has been in her family since 1815 when her ancestors came to Michigan from the Old Country. Though she has made the recipe with fresh tomatoes from the garden, her family prefers it when she makes a big batch with her home-canned tomatoes. Everyone has two big helpings of soup and several homemade baking powder biscuits—and creamy rice pudding for dessert. This is a family-request supper at least three times a month in cold weather. If there is any left over, the children take a Thermos of Mom's soup in their lunch box.

CREAM OF TOMATO SOUP

Tomatoes and potatoes are simmered to perfection in this soup

1 (1 lb.) can stewed tomatoes	1 tsp. sugar
2⅓ c. grated pared potatoes	1 tsp. salt
1½ c. chopped onion	½ tsp. summer savory leaves
2 tblsp. butter or regular margarine	¼ tsp. pepper
2 c. water	¼ tsp. baking soda
	4 c. milk

Combine tomatoes, potatoes, onion, butter and water in Dutch oven. Cover. Bring to a boil; reduce heat and simmer 50 minutes or until potatoes are tender.

Add sugar, salt, savory, pepper and baking soda; mix well. Gradually stir in milk. Heat over low heat. (Do not boil.) Makes about 1½ quarts or 5 servings.

GREEN BEAN AND PORK SOUP

A young German bride brought this recipe to this country in 1865. It was one of the treasures that she brought with her from the homeland and has survived 3 generations. Today her great-granddaughter serves this hearty soup. And it is so nourishing, with a double boost of protein in pork and navy beans. Making this soup is a family tradition when the first beans have been picked from the garden. Each serving is topped with bread cubes that have been sautéed in butter until they are crunchy and golden brown.

GREEN BEAN AND PORK SOUP

Traditionally prunes are substituted for green beans in winter

1 lb. dried navy beans	2 qts. water
2 lb. boneless pork shoulder roast	4 c. diced pared potatoes
2 c. chopped onion	4 c. cut-up green beans (1½" pieces)
2 bay leaves	2 c. chopped carrots
1½ tsp. salt	

Wash beans. Cover with water; let stand overnight.

Pour off soaking water; rinse and drain well.

Combine beans, pork, onion, bay leaves, salt and water in 6-qt. kettle. Cover. Bring to a boil; reduce heat and simmer 3 hours or until meat and beans are tender.

Add potatoes, green beans and carrots. Cook, covered, 40 more minutes or until vegetables are tender. Remove pork and cut into chunks. Add pork back to soup mixture. Makes about 3 quarts or 9 servings.

HEARTY SPLIT PEA SOUP

German cooks are artists when it comes to making soup. In Germany there is a soup for every occasion. For a first course, perhaps a clear broth that has been simmered to just the right strength and flavor or a rich, cream soup—green asparagus is a top favorite in the spring. These thrifty cooks have a knack of turning an assortment of leftovers into a rich, nourishing meal.

One of the most popular soups is the Hearty Split Pea Soup, popular with German descendants in the United States. In fact, every family has its special way of preparing this protein-rich soup. For some it must be thick with potatoes and carrots; for others it must have besides the ham some thick slices of bratwurst. Members of each family think their soup is the very best!

HEARTY SPLIT PEA SOUP

Pass lots of crisp saltines with this rib-sticking, homemade soup

3 ham hocks (1½ lbs.)	**8 c. water**
1 lb. dried split peas	**1 tsp. salt**
1¼ c. chopped carrots	**4 whole peppercorns**
(¼″ cubes)	**4 whole allspice**
½ c. sliced onion	**1 bay leaf**

Combine ham hocks, peas, carrots, onion, water and salt in Dutch oven. Cover. Bring to a boil.

Meanwhile, tie peppercorns, allspice and bay leaf in a small piece of cheesecloth. Add to pea mixture. Reduce heat and simmer 45 minutes or until peas are tender. Discard spice bag.

Remove ham hocks from soup mixture. Remove meat from bones. Discard bones. Cut ham up into chunks and add back to soup mixture. Makes 2 quarts or 6 servings.

CREAM OF POTATO SOUP

This hearty, rib-sticking soup has been served in a Wisconsin family for 3 generations. It has been the favorite cold weather supper dish since great-grandmother arrived from Germany. Potatoes, milk and cream were plentiful and it was an economical way to feed a large family. Bowls were filled to brimming and a platter of grilled cheese sandwiches rounded out the meal. Sometimes thin slices of sausage were added as garnish.

CREAM OF POTATO SOUP

Your family will welcome this soup for lunch on a cold day

3 lbs. potatoes, pared and
    cut up (9 medium)
4 whole carrots, pared
1 c. chopped onion
1½ tsp. salt

2½ c. milk
1 c. light cream
⅛ tsp. pepper
1 tblsp. minced fresh parsley

Place potatoes, carrots, onion and salt in Dutch oven. Add water to cover vegetables. Cover. Bring to a boil; reduce heat and simmer 20 minutes or until vegetables are tender.

Drain well. Remove carrots; set aside.

Mash potatoes well with potato masher. Gradually add milk and light cream, mixing well after each addition. Add pepper and parsley. Coarsely chop carrots and add to soup. Heat soup to serve (do not boil). Makes 2 quarts or 6 servings.

RED CABBAGE WITH APPLES

While the pot roast is cooking in a German household or in an American household of German descent—the red cabbage and apples are simmering to tangy goodness. These two foods taste wonderful together. All that is missing is a big bowl of fluffy mashed potatoes or giant dumplings—and deep-brown, rich gravy to ladle over meat and potatoes.

RED CABBAGE WITH APPLES

A tasty vegetable combination that accents both meat and poultry

1 medium head red cabbage, cut in ⅛" strips (about 2 lbs.)
2 medium apples, pared, cored and cut in ⅛" slices
½ c. chopped onion
2 tblsp. butter or regular margarine
½ c. red wine vinegar
1 bay leaf
2 tblsp. sugar
½ tsp. salt

Cook cabbage, apples and onion in melted butter in large skillet or Dutch oven 5 minutes, stirring often.

Add vinegar, bay leaf, sugar and salt. Cover. Bring mixture to a boil; reduce heat and simmer 35 minutes or until cabbage is tender. Remove bay leaf. Makes 12 servings.

HOMEMADE SAUERKRAUT

There are hundreds of methods for preparing sauerkraut that are regional as well as personal. Some cooks like to simmer the kraut until it's very soft and limp. Others like a bit of crunch and reduce the cooking period. The liquids that sauerkraut is simmered in are numerous. Plain water, apple juice and beef bouillon are a few favorites. Caraway seeds are a popular addition. Some cooks always grate a little raw potato into the simmering kraut while flour is often added as a thickener. Then there's the theory that kraut should *never* be thickened.

HOMEMADE SAUERKRAUT

Always rinse sauerkraut with warm water before you use it

You will need roughly 5 lbs. cabbage for every gal. of your crock. For instance, a 10-gal. crock would need about 50 lbs. of cabbage.

Quarter cabbage and shred finely. Place 5 lbs. shredded cabbage and 3½ tblsp. pickling salt in large pan. Mix well with hands. Pack gently in large crock, using a potato masher to press it down. Repeat above procedure until crock is filled to within 5" from the top.

Press cabbage down firmly with potato masher to extract enough juice to cover. Cover with clean cloth. Place a plate on top and weight it down with a jar filled with water.

Keep crock at 65° to ferment. Check kraut daily. Remove scum as it forms. Wash and scald cloth often to keep it free from scum and mold. Fermentation will be complete in 10 to 12 days. (If no bubbles rise, fermentation has ended.)

Pack in hot, sterilized jars to within 1" from top. Add enough juice to cover. If you need more juice, make a weak brine by combining 2 tblsp. salt and 1 qt. water. Cover; screw band tight. Process in boiling water bath 15 minutes. Fifty pounds of sauerkraut makes about 15 quarts.

SPRING LETTUCE SALAD

After a long winter of eating root vegetables, Germans welcomed the first tender leaves of spring lettuce. And the first batch was washed, crisped and coated with a tasty dressing made with light cream, vinegar and sugar. Then the final touch was added —a garnish of chopped eggs and crisp bits of bacon.

"The recipe has been in our family for years, can't imagine any German surviving without it," the Ohio contributor wrote us.

SPRING LETTUCE SALAD

Fresh spinach can be substituted for all or part of the lettuce

4 strips bacon	**1 c. light cream**
1 tblsp. flour	**3 qts. bite-size pieces**
1 tblsp. sugar	**romaine or leaf lettuce**
1 tsp. salt	**3 hard-cooked eggs,**
2 tblsp. vinegar	**chopped**

Fry bacon in skillet until crisp. Remove and drain on paper towels. Crumble; set aside.

Pour off bacon drippings, reserving 3 tblsp. Stir in flour, sugar, salt, vinegar and cream. Cook over low heat, stirring constantly, until mixture thickens slightly.

Pour hot mixture over lettuce, eggs and reserved bacon. Toss gently to mix. Serve immediately. Makes 10 servings.

PEARS AND POTATOES

An Oklahoma woman studied violin at the Royal Conservatory in Germany when she was a young girl. One of the dishes she enjoyed was Pears and Potatoes and she carefully copied the recipe.

We found this to be a very different dish and the combination of the fruit and vegetable was subtle and delicious. It's a wonderful accompaniment to a pork roast.

PEARS AND POTATOES

This unusual dish is even better when prepared ahead and reheated

4 strips bacon, diced	**3½ c. thickly sliced pared**
3½ c. thickly sliced pared	**pears (about 4 medium)**
potatoes (about 1¼ lbs.)	**¼ c. vinegar**
1 tsp. salt	**1 bay leaf**
1 c. hot water	**¼ tsp. ground allspice**

Fry bacon in Dutch oven until crisp. Remove and drain on paper towels. Crumble and set aside.

Add potatoes, salt and water to bacon drippings. Cover. Bring to a boil; reduce heat and simmer 25 minutes or until potatoes are tender.

Add pears, vinegar, bay leaf, allspice and reserved bacon. Cover and simmer 15 more minutes or until pears are tender. Makes 6 servings.

GERMAN HOT POTATO SALAD

This recipe for tangy potato salad has been in an Illinois family recipe file for 43 years. Every year they have met for a family reunion in August and there's always plenty of this salad on hand to eat with the grilled frankfurters.

The touch of rosemary adds an interesting flavor. There is plenty of dressing and it's perfect—not too sweet and not too tangy.

GERMAN HOT POTATO SALAD

Leftover salad is best if warmed slightly before serving

8 slices bacon, diced	⅔ c. cider vinegar
3 tblsp. flour	⅔ c. water
⅓ c. sugar	8 c. diced, cooked potatoes
3 tsp. salt	(about 4 lbs.)
1 tsp. dry mustard	½ c. chopped onion
¼ tsp. rosemary leaves	⅓ c. chopped fresh parsley
⅛ tsp. pepper	

Fry bacon in 10" skillet until crisp. Stir in flour, sugar, salt, mustard, rosemary, pepper, vinegar and water. Cook over medium heat, stirring constantly, until mixture thickens.

Pour hot sauce over potatoes, onion and parsley. Toss gently to mix. Serve warm. Makes 10 servings.

GERMAN-STYLE POTATO SALAD

Another potato salad that has been around for 75 years—every German family has a pet recipe for this zippy hot salad. And everyone has very definite ideas about ingredients and the balance of sugar and vinegar. This family's recipe calls for sliced potatoes and chopped celery for a little crunch. The thickening is cornstarch rather than flour—some cooks feel it produces a more translucent sauce.

GERMAN-STYLE POTATO SALAD

Everyone will ask for seconds when you serve this tangy salad

5 lbs. new potatoes	**1 tblsp. salt**
1 tblsp. salt	**¼ tsp. pepper**
½ lb. bacon	**2 c. water**
2 tblsp. cornstarch	**1 c. chopped onion**
½ c. vinegar	**½ c. chopped celery**
¼ c. sugar	

Cook potatoes with jackets and 1 tblsp. salt in boiling water until tender, about 30 minutes. Drain. Cool.

Remove peels. Cut potatoes into thin slices.

Fry bacon in skillet until crisp. Remove and drain on paper towels. Crumble bacon; set aside.

Pour off all but ½ c. bacon drippings. Combine cornstarch and vinegar; stir well. Add cornstarch mixture, sugar, 1 tblsp. salt, pepper and water to bacon drippings. Cook over medium heat, stirring constantly, until mixture thickens.

Pour hot sauce over combined potatoes, onion, celery and reserved bacon. Toss gently to mix. Makes 12 servings.

GERMAN POTATO PANCAKES

Crisp and crunchy around the edges, these potato pancakes are great to serve for luncheon or supper. Be sure and have a big bowl of homemade applesauce to eat along with them. Many German families make a complete meal of pancakes and applesauce. A different way to serve potatoes with thin slices of leftover pot roast.

GERMAN POTATO PANCAKES

Also good served with browned pork sausages and apple rings

2 lbs. potatoes, pared and grated (5 c.)	1 tsp. salt
	⅔ c. cooking oil
6 tblsp. flour	Applesauce
¼ c. minced onion	Pancake syrup
2 eggs, beaten	

Combine potatoes, flour, onion, eggs and salt; mix well.

Bake pancakes in hot oil in 10″ skillet, using ¼ c. mixture for each. Cook over medium heat, 4 minutes on each side, or until golden brown and potatoes are tender. Serve with applesauce or pancake syrup. Makes 14 (3½″) pancakes.

POPPY SEED ROLL

This most favorite recipe has been treasured through several generations in a Montana home. It's a great specialty of this German community and a "must" at all family reunions. Poppy seed filling is what makes this so good. The poppy seeds are ground in a coffee grinder or electric blender and mixed with sugar, corn syrup, eggs and cream or evaporated milk—the secret is to spread it thickly, at least ½″ thick on the dough before it's rolled tightly and baked. A 94-year-old German lady from Montana was thrilled when she sampled one of these Poppy Seed Rolls. Her eyes lighted up as she said, "Ah, Moon Kuchen—that's what we call it in the Old Country."

POPPY SEED ROLL

A German coffee bread that's rolled up like a jelly roll

½ c. butter or regular margarine	7 c. sifted flour
⅔ c. sugar	2 c. poppy seeds
1 tblsp. salt	1 c. sugar
2 eggs, beaten	½ c. light corn syrup
2 pkgs. active dry yeast	1 egg, beaten
1 c. lukewarm water	3 tblsp. evaporated milk
1 c. milk, scalded and cooled	

Cream together butter and ⅔ c. sugar until light and fluffy. Add salt and 2 eggs, beating well.

Sprinkle yeast on lukewarm water; stir to dissolve. Add yeast and milk to butter mixture; mix well.

Gradually add enough flour to make a very soft dough. (Dough is sticky.) Place in lightly greased bowl; turn dough over to grease top. Cover and let rise in warm place until doubled, about 1½ hours.

Meanwhile, prepare poppy seed filling. Grind poppy seeds in blender, ½ c. at a time, until smooth. Combine ground poppy seeds, 1 c. sugar, corn syrup, 1 egg and evaporated milk; mix well.

Divide dough in fourths. Roll on floured surface to 15×12″ rectangle. Spread with ½ c. of poppy seed mixture. Roll up like jelly roll and pinch seam together. Place on greased baking sheet, seam side down. Repeat with remaining dough.

Bake in 350° oven 20 to 25 minutes or until golden brown. Makes 4 rolls.

STREUSEL KUCHEN

"Just the mention of this Streusel Kuchen has been known to cause pangs of homesickness," a 90-year-old German woman from California says. She received the recipe years ago from a

German immigrant who every Thursday morning would make 3 batches of this luscious crumbed cake. Then there was plenty for anyone who dropped in for coffee or a chat for the tripled recipe made an even dozen. We baked 2 batches, one with the Streusel Topping and the other with a thick coating of brown sugar. They freeze beautifully—good to have on hand for any generation.

STREUSEL KUCHEN

Serve these crumb-topped wedges with plenty of soft, creamy butter

½ c. butter or regular margarine	2 c. milk, scalded and cooled
1 c. sugar	7 c. sifted flour
1 tsp. salt	¼ c. melted butter or regular margarine
1 egg, separated	Streusel Topping (recipe follows)
1 pkg. active dry yeast	
⅓ c. lukewarm water	

Cream together ½ c. butter and sugar until light and fluffy. Add salt and egg yolk, beating well.

Sprinkle yeast on lukewarm water; stir to dissolve. Combine yeast and milk. Add to creamed mixture alternately with flour, mixing well after each addition.

Beat egg white until stiff peaks form. Fold into mixture. Cover bowl with plastic wrap. Refrigerate 8 hours or overnight.

Divide dough in fourths. Pat dough in 4 greased 9″ pie plates. Cover and let rise in a warm place until light, about 1 hour 30 minutes.

Brush kuchens with ¼ c. melted butter. Sprinkle with Streusel Topping.

Bake in 400° oven 20 minutes or until golden. Makes 4 kuchens.

Streusel Topping: Combine ¼ c. flour, ½ c. sugar and 1 tsp. ground cinnamon. Cut in 3 tblsp. butter or regular margarine until mixture is crumbly. Add 1 tsp. vanilla and ¼ c. finely chopped walnuts; mix well.

GERMAN CHRISTMAS BREAD

While many recipes that were brought to this country from Europe remained intact through the years, some were revised and adjusted to suit the family's taste. This German Christmas Bread is an example. The recipe always had citron and white raisins as ingredients but a daughter chose to put 1 tablespoon of citron instead of ½ cup and often omitted it completely. Her family loved raisins so a cup of dark raisins was added, along with a little grated lemon rind. This Nebraska farm woman always makes several batches of fruit-studded bread during the Christmas holidays just as her mother did for years of family celebrations.

GERMAN CHRISTMAS BREAD

Decorate with bits of candied fruits for a more festive look

1½ c. milk, scalded
¼ c. sugar
1 tblsp. salt
2 pkgs. active dry yeast
½ c. lukewarm water
3 eggs
6½ c. sifted flour

1 tsp. grated lemon peel
¼ c. melted butter or
   regular margarine
1 c. golden raisins
1 c. dark raisins
Thin Glaze (recipe follows)

Combine milk, sugar and salt; cool to lukewarm.

Sprinkle yeast over lukewarm water; stir to dissolve. Add yeast, eggs and 2 c. flour to milk mixture. Beat with electric mixer at medium speed until smooth, about 2 minutes, scraping bowl occasionally. Or beat with spoon until smooth.

Add lemon peel, butter and enough remaining flour to make a soft dough that leaves the sides of the bowl.

Turn dough onto lightly floured surface. Knead in raisins. Continue kneading until smooth and satiny, about 10 minutes.

Place dough in greased bowl; turn over to grease top. Cover and let rise in warm place until doubled, about 1 hour 30 minutes.

Divide dough in thirds. Shape each into 8″ round loaf. Place on greased baking sheets. Let rise until doubled, about 1 hour 30 minutes.

Bake in 350° oven 30 to 35 minutes or until golden brown. Cool 10 minutes on racks. Frost with Thin Glaze. Makes 3 coffee cakes.

Thin Glaze: Combine 1 c. sifted confectioners sugar, 2 tsp. soft butter or regular margarine, 2 tblsp. milk and 1 tsp. vanilla; beat until smooth.

OLD-FASHIONED GERMAN KUCHEN

If you visited all the different German communities that dot the Midwest and collected kuchen recipes, you would no doubt have enough to turn out a cookbook on kuchen alone. Every one varies from the other in richness, toppings, shapes and sizes. But they are all buttery and crunchy with nuts and sugar—some of the best sweet doughs in the land. This old-fashioned kuchen is a fine-textured dough, lavish with butter and filled generously with nuts, sugar and cinnamon. Good recipe for the holiday as one batch makes 4 beautiful tea rings. For a bright holiday appearance, substitute chopped maraschino cherries for half the walnuts and decorate the glazed top with bright green citron.

OLD-FASHIONED GERMAN KUCHEN

Freeze these buttery coffee cakes for the Christmas holidays

4 c. sifted flour	½ c. melted butter or
3 tblsp. sugar	regular margarine
½ tsp. salt	1 c. sugar
1 c. shortening	1½ c. finely chopped
1 pkg. active dry yeast	walnuts
¼ c. lukewarm water	1½ tsp. ground cinnamon
1 c. cold milk	Thin Vanilla Icing (recipe
3 egg yolks, beaten	follows)

Combine flour, 3 tblsp. sugar and salt. Cut in shortening with pastry blender or two knives until mixture is crumbly.

Sprinkle yeast over lukewarm water; stir to dissolve. Add yeast, milk and egg-yolks to crumb mixture; stir until blended. Cover with aluminum foil or plastic wrap. Refrigerate 12 hours or overnight.

Divide dough into fourths. Roll each on floured surface to 14×11" rectangle. Brush with melted butter. Sprinkle with combined 1 c. sugar, walnuts and cinnamon. Roll up like jelly roll from narrow side. Pinch seam together. Place on greased baking sheets. Form into a circle; pinch ends together. With floured scissors, make cuts ⅔ of the way through ring at 1" intervals. Turn each cut section on its side. Let rise until doubled, about 2 hours.

Bake in 350° oven 20 to 25 minutes or until golden brown. Cool on racks. Frost with Thin Vanilla Icing. Makes 4 coffee rings.

Thin Vanilla Icing: Combine 1½ c. sifted confectioners sugar, 1 tblsp. soft butter or regular margarine, 2 tblsp. hot water and 1 tsp. vanilla; beat until smooth.

GERMAN PANCAKES

A New England farm woman grew up with these pancakes. She remembers how she loved to spread the golden pancake with butter, cinnamon and sugar, then roll it up and eat it out of hand. This versatile pancake can serve as dessert or as the main course. Her children love them for every meal: In the morning filled with sausage, at lunch sprinkled with grated cheese and for dessert spread thickly with homemade strawberry jam.

GERMAN PANCAKES

Protein-rich pancakes that are so versatile . . . serve them often

1½ c. sifted flour	2 c. milk
⅔ c. sugar	Red raspberry jelly
1 tsp. salt	Confectioners sugar
4 eggs, beaten	

Sift together flour, sugar and salt.

Combine eggs and milk. Add to flour mixture. Beat with rotary beater until smooth.

Pour ½ c. batter into lightly greased 10″ skillet, tilting skillet back and forth until it coats the bottom evenly. When lightly browned, loosen edges with metal spatula and turn over. Spread pancakes with raspberry jelly and roll up. Dust with confectioners sugar. Makes 6 (10″) pancakes.

BAVARIAN APPLE STRUDEL

Be sure to remove your rings before working with this delicate dough, which you stretch into a tissue-thin sheet. This is one of the most famous German desserts. The finished product with its spiced, apple-raisin filling is handsome when removed from the oven. The dough is golden brown and crisp as a parchment.

BAVARIAN APPLE STRUDEL

This flaky strudel is also delicious made with cherry pie filling

1 tblsp. cooking oil	¼ c. sugar
1 egg, beaten	1 tsp. ground cinnamon
⅓ c. lukewarm water	⅓ c. melted butter or
¼ tsp. salt	regular margarine
1½ c. sifted flour	⅓ c. dry bread crumbs
8 c. sliced pared tart apples	Confectioners sugar
1 c. raisins	

Combine oil, egg, water and salt. Gradually add flour, beating with spoon until a firm dough that pulls away from the sides of the bowl is formed.

Knead dough on floured surface until smooth and elastic, about 5 minutes. Cover and let rest 30 minutes.

Combine apples, raisins, sugar and cinnamon; set aside.

Divide dough in half. Roll each half into 18×12″ rectangle, stretching dough if necessary to make it very thin. Brush with melted butter. Sprinkle dough with half of bread crumbs. Spread half of apple mixture lengthwise in center third of dough. Fold dough over apples on one side and then the other. Brush with melted butter. Place on greased baking sheet. Repeat with remaining dough.

Bake in 400° oven 30 minutes or until golden brown and apples are tender. Serve warm or cold sprinkled with confectioners sugar. Makes 16 servings.

INDIVIDUAL SCHAUM TORTES

This delicate meringue dessert is one of the most elegant and special German desserts . . . pale amber and crunchy on the outside, soft and marshmallowy inside. When strawberries are in season this makes a mouth-watering dessert. Fill the individual meringues with strawberries and frost with a cloud of whipped cream. This tastes equally good with sliced peaches—makes a lovely party dessert to impress your guests.

INDIVIDUAL SCHAUM TORTES

Meringues store well in covered containers for up to two weeks

8 egg whites	2 qts. fresh strawberries,
½ tsp. cream of tartar	sliced and sweetened or
2 c. sugar	3 (10 oz.) pkgs. frozen
1 tsp. vanilla	strawberries, thawed
1 tsp. vinegar	2 c. heavy cream, whipped
	and sweetened

Beat egg whites with electric mixer at high speed until frothy. Add cream of tartar. Beat until egg whites are almost dry.

Slowly add sugar, 2 tblsp. at a time, beating well after each addition. (Total beating time: 20 minutes.) Add vanilla and vinegar, beat 2 minutes. (Mixture should be very stiff and glossy.) Drop mixture by spoonfuls onto greased baking sheets, making 10 tortes.

Bake in 250° oven 1 hour 15 minutes or until pale brown and crusty. Remove from baking sheets; cool on racks.

To serve: Spoon strawberries over each torte and top with whipped cream. Makes 10 servings.

SPICY MOLASSES COOKIES

A young farm girl in Wisconsin baked a batch of her great aunt's German molasses cookies. She offered several along with a glass of lemonade to a neighboring farm boy who was baling hay. After he had demolished 3 cookies and 2 glasses of lemonade he asked her for a date. "Now, I bake them for him and our children every week," she says.

SPICY MOLASSES COOKIES

Crisp and extra spicy cookies that will make a hit every time

1 c. shortening	1 tblsp. ground cinnamon
2 c. sugar	1 tblsp. ground ginger
2 eggs	1 tsp. salt
¾ c. dark molasses	1 tsp. baking powder
1½ tsp. lemon extract	1 tsp. baking soda
5 c. sifted flour	2 tblsp. vinegar

Cream together shortening and sugar until light and fluffy. Add eggs; beat well. Beat in molasses and lemon extract.

Sift together flour, cinnamon, ginger, salt, baking powder and baking soda. Add to creamed mixture with vinegar; mix well.

Roll dough out on floured surface to ⅛" thick. Cut with floured 2" cookie cutter. Place cookies about 1½" apart on greased baking sheets.

Bake in 350° oven 6 to 8 minutes or until brown. Remove from baking sheets; cool on racks. Makes about 15 dozen.

DATE/RAISIN CAKE

According to an Ohio woman's family history her German ancestors settled in Maryland. After fighting in an Ohio regiment her grandfather moved his family to an Ohio farm and raised nine children. This spicy cake was his favorite and he always raised a fuss when it was frosted—a dusting of powdered sugar was all it needed, he felt.

DATE/RAISIN CAKE

Moist-crumbed raisin cake that is great to eat out of hand

⅔ c. butter or regular margarine	1 tsp. ground allspice
2 c. brown sugar, firmly packed	½ tsp. ground ginger
	½ tsp. salt
2 eggs	1 c. warm coffee
3¼ c. sifted flour	1 c. raisins
2 tsp. baking powder	1 c. cut-up dates
1½ tsp. ground cinnamon	1 c. chopped walnuts
1 tsp. baking soda	1 tblsp. flour
	Confectioners sugar

Cream together butter and brown sugar until light and fluffy. Add eggs, one at a time, beating well after each addition.

Sift together 3¼ c. flour, baking powder, cinnamon, baking soda, allspice, ginger and salt. Add dry ingredients to creamed mixture alternately with coffee, beating well after each addition.

Combine raisins, dates, walnuts and 1 tblsp. flour; mix well. Stir into batter. Spread batter in greased 13×9×2″ baking pan.

Bake in 350° oven 35 minutes or until cake tests done. Cool. Sprinkle with confectioners sugar. Cut in 3″ squares. Makes 12 servings.

BLITZ TORTE

A typical German torte, this is a 3-layered beauty. Cake layers are topped with meringue and baked. Then the layers are filled with a rich, sour cream mixture and sliced bananas. For those who worry about calories, substitute a thin layer of whipped cream and sliced peaches for the sour cream filling. Delicious both ways!

BLITZ TORTE

A favorite in this Wisconsin family for over four generations

¼ c. butter or regular margarine	¾ c. sugar
½ c. sugar	½ c. chopped walnuts
4 eggs, separated	5 tblsp. sugar
1 tsp. vanilla	1 tblsp. cornstarch
1 c. sifted flour	1 c. dairy sour cream
1½ tsp. baking powder	1 egg, beaten
5 tblsp. milk	1 large banana, sliced

Cream together butter and ½ c. sugar until light and fluffy. Add 4 egg yolks and vanilla; beat well.

Sift together flour and baking powder. Add dry ingredients alternately with milk, beating well after each addition. Spread batter in 2 greased and floured 8" round cake pans.

Beat 4 egg whites until frothy. Gradually add ¾ c. sugar, beating until soft peaks form. Spread meringue carefully over cake batter in both pans. Sprinkle walnuts on top of each.

Bake in 350° oven 30 minutes or until cakes test done. Cool in pans 10 minutes. Remove from pans; cool on racks, meringue side up.

Combine 5 tblsp. sugar and cornstarch in small saucepan. Add sour cream and egg; mix well. Cook over low heat, stirring constantly, until mixture thickens, about 10 minutes.

Place one cake layer, meringue side up, on serving plate. Spread with cream filling. Top with banana slices. Top with other cake layer, meringue side up. Makes 10 servings.

GERMAN REFRIGERATOR COOKIES

Light, golden cookies with crackled tops—a Christmas heirloom always served during the holidays. Cardamom is used in these and many other German cookies and breads during the Christmas season. The crushed ivory-colored cardamom pod adds a special flavor.

GERMAN REFRIGERATOR COOKIES

"I don't remember a Christmas that we didn't have dozens of these"

½ c. butter or regular margarine	1 egg
½ c. lard	2 c. sifted flour
2 c. sugar	1 tsp. baking soda
	½ tsp. ground cardamom

Cream together butter, lard and sugar until light and fluffy. Add egg; beat well.

Sift together flour, baking soda and cardamom. Stir into creamed mixture; mix well. Cover and refrigerate overnight.

Shape dough into 1" balls. Place about 1½" apart on greased baking sheets.

Bake in 325° oven 10 minutes or until golden brown. Remove from baking sheets; cool on racks. Makes 5 dozen.

CARAMEL BREAD PUDDING

"My German grandmother always made this simple bread pudding for family and company. The rich caramel sauce made it extra-special," an Indiana farm woman told us. She said it was wholesome, lip-smacking good. We agree. This easy-to-fix dessert simmers for an hour and needs no stirring. Equally good hot or cold.

CARAMEL BREAD PUDDING

A three-layer bread pudding laced with a rich caramel custard

2 tblsp. butter or regular margarine	6 eggs
1 c. light brown sugar, firmly packed	½ c. light brown sugar, firmly packed
6 slices white bread, cut in ½" cubes	2 c. milk
	⅛ tsp. salt
	1 tsp. vanilla

Generously butter the inside of double boiler top. Place 1 c. brown sugar in bottom and then a layer of bread cubes. (Do not mix.)

Beat eggs well with rotary beater. Gradually beat in ½ c. brown sugar, milk, salt and vanilla. Pour over bread cubes. (Do not stir.) Place over simmering water. Cover and cook 1 hour 30 minutes. Serve hot. Makes 6 to 8 servings.

GERMAN RICE PUDDING

A very creamy pudding in spite of the fact that it contains no eggs. This handed-down recipe originated in Germany and is very popular at church suppers, a Texas farm wife told us. The family prefers it warm with a big dollop of applesauce. For church suppers she makes it early in the morning, then cools it and pours it into a big plastic bowl. Just before she leaves for the supper she dusts the top with a generous layer of cinnamon.

GERMAN RICE PUDDING

Easy-to-fix dessert cooks on top of the range . . . so creamy good

½ c. regular rice	½ tsp. salt
2 c. boiling water	1 tsp. vanilla
3 c. milk	Ground cinnamon
½ c. sugar	

Add rice to boiling water in 2-qt. saucepan. Bring to a boil again; reduce heat and cook, stirring occasionally, until all the water is absorbed.

Stir in milk. Simmer 20 minutes, stirring occasionally. Add sugar and salt; continue cooking 20 more minutes or until mixture is creamy. Stir in vanilla. Serve warm, sprinkled with cinnamon. Makes 6 servings.

Chapter 3

THE HERITAGE
OF DUTCH
COOKING

The Dutch are careful, thrifty and home-loving. Their food is straightforward, simple and hearty. The Dutch have always had a continuous battle with the sea for their land, so dikes predominate the landscape and make possible large areas of rich farmland. Dairying provides creamy milk, butter and cheese, notably the orange-yellow Edam and the pale-yellow Gouda. At one time every farm woman turned out her own cheeses. Dutch country cheese can be bought in three stages; young cheese, which is soft and creamy; old cheese which is heavy, full-bodied in flavor and golden yellow, and aged cheese which is dry and flaky with a piquant flavor.

Because Holland is so rich in coastal areas, much of the Dutch food comes from the ocean. They have been feasting on herring for centuries. In the 15th century, the day before the herring fleet sailed in May was usually a day of celebration.

Like the Germans, they love their soups, usually lusty-full of meat. The national soup in the Netherlands is pea soup. There are as many varieties as there are cooks. Every housewife has her own recipe. According to Dutch legend, any self-respecting Dutch pea soup must be so thick that the spoon will stand up in it.

When a Dutch woman plans her meal she is likely to think first of the vegetables and then the meat. They love vegetables and pride themselves on their preparation of them. Their favorites are carrots, onions, turnips, leeks, spinach, cabbage and beans—they often combine five or six vegetables in one dish. Beans form a large part of their menu and they like them any way they are fixed but especially baked with bacon and molasses. The oldest street in Amsterdam is named for the vegetable growers who lived there in the Middle Ages.

The Dutch taste for almonds, cinnamon, nutmeg and ginger, dates back to the 16th century when the Netherlands gained control of the East Indies.

For breakfast they eat a variety of breads and sliced cheeses and meat. They like pancakes on the large size with sweet or meat fillings. New Year is welcomed in with *oliebollen*. These Dutch doughnuts are a traditional treat on New Year's Eve.

The Dutch get the sharp wind from the North Sea and it builds a hunger for hearty, simple, nourishing fare; they don't go in for elaborate dishes and complicated sauces. The Dutch recipes that found their way to America via immigrants have the same hearty characteristics.

PORK CHOP/SAUERKRAUT CASSEROLE

A third-generation recipe that has been in the family and made every winter since their Dutch ancestors brought it to Ohio. This farm wife varies the meat, using pork chops, sausage or ham layered with apples and sauerkraut. A rich, nourishing meal that everyone enjoys.

PORK CHOP/SAUERKRAUT CASSEROLE

This dish simmers to perfection while you do other chores

2 large tart red apples,
   pared, cored and cut in
   ¼" slices
1 c. chopped onion
1 (1 lb.) can sauerkraut

¼ c. sugar
4 pork chops, ½" thick
Salt
Pepper

Place apples in bottom of 3-qt. casserole. Top with layer of onion and then sauerkraut. Sprinkle with sugar.

Season pork chops with salt and pepper to taste. Brown well on both sides in skillet, adding cooking oil if necessary. Place browned chops on top of sauerkraut. Cover.

Bake in 350° oven 1 hour 15 minutes. Remove cover. Bake 15 more minutes. Makes 4 servings.

PORK WITH APPLES AND POTATOES

Seventy-two years ago a farmer came to Wisconsin to operate a dairy farm and he remembered eating what he called a Dutch dinner. This robust, economical meal was prepared from all the ingredients that had been grown on their land. Pork, apples and potatoes were cooked together with a spicy bay leaf. Good eating on a cold winter night after chores.

PORK WITH APPLES AND POTATOES

So good with crusty bread to mop up the flavorful juices

1½ lbs. boneless pork shoulder, cut in 1″ cubes	6 medium potatoes, pared and cut in eighths
4 c. water	4 medium, tart red apples, pared, cored and cut in eighths
1 tblsp. salt	
⅛ tsp. pepper	
1 bay leaf	

Place pork cubes, water, salt, pepper and bay leaf in Dutch oven. Cover and bring to a boil. Reduce heat and simmer 1 hour 30 minutes or until meat is tender. Add potatoes; cook 10 minutes. Add apples and cook 20 minutes or until apples are tender. Serve with crusty bread, if you wish. Makes 4 to 6 servings.

DUTCH LETTUCE SALAD

The Dutch combine greens with skill and taste. This tasty salad, an heirloom from Michigan, is popular at family reunions and picnics. Egg and bacon garnish add an attractive note to this tangy salad.

DUTCH LETTUCE SALAD

Wash and crisp the greens ahead . . . toss at the last minute

6 strips bacon
¼ c. cider vinegar
¼ c. water
1 tblsp. sugar
4 hard-cooked eggs, sliced

4 c. bite-size pieces
   romaine lettuce
4 c. bite-size pieces fresh
   spinach

Fry bacon in small skillet until crisp. Remove and drain on paper towels. Crumble bacon.

Pour off bacon drippings; reserving 2 tblsp. Add vinegar, water and sugar to drippings. Bring to a boil, stirring constantly, cook 1 minute. Pour hot dressing over combined eggs, lettuce, spinach and bacon. Toss gently to mix. Makes 6 to 8 servings.

RAISIN PUDDING CAKE

An old-time recipe from Minnesota that was brought to this country from Holland. There were no measured amounts but through the generations, the recipe was worked up and put on a recipe card to be handed down to the next generation. A homey, old-fashioned cake that goes together quickly and bakes into a sweet pudding with a caramel sauce.

RAISIN PUDDING CAKE

Easy to fix . . . cake bakes on top with a rich sauce underneath

1 c. sifted flour
1 c. sugar
2 tsp. baking powder
¼ tsp. salt
½ c. milk
1 c. raisins

½ c. chopped walnuts
1 c. brown sugar, firmly
   packed
1 tsp. butter or regular
   margarine
1½ c. boiling water

Sift together flour, sugar, baking powder and salt into bowl. Add milk, raisins and walnuts; mix with spoon until blended. Spread batter in greased 9″ square baking pan.

Combine brown sugar, butter and boiling water; stir well. Pour over batter (do not mix).

Bake in 350° oven 35 minutes or until cake tests done. Serve warm. Makes 6 servings.

GRANDMA'S GLORIFIED GINGERBREAD

This recipe traveled from Holland to Pennsylvania and was passed on through the generations. An Oklahoma farm wife remembers her mother baking it in an old cookstove for the children. It was eaten piping hot with lots of home-churned butter. There was always plenty of sour milk and fresh eggs and when her mother would ask, "Who wants to crack some walnuts for gingerbread?" everyone would volunteer. The recipe is now in the hands of *great*-grandchildren. They use pecans from trees in their back yard.

GRANDMA'S GLORIFIED GINGERBREAD

Mildly spiced gingerbread topped with golden crumbs

2 c. sifted flour	1 tsp. baking soda
1 c. sugar	1 c. sour milk
1 tsp. ground cinnamon	1 egg
1 tsp. ground ginger	¼ c. molasses
¼ tsp. salt	½ c. chopped walnuts
½ c. butter or regular	½ c. raisins
margarine	1 tblsp. flour

Sift together 2 c. flour, sugar, cinnamon, ginger and salt into bowl. Cut in butter with pastry blender or two knives until mixture resembles coarse crumbs. Reserve 1 c. crumbs.

Combine baking soda and sour milk. Add milk mixture, egg and molasses to remaining crumbs, and mix with spoon until well blended. Combine walnuts, raisins and 1 tblsp. flour; stir into batter. Spread batter in greased 9″ square baking pan. Top with reserved 1 c. crumbs.

Bake in 350° oven 40 minutes or until cake tests done. Cool in pan on rack. Makes 9 servings.

HOLLAND SPICE COOKIES

Many homemakers in a Dutch community in Wisconsin make this cookie. Each one varies the spices and nuts, and some cover cookies with a light icing, especially during the holidays.

HOLLAND SPICE COOKIES

Ice for the holidays and decorate with bits of candied fruit

1 c. butter or regular margarine	3 tsp. ground cinnamon
1 c. lard	1 tsp. salt
2 c. brown sugar, firmly packed	½ tsp. baking soda
	½ tsp. ground nutmeg
	¼ tsp. ground cloves
½ c. dairy sour cream	½ c. chopped walnuts
4½ c. sifted flour	

Cream together butter, lard and brown sugar until light and fluffy. Beat in sour cream.

Sift together flour, cinnamon, salt, baking soda, nutmeg and cloves. Gradually add dry ingredients to creamed mixture, mixing well with a spoon. Stir in walnuts. Cover and chill 1 hour in refrigerator.

Shape dough into 4 (6″) rolls. Chill in refrigerator overnight.

Cut rolls into ¼″ slices. Place 2″ apart on greased baking sheets.

Bake in 350° oven 8 to 10 minutes or until golden brown. Remove from baking sheets; cool on racks. Makes 8 dozen.

OLIEBOLLEN

An unusual doughnut filled with apples and raisins, this is served in Holland during the holidays and always on New Year's Day, with big pitchers of milk and freshly brewed coffee. The raisins poke through the dough giving them an unusual shape. A not-too-sweet doughnut that is very moist on the inside and crisp and crusty outside.

OLIEBOLLEN

Serve these doughnuts with hot cider on Christmas Eve

1 pkg. active dry yeast	**½ c. raisins**
½ tsp. sugar	**½ c. diced pared apple**
¾ c. warm milk	**3 tblsp. chopped, mixed**
2 c. sifted flour	**candied fruit**
2 tblsp. sugar	**1 tsp. grated lemon peel**
⅛ tsp. salt	**Cooking oil**
2 eggs, beaten	**Confectioners sugar**

Sprinkle yeast and ½ tsp. sugar on milk; stir to dissolve. Let stand 10 minutes.

Sift together flour, 2 tblsp. sugar and salt into bowl. Make a well in the center. Add yeast and eggs, mix just until blended. Stir in raisins, apple, candied fruit and lemon peel. Cover and let rise in warm place until doubled, about 1 hour.

Drop batter by heaping tablespoonfuls into deep, hot oil (350°), frying until golden brown, about 3 minutes. Drain on paper towels. Dust with confectioners sugar. Makes 15.

Chapter 4

THE HERITAGE
OF SCANDINAVIAN
COOKING

Although Denmark, Norway, Sweden and Finland—usually called Scandinavia—share much in common, each country retains its own stamp of individuality, and this is true also of their cuisines. They are hospitable people and their doors are always open. They use great ingenuity, imagination and skill in preparing and presenting foods. The roots of Scandinavian eating lie with their climate. For centuries these people were forced as a matter of survival to stock supplies ahead to get them through the great blizzards of winter. Nowhere in the world will you find more ways to preserve meat and fish than in Scandinavia.

Denmark is Scandinavia's lush land. The grass is thick and luxuriant, the cows produce the richest milk and the sweetest cream. Their vegetable gardens in the springtime are works of art. Big, well-fed, pink pigs dot the fields each one looking as if it were scrubbed daily. Their foods reflect their land—rich, abundant and colorful. Coffee cakes, rolls and pastries are unequaled —fine, light and crispy and served with strong, perfectly brewed coffee. Open-face sandwiches are as handsome as a painting— breads lavishly spread with butter and heaped with meat or cheese or fish and each one garnished beautifully.

Norway on the other hand, is comprised of breathtakingly beautiful fjords, rocky seashores, huge mountains and acres of thick forests. Country people work hard in Norway; the living is tougher and it's necessary to be sturdy to battle out the long winters in the fjords and mountains.

Norwegian cooking reflects their land; it is simple, sturdy, nourishing and not too rich. They consume much fish and bushels of potatoes. Norwegian housewives make a special dish called *lutfisk* from salted, dry cod. The cod is soaked for several days in water and then put in birchwood ash, which gives it a slightly rubbery consistency. They say you must be Norwegian to like this as it is very bland. But a true Norwegian smothers the lutfisk in plenty of butter and cream and sometimes a touch of mustard and declares it is delicious. This is popular with the older Norwegians in our farm communities today but the young people generally say "no thank you." Norwegian women bake bread and cook with cheeses. Americans of Norwegian descent have adapted Norwegian ideas into American recipes and come up with some interesting dishes.

Sweden is a prosperous country and famous for the *smörgåsbord;* a buffet style of dining originated centuries ago when there were opulent country gatherings. Everyone brought food and it was spread out on a long table for each one to sample a bit of his neighbors' treasures. Smörgåsbord is found in Norway and Denmark but doesn't feature the endless dishes that the Swedish people do.

Smörgåsbord is a deeply rooted Scandinavian tradition. It goes back to the Viking feast days, weddings, christenings and funerals. Distances traveled to get together were long and because they traveled a great many miles, they planned to stay for several weeks. They brought their food with them from all areas. Cheese and greens from the farms, fish from the lake and sea areas, and those from the forest arrived with game. The tables were heavily laden with food and everyone sampled a little of each.

There are similarities in many of the Scandinavian recipes due to the geographical closeness of the countries. Often the recipe of each country has only a slight variation from the other. Recipe terminology and spelling in Scandinavia are highly controversial

—the dialects are different in the provinces and you will find their spellings are old-style, modern or colloquial. A recipe proudly proclaimed the original of one province with its own spelling will show up in other parts of the country with a different name—same ingredients.

Smörgåsbord is popular in our own country, not on as lavish a scale, but the buffet entertaining with a good variety of foods does resemble the Swedish custom. It is enjoyed by all Americans —our numerous potluck suppers so popular in the country are probably a "melting pot" adaptation of the original smörgåsbord.

We offer you a sampling of Scandinavian dishes that have passed down through generations and adaptations in this country.

DANISH PORK ROAST

Danish homemakers are thrifty but cook with imagination and skill. One of the most popular dishes in Denmark handed down through generations is pork, and the Danish cook knows how to prepare it beautifully. One recipe is pork roast stuffed with dried fruits. This recipe has a filling of prunes and a beautiful glaze of currant jelly. This is truly company fare and would be a handsome substitute for the Thanksgiving or Christmas turkey for a change of pace.

DANISH PORK ROAST

Attractive pork roast stuffed with fruits and covered with crumbs

½ tsp. salt	2 tblsp. raisins
½ tsp. ground cinnamon	¼ tsp. ground cinnamon
½ tsp. ground allspice	¼ c. brandy or apple juice
½ tsp. pepper	1½ tblsp. currant jelly,
¼ tsp. ground cloves	melted
¼ tsp. ground mace	1 c. fresh bread crumbs
3 to 3½ lb. boned pork loin	¼ c. melted butter or
12 pitted prunes	regular margarine
2 medium apples, pared,	
cored and cut into sixths	

Combine salt, ½ tsp. cinnamon, allspice, pepper, cloves and mace. Rub in surface of roast. Cover and refrigerate overnight.

Combine prunes, apples, raisins, ¼ tsp. cinnamon and brandy. Cover and refrigerate overnight.

Cut a long, deep pocket the length of the roast. Stuff with fruit. Sew closed with large needle; tie with kitchen twine. Place roast on rack in roasting pan. Brush roast with liquid left over from fruit.

Roast in 325° oven 1 hour. Remove from oven; brush with jelly. Roll in bread crumbs. Baste with butter; roast 1 hour 30 minutes more or until meat thermometer reads 185°. Let stand 15 minutes before carving. Makes 6 servings.

DANISH CARAMELIZED POTATOES

These shiny, glazed potatoes are served in all Scandinavian countries. Wreathed around a pork roast, they look handsome when brought to the table. They are easy to fix and can be glazed at the last minute.

DANISH CARAMELIZED POTATOES

Tiny potatoes with a delightful, glistening caramel glaze

24 small, new potatoes	**6 tblsp. sugar**
¼ c. butter or regular margarine	**2 tsp. salt**

Cook potatoes in their jackets in boiling water until tender. Drain and peel.

Melt butter in 10″ skillet; stir in sugar, and cook, stirring constantly, until mixture is a light caramel color.

Add potatoes; continue cooking, shaking pan so the potatoes are covered with a thin caramel coating. Sprinkle with salt during cooking. Makes 6 servings.

DANISH DUMPLING AND MEATBALL SOUP

A farm woman from Nebraska wrote us that she married a Dane who begged her to make dumplings like his mother used to make. The bigger and fluffier her dumplings were, the more disappointed her husband became. One Sunday during a visit with a Danish family they were served Danish Dumplings and her husband exclaimed, "These are the dumplings!" She was surprised to learn that the dough was basically a cream puff dough and dropped into a broth or soup along with homemade meatballs.

DANISH DUMPLING AND MEATBALL SOUP

You can also cook the dumplings in chicken broth and serve plain

6 medium potatoes, pared and quartered	**1 tsp. parsley flakes**
4 medium carrots, pared and cut in 2" strips	**¼ tsp. salt**
	1 egg, slightly beaten
2 stalks celery, cut in 1" diagonal slices	**1 tblsp. butter or regular margarine**
1 c. chopped onion	**1 c. water**
6 c. chicken broth	**½ c. butter or regular margarine**
1 (10 oz.) pkg. frozen peas	**1 c. sifted flour**
½ lb. ground beef	**¼ tsp. salt**
¼ lb. ground ham	**4 eggs**
¼ c. cracker crumbs	

Combine potatoes, carrots, celery, onion and chicken broth in 6-qt. kettle. Cover and bring to a boil. Reduce heat and simmer 30 minutes. Add peas and continue cooking 10 more minutes or until vegetables are tender.

Meanwhile prepare meatballs. Combine ground beef, ham, crumbs, parsley flakes, ¼ tsp. salt and 1 egg; mix lightly but well. Shape into ¾" balls. Brown on all sides in 1 tblsp. melted butter in 10" skillet. Cook 10 minutes, turning frequently.

Combine water and ½ c. butter in 2-qt. saucepan; bring to a boil. Stir in flour and ¼ tsp. salt. Continue stirring over medium heat until mixture leaves the sides of the saucepan and forms a ball. Remove from heat. Add 4 eggs, one at a time, beating well with spoon after each addition. Drop by rounded teaspoonfuls into boiling vegetable mixture. Cook 2 minutes or until dumplings rise to top; add meatballs. Serve immediately. Makes 6 to 8 servings.

DANISH CRULLERS

Brought to this country in 1880, these doughnuts have been a big hit in Minnesota ever since. Golden brown and tender and covered with sugar, one batch won't last long even though it makes over 5 dozen.

DANISH CRULLERS

Crisp pastry knots that look so attractive dusted with sugar

2 eggs	1 tsp. salt
½ c. sugar	½ tsp. ground nutmeg
1 c. light cream	Cooking oil
3 c. sifted flour	Confectioners sugar
2 tsp. baking powder	

Beat eggs well. Add sugar and cream, beating well to blend.

Sift together flour, baking powder, salt and nutmeg. Gradually add dry ingredients to egg mixture, stirring just enough to blend. (Do not overmix.) Dough is slightly sticky.

Divide dough in fourths. Roll each on well-floured surface to 12×8" rectangle. Cut into 16 (4×1½") strips. Cut 1" slit lengthwise in center of each strip. Pull one end of strip through slit to form knot.

Fry in deep, hot oil (350°) until golden brown on both sides. Drain on paper towels. Dust with confectioners sugar. Makes 64 crullers.

DANISH CHRISTMAS COOKIES

On Christmas day the Danes feast on goose or pork, salads and chestnuts and then when the main meal is cleared from the table, platters of cookies are brought forth. The recipe for these rich, buttery cookies was brought to this country by a 15-year-old girl years ago. Now an Illinois farm woman, she remembers her grandmother coloring the dough and decorating the cookies. It was difficult to duplicate the cookies, even with the recipe, because Grandmother cooked by "feel," but after much experimentation she believes these cookies taste just like her grandmother's.

DANISH CHRISTMAS COOKIES

Make these buttery cookies a Christmas tradition in your home

1 c. butter or regular margarine	½ tsp. almond extract
½ c. sugar	½ tsp. vanilla
½ tsp. lemon extract	2½ c. sifted flour

Cream together butter and sugar until light and fluffy. Beat in lemon extract, almond extract and vanilla. Gradually stir in flour. Cover with plastic wrap. Chill in refrigerator 30 minutes.

Shape into 13″ roll. Wrap in plastic wrap and refrigerate 8 hours or overnight. (Can be stored 2 days.)

Cut in ¼″ thick slices. Place 2″ apart on greased baking sheets.

Bake in 350° oven 8 minutes or until golden brown. Remove from baking sheets; cool on racks. Decorate with colored sugars or frost with your favorite icing, if you wish. Makes about 4 dozen.

DANISH LAYER CAKE

Desserts rank high in Denmark and they abound in rich butter, eggs and cream. And they look exquisite. This layer cake is an heirloom from Illinois—a high cake filled with pudding and raspberry jam. Surprise the family and make this beauty for a birthday treat or any special occasion. The cake is tender and light as a feather. Cut small pieces as it is rich and caloric.

DANISH LAYER CAKE

This breath-taking cake is six layers high and covered with cream

1½ c. milk	3 tblsp. flour
⅔ c. butter or regular margarine	⅛ tsp. salt
	2 c. milk, scalded
6 eggs	2 egg yolks, slightly beaten
3 c. sugar	2 tblsp. butter or regular
3 c. sifted cake flour	margarine
3 tsp. baking powder	1 tsp. vanilla
½ tsp. salt	1 c. raspberry jam
2 tsp. vanilla	1½ c. heavy cream, whipped
⅓ c. sugar	and sweetened

Heat 1½ c. milk and ⅔ c. butter to boiling point. Remove from heat.

Beat 6 eggs until thick and lemon-colored, about 5 minutes. Slowly add 3 c. sugar, beating well.

Sift together cake flour, baking powder and ½ tsp. salt. Add dry ingredients to egg mixture, beating at low speed. Continue beating at low speed, gradually adding hot milk mixture and 2 tsp. vanilla. (Batter will be bubbly and quite thin.) Pour into 3 greased and waxed-paper-lined 9″ round cake pans.

Bake in 375° oven 25 minutes or until cakes test done. Cool in pans on racks 5 minutes. Remove from pans; cool on racks.

Combine ⅓ c. sugar, flour and ⅛ tsp. salt in medium saucepan. Gradually stir in 2 c. hot milk. Cook over medium heat, stirring constantly, until mixture thickens. Remove from heat. Stir some of the hot mixture into egg yolks, mixing well. Stir back into hot mixture. Cook over low heat 2 more minutes, stirring occasionally. Remove from heat. Add 2 tblsp. butter and 1 tsp. vanilla. Cool completely.

Cut layers in half, making 6 layers. Place one layer on serving plate. Spread with ⅓ of custard filling. Top with cake layer. Spread with ½ of raspberry jam. Repeat layers. Top with cake layer; spread with remaining custard filling. Top with last cake layer. Cover with plastic wrap. Refrigerate until just before serving time.

Spread sweetened whipped cream over surface of cake. Makes 12 servings.

BEEF STEW

In Norwegian, beef stew is called *bankekjøtt* and in Denmark it is named *bankekød*. Both names mean "pounding" or "banging," which is what a Scandinavian cook always does to the cheaper cuts of meat. A typical meal to serve with this spicy stew would be boiled potatoes, pickled beets and lingonberries. Lingonberries are similar to our cranberries and are often served with meats and fish.

BEEF STEW

Basic beef dish with rich, brown gravy . . . good with potatoes

3 lbs. round steak, ½″	**¼ c. cooking oil**
thick	**2 c. hot beef broth**
¼ c. flour	**1 c. chopped onion**
1 tsp. salt	**1 bay leaf**
¼ tsp. pepper	

Pound meat well with meat mallet. Cut in serving-size pieces. Dredge with combined flour, salt and pepper.

Heat oil in Dutch oven. Brown meat on both sides. Add beef broth, onion and bay leaf. Cover and bring to a boil. Reduce heat and simmer 1 hour 15 minutes or until meat is tender. Makes 8 servings.

NORWEGIAN BEEF BIRDS

Both Danes and Norwegians have many recipes for boneless birds as they call them. There are numerous fillings. Some of the most popular variations include mushrooms or chopped anchovies or beef marrow that has been diced and mixed with a little ginger.

NORWEGIAN BEEF BIRDS

Flavorful beef rolls with ground beef and parsley tucked inside

3 lbs. round steak, ½" thick	¼ c. chopped fresh parsley
1 tblsp. salt	¼ c. flour
½ tsp. pepper	3 tblsp. cooking oil
½ tsp. ground ginger	3 c. beef broth
½ tsp. ground cloves	3 tblsp. flour
½ lb. ground beef	⅓ c. water

Pound steak well with meat mallet. Cut in 16 (5×3") pieces.

Season with combined salt, pepper, ginger and cloves. Place 1 tblsp. ground beef in center of each piece. Sprinkle with parsley. Roll up like jelly roll and secure with string. Dredge rolls with ¼ c. flour.

Brown meat rolls on all sides in hot cooking oil in Dutch oven. Return all meat rolls to Dutch oven when all are browned, pour beef broth over all. Cover and bring to a boil. Reduce heat and simmer 1 hour 25 minutes or until meat is tender.

Remove meat rolls from pan; cut string and discard. Keep warm. Skim off excess fat from pan liquid. Combine 3 tblsp. flour and water. Slowly stir into boiling liquid. Boil 1 minute. Serve meat rolls with gravy. Makes 8 servings.

NORWEGIAN-STYLE BROWN HASH

A standard way in which Scandinavian cooks use up leftovers. In some recipes meat and potatoes are browned separately and a pour of cream is added at the very end. In this recipe pork and potatoes are cooked with the onions and tasty beef broth is stirred in and cooked until all moisture is gone and only the flavor is left.

NORWEGIAN-STYLE BROWN HASH

Leftovers taste so good when used to make this great hash

4 c. diced, cooked pork	1½ c. chopped onion
4 c. diced, cooked potatoes	½ tsp. salt
½ c. butter or regular	⅛ tsp. pepper
margarine	1 c. boiling beef broth

Brown pork and potatoes in melted butter in large skillet, stirring occasionally. Add onion, salt and pepper; mix lightly. Stir in beef broth. Cover and bring to a boil. Reduce heat and simmer 45 minutes, stirring occasionally, until all the broth is absorbed. Makes 6 servings.

SAUSAGES AND POTATOES

This down-to-earth main dish is economical and delicious and popular in many Scandinavian homes. The flavor of the sausages trickles through the potatoes giving them a wonderful taste. This is a big favorite with men and field crews. Accompany with cooked carrots for a bright note of color.

SAUSAGES AND POTATOES

Country-style dish that requires little attention while cooking

2 lbs. small, pork sausage	¼ tsp. pepper
links	2 lbs. medium potatoes,
2 c. water	pared and quartered
2 bay leaves	2 tblsp. chopped fresh
10 whole allspice	parsley
1½ tsp. salt	

Place pork sausages, water, bay leaves, allspice, salt and pepper in Dutch oven. Bring to a boil. Reduce heat and simmer 20 minutes.

Add potatoes. Cover and simmer 20 minutes or until potatoes are tender. Sprinkle with parsley. Makes 6 to 8 servings.

NORWEGIAN CAULIFLOWER SOUP

Norwegians love their soups and manage to make a soup out of every vegetable. This Cauliflower Soup is a family soup often served for supper in this country with assorted cheeses and crackers. In the springtime, fresh peas are added for a colorful note. Just before serving paper-thin radish slices can be stirred into the soup for a bit of crunch.

NORWEGIAN CAULIFLOWER SOUP

An unusual cream soup featuring a favorite wintertime vegetable

2 medium cauliflower	2 tblsp. flour
(3¼ lbs.)	2 egg yolks, slightly
3 c. water	beaten
1 tblsp. salt	½ c. heavy cream
2 tblsp. butter or regular	⅛ tsp. ground nutmeg
margarine	3 c. milk

Trim cauliflower and break into flowerets. Remove stalks and cut into ½" pieces. Place cauliflower, water and salt in Dutch oven. Cover and bring to a boil. Reduce heat and simmer 20 minutes or until tender.

Drain cauliflower, reserving stock. Set aside.

Melt butter in Dutch oven. Add flour. Cook, stirring constantly, 1 minute. Slowly stir in reserved stock. Cover and simmer 10 minutes, stirring occasionally. Remove from heat.

Combine egg yolks, heavy cream and nutmeg. Add 1 c. hot soup to egg mixture; blend well. Add egg mixture back into hot soup, a little at a time, mixing well after each addition. Return to low heat. Add milk and cauliflower and heat well. (Do not boil.) Makes about 2 quarts.

YULE KAGE

Christmas bread that is served in Norway and also in Scandinavian communities in this country. A North Dakota farm woman has been making this for years. She added the glaze for an extra-festive look. Cardamom gives a different flavor which all Norwegians love—it is part of their Christmas taste.

YULE KAGE

Serve lots of soft, creamy butter with this traditional bread

½ c. milk, scalded	1 pkg. active dry yeast
½ c. butter or regular margarine	½ c. lukewarm water
	3¾ c. sifted flour
¼ c. sugar	1 egg
1 tsp. salt	1 c. raisins
¼ tsp. ground cardamom	½ c. mixed candied fruit
1 tblsp. honey	1 egg, slightly beaten

Combine milk, butter, sugar, salt, cardamom and honey. Cool to lukewarm.

Sprinkle yeast over lukewarm water; stir to dissolve.

Add yeast, 1 c. flour and 1 egg to milk mixture. Beat with electric mixer at medium speed until smooth, about 2 minutes, scraping bowl occasionally. Or beat with spoon until batter is smooth.

Stir in raisins and candied fruit. Add enough remaining flour to make a soft dough that leaves the sides of the bowl. Cover and let rise in warm place until doubled, about 1 hour 30 minutes.

Divide dough in half. Shape each into a round loaf and place on greased baking sheet. Cover and let rise 15 minutes.

Snip 1" deep cuts about 1" apart around bottom of loaf with scissors. Press down center of loaf with palm of hand. Brush with 1 beaten egg. Cover and let rise until doubled, about 45 minutes.

Bake in 350° oven 30 minutes or until golden brown. Remove from baking sheet; cool on racks. If you wish, frost with your favorite icing and garnish with bits of candied fruit. Makes 2 coffee cakes.

NORWEGIAN MOLASSES COOKIES

An heirloom recipe from Norway over 100 years old. This North Dakotan's ancestors served this spicy cookie at the Ladies' Aid Meeting. According to her grandmother, in the old days Ladies' Aid meetings started midmorning and lasted all day. Everyone brought a favorite food, big pots of coffee were brewed and the recipes shared.

NORWEGIAN MOLASSES COOKIES

This basic molasses cookie is both crunchy and chewy

1 c. lard	**5 c. sifted flour**
2 c. sugar	**3 tsp. baking soda**
2 eggs	**⅛ tsp. salt**
1 c. molasses	

Cream together lard and sugar until light and fluffy. Add eggs, one at a time, beating well after each addition. Beat in molasses.

Sift together flour, baking soda and salt. Gradually stir into creamed mixture. Cover with plastic wrap. Chill 1 hour in refrigerator.

Shape dough in 1¼" balls. Place 2" apart on greased baking sheets.

Bake in 350° oven 18 minutes or until golden brown. Remove from baking sheets; cool on racks. Makes about 7 dozen.

FATTIGMAN

Christmas is a time of great feasting in Norway. The table is groaning with food. There are always a wide array of cookies and breads. No holiday is complete without a handsome platter piled high with Fattigman. Many farm wives of Norwegian descent make this light-as-air crisp cookie at holidaytime.

FATTIGMAN

These crisp pastry knots are perfect for a coffee break

6 egg yolks	2¼ c. sifted flour
½ tsp. salt	¼ tsp. ground nutmeg
⅓ c. light cream	1 tblsp. grated lemon peel
⅓ c. sugar	Cooking oil
1 tblsp. melted butter or	Confectioners sugar
regular margarine	

Beat together egg yolks and salt until thick and light. Beat in light cream, sugar and butter.

Sift together flour and nutmeg. Add to egg yolk mixture with lemon peel, mixing well. Chill for 1 hour.

Roll out ¼ of dough at a time, keeping remaining dough chilled. Roll ¹⁄₁₆" thick and cut in strips about 1½" wide with sharp knife. Cut diagonally at 4" intervals. Make 1" slits lengthwise in center of each piece. Slip one end through slit.

Fry a few at a time in deep, hot oil at 350° for 1 to 2 minutes or until golden. Remove from oil with slotted spoon. Drain on paper towels and sprinkle with sifted confectioners sugar. Store in an airtight container. Makes 6 dozen.

STUFFED CABBAGE ROLLS

Although this recipe was originally an oriental creation from Turkey, Stuffed Cabbage Rolls have been adopted all over Europe and each country has its own style of preparation depending upon the ingredients available. Scandinavian cooks especially favor the Stuffed Cabbage Rolls using two kinds of meat and adding a little brown sugar for extra flavor and sweetness. Light cream is added to make a rich, flavorful gravy.

STUFFED CABBAGE ROLLS

This hearty supper dish is sure to please your family

1 medium cabbage	2 tblsp. brown sugar, firmly
½ c. regular rice	packed
1 c. water	½ c. beef broth
1 lb. ground beef	2 tblsp. flour
1 egg	¾ c. light cream
1 c. milk	½ tsp. salt
1½ tsp. salt	⅛ tsp. pepper
⅛ tsp. pepper	
2 tblsp. butter or regular margarine	

Cut out core of cabbage. Steam cabbage in Dutch oven to soften leaves. Remove leaves gently. Drain on paper towels. Trim center vein from each leaf; set aside.

Cook rice with water in saucepan until water is absorbed. Cool well.

Combine cooked rice, ground beef, egg, milk, 1½ tsp. salt and ⅛ tsp. pepper; mix lightly. Place ¼ c. filling on each cabbage leaf. Roll up and secure with toothpicks or string. (Makes 16 rolls.)

Brown rolls on all sides in melted butter in Dutch oven. Sprinkle with brown sugar. Add beef broth. Cover and bring to a boil. Reduce heat and simmer 45 minutes or until cabbage rolls are tender.

Combine flour and cream. Remove cabbage rolls from Dutch oven and keep warm. Slowly stir cream mixture into pan drippings, stirring constantly. Add ½ tsp. salt and ⅛ tsp. pepper. Cook over low heat until thickened (do not boil). Spoon sauce over cabbage rolls. Makes 6 to 8 servings.

SWEDISH LAMB STEW

Lamb is a particular favorite with Scandinavians and one of their family favorites is lamb stew. The flavor is very delicate and seasoned perfectly. This is a quick and easy main dish to make as the meat is not browned, but simply combined with the vegetables and stock and allowed to simmer to perfection. A shower of chopped parsley added just before serving makes a pretty garnish.

SWEDISH LAMB STEW

Lamb stew tastes especially good on a blustery winter evening

2 lbs. lamb shoulder, cut in 1½″ cubes	½ tsp. marjoram leaves
	⅛ tsp. pepper
6 medium potatoes, pared and quartered	1 bay leaf
	4 c. beef broth or bouillon
6 medium carrots, pared and sliced	4 tblsp. flour
	6 tblsp. water
3 medium onions, quartered	Chopped fresh parsley

Layer lamb, potatoes, carrots and onions in Dutch oven. Sprinkle with marjoram and pepper. Add bay leaf and beef broth. Cover and bring to a boil. Reduce heat and simmer 1 hour 30 minutes or until meat is tender.

Combine flour and water; mix well. Slowly stir into hot mixture, cook 2 more minutes. Remove bay leaf. Serve sprinkled with fresh parsley. Makes 6 servings.

SWEDISH POT ROAST

Swedish women like to cook with heavy cream, and because of their fondness for fish, they serve pot roast with a hint of anchovies in the rich gravy made with pan drippings and cream. Potatoes that have been browned in butter with a little brown sugar are a popular vegetable to present with this different and delicious pot roast. The gravy never seems to curdle even upon standing. Because of the saltiness of the anchovies, you will need less salt.

SWEDISH POT ROAST

Less expensive roasts are so tender and succulent cooked this way

4 lbs. beef round or rump roast	**1½ c. sliced carrots**
½ tsp. salt	**1 (10½ oz.) can condensed beef broth**
¼ tsp. pepper	**3 tblsp. flour**
2 tblsp. butter or regular margarine	**1 c. heavy cream**
2 c. chopped onion	**1 tsp. anchovy juice**

Season beef with salt and pepper. Brown on all sides in melted butter in Dutch oven. Remove from pan. Add onion and carrots; sauté until tender (do not brown).

Place beef back in Dutch oven. Add enough water to beef broth to make 2 c. Add to Dutch oven. Cover and bring to a boil. Reduce heat and simmer 2 hours or until meat is tender.

Remove roast from Dutch oven and keep warm. Pour off pan drippings and reserve 2 c. (Add water if necessary.) Pour back into Dutch oven.

Combine flour, heavy cream and anchovy juice. Slowly add to pan drippings, stirring constantly. Cook over low heat 2 minutes or until mixture thickens slightly. Slice roast and serve with cream gravy. Makes 8 servings.

SCANDINAVIAN HASH

Hash in our country is usually made by combining potatoes, meat and onion and browning until crusty. In Scandinavia, often each ingredient is cooked separately and then combined and seasoned to taste. This hash tastes a bit different and is a delightful way to use that leftover roast. A suggested variation often served in Swedish homes is to pour a cup of cream over the browned hash and reheat thoroughly. It then becomes a creamed hash which is quite unusual.

SCANDINAVIAN HASH

Cream is stirred in at the last minute for extra richness

¾ c. chopped onion	Salt
½ c. butter or regular margarine	Pepper
	1½ c. light cream
3 c. diced, cooked potatoes	3 tblsp. chopped fresh
3 c. ground, cooked beef	parsley

Sauté onion in melted butter in 10″ skillet until tender (do not brown). Add potatoes and beef; sauté until browned. Season with salt and pepper as needed. Pour cream over all and heat well over low heat. Serve sprinkled with parsley. Makes 6 servings.

SWEDISH MEATBALLS WITH SAUCE

If you toured farm homes in Sweden you would likely find a different meatball recipe in every kitchen. These recipes have been handed down through generations and each cook thinks her version is the very finest. They all have a hint of spice however. This version, brought to America, uses unseasoned mashed potatoes to produce a light, tender meatball. The gravy is golden brown and heavy in cream. Wonderful to serve to guests. Just pop these meatballs in a chafing dish and let guests serve themselves.

SWEDISH MEATBALLS WITH SAUCE

Makes a lovely, hot appetizer for the Christmas holiday season

⅓ c. minced onion
2 tblsp. butter or regular
  margarine
1 lb. ground beef
1 c. unseasoned mashed
  potatoes
⅓ c. dry bread crumbs
1 tblsp. minced fresh
  parsley
1 tsp. salt
1 egg

¼ c. heavy cream
2 tblsp. butter or regular
  margarine
2 tblsp. cooking oil
2 tblsp. flour
¼ tsp. ground allspice
½ tsp. bottled browning
  sauce for gravy
1½ c. heavy cream
Chopped fresh parsley

Sauté onion in 2 tblsp. melted butter in small skillet until tender (do not brown). Set aside.

Combine ground beef, potatoes, bread crumbs, 1 tblsp. parsley, salt, egg, ¼ c. heavy cream and sautéed onion. Mix until ingredients are well blended. Shape mixture into ¾" meatballs. Arrange on tray. Cover. Chill at least 1 hour.

Brown 10 meatballs at a time in 2 tblsp. melted butter and oil in heavy 10" skillet. Shake pan back and forth frequently to keep meatballs round. Add more oil if needed. Remove meatballs as they brown and place in 2-qt. casserole. Keep hot in 200° oven.

Pour off all but 2 tblsp. pan drippings. Stir in flour, allspice and bottled sauce for gravy. Cook 1 minute, stirring constantly. Remove from heat. Slowly stir in heavy cream. Cook over low heat until slightly thickened. Pour over meatballs. Garnish with chopped parsley. Makes 12 servings.

PICKLED CUCUMBERS WITH DILL

Dill is almost a staple in Swedish cooking. It lends an exquisite distinctive flavor to many foods. In the USA our most common use of dill is in making dill pickles. In Sweden the pretty green sprigs are used as a garnish and ingredient. Here dill teams with cucumbers and vinegar for a delightful sweet-sour salad that has become popular in many American homes.

PICKLED CUCUMBERS WITH DILL

Dill is a favorite herb in Sweden . . . so good with cucumbers

½ c. vinegar	⅛ tsp. pepper
¼ c. sugar	2 medium cucumbers
2 tblsp. water	2 tblsp. chopped fresh dill
½ tsp. salt	

Combine vinegar, sugar, water, salt and pepper in saucepan. Bring to a boil. Remove from heat. Cool.

Remove strips of peel lengthwise from cucumbers with vegetable peeler, leaving alternate strips of peel intact. Cut cucumbers in thin slices and place in bowl. Add vinegar mixture. Sprinkle with dill. Toss gently. Cover. Chill 2 to 3 hours. Makes 12 servings.

FISH SALAD WITH PEAS

A handsome dish to add to a buffet dinner; if you happen to have a platter shaped like a fish, this would be a conversation piece. Again the Swedish talent with fish comes through. Even those who are not too fond of fish will take seconds of this delicious dish.

FISH SALAD WITH PEAS

To make dish even more attractive, garnish with bits of pimiento

2 lbs. haddock fillets,
   cooked, drained and
   flaked
2 tblsp. lemon juice
2 tblsp. salad oil
2 c. cooked peas
2 tsp. lemon juice
2 tsp. salad oil
2 egg yolks, slightly beaten

1½ tsp. prepared yellow
   mustard
¾ tsp. salt
¼ tsp. pepper
1 tblsp. vinegar
¼ c. salad oil
⅓ c. melted butter or
   regular margarine

Combine haddock, 2 tblsp. lemon juice and 2 tblsp. oil in bowl. Toss gently to mix. Cover with plastic wrap. Chill in refrigerator.

Combine peas, 2 tsp. lemon juice and 2 tsp. oil in bowl. Toss gently. Cover with plastic wrap. Chill in refrigerator.

Combine egg yolks, mustard, salt, pepper, vinegar and ¼ c. oil in small saucepan. Stir in butter. Cook over low heat, stirring constantly, until mixture thickens. Cool well.

Pour sauce over fish mixture. Toss gently to mix. Place fish salad in center of serving dish and surround with peas. Makes 12 servings.

HERRING AND BEET SALAD

One dish that will always be found at the traditional smörgåsbord is Herring and Beet Salad. Swedish cooks have a thousand ways to fix herring but one that has become a favorite in this country is the combination of herring and beet salad with the attractive garnish of chopped egg whites and dill. A good recipe to prepare for company as it can be made several days ahead.

HERRING AND BEET SALAD

Variations of this salad are always included in a smörgåsbord

3 c. diced, cooked beets
1 c. chopped pickled
  herring
½ c. diced, cooked potatoes
½ c. diced dill pickle
½ c. chopped pared apples
⅓ c. finely chopped onion
3 tblsp. chopped fresh dill
2 tblsp. vinegar

¼ tsp. salt
⅛ tsp. pepper
3 hard-cooked eggs
2 tblsp. vinegar
1 tblsp. prepared yellow
  mustard
¼ c. salad oil
3 tblsp. heavy cream
1 tblsp. chopped fresh dill

Combine beets, herring, potatoes, pickle, apples, onion, 3 tblsp. dill, 2 tblsp. vinegar, salt and pepper in bowl. Toss gently to mix.

Remove yolks from eggs. Chop egg whites and reserve. Mash yolks with fork in bowl to a smooth paste. Add 2 tblsp. vinegar, mustard and oil; stir well. Stir in heavy cream; blend well. Pour over beet mixture. Toss gently. Cover. Chill at least 2 hours.

Garnish salad with chopped egg whites and 1 tblsp. dill before serving. Makes 8 to 12 servings.

SWEDISH COFFEE CRESCENT

A Michigan farm woman sent this heirloom recipe and told us she makes this often for Christmas bazaars. She has read many Swedish cookbooks and has never found a sweet bread quite like this pretty swirled crescent. The dough is Swedish and the filling with its crushed, vanilla-wafer base is an American adaptation. One recipe makes four crescents and they freeze well. Make several batches for the holidays to give as gifts and serve to friends.

SWEDISH COFFEE CRESCENT

A buttery-rich coffee cake with an unusual vanilla-wafer filling

4 c. sifted flour
¼ c. sugar
½ tsp. salt
1 c. butter or regular
   margarine
1 pkg. active dry yeast
1 c. milk, scalded and
   cooled
2 eggs, beaten

5½ c. crushed vanilla
   wafers
½ c. melted butter or
   regular margarine
1 tsp. almond extract
2 tblsp. water
Vanilla Icing (recipe
   follows)

Sift together flour, sugar and salt into bowl. Cut in 1 c. butter with pastry blender or two knives until mixture is crumbly.

Sprinkle yeast over milk; stir to dissolve. Add yeast and eggs to crumb mixture; stirring to mix. Cover with plastic wrap. Refrigerate overnight. (Can be stored 2 days.)

Combine vanilla wafers, ½ c. butter, almond extract and water; set aside.

Divide dough in fourths. Roll each into 15×11" rectangle on floured surface. Sprinkle with 1½ c. of wafer mixture. Roll up like jelly roll from narrow side. Place on greased baking sheet. Shape into a crescent. Snip 1½" cuts 1" apart with scissors around outside edge of crescent. Cover and let rise in warm place until doubled, about 3 hours.

Bake in 375° oven 20 minutes or until golden brown. Remove from baking sheets; cool on racks. Drizzle with Vanilla Icing while still warm. Makes 4 coffee cakes.

Vanilla Icing: Combine 4 c. sifted confectioners sugar, 2 tblsp. soft butter or regular margarine, ½ tsp. vanilla and 4 tblsp. milk; mix until smooth.

ST. LUCIA'S BUNS

In a Swedish household, on December 13 about 5 o'clock in the morning, Santa Lucia, the Queen of Light, enters each bedroom wearing a white robe and lighted crown on her head. Singing the Lucia song, she offers each family member a Lucia Bun and coffee. Traditionally Santa Lucia is one of the young daughters or a relative or friend of the family.

ST. LUCIA'S BUNS

These traditional buns are lovely with their shiny glaze

¾ c. milk, scalded
⅓ c. sugar
1 tsp. salt
¼ c. butter or regular
   margarine
¹⁄₁₆ tsp. powdered saffron
2 pkgs. active dry yeast
½ c. lukewarm water

1 egg
3½ c. sifted flour
¼ c. golden raisins
1 egg white, slightly beaten
¼ c. finely chopped
   blanched almonds
2 tblsp. sugar

Combine milk, ⅓ c. sugar, salt, butter and saffron. Cool to lukewarm.

Sprinkle yeast on lukewarm water; stir to dissolve.

Add yeast, egg and 2 c. flour to milk mixture. Beat with electric mixer at medium speed until smooth, about 2 minutes, scraping bowl occasionally. Or beat with spoon until batter is smooth.

Stir in enough remaining flour to make a soft dough that leaves the sides of the bowl. Turn onto lightly floured surface and knead until smooth and satiny, about 8 to 10 minutes.

Place in lightly greased bowl; turn dough over to grease top. Cover and let rise in warm place until doubled, about 1 hour 30 minutes.

Turn dough out on floured surface; let rest 10 minutes.

Cut dough into 18 pieces. Roll each into a 12″ long strip; cut in half. Coil both ends of each strip into center of the strip. Place

2 coiled strips back to back to make 1 bun. Place on greased baking sheets. Cover and let rise until doubled, about 30 minutes. Press a raisin in center of each coil. Brush buns with egg white. Then sprinkle with combined almonds and 2 tblsp. sugar.

Bake in 375° oven 15 minutes or until golden brown. Remove from baking sheets; cool on racks. Makes 18 buns.

SAFFRON BRAID

A variation of the Lucia Buns served throughout Sweden during the Christmas holidays. Many cooks make a double or triple batch of dough, shape their Lucia Buns for Santa Lucia Day and make several braids to have on hand when friends and relatives drop in to visit.

SAFFRON BRAID

This lovely golden bread is a must during the Christmas season

1 c. milk, scalded	¼ c. lukewarm water
½ c. sugar	1 egg
2 tblsp. butter or regular margarine	½ tsp. ground cardamom
½ tsp. salt	4¼ c. sifted flour
Pinch of powdered saffron	1 egg, beaten
1 pkg. active dry yeast	Sugar

Combine milk, ½ c. sugar, butter, salt and saffron in bowl. Cool to lukewarm.

Sprinkle yeast on lukewarm water; stir to dissolve. Add yeast, 1 egg, cardamom and 1 c. flour to milk mixture. Beat with electric mixer at medium speed until smooth, about 2 minutes, scraping bowl occasionally. Or beat with spoon until batter is smooth.

Gradually add enough flour to make a soft dough that leaves the sides of the bowl. Turn out on floured surface to knead until smooth and satiny, about 10 minutes.

Place dough in lightly greased bowl; turn over to grease top.

Cover and let rise in warm place until doubled, about 1 hour 30 minutes.

Divide dough in half. Divide each half into thirds. Roll each third into a 10″ strip. Braid three strips together. Pinch ends to seal. Place on greased baking sheet. Let rise until doubled, about 1 hour.

Brush braids with beaten egg. Sprinkle with sugar.

Bake in 375° oven 20 to 25 minutes or until loaves sound hollow when tapped. Remove from baking sheets; cool on racks. Makes 2 loaves.

SWEDISH PANCAKES

In every Swedish home you will find a special frying pan used only for making the thin pancakes that measure about 3 inches across. They are served with sugar and jam and are a favorite treat for both youngsters and adults. These thin cakes are always the standard dessert on Thursday, as that is the day many a Swedish homemaker ladles homemade pea soup into bowls for the evening meal. This custom is still followed in some Swedish-American homes.

SWEDISH PANCAKES

Traditionally served with whipped cream and plums

3 eggs	1 tsp. vanilla
1¼ c. milk	Melted butter or regular
¾ c. sifted flour	margarine
1 tblsp. sugar	Sugar
½ tsp. salt	

Blend together eggs and milk with rotary beater. Add flour, 1 tblsp. sugar and salt; blend well. Add vanilla.

Bake in lightly greased 8″ skillet, using ¼ c. batter for each. (Tilt skillet back and forth quickly when batter is added to make a thin coating.) Bake until top is dry; turn and brown other side.

Spread with melted butter and sprinkle with sugar. Roll up. Makes 8 pancakes.

SWEDISH FRUIT SOUP

The Scandinavians are famous for their fruit soups. In the summertime the cloudberry, which is shaped like the raspberry but is yellow in color, and the arctic raspberry are the fruits used to make this sweet soup thickened slightly with cornstarch. In the fall and wintertime mixed dried fruits are stirred into soups with a cinnamon stick and tart lemon juice. Instead of cookies, Swedish cooks fill a platter with crispy rusks to munch along with the soup.

SWEDISH FRUIT SOUP

A most unusual dessert to serve at your next buffet supper

1 (8 oz.) pkg. mixed dried fruit (1½ c.)	**1 c. sugar**
2 qts. water	**½ c. quick-cooking tapioca**
1½ c. diced pared apples	**2 sticks cinnamon**
½ c. raisins	**Sweetened whipped cream**

Soak dried fruit in water overnight. (Do not drain.)

Pour soaked fruit mixture into Dutch oven. Add apples, raisins, sugar, tapioca and cinnamon. Stir until sugar is dissolved. Bring to a boil, stirring constantly. Reduce heat and simmer 1 hour, stirring frequently, until fruit is tender.

Pour mixture into a large bowl. Cover and chill in refrigerator a few hours before serving. Spoon into dessert dishes and top with sweetened whipped cream. Makes 6 to 8 servings.

ALMOND RICE PUDDING

One Swedish dessert specialty is rice pudding that has been combined with lots of whipped cream, almonds, sherry and vanilla. This is often served as a company dessert with a pour of Raspberry Sauce, found in many Swedish desserts. In olden days the fruits were dried and stored until ready to be made into fruit syrups, jams and jellies. These berries form the base for desserts throughout the whole year. Berries are ladled onto every dessert from pancakes to puddings and are often made into fresh-tasting soups.

ALMOND RICE PUDDING

Most Swedish families have this for dessert on Christmas

1¼ c. regular rice	1⅓ toasted, slivered
⅔ c. sugar	almonds
1 tsp. salt	2 c. heavy cream
6 c. milk	Raspberry Sauce (recipe
⅓ c. cream sherry	follows)
3 tsp. vanilla	

Combine rice, sugar, salt and milk in 3-qt. saucepan. Bring mixture to a boil. Reduce heat; simmer uncovered 25 minutes, stirring frequently. Remove from heat.

Pour rice mixture into 13×9×2″ baking dish. Cool slightly. Stir in sherry, vanilla and almonds.

Whip cream until soft peaks form. Fold into rice mixture. Cover. Chill several hours. Serve with Raspberry Sauce. Makes 12 servings.

Raspberry Sauce: Combine 2 (10 oz.) pkgs. frozen raspberries, thawed, 2 tblsp. cornstarch and 2 tsp. lemon juice in a saucepan. Bring to a boil, stirring constantly. Boil 1 minute. Remove from heat. Strain. Cool.

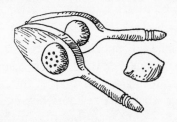

Chapter 5

THE HERITAGE OF
EASTERN EUROPEAN
COOKING

At your next coffee party pass a tray of Czechoslovakian round buns with open pockets displaying luscious fruit fillings. Set a platter of chicken, rosy with paprika and rich with sour cream, on the company dinner table. Carry a baking dish of piping hot pork and sauerkraut, flavored with sour cream, to the buffet. Or please your friends and family by presenting stroganoff for supper.

You will receive compliments on these wonderful foods, which are just a few of the superior contributions people from Eastern Europe made to American cooking. If you are in a town or city where there are bakeries, meat shops and grocery stores operated by descendants of East European immigrants, try some of the foods offered for sale. Their beautiful yeast breads, including a variety of rye loaves with caraway seeds, coffee cakes and sausages of many sizes, shapes and flavors are fascinating.

These European-Americans also continue to make in their own kitchens many of their traditional dishes for special occasions and sometimes for every-day meals. Their neighbors enjoy them so much that they also prepare some of them. The recipes in this chapter are some of the East European specialties made today in American home kitchens.

The first immigrants from Eastern Europe came from what now is Czechoslovakia as early as 1850. They settled mainly on farm lands in the Midwest—in Iowa and Nebraska particularly. Almost at once their new neighbors recognized the Czech-Americans as expert bakers, especially of yeast breads. The immigrants, glorying in the amazingly plentiful supply of wheat flour, spent many hours baking their prized breads, not only to enjoy eating them but also to help overcome homesickness and loneliness.

The big immigration from Eastern Europe started in the 1880s. Many of the families, speaking their native languages until they learned English, settled in industrial areas in closely knit ethnic groups. They had something of their own, even though they were in a new country, to tie them to their former homes and relatives and friends left behind. This was their own style of cooking. Such emotional reliance on foods was not new to them. Many of the nations from which they came had been conquered and ruled by outsiders off and on throughout their history. They had learned that their cooking was one custom they could keep. Treasuring traditions in foods was a way of life and they passed on many of those traditions from one generation to another. They continued to do this in their new American homeland.

While at first they lived in ethnic groups, they gradually entered the American mainstream and enhanced it. They welcomed the bountiful foods in their new country, which they were able to buy with money they earned. They were able to include more meat in their meals. What had been holiday food to them appeared throughout the year.

Hungarian cooking had spread to neighboring European countries in a natural exchange of food ideas and recipes before Hungarian immigrants arrived in America. Many of these dishes were so delicious that they continued to travel to one home from another on this side of the Atlantic. Among the Hungarian-

oriented dishes of the new settlers were noodle specials, goulashes or stews, especially those using paprika and sour cream.
Many Americans consider paprika a bright coloring to sprinkle
on food, but those of Eastern European descent use it for seasoning, not as a garnish. Chicken Paprika (see Index) is one of the
most widely praised specialties inspired by Hungarian-Amer-
icans.

Goulashes have enthusiastic supporters and none deserves
more praise than hearty Pork Goulash (see Index) in which
pork, sour cream and sauerkraut blend. Hungarian Beef Goulash
(see Index) is another favorite of Americans.

While the elegant stroganoff of Old Russia comes to American
dinner tables on special occasions, more frequently ready-to-use
ground beef will substitute for the tiny strips of the most tender
and costly beef cuts (see Hamburger Stroganoff). And sometimes in this burger-loving country, the stroganoff appears in
delicious and satisfying sandwiches (see Beef Stroganoff Sandwiches).

Polish-Americans added many tasty touches to American
meals. Polish sausage (kielbasa) is highly prized and exceedingly popular. And Polish-Americans, as well as Americans from
other Eastern European countries, demonstrate that marvelous
dishes can be fashioned with a humble head of cabbage. Cabbage
with Polish Sausage is wonderfully good, as is Polish-American
Stew (see Index) which in addition to cabbage features sausage,
potatoes, sauerkraut and apples. In fact, all Eastern Europeans
excel in creating splendid dishes with vegetables; they showed
Americans how to use their favorites—especially beets—in interesting combinations. Polish Hot Beet Relish (see Index) is a
good example. It is served as a vegetable dish rather than as a
relish.

Some of the inspiration for cooking meat and vegetables on
skewers derives from southeastern Europe, Georgia and Ar-
menia, as well as from Turkey and other countries in the
Mideast. Our recipe for Midwestern Kabobs from the Mideast
(see Index) is an example.

No consideration of Eastern European contributions to the

American cuisine can omit paying tribute to the superlative and sometimes intricate yeast breads. Many of them are holiday traditionals and they bring happiness to many a Christmas and Easter celebration on this side of the Atlantic. One cf the most distinctive breads baked in America is kulich, an old Russian Easter special—tall, stately loaves with dome-shaped tops.

Probably no food contribution of the Czechs (also famous for their noodle dishes and dumplings) is superior to kolaches. These yeast-leavened buns are light in texture and hold a variety of fruit fillings dusted with confectioners sugar. One of the fillings Czech-Americans like best consists of ground poppyseeds cooked with milk and honey. Some home kitchens in Nebraska prize and use poppyseed grinders; others depend on old-fashioned coffee grinders to prepare the seeds. Other Americans, as a rule, prefer the fillings made with dried apricots or prunes, or a combination of the two. These buns are perfect companions to coffee.

MIDWESTERN KABOBS FROM THE MIDEAST

Cookout kings across the United States pay tribute to the kabobs of southwestern Russia, Turkey and other nationalities in the Mideast. They have taken the ancient techniques for cooking vegetables and meats on sticks or skewers and adapted them for use in their own back yards. Americans frequently substitute beef for the lamb universally cooked in the Mideast. And some of the American experts grill the cubes of meat and the vegetables on separate skewers because the cooking times differ.

With beef, only the tender cuts, such as sirloin steak, usually are grilled. In our recipe for Midwestern Kabobs, we use round steak cubes. It is tender enough after chilling overnight in a marinade. This also adds pleasing flavor.

Small onions, green pepper and zucchini slices are parboiled before stringing on skewers. Dip cherry tomatoes and mushrooms in boiling water to prevent splitting. Serve the grilled meat and vegetables on rice.

MIDWESTERN KABOBS FROM THE MIDEAST

You can also cook these over the coals in the summer

2½ lbs. round steak, cut
   1" thick
¾ c. cooking oil
⅓ c. soy sauce
2 tblsp. Worcestershire
   sauce
¼ c. minced onion
3 tblsp. minced fresh
   parsley
1 clove garlic, minced

⅓ c. lemon juice
¼ tsp. pepper
1 large green pepper, cut in
   1½" chunks
12 small onions
3 small zucchini squash,
   cut in 1" slices
16 cherry tomatoes
1 (13½ oz.) can pineapple
   chunks, drained

Cut beef in 32 (1") pieces. Combine oil, soy sauce, Worcestershire sauce, onion, parsley, garlic, lemon juice and pepper; mix well. Pour over beef in bowl. Cover and marinate in refrigerator 24 to 48 hours.

Cook green pepper, onions and squash in water until tender crisp. Drain.

Thread 8 (12") skewers with alternate pieces of beef, vegetables and pineapple, using 4 pieces of meat on each. Broil 4 skewers at a time, 3" from the source of heat, 5 minutes. Turn as needed. Baste with marinade frequently. (Meat will be medium done.) Repeat with remaining skewers. Serve with either Bulgur Wheat Pilaf or Rice Pilaf (recipes follow). Makes 6 to 8 servings.

RICE PILAF

Cook rice and onions in butter until golden—enhances flavors

½ c. chopped onion
1 c. uncooked rice
¼ c. butter or regular
   margarine

1 tsp. salt
2 c. chicken broth, or 1
   (13¾ oz.) can chicken
   broth plus ¼ c. water

Cook onion and rice in butter in heavy saucepan until rice is golden. Stir frequently. Add salt and chicken broth. Bring to a boil. Reduce heat; cover and simmer 20 minutes. Makes 6 servings.

BULGUR WHEAT PILAF

Use bulgur or cracked wheat to make this tasty nut-flavored pilaf

2 c. bulgur wheat
¼ c. butter or regular
    margarine
1 c. chopped onion
1 (8 oz.) can mushroom
    stems and pieces
2 (13¾ oz.) cans chicken
    broth, or 3½ c. chicken
    broth

1 tsp. salt
½ tsp. dried oregano leaves,
    crushed
⅛ tsp. pepper

Cook wheat in butter in 10″ skillet until slightly toasted. Stir frequently. Add onion, mushrooms, chicken broth, salt, oregano and pepper. Cover and simmer about 20 minutes or until tender. Makes 8 servings.

PORK AND BEAN CASSEROLE

The recipe for Pork and Bean Casserole comes from an Illinois woman who obtained it from her grandmother while visiting her in Yugoslavia. When she returned, she duplicated the dish, which she describes as "solid farm food," and shared it with neighbors.

Chicken broth is the unusual ingredient. If you have a supply in the freezer, this is a splendid use for it, but commercially canned chicken broth or bouillon also fills the bill. It imparts a subtle flavor, which taste testers usually do not identify. But they agree the dish has an exceptional richness. Wonderful recipe for using dry beans.

PORK AND BEAN CASSEROLE

Unusually good, hearty dish made with dry beans and chicken broth

2 c. navy or Great Northern beans	2 c. chicken broth, or 1 (13¾ oz.) can chicken broth plus ¼ c. water
Water	
1 c. chopped onion	2 tsp. paprika
2 cloves garlic, minced	¼ tsp. crushed, dried red pepper
2 lbs. smoked pork shoulder roll, cut in ½" cubes	

Wash beans. Place beans in Dutch oven and cover with cold water. Bring to a boil; boil 2 minutes. Remove from heat; cover and let stand 1 hour. (Or soak beans overnight.)

Drain beans. Combine with onion, garlic, pork, chicken broth, paprika and red pepper. Bring to a boil; reduce heat, cover and simmer 1 hour 15 minutes. Uncover and simmer about 15 minutes or until most of liquid has cooked away. Stir occasionally. Makes 8 servings.

HAMBURGER STROGANOFF

No other dish imported from Russia pleases American tastes more than beef stroganoff. The magnificent classic, when created in Imperial Russia, was named for the famous Stroganoff family. Slender strips of tender beef, often the filet, take the meat role in the dish, which in Russia is served with potatoes cut exceptionally fine and fried very crisp, similar to our shoestring potatoes.

Americans usually serve their versions of stroganoff over rice, noodles or mashed potatoes. The noodles in the simplified Hamburger Stroganoff are folded into the meat and sour cream mixture just before serving.

For special occasions, many people use sirloin steak to make stroganoff, but for frequent, every-day meals you can make the dish quickly, and thriftily and deliciously with ground beef.

HAMBURGER STROGANOFF

Use this recipe to skip the tedious cutting of tiny meat strips

1 lb. ground beef
½ c. chopped onion
2 tblsp. flour
1 tsp. salt
¼ tsp. pepper
1 (8 oz.) can mushroom
   stems and pieces, drained
1 (10¾ oz.) can condensed
   cream of chicken soup

2 tblsp. ketchup
2 tsp. Worcestershire sauce
1 (8 oz.) pkg. noodles
1 c. dairy sour cream
2 tblsp. chopped fresh
   parsley

Cook ground beef and onion in 10″ skillet until beef is browned. Stir in flour, salt, pepper, mushrooms, chicken soup, ketchup and Worcestershire sauce. Cover and simmer 10 minutes, stirring occasionally.

Meanwhile, cook noodles as directed on package; drain. Stir sour cream into meat mixture. Heat thoroughly, but do not boil. Stir in hot noodles. Turn into serving dish. Sprinkle with chopped parsley. Makes 6 servings.

BEEF STROGANOFF SANDWICHES

Americans have adapted Russian stroganoff, sometimes in ways quite far afield from the original dish. A good example is Beef Stroganoff Sandwiches, which have the good taste of beef plus sour cream.

This is an economical sandwich filling. One pound of ground beef, bolstered by cheese, makes 8 servings. If you are in a rut with supper menus, try these hearty and delicious sandwiches for your main dish. You can make them in less than 30 minutes.

BEEF STROGANOFF SANDWICHES

Complete menu with buttered peas, tossed salad and raspberry parfaits

1 loaf French bread	1 tsp. salt
1 lb. ground beef	⅛ tsp. pepper
¼ c. finely chopped onion	1 tsp. Worcestershire sauce
1 c. dairy sour cream	1½ c. shredded process
1 tblsp. milk	American cheese (6 oz.)
¼ c. chopped fresh parsley	

Cut bread in half lengthwise. Wrap in foil and heat in 375° oven 10 minutes.

Meanwhile, brown beef with onion, drain off excess fat. Stir in sour cream, milk, parsley, salt, pepper and Worcestershire sauce. Heat, but do not let boil.

Spread meat mixture over cut surface of bread. Sprinkle with cheese. Place on baking sheet and return to oven for 5 minutes. Makes 8 servings.

POLISH-AMERICAN STEW

The Poles, like their neighbors in Eastern European countries, make many marvelous dishes with pork. They are famed internationally for their sausages. Polish-American Stew combines the two meats most successfully. Such dishes are gaining favor because some supermarkets now sell the sausage, usually called *kielbasa*. High school and college students in many Midwestern communities are fond of "hot dogs" using Polish sausage instead of the conventional frankfurter. Cut sausage into frankfurter lengths (sometimes kielbasa is made in individual sausages), heat them, top with sauerkraut and serve in long buns.

Polish-American Stew also contains sauerkraut, as do many dishes in Eastern Europe. The Chinese invented the fermented cabbage long ago; it was an important food in the diet of workers who built the Great Wall. The Tartars carried it to Eastern

Europe and sometime later it was introduced by Austrians into what is now Germany.

Polish people cook all stew ingredients together, but in most American kitchens the potatoes, apples, cabbage and sausage are added toward the end of the cooking. This ends up as a cross between a stew and soup. Serve it in bowls with crusty French bread or arrange the bread slices on individual serving plates and ladle stew over them.

POLISH-AMERICAN STEW

This is a one-pot meal. Good served with a fruit salad

2 lbs. pork, cut in 1" cubes	2 tsp. salt
2 tblsp. cooking oil	¼ tsp. pepper
1 c. chopped onion	1 bay leaf
1 clove garlic, minced	4 medium potatoes, pared and quartered
1 (1 lb.) can sauerkraut	3 c. shredded cabbage
1 c. beef broth, or 1 beef bouillon cube dissolved in 1 c. boiling water	2 apples, pared and sliced
	1 lb. Polish sausage, cut in 1" slices
1 (8 oz.) can tomato sauce	French bread slices

Brown pork in oil in Dutch oven. Add onion, garlic, sauerkraut, beef broth, tomato sauce, salt, pepper and bay leaf. Bring to a boil. Reduce heat; cover and simmer 30 minutes.

Add potatoes; continue simmering 30 minutes. Add cabbage, apples and Polish sausage; simmer 20 minutes. Remove bay leaf. Serve in bowls with French bread. Makes 12 servings.

CABBAGE WITH POLISH SAUSAGE

Of all the ways Polish-Americans have contributed to American kitchens with food, those with cabbage and sauerkraut have caught on most extensively on this side of the Atlantic. You scarcely can miss on a dish when either of these forms of cabbage teams with Polish sausage, available in many markets.

Americans usually adapt the recipes from Eastern Europe. Perhaps the most common change is to cook cabbage a shorter time. The original recipe for Cabbage with Polish Sausage was contributed by a homemaker of Polish descent who lives in the Green Bay area of Wisconsin. It calls for cooking the cabbage 1 hour, while our recipe reduces the time to 20 minutes.

The first step in making the thrifty main dish is to cook the onions in butter or margarine until soft and very lightly browned (in Poland lard usually is used for the fat). The sausage seasons the vegetable delightfully. Even people who normally do not like cabbage are enthusiastic about this dish.

CABBAGE WITH POLISH SAUSAGE

Good with baked potatoes, rye bread and apple salad or dessert

1 c. chopped onion	¾ tsp. salt
2 tblsp. butter or regular margarine	½ tsp. sugar
	¼ tsp. pepper
2 tblsp. flour	3 qts. shredded cabbage
1 c. water	6 Polish sausages, cut in
¼ c. white vinegar	1″ slices

Cook onion in butter in Dutch oven until soft and lightly colored. Blend in flour. Add water and vinegar, and cook, stirring constantly, until mixture comes to a boil. Blend in salt, sugar and pepper. Stir in cabbage and sausage. Cover and simmer about 20 minutes or until cabbage is tender. Stir occasionally. Makes 6 servings.

HUNGARIAN BEEF GOULASH

The national dish of Hungary is *gulyás,* a beef stew that in America we call goulash. Of all meat dishes it is the one most borrowed from Hungarian kitchens. An essential ingredient of the stew is paprika. The production of most Hungarian paprika is mechanized, but in the southern part of Hungary you will sometimes see strings of brilliant red peppers hanging from the eaves of farm houses and drying in the sunshine. This sight reminds one of equally bright peppers hanging from adobe houses in New Mexico.

Hungarian paprika is mild in comparison with some of the pepper products made in America—cayenne, for instance. One reason is that Hungarians grind only the pulp of pepper pods while in cayenne the seeds and pithy interior, the hottest part of peppers, are included. In the Americas, some people combine different kinds, mild to fiery, to obtain the exact taste desired.

Americans make some changes in the goulash recipes that Hungarian immigrants brought to their new home. One is that they usually add sour cream, which is not included in the true Hungarian dish made with beef. And they often omit the caraway seeds, so much used and appreciated in Eastern Europe.

HUNGARIAN BEEF GOULASH

Add ½ tsp. caraway seeds with other seasoning, if you like

2 lbs. stewing beef, cut in 1½" cubes	½ c. water
½ c. flour	1 tblsp. paprika
3 tblsp. cooking oil	2 tsp. salt
2 c. chopped onion	¼ tsp. pepper
2 cloves garlic, minced	¼ tsp. dried thyme leaves
1 (1 lb.) can tomatoes, cut up	1 c. dairy sour cream
	12 oz. noodles, cooked and drained

Shake stew meat in bag containing flour. Brown meat on all sides in hot oil in Dutch oven. Add onion, garlic, tomatoes, water, paprika, salt, pepper and thyme. Cover and simmer 1 hour 30 minutes, stirring occasionally. Then simmer uncovered about 30 minutes or until meat is tender. Stir frequently.

Stir in sour cream. Heat thoroughly, but do not boil. Serve over hot noodles. Makes 6 to 8 servings.

PORK GOULASH

Women in a Wisconsin club, seeking a new approach to the annual supper given for their husbands, agreed to contribute a dish their ancestors brought to America. Among the dishes that captured the spotlight at the "melting-pot potluck" was Pork Goulash of Hungarian descent. "It was a big surprise to me," one of the hostesses said, "that the ordinary pork and sauerkraut stew which my great-grandmother learned to make in Eastern Europe won so many bouquets."

Our modified recipe for Pork Goulash omits the caraway seeds and tomato purée listed in many European recipes, and calls for marjoram and less sour cream. The rule in Hungary is to cook the onions in lard instead of oil; either may be used—whichever is more available. If your family and friends enjoy sauerkraut, Pork Goulash offers you a good way to please them.

PORK GOULASH

Good served with parsley potatoes, beet relish, celery and a baked apple dessert—cobbler, crisp, pie or dumplings

3 lbs. pork shoulder, cut in
    1" cubes
2 tblsp. cooking oil
3 large onions, sliced
2 cloves garlic, minced
1 tblsp. paprika
1 tsp. salt
½ tsp. dried marjoram
    leaves

½ c. chicken broth, or 1
    chicken bouillon cube
    dissolved in ½ c. boiling
    water
2 (1 lb.) cans sauerkraut,
    drained and rinsed
1 c. dairy sour cream

Brown pork cubes in hot oil in Dutch oven. Remove meat from pan. Cook onions in drippings until golden, stirring frequently. Add pork, garlic, paprika, salt, marjoram and chicken broth. Cover and simmer 30 minutes.

Add sauerkraut; continue simmering 30 minutes or until pork is tender. Stir in sour cream. Heat, but do not boil. Makes 8 to 10 servings.

GROUND BEEF/EGGPLANT CASSEROLE

If members of your family are less than enthusiastic about eggplant, chances are good that you can change their minds with Ground Beef/Eggplant Casserole. It is an autumn favorite in many country homes. Slices of the vegetable are browned and layered in a baking dish with tomatoes, onions and ground beef. The flavors blend delightfully during the baking.

This casserole is a distant relative of the famous Greek moussaka for which there are many recipes. The recipe for Ground Beef/Eggplant Casserole came to Michigan from Romania where ground lamb is more commonly used than beef. This is also true in Greece. Either meat may be used, whichever is the more available.

GROUND BEEF/EGGPLANT CASSEROLE

Serve with green beans and Perfection Salad (see Index)

1 large eggplant (1½ lbs.)	⅓ c. uncooked rice
⅓ c. cooking oil	1½ tsp. garlic salt
1 lb. ground beef	1 tsp. salt
2 c. chopped onion	¼ tsp. pepper
1 (1 lb.) can tomatoes, cut up	

Peel eggplant; cut in 1" slices. Lightly brown eggplant slices in hot oil in large skillet. Remove from skillet. Add ground beef and onion to skillet; cook, stirring frequently, until beef is browned. Add tomatoes, rice, garlic salt, salt and pepper; bring to a boil.

Place half of eggplant slices in greased 2½-qt. casserole. Top with half of beef mixture. Repeat layers. Cover and bake in 350° oven 1 hour. Makes 6 servings.

CHICKEN PAPRIKA

Mention Hungarian cooking almost any place in America and you'll bring to mind rich chicken or meat gravy spiced and tinted by paprika and enhanced by sour cream. Chicken Paprika is a highly esteemed Hungarian-American dish. Its marvelous taste contributes to its popularity, but there is another reason for its wide acceptance. Country women are the world's champions when it comes to collecting and trying promising chicken recipes.

Hungary's best grade of paprika is known as "the rose," which you can find in some specialty food stores. Most women make do with the kind they can buy in the supermarkets. They frequently add seasonings of their own to make up for possible lack of flavor. Bacon is the extra ingredient in the recipe that follows. Everyone who tastes the main dish with the American addition likes the faint, smoky flavor it adds.

CHICKEN PAPRIKA

Serve the chicken and luscious gravy over homemade noodles

8 slices bacon, chopped
1 c. chopped onion
1 clove garlic, minced
1 (3 lb.) broiler-fryer,
   cut up
¾ c. flour
1 tblsp. paprika
1 tsp. salt

1 c. chicken broth, or 2
   chicken bouillon cubes
   dissolved in 1 c. boiling
   water
1 c. dairy sour cream
12 oz. noodles, cooked
   and drained

Cook bacon in 12″ skillet until crisp. Remove and drain on paper toweling. Cook onion and garlic in bacon drippings until soft. Remove and reserve.

Shake chicken pieces, a few at a time, in mixture of flour, paprika and salt in plastic bag. Reserve excess flour mixture. Brown chicken on all sides in bacon drippings in skillet. Pour off all drippings.

Add chicken broth and reserved onion and garlic to skillet; cover and simmer 25 to 30 minutes or until chicken is tender. Remove chicken.

Blend together sour cream and reserved flour mixture. Add to skillet. Cook and stir until mixture is thickened and hot. Do not boil. Add chicken pieces and bacon. Spoon sauce over and heat. Serve over hot noodles. Makes 5 servings.

CABBAGE SKILLET

Cabbage dishes appear in Hungarian meals as often as potatoes do in American country dinners and suppers. Among the Eastern European favorites adopted on this side of the Atlantic Ocean with little or no change is pan-fried cabbage, seasoned with onion, bacon drippings, paprika and sour cream.

For an easy, quick and tasty vegetable dish, make Cabbage Skillet. It is especially good with pork, chicken, ham loaf and other meat dishes. Youngsters insist it is best of all served with hamburgers or frankfurters.

CABBAGE SKILLET

You can make this from start to finish in 15 minutes

8 c. shredded cabbage	1½ tsp. salt
2 tblsp. chopped onion	1 tsp. paprika
2 tblsp. bacon drippings	½ c. dairy sour cream

Cook cabbage and onion in bacon drippings in 10″ skillet about 7 minutes or until tender. Stir frequently. Add salt, paprika and sour cream. Heat thoroughly, but do not boil. Makes 6 servings.

GREEN BEANS AND TOMATOES

Practically all nationalities have vegetable twosomes. Favorite American specials are carrots and peas, corn and lima beans, new potatoes and peas. Green beans and tomatoes get together in Polish kitchens to make a dish called *yelni*. Americans welcome the combination as a way to introduce variety in meals.

The green and red vegetables have the flavorful support of a bit of ham and onion. If you do not have fresh tomatoes, use canned, firm, whole tomatoes, drained and cut up.

GREEN BEANS AND TOMATOES

Attractive way to blend the flavors of two common vegetables

1 (1 lb.) can whole green
beans
2 small tomatoes, peeled
and cut up
⅓ c. chopped onion

⅓ c. chopped, cooked ham
⅛ tsp. salt
⅛ tsp. pepper
1 tblsp. butter or regular
margarine

Drain beans, reserving ¼ c. liquid. Combine beans, bean liquid, tomatoes, onion, ham, salt and pepper in saucepan. Bring to a boil. Reduce heat; cover and simmer about 20 minutes or until flavors are blended. Stir in butter. Makes 5 servings.

CAULIFLOWER POLONAISE

The Polish way of elevating buttered cauliflower above the commonplace has become popular on this side of the Atlantic. The trick is to brown butter lightly, add bread crumbs, chopped hard-cooked egg and seasonings, and spoon the mixture over hot, cooked cauliflower in the serving dish. The vegetable is attractive and the topping enhances its taste and appearance.

CAULIFLOWER POLONAISE

This same topping is also good on cooked green beans

1 medium head cauliflower
⅓ c. butter or regular
margarine
½ c. fine, dry bread crumbs
chopped
1 hard-cooked egg, finely

1 tblsp. chopped fresh
parsley
½ tsp. salt
⅛ tsp. pepper
⅛ tsp. paprika

Trim base from cauliflower and remove leaves. Break into flowerets. Cook in boiling, salted water 10 to 15 minutes or until tender. (Or cook whole for 15 to 20 minutes.) Drain thoroughly and place in serving dish.

Lightly brown butter. Stir in bread crumbs, egg, parsley, salt, pepper and paprika. Spoon over cauliflower. Makes 6 servings.

POLISH HOT BEET RELISH

Although this well-seasoned, hot beet dish is called a relish by Polish-Americans, many meal planners consider it the second vegetable in the dinner menu. It enjoys special popularity during the hunting season in autumn. The sweet-sour taste complements game, but the beets are equally good in meals when chicken or pork is on the platter.

POLISH HOT BEET RELISH

Serve beets this new way for a delicious change of pace

4 c. shredded, cooked beets (8 medium)	1 tblsp. sugar
	¾ tsp. salt
2 tblsp. melted butter or regular margarine	½ c. dairy sour cream
1 tblsp. flour	1 tblsp. vinegar

Heat beets in melted butter in saucepan. Stir in flour, sugar and salt. Add sour cream and vinegar. Heat thoroughly, stirring frequently, but do not boil. Makes 6 to 8 servings.

CUCUMBERS IN SOUR CREAM

People of many countries enjoy thinly sliced cucumbers, seasoned and dressed with sour cream. The Poles are no exception, but they prepare the cucumbers somewhat differently. American women who are exposed to the Polish method almost always adopt it in their kitchens. Boiling water is poured over the cucumbers to cover and allowed to stand for 20 minutes. Drain, plunge in cold water for a minute or two, drain again and refrigerate for 30 minutes before combining the slices with the sour cream dressing.

CUCUMBERS IN SOUR CREAM

You can substitute lemon juice for vinegar, chives for dill

2 large cucumbers, peeled	1 tsp. salt
and thinly sliced	½ tsp. dried dill weed
½ c. dairy sour cream	⅛ tsp. pepper
2 tsp. sugar	2 tsp. vinegar

Cover cucumbers with boiling water; let stand 20 minutes. Drain. Cover with cold water; let stand 1 minute. Drain again. Refrigerate 30 minutes.

Stir in sour cream, sugar, salt, dill weed, pepper and vinegar. Refrigerate at least 1 hour to blend flavors. Makes 6 servings.

KULICH

Perhaps the Russian food specialty that most fascinates American women who like to bake bread is kulich, a traditional Russian Easter bread. One Midwestern hostess of Russian ancestry teams the bread with hot tea, which she serves in tall glasses as her grandmother did. It is a good idea to slice one loaf and stand the other in the background to dramatize the tall and stately bread. Place it on a tray and, if served during the Easter season, arrange Easter eggs of bright colors around its base.

One Russian way, and a good one, to cut the loaf is to slice off the puffed-up, rounded top that resembles the dome of a Russian Orthodox church. Cut the loaf, minus its top, in lengthwise halves. Slice each half in pieces about 1½″ thick. Center the top on the serving plate or tray and lay the slices around it.

Our recipe for kulich is for a sweet yeast dough baked in two one-pound coffee cans instead of the Russian pans, shaped like a 12″ piece of stove pipe, which is not generally available. Spread the confectioners sugar frosting over the top and let it dribble down the sides of the loaf; or frost both the top and sides. Sprinkle on tiny, multicolored candies for a final touch.

KULICH

Keep one loaf and give the other for a lovely Easter gift

4½ to 5 c. sifted flour
2 pkgs. active dry yeast
1 c. milk
½ c. sugar
1 tsp. salt
½ c. shortening
2 eggs
½ tsp. vanilla

½ c. raisins
¼ c. chopped, blanched
  almonds
Snowy Frosting (recipe
  follows)
Tiny, multicolored
  decorating candies

Combine 2½ c. flour and yeast in large mixer bowl.

Heat milk, sugar, salt and shortening in saucepan just until warm, stirring to melt shortening. Add to flour-yeast mixture along with eggs and vanilla. Beat at low speed 30 seconds, scraping sides of bowl constantly. Beat at high speed 3 minutes.

Stir in raisins and almonds by hand. Stir in enough remaining flour to make a soft dough. Turn out on lightly floured surface and knead until smooth and elastic, about 5 minutes. Place in greased bowl; turn dough over to grease top. Cover and let rise in warm place until double, 1 to 1 hour 30 minutes. Punch down dough. Let rise again 30 to 40 minutes or until almost double.

Divide dough in half. Form each half into a ball, sealing edges at bottom with fingers. Gently press each ball into well-greased 1-lb. coffee can. Cover and let rise until dough starts to puff over can top.

Bake in 375° oven 40 to 45 minutes. Remove from cans at once; cool on rack. Spread tops with Snowy Frosting, letting it drizzle down sides. Sprinkle with tiny, multicolored decorating candies (or with 2 tblsp. slivered almonds and 2 candied cherries, sliced). Makes 2 loaves.

Snowy Frosting: Mix ½ c. sifted confectioners sugar with 2 to 2½ tsp. milk or light cream, or enough to make frosting of spreading consistency.

KOLACHES

Americans who know kolaches are grateful to the Czechoslovakian-Americans for this taste gift. You sometimes encounter the fruit-topped, yeast-leavened buns in bake shops where many of these people live, such as in Nebraska, Iowa, Minnesota and Wisconsin. You are likely to have them served to you with coffee in the homes in these ethnic neighborhoods. Since American women have a knack for obtaining recipes for a food new to them that tastes exceptionally good, these Bohemian buns are baked by many American women not of Czech descent.

It may not be too easy to achieve perfection in the shape of kolaches baked the first time, but if you follow this recipe faithfully, you should have good results. To make the work easier on baking day, make the filling (or fillings if you want to use more than one) a day ahead, cover and refrigerate. Or you can bake the filled kolaches several days ahead and freeze. (If you do, omit brushing tops of buns with melted butter and sprinkling on confectioners sugar until after you have warmed them just before serving. This last-minute treatment gives them a freshly baked taste.)

KOLACHES

Tempting coffee go-withs—always the talk of the party

½ c. milk	1 tsp. salt
2 pkgs. active dry yeast	4 egg yolks
½ c. warm water (110 to 115°)	4½ c. sifted flour
	Fillings (recipes follow)
¾ c. butter or regular margarine	2 tblsp. melted butter
	2 tblsp. sifted confectioners sugar
½ c. sugar	

Scald milk; cool to lukewarm.

Sprinkle yeast on warm water; stir to dissolve.

Cream together butter, sugar, salt and egg yolks until light and fluffy. Add yeast, milk and 1½ c. flour. Beat at medium speed 5 minutes, scraping bowl occasionally. Batter should be smooth.

Stir in enough remaining flour, a little at a time, to make a soft dough that leaves the sides of bowl. Place in lightly greased bowl; turn dough over to grease top. Cover and let rise in warm place until doubled, 1 to 1 hour 30 minutes.

Stir down; turn onto lightly floured board and divide into 24 equal pieces. Shape each piece into a ball. Cover and let rest 10 to 15 minutes.

Place dough balls 2" apart on greased baking sheets; press each ball of dough from center outward with fingers of both hands to make a hollow in center with a ½" rim around edge. Fill each hollow with 1 level tblsp. filling. Cover and let rise in warm place until doubled, 30 to 40 minutes.

Bake in 350° oven 15 to 18 minutes or until browned. Brush tops of rolls lightly with melted butter and sprinkle lightly with confectioners sugar. Remove from baking sheets and place on racks. Makes 2 dozen.

FILLINGS FOR KOLACHES

Prune: Cook 30 prunes in water to cover until tender; drain. Mash with fork; stir in ¼ c. sugar and ¼ tsp. ground allspice. Filling should be thick. Makes enough for 14 kolaches.

Thick Apricot: Cook 25 dried apricot halves in water to cover until tender; drain. Press apricots through strainer or food mill (or blend in blender). Stir in ¼ c. sugar. Filling should be thick. Makes enough filling for 10 kolaches.

Prune/Apricot: Simmer 1 c. prunes and ¾ c. dried apricot halves in water to cover until tender; drain. Chop and mash with fork. Stir in ½ c. sugar, 1 tblsp. orange juice and 1 tblsp. grated orange peel. Filling should be thick. Makes enough filling for 24 kolaches.

RUSSIAN-AMERICAN CHARLOTTE RUSSE

Collecting recipes for glamorous desserts once popular but largely forgotten is a hobby with some women who like to entertain. Charlotte Russe, the rave of the Gay Nineties, is a good candidate. The beginning of the dessert is obscure, but Americans—especially the Southerners—served it elegantly, garnished with puffs of whipped cream, on antique silver trays or footed, glass cake stands. That was when the South's major industry was agriculture and farm produce plentiful and cheap so that cream and eggs were used lavishly in cooking.

One legend states that a French chef working in Russia created the dessert for a special occasion. Another story is that a French chef invented it for a Russian Czar who was in France on a visit. It was, at any rate, quite the vogue in aristocratic society in the old Imperial Empire.

Our recipe for Russian-American Charlotte Russe, decorated with Ruby Raspberry Sauce, is an adaptation of the old-time dessert. Here's the recipe from an old Maryland cookbook:

MRS. GRAY'S CHARLOTTE RUSSE

Dissolve gelatin in ½ c. water. When dissolved, beat up yolks of 6 eggs and a good-sized cup of sugar. Put in double saucepan with gelatin, and cook until eggs are cooked. Pour into a large bowl to cool. While it cools, beat up 1 quart cream and add to egg yolks and keep stirring until cold enough to mold. Flavor with vanilla. Set ladyfingers in tin or china mold, then pour in the mixture and set away in a cold place.

Now, contrast Mrs. Gray's recipe with our Russian-American Charlotte Russe. Tested recipes of today are easier to use, give better results and avoid waste because guessing has been eliminated.

RUSSIAN-AMERICAN CHARLOTTE RUSSE

Sour cream and raspberry sauce enhance this elegant dessert

2 envelopes unflavored gelatin	1 c. dairy sour cream
¾ c. sugar	2 tsp. vanilla
¼ tsp. salt	12 ladyfingers, split
4 eggs, separated	1 c. heavy cream, whipped
2 c. milk	Raspberry Sauce (see Index)

Stir together gelatin, sugar and salt in heavy saucepan.

Beat egg yolks slightly; add to gelatin mixture along with milk. Cook over low heat, stirring constantly or until mixture coats a spoon. Remove from heat. Blend in sour cream and vanilla. Chill until mixture mounds slightly.

Arrange ladyfingers, rounded sides out, around edge of 9" springform pan.

Beat egg whites until stiff; fold into custard mixture. Fold in whipped cream. Spoon into pan. Chill until firm, 6 hours or overnight. To serve, remove sides of pan and drizzle dessert with part of the Raspberry Sauce. Pass remaining sauce. Makes 12 to 16 servings.

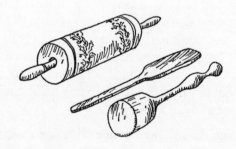

Chapter 6

THE HERITAGE OF
ITALIAN AND OTHER
MEDITERRANEAN
FAVORITES

Hungry Americans love spaghetti in tomato sauce sprinkled with Parmesan cheese. The teen-age crowd gathers at the favorite hangout for hot servings of pizza, dripping melted cheese. No doubt about it, Italian-type foods are a part of the American cuisine.

Since there are many more Italian-Americans than people descended from other nationalities that touch Mediterranean waters, we are including mainly recipes for some of the dishes brought by Italian immigrants to our shores. Most of them, however, have been naturalized in American kitchens. Spain's contributions to our cooking appear in Southwestern Specialties for they came mainly by way of Mexico and South America.

Certain food customs are common to all southern European people, such as the use of olive oil, lemon juice, fresh herbs and local fish. Eggplant dishes are highly regarded (see Index for Eggplant Parmesan).

Many Italian emigrants lived in poverty before they came to America in the early 1900s. Through hard work they were able to buy plentiful foods that previously were luxuries they could not afford. To these Italian-Americans eating was enjoyment.

Italian women in the United States sometimes took paying boarders and served Italian-American dishes that were tasty, substantial and comparatively inexpensive. Reports of these meals circulated and gradually Americans gravitated to them. This was the modest beginning of Italian-American restaurants that today are popular the country over.

The wonderful world of pasta, introduced by Italian-Americans, makes a valuable contribution to meals, particularly when food costs are high. Spaghetti, noodles and macaroni of various shapes and sizes are great "stretchers." Our recipes reflect Italian seasonings and combinations of foods, such as fish and macaroni and cheese in Tuna Bake Italian Style (see Index).

Easy Chicken Tetrazzini, Noodles Parmesan and Two-pan Lasagne are other Italian-American favorites that fit today's lifestyle. Our Pizza Crust is the thin, crisp Neopolitan type and the fillings are exciting and delicious. One is as American as hamburger, another is as Italian as pepperoni, and a third, Texas Pizza, is an example of the "melting pot" influence on food. The pizza is an Italian inspiration and the taco topping of finely shredded lettuce and chopped green onions and tomatoes is a Texas-Mexico addition. Pizzas introduced mozzarella cheese to American kitchens, while pastas established Parmesan as a staple item.

Geography has much to do with what people eat. Mediterranean countries have a climate similar to parts of California. Olives, citrus fruits, figs, grapes and a variety of vegetables, including Italian specials like multiflowered broccoli, artichokes and slim zucchini, grow in both places commercially. Crisp green salads are served with lemon juice or wine vinegar and salad oil dressing. Wine making is a big industry in both Italy and California; raisins are another vineyard product.

Bread loaves frequently are long, slender and crusty; sometimes they are sliced, spread with garlic butter and heated. Italian-type sausages—salami, pepperoni, bologna and others—

are popular in sandwiches and cold plates. Italian-Americans' enthusiasm for good food and the pleasures of cooking have had a great influence in the Golden State particularly.

Italian-American women have the Italian hand in using fresh herbs, such as parsley with flat leaves, sweet basil, oregano, chives, marjoram, tarragon, thyme and bay leaves. They are skilled in using anise-flavored fennel seeds and garlic. These seasonings in Italian-American dishes led to the packaging of mixed Italian spices.

Try the recipes in this sampler of naturalized Mediterranean favorites now enjoyed in homes across the country. America's cuisine is the better for them.

EASY CHICKEN TETRAZZINI

Hostesses have depended on Chicken Tetrazzini to delight their guests since the early 20th century when Luisa Tetrazzini thrilled Americans with her magnificent voice. The dish was created in America for the Italian opera star.

We adapted our version, Easy Chicken Tetrazzini, from the original recipe. Dairy half-and-half substitutes for heavy cream in making the sauce and chicken broth serves as part of the liquid instead of sherry.

EASY CHICKEN TETRAZZINI

We omitted sherry, but you may substitute ⅓ cup for equivalent chicken broth. Leftover turkey also can substitute for chicken

6 tblsp. butter or regular margarine	1 (8 oz.) can mushroom stems and pieces, drained
6 tblsp. flour	12 oz. spaghetti, cooked and drained
¾ tsp. salt	½ c. grated Parmesan cheese
¼ tsp. pepper	
2 c. dairy half-and-half	
1 c. chicken broth	
3 c. cubed, cooked chicken	

Melt butter in 3-qt. saucepan. Blend in flour, salt and pepper. Add half-and-half and chicken broth; cook, stirring constantly, until mixture comes to a boil. Remove from heat.

Stir in chicken and mushrooms. Toss gently with drained spaghetti. Turn into greased 3-qt. casserole. Top with cheese.

Bake in 350° oven 30 minutes. Makes 8 servings.

CHICKEN CACCIATORE

Cacciatore is Italian for a stew in which meat, game, fish or chicken cook in a sauce. The Italian version that Americans like features chicken in a beautifully seasoned tomato sauce. You fry the chicken pieces to a golden brown and then cook it slowly in the sauce.

CHICKEN CACCIATORE

Serve with rice or buttered noodles and broccoli

1 (3 lb.) broiler-fryer, cut up
½ c. flour
½ c. cooking oil
1 medium onion, sliced and separated into rings
½ c. chopped green pepper
2 cloves garlic, minced
1 (1 lb.) can tomatoes, cut up

1 (6 oz.) can tomato paste
1 (4 oz.) can sliced mushrooms, drained
1 tsp. salt
¼ tsp. dried oregano leaves
⅛ tsp. pepper
1 bay leaf

Shake chicken, a few pieces at a time, in bag with flour. Brown chicken on all sides in hot oil in 12″ skillet, removing pieces as they brown. Add onion rings, green pepper and garlic to skillet; sauté until tender (do not brown). Drain off excess oil.

Stir in tomatoes, tomato paste, mushrooms, salt, oregano, pepper and bay leaf. Return chicken pieces to skillet, spooning sauce over. Cover tightly and simmer about 30 minutes or until chicken is tender. Remove bay leaf. Makes 4 servings.

TUNA BAKE ITALIAN STYLE

Sicilian fishermen catch almost half the Italian tuna. Many dishes in the island homes are made with the fish. And many of them are seasoned with tomatoes. Dishes made with tuna, fresh or canned in olive oil, are favorites in all parts of Italy.

Tuna Bake Italian Style is exactly what its name implies. It carries some of the same flavors of similar dishes in Italy.

TUNA BAKE ITALIAN STYLE

The tuna-macaroni combination contains tomato sauce and overtones of mixed Italian seasonings and cheese

1 (8 oz.) pkg. macaroni, cooked and drained	1 tsp. instant minced onion
1 (7 oz.) can tuna, drained and flaked	½ tsp. mixed Italian seasoning
1 (15 oz.) can tomato sauce	1 chicken bouillon cube
½ c. grated Parmesan cheese	¼ c. boiling water
1 tblsp. parsley flakes	1 c. shredded mozzarella cheese (4 oz.)

Combine macaroni, tuna, tomato sauce, Parmesan cheese, parsley, onion and Italian seasoning.

Dissolve bouillon cube in boiling water; add to macaroni mixture. Turn into greased 2-qt. casserole.

Bake in 350° oven 30 minutes. Sprinkle with mozzarella cheese. Continue baking 3 to 5 minutes or until cheese is melted. Makes 6 servings.

TUNA/CHEESE CASSEROLE

Inland Americans depend on canned tuna for much of the fish in their meals. They lean heavily on ideas borrowed from Italian kitchens, where tuna was used plentifully. Tuna/Cheese Casserole is a lasagne-type dish in that it contains pasta and three kinds of cheese—but cream, cottage and process American, rather than Italian types. The final touch of genius is sour cream.

TUNA/CHEESE CASSEROLE

This fish special wins praise every time it comes to the table

1 (8 oz.) pkg. cream cheese, softened
½ c. dairy sour cream
½ c. creamed cottage cheese
¼ c. sliced green onions and tops
¼ tsp. garlic salt
1 (8 oz.) pkg. macaroni shells, cooked and drained

1 (7 oz.) can tuna, drained and flaked
2 tomatoes, peeled and sliced
¼ tsp. salt
1½ c. shredded sharp process American cheese (6 oz.)

Stir together cream cheese, sour cream, cottage cheese, green onions and garlic salt.

Place half of hot macaroni in bottom of greased 2-qt. casserole. Top with half the cream cheese mixture, all of the tuna, remaining macaroni, then remaining cream cheese mixture. Arrange sliced tomatoes over top; sprinkle with salt.

Bake in 350° oven 30 minutes. Sprinkle cheese over tomatoes. Continue baking 3 to 5 minutes or until cheese is melted. Makes 6 to 8 servings.

TWO-PAN LASAGNE

Americans of all ages often carry a main dish to co-operative meals and lasagne often is the first choice. This recipe for Two-pan Lasagne allows one lasagne to go while the other can stay at home for the family's supper or be frozen for future use.

TWO-PAN LASAGNE

All the ingredients in Two-pan Lasagne are used in Italy, except the cottage cheese, which is a substitute for their fresh ricotta

1½ lbs. ground beef
1 c. chopped onion
1 clove garlic, minced
1 (1 lb. 12 oz.) can
    tomatoes, cut up
1 (12 oz.) can tomato
    paste
1½ tsp. salt
1 tsp. dried basil leaves
1 tsp. dried oregano leaves
¼ tsp. pepper

4 c. creamed cottage cheese
3 eggs, beaten
½ c. grated Parmesan
    cheese
2 tblsp. chopped parsley
1½ tsp. salt
1 (1 lb.) pkg. lasagne
    noodles, cooked and
    drained
1 lb. mozzarella cheese,
    thinly sliced

Cook ground beef, onion and garlic in large skillet until beef is browned. Add tomatoes, tomato paste, 1½ tsp. salt, basil, oregano and pepper. Simmer 30 minutes, stirring occasionally.

Combine cottage cheese, eggs, Parmesan cheese, parsley and 1½ tsp. salt.

Divide ⅓ of lasagne noodles evenly between two greased 9″ square pans. Trim noodles to fit and place trimmings over noodles. Top with ⅓ cottage cheese mixture, ⅓ tomato sauce and ⅓ mozzarella cheese, dividing evenly between the two pans. Repeat layers.

Bake in 375° oven 30 minutes. (If made ahead and refrigerated, bake 45 minutes.) Let stand 10 minutes before cutting in 3″ squares. Each pan makes 9 servings.

LASAGNE FLORENTINE

To Americans, as to the French, Florentine in the name of a dish signifies it contains spinach. Sometimes this designation holds in Italy, but not always. It is as likely to indicate that the dish is prepared the same way as in Florence.

Lasagne Florentine is an Italian-American creation that features a layer of spinach which adds a new flavor note to the baked noodle-cheese dish. This is one easy way to get youngsters to eat spinach.

LASAGNE FLORENTINE

This can be prepared in advance and refrigerated

2 (10 oz.) pkgs. frozen
  chopped spinach, thawed
1 lb. ground beef
1 c. chopped onion
1 (8 oz.) can mushroom
  stems and pieces, drained
1 (15 oz.) can tomato sauce
1 tsp. salt
1 tsp. dried oregano leaves
½ tsp. dried basil leaves
¼ tsp. pepper
1 egg, beaten

½ tsp. salt
1½ c. creamed cottage
  cheese (12 oz.)
1 egg, beaten
1 (8 oz.) pkg. lasagne
  noodles, cooked and
  drained
1 (6 oz.) pkg. sliced
  mozzarella cheese
2 tblsp. grated Parmesan
  cheese

Drain uncooked spinach on paper towels.

Meanwhile, cook ground beef and onion in skillet until beef is browned. Add mushrooms, tomato sauce, 1 tsp. salt, oregano, basil and pepper. Cover and simmer 15 minutes.

Mix together spinach, 1 egg and ½ tsp. salt; set aside.

Combine cottage cheese and 1 egg; mix well. Set aside.

Place ½ of noodles in bottom of greased 13×9×2" baking dish. Cover with ½ of the cottage cheese mixture, mozzarella cheese slices and meat sauce. Spread all of spinach mixture over sauce. Repeat layers. Sprinkle with Parmesan cheese.

Bake in 375° oven 30 minutes. (If prepared in advance and refrigerated, bake 45 minutes.) Let stand 10 minutes before serving. Makes 8 to 10 servings.

BAKED POLENTA

Early English settlers in New England learned from the Indians that when making cornmeal mush the kernels crushed easier if first heated. Many new Americans ate mush twice a day as the Indians had for many centuries. The colonists named their new food hasty pudding because it reminded them of a grain porridge by that name eaten in their former homeland. Years later, during the Revolutionary War, people were singing:

> Fath'r and I went down to camp
> Along with Captain Goodwin,
> And there we saw the men and boys
> As thick as hasty puddin'.

Colonial women invented dishes made with cornmeal, such as fried mush and Indian pudding. The latter was not named for the Indians but to distinguish their Indian corn from the wheat called corn in England.

Corn reached Italy from the Americas, and the Italians started to make polenta (their name for mush) with it. People in Italy had used mush since ancient days—first made with water and millet, primitive wheat or the flour from chick-peas. Polenta was the field ration of the Roman legions who conquered the ancient world. They heated grain on stones in campfires, crushed it and put it in their haversacks. They added water to it and cooked the mush wherever they might bivouac.

Baked Polenta is an adaptation of a dish introduced in this country by Italian-Americans. The polenta with cheese added is baked and served with a tasty meat-tomato sauce. This main dish is gaining prestige because it is substantial and tasty, also thrifty and nutritious.

BAKED POLENTA

Cook cornmeal in chicken broth to impart a fine flavor to polenta

½ lb. ground beef
1½ c. sliced fresh
   mushrooms (optional)
½ c. chopped onion
1 clove garlic, minced
1 (15 oz.) can tomato
   sauce
½ tsp. salt
1 small bay leaf
¼ tsp. mixed Italian
   seasoning

1 (13¾ oz.) can chicken
   broth
1 c. yellow cornmeal
1 c. water
½ tsp. salt
½ c. grated Parmesan
   cheese
Grated Parmesan cheese

Cook ground beef, mushrooms, onion and garlic in skillet until meat is browned. Add tomato sauce, ½ tsp. salt, bay leaf and Italian seasoning. Cover and simmer 20 minutes. Remove bay leaf. Set aside.

Meanwhile, bring chicken broth to a boil in large saucepan.

Stir together cornmeal, water and ½ tsp. salt. Gradually stir into chicken broth. Cook until thick, stirring frequently. Cover and simmer over low heat 10 minutes. Remove from heat and add ½ c. Parmesan cheese. Turn into greased 11×7×1½" baking dish.

Bake in 350° oven 15 minutes. To serve, cut in squares. Spoon hot meat sauce over top. Sprinkle with additional Parmesan cheese. Makes 6 servings.

PIZZA-STYLE STEAK

When is steak a pizza? Never, of course, but Pizza-style Steak capitalizes on the appeal both the Italian favorite and beef have for Americans. A well-seasoned tomato sauce tenderizes chuck steak, browned first on both sides, then gently simmered in it.

Little pot-watching is required. The topping of cheese, added as the final touch, gives the dish a wonderful taste medley.

PIZZA-STYLE STEAK

The best flavors of pizza and steak are blended to perfection

2 lbs. chuck steak, cut 1" thick	1 tsp. parsley flakes
1½ tblsp. flour	1 clove garlic, minced
2 tblsp. cooking oil	1 tsp. salt
1 (1 lb.) can tomatoes, cut up	½ tsp. dried oregano leaves
¼ c. chopped onion	⅛ tsp. pepper
	4 slices mozzarella cheese (3 oz.)

Coat steak with flour. Brown on both sides in hot oil in 10" skillet.

Combine tomatoes, onion, parsley, garlic, salt, oregano and pepper. Pour over steak. Bring to a boil. Place in 11×7×1½" baking dish.

Cover with foil and bake in 350° oven 1 hour 30 minutes to 2 hours or until tender. Top with cheese. Continue baking 2 to 3 minutes or until cheese melts. Makes 6 servings.

SPAGHETTI WITH MEAT SAUCE

One characteristic of the pasta in Southern Italy is the variety of superior sauces served with it. (Naples is called the spaghetti city.) Many of the best ones contain tomatoes. Tomatoes grown in the southern areas are smaller in size than American varieties, and are sweet and flavorful. You sometimes see them hanging in the sunshine on Italian houses. This supply keeps the sauces simmering until the new crop is ready.

Among the tomato sauces that especially appeal to Americans are those that contain beef. Meat sauce on hot, freshly cooked spaghetti was the first Italian ethnic dish Americans adopted widely. American pasta comes largely from Durum wheat, high in protein, grown in North Dakota.

Almost all American kitchens favor a special recipe for the meat sauce, but our recipe definitely is one of the best. Quick-to-use mixed Italian seasonings give our sauce fine flavor.

SPAGHETTI WITH MEAT SAUCE

Double the recipe and freeze half of sauce, ready to use later

1 lb. ground beef	¼ c. chopped fresh parsley
1 c. chopped onion	1½ tsp. mixed Italian
½ c. chopped green pepper	seasoning
2 cloves garlic, minced	1½ tsp. salt
1 (1 lb.) can tomatoes,	1 tsp. sugar
cut up	¼ tsp. pepper
1 (15 oz.) can tomato sauce	Hot, cooked spaghetti
1 (4 oz.) can mushroom	Grated Parmesan cheese
stems and pieces	

Cook ground beef, onion, green pepper and garlic in Dutch oven until meat is browned. Add tomatoes, tomato sauce, undrained mushrooms, parsley, Italian seasoning, salt, sugar and pepper. Cover and simmer 1 hour.

Uncover and continue simmering 20 to 30 minutes or until thick. Stir occasionally.

Spoon meat sauce over hot spaghetti. Pass Parmesan cheese. Makes 6 servings.

AMERICAN SPAGHETTI WITH MEATBALLS

History does not record who first included meatballs in spaghetti sauce. Perhaps it was one of the new Americans who, back home in Italy, sometimes added scraps of meat or fish to the spaghetti sauce. Or it may have been an adaptation of Swedish meatballs to the Italian dish. At any rate, American Spaghetti with Meatballs from FARM JOURNAL COUNTRYSIDE TEST KITCHENS produces a dish that always wins compliments.

AMERICAN SPAGHETTI WITH MEATBALLS

Serve with crusty bread and greens tossed with Italian dressing

1 c. chopped onion
1 clove garlic, crushed
2 tblsp. olive or cooking oil
1 (1 lb. 12 oz.) can
  tomatoes, cut up
1 (12 oz.) can tomato paste
1½ c. water
¼ c. chopped fresh parsley
1 tsp. salt
1 tsp. dried oregano leaves
½ tsp. dried basil leaves
¼ tsp. pepper
1 bay leaf

1 lb. ground beef
2 eggs, beaten
½ c. milk
¾ c. dry bread crumbs
¼ c. grated Parmesan
  cheese
1 clove garlic, minced
1 tsp. salt
¼ tsp. dried oregano
  leaves
⅛ tsp. pepper
Hot, cooked spaghetti
Grated Parmesan cheese

Sauté onion and 1 clove garlic in hot oil in Dutch oven until soft. Add tomatoes, tomato paste, water, parsley, 1 tsp. salt, 1 tsp. oregano, basil, ¼ tsp. pepper and bay leaf. Cover and simmer 1 hour.

Meanwhile, combine ground beef, eggs, milk, bread crumbs, ¼ c. Parmesan cheese, 1 clove garlic, 1 tsp. salt, ¼ tsp. oregano and ⅛ tsp. pepper. Mix lightly, but well. Shape mixture by rounded tablespoons into balls. Place in 15½ × 10½ × 1" jelly roll pan. Bake in 375° oven 35 minutes.

Add meatballs to sauce; cover and simmer 30 minutes. Remove bay leaf.

Place hot spaghetti on large, deep platter. Top with meatballs and sauce. Pass grated Parmesan cheese. Makes 6 to 8 servings.

MACARONI AND CHEESE WITH BEEF

Among the most tasty macaroni and cheese specials developed in this country are those in which ground beef is an ingredient. Such main dishes are hearty enough to satisfy appetites of hungry men and boys.

Macaroni and Cheese with Beef retains the influences of Italian kitchens since it includes some ingredients frequently used in lasagne—cottage cheese, oregano and tomato sauce. But it is an American dish in its own right, with process American cheese substituting for an Italian type.

MACARONI AND CHEESE WITH BEEF

Great dish to take to church and other co-operative suppers

1½ lbs. ground beef
1 c. chopped onion
½ c. chopped green pepper
1 (15 oz.) can tomato sauce
1½ tsp. salt
1 tsp. dried oregano leaves

¼ tsp. pepper
1 (8 oz.) pkg. macaroni
1 c. creamed cottage cheese
1 c. shredded process
   American cheese (4 oz.)

Cook ground beef with onion and green pepper in skillet until meat is browned. Drain off excess fat. Add tomato sauce, salt, oregano and pepper. Cover and simmer 30 minutes, stirring occasionally. Meanwhile, cook macaroni according to package directions. Drain.

Combine meat mixture with macaroni, cottage cheese and half the American cheese. Turn into greased 2½-qt. casserole.

Bake in 350° oven about 30 minutes or until bubbly. Sprinkle with remaining American cheese. Return to oven about 3 minutes or until cheese melts. Makes 8 servings.

TIMBALLO WITH CHEESE SAUCE

Pasta is the basic food of Southern and Middle Italy. There are endless ways to prepare this favorite, some very plain and others rich and fancy. Our Timballo is a "dressed up" dish that looks and tastes downright elegant.

TIMBALLO WITH CHEESE SAUCE

An unusual pasta main dish in traditional Italian style

1 lb. spaghetti (break
    strands in half)
⅓ c. butter or regular
    margarine
1 lb. bulk pork sausage
1 (4 oz.) can sliced
    mushrooms, drained
3 tblsp. finely chopped
    onion
⅓ c. sliced stuffed olives
½ c. grated Parmesan
    cheese

2 tblsp. chopped fresh
    parsley
½ tsp. salt
¼ tsp. pepper
¼ c. dry bread crumbs
2 eggs, well beaten
¼ lb. mozzarella cheese,
    shredded
Cheese Sauce (recipe
    follows)

Cook spaghetti for 10 minutes in boiling salted water. Drain. Toss with butter; coat well.

Sauté sausage in skillet until amost done. Pour off all fat except 2 tblsp. Add mushrooms and onion. Sauté in fat until tender (do not brown).

Toss together spaghetti, sausage mixture, olives, Parmesan cheese, parsley, salt and pepper.

Coat a buttered 9″ springform pan with bread crumbs; reserve some for top. Place half the spaghetti mixture in pan; pour eggs evenly over all. Sprinkle with mozzarella cheese; put remaining mixture on top. Sprinkle with remaining crumbs. Cover with aluminum foil.

Bake in 375° oven 40 minutes. Let stand for 5 minutes. Serve with Cheese Sauce. Makes 6 to 8 servings.

Cheese Sauce: Stir ¼ c. Parmesan cheese and 1 tblsp. chopped fresh parsley into 2 c. of medium white sauce.

McPHERSON COUNTY MACARONI

When soldiers sang of Yankee Doodle and the feather in his cap that he called macaroni, it is doubtful that anyone dreamed that the Italian pasta would be a staple in American homes. This occurred at the end of the 19th century, when cookbooks began including a variety of recipes using pasta. Interestingly enough, this recipe came from a Kansas community ethnically Swedish, further reflecting our melting-pot cuisine.

McPHERSON COUNTY MACARONI

Sour cream gives the casserole a different, distinctive taste

12 oz. macaroni	1 tsp. salt
3 c. shredded process sharp American cheese (12 oz.)	¼ tsp. pepper
	1 tsp. Worcestershire sauce
1½ c. dairy sour cream	½ c. dry bread crumbs
2 tblsp. melted butter or regular margarine	2 tblsp. melted butter or regular margarine
1 tsp. instant minced onion	

Cook macaroni according to package directions; drain.

Stir together cheese, sour cream, 2 tblsp. butter, onion, salt, pepper and Worcestershire sauce. Combine with macaroni. Turn into greased 2-qt. casserole.

Toss bread crumbs with 2 tblsp. butter. Sprinkle on top of casserole.

Bake in 350° oven 30 minutes or until heated through. Makes 6 servings.

NOODLES PARMESAN

In China, noodles—called *mein*—were made and enjoyed for thousands of years before America was discovered. It is believed that Marco Polo on his return home over the Old Silk Route introduced the pasta to Italy. Regardless of how the southern Europeans learned to make noodles, they invented many glorious dishes including them, such as those containing cheese, made in and near the city of Bologna. Noodles Parmesan is one American interpretation of these rich and delicious noodle-cheese combinations which Italian immigrants brought with them to

America. Be sure to serve the noodles promptly after tossing the hot, seasoned pasta with the cheese.

NOODLES PARMESAN

Marvelous with chicken—cheese extends protein content

1 (8 oz.) pkg. thin noodles	1 c. grated Parmesan cheese
6 tblsp. butter	½ c. dairy half-and-half
½ c. dairy half-and-half	

Cook noodles according to package directions; drain.

Melt butter in skillet; cook over low heat until lightly brown. Stir in ½ c. half-and-half; heat until bubbly. Add noodles and toss with two forks. Add cheese and ½ c. half-and-half in three additions, tossing after each. Makes 8 servings.

SKI COUNTRY VEGETABLE SOUP

Wedges of ducks honking overhead signal cold weather on the way and soup-making days at hand. Soups are as varied as the people of the world.

Italian vegetable soups not only vary from region to region but also with the foods on hand at the moment. Ski Country Vegetable Soup contains two varieties of canned beans, a can of condensed onion soup and canned tomato paste. The tomato and the Parmesan cheese tie it to soups of Italy.

SKI COUNTRY VEGETABLE SOUP

This Italian-type soup is filling after a day on the slopes

2 lbs. stewing beef, cut in 1″ cubes	¼ tsp. pepper
1 (6 oz.) can tomato paste	2 c. sliced pared carrots
1 (10 oz.) can condensed onion soup	1 c. sliced celery
5 c. water	1 (1 lb.) can green beans
1½ tsp. salt	1 (15 oz.) can kidney beans
1 tsp. dried basil leaves	½ c. grated Parmesan cheese

Combine meat and tomato paste in Dutch oven. Stir in onion soup, water, salt, basil and pepper. Bring to a boil. Reduce heat; cover and simmer about 1 hour 30 minutes or until meat is tender.

Add carrots, celery, undrained green beans and kidney beans. Continue simmering 30 to 40 minutes or until all vegetables are tender. Stir in Parmesan cheese. Makes 3¾ quarts.

PASTA AND BEAN SOUP

At least once a week in Southern Italy, this hearty, thick soup is served in Italian homes. Some regions feature a thinner soup, using more liquid. Our recipe has been handed down through several generations of good Italian cooks.

PASTA AND BEAN SOUP

Nourishing main dish soup that will please the heartiest appetite

1 lb. dry Great Northern beans	1 (1 lb.) can stewed tomatoes
2 qts. water	½ bay leaf
2½ tsp. salt	½ tsp. dried oregano leaves
1 large, whole carrot	½ tsp. salt
6 strips bacon	¼ tsp. pepper
½ c. chopped onion	¼ c. water
½ c. chopped celery	1 c. ditalini, or small elbow macaroni
1 small clove garlic, minced	

Soak beans 8 hours or overnight. Rinse and drain. Combine beans, 2 qts. water, 2½ tsp. salt and carrot; simmer in 6-qt. pot for 2 hours or until beans are tender.

Fry bacon in skillet until crisp. Remove and drain on paper towels. Crumble and set aside.

Reserve ¼ c. bacon drippings. Add onion, celery and garlic. Sauté until tender (do not brown). Stir in tomatoes, bay leaf, oregano, ½ tsp. salt, pepper and ¼ c. water. Bring to a boil; reduce heat. Simmer 30 minutes.

Cook macaroni according to package directions. Drain.

Purée half of the beans. Remove carrot and cube. Combine all ingredients in pot. Heat thoroughly. Makes 3½ quarts.

GREEN BEANS ITALIAN

Italians were quick to accept the New World vegetables, including snap beans. They planted seeds and were gratified to discover that they grew successfully. The art of cooking them developed over many years. Green Beans Italian illustrates what seasonings can do to a commonplace vegetable.

GREEN BEANS ITALIAN

Cheese, lemon juice and garlic bring out the best bean flavor

2 lbs. green beans, cut up, or 2 (9 oz.) pkgs. frozen cut green beans
½ c. chopped onion
1 clove garlic, minced
3 tblsp. butter or regular margarine

3 tblsp. lemon juice
½ c. grated Parmesan cheese
¼ tsp. pepper

Cook beans in boiling salted water until tender; drain.

Meanwhile, sauté onion and garlic in butter until tender. Add lemon juice, cheese and pepper. Pour over hot beans. Makes 6 to 8 servings.

EGGPLANT PARMESAN

Supermarket shoppers selecting a shiny, purple eggplant probably are planning to prepare a dish of Mediterranean origin. Eggplant Parmesan is a favorite on the west side of the Atlantic. The recipe for this herb-seasoned casserole underwent almost no change in American kitchens although vegetable oil, due to cost and taste differences, usually replaces olive oil. Americans generally use oils from crops they grow on a large scale, such as soybeans, corn and cotton (seed), while Italians and people of other nationalities in the Mediterranean region use the oil their olive groves provide.

EGGPLANT PARMESAN

The vegetable-cheese casserole is a good main dish for lunch. Serve with fruit salad and hard rolls

1 large eggplant (1½ lbs.)	1 tsp. dried oregano leaves
2 eggs, beaten	1 tsp. dried basil leaves
2 tblsp. water	½ tsp. salt
¾ c. dry bread crumbs	½ lb. mozzarella cheese,
¾ c. cooking oil	sliced
½ c. grated Parmesan	3 (8 oz.) cans tomato sauce
cheese	

Peel eggplant; cut in ¼" slices. Dip slices in mixture of beaten eggs and water, then in bread crumbs. Brown on both sides in hot oil, removing slices as they brown.

Combine Parmesan cheese, oregano, basil and salt. Place ⅓ of eggplant in greased 2-qt. casserole; sprinkle with ⅓ of Parmesan cheese mixture. Top with ⅓ of mozzarella cheese slices and 1 can tomato sauce. Repeat layers twice.

Bake in 350° oven 30 minutes or until sauce is bubbly. Makes 6 servings.

EASTER EGG BREAD

The fascinating Easter egg breads in Italian bakery windows can be baked at home—as easy to make as to bake sweet rolls. Our Easter Egg Bread consists of the sweet-roll dough baked around individual eggs tinted in bright colors. Italian-American bakers form the dough in fancy shapes, such as lambs, other animals, little men and roses. They then place the colorful eggs in the desired positions and frame them with strips of dough.

Our Easter Egg Bread is easier. You shape the dough in rings around the eggs, which make individual rolls. The only decoration is a sprinkling of tiny, multicolored candies.

EASTER EGG BREAD

Combination main dish for a gala Easter Sunday breakfast

12 eggs	**½ c. shortening**
Easter egg coloring	**Grated peel of 2 lemons**
4½ c. flour	**2 eggs**
2 pkgs. active dry yeast	**1 egg, beaten**
1 c. milk	**Tiny, multicolored**
½ c. sugar	**decorating candies**
1 tsp. salt	

Wash 12 raw eggs. Tint shells with egg coloring; set aside.
Combine 2½ c. flour and yeast in large mixing bowl.

Heat milk, sugar, salt and shortening just until warm, stirring occasionally to melt shortening. Add to flour mixture along with lemon peel and 2 eggs. Beat at low speed 30 seconds, scraping sides of bowl constantly. Beat at high speed 3 minutes, scraping bowl occasionally. By hand stir in enough remaining flour to make a soft dough. Turn out on lightly floured surface, knead until smooth and elastic, about 5 minutes. Place in greased bowl; turn dough over to grease top. Cover and let rise in warm place until double, about 1 hour. Punch down; cover and let rise again until almost double, about 30 minutes.

Divide dough into 12 equal balls. Form each into a ring around a tinted egg. Cover and let rise until double, about 30 minutes.

Brush 1 egg evenly over dough. Sprinkle with decorating candies. Bake in 375° oven about 15 minutes or until lightly brown. Serve warm. Makes 12.

PIZZA CRUST

Pizza and spaghetti are the two Italian food contributions young Americans today most enjoy and many grownups endorse this selection. Pizza, according to food historians, dates back to the Neolithic Age, but it became really popular in Italy when tomatoes were introduced from the New World in the 16th century. Italians improved on the Inca tomato and created the fabulous sauces made in America 200 years later.

Although many American communities have thriving "pizza parlors," the "made-from-scratch" version is favored in many households. After numerous tests in FARM JOURNAL KITCHENS, the final choice of taste panels was for the Pizza Crust recipe that follows.

The dough is partially baked 6 to 8 minutes and cooled. The crust is later filled and baked. Or the crusts can be frozen for later use. The pizza can also be prepared and frozen before final baking for meals or snacks.

PIZZA CRUST

A baking sheet is a handy, giant spatula to lift pizza from oven

2 pkgs. active dry yeast	**1 tsp. salt**
7 c. sifted flour	**2½ c. warm water (110 to 115°)**

Combine yeast, 2½ c. flour, salt and warm water in large bowl. Beat at low speed 30 seconds, scraping sides of bowl constantly. Beat at high speed 3 minutes. Stir in enough remaining flour to make a very stiff dough. (As dough becomes stiff, flour can be kneaded in.)

Knead on lightly floured surface until smooth and elastic, 8 to 10 minutes. Shape into a ball; place in greased bowl and turn dough over to grease top. Cover and let rise in warm place until doubled, about 45 minutes.

Punch down dough; divide in fourths. Roll each part to make an 11" circle. Stretch each circle to fit a greased 12" pizza pan or place on greased baking sheet and make ½" rim around edges.

Bake in 500° oven 6 to 8 minutes or until crust starts to brown. (Crust will be somewhat uneven due to baked-in air bubbles, but they will not affect finished pizza.) Remove from pans; cool on racks. You can leave partially baked crusts at room temperature 24 hours before making pizza. Makes 4 pizza crusts.

To freeze Pizza Crusts: Freeze Pizza Crusts in pans or on baking sheets. When frozen, remove from pans or sheets. Wrap each crust separately in foil or freezer paper and freeze. Thaw before using in one of the following recipes.

To freeze prepared pizzas: Top Pizza Crusts with fillings using the following recipes. Freeze in pans or on baking sheets. When frozen, remove from pans or sheets. Wrap each pizza separately in foil or freezer paper and freeze.

To heat: Place frozen pizza on baking sheet. Place on oven rack at lowest position. Bake in 500° oven 10 minutes or until bottom of pizza is golden brown.

CHEESE/MUSHROOM PIZZA

In every crowd there are mushroom fans who prefer this one

1 Pizza Crust
1 (8 oz.) can pizza sauce
¼ c. grated Parmesan
   cheese

1 (4 oz.) can mushroom
   stems and pieces, drained
1½ c. shredded mozzarella
   cheese (6 oz.)

Place Pizza Crust on baking sheet. Spread with pizza sauce. Sprinkle with Parmesan cheese and mushrooms. Top with mozzarella cheese. Place on lowest rack in oven.

Bake in 500° oven 7 to 8 minutes or until bottom of pizza is golden brown. Makes 1 (12″) pizza.

HAMBURGER PIZZA

Excellent way to extend ground beef—a change from burgers

1 Pizza Crust
1 (8 oz.) can pizza sauce
¼ c. grated Parmesan
   cheese
½ lb. ground beef, cooked
   and drained

½ c. chopped green pepper
½ c. chopped onion
½ tsp. salt
1½ c. shredded mozzarella
   cheese (6 oz.)

Place Pizza Crust on baking sheet. Spread with pizza sauce. Sprinkle evenly with Parmesan cheese, ground beef, green pepper, onion, salt and mozzarella cheese. Place on lowest rack in oven.

Bake in 500° oven 7 to 8 minutes or until bottom of pizza is golden brown. Makes 1 (12″) pizza.

SAUSAGE/CHEESE PIZZA

Tastes good—like pizzas baked in the best Italian restaurants

1 Pizza Crust	**½ lb. bulk pork sausage,**
1 (8 oz.) can pizza sauce	**cooked and drained**
¼ c. grated Parmesan	**1½ c. shredded mozzarella**
cheese	**cheese (6 oz.)**

Place Pizza Crust on baking sheet. Spread with pizza sauce. Sprinkle with Parmesan cheese, sausage and mozzarella cheese. Place on lowest rack in oven.

Bake in 500° oven 7 to 8 minutes or until bottom of pizza is golden brown. Makes 1 (12″) pizza.

PEPPERONI PIZZA

Sliced, "hot" Italian sausage makes this a sure winner

1 Pizza Crust	**1 small green pepper, cut in**
1 (8 oz.) can pizza sauce	**strips**
½ c. grated Parmesan	**1½ c. shredded mozzarella**
cheese	**cheese (6 oz.)**
2 oz. thinly sliced pepperoni	

Place Pizza Crust on baking sheet. Spread with pizza sauce. Sprinkle with Parmesan cheese. Arrange pepperoni and green pepper over top. Sprinkle with mozzarella cheese. Place on lowest rack in oven.

Bake in 500° oven 7 to 8 minutes or until bottom of pizza is golden brown. Makes 1 (12″) pizza.

INTRODUCTION

INFORMAL ENTERTAINING COUNTRY STYLE

The trend to easy, casual living is changing the lifestyle of all America. Growing interest even among urban dwellers in the good earth and its produce is making country-style cooking and hospitality the popular way to welcome guests. Sharing food informally and unpretentiously with the warmth and natural graciousness born from generations of farm neighborliness fills a need in our society today. And the time-tried dishes for which country women have developed a well-deserved reputation are served with enthusiasm.

Women all across the country, especially young hostesses, strive to capture the natural, casual charm of country entertaining. They ask many questions: What kind of menus do you use? What makes country food so good? Where do you get recipes? How do busy women find time to prepare them?

Country entertaining has changed, too, with changes in farming and in farm family life and interests. Over the years, farm women have adapted country-style entertaining to changing living conditions in a remarkable way. They have kept the warmth and ease with which guests are served but have prepared meals by more efficient timetables. They are experts at planning ahead—with the unpredictable schedules of farm life, they have had to be!

The main purpose of this book is to share their experiences and at the same time give the hostess who already entertains country style some new and exciting menus and recipes. It's really a hostess handbook because in addition to superior recipes there are tips on meal management.

In the country, people always have shared food—an important part of neighborliness, family life and community get-togethers. For the latter, the meals are likely to be "planned potluck"—actually a contradiction. But it is an improvement farm women have made over the old custom: "Bring a covered dish." This could result in a dozen bowls of coleslaw and only one main dish! Cooperative meals appropriated the name "potluck" even though every woman is assigned food to bring.

So now when cars stop in a farmyard, men and women, and often children, emerge carrying packages of different sizes and shapes, holding some of the most delicious homemade country food prepared today. These planned potlucks divide the work and cost of a dinner or supper party. And they practically eliminate much of the large-quantity cooking once done by clubs and other country groups.

Here's how the potlucks are planned. Take a recipe in this cookbook. Notice the number of servings it makes and then figure out how many times it would have to be made to get the total servings you need for the guests expected. This tells you the number of women required to prepare this dish. The hostess (or a committee) plans the entire menu this way. Large utensils for big-quantity cooking are no longer needed. But do select foods that travel well.

Much country hospitality is impromptu, which means having something on hand to heat and serve quickly. A farm business caller often arrives midmorning (and not always without a secondary motive—coffee break!). Or perhaps it is a neighbor down the road who has the earliest garden in the neighborhood and shares the first garden lettuce. Whoever it is will likely be invited to the kitchen table for hot coffee and heated homemade coffee bread, or whatever the freezer yields. The coffee break originated in the country!

Every farm woman can share tales of unexpected friends or relatives from a distance descending without notice. An advantage of modern travel: These guests often are equipped for camping so have their own beds, cooking facilities and some of their food. But meals are usually shared. The hospitable host may take over breakfast and bake pancakes for everyone on the outdoor grill.

Farm women are expert at stretching a meal to accommodate one or more unexpecteds. When the school bus stops at the front gate, the family schoolboy may bring friends, and suppertime approaches with the familiar question: "Mom, may David and John stay for supper?" Extra plates go on the table and the menu is quickly enlarged. Young people, especially teen-agers, are frequent unexpected guests in today's country homes.

Guest participation in cooking, serving or clean-up is a country custom. This is one reason why fondue suppers are a popular current way of entertaining. Fondue parties are easy to give; with one or more pots on the table, everyone cooks for himself. The informality promotes lively conversation.

These are a few of the occasions in this changing world in which country-style food lives up to its fabulous reputation as the best in America. Frequently the guests come family style and the hospitality and service are family style.

We compiled this cookbook with the help of homemakers who are experts in entertaining country style. In it we share tested recipes and menus, many of which they suggested. Here are some pointers for successful informal entertaining:

DEPEND ON GOOD HOME-COOKED FOODS to lift your meals and refreshments for guests above the commonplace. You can serve simple food if you prepare and season it with care. Then—if your guests are comfortable and feel welcome—they will enjoy what you serve them. Hamburgers with an extra touch, like our Home-made Burger Buns, can please more than a fancy dish.

PLAN AHEAD WHAT YOU WILL SERVE and stick to your menu. In this book we accompany our menus with a timetable—tips on what to do ahead and what to do on guest day—plus suggestions for serving. The women who contributed their favorite menus for country-style entertaining believe it is wise, whenever possible, to include few dishes that require last-minute cooking. If you have a freezer, make it work for you. Give the refrigerator its share of responsibility. This book makes maximum use of these appliances.

MAKE AND SERVE YEAST BREADS. They are the trump card for many country hostesses. Fortunately, breads keep successfully for months in the freezer. You can dramatize the serving of bread by placing it on a board and cutting and serving it at the table or buffet. This service is a direct takeover from the old-fashioned family table in the country kitchen. Our thrifty grandmothers served bread this way, not to glamorize it (good homemade bread was usual those days) but to avoid cutting more slices than would be eaten because they would dry out. With freezers and plastic wraps and bags, this is no problem today.

STOCK AT LEAST A FEW SHELVES in the cupboard or fruit closet with jellies, jams, preserves and other fruit spreads, spiced fruits, vegetable relishes and pickles. Use them to point up flavors in company meals and to add the magic country touch—especially if homemade. Another good idea borrowed from our grandmothers!

FEATURE GARDEN VEGETABLES AND FRESH FRUITS

when in plentiful supply. That's when they reach their flavor peak. One classic example of such a meal in this cookbook is the Iowa Corn Dinner. Sweet corn at the right stage of maturity, freshly picked and cooked promptly is always welcome. Notice, too, how Marinated Tomatoes, Fruit-Jar Tomato Relish, Fresh Cucumber/Onion Relish, Garden-Patch Salad and other garden treats show up in our menus.

FREEZE SOME OF SUMMER'S FLAVORS, if you have a freezer, to brighten guest meals out of season. One country hostess' favorite company dessert always ready in her freezer is a mixture of two—often more—packages of frozen fruits and berries. She places the frozen packages in a large bowl in the refrigerator to partially thaw by serving time. Then she tops the bowl with scoops of sherbet and invites guests to help themselves. The chance to help yourself makes the buffet style of serving so popular.

SERVE APPETIZERS IN THE LIVING ROOM before dinner or supper to lighten your last-minute activities. Make your husband a part of the hospitality by asking him to assume responsibility by serving and keeping guests happy during this course, while you are in the kitchen. If the children are old enough, they will enjoy helping their father to host. Our Christmas Snack Tree, from which guests have fun picking their snacks, is a great conversation piece. See also recipes for Sauerkraut Balls, Chicken Nuggets and spreads and dips.

MAKE ENTERTAINING A FAMILY ADVENTURE. Even small boys and girls can shell peas, pull radishes and do other simple chores. The teen-agers can do some of the cooking—even the baking. Don't call on them only for clean-up chores. Many hosts like to take an active role such as grilling meats, poultry and fish over coals for indoor or outdoor eating. We kept this in mind when we included recipes for Grilled Halibut Steaks, Barbecued Chicken Halves, Grilled Minute Steak Rolls, Grilled or Broiled Pot Roast and many other main-dish specialties. If your husband dislikes to carve roasts at the table, give him a second choice—to carve in the kitchen without spectators. An interested family greatly helps hospitality atmosphere, for which there is no substitute.

We hope this handbook on how to be a successful hostess country style will make your entertaining easier and more pleasant.

CHAPTER 1

Entertaining Before Noon

COFFEE BREAKS . . .
COFFEE PARTIES . . . BRUNCHES

The coffee break originated in pioneer country kitchens; today its popularity is universal. In the home, there is no more gracious and spontaneous way to extend a cordial welcome to midmorning guests. Regardless of how busy neighbors, friends and business callers are when they stop by on an errand, they will take at least a few minutes off to relax around the hospitable kitchen table and exchange ideas or news while they sip coffee and eat a tasty accompaniment.

Not all guests arrive unannounced, for women in town and country alike often telephone friends and invite them over for coffee. With advance notice, the hostess has time to make the coffee and bring out or fix something good to serve with it.

The perfect country coffee break creates the impression that the food is unplanned—the hostess serves what she has on hand and makes coffee. This carefree atmosphere contributes to the charm and success of the occasion. Thoughtful, busy guests like to believe they are not making extra work for their equally busy hostess. But most women actually do prepare appropriate food ahead to serve at coffeetime. They hide it in their freezers to bring out and run through the oven for a fast reheat.

Homemade breads excel as coffee companions. Try the recipes in this chapter for Square Doughnuts, Butter-Bright Pastries, Cottage Cheese Crescents and Golden Crown Coffee Cake—these are from country kitchens and will testify to the popularity of the country coffee break. You will also want to look in the Index under Breads for other homemade specialties that are great coffee go-withs.

Keep a special file of recipes for coffee accompaniments you can fix in a hurry. This is especially important for women without freezers. Quick Danish Pastry made with packaged rolls from the refrigerator and Pineapple Muffins are two good examples. Remember, too, how good homemade bread, toasted and buttered, tastes when served with jam, jelly or preserves—homemade, if you have them.

Coffee breaks sometimes evolve into full-fledged midmorning parties for invited guests. The scene shifts from the kitchen to the dining and living rooms and the menu expands to include fruit or fruit juice and often cake or cookies as well as bread. Our Mother's Day Coffee menu is an excellent example. If fresh strawberries are unavailable, substitute chilled fruit juice. Coffee parties also provide pleasing refreshments for afternoon entertaining.

Brunches are a more substantial way to entertain before noon. Regardless of what you call these late morning gatherings, the food consists of two meals in one, breakfast and luncheon. Youthful late sleepers call them breakfast (see Late Saturday Breakfast), but they skip lunch.

You can use the brunch menus in this chapter for informal suppers as well. Try Pancake Buffet and if you have a fondue pot, the Cook-at-Table Brunch menu. You'll find that many guests who fry their own French toast and eat it piping hot believe it tastes better than any they ever ate previously. Helping with the cooking and serving of food is a country tradition. It deserves much credit for the fame of country hospitality.

Recipes for all dishes starred (*) are in this cookbook.

NEIGHBORHOOD COFFEE

Square Doughnuts*   Coffee

Drop-in guests are an accepted country tradition. "Friends stop by so often," a Maryland farm woman says, "that I'm an expert at quickly putting on the coffeepot and running homemade bread of some kind in the oven to warm."

The kitchen usually is the setting for this midmorning or afternoon impromptu entertaining. No room in country homes is more friendly or attractive than the kitchen. Why not ask your visiting neighbors to sit down at the table and pour the coffee while you take the piping hot doughnuts from the oven and shake them in a bag containing sugar or dip them in a glaze?

TIMETABLE

Do-Ahead: You can fry the doughnuts, package and freeze them, but if you do, sugar or glaze them just before serving. (Like all fried foods, they have a comparatively short life in the freezer in comparison with other baked breads. The fat they contain may become rancid if they are held too long. The recommended maximum storage time is 2 months.)

On Guest Day: Spread a single layer of doughnuts in a big pan and warm in a slow oven (300°) about 20 minutes, or until hot. Then glaze or sugar them.

SERVING SUGGESTIONS

If you have mugs, serve the coffee in them. Coffee stays warm longer in any cup with straight sides. Bring out colorful paper napkins to brighten the scene. Guests will need them, for doughnuts are finger food.

SQUARE DOUGHNUTS

Try raisin doughnuts for a change—they're a pleasant surprise

¾ c. milk	1 pkg. active dry yeast
¼ c. sugar	1 egg, beaten
1 tsp. salt	3¼ to 3½ c. unsifted flour
¼ c. butter or regular margarine	Glaze
¼ c. lukewarm water (110 to 115°)	

Scald milk; stir in sugar, salt and butter. Cool until lukewarm.

Measure lukewarm water into a large warm mixing bowl (warm by rinsing out bowl with hot water). Sprinkle in the yeast and stir until yeast dissolves.

Add lukewarm milk mixture, egg and half the flour. Beat until smooth. Stir in enough remaining flour to make a soft dough. For lightness, add only enough flour to make a dough you can handle.

Turn dough onto a lightly floured board or pastry cloth. Knead until smooth and elastic, about 5 to 10 minutes. (If dough sticks to the hands, grease them lightly with shortening or oil.)

Place dough in a greased bowl, then turn the bottom side up. Cover with a damp cloth; let rise in a warm place until doubled, about 1 hour.

Punch down dough. On a lightly floured surface, roll about ½" thick to make a rectangle 12×10". With a sharp knife, cut in 2½" squares (cut in rounds if you prefer round doughnuts); cut holes in centers with a 1" cutter or bottletop. Place doughnuts about 2" apart on oiled baking sheets or waxed paper. Cover with inverted baking pans (allow room for dough to rise), or with a cloth. Let rise until doubled, about 1 hour.

About 15 minutes before end of rising period, heat fat in deep fryer or electric skillet to 375°. (You will be more confident of temperature if you use a deep fat frying thermometer.)

Handle the doughnuts as gently as possible so they will not fall. Fry them, a few at a time, in deep fat 2 to 3 minutes, or until brown on both sides. Turn doughnuts only once. Drain on absorbent paper; dip while still warm, in a glaze or granulated sugar. (You can fry the center cutouts.) Makes about 20 doughnuts.

Variation

Raisin Doughnuts: Follow the recipe for Square Doughnuts, except use 2 pkgs. active dry yeast instead of 1 pkg., and stir in 1 c. chopped raisins with first half of the flour. Dough may rise slower.

Glazes for Doughnuts

Vanilla Glaze: Blend 2 c. confectioners sugar, ⅓ c. milk and 1 tsp. vanilla. Dip warm doughnuts into glaze and drain them on a rack over waxed paper. Reuse the glaze that drips off.

Spicy Glaze: Make like Vanilla Glaze, but omit the vanilla and add ½ tsp. ground cinnamon and ¼ tsp. ground nutmeg.

Orange Glaze: Follow recipe for Vanilla Glaze, but omit vanilla and substitute orange juice for milk.

To Glaze Doughnuts: Dip warm doughnuts in glaze and drain them on cooling racks over waxed paper. You can reuse the glaze that drips onto the waxed paper.

To Sugar Doughnuts: Drop drained, warm doughnuts into a paper bag of sugar and shake to coat. Or add 2 tsp. ground cinnamon to each ½ c. sugar when coating doughnuts.

SHORT-NOTICE COFFEE

Quick Danish Pastry*   Coffee

You could spend hours baking a go-with for coffee without getting results half as tasty as Quick Danish Pastry. You can make it from start to finish in a half hour. That is, you can if you have a can of crescent dinner rolls from the supermarket in your refrigerator and some fruit preserves in your cupboard. The North Dakota home-maker who first baked this coffee bread for a gathering of Girl Scout leaders, now considers it a standby when she plans to entertain and time is at a premium. We predict you'll do the same once you taste this treat and hear what your friends say about it.

TIMETABLE

On Guest Day: About 25 minutes before you wish to serve the coffee bread, put it in the oven. Make the coffee while it bakes.

SERVING SUGGESTIONS

The bread needs no accompaniment other than coffee. Be sure to serve it piping hot. If you wish to garnish the top of the bread, scatter dabs of the apricot preserves here and there on the sour cream topping just before returning bread to oven for the last 6 minutes of baking.

QUICK DANISH PASTRY

Crust is crisp and brown, in layers like Danish pastry—good

1 (8 oz.) can refrigerated crescent dinner rolls	1 c. dairy sour cream
	1 tblsp. sugar
½ c. apricot or peach preserves	1 tsp. vanilla
1 egg, beaten	

Press crescent rolls over bottom of ungreased 13×9×2" pan to cover. Spread with preserves. Bake in hot oven (425°) 15 minutes. Remove from oven; turn temperature to slow (325°).

Combine egg, sour cream, sugar and vanilla; mix gently, but well. Spread over top of baked crust. Return to oven and bake 6 minutes. Cut in 4×3" pieces and serve warm. Makes 12 servings.

MORNING COFFEE

Golden Crown Coffee Cake*   Coffee

When the chairman of the committee to which you belong telephones and asks if a special meeting can be held at your house next morning, chances are you'll immediately wonder what to serve with coffee. This coffee cake is a good one; it's easy to make. Time the baking so it will come out of the oven just before guests arrive. They'll sniff that marvelous aroma of yeast bread baking and be glad they came.

TIMETABLE

Do-Ahead: Make the dough for the coffee cake in the evening; cover and refrigerate.

On Guest Day: Put dough in the pan early in the morning. It will double in 1 to 1½ hours and be ready for baking.

SERVING SUGGESTIONS

If you and your guests sit around the table, serve the coffee cake on a large plate and let everyone pull off his servings. Pass butter for those who are not weight-watchers. And keep the coffee cups filled.

GOLDEN CROWN COFFEE CAKE

Made with same dough used for the refrigerator pan rolls in Harvest Festival Dinner menu in Chapter 4—an attractive coffee go-with

¾ c. sugar	½ dough for Overnight
2 tsp. ground cinnamon	Refrigerator Pan Rolls (see
½ c. chopped walnuts	Index)
½ c. seedless raisins	Melted butter

Combine sugar, cinnamon, walnuts and raisins.

Cut off pieces of dough about the size of a walnut. Roll each piece in melted butter, then in sugar-cinnamon mixture.

Arrange the first layer of dough pieces in a well-greased 9″ tube pan; place a second layer over the spaces. Continue building layers until all dough pieces are used. Sprinkle remaining sugar mixture over top.

Cover with a clean towel and let rise in warm place until doubled, 1 to 1½ hours. Bake in moderate oven (350°) 40 to 55 minutes. Take from oven, cool 10 minutes and then remove from pan. Makes 12 servings.

COFFEE FOR DROP-IN GUESTS

Pineapple Muffins*   Coffee

Take a pan of golden, fragrant muffins from the oven with your guests watching. Pour the coffee, pass the hot bread and butter and relax while you visit. A country coffee break is in session. The friendly custom started long ago in pioneer farm kitchens and it flourishes to this day. Usually the refreshments consist of coffee with one accompaniment, frequently from the freezer.

If you are too busy to stock your freezer with baked foods, or do not have one, depend on your cupboard to help you entertain unexpected drop-in guests. You can bake marvelous muffins with little fuss—and fast—from staple ingredients on hand. You can stir up the batter in a jiffy and get it in the oven. The muffins, when delivered to guests, are hot enough to melt, almost instantly, butter spread on them.

PINEAPPLE MUFFINS

Muffins are cake-like because of creaming method of mixing batter

2 c. sifted flour	¼ c. shortening
3 tsp. baking powder	1 egg, beaten
½ tsp. salt	1 c. crushed pineapple, undrained
½ c. sugar	

Sift together flour, baking powder and salt.

Cream sugar and shortening until light and fluffy. Add egg and beat well. Stir in undrained pineapple. Add dry ingredients and stir just enough to moisten flour. Do not beat.

Fill greased muffin-pan cups two thirds full. Bake in hot oven (400°) 20 to 25 minutes, or until golden. Remove from pans at once. Makes 12 to 15 medium muffins.

MOTHER'S DAY COFFEE

Strawberry Send-off
Superfine Sugar   Sour Cream/Brown Sugar Dip
Apricot/Almond Torte*
Orange Spice Cake*
Coffee   Tea

Inviting your mother, your husband's mother and their friends to share a few Maytime hours in your home shortly before Mother's Day contributes genuine pleasure to hostess and guests. The food for such celebrations is best if simple, but it must be exceptionally tasty. And a thoughtful hostess makes certain there is something, regardless of diets, for everyone to eat and enjoy.

Apricot/Almond Torte definitely meets the challenge of a special-occasion treat. Orange Spice Cake contains no egg yolk and with salad oil as the shortening, it's designed especially for guests restricted to low-cholesterol foods. The strawberry appetizer is as luscious as it looks. The hulls serve as handles when dunking the berries in the dips. Serve for the first course in the living room.

TIMETABLE

Do-Ahead: Bake the torte a day or two ahead, cool, wrap and freeze if you like, but glaze it shortly before serving. Bake the cake a day ahead, cool, wrap in foil and store overnight in a cool place. Frost when you glaze the torte.

On Guest Day: If the torte is frozen, thaw it in its heavy-duty aluminum foil wrap in a moderate oven (350°); it will thaw in 20 to 25 minutes. Remove from oven and glaze. Frost the cake. Fill a bowl with dairy sour cream and sprinkle liberally with brown sugar; fill a similar bowl with superfine sugar. Wash and drain choice ripe strawberries.

SERVING SUGGESTIONS

Arrange strawberries on tray in a wreath or any desired pattern around the twin bowls of dips and serve as an appetizer. Cut the torte and the cake and place on trays or large plates. Let everyone help herself. Give guests a choice of tea or coffee.

APRICOT/ALMOND TORTE

Elegant, yeast-flavored coffee bread made in three layers with sugar and almonds, and apricot preserves between, a glaze on top

1 pkg. active dry yeast	½ c. dairy sour cream
¼ c. warm water (110 to 115°)	1 c. chopped almonds
1⅓ c. butter, softened	¾ c. sugar
3½ c. flour	1 (12 oz.) jar apricot preserves
4 egg yolks	(about 1 c.)
½ tsp. almond extract	Glaze

Sprinkle yeast on warm water; stir to dissolve.

Combine butter and flour in large mixing bowl until mixture resembles coarse crumbs. Add egg yolks, beaten slightly, almond extract, sour cream and yeast. Mix until a dough forms. Do not let dough rise. Divide into 3 equal parts.

Roll out each third of dough on lightly floured surface to a 13×9″ rectangle. Fit one rectangle into bottom of greased 13×9×2″ pan.

Combine almonds and sugar; sprinkle over dough in pan. Top with second dough rectangle and spread with apricot preserves. Top with remaining dough. Bake at once in moderate oven (350°) 50 to 55 minutes. While warm, spread with Glaze. Makes 12 servings.

Glaze: Blend together ½ c. confectioners sugar, 2 to 3 tblsp. milk and 1 tsp. butter.

ORANGE SPICE CAKE

Orange peel and raisins enhance this spice cake. While tailored to fit low-cholesterol diets, it tastes too good to be limited to them

2 c. sugar	1 tsp. ground nutmeg
½ c. salad oil	2 c. buttermilk
1 tblsp. baking soda	1 tblsp. grated orange peel, or ½
3 c. flour	tsp. dehydrated orange peel
1 tsp. ground cinnamon	1 c. seedless raisins
½ tsp. ground cloves	Brown Sugar Frosting

Blend sugar and oil.

Sift together baking soda, flour and spices; add alternately with buttermilk to sugar-oil mixture, beating after each addition. Add orange peel and raisins. Pour into two greased 9″ round layer cake pans.

Bake in moderate oven (375°) 40 minutes, or until cake tests done. Frost with Brown Sugar Frosting. Makes about 12 servings.

Brown Sugar Frosting: Melt ½ c. regular margarine in saucepan; stir in 1 c. brown sugar, firmly packed. Heat to boiling, stirring constantly. Boil and stir over low heat for 2 minutes. Remove from heat; stir in ¼ c. milk. Return to heat and bring to a boil, stirring.

Remove from heat and gradually stir in 2 c. confectioners sugar. Place pan of frosting in a bowl of ice water and beat until of spreading consistency. If frosting becomes too stiff, heat it slightly, stirring all the time.

EVER-READY COFFEE PARTY

Butter-Bright Pastries*   Coffee

Most country women plan to have something tasty to serve friends who stop by at any time without advance warning. Home-baked bread is always welcome, and if it's yeast-leavened Butter-Bright Pastries, compliments are bountiful.

You can vary the pastries in many ways, as the recipe suggests. And you can keep them in the freezer in readiness for the days when the doorbell rings unexpectedly.

TIMETABLE

Do-Ahead: Bake the pastries several days or weeks ahead if you wish. Cool them, wrap in heavy-duty aluminum foil and freeze. You may prefer to glaze the pastries after freezing. It gives them a fresh-baked taste.

On Guest Day: Heat the frozen pastries in their wrap in a moderate oven (350°) 20 to 25 minutes. Or if you have time, you can let them thaw in their wrap at room temperature for 2 to 3 hours. If you add the icing after thawing, let your guests watch you spread it on the heated pastries. It will make them more eager than ever for a taste.

SERVING SUGGESTIONS

One of the friendliest places to serve the pastries is at the kitchen table with a full coffeepot nearby.

BUTTER-BRIGHT PASTRIES

Our Countryside Test Kitchens developed five excellent variations

2 pkgs. active dry yeast	4 to 4½ c. sifted flour
¼ c. warm water (110 to 115°)	2 eggs
⅓ c. sugar	1 c. butter
⅛ tsp. salt	Glaze
1 c. cold milk	

Dissolve yeast in warm water. Combine yeast mixture, sugar, salt and milk. Beat in 2 c. flour; add eggs, beating well. Stir in enough remaining flour to make a soft dough. Cover and refrigerate 15 minutes.

On a lightly floured surface, roll dough into an 18×15" rectangle. Cut ⅓ c. butter into small pieces. Dot surface of dough with butter pieces, leaving a 1" margin. Fold 18" side into thirds and then fold 15" side into thirds. Wrap in floured aluminum foil; chill 15 minutes. Repeat procedure twice, using remaining butter. (When you roll dough second and third times, turn dough so narrow side faces you.) Chill 15 more minutes.

Divide dough in fourths. Roll and cut into desired shapes (directions follow). Let rise until doubled. Bake in hot oven (400°) 8 minutes or until golden. Cool. Drizzle with Glaze. Makes 24 pastries.

Glaze: Combine 1 c. sifted confectioners sugar, 2 tblsp. butter, 2 tblsp. evaporated milk and ½ tsp. vanilla.

Crescents: Combine ¼ c. brown sugar, firmly packed, ¼ c. chopped nuts and ¼ tsp. ground cinnamon. Melt 2 tblsp. butter. Cut dough into 5×2×⅛" rectangles and spread with butter. Sprinkle with filling. Roll like a jelly roll. Shape into crescent with seam side down. Snip at 1" intervals.

Butterflies: Cut into 3×¼" squares. Fold opposite corners to the center and press down. After baking and adding Glaze, fill with assorted jams or jellies.

"S" Shapes: Cut into 8×1×¼" strips. Roll back and forth to form

evenly shaped sticks. Shape into an "S" with sides of "sticks" touching. After baking and adding Glaze, fill with assorted jams or jellies.

Whirls: Cut into 8×1×¼″ strips. Roll back and forth to form evenly shaped sticks. Place one end in center and wind dough pinwheel fashion. Tuck loose end under. After baking and adding Glaze, fill with assorted jams or jellies.

Twists: Cut into 8×1×¼″ strips. Roll to form evenly shaped sticks. Fold in half; cross ends over each other to form twists.

N O T E : If pastries are made more than one day before serving them, do not add glaze. Wrap the baked pastries in aluminum foil and freeze. To serve, heat frozen pastries in their wrap in a moderate oven (350°) 20 to 25 minutes. Add Glaze (and filling) before serving.

PLANNED COFFEE PARTY

Cottage Cheese Crescents*   Coffee

Recipes for new delicacies to serve with coffee are a popular search project among thousands of women who like to have their friends stop by. One Wisconsin farm woman discovered an unusual bread her guests enjoy; try her Cottage Cheese Crescents.

TIMETABLE

Do-Ahead: Make the dough for the rolls a day ahead (or at least several hours) and refrigerate.

On Guest Day: Shape, bake, cool and glaze the rolls.

SERVING SUGGESTIONS

Cottage Cheese Crescents need no accompaniment other than cups of steaming coffee. You can serve currant or other tart jelly with them if you wish.

COTTAGE CHEESE CRESCENTS

No one will guess cottage cheese imparts the fascinating flavor

1 c. butter	⅛ tsp. salt
2 c. small curd creamed cottage cheese	2 c. sifted flour
	Vanilla Glaze

Have butter and cottage cheese at room temperature. Combine in bowl with salt and flour, and beat until smooth and elastic. Cover and chill for several hours, or overnight.

Divide dough into 4 equal parts. Roll 1 part in circle about ½" thick, 6" in diameter. Cut in 8 wedges. Roll up each wedge, starting at rounded edge. Place point side down on ungreased baking sheet and curve slightly. Repeat with remaining portions of dough.

Bake in moderate oven (350°) about 20 minutes. Cool on racks. Spread tops with Vanilla Glaze. Makes 32.

Vanilla Glaze: Mix 1½ tblsp. light cream or 1 tblsp. milk into 1 c. confectioners sugar and ½ tsp. vanilla until of spreading consistency.

N O T E : For a change, lightly brush circles of dough with melted butter and sprinkle with a little sugar-cinnamon mixture before rolling the wedges of dough into crescent shapes.

LATE SATURDAY BREAKFAST

Fruit Juice
Fluffy Omelet with Cheese Sauce*
Lacy Potato Cakes*
Coffee

When a daughter away at school returns home for the weekend, bringing a friend or two with her, an opportunity to get into the kitchen again usually appeals, but the timing is important. Up late on Friday night, the girls welcome a chance to "sleep in" Saturday morning until the family have breakfasted. While the girls call the meal they fix for themselves breakfast, it's really brunch. By evening they're ready for Mom's wonderful cooking.

The menu that pleases most consists of foods not served in the school dining hall. A fluffy omelet, for example, is a mighty fine country dish, but a difficult one to handle for a crowd. And crisp Lacy Potato Cakes, made by the recipe from a California girl of college age, are a good companion for omelet and other egg dishes. Something men and boys like too, so don't necessarily use the recipe for girls only!

TIMETABLE

Do-Ahead: If Mother has a loaf of homemade bread on hand, toast made with it and spread with butter and fruit or berry preserves from the fruit closet may prove irresistible even to ardent young weight-watchers.

On Guest Day: The hostess makes the cheese sauce and then the omelet, while a guest fixes the potato cakes.

SERVING SUGGESTIONS

The kitchen provides the homey setting girls home from school appreciate. Let them eat there too. They can bake potato cakes on an electric griddle or in an electric skillet placed on the kitchen table.

FLUFFY OMELET WITH CHEESE SAUCE

With fresh country eggs and the right techniques, this is a great dish

4 eggs, separated	1 tblsp. butter or regular
2 tblsp. water	margarine
¼ tsp. salt	Cheese Sauce

Beat egg whites until frothy. Add water and salt and beat until stiff, but not dry. Beat egg yolks until lemon-colored and very thick. Gently fold into the whites.

Heat butter in a 10″ skillet with ovenproof handle. Shake a few drops of water into the skillet. If they sizzle, pour in the egg mixture, spreading it evenly, but slightly higher around the edges. Reduce heat and cook *slowly* about 8 to 10 minutes, or until omelet is puffed up and set. Gently lift up one edge of it with a spatula; it should be golden on the underside.

Bake in a slow oven (325°) about 10 minutes, or until a knife inserted in omelet center comes out clean.

Loosen omelet around edges with spatula. Make a shallow cut across omelet shortly above center and parallel to skillet handle.

Tilt pan and fold the smaller, or upper half, over the lower half. With the aid of spatula and spoon, slip omelet onto hot platter. Spoon Cheese Sauce on it and serve at once. Makes 2 or 3 servings.

Cheese Sauce: Melt 2 tblsp. butter in saucepan over low heat. Blend in 2 tblsp. flour, ¼ tsp. salt and a dash of white pepper. Add 1 c. milk all at one time; cook and stir until mixture bubbles and thickens. Add 1 c. shredded sharp cheese and stir until it melts. Makes 1½ cups.

LACY POTATO CAKES

Potatoes and eggs team as well as peaches and cream in country meals. Make these for the entire family to enjoy

2 medium baking potatoes	Freshly ground pepper
1 tblsp. chopped fresh chives	Butter
1 tsp. salt	Salad oil

Peel potatoes, and shred coarsely into a medium mixing bowl. Add chives, salt and pepper and toss to mix. Heat equal parts butter and salad oil in a skillet over medium high heat until mixture stops foaming (should be hot, but not smoking).

Use 2 tblsp. of potato mixture for each cake and pan-fry 3 or 4 cakes at a time, flattening each to about 3″ in diameter with a spatula. Cook over medium-high heat 2 to 3 minutes on each side, or until golden. Serve at once. Use equal amounts of butter and oil as needed in baking the remainder of the cakes. Makes 9 or 10 potato cakes.

N O T E : This is an easy recipe to double.

PANCAKE BUFFET

Chilled Fruit Juice
Sour Cream Pancake Puffs*   Blueberry Pancakes
Maple Syrup   Pineapple Sauce*
Bacon Platter   Coffee

For a happy, relaxed way to entertain friends at brunch try this pancake buffet, featuring exceptionally light and tender sour cream pancakes. They'll disappear like magic—proof of how delicious they are. Flatter your guests by offering them a choice of pancakes;

the second kind could be made with a packaged mix. It might be blueberry cakes.

This meal plan gives the host a chance to star as the chef presiding over the electric griddle or skillet. Relief will come his way for some of the guests likely will ask to bake their own seconds, or, eventually, the hostess may take her turn at the griddle. You can handle up to 8 people with this meal.

TIMETABLE

On Guest Day: About an hour before mealtime, set up the buffet and combine juices for appetizer; refrigerate. One excellent choice is 1 (6 oz.) can frozen orange juice concentrate reconstituted with 3 cans cold water and mixed with 1 (1 lb. 13 oz.) can chilled apricot nectar. Make pancake batters and pour into pitchers or attractive bowls with ladles. While the bacon bakes and coffee drips or percolates, serve the fruit juice. Lay bacon, 2 or 3 strips per person, on rack in broiling pan; be sure not to overlap them. Bake in hot oven (400°) 10 minutes; allow 20 minutes for thick bacon slices. There's no turning or draining. Heat Pineapple Sauce.

SERVING SUGGESTIONS

Set pitcher of chilled fruit juice and juice glasses on a side table or coffee table so everyone can help himself. Float thin orange slices in pitcher. Place electric griddle (or electric skillet) on one end of buffet, with pancake batters nearby, the coffeemaker, cups, sugar and cream at the opposite end. Arrange serving plates, bacon, butter, Pineapple Sauce and maple syrup in between. You may wish also to serve other pancake toppings, such as honey and berry syrup from the supermarket. If you have a lazy susan, arrange pancake trimmings on it. The host asks the first guest to be served for her choice of pancakes and bakes them. She helps herself to the toppings and bacon; the hostess pours the coffee. This scene repeats until everyone has eaten his fill.

SOUR CREAM PANCAKE PUFFS

Superlative dollar-size griddlecakes that contain 4 eggs and only ⅓ cup flour—they're light, tender and wonderfully delicious

⅓ c. flour	¼ tsp. salt
3 tblsp. sugar	4 eggs
1 tsp. baking soda	2 c. dairy sour cream

Sift together flour, sugar, soda and salt.

Beat eggs; stir in sifted dry ingredients. Gently blend in sour cream (a wire whip is a good tool to use).

Drop tablespoonfuls of batter onto greased griddle heated to 375°, or hot enough to sizzle when a few drops of water are sprinkled on it. When bubbles appear in pancakes, but before they break, slip spatula halfway under each and turn to brown on other side. Serve at once. Makes about 72 pancakes, or 8 servings.

PINEAPPLE SAUCE

This is best served warm—perfect accompaniment for pancakes

3 tblsp. butter or regular margarine	2 tblsp. brown sugar
1 (8¼ oz.) can crushed pineapple	

Melt butter in small saucepan. Add undrained crushed pineapple and brown sugar. Heat about 5 minutes, or until sauce cooks down a little. Makes about 1 cup.

N O T E : Add a dash of spice, if you like. Try ground nutmeg.

COOK-AT-TABLE BRUNCH

Chilled Fruit Juice
French Toast Nuggets*
Honey   Confectioners Sugar   Maple Syrup
Little Pig Sausages
Coffee

Spear a cube of crisp-crusted French bread on your fondue fork, transform it into a golden nugget in the fondue pot, dunk in honey or maple syrup, or sprinkle with confectioners sugar—m'm, good! Your guests will agree.

One or two guests in a group often come to brunch carrying an extra fondue pot. Fondue parties are popular in the country—guests, host and hostess enjoy sitting around the table, doing their own "cooking." It's part of the entertainment.

Always use a metal fondue pot (not earthenware—it may crack) when you cook with oil; it will handle high temperatures adequately. Provide one cooker for every four people if you can, so the oil will stay hot enough. The electric fondue cooker with more easily controlled heat helps to avoid temperature problems and is safer with crowds than the open burner. Or use your electric skillet. Buffet-style skillets are attractive and convenient for cooking at the table. They come in many colors, are deep, have two comfortable handles for carrying and temperatures are controlled.

Regardless of the kind of cooking utensil you use to make French toast, play safe and place a protective mat or tray under it to keep spatters and spills off the table.

TIMETABLE

Do-Ahead: The day before the brunch, cut a long loaf of French bread in about 50 bite-size pieces, every piece with crust on one side. Cover and keep in a cool place.

On Guest Day: Before the guests arrive, stir up the batter for dipping toast. A few minutes before serving time, pour orange juice or equal parts grapefruit and tangerine juices (reconstituted frozen juice concentrates) over cracked ice in a pitcher. Cook the sausages and make the coffee. Heat the oil in the fondue cooker.

SERVING SUGGESTIONS

Set the juice and juice glasses on the buffet or side table and ask guests to help themselves while you finish your chores. Arrange a bowl of the batter (or two bowls if you're using two fondue pots), bowls of bread pieces, honey, maple syrup and a shaker of confectioners sugar on the table. Provide a dinner fork, fondue fork and a serving plate for each person. Keep the sausages warm in a chafing dish or electric skillet alongside the fondue pot.

FRENCH TOAST NUGGETS

Anticipating amount of food needed is difficult but allow at least 8 bread cubes per person. Increase amount if appetites are ravenous

1 long loaf French bread (1 lb.) ¼ tsp. salt
2 eggs, well beaten Salad oil
½ c. milk

Cut bread in bite-size pieces, each with crust on one side.

Combine eggs, milk and salt until smooth. Pour into bowl.

Pour oil to depth of 2″ (no more) in metal fondue cooker. Heat to 375° (using fat thermometer) on kitchen range; set over fondue burner. Or, if using an electric fondue pot, follow manufacturer's directions. Add 1 tsp. salt to hot oil to help reduce spatters. Adjust heat throughout cooking as needed to keep the oil at a satisfactory temperature.

Spear a piece of bread through the crust side with a fondue fork, dip in batter and let the excess drip off. Fry it in the hot oil until golden brown. Transfer to dinner fork and dunk in maple syrup or honey, or shake on confectioners sugar. Makes about 6 servings.

MAYTIME BRUNCH

Fruit-in-the-Pink*
Cheese Strata Soufflé*   Glazed Ham Strips
Hard Rolls
Coffee   Tea   Milk

Call this brunch or supper, as you like. The tempting food tastes equally good on a beautiful late Sunday morning in spring and early in the evening. It's a sit-down partnership meal with husband and wife involved in the cooking. The host grills the ham outdoors over coals and the hostess prepares the remainder of the food.

Use two slices of fully cooked center-cut smoked ham 1″ thick. Score each side of ham slices ¼″ deep, forming diamonds to help hold the barbecue sauce. Brush surface of ham with your favorite barbecue sauce or with ½ c. syrup drained from pickled peaches mixed with 1 c. brown sugar, firmly packed, and ¼ c. prepared horse-radish and brought to a boil. Lay slices on lightly greased grill over low to medium coals; the trick is to keep meat moist. Brush frequently with sauce and cook 10 to 15 minutes, or until underside is browned. Brush with sauce, turn and cook about 10 minutes longer. Keep warm on platter until serving.

TIMETABLE

Do-Ahead: Pour ginger ale over little red cinnamon candies (red hots) a day or several hours ahead. Stir occasionally and chill. Combine ingredients for casserole a day or a couple of days ahead, cover and refrigerate.

On Guest Day: Add pineapple to ginger ale-candy mixture at least 1 to 2 hours before serving time. About an hour before you want to serve the casserole, put it in the oven to bake. At that time, light the coals so the embers will be ready to cook the ham the last half hour before time to sit down to eat. Combine the fruit for the first course and serve.

SERVING SUGGESTIONS

Serve the fruit in chilled stemmed dessert glasses to display its lovely color. Cut the ham in strips and garnish the platter with water cress.

FRUIT-IN-THE-PINK

Candy teams with strawberries to tint and flavor this eye-opener

1 (7 oz.) bottle ginger ale	1 (1 lb. 4 oz.) can pineapple
¼ c. cinnamon candies (red hots)	chunks
	1 qt. strawberries

Pour ginger ale over cinnamon candies and let stand several hours. Pour over pineapple and chill at least 1 to 2 hours.

Add hulled, ripe strawberries and serve in chilled dessert glasses. Makes 8 servings.

CHEESE STRATA SOUFFLÉ

Blended seasonings, rich flavor distinguish this country-type soufflé

12 slices sandwich bread, crusts
   removed
¾ lb. sharp Cheddar cheese,
   shredded
6 eggs, beaten
1¼ c. light cream
1¼ c. milk

¾ tsp. salt
⅛ tsp. pepper
¼ tsp. dry mustard
⅛ tsp. ground red pepper
½ tsp. seasoned salt
1 green onion, minced

Butter bread slices and dice. In greased 2-qt. baking dish arrange alternate layers of bread and cheese, beginning and ending with bread.

Combine eggs, cream, milk, seasonings and onion. Pour over bread and cheese. Cover and chill in refrigerator at least 1 hour, but better overnight or for a day or two.

Bake uncovered in moderate oven (350°) 1 hour, or until no particles adhere to a metal knife inserted into soufflé. Serve at once. Soufflé puffs up but falls somewhat if allowed to stand more than a few minutes. Makes 6 to 8 servings.

CHAPTER 2

Entertaining at Midday

. . . LUNCHEONS WITH FEMININE APPEAL

Country men are often called meat-and-potatoes men. Perhaps the old—and enduring—custom in farm communities of serving husbands the noon meal before wives drive off to join friends at luncheon helped to build this masculine reputation. And it established 1:00 to 1:30 afternoon time for country women's luncheons.

Although we planned most of the luncheon menus in this chapter primarily for women, you will find that some menus produce meals men accept—and praise. Our Autumn Picnic is one; success of this meal depends on the entire family's cooperation, including Father's. Certainly the Welcoming Lunch with its homemade bread, cheese, applesauce and coffee will please most men. But for the most part, our supper menus would be better menus for luncheons attended by men. Two of the menus, Vegetarian Luncheon and Accent-on-Youth Lunch, will please young people.

In the main, our menus feature salads and desserts designed for women. Melon Salad Plate presents a colorful picture plate. Plantation Chicken Salad in Women's Luncheon is another favorite. Our Buffet Luncheon is excellent for 8 to 10 guests. For a larger group, make as many recipes of the salad, hot rolls and dessert as you need.

Sit down in a comfortable chair and peruse this chapter while you make plans for luncheons in the months ahead. Choices from our menus will boost your reputation as a hostess—we guarantee it!

Recipes for all dishes starred (*) are in this cookbook.

SUMMER LUNCHEON

Melon Salad Plate*   Special Blue Cheese Dressing*
Parkerhouse Rolls   Hot Tea

Guests describe this luncheon, tailored to fit a hot, humid day, as both beautiful and refreshing. The hostess who prepares the meal keeps cool. All the cooking she needs to do is put rolls in the oven to warm and heat water for the tea. Water cress makes a charming garnish for the colorful melon and fruit, especially if its leaves are dark green. Romaine also adds a pleasing touch, and in summer is more widely available than the cress. Look for a head with as few blemishes as possible.

TIMETABLE

Do-Ahead: Wash water cress a day ahead. Place it in a glass jar containing a little water; let the stems, but not the leaves touch the water. Cover with plastic wrap and chill. If you use romaine instead of cress, hold it under running cold water, shake off excess and chill in a plastic bag.

On Guest Day: At least 3 hours before luncheon add ingredients to salad dressing and chill. Peel rind from melons and cut pulp in shapes, as recipe designates. Wash stemmed grapes and drain. Refrigerate different kinds of melon and grapes in separate containers. Pull rolls far enough apart to spread with butter; wrap them in foil. About 20 minutes before luncheon time, put them in a moderate oven (350°) to heat for 10 to 15 minutes. Arrange melons and grapes on plates and garnish. (If refrigerator space permits, first chill the plates.) Just before serving, put a dip of sherbet on each salad plate.

SERVING SUGGESTIONS

Place sprays of water cress around border of each salad. Or, if using romaine, cut off base of head, break off leaves, wash, pat dry with paper towels and use scissors to cut each leaf into a point. Tuck a few of these green petals under edge of salads. Pass salad dressing so guests may help themselves. Also pass the hot, buttered rolls.

MELON SALAD PLATE

You can substitute cottage cheese or chicken salad for lime sherbet

1 medium honeydew melon
4 c. watermelon chunks
4 c. cantaloupe balls
4 c. stemmed seedless green
   grapes

Salad greens
1 qt. lime sherbet
Special Blue Cheese Dressing

Peel rind from chilled melons and cut honeydew in 18 wedges. Place 3 of them on each salad plate to divide it in three sections of equal size. In one section, place watermelon chunks, cantaloupe balls in another and grapes in the third section. Garnish with water cress or romaine, or with other lettuce. Place a scoop of sherbet in center of salads. Serve with Special Blue Cheese Dressing. Makes 6 servings.

Special Blue Cheese Dressing: Shake 1 (8 oz.) bottle blue cheese salad dressing with ¼ c. orange juice and 1 tsp. lemon juice. Chill at least 3 hours before serving. Makes 1¼ cups.

WINTER LUNCHEON

Hot Chicken Salad Casserole*   Buttered Peas (optional)
Sautéed Cherry Tomatoes   Watermelon Pickles
Hot Rolls   Broiled Pink Grapefruit*

Some women prefer chicken salad hot, others prefer it cold, but just about everyone likes it both ways. The weather has much to do with the choice. For a luncheon in winter, when bitter-cold winds are blowing, the hot salad makes an appetizing, satisfying main dish. Team it with colorful foods, as in this menu, and you have a superb guest meal.

TIMETABLE

Do-Ahead: Cook chicken the day before the luncheon, cool and refrigerate. Or cook it several days ahead and freeze. In either case, after cooling, remove meat from bones, pour a little broth on to moisten and package the remaining broth separately.

On Guest Day: Assemble salad casserole at your convenience, cover and refrigerate. Thirty minutes before serving time put it in oven. Place the foil-wrapped rolls in oven alongside salad for the last 10 to 15 minutes. Cook frozen peas by package directions.

Melt 2 tblsp. butter in skillet, add 1 pint cherry tomatoes, washed, stems removed and each tomato pricked several times to prevent skin breaking when heated. Cook and stir gently over medium heat just long enough to heat thoroughly, about 3 minutes. Sprinkle with seasoned salt, if desired. Broil grapefruit between main and dessert courses, while removing dishes, filling water glasses and coffee cups, but watch it. It's easy to brown the tops too much.

SERVING SUGGESTIONS

Serve plates in kitchen and carry to table. On each warm luncheon plate, arrange a mound of the hot salad, a ramekin filled with the peas and a few of the cherry tomatoes. Pass the rolls and watermelon pickles. Garnish each grapefruit half with a fresh strawberry or a maraschino cherry.

HOT CHICKEN SALAD CASSEROLE

Requires no attention while baking—delicious for lunch in winter

2 c. chopped cooked chicken	3 tblsp. chopped onion
2 c. chopped celery (green if available)	½ tsp. salt
	2 tblsp. lemon juice
½ c. chopped salted almonds (blanched)	½ c. mayonnaise
	⅓ c. grated Swiss cheese
2 tblsp. chopped pimiento	2½ c. crushed potato chips
⅓ c. chopped green pepper	

Blend together chicken, celery, nuts, pimiento, green pepper, onion, salt, lemon juice and mayonnaise. Turn into a buttered 2-qt. casserole. Top with cheese and potato chips.

Bake in moderate oven (350°) about 25 minutes, until cheese melts. Makes 6 servings.

BROILED PINK GRAPEFRUIT

Treat your guests to this pretty, tasty, easy, light dessert

3 pink grapefruit	6 tblsp. flaked coconut
6 tblsp. dark brown sugar	

Cut each grapefruit in half; remove seeds. Loosen sections with grapefruit knife and cut out center. Sprinkle each half with 1 tblsp. brown sugar. Place in shallow pan.

Broil 4 to 6″ from heat until hot or until juice bubbles, 5 to 10 minutes. Sprinkle 1 tblsp. coconut on each half and broil 1 minute longer, or just long enough to lightly brown coconut. Serve hot. Makes 6 servings.

WOMEN'S LUNCHEON

Plantation Chicken Salad* Whole Wheat Refrigerator Rolls*
Cranberry Sherbet* Hot Tea or Coffee

The salad country hostesses most often serve to their women friends is chicken. There are almost as many versions of this classic in a neighborhood as there are homes. Plantation Chicken Salad, a southern special, certainly deserves the praise it always generates. You will note that it contains hard-cooked eggs and that chopped sweet pickles and other seasonings, discreetly added, point up flavors. Team the salad with piping hot, homemade whole wheat rolls and cranberry sherbet and you have a feast for the palate and the eyes.

In days gone by, cranberry or lemon sherbet in stemmed crystal dessert dishes accompanied the main course of country chicken and turkey dinners. Revive the custom by serving the sherbet alongside the chicken salad, and you'll please your guests with the harmonious blending of flavors. Often something so old in meal planning has the freshness of something new. After all, holding on to the best of the old and adding the best of the new is the key to successful meal planning.

TIMETABLE

Do-Ahead: Cook the chicken a day ahead, cool. Remove from bones, cut in cubes, and chill chicken and broth separately. (Freeze the broth for future use.) Make the dough for the refrigerator rolls and chill overnight. Make the sherbet, or buy it if you prefer.

On Guest Day: Make the chicken salad, cover and chill at least 2 hours. Shape dough for rolls and let rise until double in bulk; it will take from 1½ to 2 hours. Bake them the last 15 minutes before time to serve the luncheon. Arrange chicken salad in lettuce cups and garnish. Make the tea or coffee.

SERVING SUGGESTIONS

Garnish salad with sliced hard-cooked eggs and thin slices of pimiento-stuffed olives. Either serve the sherbet with the salad or as the dessert.

PLANTATION CHICKEN SALAD

Seasonings added with a light hand round out the salad's flavor

3 c. cubed cooked chicken	¼ tsp. onion salt
1½ c. diced celery	¾ tsp. salt
3 hard-cooked eggs, quartered	Salad dressing
3 tblsp. chopped sweet pickle	Lettuce
¼ tsp. poultry seasoning	

Combine all ingredients, except salad dressing and lettuce, in a bowl. Moisten with salad dressing and toss to mix. Cover and chill. Serve on lettuce. Makes 6 to 8 servings.

WHOLE WHEAT REFRIGERATOR ROLLS

Dough keeps up to 5 days if refrigerator temperature is 45° or below

2 pkgs. active dry yeast	½ c. sugar
½ c. warm water (110 to 115°)	2 eggs, beaten
1 c. milk, scalded	2 c. whole wheat flour
⅓ c. shortening	4 c. sifted flour (about)
2 tsp. salt	

Sprinkle yeast on warm water; stir to dissolve.

To the hot milk, add shortening, salt and sugar; stir until shortening melts and sugar dissolves. Cool to lukewarm.

Add eggs and yeast to lukewarm milk mixture and mix thoroughly. Beat in whole wheat flour. Gradually add all-purpose white flour to make a soft dough that leaves the sides of bowl. Place on lightly floured board. Let rest 10 minutes. Knead until smooth and elastic, about 8 minutes. Place in lightly greased bowl, turn dough over to grease top; cover and refrigerate overnight.

Punch down dough, and take out half of it. (Cover and return other half to refrigerator to use later.) Divide in small 1″ balls;

place 3 in each greased muffin-pan cup. Balls should half-fill cups. Let rise until doubled. Bake in hot oven (400°) 12 to 15 minutes. Half of dough makes 18 cloverleaf rolls.

CRANBERRY SHERBET

Recommended for its tart-sweet flavor and its brilliant red color

1½ tsp. unflavored gelatin (½ envelope)
¾ c. sugar

Dash of salt
2 c. cranberry juice cocktail
2 tblsp. lemon juice

Mix gelatin with sugar and salt in saucepan; add 1 c. cranberry juice cocktail. Stir and cook over medium heat until gelatin and sugar dissolve. Remove from heat.

Add remaining 1 c. cranberry juice cocktail and lemon juice. Pour into refrigerator tray and freeze until firm. Break in chunks and turn into mixer bowl. Beat until smooth. Return to tray and freeze at least several hours. Makes 6 to 8 servings.

COOPERATIVE CLUB LUNCHEON

Special Chicken Salad*   Cucumber Swirl*
Assorted Sandwich Triangles
Coffee or Tea

One of the signs of the times is the way in which women's organizations share the preparation of refreshments for their meetings. In one Florida committee group of 8 members, 7 of them bring a sandwich each and the hostess provides a choice of two salads and coffee or tea.

Each sandwich has been cut diagonally in half and the halves cut again to make little triangles. Sandwiches are arranged on a large plate or tray, and making the selections is fun. You don't know what you'll draw, but as one of the women says: "All of us try to bring our best sandwiches."

Usually the hostess molds one salad and makes a protein-rich chicken, fish or meat salad also. This menu features a pretty, marbled molded salad and the old country special, chicken salad, with a new note—bright orange sections.

TIMETABLE

Do-Ahead: The hostess cooks the chicken for the salad unless she has it in the freezer. And she molds the gelatin salad (Cucumber Swirl) a day ahead.

On Guest Day: Fix the chicken salad, cover and chill for a minimum of 2 hours before serving. Wash lettuce leaves for placing under salads, drain and chill them in a plastic bag.

SERVING SUGGESTIONS

Serve the luncheon buffet style, or if you prefer, place salads on individual serving plates. Pass the sandwiches.

SPECIAL CHICKEN SALAD

Tiny orange sections add color, a juicy note and they enliven flavors

6 c. cubed cooked chicken
1½ c. sliced celery
¾ c. mayonnaise or salad dressing
1¼ tsp. salt
Dash of pepper

2 tsp. onion juice
2 (11 oz.) cans mandarin oranges, drained
Lettuce

Combine chicken and celery in bowl. In another bowl mix mayonnaise, salt, pepper and onion juice. Pour over chicken-celery mixture and toss to mix. Cover and chill at least 2 hours to blend flavors.

At serving time, fold in orange sections. Serve on lettuce. Makes 8 servings.

CUCUMBER SWIRL

Delight guests with this decorative marbled salad—marvelous flavor

2 (3 oz.) pkgs. lime flavor gelatin
3 c. hot water
¼ tsp. salt
¼ c. lemon juice
1 c. grated cucumber, drained
2 (3 oz.) pkgs. cream cheese, softened at room temperature

2 tblsp. mayonnaise
2 to 3 tblsp. milk
1½ tsp. prepared horse-radish
¼ c. finely snipped fresh chives or thinly cut green onion

Dissolve gelatin in hot water (scant measurement); cool. Add salt, lemon juice and cucumber, and stir. Chill until partially set, or until mixture molds slightly when dropped from a spoon.

Combine cream cheese, mayonnaise, milk, horse-radish and chives to make a smooth mixture. Swirl gently into the gelatin mixture for marbled effect. Pour into a 9″ square pan and chill until firm. To serve, cut in squares. Makes 8 to 10 servings.

THREE-PIECE LUNCHEON

Chicken Treasure*
Hot Buttered Rolls
Black Cherry Salad*

You'll find it easy to be both cook and hostess if you use this three-piece menu when you give a luncheon for members of your Homemakers Club or some other group of women friends. The casserole, which is a treasure chest of fine flavors, combines the meat (chicken) and vegetable (asparagus). The salad does double duty and also serves for dessert. If you prefer, you can have a fresh fruit salad instead of molded. And it's easy to change the menu into a dinner for men and women—we tell you how.

TIMETABLE

Do-Ahead: Cook chicken breasts a day ahead, cool, remove meat from bones and refrigerate chicken and broth separately. Make the salad a day ahead and chill.

On Guest Day: About 1¼ hours before serving time, prepare casserole. Bake it the last 45 minutes before luncheon. About 10 minutes before serving time, put foil-wrapped rolls in oven to heat. Serve the salad on individual plates and make the coffee.

SERVING SUGGESTIONS

Unmold salad on lettuce and garnish each serving either with a spoonful of salad dressing or mayonnaise.

NOTE: To convert luncheon to a dinner, serve chilled cranberry juice cocktail for an appetizer in small glasses containing a spoonful of lemon sherbet. Pass nibblers. Add buttered lima beans to menu.

Cook 3 (10 oz.) pkgs. frozen limas by package directions; drain. Add ¼ c. melted butter, 1 to 2 tblsp. lemon juice and ½ tsp. dill weed; stir to mix. Serve the cherry mold, topped with spoonfuls of salad dressing, in the main course. For dessert, have a chocolate-frosted sour cream yellow cake, using packaged mixes for cake and frosting.

CHICKEN TREASURE

Mayonnaise contributes rich flavor to this chicken-asparagus bake

4 whole chicken breasts	2 c. chicken broth
Water	1 tsp. lemon juice
⅓ c. butter or regular margarine	1 c. mayonnaise
½ c. flour	2 (15 oz.) cans green asparagus
1 tsp. salt	½ c. toasted bread crumbs
1 c. milk	

Simmer chicken in boiling salted water to cover 1 hour, or until tender. Save broth (you'll need 2 c.). Spread chicken on plate to cool. Discard bones, fat and skin; pull chicken into bite-size pieces.

Melt butter and stir in flour and salt; stir to mix. Add milk and chicken broth; cook until creamy and thick, stirring constantly.

Beat lemon juice and mayonnaise together and stir into the creamy sauce. Remove from heat and stir well.

Lightly grease a 2½-qt. casserole and layer chicken and asparagus alternately in it. Pour sauce over and top with bread crumbs. Bake in moderate oven (375°) 45 minutes, or until mixture bubbles in center. Makes 8 to 10 servings.

BLACK CHERRY SALAD

Celery and nuts add crunchy texture to this black-red fruit salad

1 (1 lb.) can dark sweet cherries	1 (8½ oz.) can crushed pineapple
Juice drained from cherries	½ c. thinly sliced celery
Water	½ c. chopped walnuts
1 (3 oz.) pkg. dark cherry flavor gelatin	Romaine or other lettuce

Drain cherries; measure juice and add enough water to make 1¾ c. Heat half of liquid and add to gelatin; stir until gelatin is dissolved. Add remaining liquid (mixture of water and cherry juice). Chill until mixture starts to thicken.

Meanwhile, cut cherries in halves and combine with drained

pineapple, celery and nuts. Fold into gelatin and turn into individual molds. Chill until firm.

To serve, unmold on romaine or other lettuce. Makes 9 servings.

JULY LUNCHEON

Peachy Cherry Salad Mold*
Whole Wheat Berry Muffins*
Iced Tea

When wild fruits ripen, country women like to share with their friends these free gifts from their land. Juneberries come to Montana tables in July. After the family enjoys the first fresh berries of the year, plain with sugar and cream, they begin to find their way into recipes like these whole wheat muffins. (If you don't have Juneberries try blueberries, or another berry—muffins are also delicious plain, of course.)

Serve a salad worthy of the muffins for luncheon. In this menu, lovely gold and red Peachy Cherry Salad Mold comes highly recommended.

TIMETABLE

Do-Ahead: Make the salad a day ahead. Wash and drain lettuce to serve under it and chill in a plastic bag.

On Guest Day: Make muffins at the last minute and serve them so hot that butter spread on them melts almost instantly.

PEACHY CHERRY SALAD MOLD

Cut the servings so each contains a peach half in orange gelatin

1 (3 oz.) pkg. black cherry flavor gelatin	2 tblsp. chopped nuts
1 c. boiling water	1 (3 oz.) pkg. orange flavor gelatin
1 c. cold water	1½ c. boiling water
1 (3 oz.) pkg. cream cheese	½ c. peach syrup
2 tblsp. orange marmalade	2 tblsp. lemon juice
1 (1 lb. 13 oz.) can cling peach halves	Dash of salt
	Lettuce

Dissolve cherry gelatin in 1 c. boiling water. Add 1 c. cold water. Pour into an 11×7×1½″ glass dish; chill until partially thickened.

Mix together cream cheese and orange marmalade.

Drain peach halves, reserving syrup (you should have ½ c.). Fill cavities in peach halves with cream cheese mixture. Sprinkle with nuts. Arrange peaches cut side up in partially thickened gelatin. Return to refrigerator; chill until almost set.

Dissolve orange gelatin in 1½ c. boiling water; add peach syrup, lemon juice and salt. Cool until partially set. Pour over peaches in cherry gelatin. Chill until set. Cut in squares and serve on lettuce. Makes 8 servings.

WHOLE WHEAT BERRY MUFFINS

If you do not add berries to these muffins you may wish to use only 3 tblsp. each brown and white sugars for a slightly less sweet bread

1 c. flour	1 egg, well beaten
½ tsp. salt	1 c. milk
¼ c. sugar	¼ c. melted butter or regular
¼ c. brown sugar, firmly packed	margarine
3 tsp. baking powder	1 c. fresh Juneberries or
1 c. whole wheat flour	blueberries

Sift all-purpose flour, salt, sugars and baking powder into a bowl. Stir in the whole wheat flour.

Add egg to milk and add with melted butter all at one time to flour mixture. Use care not to overmix batter. Batter will not be smooth. Fold in berries.

Pour batter into greased muffin-pan cups, filling two thirds full. Bake in hot oven (400°) 20 to 25 minutes. Remove from pan immediately and serve hot. Makes 12 medium muffins.

SALAD LUNCHEON

Carrot/Coconut Salad*

Cheese Muffins*   Toasted Party Rye Bread

Almond Butter Crunch*

When a salad is the main dish in a meal, it needs to look beautiful, taste wonderful and satisfy appetites. Carrot/Coconut Salad meets these requirements. And it stands alone; you serve no salad dressing with it. Hostesses rate this a perfect choice for the buffet supper. In this luncheon you can serve the salad in a big ring at the table or you can chill it in individual molds.

Hot breads lift guest meals above the commonplace. This menu pampers the guests by offering them two kinds, muffins and toasted rye bread slices. You can skip a dessert, but a piece of Almond Butter Crunch provides a much enjoyed sweet-tooth ending. If you prefer, you can pass candy mints or assorted salted nuts.

TIMETABLE

Do-Ahead: Make the almond treat a day or two ahead, put it in an airtight container and store in a cool place. The delicacy often gets sticky in an hour or less if not protected from air exposure. Make salad a day ahead and refrigerate.

On Guest Day: Butter slices of party rye bread, spread on baking sheet and toast in a slow oven (325°) until crisp, 10 to 12 minutes. Get the muffins in the oven about 10 minutes before lunchtime. Stir up the batter at the last minute—no need to use your electric mixer because you can mix it by hand in 2 to 3 minutes. Remove muffins from pans as soon as baked; serve piping hot. If they must wait, remove them and place on their sides in the muffin cups; keep warm in a very low oven.

SERVING SUGGESTIONS

Garnish salad with green leaves; make a wreath of them around base of ring or tuck a jaunty bouquet of them in center opening. Use water cress, curly endive or lettuce—even spinach. Pass muffins in napkin-lined basket or roll warmer, rye toast on a large plate. When making Almond Butter Crunch, go artistic and form it into flower shapes. Arrange clusters of toasted almond halves in petal fashion on baking sheet. With a teaspoon drop hot candy mixture on them.

CARROT/COCONUT SALAD

It's pale yellow with orange flecks; lemon juice gives it extra zip

4 c. finely grated carrots	2 c. boiling water
2 tsp. grated lemon peel	2 (3 oz.) pks. lemon flavor gelatin
¼ c. lemon juice	2 c. cold water
1 c. flaked coconut	1 c. dairy sour cream
¼ tsp. salt	Greens

Mix carrots, lemon peel, lemon juice, coconut and salt in a large bowl; toss. Cover and set aside.

Stir boiling water into gelatin; stir until it dissolves. Add cold water. Cover and refrigerate until mixture mounds when dropped from a spoon. Fold in carrot mixture and sour cream.

Turn into a 2-qt. ring mold. Chill until set. To serve, unmold on large plate and garnish with salad greens. Makes 10 to 12 servings.

CHEESE MUFFINS

Key secret to success with muffins is to avoid overmixing the batter

2 c. sifted flour	1 egg, beaten
3 tsp. baking powder	1 c. milk
½ tsp. salt	¼ c. salad oil
¼ c. sugar	½ c. grated sharp Cheddar cheese

Sift flour, baking powder, salt and sugar into a big bowl. Make a well in the center.

Combine egg, milk and salad oil; stir to mix. Pour all at once into the well in flour mixture. Mix quickly with fork or spoon until flour is moistened, but do not beat. The batter will contain some lumps. Fold in cheese with a few strokes.

Pour into greased muffin-pan cups, filling them two thirds full. Bake in hot oven (400°) 20 to 25 minutes, until muffins are golden. Serve at once. Makes 12 medium muffins.

ALMOND BUTTER CRUNCH

Candied nuts add texture contrast—shape like stars at Christmastime

1½ c. blanched almond halves	1 tblsp. light corn syrup
¾ c. butter	3 tblsp. water
1½ c. sugar	

To halve almonds, pour boiling water over nuts and simmer 2 minutes. Drain and split in halves.

Toast almonds on baking sheet in slow oven (300°) until golden brown.

Melt butter in 2-qt. heavy saucepan; add sugar, corn syrup and water. Cook to soft crack stage (290°) without stirring.

Remove from heat and pour in thin stream over nuts on baking sheet. Cool. Break into pieces. Makes about 1½ pounds.

Variation

Christmas Stars: Arrange clusters of 5 toasted almond halves in star patterns on baking sheets. Drop teaspoonfuls of hot candy on clusters of almonds. Cool.

SUPERB SPRING LUNCHEON

Ham/Asparagus Roll-Ups*
Summer Squash Parmesan*
Relish Tray
Orange Pinwheels*
Grapefruit Halves

No need to suggest to the country hostess that she feature seasonal foods in company meals; it's a traditional habit. What better time to serve asparagus than when it takes almost daily cutting to keep up with the delicate spears that shoot up overnight?

In this menu asparagus teams with smoky-flavored ham and bakes briefly in a special mustard sauce. To maintain the pace for fascinating food, cook thin slices of young, green-skinned zucchini and yellow crookneck squash in the same saucepan. The vegetable combination is much more exciting than either vegetable cooked singly.

The orange rolls are an illustration of what makes country guest meals famous—homemade yeast bread. Center each chilled grapefruit half with a particularly lush fresh strawberry.

You can serve a replica of this luncheon when snow drifts and arctic winds blow, by using canned asparagus and frozen squash. And you will find another garnish for the grapefruit. It might be maple syrup, or possibly frozen strawberries. Not that such a luncheon equals the springtime meals, but it is highly acceptable.

You can expand this menu into a full-fledged spring dinner that both women and men will enjoy. Just add parslied new potatoes to the bill of fare and substitute fresh strawberry-rhubarb pie for the grapefruit. You may want to buy (and heat) rolls if you're baking pies.

TIMETABLE

On Guest Day: Start the rolls early—before you wash the breakfast dishes. It takes 3 hours to make and bake them, but you do not have to stand over them. While the dough doubles, attend to other preparations. Assemble relishes and chill. Make the mustard sauce. Pull the green onions for the main dish and relish tray when you cut the asparagus. Cook asparagus and wrap the ham around it. If refrigerator space permits, cut grapefruit in half, cut out centers, loosen sections from membrane, but leave them in the yellow shells; chill. Stem, wash, crush, sweeten and chill berries. While the roll-ups bake, cook squash.

SERVING SUGGESTIONS

Serve the plates for this sit-down meal in the kitchen, but pass the relishes and second helpings (maybe thirds) of the rolls. Spoon strawberries over grapefruit at serving time, and if you have fresh mint, garnish with a few fragrant leaves.

HAM/ASPARAGUS ROLL-UPS

Give the sauce credit for its part in seasoning this pretty main dish. You can easily double this recipe to serve more guests

24 cooked fresh asparagus spears (or canned)	Creamy Mustard Sauce
6 slices boiled ham, ¼″ thick	¼ c. chopped green onions

Place 4 asparagus spears on each ham slice. Roll up cornucopia fashion and secure with toothpicks.

Pour Creamy Mustard Sauce into shallow baking dish. Lay roll-ups in sauce. Bake in moderate oven (350°) 20 to 25 minutes. Just before serving, garnish with onions. Makes 6 servings.

Creamy Mustard Sauce: Heat ¾ c. light cream in top of double boiler. Beat 1 egg yolk with ¼ c. light cream. Mix ½ c. sugar, 4 tsp. dry mustard, ¼ tsp. salt and 1 tblsp. flour; add to egg yolk mixture.

Stir into heated cream in double boiler; cook, stirring constantly, until mixture thickens. Heat ⅓ c. vinegar; blend into sauce and beat.

SUMMER SQUASH PARMESAN

Quick-cooking squash require no peeling—just washing and slicing

4 c. thinly sliced unpeeled, fresh or frozen summer squash
1 small onion, sliced
1 tblsp. water
2 tblsp. butter
½ tsp. salt
⅛ tsp. pepper
3 tblsp. Parmesan cheese

Put all ingredients except cheese in a skillet. Cover and cook 1 minute over high heat. Uncover, continue to cook over low heat, turning with spatula, until barely tender.

Sprinkle with cheese and serve. Makes 6 to 8 servings.

ORANGE PINWHEELS

Feather-light yeast dough rolled around orange filling and baked

Dough:
1 pkg. active dry yeast
¼ c. warm water (110 to 115°)
¾ c. milk
¼ c. sugar
1 tsp. salt
3 eggs
3 tblsp. soft butter
4 to 4½ c. flour
Orange Filling:
⅓ c. soft butter
½ c. sugar
2 tsp. grated orange peel

To make dough, dissolve yeast in warm water in mixing bowl.

Scald milk; cool to lukewarm. Add milk, sugar, salt, eggs, butter and half the flour to yeast mixture. Stir with a spoon until smooth. Mix in enough of remaining flour to make a soft dough. (The consistency of the dough is important. When you first make these rolls, you may have difficulty handling the soft dough, but it's the softness that makes these rolls so very light and tender.)

Knead on a lightly floured board until smooth and elastic, about 5 minutes. Place in a greased bowl; turn dough over to grease top. Cover with a clean towel; let rise in a warm place until doubled, about 1½ hours. Punch down; let rise until amost doubled, about 30 minutes.

Roll dough in a 15×9″ rectangle. Mix ingredients for Orange Filling and spread over the dough. Roll as for jelly roll, pinching edges together. Cut roll in 1″ slices.

Place cut side down in a greased 13×9×2″ pan. Cover and let rise until doubled, 35 to 40 minutes. Bake in moderate oven (375°) 25 minutes, or until lightly browned. Makes 18.

MAYTIME LUNCHEON

Chilled Pineapple Juice
Baked Asparagus/Cheese Sandwiches*
Celery Hearts   Radish Roses   Cucumber Pickle Slices
Angel Food Cake   Pink Party Topping*

Spring delivers tender stalks of asparagus to country kitchens either from home gardens or markets. Appetites start to crave other seasonal treats soon to appear, such as strawberries and red raspberries to serve with tall, stately angel food cakes. Why not cash in on this prevailing mood and entertain friends at a lovely luncheon? This menu will help you do it easily.

The pink berry topping for the snowy angel food cake uses frozen strawberries or raspberries, universally available, but if you have even a few plump fresh berries, generously garnish with them to glamorize the cake.

TIMETABLE

Do-Ahead: Bake the angel food cake a day ahead, or several days ahead and freeze. Combine in a bowl the ingredients for the cake topping (except for whipped cream), cover and chill overnight.

On Guest Day: You can fix and bake the sandwich in less than an hour. While it bakes, wash celery and radishes, make radish roses and chill in ice water. At dessert time, cut cake, whip cream and fold it into topping and put the two together for a wonderful ending to a delightful meal.

SERVING SUGGESTIONS

Serve chilled pineapple juice in small glasses for an appetizer to sip in the living room or at the dining table. Garnish with perky mint sprigs. Arrange sandwich servings on individual plates in kitchen with celery hearts, radish roses and pickles.

BAKED ASPARAGUS/CHEESE SANDWICHES

You may need to bake two dishes of the hot sandwiches—depends on how many people you're having for lunch

6 thick (¾") slices firm-textured bread (like home-baked)
6 (3½" square) slices process Swiss cheese
4 eggs
2 c. milk

1 tsp. salt
⅛ tsp. pepper
¼ tsp. ground nutmeg
1 tblsp. finely chopped onion
18 cooked asparagus spears
½ c. shredded Cheddar cheese

Trim crusts from bread slices. Arrange bread slices in bottom of 13×9×2" pan or glass dish. Top each bread slice with a slice of process Swiss cheese.

In a bowl, beat eggs slightly; add milk, stir in seasonings and onion. Pour this mixture over sandwiches and bake in slow oven (325°) 25 minutes.

Remove from oven. Top each bread slice with 3 cooked asparagus spears. Sprinkle on shredded Cheddar cheese. Return dish to oven and continue to bake 10 to 15 minutes, until custard sets and top is golden. Allow to stand 5 minutes before serving. Makes 6 servings.

PINK PARTY TOPPING

Pretty pink fluffy sauce on cake slices is so good and so easy to fix

1 c. miniature marshmallows
1 (10 oz.) pkg. frozen red raspberries or strawberries

1 c. heavy cream, whipped

Pour marshmallows and frozen berries in a bowl. Cover; refrigerate overnight. Before serving, fold in whipped cream. Serve on angel food cake slices. Makes 3 cups.

BUFFET LUNCHEON

Hearty Buffet Salad*
Bran Refrigerator Rolls*
Assorted Olives
Blancmange Ring with Fresh Peaches (or Berries)*

This luncheon menu is of blue-ribbon caliber—select it when you entertain a group of friends whom you want to impress and please. The bowl salad, with ingredients arranged as the serving suggestions describe, makes a pretty buffet. And it's neither too light to qualify as a main dish salad nor too heavy to refresh. The homemade bran rolls, yeast-leavened, are the perfect go-with. And the molded dessert ring holds fresh peaches, sliced and lightly sugared.

TIMETABLE

Do-Ahead: Cook the turkey a day ahead and refrigerate. The salad recipe starts with the turkey cooked and cut in julienne strips. Make the dough for the rolls and cover; fix the dessert mold. Chill both the dough and mold. Wash the salad greens, drain and refrigerate each kind in a plastic bag.

On Guest Day: Shape the dough for rolls, let rise and bake. It will be easier to do this first in the day and reheat the rolls at mealtime in order to serve them piping hot. Cook the bacon.

Chop the three kinds of lettuce, chives and water cress; do not mix. Chop finely the tomatoes, avocado (sprinkle with a little lemon juice if it must wait) and bacon. To arrange salad, alternate layers of the different kinds of lettuce and water cress in a *big* (wide) salad bowl. On top place alternate rows of the chopped foods for a striking effect. Take time to build this salad by the culinary artist's pattern (allow about 30 minutes!).

If you use fresh peaches with the dessert mold, peel, slice and lightly sugar them. Then sprinkle with ascorbic acid powder, the kind you use when freezing peaches, dissolved in a little cold water to retain color. Follow label directions, or use 2 tsp. of powder to 3 tblsp. water for 1 qt. fruit. Or sprinkle with lemon juice. Cover peaches and keep in refrigerator until time to serve the dessert. Serve them in center and around base of the mold. Heat the rolls, wrapped in foil, in a moderate oven (350°) 10 to 15 minutes.

SERVING SUGGESTIONS

The menu is designed for food to be served buffet style. Don't worry about garnishes—the food is so beautiful that decorating is unnecessary. An attractive way to build the salad, after adding alternate layers of the different kinds of lettuce and water cress, heaping the greens a little in the center, is to place a row of turkey strips at the center across the bowl. On one side arrange rows of chopped tomato, egg and bacon, with rows of grated cheese, cubed avocado and chopped chives on the other side.

After guests see the spectacular salad, sprinkle one side, including all toppings, with salad dressing and toss lightly; repeat with the other half later. This helps to maintain part of the attractive design while serving.

HEARTY BUFFET SALAD

You can use chicken instead of turkey for this handsome salad

½ head lettuce	½ lb. bacon, cooked crisp
1 small bunch red lettuce or chicory	3 c. julienne strips cooked turkey or chicken breast
1 head romaine	½ c. finely grated Cheddar or crumbled blue cheese
½ bunch water cress	
2 medium tomatoes, peeled	2 tblsp. finely chopped fresh chives
1 medium avocado, peeled	
3 hard-cooked eggs	1 c. garlic French dressing

With a sharp knife, chop each of the greens very fine. Spread in layers in large salad bowl, heaping up slightly in center.

Finely chop tomatoes, avocado, eggs and bacon. Arrange the turkey, tomatoes, avocado, eggs, bacon, cheese and chives in rows in pretty, contrasting colors over top of the greens. (See Serving Suggestions.)

Sprinkle part of salad dressing across only one end at a time, toss lightly and serve from that section. Makes 3½ quarts salad, or 8 to 10 large servings.

BRAN REFRIGERATOR ROLLS

Cloverleaf yeast rolls provide a charming homemade country touch

½ c. shortening	1 pkg. active dry yeast
⅓ c. sugar	½ c. warm water (110 to 115°)
¾ tsp. salt	1 egg, beaten
½ c. boiling water	3 to 3¼ c. sifted flour
½ c. ready-to-eat bran cereal	

Combine shortening, sugar and salt with boiling water; stir until shortening is softened. Add bran, stir and cool to lukewarm.

In the meantime dissolve yeast in warm water; stir into cooled bran mixture. Blend in egg. Stir in enough flour to make a soft dough and mix thoroughly. Cover, and store in refrigerator.

When needed, remove dough from refrigerator and allow to stand in warm place (85°) 15 minutes. Form dough into small balls. Place in groups of 3 in greased muffin-pan cups. Allow to rise until almost doubled.

Bake in hot oven (425°) 15 to 20 minutes. Makes 12 to 18 rolls.

N O T E : Recipe may be doubled or tripled for more servings.

BLANCMANGE RING WITH FRESH PEACHES (OR BERRIES)

An old-fashioned pudding presented in a new-fashioned way

1½ envelopes unflavored gelatin (1½ tblsp.)	3¾ c. cold milk
¼ c. cold water	¼ tsp. almond extract
2 (3¾ oz.) pkgs. vanilla instant pudding	4 c. fresh peach slices
	1 c. heavy cream, whipped and sweetened to taste

Soften gelatin in cold water; set in pan of boiling water to dissolve.

Combine vanilla pudding and cold milk according to package directions, then stir in dissolved gelatin and almond extract. Pour into oiled 1-qt. ring mold and chill until set.

Unmold ring onto large serving platter. Fill center with peach slices and arrange remaining fruit around edge. Garnish with whipped cream. Makes 8 to 10 servings.

N O T E : You can use 4 c. fresh berries instead of the peaches.

AUTUMN PICNIC

Rancho Beans*   Spaghetti Bake*
Dutch Slaw*
Sliced Tomatoes
Homemade Cucumber Pickles
Sourdough Bread*
Pears   Chocolate Fudge
Coffee   Milk

Aspen trees changing from green to gold on western mountain sides signal it's time for those last fall picnics—winter's on the way. This is when a ranch wife will call a neighbor and invite her family to join them for lunch at noon in the cottonwood grove by the stream. Usually such an impromptu picnic turns into a cooperative meal: "I'll bring my beef-spaghetti casserole and the girls will make a batch of fudge."

Food for the noon meal needs to be easy to fix and to carry in car or jeep, substantial enough to satisfy hungry people and so good that memories will brighten winter days. This menu meets the requirements regardless of where the two families dine, in the shadow of the Rocky Mountains or in Vermont where the hills are a riot of fall color.

Rancho Beans, the recipe contributed by a Montana homemaker, and Spaghetti Bake, a favorite picnic food of a Vermont family, provide a hearty and delicious choice which a cooperative meal affords. Dutch Slaw (from Illinois) fits perfectly into the meal, plus the last of the season's homegrown tomatoes, sliced and sprinkled with a bottled salad seasoning.

Sourdough Bread and a jar of homemade pickles are tasty testimony of time well spent in advance in the country kitchen. Juicy fresh pears, a pan of smooth chocolate fudge and vacuum containers of hot coffee and cold milk round out the meal.

TIMETABLE

Do-Ahead: Only the bread and pickles were ready when picnic day dawned.

On Guest Day: All the other foods are prepared or collected by the participating families.

SERVING SUGGESTIONS

Picnic baskets hold plates, cups, spoons, forks and knives along with napkins and a tablecover to spread on a portable table or the ground. The casseroles, wrapped in several layers of newspapers, retain their heat on the short drive to the picnic spot.

RANCHO BEANS

Well seasoned beef-and-bean hot dish that men especially like

1 lb. lean ground beef	2 tsp. cider vinegar
1 envelope dry onion soup mix	2 (1 lb.) cans pork and beans in
1 c. ketchup	tomato sauce
2 tblsp. prepared mustard	1 (1 lb.) can kidney beans
½ c. water	

Stir and brown beef in large skillet over medium heat. Add the remaining ingredients; mix well. Heat thoroughly. Pour into 3-qt. casserole and bake in hot oven (400°) about 30 minutes, until bubbling hot in center. Makes 8 to 10 servings.

SPAGHETTI BAKE

Seasonings are mild in this tasty beef-spaghetti casserole

1 lb. ground beef	1 soup can water (1¼ c.)
¾ c. finely chopped onion	1 (8 oz.) can tomato sauce
½ c. finely chopped green pepper	½ tsp. salt
1 can condensed cream of mushroom soup	1 clove garlic, minced
	1 (8 oz.) pkg. spaghetti
1 can condensed tomato soup	1 c. shredded sharp process cheese

Combine beef, onion and green pepper in skillet. Stir and cook to lightly brown meat. Add soups, water, tomato sauce, salt and garlic. Heat.

Meanwhile, cook spaghetti by package directions; drain. Blend ½ c. cheese and spaghetti into soup mixture. Turn into greased 3-qt. casserole. Top with remaining ½ c. cheese.

Bake in moderate oven (350°) about 45 minutes, until bubbling hot in center. Makes 8 to 10 servings.

DUTCH SLAW

Bacon and lemon juice do wonders flavor-wise for cabbage slaw

¾ c. chopped bacon

2 tblsp. lemon juice

½ tsp. salt

½ tsp. dry mustard

½ c. salad dressing or mayonnaise

2 c. finely shredded cabbage

¼ c. chopped green pepper

2 tblsp. chopped parsley

1 medium onion, finely chopped

Cook bacon in skillet to a light golden brown. Remove from heat; add lemon juice, salt and mustard. Mix in the salad dressing. Add vegetables and toss. Makes about 3 cups.

SOURDOUGH BREAD

It takes time to make this, but keeping the starter in the refrigerator will shorten the procedure. Toast it for a treat

1 c. warm water (110 to 115°)

1 pkg. active dry yeast

2 tblsp. sugar

2 tsp. salt

1½ c. Sourdough Starter

5 c. flour

Put warm water, yeast, sugar and salt in blender and blend at low speed until yeast is dissolved (or in large bowl and beat at low speed on mixer). Add starter (if you don't have some in your refrigerator, see recipe which follows). Continue blending to mix. Turn the control high and gradually blend in 1½ c. flour, using rubber spatula to scrape down sides of blender.

When smooth, pour into bowl and gradually add 2½ c. flour, mixing with spoon until smooth. Cover bowl with damp towel and let stand in a warm place until doubled, about 1½ hours.

Turn onto lightly floured surface and work in about 1 c. more of remaining flour, or enough so that the dough no longer is sticky. Knead until elastic and satiny; shape into large round loaf (or in two long oval loaves).

Sprinkle a little cornmeal on ungreased baking sheet and place loaf on it. Cover lightly with a towel and let rise again in warm place until doubled, or about 1½ hours.

Put shallow pan of water on lower shelf in oven. Preheat oven to hot (400°). With razor blade, make diagonal slashes on loaf about 2″ apart.

Bake 40 to 50 minutes until crust is a dark brown. Cool on rack. Makes 1 big round loaf.

N O T E : If you freeze bread, for a picnic, thaw it, wrapped in heavy-duty foil in moderate oven (350°) about 30 minutes. Slice, butter and put together in sandwich style.

SOURDOUGH STARTER

This is the magic that gives sourdough its characteristic flavor

2 c. warm water (110 to 115°)   2 c. flour
1 pkg. active dry yeast

Put ingredients in blender, cover and blend on low speed until smooth, or blend in large bowl of electric mixer. Pour into a 2-qt. mixing bowl, cover with cheesecloth and leave in a warm place 48 hours, stirring two or three times. Then pour into jar with a tight-fitting lid and refrigerate.

To use, stir starter and pour off 1½ c. or the amount the bread recipe specifies. Add 1 c. flour and 1 c. warm water (110 to 115°) to the remaining starter, using blender or electric mixer to blend smooth.

Cover with cheesecloth and let stand at room temperature for 5 to 6 hours, or until mixture bubbles. Then pour into jar, cover tightly and refrigerate. Always add an equal amount of flour and water after using some of the starter.

WELCOMING LUNCH

Homemade 100% Whole Wheat Bread*
Whipped Butter
Sharp Cheddar Cheese   Applesauce
Coffee   Milk

Visitors, traveling by car, often arrive between meals. The farm hostess and host, always suspecting that their guests may be hungry, welcome them with a lunch. Frequently the food is spread on a neat table in a cheerful kitchen. This traditional country custom rates the same popularity it enjoyed in horse-and-buggy days. Everyone in the house gathers around the table to share in the talk and simple feast.

The super star in this menu is the rich-flavored, nut-brown whole wheat bread. It glorifies the other foods. You'll want to bake these loaves soon.

TIMETABLE

Do-Ahead: All the food is ready before the friend-filled car shows up in the driveway. You can fix the butter a day or a few days ahead and store it in covered bowls in the refrigerator to serve with pancakes, waffles, hot rolls, biscuits, muffins and all hot breads. To fix the spread, whip 1 lb. butter with electric mixer on medium speed, scraping down sides of bowl several times with rubber spatula. Beat until light and fluffy. It will almost double in volume.

SERVING SUGGESTIONS

Add glamor to this homespun food by the way you serve it. Place the loaf of bread on a bread board and slice it at the table. Set a bowl of butter nearby and alongside place the cheese on cutting board with knife. Bring out a big bowl of freshly made or home-canned applesauce and let your guests ladle it into their sauce dishes. Have the coffee or teapot (your guests' preference) and a pitcher of cold milk ready to pour.

HOMEMADE 100% WHOLE WHEAT BREAD

This bread created by the hostess' own hands makes lunch special

1 pkg. active dry yeast	4 tsp. salt
¼ c. warm water (110 to 115°)	2 c. milk, scalded
¼ c. sugar	5 c. stone-ground whole wheat
¼ c. molasses	flour
2 tblsp. shortening	

Sprinkle yeast on warm water; stir to dissolve.

Add sugar, molasses, shortening and salt to warm milk; stir to blend. Pour into large mixing bowl and cool until lukewarm. Stir in yeast.

Add flour, beating until well mixed. Turn dough out onto lightly floured surface; knead until smooth and elastic, 8 to 10 minutes. Place in lightly greased bowl, turn dough over to grease top. Cover and let rise in warm place until doubled. Punch down dough and divide in half; shape into loaves.

Place in two lightly greased 9×5×3″ or 8½×4½×2½″ loaf

pans. Let rise until doubled. Bake in hot oven (400°) 20 to 25 minutes. Makes 2 (1½ lb.) loaves.

VEGETARIAN LUNCHEON

Hearty Mushroom/Barley Soup*   Garden Sandwiches*
Homemade Mayonnaise*
Fresh Apple Cake*

If your college-age daughter decides to invite friends to lunch, don't be surprised if she selects a vegetarian menu. Times change; mothers fretted for years because their children often balked at eating their full vegetable quota. Now these foods enjoy great popularity with many young people. You don't need to be a vegetarian, though, to like this meal, for it's flavorful and satisfying.

The sandwiches are made with a filling of several vegetables, held together with mayonnaise (homemade is nice!) and whole wheat bread. The soup has a pleasing blend of flavors, and the moist, apple spice cake is as easy to eat as it is to make. A crisp topping bakes right on the cake.

TIMETABLE

Do-Ahead: Make the mayonnaise a day or two ahead and refrigerate. Make the sandwich filling (all but adding tomatoes) the day before the luncheon.

On Guest Day: Bake the cake. Start making soup about 1½ hours before lunchtime. While the soup vegetables cook, make the sandwiches. If you want 6 instead of 12 sandwiches, halve the recipe.

SERVING SUGGESTIONS

Serve sandwiches pointed ends toward center of plate to show off the color of sandwich filling. If you have fresh dill, sprinkle a bit into the bowls of soup just before serving.

HEARTY MUSHROOM/BARLEY SOUP

Almost filling enough for a meal if served with a tossed green salad

10 to 12 fresh mushrooms	2 qts. boiling water
⅓ c. large pearl barley	1½ tblsp. butter
2 tsp. salt	¼ c. diced onion
¼ tsp. pepper	2 tblsp. flour
1½ tblsp. butter	½ c. milk
½ c. diced celery	Chopped fresh dill
½ c. diced carrots	

Wash mushrooms under gently flowing cold water; wipe dry and slice. Add mushrooms, barley, salt, pepper, 1½ tblsp. butter, celery and carrots to boiling water. Cover and simmer gently 1 hour, or until barley is tender. Stir every 20 minutes while cooking.

Meanwhile melt 1½ tblsp. butter in skillet; add onion and sauté until transparent (do not brown). Add flour and blend well. Add milk; cook and stir to make a smooth sauce. Add to soup, mixing well. Serve hot, garnished with dill. Makes about 6 servings.

GARDEN SANDWICHES

Texture contrast, flavor and gala color of filling appeal to almost everyone—it's a pleasing, attractive way to put vegetables in meals

2 c. frozen peas	1 c. cut-up peeled, firm tomatoes
2 c. cut-up peeled carrots	Homemade Mayonnaise
2 c. finely cut celery	24 slices bread

Cook peas by package directions in salted water, only cook less time; they should be slightly *undercooked*.

Cut carrots in small squares, the size of peas, and slightly undercook. Cut celery in pieces of the same size; do not cook.

Mix peas, carrots and celery to distribute vegetables evenly. Cover and refrigerate overnight.

At serving time, cut tomatoes in pieces the size of peas; add to vegetable mixture and toss lightly with just enough homemade or other mayonnaise to moisten vegetable mixture.

Spread on 12 whole wheat or other bread slices; top with remaining bread slices. Cut sandwiches diagonally in fourths. Makes 12 sandwiches.

HOMEMADE MAYONNAISE

Keep a jar of this in the refrigerator. It improves many salads

2 tblsp. flour	1¼ c. hot water
3 tblsp. cornstarch	1 egg
2 tblsp. sugar	2 c. salad oil
½ tsp. dry mustard	2 tblsp. lemon juice
1 tsp. salt	2 tblsp. vinegar

Mix flour, cornstarch, sugar, dry mustard and salt in saucepan. Add hot water; stir and cook to a thick paste. Cool.

Add egg to cooled mixture and beat well. Continue to beat while slowly and alternately adding oil, lemon juice and vinegar. Makes about 1 quart.

N O T E : If you wish to make mayonnaise in blender, start with the cooked paste when cooled. Put it in blender and add the other ingredients as directed in recipe.

FRESH APPLE CAKE

This is a moist spice cake with crisp top. It contains chopped apples

½ c. shortening	1 tsp. ground cinnamon
½ c. brown sugar, firmly packed	¾ tsp. ground nutmeg
1 c. sugar	½ tsp. ground cloves
2 eggs	1 c. buttermilk
2 tsp. baking soda	2 c. finely diced apples
2¼ c. flour	Topping

Cream together shortening and sugars until light and fluffy. Add eggs, one at a time, beating well after each addition.

Sift together baking soda, flour and spices. Add alternately with buttermilk to creamed mixture. Fold in apples. Pour into a greased and floured 13×9×2″ baking pan. Sprinkle with Topping.

Bake in moderate oven (350°) 45 to 50 minutes. Makes 12 servings.

Topping: Mix together ¼ c. brown sugar, firmly packed, ¼ c. sugar, ½ c. chopped nuts and 1½ tsp. ground cinnamon.

ACCENT-ON-YOUTH LUNCH

Egg Salad Dip   Crackers
Miniature Drumsticks   Corn Chips
Chilled Pineapple Juice   Baked Tuna Sandwiches*
Overnight Vegetable Salad*   Alabama French-Style Dressing*
Chocolate Ice Cream Float

The success of this meal depends to a large extent on making plenty of sandwiches. They're so good you may want to bake more than one batch. Active teen-age boys and girls often arrive at the table with ravenous appetites. Boys may say what they like is quantity, but when they and girls plan menus for their guests, they have decided ideas about what to serve and how a food tastes.

If the teen-ager has only a guest or two, the remainder of the family can join them at the table. So this menu is for a family lunch or supper, with the spotlight on youth favorites.

Egg salad, usually served as a sandwich filling, makes a great spread for crackers. The large joints of chicken wings (broiler-fryers), which resemble little drumsticks, rolled in seasoned flour and pan-fried in a little salad oil until golden, also win praise from young people. And always there are nibblers who like to munch on peanuts, potato and corn chips and other crisp foods.

TIMETABLE

Do-Ahead: Make sandwiches a day ahead and chill; they'll be ready to dip in batter and bake. Make the vegetable salad at least a day ahead, cover and chill. It stays in good condition for several days.

On Guest Day: Fry the chicken at any time convenient. Drain on paper toweling. Start dipping and baking sandwiches about an hour before time to serve them, especially if you bake two batches. Set out appetizers on buffet or on table in living room. Let the teen-age host or hostess fix and serve the dessert at serving time. For each cup of cold milk, beat in 2 tblsp. chocolate syrup and a small scoop of vanilla ice cream. Use the electric blender for the mixing if you have one. Serve in glasses with scoops of ice cream on top.

SERVING SUGGESTIONS

Serve the plates in the kitchen. Arrange a double sandwich (2 slices bread) on each plate and place the salad, well drained, in lettuce cups alongside. Have extra warm sandwiches waiting in a very low oven to pass for second helpings. If you wish to dress up the drumsticks, put paper frills on them (the kind used on lamb chops). A ketchup dip for the chicken wins the approval of most youngsters. If you wish to make it, stir (do not beat) 2 tblsp. prepared mustard into 1 c. ketchup. Serve in small bowls. Frost the egg salad in the bowl with dairy sour cream and sprinkle a finely chopped hard-cooked egg over the top for a party look. Serve teaspoons or iced beverage spoons with the dessert, the size depending on the size of the serving glasses.

BAKED TUNA SANDWICHES

Hot sandwiches are crusty and brown on outside with moist filling

1 can condensed cream of chicken soup	¾ c. milk
	8 slices white bread
1 tblsp. minced onion	2 eggs, beaten
2 tblsp. chopped pimiento	3 tblsp. milk
2 (7 oz.) cans water pack tuna, flaked	2 c. crushed potato chips
	½ c. chopped pecans
3 tblsp. flour	

Mix soup, onion, pimiento and tuna in saucepan. Blend flour with ¼ c. milk and add with remaining ½ c. milk to soup mixture. Cook, stirring, until thick. Cool; then chill.

Remove crusts from bread. Place 4 slices in bottom of any shallow baking pan. Spread with tuna mixture. Top with remaining bread slices. Cover and refrigerate overnight or at least several hours.

Blend eggs with 3 tblsp. milk. Cut each sandwich in half. Dip both sides into egg mixture, then in potato chips. Spread on greased baking sheet sprinkled with pecans. Bake in moderate oven (350°) 25 to 30 minutes. Makes 4 sandwiches (8 halves).

OVERNIGHT VEGETABLE SALAD

A tasty way to include a satisfactory quota of vegetables in a meal

1 (1 lb.) can peas, drained	4 c. celery cut in 1" matchsticks
2 (1 lb.) cans whole green beans	6 green onions, thinly sliced
½ c. sliced pimiento-stuffed olives	(about ¾ c.)
4 carrots, cut in 1" matchsticks	1½ c. Alabama French-Style
4 oz. slivered almonds	Dressing

Combine all ingredients, except dressing. Toss with Alabama French-Style Dressing. Cover and refrigerate overnight. Salad will keep several days in refrigerator. Makes about 3 quarts.

ALABAMA FRENCH-STYLE DRESSING

Keep handy in refrigerator—good served on green and fruit salads

1 c. salad oil	1 clove garlic, crushed
¼ c. vinegar	⅓ c. orange juice
1 tsp. Worcestershire sauce	¼ c. lemon juice
½ tsp. paprika	⅓ c. confectioners sugar
2 tsp. salt	½ tsp. dry mustard

Combine all ingredients; shake to mix well. Chill. Shake before using. Makes about 2 cups.

CHAPTER 3

Entertaining at Supper

. . . *GREAT EVENING MEALS*

When you ask country women the difference between a company supper and dinner, you get a variety of answers. But on one point everyone agrees . . . it is easier to invite friends to supper than dinner because the menu is less pretentious. For example, steaming hot, homemade Pleasant Valley Cheese/Vegetable Soup, a recipe in this chapter, takes the main-dish role in one of our supper menus.

Supper is expected to be a lighter meal than dinner and contains fewer foods, which makes it easier to get. Boys' Burger Supper, Chili Supper, Cook-In, Eat-Out Supper and Fondue Supper are hearty. And you'll notice that many of our suppers are more considerate of a tight food budget than those for company dinners. For instance, Barbecued Turkey Wings taste great and cost less than other turkey pieces.

The menus that follow are exceedingly good family meals, with a few touches that create a company atmosphere. Fruit-Jar Tomato Relish, for example, is really a fresh-from-the-garden, mixed vegetable salad you fix a day ahead in a glass fruit jar and chill until serving time. The varicolored layers add charm to the dish. Eliminates tossing a salad at the last minute, too.

So does Garden-Patch Salad, which consists of an expertly seasoned gelatin mixture that holds color-bright vegetables. It represents the many fix-ahead salads in this chapter that make clever and delicious use of vegetables when they are in bountiful supply. Consider Easygoing Summer Supper to share with friends on a sultry evening when cooking appeals to no one. Notice how again gelatin traps a variety of garden vegetables in a salad that refreshes.

The recipe for Chili con Carne in the Chili Supper comes from a ranch kitchen in southern Colorado, an area in which Spanish-Americans have farmed for many generations. The unusual addition is hominy, which makes a delicious difference.

There are many other distinctive recipes in this chapter. Grilled

Halibut Steaks and Grilled Minute Steak Rolls (the beef is rolled around butter) are two wonderful examples . . . and the handsome Salmon Loaf with Shrimp Sauce.

Look through this chapter and you'll make other discoveries for easy, successful entertaining.

Recipes for all dishes starred (*) are in this cookbook.

BOYS' BURGER SUPPER

Peanuts in Shell
Ground Beef Patties   Homemade Burger Buns*
Tomatoes   Dill and Sweet Pickles   Onions   Cheese
Ketchup   Mustard
Mom's Best Baked Beans*
Caramel Fondue* with Dippers
Milk   Soft Drinks

Forget your creative urge when your senior and junior high school sons entertain their friends. Give them hamburgers and make them happy. If you want to add a special touch, bake the buns yourself. The boys will appreciate the homemade taste. Set out the trimmings and let everyone build his own burger.

To help satisfy hungry boys fix our recipe for dressed up canned baked beans; heat them to blend flavors. End the meal with a dessert fondue with chunks of fruit and marshmallows to dip. Such a menu pleases 99 out of 100 boys, and especially if bowls of peanuts in shell are on hand to satisfy the nibblers.

TIMETABLE

Do-Ahead: Bake the buns the day before (or several days ahead and freeze them).

On Guest Day: If buns are frozen, thaw them at room temperature in their wrap; this will take from 2 to 3 hours. Put the beans in the oven about an hour before serving time. Shortly before supper, slice the tomatoes, pickles, onions and cheese (unless you buy packaged slices). Cook the beef patties the last half hour before mealtime. Use an electric grill or a skillet, or broil them if you prefer. Make them about ½″ smaller than buns. While the boys eat, get the fondue ready. Cut the unpeeled apples and bananas in bite-size chunks;

sprinkle with lemon juice diluted with water to prevent discoloration if they have long to wait. Set out a bowl of marshmallows. Make a second batch of Caramel Fondue and keep warm in double boiler over hot water so you'll be ready to replenish it if needed. Or use two fondue pots if there are more than four or five boys.

SERVING SUGGESTIONS

Serve the supper buffet style indoors or out, as weather and situation dictate. Place the hot burgers in the buns and arrange them on a platter alongside serving plates (these can be paper). On a tray arrange alternate rows of tomato, onion, pickle and cheese slices. Set a bottle of ketchup and a jar of prepared mustard nearby. If you have a bean pot, bake and serve the beans in it; a casserole will do. Place drinking glasses and bottles of soft drinks, inserted in an ice-filled bucket, within easy reach. And don't forget the pitcher of milk, for many boys are great milk drinkers. When the main course is eaten, bring out the fondue, set it over the burner (or at low heat if using an electric pot or skillet—which is safer), and then carry out the dippers—marshmallows, apples and bananas. Provide bowls or trays to hold peanut shells.

HOMEMADE BURGER BUNS

Boys prefer plain buns, so you may omit sesame and poppy seeds

2 pkgs. active dry yeast	2 c. water
¼ c. sugar	2 eggs, beaten
½ c. warm water (110 to 115°)	½ c. salad oil or melted
6 c. sifted flour	shortening
½ c. nonfat dry milk (not	1 egg, beaten
reconstituted)	Milk
1 tblsp. salt	Sesame or poppy seeds (optional)

Combine yeast, sugar and water; let stand until yeast softens. Stir to dissolve.

Sift together flour, dry milk and salt into large bowl. Make a well in center and pour in the water, yeast, 2 beaten eggs and oil. Mix well; cover and let rise in a warm place 1 hour.

Turn dough onto well-floured board (dough may be sticky), turn a few times to coat dough well with flour. Pinch off pieces about the size of an egg; place smooth side up about 3″ apart on greased baking sheet. Brush with mixture of 1 beaten egg (or egg yolk) and a little milk; then sprinkle with sesame or poppy seeds, if desired.

Let rise 20 minutes. Bake in hot oven (425°) 8 to 12 minutes, or until done. Makes about 30 buns.

MOM'S BEST BAKED BEANS

You can fix these beans in an uncovered skillet in about 20 minutes. Bring them to a boil, then simmer gently, stirring occasionally

6 bacon slices
1 c. finely chopped onions
⅓ c. ketchup

2 tsp. prepared mustard
3 (about 1 lb. 3 oz.) cans pork and beans

Cut bacon in small pieces with kitchen scissors; cook with onions in skillet, stirring until bacon is crisp. Stir in ketchup, mustard and beans. Pour into ungreased 2-qt. casserole or bean pot and bake uncovered in moderate oven (350°) 40 to 45 minutes. Serves 8.

CARAMEL FONDUE

Caramel sauce coats the dippers with a delicious glaze. Keep it warm; if it gets too hot fondue runs off dippers and also may scorch

1 (14 oz.) pkg. vanilla caramels
⅓ c. water
Dash of salt

Marshmallows, apple and banana pieces

Place caramels and water in top of double boiler and heat over water until melted. Stir in salt. Pour sauce into fondue pot and set over fondue burner. (If boys are young teens, stick around for safety's sake—boys will be boys.) Keep warm (not hot) over low heat. If sauce gets too thick, stir in a little warm water.

Let boys spear marshmallow or bite-size chunks of unpeeled apple or banana (if fruit has been dipped in lemon juice diluted with water, it should be dry and at room temperature) on fondue forks or bamboo skewers and dip into the fondue. Makes 1⅓ cups sauce, about 4 servings.

TEEN-AGE SUPPER

Sardine/Egg Spread*
Crackers   Cherry Tomatoes
Orange Fizz
Southwestern Ham Rolls*
Speedy Bean Skillet*
Choco/Date Squares*
Snack Bowl*

The girl who planned this menu thinks young. That's not surprising for she's sweet sixteen. Proof of her wisdom in selecting the right foods was the speed with which the supper disappeared after the high school crowd arrived. And it's a meal a girl can get without her mother's help.

TIMETABLE

Do-Ahead: Either make the cookies a day ahead, cool and place in tightly covered container, or bake them the morning of the supper.

On Guest Day: Fix the ham rolls, wrap in foil and refrigerate. Make the sardine spread at any time convenient; cover and chill. Put the ham rolls in the oven to heat 1 hour before supper. Put the beans on to heat about 20 minutes before you want to serve them. Reconstitute frozen orange juice for the Orange Fizz, pour into a pitcher and chill. Finish the Orange Fizz just before serving: Usually a boy will volunteer to open the chilled ginger ale and add an equal amount of it to the orange juice, while one of the girls adds a spoonful of orange sherbet to each glass. Young guests like to help their hostess.

SERVING SUGGESTIONS

Serve the food buffet style. Bring out the Sardine/Egg Spread in a bowl along with a tray of crackers and knives for spreading. To give the spread color, scatter snipped fresh parsley over it. Set out a bowl of cherry tomatoes; have a shaker of seasoned salt nearby. Serve the orange drink with straws. Serve the ham rolls in their foil wrap; the beans in an attractive casserole. And to end the feast, serve the Snack Bowl and Choco/Date Squares.

SARDINE/EGG SPREAD

Ingredients for this tasty appetizer usually are on hand

2 (3¾ oz.) cans sardines in oil
2 hard-cooked eggs, finely
 chopped

¼ c. mayonnaise
2 to 3 tblsp. lemon juice
¼ c. finely chopped pecans

Drain oil from sardines. Place them in a bowl and mash with a fork. Add remaining ingredients and blend well. Makes 2 cups.

SOUTHWESTERN HAM ROLLS

If you prefer a milder filling, split buns, insert a slice each of baked ham and process American cheese, wrap in foil; chill. To serve, heat in moderate oven (350°) 25 minutes; serve in foil, opened at top

1 (12 oz.) can chopped ham, or
 2 c. cubed cooked ham
¾ lb. grated or cubed sharp
 Cheddar cheese
1 large onion, chopped
1 (4½ oz.) can chopped ripe
 olives

1 (4 oz.) can whole green chili
 peppers
1 (8 oz.) can tomato sauce
2 tblsp. vinegar
Hard rolls (10 to 12)

Mix all the ingredients, except the rolls.

Slice off tops of hard rolls, scoop out inside (save for crumbs) and fill with ham-cheese mixture. Replace tops on rolls and wrap individually in foil. Bake in very slow oven (275°) 1 hour. Makes 10 to 12 servings.

SPEEDY BEAN SKILLET

A bean bowl accented with franks pleases the boys and fills them up

2 tblsp. butter or regular
 margarine
1 c. diced peeled tomatoes

¼ tsp. crushed orégano leaves
2 (1 lb.) cans beans and franks in
 tomato sauce

Melt butter in skillet; add tomatoes and orégano. Cook a couple of minutes to blend flavors. Stir in beans. Heat, stirring frequently, until piping hot. Makes 6 servings.

CHOCO/DATE SQUARES

Cookies made with ready-to-eat cereals rate high with young people

1 c. chopped dates
½ c. butter or regular margarine
⅓ c. sugar

2 c. crisp rice cereal
6 squares semisweet chocolate

Combine dates, butter and sugar in saucepan; heat until butter is melted and dates are tender; remove from heat and add crisp rice cereal. Mix well with spoon.

Press mixture into 8″ square pan and cool.

Melt chocolate over very low heat and spread over date cookies. When completely cool, cut in small squares. Makes about 24 small cookies.

SNACK BOWL

The teen-age crowd goes for fruit-nut-candy mixes

2 c. light or dark raisins
2 c. salted redskin peanuts

2 c. candy-coated chocolate pieces

Stir ingredients to distribute evenly. Serve in attractive glass bowl. Makes 6 cups.

EASYGOING SUMMER SUPPER

Platter of Cold Cuts   Vegetable Salad Mold*
Buttered Hot Rolls
Lemon Sherbet   Brownies

Collect some fresh vegetables in a salad that you can make ahead and you have a good start on a delightful summer company meal. The salad in this menu is a California special inspired by the famous cold Spanish vegetable soup, gazpacho. Add a generous platter of cold meats that have variety in color, flavor and texture—slices of liver sausage, salami and large bologna, for instance—and Swiss cheese. If you have a meat loaf in the freezer, by all means include slices of that.

Add buttered hot rolls and you have the main course planned. If the weather isn't too hot, bake a batch of baking powder biscuits instead of warming ready-made rolls. It's fast work with packaged biscuit mix. Generations of farm women have relied on hot bread to give meals a special appeal. You'll want to open a jar of berry jam or peach preserves. And do remember how good honey is on hot, buttered biscuits.

For dessert, we give you two suggestions: lemon sherbet with some kind of chocolate cookies, or chilled small cantaloupe halves with a scoop of lime sherbet in the center.

N O T E : To convert this supper into a dinner, add sweet corn on the cob to the menu.

TIMETABLE

Do-Ahead: Make salad a day ahead, or at least in the morning for evening serving. For serving more than 5, make two molds of salad.

On Guest Day: Shortly before suppertime, heat buttered rolls (wrapped in foil) in moderate oven (350°) 10 to 15 minutes. Arrange cold cuts and cheese on platter. Unmold the salad on lettuce or other greens.

SERVING SUGGESTIONS

Garnish ends and center of cold meat platter with spiced crab apples, your best sweet pickles or small clusters of seedless green grapes. Or use perky sprigs of parsley. Serve salad at table or individual servings on salad plates lined with crisp lettuce. Pass salad dressing to make it optional. Try to serve the rolls piping hot in a napkin-lined and covered basket, or in a roll warmer.

VEGETABLE SALAD MOLD

Western hostesses use hot green chili peppers in this but you can use the more widely available and milder green pepper

1 envelope unflavored gelatin
1½ c. tomato juice
1 large ripe tomato, peeled
2 tblsp. vinegar or pickle juice
1 medium cucumber, peeled and finely chopped
1 peeled and seeded green chili pepper, finely chopped, or about ¼ c. chopped sweet green pepper

½ c. finely chopped celery
¼ c. finely chopped onion
1 tsp. garlic salt
⅛ tsp. pepper
¼ tsp. orégano leaves
Greens

Soften gelatin in ¼ c. tomato juice 5 minutes.

Meanwhile, heat 1 c. tomato juice; add the gelatin mixture and stir to dissolve.

Chop fresh tomato, saving the juice. Combine vinegar, remaining ¼ c. tomato juice and juice from tomato (add water if necessary to make ½ c. liquid). Add fresh tomato and add to hot gelatin mixture with cucumber, green chili, celery, onion, garlic salt, pepper and orégano. Pour into 1-qt. mold. Chill until firm. To serve, unmold on greens. Makes about 6 servings.

WESTERN BUFFET SUPPER

California Chicken*   Baked Almond Rice*
Garden-Patch Salad*
Hot Roll Ring*   Berry Preserves
Orange-Glazed Cake*

You can almost hear the Pacific breakers when you serve and eat this wonderful meal . . . it consists of the kinds of food highly esteemed in California. The chicken has an exciting Americanized oriental taste. This comes from the soy sauce and faint sweet-sour flavor of pineapple juice and sugar. It is a main dish that can wait in the oven a bit without deteriorating when dinner is delayed.

Rice cooked in the oven in a *tightly* covered casserole is easy, fluffy and flavorful with almonds, butter and chicken broth. It bakes at the same temperature as the chicken.

Amazing how good the salad tastes. It assumes the role of vegetables in the menu. The ring of little hot rolls always fascinates— guests like to pull off a roll, drop a bit of melted butter and a sweet spread on it. You'd better bake two rings!

The Orange-Glazed Cake tops off the meal in great country style. All that's needed to make the supper a huge success is a big pot of hot coffee.

TIMETABLE

Do-Ahead: Get the salad in the refrigerator a day ahead. You can bake the cake and rolls a day or several days ahead, wrap in foil and freeze.

On Guest Day: All you have to cook is the chicken dish, which needs an hour in the oven, and the rice, which bakes only half an hour. You do baste the chicken four times while it cooks, but the taste results are worth the effort. If the rolls are baked ahead, reheat them in a moderate oven (350°) 20 to 25 minutes if frozen, 10 to 15 minutes if at room temperature. Remove foil wrapping after heating.

SERVING SUGGESTIONS

Raid your cupboard for your most delectable jam, preserves or marmalade. If you have a divided relish dish, you can generate a lot of praise by offering more than one kind.

CALIFORNIA CHICKEN

Excellent dish to serve a crowd. Double or triple the recipe. It's important to be faithful in the basting while the chicken cooks

⅔ c. flour	4 whole chicken breasts, split,
1 tsp. salt	skinned and boned
½ tsp. celery salt	¼ c. melted butter
½ tsp. garlic salt	1 c. pineapple juice
½ tsp. ground nutmeg	½ c. soy sauce
	2 tblsp. sugar

Mix together flour, salt, celery salt, garlic salt and nutmeg; dredge chicken in mixture. Brown chicken in melted butter in skillet. Transfer to roasting pan.

Combine pineapple juice, soy sauce and sugar; mix well and pour over chicken. Bake uncovered in moderate oven (350°) 1 hour, basting every 15 minutes. Makes 4 servings.

BAKED ALMOND RICE

Ideal way to cook rice for an oven meal. It's easy and tastes good

3 c. boiling chicken broth or
    water
1½ c. regular rice, uncooked
1¼ tsp. salt

¾ c. slivered almonds
3 tblsp. butter or regular
    margarine

Mix broth, rice and salt in ungreased 3-qt. casserole (or a 13×9×2″ baking pan). Cover *tightly*—use aluminum foil to cover pan. Bake in moderate oven (350°) 25 to 30 minutes, until liquid is absorbed and rice is tender.

Meanwhile, lightly brown almonds in butter. Add to hot, cooked rice and toss to mix. Makes 6 to 8 servings.

GARDEN-PATCH SALAD

Lemon gelatin accented with tarragon vinegar holds six vegetables

2 (3 oz.) pkgs. lemon flavor
    gelatin
2 c. hot water
1½ c. cold water
¼ c. tarragon vinegar
½ tsp. salt
2 c. finely chopped cabbage

½ c. thinly sliced carrots
½ c. chopped celery
¼ c. chopped green pepper
¼ c. thinly sliced radishes
2 tblsp. thinly sliced green onion,
    including some of green top
2 tblsp. pickle relish

Dissolve gelatin in hot water. Add cold water, vinegar and salt; pour into 2-qt. mold or an 11×7×1½″ glass dish and chill until mixture is partially set (the consistency of unbeaten egg white).

Add vegetables and pickle relish to gelatin and chill until firm. Serve with salad dressing if you like. Makes 8 to 10 servings.

HOT ROLL RING

Have a bowl of melted butter in open center of the ring—spoon it on

1 (13¾ oz.) pkg. hot roll mix
¾ c. warm water

1 egg
⅓ c. melted butter

Follow package directions for mixing dough with water and egg. Place dough in lightly greased bowl, invert to grease top; cover and let rise until doubled.

Roll dough ¼" thick on lightly floured board. The rectangle will be about 16×12". Cut in diamond-shaped pieces about 3×2". Dip each piece in melted butter and arrange in ungreased 9" ring mold, overlapping pieces. Let rise until doubled, about 30 minutes.

Bake in moderate oven (375°) 20 to 25 minutes. Remove from oven, unmold while very warm and brush lightly with butter. Serve top side up. Makes one 9" ring, 40 diamonds or rolls.

ORANGE-GLAZED CAKE

A pour-on orange glaze dresses up and flavors this raisin-nut cake

½ c. shortening	½ tsp. salt
1 c. brown sugar, firmly packed	½ tsp. baking soda
2 eggs	1 c. buttermilk
1 tsp. lemon extract	1 c. seedless raisins
½ tsp. maple flavoring	½ c. chopped walnuts
2 c. sifted cake flour	Peel of 1 orange
1 tsp. baking powder	Orange Glaze

Cream shortening and brown sugar thoroughly. Add eggs one at a time, beating well after each addition. Add flavorings.

Sift together flour, baking powder, salt and soda. Add alternately with buttermilk to creamed mixture. Put raisins, walnuts and orange peel through food chopper and stir into cake batter. Pour into greased 9" square cake pan.

Bake in moderate oven (350°) 40 minutes. Remove from oven and let stand in pan 5 minutes. Pour Orange Glaze over cake while it is still in pan. Cool on rack.

Orange Glaze: Combine 1 c. sugar and ⅓ c. orange juice; stir to dissolve. Pour over warm cake.

SUPPER DELICIOUS

Broiled Ham/Pineapple Patties*
Tart Barbecue Sauce*
Maple Sweet Potatoes*
Tossed Green Salad
Nutmeg Cake*
Green Grapes with Sour Cream and Brown Sugar

If you've been looking for a distinctively different supper that's exceptionally delicious, use this menu. The patties of smoky ham and ground beef with juicy pineapple rings on top have both eye and taste appeal. The fruity basting sauce heightens flavor.

The golden cake powdered with confectioners sugar is out of this world in flavor. And it's so easily baked. Chilled green grapes in a sour cream and brown sugar sauce are an eating experience your guests will not forget.

TIMETABLE

Do-Ahead: Bake the cake a day ahead if you like. Make the basting sauce for the meat patties; cool, cover and chill. Wash, drain and chill salad greens in plastic bag.

On Guest Day: Prepare seedless green grapes several hours before suppertime. Remove from stems, wash, drain and place in an 8" square baking pan. Cover with dairy sour cream and sprinkle generously with brown sugar. Start cooking the meat patties about 25 minutes before time to serve. Meanwhile, glaze canned sweet potatoes. Toss the salad just before serving.

SERVING SUGGESTIONS

This is a sit-down dinner. At dessert time, spoon the grapes into stemmed dessert glasses, or in goblets, filling half full. Serve on plate with cake alongside.

BROILED HAM/PINEAPPLE PATTIES

An unusual feature of these patties is that they contain ground beef and ham. Fruit juices and chopped vegetables make sauce special

1½ lbs. ground cooked ham	6 slices pineapple
½ lb. ground beef	Tart Barbecue Sauce

Mix together ground ham and beef. Shape into 6 patties about ¾" thick. Press a pineapple slice firmly into the top of each patty. Place patties, pineapple side down, on cold broiler grid.

Broil 12 to 15 minutes on one side, brushing occasionally with Tart Barbecue Sauce. Carefully turn and broil 4 to 6 minutes on other side, brushing occasionally with sauce. Makes 6 servings.

TART BARBECUE SAUCE

Blend of flavors that can't be surpassed for ham and pineapple

1 onion, grated	1 tsp. prepared mustard
2 tblsp. salad oil	½ c. pineapple juice
¼ c. lemon juice	½ c. chopped celery
2 tblsp. brown sugar	½ c. finely chopped green pepper
1 c. ketchup	2 tblsp. Worcestershire sauce

Combine all ingredients in medium-size saucepan. Stir to blend. Cover and simmer gently 30 to 40 minutes, stirring occasionally. Makes about 1½ cups.

MAPLE SWEET POTATOES

Maple syrup enhances flavor and gives attractive glaze

1 c. maple-blended syrup	2 (17 oz.) cans vacuum pack
½ c. butter or regular margarine	sweet potatoes, drained

Combine syrup and butter in 2-qt. saucepan; bring to a boil and cook until thickened.

Add sweet potatoes; simmer until hot, basting occasionally with glaze. Makes 8 servings.

NUTMEG CAKE

Surprisingly easy cake to make and surprisingly good eating

1 pkg. yellow cake mix (for
  2-layer cake)
¾ c. salad oil
¾ c. dry sherry or sauterne
4 eggs

1 (3¾ oz.) pkg. vanilla instant
  pudding
¾ tsp. ground nutmeg
Confectioners sugar

Combine cake mix, oil and wine in mixing bowl. Blend thoroughly. Add eggs, one at a time, mixing well after each addition. Add vanilla pudding and nutmeg; beat 3 minutes at medium speed on mixer.

Pour into greased and floured 10″ tube or fluted tube pan. Bake in moderate oven (350°) about 45 minutes, or until cake tests done. Cool on rack.

When cool, remove cake carefully from pan and lightly dust with confectioners sugar.

GARDEN SUPPER

Melon Appetizer
Crab/Zucchini Casserole*
Buttered Peas
Cucumber Bowl*
Lemon/Raspberry Parfait*

This meal is not served in the garden, but comes from there. It features one of the most prolific vegetables, zucchini. When your vines are producing more of the squash than you know how to use, entertain your friends at this supper. The zucchini combined with crabmeat and Swiss cheese is so delicious that you'll want to serve it again and again. Your guests will ask for the recipe and if they don't have a garden will hope for a handout of the plentiful zucchini. The casserole is filling and its red (diced tomato) and brown top gives it eye appeal.

The cucumbers make a perfect accompaniment. You can substitute asparagus for peas, if you wish.

Start the meal with cubes of watermelon, cantaloupe and honeydew. Squeeze lime or lemon juice over them. For dessert, serve chilled lemon tapioca cream pudding, a country favorite, teamed with raspberries.

TIMETABLE

On Guest Day: Prepare the cucumbers at any time during the day and chill. Make the tapioca and chill; assemble the dessert at serving time. About 35 minutes before dinnertime, put the casserole in the oven to bake. Meanwhile, cook and season the peas.

CRAB/ZUCCHINI CASSEROLE

For a women's luncheon you can bake this in buttered scallop shells

1¼ lbs. zucchini (about 5 small)	2 cloves garlic, crushed
1 medium onion, chopped	1 (7½ oz.) can crabmeat
1 stick butter (¼ lb.)	1⅓ c. small sticks of Swiss cheese
½ tsp. salt	1 tsp. sweet basil leaves
Dash of pepper	1 c. fresh bread crumbs
3 medium tomatoes, peeled	

Wash unpeeled zucchini, cut in ½" slices. Sauté with chopped onion in two thirds stick of butter, but do not brown. Add salt and pepper.

Cut tomatoes coarsely.

Sauté garlic and crabmeat briefly in remaining one third stick of butter. Discard garlic. Fold crabmeat into zucchini-onion mixture. Add cheese (in matchlike strips), tomatoes, basil and bread crumbs. Pour into a greased 2-qt. casserole.

Bake, uncovered, in moderate oven (350°) 30 to 35 minutes. Makes 8 servings.

CUCUMBER BOWL

Dill weed, wine vinegar and thorough chilling make this special

4 medium cucumbers, peeled and thinly sliced	1 tsp. salt
	1 tsp. wine vinegar
1½ c. dairy sour cream	½ tsp. dill weed
2 tblsp. salad oil	Chopped fresh parsley or chives
2 tsp. sugar	

Slice cucumbers into a bowl.

Mix sour cream, salad oil, sugar, salt and vinegar. Pour over cucumbers. Toss gently to mix. Sprinkle with dill weed. Cover and chill at least 1 hour, or a few hours.

To serve country style, leave in bowl and sprinkle with chopped parsley or chives. Makes 8 servings.

LEMON/RASPBERRY PARFAIT

If you don't have parfait glasses serve in stemmed dessert glasses; place a layer of raspberries in the bottom of glass and on top

¼ c. quick-cooking tapioca	Grated peel of 1 lemon
¾ c. sugar	½ c. heavy cream
¼ tsp. salt	1 c. sweetened red raspberries, or
2¼ c. water	1 (10 oz.) pkg. frozen
¼ c. lemon juice	raspberries

Combine tapioca, sugar, salt and water in saucepan; let stand 5 minutes. Bring just to a boil over medium heat, stirring occasionally. Remove from heat and stir in lemon juice and peel; cool.

Whip cream and fold into tapioca mixture. Chill. Spoon alternate layers tapioca and raspberries in parfait glasses, ending with raspberries. Makes 6 servings.

IMPROMPTU FISH BARBECUE

Grilled Halibut Steaks*
Tomato/Macaroni Salad*
Hard Rolls
Honeyed Fruit Compote*
Homemade Cookies
Hot Coffee   Iced Tea

Impromptu entertaining radiates an easygoing charm of its own. You telephone the invitations on the day of the party when you are in a social mood and no rain is predicted. Advance preparations are impossible, but you can make do with what you have or can get in a hurry. Few ways of sharing food with friends excel the spontaneous cookout.

Actually, with this menu, all you cook is the macaroni for the salad, and the fish. You (or your husband) can pick up the halibut steaks and any other needed supplies at the supermarket. Of course he will check the charcoal supply.

The substantial salad, enlivened by ripe tomatoes, complements the fish. All you need to round out the meal is a compote of melons and fruits. If you have homemade cookies in the freezer or cookie jar, by all means bring out a plate full. (Perhaps you have a daughter who can bake a batch of cookies for you.)

TIMETABLE

On Guest Day: Cook the macaroni and fix the salad as early in the day as you can, to give flavors a chance to blend. Add the tomato quarters just before serving. Make the fruit compote at least an hour, or several hours ahead, cover and chill. When the host has the coals at the right stage for cooking the fish, bring the other foods to the table. Fish cooks in about 10 minutes.

SERVING SUGGESTIONS

Eat indoors or out, whichever place seems more inviting.

GRILLED HALIBUT STEAKS

The smoky flavor makes fish taste good; lemon, parsley add color

8 halibut steaks (about ¼ lb. each)	Salt
2 small cloves garlic, cut in halves	Paprika
6 tblsp. salad oil	4 to 6 tblsp. Toasted Sesame
6 tblsp. lemon juice	Seeds (see Index)

Rub halibut on both sides with cut garlic clove; brush with salad oil. Sprinkle with lemon juice (bottled lemon juice is easy to use) and salt. Place on grill about 4″ above medium-hot coals.

Cook about 5 minutes; turn. Sprinkle top of steaks with paprika and Toasted Sesame Seeds. Cook 5 minutes longer, or until the fish is done. Test for doneness with a fork; if the fish flakes easily, it is ready to serve. Serve at once with lemon wedges and chopped parsley. Makes 8 servings.

TOMATO/MACARONI SALAD

Young boys coming to the barbecue? If so, use bow-tie macaroni

½ lb. bow-tie or seashell macaroni	¼ tsp. pepper
1 c. diced celery	½ tsp. celery seeds
1 green pepper, chopped	¼ c. mayonnaise
2 tblsp. finely chopped onions	⅓ c. creamy French dressing
3 tblsp. finely chopped fresh	4 large tomatoes, peeled and cut
parsley, or 1½ tblsp. dried	in wedges and sprinkled lightly
parsley flakes	with salt
1¼ tsp. salt	Lettuce

Cook macaroni in boiling salted water by package directions; rinse under cold water, drain and cool. Combine macaroni and all ingredients except tomatoes and lettuce. Cover and chill until serving time. Fold in tomato wedges, serve on lettuce. Makes 8 servings.

HONEYED FRUIT COMPOTE

Serve in a big bowl and let everyone help himself. Set a filled cookie jar on table. Refill coffee cups and iced tea glasses

1 cantaloupe	1 c. strained honey
1 honeydew or casaba melon	1 (1 lb.) can apricots (about 2 c.)
2 large peaches	1 c. juice from apricots (about)
2 Bartlett pears	

Cut each melon in half, remove seeds and peel off rind and unedible portions. Cut each melon half in eighths. Peel peaches, remove pits and cut in serving-size pieces. Cut pears in halves (no need to peel) and remove cores; cut in serving-size pieces.

Add honey to canned apricots. Stir in liquid drained from apricots. Mix all the ingredients together with a light hand, cover and let stand 30 minutes to 1 hour. Let guests help themselves. Makes 8 servings.

SUNDAY SUPPER

Seafood Supper Soup*
Toasted French Bread Slices
Assorted Relishes
Easy Pear Torte*
Hot Tea or Coffee

Keep the ingredients for this meal in your kitchen and you'll always be ready for a good family meal to share with guests. When friends telephone late on a dreary Sunday afternoon and suggest dropping in for a brief visit, rise to the occasion and invite them to stay for an early supper. That's true country hospitality.

TIMETABLE

Do-Ahead: Before your guests arrive, get the torte in the oven. It's easy, fast, delicious and different. Check the freezer to find out if you have a jar of hard sauce. If not, bring out the mixer and beat up the fluffy sauce in a jiffy. Put in refrigerator. Take fish filets from freezer to thaw partially so you can cut them in slices. Thaw the frozen bread in its foil wrap. And if there is time, start opening cans from the cupboard shelf and some of your choice relishes.

On Guest Day: For the finishing touches, put the soup on to cook, open the bread and spread it on the grid to toast later in the broiling oven. (Be glad you sliced the loaf before you wrapped and froze it.) Arrange some of your choice pickles and a spiced fruit on a tray. Take the torte from the oven and toast the bread. Make tea or coffee.

SERVING SUGGESTIONS

Carry the relishes and toast to the table. Ladle the steaming soup into bowls in the kitchen, or if you prefer, turn it into a tureen and serve it at the table. A good way to brighten the evening for friends.

SEAFOOD SUPPER SOUP

After one spoonful you'll know people do not have to live near an ocean to enjoy tasty seafood dishes. Expert seasonings help

1 (1 lb. 12 oz.) can tomatoes, cut up
2 c. water
1 (7½ oz.) can minced clams
1 medium onion, chopped
½ c. chopped celery
¼ c. chopped green pepper
1 clove garlic, minced
1 tsp. salt
¼ tsp. thyme leaves, crushed
⅛ tsp. pepper
1 lb. frozen fish filets, partially thawed
1 (10 oz.) pkg. frozen green beans
Parmesan cheese

In a large kettle, combine tomatoes, water, clams, onion, celery, green pepper (maybe some you froze), garlic, salt, thyme and pepper. Cover; bring to a boil and simmer gently 15 minutes.

Meanwhile, cut block of fish filets in half lengthwise, then crosswise in ½" slices. Add to kettle along with green beans. Bring to a boil and simmer 15 minutes, or until green beans are tender. Pass Parmesan cheese at table to sprinkle over top. Makes 6 servings.

EASY PEAR TORTE

Dried fruits have been important in country cooking from pioneer days. Many heirloom dishes depend on them for flavor. This is a combination of the old and the new. It is surprisingly delicious

¼ c. butter or regular margarine
¾ c. sugar
3 eggs
1 tsp. vanilla
¼ tsp. ground cinnamon
1 pie crust stick, finely crumbled
1 c. snipped dried pears
½ c. snipped dates
½ c. chopped nuts
Fluffy Hard Sauce

Cream butter with sugar; add eggs, vanilla and cinnamon and beat well. Stir in crumbled pie crust stick, pears, dates and nuts.

Spread in greased 9" pie pan. Bake in slow oven (325°) 45 to 50 minutes. Serve warm, cut in wedges and topped with Fluffy Hard Sauce. Makes 6 servings.

Fluffy Hard Sauce: Cream ½ c. butter or regular margarine with 2 c. sifted confectioners sugar until fluffy. Add 1 tsp. vanilla and 1 egg yolk; beat well. Fold in 1 egg white, stiffly beaten. Chill.

FRESH-AS-A-DAISY SUPPER

Artichoke/Tuna Casserole*
Marinated Tomatoes*   Bread Sticks
Lemon Angel Pie*

A hostess who serves this meal to friends calls it her fresh-as-a-daisy menu. This, she insists, is the way she feels when she greets her company—after getting the supper. And it describes the way the food tastes and looks.

The menu wanders off the beaten path a bit: Artichoke hearts and cashews are not everyday ingredients but they lift the tuna, rice and cream of celery soup casserole above the commonplace. Chilling thick, ripe tomato slices in salad dressing gives them time to absorb and blend flavors. This is an old trick in country kitchens, where layers of sliced tomatoes, cucumbers and onions often chill several hours in seasoned vinegar.

Lemon Angel Pie, correctly named, is not a new dessert, especially to anyone who ever has lived in or visited Milwaukee or other areas along Lake Michigan's shores to the north where people of German ancestry live. Our version is a revised one, which is superlative, we think—queen of make-ahead desserts.

TIMETABLE

Do-Ahead: Make the dessert a day ahead (all but adding whipped cream) and refrigerate.

On Guest Day: Pour the salad dressing over the tomatoes and chill several hours, or until very cold. You can also fix the casserole several hours ahead and refrigerate. It needs to bake at least 1½ hours to heat (until the center bubbles). While it bakes, you have ample time to set the table and arrange a centerpiece.

SERVING SUGGESTIONS

This meal needs no garnishes because the food itself has eyes appeal—the browned casserole, the ripe red tomatoes, buttercup-yellow pie filling in a brown-tipped meringue shell.

NOTE: To convert this supper or luncheon into a dinner, add buttered asparagus or peas to the menu and substitute hot buttered rolls for the bread sticks.

ARTICHOKE/TUNA CASSEROLE

This is a very pretty dish—one you'll add to your list of favorites. You can substitute ⅓ cup fresh lemon juice for the ½ cup wine

2 (10 oz.) pkgs. frozen artichoke hearts

2 cans condensed cream of celery soup

½ c. dry white wine or ⅓ c. lemon juice

2 (7 oz.) cans tuna, drained and flaked

¾ c. coarsely chopped cashew nuts

¾ c. regular rice (uncooked)

1 c. water

1 tsp. salt

⅔ c. bread crumbs

1½ tblsp. melted butter

Cook artichoke hearts as directed on package; drain.

Combine soup and wine in a small saucepan; bring to a boil, stirring occasionally.

Layer half the artichokes, tuna, cashews and soup mixture in a 2-qt. casserole. Add all the rice, water and salt. Repeat with layers of remaining artichokes, tuna, cashews and soup mixture.

Toss bread crumbs with melted butter and sprinkle over casserole. Cover and bake in slow oven (325°) 1 to 1½ hours. Makes 6 to 8 servings.

MARINATED TOMATOES

Stir tomatoes in the marinade a few times to distribute flavor

5 large ripe tomatoes

¼ c. salad oil

1½ c. red wine vinegar

½ clove garlic, minced

¼ tsp. salt

½ tsp. orégano leaves

¼ tsp. pepper

Greens (optional)

Peel tomatoes, cut in thick slices and put in bowl.

Combine remaining ingredients, except greens, and pour over tomatoes. Cover and chill thoroughly. Serve on greens, or if you prefer, in bowl. Makes 6 to 8 servings.

LEMON ANGEL PIE

This meringue shell is a versatile dessert base—for a change from lemon, fill meringue at serving time with vanilla ice cream and top with fresh strawberries or sliced fresh peaches, sugared lightly

Meringue Shell:
  3 egg whites (⅓ to ½ c.)
  ¼ tsp. cream of tartar
  ¾ c. sugar
Lemon Filling:
  ¾ c. sugar
  3 tblsp. cornstarch

  ¼ tsp. salt
  3 egg yolks, slightly beaten
  ¼ c. water
  1 tblsp. butter or regular
    margarine
  1¼ tsp. grated lemon peel
  ⅓ c. fresh lemon juice
  1 c. heavy cream, whipped

To make shell, beat egg whites with cream of tartar until frothy. Gradually beat in sugar, 1 tblsp. at a time. Beat until glossy and very stiff (do not underbeat). Use your electric mixer.

Spread on heavy brown paper covering baking sheet to make a 9″ round, building up sides with spoon to make a rim as for a pie shell. Bake in very slow oven (275°) 1½ hours; turn off heat and leave meringue in oven, door closed, for 1 hour. Remove and cool completely away from drafts.

Meanwhile, prepare filling. Blend sugar, cornstarch and salt in saucepan. Combine egg yolks with water; gradually stir into mixture in saucepan. Cook over medium heat, stirring constantly, until mixture thickens and comes to a boil. Boil 1 minute, stirring. Remove from heat and stir in butter, lemon peel and juice. Cool to room temperature.

Spread cooled filling in meringue shell and refrigerate overnight, or at least 12 hours. Top with whipped cream before serving. Makes 8 servings.

SUPPER SPECIAL

Salmon Loaf with Shrimp Sauce*
Buttered Peas and Carrots
Hot Rolls
Homemade Pickles
Pineapple/Cheese Salad*

When you return home from an afternoon meeting, bringing guests for supper, you want to serve a superior meal with a minimum of work at the last minute. This menu has that kind of timetable. While many recipe files contain directions for making salmon loaves, this one we consider champion of them all. Seasoned expertly and subtly, it tastes extra good.

The fruit salad is substantial enough to serve as both salad and dessert.

TIMETABLE

Do-Ahead: Make the salad a day ahead; chill.

On Guest Day: Before you leave home, fix salmon, place in loaf pan ready to bake, cover and chill. On your return home, or a little more than an hour before suppertime, put the salmon loaf in the oven. You can forget about it. Since the loaf is chilled, you may need to bake it a few minutes longer than the recipe specifies. After the salmon bakes 30 minutes, set the table, cut the salad in individual servings, cook the carrots and frozen peas separately, drain if necessary, combine and season with butter. Heat the shrimp sauce and make the coffee or tea.

SERVING SUGGESTIONS

This is a sit-down dinner. Slice the salmon loaf at the table or cut it in the kitchen and arrange slices on platter. Garnish platter with celery leaves or parsley and lemon slices (see photo).

SALMON LOAF WITH SHRIMP SAUCE

Loaf slices hold their shape and display that lovely salmon color

2 (1 lb.) cans salmon
¼ c. finely minced onion
¼ c. chopped parsley
¼ c. lemon juice
½ tsp. salt
½ tsp. pepper

½ to 1 tsp. ground thyme
2 c. coarse cracker crumbs
½ c. milk (about)
4 eggs, well beaten
¼ c. melted butter
Shrimp Sauce

Drain salmon, saving liquid.

Flake salmon into bowl; add onion, parsley, lemon juice, seasonings and cracker crumbs; mix lightly.

Add salmon liquid plus enough milk to make 1 cup; add eggs and melted butter. Mix lightly.

Spoon into greased 2-qt. loaf pan or casserole. Bake in moderate oven (350°) 1 hour or until loaf is set in center. Spoon Shrimp Sauce over top. Makes 8 servings.

Shrimp Sauce: Heat 1 can condensed cream of shrimp soup according to directions on label. Add ¼ c. milk, stir until smooth.

PINEAPPLE/CHEESE SALAD

Decorative, flavorful topping chills on salad—no dressing needed

2 pkgs. lemon flavor gelatin
2 c. boiling water
2 c. cold water
6 bananas, peeled and sliced
2 c. miniature or cut-up
    marshmallows

½ c. sugar
3 tblsp. cornstarch
2 (8¼ oz.) cans crushed pineapple
1 c. heavy cream
1 c. shredded Cheddar cheese

Dissolve gelatin in boiling water; add cold water and chill until syrupy. Stir in sliced bananas and marshmallows. Pour into 13×9× 2″ pan. Chill until set.

Mix sugar and cornstarch; add to undrained pineapple. Cook over medium heat, stirring constantly, until thickened. Cool.

Whip cream and fold into cooled pineapple mixture along with half the shredded cheese. Spread mixture on congealed lemon gelatin.

Sprinkle remainder of shredded cheese over top. Chill overnight. Cut into squares. Makes 12 to 15 servings.

INLAND CLAM CHOWDER SUPPER

Famous Clam Chowder*
Hearts of Lettuce and Tomato Salad
Vinegar and Oil Dressing
Sourdough Bread
Elegant Chocolate Log

To dramatize the food in this menu and tempt guests, serve it at the table. They never will dream that this might rightfully be called a kind-to-the-budget supper. Canned clams are a good buy. The Elegant Chocolate Log reflects a graceful elegance that gave the dessert its name.

This is the kind of simple supper members of a family like to come home to at the end of a busy, frustrating day, and especially on a rainy, chilly evening. Guests fortunate enough to share it feel that the hostess merely put extra plates on the table for them and went to no extra work. That gives an at-home feeling.

TIMETABLE

Do-Ahead: See Index for Elegant Chocolate Log recipe (featured in "February Dessert Party" menu) and directions for baking it ahead and freezing; also for baking it on guest day. Also see Index for Sourdough Bread and directions for baking it—included in Autumn Picnic menu.

On Guest Day: If you have made the dessert and bread previously, you can get this supper ready in less than an hour from start to finish.

SERVING SUGGESTIONS

Serve the chowder from a soup tureen or large bowl at the table to add glamor to the homespun dish. Slice and serve the lovely dessert at the table.

FAMOUS CLAM CHOWDER

Taste a spoonful of this flavorful inland clam chowder and you'll know why it's famous and always brings compliments from guests

2 (6½ oz.) cans minced clams	¾ c. flour
1 c. finely chopped onions	1 qt. dairy half-and-half
1 c. finely diced celery	1½ tsp. salt
2 c. very finely diced potatoes	Few grains white pepper
¾ c. butter	2 tblsp. red wine vinegar

Drain juice from clams and add to vegetables in small saucepan. Add enough water to barely cover vegetables. Simmer, covered, over medium heat until just tender.

In the meantime, melt butter; add flour, blend and cook, stirring for 2 to 3 minutes. Add dairy half-and-half; cook and stir with wire whisk until smooth and thick.

Add undrained vegetables and clams and heat through. Add salt, pepper and vinegar. Makes 8 servings.

SUPPER IN LILAC TIME

Pleasant Valley Cheese/Vegetable Soup*   Assorted Crackers
Radishes   Wilted Garden Lettuce*
Rhubarb Crisp*

A perfect setting for this supper is a chilly, Sunday evening in spring when the fragrant breath of lilacs along the drive greets arriving guests. If you have a garden, now is the time to make the most of the early vegetables and foods that complement them, such as cheese and bacon. Start off with a hearty soup and wind up with slender, red-pink rhubarb stalks, cut up, sweetened and baked in a simple dessert. Punctuate the meal with tiny, crisp, red radishes fresh from the earth and a big bowl of delicate leaf lettuce tossed with hot bacon-vinegar dressing. What country feast could be better?

TIMETABLE

Make-Ahead: You did your advance work when you planted your garden!

On Guest Day: Gather the radishes and green onions, cut the lettuce and rhubarb, wash and prepare them. If they must wait more than an hour, chill them in plastic bags. Make the soup at any convenient time during the afternoon, or just before supper. The important point is never to let it boil in the making or reheating. Put the dessert in the oven to bake about 30 minutes before you wish to serve supper. It will be ready when the main course is finished. Dress the lettuce at the last minute.

SERVING SUGGESTIONS

Serve the lettuce in individual salad bowls or on plates. Or pass it in a big bowl and let everyone help himself. If you have a tureen, you can ladle the soup into bowls at the table while guests serve themselves lettuce.

PLEASANT VALLEY CHEESE/VEGETABLE SOUP

Rich, substantial, delicious and attractive—serve it piping hot

1 c. finely cut celery	1½ lbs. process American cheese,
½ c. finely cut carrot	cut up
¼ c. finely chopped onion	½ c. butter or regular margarine
2 tblsp. instant chicken bouillon	½ c. flour
crystals	½ tsp. dry mustard
1 qt. water	Salt (optional)
1 qt. milk	

Place celery, carrot, onion, bouillon and water in saucepan. Cook until vegetables are tender.

Meanwhile, scald the milk but do not let it boil. Add cheese, stir until melted.

Melt butter. Add flour and mustard; mix until smooth. Stir into cheese-milk mixture and heat. Stir in hot vegetables and the water in which they cooked. Check for salt. Serve hot. Makes 2 quarts.

WILTED GARDEN LETTUCE

For a pretty, springtime garnish top with 2 hard-cooked eggs, chopped

3 qts. bite-size pieces leaf lettuce	5 slices bacon, diced
1 tsp. salt	¼ c. vinegar
2 tsp. sugar	2 tblsp. water
2 green onions, sliced	

Place torn lettuce in a 3-qt. bowl. Sprinkle with salt, sugar and onions (use some of the green tops).

Cook bacon until crisp (not brittle). Drain bacon on paper towels. To bacon drippings add vinegar and water. Heat to boiling point and at once pour over lettuce. Toss until all the lettuce is slightly wilted. Check for salt. Sprinkle with bacon and serve immediately. Makes 8 servings.

RHUBARB CRISP

Serve topped with vanilla ice cream or pass pitcher of light cream

4 c. cut-up rhubarb	1 tsp. ground cinnamon
½ tsp. salt	2 tsp. grated orange peel
1⅓ to 2 c. sugar	⅓ c. butter or regular margarine
¾ c. flour	

Put rhubarb in ungreased 10×6×1½" baking dish. Sprinkle with salt.

Combine sugar (amount depends on tartness of rhubarb), flour, cinnamon, orange peel and butter in small bowl and mix until crumbly. Sprinkle evenly over rhubarb.

Bake in moderate oven (350°) about 45 minutes, or until topping is golden brown. Serve warm in bowls. Makes about 6 servings.

N O T E : For more servings, make the recipe 2 times.

CHILI SUPPER

Chili con Carne*	Assorted Crackers
Carrot Sticks	Pickles
Fruit Salad/Dessert*	Iced Tea

In thousands of western homes chili con carne rates high on the list of favorite main dishes to serve to company. It is to the west what baked beans are to New England. Americans shorten the name of this cross between a stew and a soup to chili. It's a shortcut version of Mexico's chili con carne in which the first step in preparation is to cook beef in water until almost tender, cut in tiny cubes and pan-fry them in a little fat. And beans accompany the dish, but are not a part of it. Speedy ground beef substitutes in our country kitchens for the precooked meat. The beef and the hearty ingredients, including beans, simmer together gently in an electric skillet.

Our recipe comes from a ranch in Rio Grande County, Colorado, the home of Mexican-Americans who are the fourth generation of the family (the fifth if you count the children) to live on the same land. An unusual feature of the main dish is the inclusion of hominy. It imparts that special taste south-of-the-border cornmeal gives to certain dishes.

Try this menu when your youngsters are having supper guests. You may wish to use less chili powder than the recipe specifies, but do taste the chili before you ladle it into serving bowls to make certain it is "hot" enough. If it isn't, stir in a little more of the lively powder. Serve the main dish with cooling fruit. Our Fruit Salad/ Dessert fills the bill. The salad dressing is the traditional kind country women like to cook for fruit salads and keep in the refrigerator. It adds a special-occasion taste.

TIMETABLE

Do-Ahead: Make the salad dressing a day ahead and chill, but fold the whipped cream into it at serving time.

On Guest Day: You can get the supper in an hour. While the chili simmers, make the salad and fix the iced tea.

SERVING SUGGESTIONS

Serve the chili in bowls, the salad/dessert on lettuce-lined individual salad plates, or pass it in a lettuce-lined bowl. Add sprigs of fresh mint to tall glasses of iced tea; accompany them with lemon slices or wedges.

CHILI CON CARNE

Double this recipe to serve a crowd of twelve; triple or quadruple for a bigger crowd—you'll have good results

1 lb. ground beef	1 tsp. salt
¾ to 1 c. chopped onions	2 tblsp. chili powder
1 (1 lb. 13 oz.) can tomatoes	¼ tsp. ground cumin seeds
1 (1 lb.) can hominy	(optional)
1 (15½ oz.) can red, pinto or kidney beans	

Cook and stir beef and onions until beef is lightly browned and onions are almost tender. Pour off fat. Add remaining ingredients and simmer, covered, about 30 minutes. Check seasonings, especially salt. Serve piping hot. (If chili is not as thick as you like it, simmer, uncovered, an additional 15 minutes.) Makes 6 servings.

FRUIT SALAD/DESSERT

Combine shortly before serving to prevent discoloration of fruits

4 unpeeled red apples, diced	½ c. heavy cream, whipped
¼ c. lemon juice	6 tblsp. Fruit Salad Dressing
1 (14¼ oz.) can sliced pineapple, diced	Lettuce
4 bananas, sliced	⅓ c. chopped walnuts

Toss diced apples with lemon juice; let stand while preparing other fruits.

Drain apples and combine with pineapple and bananas. Fold whipped cream into Fruit Salad Dressing; fold into fruits. Serve on lettuce and sprinkle with nuts. Makes 6 servings.

Fruit Salad Dressing: Mix ⅓ c. orange juice, ⅓ c. pineapple juice and 2 tblsp. lemon juice. Add 2 eggs, beaten slightly, then add ½ c. sugar and ¼ tsp. salt. Cook in top of double boiler 3 to 5 minutes, until dressing thickens. Cool; cover and refrigerate. Use as directed in Fruit Salad/Dessert recipe, folding in whipped cream before serving. Store covered in refrigerator and use as needed, adding whipped cream as desired. Makes about 2½ c. salad dressing with 1 c. heavy cream, whipped, folded in.

MINUTE STEAK BARBECUE

Grilled Minute Steak Rolls*
Hominy/Bean Barbecue*   Fruit-Jar Tomato Relish*
Buttered French Bread
Watermelon Wedges
Hot Coffee

While this barbecue menu is on the new side, it scores success with guests. The foods are familiar favorites handled in an unusual way.

Take the scored cube or minute beef steaks for example: The

trick is to wrap the beef around sticks of cold, hard butter and grill quickly over coals. The vegetable relish reminds you in flavor of the floating vegetable salads in old-time country kitchens. They consisted of vegetables, usually tomatoes, cucumbers and onions, in a sweet-sour vinegar sauce. For this meal you make the salad in a glass fruit jar.

The hearty casserole, which bakes without attention, almost always brings ovations. Among the ingredients is a pioneer special, hominy. And what could be better to wind up the meal on a summer evening than cold watermelon? Watermelon with bowls of buttered, salted, warm popped corn—a great taste combination.

TIMETABLE

Do-Ahead: Make the vegetable relish a day ahead and chill.

On Guest Day: In the morning combine foods in casserole ready to bake; cover and refrigerate. Slice the French bread at your convenience, butter, reassemble loaf and wrap in heavy foil. Wrap cold minute steaks around butter as recipe directs and chill until about 15 minutes before suppertime, when the coals should be ready for grilling the steaks over them. During the last 10 to 12 minutes before mealtime, put the bread in its foil wrap alongside the casserole to heat.

SERVING SUGGESTIONS

If you want to show off the striped relish, serve it in the glass jar picnic style. It will intrigue your guests. If you have an electric corn popper, ask the children to pop a big bowl of corn, add salt and melted butter and deliver it warm to the picnic table to serve with the melon.

GRILLED MINUTE STEAK ROLLS

These steaks cost less than those usually grilled but they taste superb

8 minute steaks (cube beef)	Pepper
½ tsp. marjoram leaves, crushed	5 tblsp. cold, hard butter (about)
Garlic salt	

Sprinkle steaks with marjoram, garlic salt and pepper. Cut butter in 8 sticks of equal size. Place 1 stick on each steak and roll, turning ends to completely cover butter. Skewer to keep closed.

Broil over medium coals, turning often, until steak is browned on the outside, but rare inside, about 10 to 12 minutes. Makes 8 servings.

HOMINY/BEAN BARBECUE

This substantial dish features four American originals: beans, hominy, tomatoes, chili peppers—they all come from cans

6 slices bacon, chopped	¼ c. chopped canned green chili
1 c. chopped onion	peppers
2 (20 oz.) cans yellow hominy,	2 tblsp. cider vinegar
drained	2 tsp. Worcestershire sauce
2 (15½ oz.) cans kidney beans,	2 tsp. prepared mustard
drained	1 tsp. salt
1 (15 oz.) can tomato sauce	

Cook bacon in skillet until crisp. Remove and set aside. Pour off all but 2 tblsp. drippings.

Add onion to skillet and cook until tender, but do not brown. Combine onion and bacon with remaining ingredients. Pour into a greased 2-qt. casserole; cover and bake in moderate oven (350°) 1½ hours. Makes 8 servings.

FRUIT-JAR TOMATO RELISH

Seeing and tasting is believing how pretty and good this relish is

2 tomatoes, peeled and chopped	2 tblsp. wine vinegar
1 cucumber, peeled and chopped	1 tblsp. snipped fresh parsley
1 green pepper, seeds removed	1 small clove garlic, minced
and chopped	½ tsp. salt
¼ c. chopped onion	Dash of pepper
¼ c. olive or salad oil	

In a 1-qt. glass jar, alternate layers of tomatoes, cucumber, green pepper and onion to make stripes when viewed from the side.

Combine remaining ingredients and pour over vegetables; cover and chill overnight. Turn jar upside down during part of the chilling to marinate vegetables evenly. Makes 1 quart.

COOK-IN, EAT-OUT SUPPER

Green Soup*   Crackers
Lasagne Roll-ups*
Garlic Green Beans   Fiesta Salad Bowl
Warm French Bread
Strawberry-Almond Sundaes

Cook indoors and eat under the maple tree in the yard. Or drive the family, guests and supper to a favorite picnic spot on the farm. How about the pond so the children, after eating, can fish while the adults visit?

This menu is for a meal you can serve indoors or out, whichever you think your guests will enjoy more. No doubt the weather will dictate where to dine, saving you from making a decision. The supper is better adapted to serving near the house so you can return to the kitchen to get the dessert.

But you can easily alter the menu for the situation. Eliminate the soup, change the dessert to fresh fruit—such as apples, pears, grapes or whatever is available—and add a jar of homemade cookies, a vacuum container of iced tea or hot coffee and bottles of ice cold milk. No one will wish for more.

TIMETABLE

Do-Ahead: You can, if you like, combine the casserole ingredients a day ahead and refrigerate.

On Guest Day: Wash the salad greens. Be sure to include some young, tender spinach leaves with the lettuce. Drain well and chill in plastic bags. Cut a 1-lb. long loaf of French bread in 1″ slices, butter, reassemble, wrap in heavy-duty aluminum foil. About 45 minutes before serving time, put the lasagne in oven to bake. Heat the foil-wrapped bread alongside the last 20 minutes. Make the soup. Toss the greens in a big bowl with Italian salad dressing and, if eating indoors, serve in individual bowls. Garnish tops of salads. If toting salad outdoors, place garnishes on top of big bowl of salad.

Cook 2 (10 oz.) pkgs. frozen green beans by package directions, drain and dress with garlic butter. To make it, melt ¼ c. butter and add 1 clove garlic, crushed. Heat, but do not brown garlic. Discard garlic and pour butter over beans. Make the dessert at serving time. Prepare the Strawberry-Almond Sundaes at the last minute. Drizzle bottled strawberry-flavored syrup over vanilla ice cream in sherbet glasses and top each serving with a few toasted slivered almonds.

SERVING SUGGESTIONS

If serving soup in the yard, carry it out in a tureen or bowl and ladle into cups or bowls. Set up a portable table for a buffet and let everyone help himself. Use slivers of pickled beets, bits of green pepper, shredded carrots, green or ripe olives and peeled tomato quarters, lightly salted on both sides, for the salad garnish. Serve the sundaes in dessert bowls.

GREEN SOUP

Easy to fix, refreshing and pretty. Garnish with chopped chives

2 c. frozen peas, thawed
2 (14 oz.) cans chicken broth

2 tsp. onion juice
Dash of curry powder (optional)

Put peas through a sieve or food mill, or whirl in blender. Add broth and heat to simmering point. Add onion juice and curry powder. Check for salt. Makes 8 servings.

LASAGNE ROLL-UPS

A delicious new way to fix and serve lasagne—freezes well too!

Meat Sauce:
1½ lbs. ground beef
⅓ c. salad oil
⅓ c. finely chopped onion
1½ cloves garlic, minced
2 tsp. salt
¼ tsp. pepper
2 whole cloves
½ bay leaf
3 (1 lb. 1½ oz.) cans plum
   tomatoes, sieved
2 (6 oz.) cans tomato paste
1¼ c. water
1 tsp. orégano leaves, crushed

¼ tsp. monosodium glutamate
2 tsp. sugar
Filling:
2 lbs. ricotta cheese
½ tsp. salt
⅛ tsp. pepper
½ tsp. ground nutmeg
¼ lb. mozzarella cheese,
   shredded
4 tblsp. grated Parmesan or
   Romano cheese
1 tblsp. chopped fresh parsley
1 (1 lb.) pkg. lasagne noodles

Partially brown ground beef in oil. Add onion, garlic, salt, pepper, cloves and bay leaf. Continue to brown over medium heat for 10 minutes or until well browned.

Stir in tomatoes, tomato paste, water, orégano, monosodium glutamate and sugar. Let come to a boil, then simmer gently, loosely covered, for about 1 hour; stir occasionally.

In the meantime, whip ricotta cheese. Add salt, pepper, nutmeg, mozzarella cheese, grated cheese and parsley. Set aside.

Cook lasagne noodles according to package directions. Rinse with cold water; drain well. Lay noodles on clean dish towels.

On each noodle, spread ¼ c. filling. Fold over 1″ and continue to fold, making a slightly flat roll.

Place 1 c. meat sauce in each of 2 (2-qt.) rectangular baking dishes. Place roll-ups, seam side down, in baking dishes. Add ⅓ c. hot water to each dish and enough meat sauce to almost cover roll-ups. Reserve rest of sauce.

Bake in moderate oven (350°) 45 minutes, or until sauce bubbles in center of dish.

Serve with rest of sauce and grated cheese. Makes 16 party rolls (8 main dish servings, or 16, if served as meat accompaniment).

OUTDOOR SUPPER

Cornucopias*   Pineapple Sparkler   Popcorn Bowl
Tamale Pie Santa Fe*   Fresh Cucumber Relish*
Quartered Tomatoes   Warm Vienna Bread
Sundae Ice Cream Cones

When the weather is right—neither too hot nor too cold—call friends and invite them to supper. Serve the meal on the porch or patio, or set up card tables and chairs on the lawn. This easy meal requires no make-ahead preparations—good for spur-of-the-moment entertaining.

Provide an appetizer course to put everyone in a social mood. For the Pineapple Sparkler, reconstitute frozen pineapple juice concentrate with chilled ginger ale instead of water. Or substitute frozen orange juice concentrate for the pineapple. Fix the cornucopias with slices of cold meat; pop some corn and sprinkle with seasoned salt.

Ice cream cones fit the occasion. Some guests at outdoor meals prefer mobile desserts—finger food they can eat while moving around to look at the garden or flowers in bloom.

TIMETABLE

On Guest Day: Make the cucumber relish early in the day and chill. Cut the loaf of bread in ½″ slices, spread with butter, reassemble loaf and wrap in heavy-duty aluminum foil. Put the tamale pie in the oven about 30 minutes before serving time; then add the bread alongside to heat the last 15 or 20 minutes. Keep warm until served. While you fix the cornucopias, encourage your husband or children to pop the corn, add melted butter and sprinkle with seasoned salt. The dessert can be made up quickly just before serving.

SERVING SUGGESTIONS

Depend on the family or willing friends to help carry the platter of cornucopias and crackers, pitcher of Pineapple Sparkler and the big bowl of popcorn outdoors to the assembled guests. Set up the main-course buffet in the house and let everyone carry his food outdoors. Or if you prefer, arrange the buffet on the porch or patio, or in the yard.

When it's dessert time, excuse yourself and invite guests to follow and pick up their dessert. Fill ice cream cones with chocolate ice cream, dip the top of the ice cream in fudge sauce. (Vanilla ice cream and butterscotch sauce are also a good combo.) If desired, sprinkle frosted ice cream tops with chopped nuts. Repeat until everyone is served. Set out a pot of coffee so that guests can fill their own cups or mugs for a finish.

Cornucopias: Cut thin bologna or salami slices in halves; roll each semicircle around a tiny stuffed olive or pickled onion to make a cornucopia. Fasten with a toothpick and fill with a dab of softened cream cheese.

TAMALE PIE SANTA FE

Inviting crust on top of this tasty meat pie is yellow and crisp

1½ lbs. ground beef	2 tsp. salt
1½ tsp. salt	½ tsp. chili powder
½ tsp. orégano leaves	2 tblsp. butter or regular
½ tsp. pepper	margarine
⅔ c. finely chopped onion	1 c. yellow cornmeal
1 (1 lb.) can tomatoes	½ c. shredded process American
1 (12 oz.) can Mexicorn, drained	cheese
2 c. water	

In a 10″ skillet brown beef lightly; drain off excess fat. Add 1½ tsp. salt, orégano, pepper, onion and tomatoes. Stir to mix; bring to a boil. Simmer 10 minutes or until excess liquid evaporates and mixture thickens. Stir in corn; cook just to heat. Pour into greased 2½-qt. casserole.

For topping, mix water, 2 tsp. salt, chili powder, butter and cornmeal in saucepan. Cook until mixture thickens, stirring frequently. With spoon and rubber spatula, gently drop spoonfuls on top of hot mixture in casserole. Spread thinly over the top.

Bake, uncovered, in moderate oven (375°) 30 minutes. Sprinkle cheese over top and bake 10 to 15 minutes longer, or until cheese melts. Makes 8 servings.

FRESH CUCUMBER RELISH

Garnish with small chilled tomato quarters or whole cherry tomatoes for bright color. The cooling cucumber-tomato flavors always please

3 medium cucumbers	1 tsp. dill seeds
¼ c. minced onion	1½ tsp. salt
¼ c. cider vinegar	½ tsp. pepper

Peel cucumbers and chop fine. Let stand a few minutes; drain. Add remaining ingredients; chill several hours so flavors will blend. Makes about 2 cups.

BARBECUE SUPPER

Barbecued Turkey Wings*

Savory Baked Beans   Scalloped Corn

Tossed Green Salad

Homemade French Bread*

Fresh Lemon Ice Cream*

Coconut Cookies

This menu for a supper with cooked turkey, brushed with barbecue sauce and grilled over coals until hot and crusty, will help keep down food costs. At the same time it will enable you to serve a superior meal.

Using turkey wings (many markets now carry turkey parts) stretches food dollars. You can barbecue turkey thighs instead of wings if you prefer them.

To round out the meal, toss a big green salad, bake long loaves of French bread, add your own seasonings to canned baked beans and fix a casserole of Scalloped Corn (we feature it in the menu "A Dinner to Tote"—see Index for recipe). And for dessert freeze a gallon of Fresh Lemon Ice Cream and offer a choice of cold milk or coffee for the beverage. Have plenty of all foods and your guests will rate you a genius with food. Not a thought of economy will cross their minds.

TIMETABLE

Do-Ahead: Most of the food preparation takes place a day ahead. That's the time to cook the turkey wings or thighs in salted water until tender, drain and chill. Make the barbecue sauce; refrigerate. Also wash, drain and store the lettuce in plastic bags; chill. Bake the bread a day or several days ahead and freeze.

On Guest Day: About 4 hours before suppertime, start freezing the ice cream and let it ripen in the freezer. At least 30 minutes before time to serve supper, have the coals ready for grilling the turkey and heat casseroles of corn and baked beans in a moderate oven (350°). Heat the foil-wrapped bread in oven 25 to 30 minutes if frozen. Meanwhile, get the beverages ready and toss the salad.

BARBECUED TURKEY WINGS

Different and delicious way to cook turkey—serve it sizzling hot

10 turkey wings (or 5 turkey thighs)	½ tsp. chili powder
¾ c. water	2 tblsp. instant minced onion
¾ c. ketchup	2 tblsp. vinegar
1 tsp. salt	1 tblsp. Worcestershire sauce

Separate wing pieces at joints and discard wing tips. Cook turkey wings in small amount of boiling salted water 1 to 1½ hours, or until tender. Or cook in pressure cooker according to manufacturer's directions. Drain cooked turkey and chill.

Combine water, ketchup, salt, chili powder, onion, vinegar and Worcestershire sauce in small saucepan; cover and simmer about 45 minutes. Store in covered jar in refrigerator to use as needed.

Place turkey pieces over hot coals and broil 15 minutes; turn. Brush with barbecue sauce and continue cooking 15 minutes more, basting frequently, or until turkey is hot and crusty. Makes about 5 servings.

N O T E : This recipe can be doubled for more servings.

HOMEMADE FRENCH BREAD

Everyone's favorite—it's crusty and crunchy with a shiny glaze

2 pkgs. active dry yeast	1 tblsp. salt
½ c. warm water (110 to 115°)	⅓ c. salad oil
2 c. hot water	6 c. flour, stirred before measuring
3 tblsp. sugar	1 egg white, slightly beaten

Dissolve yeast in warm water.

Combine 2 c. hot water, sugar, salt, oil and 3 c. flour; stir well. Stir in yeast. Add remaining flour, stirring well with a heavy spoon. Leave spoon in batter and allow dough to rest 10 minutes. Stir down batter, let dough rest another 10 minutes. Repeat this process 3 more times (making 5 times in all).

Turn dough onto lightly floured board. Knead only enough to coat dough with flour so it can be handled, then divide it into two equal parts. Roll each part into a 12×9″ rectangle; roll up like a jelly roll, starting on the long side. Arrange lengthwise on greased baking sheet, seam side down, allowing room for both loaves. Let rise in warm place 30 minutes.

With a very sharp knife cut 3 diagonal gashes in the top of each loaf; brush with egg white. Bake in hot oven (400°) about 30 minutes, or until crusty brown. (For added crustiness, put a pan of hot water on floor of oven during baking.) Makes 2 loaves.

FRESH LEMON ICE CREAM

Light, refreshing dessert—perfect to serve on a hot summer night

2 qts. milk	2 tsp. lemon extract
1 c. heavy cream	4 c. sugar
¾ c. lemon juice (3 large)	

Combine all ingredients in a 1-gal. ice cream freezer can, filling about three fourths full. Adjust dasher and cover. Pack crushed ice and rock salt around can, using 6 parts ice to 1 part salt.

Turn dasher slowly until the ice melts enough to make a brine. Add more ice and salt, mixed in the proper proportion, to maintain the ice level. Turn the handle fast and steadily until it turns hard. Then remove ice until the level is below the lid of can; take off lid and remove the dasher.

Plug the hole in lid and cover can with several thicknesses of waxed paper or foil to make a tight fit for the lid. Pack more ice-salt mixture, using 4 parts ice to 1 part salt, around can and filling the freezer. Cover with a blanket, canvas or other heavy cloth, or with newspaper. Let the ice cream ripen 4 hours before serving. Or put it in the home freezer for an hour. Makes 1 gallon.

N O T E : If you use an electric ice cream freezer, follow the manufacturer's directions.

MAIN-DISH QUICHE SUPPER

Hot Tomato Bouillon   Crackers
Quiche*
Tossed Green Salad
Fruit Compote
Candy Mints

Quiche is a French gourmet dish that will delight a group of women as the main dish at a luncheon—or the family plus guests at supper. We give you a basic recipe with three delicious substantial fillings. Make all three and cut small wedges—guests enjoy tasting all three and comparing preferences. The pastry and ingredients can all be ready and combined with cream and eggs just before putting in the oven.

TIMETABLE

Do-Ahead: You can make the pastry a day before you entertain. Fit it into the pan, cover with plastic wrap and refrigerate. (Or if you wish, make it a week or more ahead and keep, unbaked, in freezer.) Wash and drain salad greens and chill in a plastic bag.

On Guest Day: About an hour before supper, make filling, pour into pastry-lined pan and bake. You can get the ham and cheese cut up or spinach cooked and ready earlier in the day. Make the fruit compote and chill. Use your favorite combinations of fruits. Grapefruit sections, sliced bananas and frozen peaches are delicious—especially when topped with frozen red raspberries. Heat the bouillon. A good way to make it is to combine 1 (1 lb.) can tomato juice and a can of condensed beef broth. Point up flavors with a dash of celery salt. Toss the salad just before the Quiche is ready to serve.

SERVING SUGGESTIONS

If you do not use a colorful fruit such as raspberries in the compote, decorate each-serving with a maraschino cherry and pour on a little of the cherry juice. Serve very cold in dessert glasses.

QUICHE

The crust is rich with butter, filling is rich with cream

1½ c. sifted flour
¼ tsp. salt
½ c. butter
1 egg, slightly beaten

Filling
3 eggs
1 c. heavy cream

Sift together flour and salt. Cut in butter with pastry blender until mixture resembles coarse cornmeal. Add the slightly beaten egg and toss with a fork to mix. Gather dough into a ball and chill.

Roll dough out on a well-floured board. Fit into 10″ pie pan, or a 10″ fluted tart pan. Measure depth of pan and trim pastry 1″ wider. Fold dough over and press it firmly against the pan sides. Arrange the filling ingredients (directions follow) in the crust.

To make custard, beat the 3 eggs; beat in cream. (See Fillings for seasonings.) Pour over filling in crust.

Bake in hot oven (425°) 10 minutes; reduce heat to slow (325°) and continue baking about 30 minutes, or until custard is set. To test for doneness, insert a knife in center of pie. If it comes out almost clean, remove pie from oven. It will set completely in a few minutes. Cut in wedges and serve warm. Makes 6 to 8 servings.

Fillings

Ham/Cheese Filling: Sprinkle ¼ lb. shredded Cheddar cheese and ¾ c. finely diced cooked ham in the crust. Blend 1 tsp. Worcestershire sauce, ¼ tsp. salt, ¼ tsp. dry mustard and ⅛ tsp. pepper into the custard. Pour over the cheese-ham mixture. If you like, sprinkle 1 tsp. caraway seeds over the pie before baking.

Chicken/Cheese Filling: Sprinkle ¼ c. grated Parmesan cheese in the crust. Top with 1 c. finely diced cooked chicken and 2 small green onions with tops, finely chopped. Add ¼ tsp. salt, ⅛ tsp. dry mustard and ⅛ tsp. pepper to the custard and pour it over the chicken-onion mixture. Sprinkle top of pie with ¼ c. sliced almonds and ¼ c. grated Parmesan cheese and bake.

Cheese/Spinach Filling: Cook 1 (10 oz.) pkg. frozen chopped spinach (or 1 c. finely chopped fresh spinach leaves) until tender. Drain and squeeze dry. Cook 4 small green onions with tops, thinly sliced, in 1 tblsp. butter until soft. Remove from heat and combine with the spinach and ¼ c. finely chopped (or snipped with scissors) parsley. Blend ½ tsp. salt, ½ tsp. rubbed sage and ⅛ tsp. pepper into the custard and stir into it the spinach mixture. Pour into the crust. Sprinkle top of pie with ¼ c. grated Parmesan cheese and bake.

COUNTRY KITCHEN SUPPER

Chilled Cocktail Vegetable Juice   Baked Cheese Fondue*
Apple/Grape Salad*   Brownies à la Mode

Most good hostesses treasure at least a few recipes for old-fashioned dishes too taste-rewarding to forget. They appreciate the enthusiasm their guests almost always show over old-time favorites that remind them of what their mothers used to make. Baked Cheese Fondue, an American original, is an excellent example. Created in country kitchens when women considered it their duty to salvage scraps of bread no longer fresh, and cheese somewhat hardened, it bears little resemblance to European-type fondues which skip the oven and cook in pots—also much in vogue in America now.

A California woman who entertains often says that Baked Cheese Fondue, which she sometimes calls cheese pudding, is a main dish her friends enjoy. You may prefer to think of it as a substantial, three-decker sandwich. We share her recipe with you.

Why not save the dessert to serve at the end of the evening just before guests leave? It gives them a well-fed feeling as they step out into the night to return home—and it's a country custom.

TIMETABLE

Do-Ahead: Get the main dish ready to bake a day ahead and refrigerate. Bake the brownies.

On Guest Day: Put the canned vegetable juice in refrigerator to chill; it is expertly seasoned and is flavorful served as it comes from the can. Put the fondue in the oven an hour before you wish to serve supper. Make and chill the salad, using tart, red apples and whatever grapes are available. If they are not seedless, cut them in halves and remove seeds.

SERVING SUGGESTIONS

This is a good supper to serve buffet style, especially if you bake the fondue in a glass baking dish. Arrange salad in lettuce-lined bowl and garnish the top with nuts and wedges of unpeeled red apples sprinkled with lemon juice to prevent discoloration. Or serve on the supper plates. Cut the brownies in somewhat larger pieces than usual, or bake them in a pie pan and cut in pie-shaped pieces. Top with vanilla or coffee ice cream at serving time.

BAKED CHEESE FONDUE

It's as American as the Fourth of July—and you can have it all ready in advance, except for the baking

18 slices dry bread	8 eggs
Butter or regular margarine	5 c. milk
Salt	1½ tsp. dry mustard
Pepper	2 tsp. Worcestershire sauce
2 lbs. process sharp cheese, shredded	

Butter bread slices. Arrange 6 slices, buttered side up, in greased 13×9×2" ovenproof glass dish. Sprinkle lightly with salt and pepper and one third of cheese. Press down and add another layer of buttered bread and cheese, and press down; repeat. (You will have three layers and the pan will be full.)

Beat eggs; add milk, dry mustard and Worcestershire sauce. Pour over the bread-cheese layers in pan. Cover with foil and let stand in refrigerator at least 8 hours, or overnight.

Baked uncovered in moderate oven (350°) about 1 hour, or until a knife inserted in center comes out clean. Serve at once. Makes 8 or 9 servings.

APPLE/GRAPE SALAD

Apples, grapes and black walnuts unite in this great farm salad

6 tart unpeeled red apples, diced
2 tblsp. lemon juice
1½ c. diced celery
1½ c. halved and seeded Tokay or
    Emperor grapes

1 c. miniature marshmallows
¾ c. salad dressing
½ c. broken black walnuts or
    hickory nuts
Lettuce

Sprinkle diced apples with lemon juice. Combine with celery, grapes, marshmallows and salad dressing. Cover and chill. At serving time add the nuts. Serve on lettuce. Makes 8 servings.

N O T E : You can use pecans, toasted almonds or walnuts if black walnuts or hickory nuts are not available. Some country salad makers use ½ c. salad dressing with ¼ c. heavy cream, whipped, folded into the salad.

FONDUE SUPPER

Cheese Fondue*
French Bread   Rye Bread
Lettuce Salad Cups*
Fresh Fruit
Butterscotch Wafers*
Coffee

Nothing surpasses gathering with several favorite friends around a pot of cheese fondue, to add warmth and brightness to a freezing-cold winter evening. And this supper featuring hearty food is a meal a busy woman, even though she may work away from home, can prepare quickly after she returns late afternoon. It is important, however, to do some of the food preparation ahead. Our timetable is a guide.

Many treasured recipes for cheese fondue, patterned after the Swiss classic, circulate around the countryside, but most of them—like the one we give you—are Americanized. You can follow this menu even if you wish to use your own favorite fondue recipe. It may be one from the manufacturer's leaflet that came with your fondue pot.

This menu features some pleasing variations from those for most fondue suppers. Long-loaf rye, as well as French bread, awaits dunking, and fresh fruit, such as apples, pears and/or grapes contribute flavors that complement cheese. You can omit the wafers, which are really refrigerator cookies, but they contribute a typical country-style, homemade, sweet addition almost everyone enjoys. Perhaps your young cook can help by baking the cookies for you. If you do serve them, you'll notice that practically everyone happily eats a crunchy wafer or two as he sips the last cup of coffee.

TIMETABLE

Do-Ahead: Prepare rolls of cookie dough a couple of days ahead, wrap tightly in waxed paper or plastic wrap and refrigerate. Or freeze the rolls several days or weeks ahead. If you bake the wafers the evening before guest day, cool them and store in an airtight container. Fresh-from-the-oven cookies, of course, always score a hit, but day-old ones also taste good.

Wash and drain the salad greens and chill in plastic bags. Make the salad dressing and store, tightly covered, in refrigerator.

On Guest Day: Cut bread in bite-size pieces with crust on one side of each if possible; place in baskets. Cover with napkins to prevent drying. If you are hurried, assign this chore to your husband, an older child or to a guest. Wash and drain chilled fruits and divide grapes into small clusters. Arrange on a tray. Slice and bake as many cookies as you think you will need (you may have baked them the previous evening). Make the fondue after guests arrive and toss the salad at the last minute.

SERVING SUGGESTIONS

Center fondue pot on table and place individual salads at each plate. Set baskets or bowls of bread within easy reach of everyone. Bring the tray of fruit and plate of wafers to the table when you pour the second cup of coffee.

CHEESE FONDUE

This fondue is made with one kind of cheese—aged natural Swiss

French bread (long loaf)
Rye bread (long loaf)
1 lb. natural Swiss cheese,
   shredded (about 4 c.)
1½ tsp. cornstarch

1 clove garlic
1¼ c. dry white wine
1 tblsp. lemon juice
Dash of pepper

Cut bread in bite-size pieces with crust on one side.

Combine cheese and cornstarch and mix.

Rub inside of metal fondue cooker or heavy skillet with cut garlic clove. Pour in wine and lemon juice. Heat on low to medium heat until air bubbles rise and cover surface of wine-lemon juice mixture. Do not let come to a boil.

Add about ½ c. cheese at a time, stirring vigorously all the time with a wooden spoon. Keep on low to medium heat; do not let mixture boil. When cheese melts, add another ½ c. cheese, stirring constantly. Be sure to let each addition of cheese melt before adding another. Repeat until all the cheese is added and melted. Stir in pepper. Place fondue on heating unit if using electric fondue pot in case the fondue was not made on it. Keep warm over low heat. If making fondue in skillet, pour into the fondue pot's ceramic cooker and set over burner. Keep over low heat.

Spear bread pieces through the crust side with fondue fork and swirl in fondue. The swirling is important because it keeps the cheese mixture moving so it will not thicken and stick to bottom of cooker. Transfer dipped bread to dinner fork and eat. Makes 4 to 6 servings.

LETTUCE SALAD CUPS

Salad adds color, crispness and piquant flavor to the supper

1 large head iceberg lettuce
⅓ c. salad oil
2 tblsp. wine vinegar
1 tsp. paprika
½ tsp. seasoned salt

⅛ tsp. pepper
⅛ tsp. dry mustard
2 c. bite-size spinach
12 cherry tomatoes

Remove outer leaves of lettuce to use for lettuce cups. Arrange cups in individual salad bowls. Shred remaining lettuce.

In a large salad bowl make the salad dressing by beating together with fork or wire whisk, salad oil, vinegar, paprika, seasoned salt, pepper and dry mustard. Add lettuce and spinach and toss well.

Cut tomatoes in halves and fold gently into salad. Makes 6 to 8 servings.

BUTTERSCOTCH WAFERS

Keep rolls of dough in freezer and you'll be ready to fast-bake wafers

1 c. softened butter or regular margarine

1 c. brown sugar, firmly packed

2 eggs

1½ tsp. vanilla

3 c. sifted flour

1 tsp. salt

½ c. finely chopped nuts (optional)

Thoroughly mix together butter, brown sugar, eggs and vanilla. Stir in flour, salt and nuts. Divide dough in thirds. With hands, firmly shape each portion in a roll 1½" in diameter. The rolls will be about 7" long. Wrap each roll tightly in waxed paper, lightweight aluminum foil or plastic wrap. Twist ends to make seal. Chill in refrigerator until firm, about 4 hours, or no longer than 2 or 3 days before baking. Or overwrap rolls, if covered with waxed paper, in aluminum foil and freeze. (Frozen dough may be kept up to 6 months before baking.)

To bake, cut roll in slices ¼" thick. (For crisper wafers, slice them ⅛" thick.) Be sure slices are the same thickness to insure even baking. Place about 1" apart on ungreased baking sheet; bake in hot oven (400°) 8 to 10 minutes, until light brown. Remove from baking sheet immediately and spread on wire racks to cool. One roll makes about 28 cookies.

CHAPTER 4

Entertaining at Dinner

. . . *MIDDAY OR EVENING MEALS*

Much of country cooking's fame was earned around the dinner table. "Dinnertime" in the country usually has been synonymous with noon, when it has been customary to serve the day's heartiest meal.

Regardless of the time of day you serve the dinner menus in this chapter to guests, you will find the food lives up to the long-established reputation for superior flavor and eye appeal. Definitely on the hearty side with a wide variety of foods in every menu, these dinners are not difficult if you plan ahead. Our timetables incorporate some make-ahead dishes to relieve the hostess of last-minute pressures.

Serving of predinner appetizers in the living room also pleasantly occupies the host and guests while the hostess returns to the kitchen to put the finishing touches on the meal. Greater use of help-yourself foods, buffet style of service, and other techniques used by country women for easy company dinners are included.

The menus will make you hungry for a good country dinner. Notice that the recipes feature some of the old-time country favorites with up-to-date touches. This is true in the many chicken specials— Sesame Chicken, Summer Chicken with Peas and New Potatoes, Royal Chicken Pie, Southern Stuffed Chicken Breasts and others.

Men's liking for meat and potatoes is considered in country dinners. You'll find directions for cooking to perfection the king of the platter, a standing rib beef roast. And you will get a new concept of how versatile, intriguing and delicious pot roasts can taste. For instance, you can broil them in the oven or grill them over coals. The secret is the marinade in which the beef chills 24 to 48 hours. Ground beef and meat balls show up in delicious variety. Pork Roast Danish Style is elegant. Pork/Sauerkraut Skillet wins praise as do Party Pork Rolls.

It seems unfair to single out a few dishes for honorable mention from a chapter overflowing with them. Special salads include FARM

JOURNAL's famed beauty, Three-Row Garden Salad, and a brand new Green Pea Salad. And farm women are experts with vegetables and at serving potatoes in many ways—many of these recipes came from their kitchens.

Homemade breads are so good . . . Overnight Sourdough Bread, for instance. Desserts include FARM JOURNAL's lovely Strawberry Satin Pie, Orange Meringue Pie, spicy Pumpkin Cake and Orange/Peanut Cake.

Don't miss the Wild Duck Dinner, Summer Fish Dinner and Iowa Corn Dinner. Sweet corn, of course, rushed from the patch, cooked and served at once with plenty of butter.

Recipes for all dishes starred (*) are in this cookbook.

IMPORTANT CHICKEN DINNER

Chilled Tomato Juice
Sauerkraut Balls*   Crackers
Southern Stuffed Chicken Breasts*
Buffet Cheese Potatoes*
Baby Beet Salad*
Lemon Sherbet
Coconut Pound Cake*

Some occasions challenge the country hostess to serve an elegant chicken dinner. The guest of honor often is the visiting speaker at a community meeting or a returned native who achieved success in faraway places. An exceptional chicken dish frequently is the center of interest in the meal.

In this menu the main dish consists of stuffed chicken breasts pan-fried in butter until golden. The meal starts in the living room with chilled tomato juice (home-canned if available), crisp crackers and intriguing appetizer balls tangy and flavorful with sauerkraut and corned beef.

The dinner continues with potatoes with cheese sauce, a salad of little beets from the garden (or canned midget beets) touched up with a yellow and white country garnish of chopped hard-cooked eggs. By dessert time appetites no longer are ravenous, but a southern-accented meal ending, lemon sherbet with small wedges of homemade coconut pound cake, is just right.

TIMETABLE

Do-Ahead: Bake cake a day, or several days ahead and freeze. Cook beets for salad, or drain canned beets, pour on salad dressing, cover and chill. Prepare potatoes, place in loaf pan, cover and refrigerate; chill sauce separately. Get chicken ready for browning, cover and chill. Make mixture for appetizer balls, shape, roll in crumbs and refrigerate.

On Guest Day: Whenever convenient, set cake on kitchen counter to thaw in its wrap. Unmold potatoes ready for baking; refrigerate. Chop eggs for salad, cover and chill. Put potatoes in oven 1 hour before dinner. Cook and brown chicken the last half hour before mealtime. When guests arrive, remove potatoes from oven and broil appetizer balls just long enough to brown lightly. Carry them and tomato juice to the living room, but before you leave kitchen, put potatoes and chicken, uncovered, in very slow oven (275°) with door open to keep warm. When you return to the kitchen to put the final touches on the food for the main course, enlist a friend or relative to help you. Ask her to assemble the salad. Heat the cheese sauce.

SERVING SUGGESTIONS

Serve the chicken, potatoes and salad buffet style. Put salad in lettuce-lined salad bowl, or if you prefer, spoon it into individual bowls or on individual plates and set in place on the dinner table. Serve hot cheese sauce in gravy boat or bowl. At dessert time, cut the cake at the table and pass it. Serve sherbet in stemmed dessert glasses.

SAUERKRAUT BALLS

Men always single out these appetizers as especially praiseworthy

¼ c. shortening	1 (12 oz.) can corned beef, finely
1 medium onion, minced	chopped
2 tblsp. minced parsley	1 (1 lb.) can sauerkraut, well
¼ c. flour	drained (about 2 c.)
1 tsp. dry mustard	1 egg, well beaten
½ c. milk	2 tblsp. cold water
	¾ c. fine bread crumbs

Melt shortening in small skillet; add onion and parsley. Cook over low heat, stirring until lightly browned. Stir in flour, mixed with mustard. Gradually add milk, stirring to blend well. Cook until smooth and thick, stirring constantly.

Add corned beef and sauerkraut, blending well. Cool and chill several hours or overnight. Shape in 50 small balls.

Combine beaten egg with water and blend thoroughly. Roll sauerkraut balls in egg mixture, then in bread crumbs. (If made ahead, chill until serving time.) Place on cold broiler grid and broil to brown lightly on all sides, turning as necessary to brown entire surface. Makes about 50 appetizers.

SOUTHERN STUFFED CHICKEN BREASTS

Delicious adaptation of chicken Kiev omits the deep fat frying

4 large chicken breasts, boned and cut in halves lengthwise	Flour
	1 egg, well beaten
Salt	1 tblsp. water
½ c. softened butter	½ c. fine bread crumbs
½ c. chopped onion	¼ c. butter or regular margarine
½ c. chopped parsley	

Remove skin from chicken breasts; pound with wooden mallet or rolling pin to flatten to ¼" thickness. Sprinkle with salt.

Cream ½ c. softened butter; add onion and parsley. Divide mixture into 8 even portions. Spread butter mixture at the end of each chicken breast. Roll as for jelly roll; tuck in sides of meat. Press to seal; fasten with toothpicks, or tie with string to secure.

Dust each chicken roll with flour; dip into egg beaten with the water, and roll in bread crumbs. Chill at least 1 hour.

Melt ¼ c. butter in a skillet; brown the chicken rolls on all sides. Cover and cook gently 12 minutes; uncover and cook 5 minutes longer, or until crisp, turning the rolls once. Remove toothpicks or string. Serve hot. Makes 6 to 8 servings.

BUFFET CHEESE POTATOES

You can make these in a ring mold but a loaf is easier to unmold

6 c. cubed cooked potatoes (6 or 7)
½ tsp. salt
¼ tsp. pepper
¼ c. butter or regular margarine
¼ c. flour
½ tsp. salt
⅛ tsp. pepper

½ tsp. dry mustard
2 c. milk
½ lb. sharp Cheddar cheese, shredded
2 tblsp. crushed round buttery crackers
½ c. grated Cheddar cheese
1 to 2 tblsp. milk

Combine potatoes, ½ tsp. salt and ¼ tsp. pepper in mixing bowl.

Melt butter in saucepan, blend in flour, ½ tsp. salt, ⅛ tsp. pepper and dry mustard. Add milk and cook over low heat until sauce is thickened. Stir in shredded cheese and continue cooking until cheese melts. Remove sauce from heat.

Mix just enough cheese sauce into potatoes to hold them together. Place in a well-greased 9×5×3″ loaf pan. Cover and refrigerate several hours or overnight.

Refrigerate remaining cheese sauce.

Remove potatoes from refrigerator, run knife carefully around edges of pan. Place ovenproof platter or baking sheet on top of loaf pan. Invert and let stand a few minutes. Tap gently to loosen potatoes. Remove loaf pan. Sprinkle potatoes with cracker crumbs and grated cheese. Bake in hot oven (400°) about 25 minutes, until potatoes are lightly browned and heated through.

Serve with remaining cheese sauce. To heat sauce, add 1 to 2 tblsp. milk to cold sauce and place over medium heat, stirring frequently. Makes 8 servings.

BABY BEET SALAD

Beets the size of ping-pong balls are ideal for this colorful salad

1 c. French dressing
2 drops Tabasco sauce
½ tsp. minced fresh thyme leaves, or ¼ tsp. dried thyme leaves

3 c. cooked baby beets, quartered
Lettuce
2 hard-cooked eggs, chopped

Mix French dressing, Tabasco and thyme in saucepan; simmer 5 minutes. Add beets, cover and refrigerate overnight. Drain.

Arrange beets on lettuce or other crisp greens. Sprinkle with chopped eggs. Makes 6 servings.

COCONUT POUND CAKE

A big cake that's a favorite of a charming Virginia hostess

1 c. butter	1 c. milk
2 c. sugar	1 (3½ oz.) can flaked coconut
5 eggs	(1⅓ c.)
3 c. sifted flour	1 tsp. lemon extract
¼ tsp. salt	½ tsp. vanilla

Using medium speed on mixer, cream together butter and sugar until light and fluffy. Add eggs, one at a time, beating well after each addition (this takes about 10 minutes).

Sift flour with salt; add alternately with milk to creamed mixture, beating after each addition. Add remaining ingredients. Pour into greased and floured 10″ tube pan.

Bake in slow oven (325°) 1 hour and 30 minutes, or until cake tests done. Cool 10 minutes, then remove from pan and complete cooling on rack. Makes 12 servings.

CHICKEN BARBECUE DINNER

Hawaiian Dip* Sesame Seed Crackers
Rye Crackers Chilled Fruit Juices
Barbecued Chicken Halves* Rice Pilaf*
Buttered Asparagus Fruit Salad
Homemade Vanilla Ice Cream*

The charm of entertaining along palm-fringed Hawaiian shores or island cattle ranches has been copied in country homes on the mainland in this flavorful dinner. Teamwork is the key to getting this meal ready; everyone in the family will feel he's an important part of the party. The menu divides readily into three parts.

The host assumes the responsibility for building the fire and cooking the chicken to perfection. The hostess takes on the cooking in the kitchen. How the children help depends largely on their age. An ideal assignment for them is to turn the ice cream freezer. The reward for them on the completion of this job is to sample the ice cream that clings to the dasher. A teen-age daughter or son will be expert at fixing the dip and fruit juice.

TIMETABLE

On Guest Day: Freeze the ice cream at least 4 hours before dinnertime so it will ripen. Make the barbecue sauce 2 or more hours before you want to use it. Allow a minimum of 1½ hours for getting the coals ready for cooking and grilling the chicken. During that time, fix the dip and chill it; arrange crackers on trays. Break cauliflower into flowerets; place in cold water ready to drain and serve. Combine equal parts of reconstituted frozen lemonade and pineapple juice concentrates (or pineapple and grapefruit concentrates). Cook the frozen asparagus and the rice during the last few minutes before serving.

SERVING SUGGESTIONS

Serve the food from a buffet table set up near the grill, or, if it is warm and the house is air-conditioned, serve and eat indoors. Pour the beverage, icy cold, from a pitcher. Set the bowl of dip on a tray and surround with the crackers. Place drained cauliflowerets in a bowl for dipping.

HAWAIIAN DIP

Ranch hostesses in our newest state excel in informal entertaining; try this Hawaiian-inspired dip and its interesting accompaniments

1 c. mayonnaise, chilled	2 tblsp. finely chopped candied
1 c. dairy sour cream	ginger
¼ c. finely minced onion	1 tblsp. soy sauce
¼ c. minced parsley	1 clove garlic, crushed
½ c. finely chopped canned water	Salt
chestnuts	

Combine mayonnaise and sour cream; add remaining ingredients and mix well. Cover and chill. Serve with sesame seed crackers, rye crackers and cauliflowerets for dunking. Makes about 3 cups.

BARBECUED CHICKEN HALVES

*Lemon barbecue sauce and unhurried cooking give delicious results.
Recipe is for one chicken but you can increase it to fit your crowd*

1 clove garlic, crushed (optional)	2 tblsp. grated onion
½ tsp. salt	¼ tsp. pepper
¼ c. salad oil	Salt
½ c. lemon juice	1 broiler-fryer, split in half
1 tsp. Worchestershire sauce	

Put garlic and ½ tsp. salt in bowl; stir in oil, lemon juice, Worcestershire sauce, onion and pepper. Let this sauce stand 1 to 2 hours to blend flavors.

When the charcoal has a white covering, it is ready for the grilling. (It takes about 30 minutes after igniting to reach this stage.) Spread the coals out about the size of the area the chicken will occupy. Salt chicken halves lightly. Then brush skin side of chicken lightly with barbecue sauce and place this side down on grill, 8 to 10″ above the coals. Grill 15 minutes. Brush top side of chicken generously with sauce while skin side cooks. Turn chicken and cook other side about 15 minutes, brushing top with sauce. Repeat turning and brushing with sauce until chicken has broiled at least 1 hour. The chicken is done when its juices stop dripping. Makes 2 or 4 servings. Most people will eat a half chicken, although others prefer a quarter. If quarters are desired, divide halves after cooking.

RICE PILAF

You can make this skillet version of pilaf with canned chicken broth

1 medium onion, finely chopped	1½ tsp. salt
¾ c. thinly sliced celery	¼ tsp. pepper
1½ c. long grain rice	½ tsp. thyme leaves
¼ c. butter or regular margarine	3½ c. chicken broth

Sauté onion, celery and rice in butter over low heat until vegetables are transparent and rice is golden. Add salt, pepper, thyme and chicken broth.

Cover skillet with a tight-fitting lid and cook over low heat until broth is absorbed, about 20 to 25 minutes. Makes 8 servings.

HOMEMADE VANILLA ICE CREAM

Easy-to-make, velvety ice cream—there's no cooking of ingredients

4 eggs, beaten well	1½ qts. dairy half-and-half
1 c. plus 2 tblsp. sugar	1 qt. milk
1 (14 oz.) can sweetened	2 tblsp. vanilla
condensed milk	Dash of salt

Mix all ingredients in a 1-gal. ice cream freezer can, adding a little milk if necessary to fill can almost three fourths full. Adjust dasher and cover. Pack crushed ice and rock salt around can, using 6 parts ice to 1 part salt.

Turn dasher slowly until the ice melts enough to make a brine. Add more ice and salt, mixed in the proper proportion, to maintain the ice level. Turn the handle fast and steadily until it turns hard. Then remove ice until the level is below the lid of can; take off lid and remove the dasher.

Plug the hole in lid and cover can with several thicknesses of waxed paper or foil to make a tight fit for the lid. Pack more ice-salt mixture, using 4 parts ice to 1 part salt, around can and filling the freezer. Cover with a blanket, canvas or other heavy cloth, or with newspaper. Let the ice cream ripen 4 hours before serving. Or put it in the home freezer for an hour. Makes 1 gallon.

N O T E : If you use an electric ice cream freezer, follow the manufacturer's directions.

SIT-DOWN DINNER

Orange/Cranberry Juice   Corn Chips

Royal Chicken Pie*   Mashed Winter Squash

Lima Beans with Mushrooms   Pickled Beets

Sun Gold Fruit Salad*   Cookie Tray

Milk   Coffee

When the guest list includes children, consider this dinner menu. All the food, from the chilled juice at the beginning to the cookies at the end, appeals to people of all ages. And children can easily manage it. They like chicken pie—this country way with chicken never goes out of style. It changes with the years, but the delicious old-fashioned taste remains.

The salad mold answers both for salad and dessert, but, because youngsters, as well as many grownups, like to end meals on a sweet note, we include a tray of homemade cookies. Be sure to have milk for the children and-coffee for adults—plenty of milk because some adults will likely choose it for their beverage too.

TIMETABLE

Do-Ahead: A day before the company dinner make and pour the salad into a mold and chill. Cook the chicken, cool; remove meat from bones, dice and refrigerate meat and broth separately (fat will rise to top of broth for use in sauce). Bake cookies unless you have a supply in the freezer.

On Guest Day: Frost salad; return to refrigerator. Cook squash, drain and mash; season at your convenience to reheat before serving. You will need about 9 c. diced peeled butternut or Hubbard squash for 8 or 9 servings. Prepare chicken filling for pie when you have time, but be sure to reheat it until bubbly hot before putting on the crust to bake. Cook 3 (10 oz.) pkgs. frozen lima beans by package directions, drain; add 1 (6 oz.) can sliced mushrooms, drained, and ¼ c. butter or regular margarine. Reheat. Combine equal parts reconstituted frozen orange juice concentrate and canned cranberry juice cocktail.

SERVING SUGGESTIONS

Pour fruit juice mixture into pitcher over cracked ice, carry with bowl of corn chips on tray to living room and serve in juice glasses. Since the salad is beautiful, it's a good idea to serve it at the dinner table. Sugar cookies and chocolate chip cookies make an attractive tray—children love a chance to make a choice.

ROYAL CHICKEN PIE

Cheese and olives impart special flavor to biscuit crust spirals

¼ c. chopped onion	2½ c. chicken broth
1 branch celery, chopped	½ tsp. soy sauce
¼ c. chicken fat	¼ tsp. pepper
½ c. chopped pimiento	¼ tsp. garlic salt
3 c. diced cooked chicken	Crust
3½ tblsp. flour	

Sauté onion and celery in 2 tblsp. chicken fat until onion is transparent, but not brown; add pimiento. Add chicken and pour into 2-qt. casserole.

Melt remaining 2 tblsp. chicken fat in skillet. Add flour and stir until smooth. Add chicken broth, soy sauce, pepper and garlic salt; cook and stir over medium heat until sauce thickens. Pour over chicken in casserole, cover and place in hot oven (425°) about 20 minutes, or until bubbly hot. Remove from oven.

Arrange slices of crust over top of hot chicken in casserole. Return to oven and bake about 12 minutes more, or until crust is light golden brown. Makes 8 servings.

Crust: Make biscuit dough with 2 c. all-purpose buttermilk biscuit mix following package directions. Roll in 10×9″ rectangle. Sprinkle with ¾ c. shredded Cheddar cheese and ¼ c. finely chopped pimiento-stuffed olives. Roll as for jelly roll; cut in ½″ slices and place on hot chicken mixture. Brush top with 1 tblsp. melted butter or regular margarine.

N O T E : You can substitute chopped green pepper for the pimiento; sauté it with onion and celery.

SUN GOLD FRUIT SALAD

Frosting with shredded cheese trim substitutes for salad dressing

2 (3 oz.) pkgs. orange flavor gelatin
2 c. boiling water
1½ c. cold water
1 (11 oz.) can mandarin oranges
1 (8¾ oz.) can apricot halves
1 c. seedless white grapes, fresh or canned
2 large bananas, sliced
Fluffy Topping
¼ c. grated American cheese

Dissolve gelatin in boiling water; add cold water. Refrigerate until syrupy.

Drain fruit, reserving 1 c. liquid. Fold fruit into gelatin mixture; pour into 9×5×3″ loaf pan or 11½×7⅜×1½″ glass dish. Refrigerate overnight.

Unmold salad and frost with Fluffy Topping. Sprinkle top with cheese. Refrigerate until topping sets, about 1 hour. Makes 12 servings.

Fluffy Topping: Combine 6 tblsp. sugar and 2 tblsp. cornstarch in a heavy saucepan. Blend in 1 egg, slightly beaten, and the 1 c. reserved fruit liquid. Cook, stirring constantly, over low heat until thickened. Remove from heat; stir in 2 tblsp. butter and 1 tblsp. lemon juice. Cool. Whip 1 c. heavy cream, or 1 envelope dessert topping mix; fold into the cooled mixture.

COLORFUL CHICKEN DINNER

Golden Broiled Chicken* Cranberry/Orange Garnish
Broccoli/Cauliflower Scallop*
Green Pea Salad*
Hot Rolls Apricot Preserves
Glorified Rice with Green Grapes*

Broiled chicken requires some attention while cooking, but it is ready to serve when you take it from the oven (no carving). It cooks only 45 minutes—tastes great. To the delight of weight-watching guests, it is lower in calories than many other platter favorites.

In this menu two old-time friends, chicken and rice, appear but the rice assumes the dessert role. It's really a glamorized edition of a country rice pudding. Broccoli and cauliflower teamed together in a baking dish make a pretty green and white combination. And the vegetable salad provides a change from the universal tossed greens.

TIMETABLE

Do-Ahead: Make the dessert the evening before the dinner party or, if easier, the next morning. It needs to chill several hours.

On Guest Day: Make the salad at least 2 to 3 hours before you want to serve it; cover and refrigerate. Get the broccoli and cauliflower ready to bake; refrigerate. About 1¾ hours before dinnertime, add the marinade to the chicken. And 45 minutes before you want to serve it, place chicken in preheated broiler oven. When you remove it from oven, set the regulator at 350° and put the Broccoli/Cauliflower Scallop in oven to heat for 15 to 20 minutes. Put the foil-wrapped rolls alongside the last 10 minutes.

SERVING SUGGESTIONS

Serve chicken on a warm platter and garnish with orange slices topped with circles (round slices) of canned jellied cranberry sauce. The scallop requires no trim—it's decorative by itself. Serve the salad in a bowl, or if you prefer, in lettuce cups on individual salad plates. When it's time for dessert, fold in whipped cream and spoon rice into stemmed dessert glasses; garnish each serving with a tiny cluster of green grapes. This is an ideal dinner to serve buffet style.

GOLDEN BROILED CHICKEN

Weight-watchers rejoice! One 3-ounce serving has only 185 calories

1 c. cider vinegar	½ tsp. white pepper
¾ c. salad oil	1 egg, beaten
4½ tsp. salt	½ c. sliced onion
1 tblsp. poultry seasoning	2 (3 lb.) broiler-fryers, quartered

Combine vinegar, oil, salt, poultry seasoning, pepper, egg and onion in a 2-qt. saucepan. Stirring constantly, bring mixture to a boil. Pour over chicken and let stand at room temperature 1 hour.

Place chicken skin side down on broiler pan. Place pan in broiler, 7 to 9″ from heat. Broil 30 minutes, basting frequently with marinade. Turn chicken and baste. Broil another 15 minutes or until chicken is tender and golden. Makes 4 to 8 servings.

BROCCOLI/CAULIFLOWER SCALLOP

Contrast in color gives this vegetable combination a party look

2 (10 oz.) pkgs. frozen broccoli (spears)	1½ c. milk
1 (10 oz.) pkg. frozen cauliflower	1 c. cut-up process American cheese
2 tblsp. flour	⅛ tsp. salt
2 tblsp. melted butter or regular margarine	Dash of pepper
1 (4 oz.) can mushrooms	2 tblsp. butter
	1 c. bread crumbs

Cook broccoli and cauliflower separately by package directions; do not overcook. Drain and cool.

Add flour to 2 tblsp. melted butter and stir over low heat to make a smooth paste, but do not brown.

Drain mushrooms. Mix liquid drained from mushroom with milk; gradually add to flour-butter mixture, and cook, stirring. As mixture thickens, add cheese. Season with salt and pepper. Stir until cheese melts. Remove from heat and add mushrooms.

Arrange broccoli and cauliflower in alternate rows in shallow 11×7×1½″ glass baking dish or shallow casserole. Pour cheese sauce over top.

Melt 2 tblsp. butter in small skillet, add crumbs and cook, stirring until crumbs are golden brown. Spoon crumbs around edge of Broccoli/Cauliflower Scallop to make a border. Heat in moderate oven (350°) 15 to 20 minutes, or until bubbly. Serves 8 to 10.

GREEN PEA SALAD

Avoid overcooking peas or you will lose bright green color. Just heat them well. Perfect escort for lamb roasts and chops

2 (10 oz.) pkgs. frozen peas	1 tsp. sugar
½ c. salad oil	1 tblsp. minced fresh mint leaves
⅓ c. red wine vinegar	½ c. chopped celery
1½ tsp. salt	½ c. redskin peanuts
¼ tsp. pepper	¼ c. dairy sour cream

Cook peas by package directions, only to heat through. Drain.

Combine salad oil, vinegar, salt, pepper, sugar and mint leaves. Pour over peas; cover and chill at least 2 to 3 hours. Just before serving stir in celery, peanuts and sour cream. Makes 6 to 8 servings.

GLORIFIED RICE WITH GREEN GRAPES

No rice pudding ever tasted better than this luscious chilled version

2 c. cooked regular rice	½ c. sugar
1 c. canned crushed pineapple, drained	1 tsp. vanilla
	1 c. seedless green grapes
2 c. miniature marshmallows	1 c. heavy cream, whipped

Combine rice, pineapple, marshmallows, sugar, vanilla and grapes. Cover and chill at least 1 hour, or several hours in refrigerator. Just before serving fold in whipped cream. Makes 6 to 8 servings.

A DINNER TO TOTE

Sesame Chicken*
Scalloped Corn* or Honey-Glazed Sweet Potatoes*
Tomato Salad Ring*   Herb Bread*
Chocolate Cake

Picture the food for this cooperative dinner on your buffet: golden-crusted chicken; casserole of yellow corn with a crunchy, brown top; the scarlet salad ring; homemade bread, and a lovely chocolate cake. Members of the club will feel proud of this cooperative meal to which they contributed.

All the dishes in this menu travel successfully, although if the weather is warm, substitute a fresh tomato-cucumber salad for the molded ring. Wrap the bread in foil and heat it before taking it to the gathering place, where you'll want to put it in a low oven to keep warm until serving time. Do the same with the corn.

This is also a menu which one woman can prepare and serve to guests in her home. The following timetable is for her rather than for the cooperative, share-the-load dinner. If serving more than 6 people, the chicken recipe needs to be doubled and there will not be room for two pans and the corn casserole in the oven at the same time. Fix Honey-Glazed Sweet Potatoes instead of the corn.

TIMETABLE

Do-Ahead: Make the salad ring a day ahead and refrigerate. Bake the bread and cake a day or several days ahead and freeze.

On Guest Day: Put the chicken in the oven about 1¼ hours before serving time. The sweet potatoes are a fast-fix dish, but allow 15 to 20 minutes for them. Heat the foil-wrapped bread 15 to 20 minutes, or 25 to 30 minutes if frozen.

SERVING SUGGESTIONS

This is an excellent dinner to serve buffet style.

SESAME CHICKEN

A sophisticated main dish that's tasty. It will impress your guests

Breasts, thighs and legs of 2
    broiler-fryers
1 tblsp. melted butter
1 tsp. prepared mustard
2 tblsp. lemon juice
1 tsp. salt
2 tblsp. flour

⅓ c. Toasted Sesame Seeds
1 pkg. cheese-flavored salad
    dressing mix
¾ c. evaporated milk
1½ c. prepared pancake mix
1 tblsp. paprika
½ c. shortening

Wash chicken; pat dry with paper towels. Mix butter, mustard, lemon juice, salt, flour, sesame seeds and salad dressing mix to make a paste. Spread on the chicken to coat pieces.

Dip chicken in milk, then in pancake mix combined with paprika. Lightly brown in hot shortening; turn carefully with tongs.

Place in 13×9×2" baking pan. Cover pan with aluminum foil. Bake in moderate oven (375°) 35 minutes. Then bake uncovered 25 minutes, or until chicken is tender. Makes 6 servings.

Toasted Sesame Seeds: Spread sesame seeds in shallow baking pan; bake in moderate oven (350°) about 20 minutes, until seeds turn a pale brown. Watch them to prevent overbrowning, which destroys the seeds' finest flavor.

SCALLOPED CORN

Corn vies with scalloped potatoes for top honors in country kitchens

½ c. chopped onion
½ c. chopped green pepper
¼ c. butter or regular margarine
¼ c. flour
1½ tsp. salt
¼ tsp. pepper

½ tsp. dry mustard
1½ c. milk
2 (1 lb.) cans whole kernel corn
2 eggs, slightly beaten
¾ c. cracker crumbs
2 tblsp. melted butter

Cook and stir onion and green pepper in ¼ c. melted butter until onion is tender; do not brown. Remove from heat and stir in flour, salt, pepper and mustard. Cook and stir over low heat until mixture is bubbly hot. Remove from heat and gradually stir in milk. Stir and heat to boiling; boil 5 minutes. Stir in corn and eggs.

Pour into greased 2-qt. casserole. Combine cracker crumbs with

2 tblsp. melted butter; sprinkle over top of corn. Bake in moderate oven (350°) 40 to 45 minutes. Makes 8 servings.

HONEY-GLAZED SWEET POTATOES

Take your choice of candying these in oven or on top of range

¼ c. strained honey

2 tblsp. brown sugar

2 tblsp. butter or regular margarine

¼ tsp. salt

1 (17 oz.) can vacuum pack sweet potatoes, drained

Combine honey, brown sugar, butter, salt and the liquid drained from sweet potatoes in saucepan. Boil until thickened. Add sweet potatoes and heat; spoon glaze over potatoes occasionally. Or put sweet potatoes in an oiled shallow baking dish (if sweet potatoes are large, cut in halves). Pour the syrup over and bake in moderate oven (375°) about 30 minutes. Makes 4 servings.

TOMATO SALAD RING

Set out salad dressing to spoon over colorful salad if desired

4 c. tomato juice

⅓ c. chopped onion

¼ c. chopped celery leaves

2 tblsp. brown sugar

1 tsp. salt

1 small bay leaf

3 whole cloves

2 envelopes unflavored gelatin

3 tblsp. lemon juice

1 c. finely chopped celery

Lettuce

Combine 2 c. tomato juice, onion, celery leaves, brown sugar, salt, bay leaf and cloves. Simmer 5 minutes; strain.

Soften gelatin in 1 c. remaining tomato juice. Add to hot tomato juice mixture and stir until gelatin dissolves. Add remaining 1 c. tomato juice and lemon juice. Chill until mixture is consistency of unbeaten egg white. Fold in celery and pour into a 5-c. ring mold. Chill until firm. Unmold and serve on lettuce. Makes 8 servings.

HERB BREAD

Herb seasoning does something good to the chicken it accompanies

2 pkgs. active dry yeast

¼ c. warm water (110 to 115°)

⅓ c. shortening

¼ c. sugar

1 tblsp. salt

1 c. scalded milk

2 eggs

4½ to 5 c. flour

Herb Butter

Sprinkle yeast on warm water; stir to dissolve.

In mixing bowl, combine shortening, sugar, salt and hot scalded milk; stir until shortening melts and sugar dissolves. Cool to lukewarm.

Blend unbeaten eggs and yeast into lukewarm mixture. Gradually add flour to make a soft dough that leaves the sides of bowl.

Turn onto lightly floured board and knead until smooth and elastic. Place in lightly greased bowl; turn dough over to grease top. Cover and let rise in warm place until doubled, about 1½ hours.

Roll out half of dough ⅛" thick. Cut in 3 to 3½" rounds. Spread top of each round with Herb Butter. Fold dough in half (buttered side inside) and lay on greased baking sheet. Spread top with Herb Butter. Continue placing buttered and folded rounds on baking sheet, folded side down, overlapping previous folded round three fourths of the way. You will have about 14 folded rolls, which make a loaf. Spread top of this loaf with Herb Butter. Let rise 30 to 40 minutes. Repeat with second half of dough.

Bake in moderate oven (350°) 20 to 25 minutes. Makes 2 loaves.

Herb Butter: Combine ½ c. softened butter or regular margarine, ½ tsp. caraway seeds, ½ tsp. sweet basil leaves, ½ tsp. grated onion, ¼ tsp. orégano leaves and ⅛ tsp. garlic powder. Mix.

GARDEN DINNER

Summer Chicken with Peas and New Potatoes*
Wilted Garden Lettuce
Strawberry Satin Pie*

June, the time of roses, is also the time for the first batch of succulent peas. Berry patches redden with ripe strawberries and new potatoes appear more abundantly in supermarkets. It's the perfect time to ask friends to a dinner of wonderful country foods.

This menu is an easy one to execute. The chicken, potatoes and peas cook together in the same skillet. You can get the meal ready from start to finish, if you bake the pie ahead, in an hour. The pie is something to remember with pleasure—both visually and gastronomically!

TIMETABLE

Do-Ahead: Bake and cool pie shell. Make the cream filling, pour it into the pie shell and chill overnight.

On Guest Day: Arrange berries with precision on top of filling in pie shell, glaze and return to refrigerator. Chill at least 3 hours. Look in Index for recipe for Wilted Garden Lettuce (included in "Supper in Lilac Time" menu). Gather leaf lettuce, wash, place in plastic bags and chill. About 1 hour before dinnertime, start cooking chicken and potatoes. Shell peas. Add them after the chicken has cooked 30 minutes. When chicken and vegetables are cooked, remove from skillet and make the sauce or gravy. Wilt the lettuce.

SERVING SUGGESTIONS

This is a sit-down dinner. Serve chicken, potatoes and peas on one large platter. If peas are not overcooked, they will retain their bright green color to contrast with the red skins of the small potatoes. Pour sauce over chicken or pass it in gravy boat or bowl. Garnish with snipped fresh parsley if you wish.

SUMMER CHICKEN WITH PEAS AND NEW POTATOES

Perfect combination of late spring or early summer country foods

6 tblsp. butter or regular margarine

1 broiler-fryer (about 2½ lbs.) cut in serving pieces

1 lb. small new potatoes, scrubbed, with a strip peeled around the centers

Salt

Freshly ground pepper

2 tblsp. lemon juice

3 green onions with tops, thinly sliced

1 lb. fresh peas, shelled (about 1 c.), or 1 (10 oz.) pkg. frozen peas

¼ c. chopped fresh parsley

1 c. dairy sour cream

1 tsp. thyme leaves, crumbled

½ tsp. salt

¼ tsp. pepper

Parsley (for garnish)

Melt butter in a large skillet. Add chicken and potatoes and brown slowly on all sides; season with salt and pepper. (Be generous with pepper.) Sprinkle chicken with lemon juice; reduce heat, cover pan and simmer 30 minutes.

Add green onions to butter in bottom of skillet; sprinkle peas and parsley over chicken and potatoes; cover again and simmer 10 minutes more, or until chicken and potatoes are tender.

Remove chicken and vegetables to serving platter; keep warm.

Remove skillet from heat. Add sour cream, thyme, ½ tsp. salt and ¼ tsp. pepper; stir to mix well and to loosen pan drippings.

Pour over chicken or pass as sauce. Garnish with additional parsley; serve immediately. Makes 4 servings.

NOTE: You may want to make two skilletfuls for 8 servings.

STRAWBERRY SATIN PIE

The beauty of the pie depends on artistic arrangement of the berries

Baked 9″ pie shell

½ c. sliced toasted almonds

Creamy Satin Filling

1½ c. fresh strawberries

Shiny Glaze

Cover bottom of baked pie shell with almonds.

Cover almonds with Creamy Satin Filling. Chill thoroughly at least 3 hours, or overnight.

Slice strawberries in halves, reserving a few perfect berries for center of pie. Arrange on filling in layers, starting at outer edge.

Place some berries cut side up to make a pattern. Cover with Shiny Glaze. Refrigerate 1 hour, or until serving time. Makes 8 servings.

CREAMY SATIN FILLING

Perfect filling for strawberry pie—so smooth—it deserves its name

½ c. sugar
3 tblsp. cornstarch
3 tblsp. flour
½ tsp. salt

2 c. milk
1 egg, slightly beaten
½ c. heavy cream, whipped
1 tsp. vanilla

Combine sugar, cornstarch, flour and salt in saucepan.

Gradually add milk, stirring until smooth. Cook, stirring constantly, until mixture is thick and bubbling.

Stir a little of this hot mixture into egg, then add to hot mixture and cook until just bubbling hot again.

Cool, then chill thoroughly. This mixture will be very thick. Beat with mixer or rotary beater until smooth.

Fold in whipped cream and vanilla.

Shiny Glaze: Crush ½ c. fresh strawberries. Add ½ c. water and cook 2 minutes; strain through sieve. Combine ¼ c. sugar and 1 tblsp. cornstarch in small saucepan; stir in berry juice. Cook, stirring constantly, until thick and clear. Cool; spoon carefully over strawberries in the pie.

SUMMER CHICKEN DINNER

Chicken Parmesan*   Dilly Potato Salad*
Corn on the Cob   Ripe Tomato Platter
Vanilla Ice Cream   Chocolate Peppermint Sauce*

When plump, juicy tomatoes hang heavy on vines and sweet corn is ready in the garden or field, it's a great time to invite friends to dinner. Team these vegetables with new-potato salad and chicken and you have a feast. A country dinner like this makes everyone wish summer never would end.

TIMETABLE

Do-Ahead: Make the potato salad and chocolate sauce a day ahead and refrigerate.

On Guest Day: Since the chicken needs to cook 1 hour, put it in the oven about 1¼ hours before mealtime. Bring the corn to the kitchen as near the dinner hour as you can. Allow 2 ears per person. If you buy it, select ears with deep green husks. To test it, puncture a kernel with the thumbnail. If a thin, milky liquid spurts out, the corn is in its prime. If the milky juice is thick and the skin on kernels tough, the corn is too old. When it must wait in the kitchen, keep it, unhusked, in the refrigerator. Husk and remove silk just before cooking. Cook briefly at the last minute. One good way is to place the ears in a large kettle, cover with cold, unsalted water and bring quickly to a boil. Lift ears from the hot water with tongs, drain and rush to table. While it cooks, peel, quarter and arrange tomatoes on platter or tray and carry, along with the potato salad, to the table. Move ice cream from freezer to refrigerator when dinner is served. If you like warm sauce on ice cream, set it over low heat while you dish up the ice cream.

SERVING SUGGESTIONS

Sprinkle tomatoes with chopped parsley. For attractive service, center olives and pickle slices on tomato platter. Garnish potato salad with hard-cooked egg slices. Either spoon chocolate sauce on the ice cream or pass it in a pitcher so everyone can help himself. For dessert you can serve chilled watermelon or other melon instead of ice cream.

CHICKEN PARMESAN

The coating on this chicken turns golden—guests like the flavor

1⅓ c. packaged herb-seasoned stuffing	⅛ tsp. pepper
	1¼ tsp. monosodium glutamate
½ c. shredded Parmesan cheese	¾ c. butter
¼ tsp. garlic salt	16 pieces chicken (breasts, thighs
1¼ tsp. salt	and legs)

Roll stuffing to make fine crumbs; put in pie pan. Mix in cheese and seasonings.

Melt ½ c. butter (1 stick) in shallow pan. Dip chicken pieces, one at a time, in butter, then roll in crumbs to coat.

Arrange chicken in large, shallow baking pan lined with foil. Do not overlap pieces. Dot with remaining butter, breaking it in bits.

Bake, uncovered, in moderate oven (350°) 1 hour. Serves 8.

DILLY POTATO SALAD

Chilling enhances the good taste—permits flavors to blend

5 c. cubed cooked potatoes	2 tsp. sugar
4 hard-cooked eggs, chopped	½ tsp. pepper
¼ c. chopped dill pickle	1 tsp. chopped fresh dill, or ¾ tsp.
½ c. chopped onion	dried dill weed
¼ c. vinegar	½ c. mayonnaise
1 tsp. salt	Paprika

Toss together potatoes, eggs, pickle and onion. Mix vinegar, salt, sugar, pepper, dill and mayonnaise; pour over the potatoes. Toss lightly. Sprinkle with paprika. Cover and chill. Makes 8 servings.

CHOCOLATE PEPPERMINT SAUCE

Most everyone prefers the sauce warm—try it on chocolate ice cream

2 squares unsweetened chocolate	2 tblsp. butter or regular
⅓ c. water	margarine
½ c. sugar	½ tsp. peppermint extract
Dash of salt	½ c. chopped nuts

Combine chocolate and water in small saucepan. Stir over low heat until smooth. Add sugar and salt. Cook, stirring constantly until sugar dissolves. Add butter, extract and nuts; stir to mix. Serve warm or cold. Makes about 1 cup.

HARVEST FESTIVAL DINNER

Oven-Fried Pecan Chicken*   Potato Roses*
Smoky Green Beans
Ripe Tomato Salad*   Overnight Refrigerator Pan Rolls*
Corn Relish   Peach Pickles   Raspberry Jam
Melon Compote*

When the days are cooler, but before frost strikes, the generous bounty of food in country places inspires many women to ask friends over to dinner. They never underestimate the appeal of fried chicken, mashed potatoes, sliced tomatoes, green beans and piping hot, home-made rolls.

Our menu gives new and easier versions of these old-time favorites. It's a good idea to point up the flavors of food in the main course with relishes. End the dinner with a luscious melon compote as a bow to a departing season; melons soon will be a memory of summer. Or substitute apple pies for them if you have time to bake them. Made with freshly harvested fruit, they are hard to beat.

TIMETABLE

Do-Ahead: Make dough for rolls and cook and shape Potato Roses a day ahead; refrigerate.

On Guest Day: Shape dough for rolls, let rise until doubled, 1 to 1½ hours, and bake 15 to 20 minutes. You can bake them early in the day and reheat at mealtime after you take the potatoes from the oven. Or you can bake them while serving the main course. They will be ready to pass shortly after everyone starts to eat.

Peel melon, cover and refrigerate at any convenient time. Combine honey and lime juice, cover and chill. Cook the chicken 1 or 2 hours, whichever time is best for you (see recipe directions). While it is in the oven, cook the green beans. If you have fresh beans, cook them in a little water, lightly salted, until just tender, 10 to 15 minutes. Drain and season with 6 tblsp. butter or margarine and ¾ tsp. smoky salt. Or cook 3 (10 oz.) pkgs. frozen green beans by package directions and season like the fresh beans.

SERVING SUGGESTIONS

Serve this dinner buffet style if you like. Heap the golden fried chicken on a platter, serve the pretty potatoes on another platter, the green beans and salad in bowls. Display the relishes on a lazy susan if you have one. If you have a sit-down meal, you may wish to serve the plates in the kitchen. Enlisting the help of one of your guests simplifies and speeds up the serving. Serve the melon in compote dishes, or if you have a sit-down dinner, stemmed dessert glasses are a good choice. Use sprigs of fresh mint to garnish the inviting melon.

OVEN-FRIED PECAN CHICKEN

Crisp-coated, golden brown chicken has a rich, pecan taste

1 c. all-purpose buttermilk biscuit mix	1 (2½ to 4 lb.) broiler-fryer, cut in serving pieces
½ tsp. salt	½ c. evaporated milk
2 tsp. paprika	½ c. melted butter or regular margarine
½ tsp. poultry seasoning	
½ c. finely chopped pecans	

Combine biscuit mix, seasonings and pecans. Dip chicken into evaporated milk; then coat well with the flour mixture. Place in 13×9×2" baking pan.

Pour melted butter over the chicken, completely covering every piece. Bake in moderate oven (375°) 1 hour or in very slow oven (200°) for 2 hours, or until chicken is fork tender. Makes about 5 servings.

N O T E : To oven-fry chicken for 8 to 10 servings, double the recipe and arrange chicken pieces in two 13×9×2" baking pans. Bake, uncovered, on 2 racks in a moderate oven (375°) 30 minutes; reverse position of pans on shelves in oven and bake 30 minutes longer, or until chicken is tender.

POTATO ROSES

They sound fancy but are easier to make than you may think

4 lbs. baking potatoes	2 tblsp. grated Parmesan or Romano cheese
¼ c. butter	1 egg
1 tblsp. minced onion	Paprika
1½ tsp. salt	½ c. melted butter
⅛ tsp. pepper	
1 tblsp. minced parsley	

Peel potatoes; cut in halves and cook in boiling, lightly salted water until tender. Mash slightly.

Place potatoes in large mixer bowl; beat until light and fluffy. Add ¼ c. butter, onion, salt, pepper, parsley, cheese and egg. Whip until well mixed. Cool.

Moisten hands; shape potato mixture into balls, about ¾ c. each. Place on greased baking sheet; flatten slightly on bottom.

To form roses, dip forefinger in water; make an indentation in center of each potato ball. Swirl finger clockwise to make a spiral. If you wish, cover and chill overnight.

Before baking, sprinkle lightly with paprika and drizzle ½ c. melted butter over roses. Bake in very hot oven (450°) 8 minutes. Let set a few minutes. Makes 10 servings.

RIPE TOMATO SALAD

This salad features famous teammates, juicy red tomatoes and basil

4 ripe tomatoes, cut in wedges
Salt
2 tblsp. finely chopped fresh basil leaves or ½ tsp. dried basil leaves

2 tblsp. salad oil
Juice of ½ lemon

Sprinkle tomatoes with salt to season. Add basil to salad oil (if you use dried basil, crumble it). Sprinkle over tomatoes. Chill at least 1 hour.

Squeeze lemon juice over top just before serving. Serve on large plate or in shallow bowl. Lemon quarters and chopped parsley make an attractive garnish. Makes 6 to 8 servings.

OVERNIGHT REFRIGERATOR PAN ROLLS

Puffy, light, homemade rolls from dough that requires no kneading

2 pkgs. active dry yeast
2½ c. warm water (110 to 115°)
¾ c. soft or melted shortening
¾ c. sugar

2 eggs, well beaten
8 to 8½ c. flour
2½ tsp. salt

Soften yeast in warm water. Add shortening, sugar, eggs, 4 c. flour and salt. Stir to mix and then beat until smooth, about 1 minute.

Stir in remaining flour. (You may want to use your hands to mix in the last 2 cups.) This will be a soft dough.

Place in a greased bowl and lightly grease surface of dough. Cover tightly. Store in the refrigerator overnight or until needed. (Dough will keep about 4 days, but punch it down daily. Count days from time dough is placed in refrigerator.) Make pan rolls according to directions that follow. Dough makes 36 rolls. (This dough also will make two Golden Crown Coffee Cakes, included in Morning Coffee menu—see Index.)

Punch down refrigerated dough and pinch off one third. Cover the remaining dough and put back in the refrigerator.

Shape the one third dough into 12 rolls and place them in a greased 9×9×2″ baking pan. Cover with a clean towel and let rise until doubled, 1 to 1½ hours.

Bake in a hot oven (400°) 15 to 20 minutes. Turn out on wire rack. Serve hot.

MELON COMPOTE

Lime juice and honey complement melons—especially honeydews

8 c. bite-size melon pieces   ¼ c. honey
Juice of 2 limes

Use honeydew melon or a combination of honeydews and cantaloupe. Chill. Combine lime juice and honey; cover and chill. Just before serving, mix gently with melon. Makes 8 servings.

WILD DUCK DINNER

Tomato Juice Starter*   Country Cheese/Bacon Dip*
Carrot Sticks   Celery   Chips
Texas Barbecued Ducks* or California Rare Duck*
Stuffed Baked Sweet Potatoes*   Buttered Broccoli
Hard Rolls   Currant Jelly   Lemon Velvet Pie*

When the duck hunter returns home with his bounty, he'll be eager to share the treat with friends. Chances are good that his wife knows (from experience) how to meet the challenge. She plans a dinner menu that gives the ducks the spotlight, with all food accompaniments taking a secondary role.

Her menu is a blueprint for a delicious country-style duck dinner. You may wish to substitute traditional wild rice for the sweet potatoes, but the strain will be greater on your pocketbook if you do. The potatoes, a special favorite in southern game dinners, taste wonderful and add color to the meal. The appetizers are of course optional.

TIMETABLE

Do-Ahead: Bake and stuff sweet potatoes and make the barbecue sauce for the duck the day before your dinner. Cover and refrigerate.

On Guest Day: Make the pie in the morning and refrigerate. (You may need to bake two pies; it depends on the size of your family and guest list.) Fix the tomato juice drink; cover and chill. Blend the dip any convenient time in the afternoon (for serving in evening); cover and chill.

About 1½ hours before dinner put the ducks in the oven to bake. There are regional preferences for ways to cook wild ducks. You may choose to have California Rare Duck; it spends only 25 to 35 minutes in the oven. Reheat sweet potatoes 30 to 40 minutes alongside ducks if oven space permits. Otherwise increase the oven temperature to 400° and heat them after you remove the ducks from the oven, while you are getting the ducks ready to serve and cooking the frozen broccoli. You will need 3 (10 oz.) pkgs. for 8 to 9 servings; cook by package directions.

SERVING SUGGESTIONS

Serve the tomato juice drink and accompaniments in the living room before dinner. Join the guests there if you can spare time from the kitchen, but make your duck hunter responsible for serving this course and keeping guests happy. Many farmers consider it ideal to serve each person a whole duck, while others believe half a duck is adequate. The size of the birds influences the size of serving portions. Be sure to split birds in half lengthwise.

Display the ducks on a big platter if you have one. Clusters of seedless grapes make an interesting garnish (see photo). Another good way to serve this dinner is to arrange the food on the plates in the kitchen. Assign specific duties to your helper if you have one. How about asking a guest to help? She can serve the sweet potatoes and broccoli and garnish tops of sweet potatoes with half an orange slice.

TOMATO JUICE STARTER

Colorful start for a game dinner; this recipe can be doubled

2 (14 oz.) cans tomato juice	1 tsp. sugar
2 tsp. instant minced onion	1 tsp. salt
3 tblsp. celery seeds	2" stick cinnamon (optional)
½ tsp. Worcestershire sauce	1 tsp. prepared horse-radish

Combine all ingredients; cover and chill at least 3 hours to blend flavors. Strain and serve over cracked ice in juice glasses (also good heated and served in mugs). Makes 6 servings.

COUNTRY CHEESE/BACON DIP

Good with potato chips and vegetables—an easy recipe to double

1 c. creamed cottage cheese	1 tsp. lemon juice
3 slices crisp-cooked bacon, crumbled	1½ tblsp. milk
	1 clove garlic, cut
½ tsp. onion salt	Paprika
2 tblsp. salad dressing	

Combine cottage cheese, bacon, onion salt, salad dressing, lemon juice and milk; mix well.

Rub a small bowl with cut garlic; fill with cottage cheese mixture. Sprinkle lightly with paprika. Cover and chill. Makes about 1 cup.

TEXAS BARBECUED DUCKS

Roasting in foil is a safe bet—it tenderizes and keeps birds moist

2 wild ducks	Barbecue Sauce
2 tblsp. salad oil	

Rub ducks with oil; brown under broiler. Brush ducks with half the Barbecue Sauce; place 1 tblsp. sauce in cavity. Wrap each bird closely in heavy foil; bake in shallow pan in slow oven (325°) 1 hour, or until tender. Remove foil last 15 minutes, and spoon over remainder of sauce.

To Grill Outdoors: Proceed as above, browning over hot coals and finishing over slow coals.

Barbecue Sauce: Sauté 2 tblsp. chopped onion in ¼ c. butter. Add ½ c. ketchup, ½ c. lemon juice, ¼ tsp. paprika, ½ tsp. salt, ¼ tsp. pepper, ¼ tsp. ground red pepper, 2 tblsp. brown sugar and 2 tblsp. Worcestershire sauce. Simmer 15 minutes.

CALIFORNIA RARE DUCK

Glaze makes skin crisp and shiny—pink flesh tastes like beef

1 wild duck	¼ tsp. garlic salt
1 tsp. salt	Glaze
½ tsp. pepper	

Rub cavity and outside of duck with seasonings. Bake on rack in shallow pan, uncovered, in extremely hot oven (500°) 25 to 35 minutes, brushing with Glaze.

Glaze: Ten to 15 minutes after placing duck in oven, brush several times with mixture of 2 tblsp. light or dark corn syrup and 1 tsp. bottled browning sauce.

STUFFED BAKED SWEET POTATOES

The orange flavor is great with duck—make ahead if time is short

8 medium sweet potatoes	1½ tsp. salt
½ c. butter or regular margarine	Orange juice
2 tblsp. grated orange peel	

Bake sweet potatoes in hot oven (400°) 30 to 40 minutes, until soft. Cut a slice from top of each potato. Scoop out hot pulp (save shells) and mash; add butter, orange peel, salt and enough orange juice to moisten (the way you add milk when mashing white potatoes). Beat with electric mixer until smooth and fluffy. You should have about 8 c. mashed potatoes.

Refill shells, piling the mixture lightly. For a fancy look, put mashed, seasoned sweet potatoes through pastry tube. Makes about 8 servings.

LEMON VELVET PIE

This luscious pie filling has two layers, one like a good lemon meringue, the other like a fine lemon chiffon pie

Baked 9″ pie shell	1 tsp. grated lemon peel
1⅓ c. sugar	1 tsp. vanilla
6 tblsp. cornstarch	1 envelope unflavored gelatin
½ tsp. salt	¼ c. cold water
1½ c. cold water	1 c. light cream
2 egg yolks, slightly beaten	2 egg whites, stiffly beaten
2 tblsp. butter	1 c. heavy cream, whipped
⅓ c. lemon juice	

Combine sugar, cornstarch and salt in saucepan. Gradually stir in 1½ c. water. Cook over medium heat, stirring constantly, until mixture is smooth and thick enough to mound when dropped from a spoon. Stir some of the hot mixture into egg yolks. Slowly stir yolks and butter into remaining hot mixture; cook 2 minutes. Remove from heat and stir in lemon juice, peel and vanilla. Remove 1 c. filling (for top layer) and set it aside to cool.

Soften gelatin in ¼ c. water. Add to remaining hot filling and stir until dissolved. Gradually stir in light cream. Cool.

When mixture begins to thicken, fold in egg whites. Pour into pie shell. Chill 15 minutes. Spread with reserved filling. Chill well. Decorate with whipped cream. Makes 6 to 8 servings.

REGAL BEEF DINNER

Standing Rib Roast*
Special Stuffed Baked Potatoes*
Favorite Green Beans*
Fiesta Relish Tray
Strawberry/Cheese Pie*

This is a splendid menu for your husband's birthday dinner, an impressive selection for many other special occasions. You get off to a good start with the meal because a standing rib roast commands great respect. Country men and women know that in comparison with other cuts, it is not the extravagant luxury for an important dinner party that some people think. With a good piece of meat and plenty of it, the remainder of the meal can be less expensive and simple. And even a new cook can take a perfect roast from the oven if she follows the easy rules.

When there are 8 people at a dinner, the country host and hostess tend to choose a 7- to 8-lb. roast. It's a tradition to have more beef than is absolutely necessary and to be able to give generous servings. (The leftovers are used later in many interesting ways.)

This dinner, in addition to the regal roast, features marvelous stuffed baked potatoes, flavored with sour cream and cumin. You can get them ready ahead to reheat shortly before serving. Green beans, expertly seasoned, ably support the potatoes. A tray of assorted colorful relishes carries the salad role with attractive distinction.

You can skip dessert or have a mini-sweet ending, like small scoops of ice cream, but Strawberry/Cheese Pie is so lovely to look at and delicious to eat that you may wish to end the dinner with it, even if you postpone serving it. By the time forks cut the second bite of this pie, compliments for it circulate round and round the table like gentle breezes.

TIMETABLE

Do-Ahead: Make pie filling and pour into crust; chill overnight. Bake, stuff and cool potatoes a day ahead and refrigerate, or wrap and freeze several days before the dinner party.

On Guest Day: Cook and cool strawberry topping for pie; spread on the pie and return to refrigerator. Early in the day fix the vegetables for the relish tray. Cut carrots, celery and green pepper in strips and break flowerets from the cauliflower head. Wash and chill cherry tomatoes. Put carrots, celery and cauliflower in separate jars, add a little water to each, cover and chill. Place green pepper in a plastic bag and refrigerate.

The time to put the roast in the oven depends on its weight and to what stage of doneness you wish to cook it. Consult the roasting guide that follows. The cardinal rule is to let the meat thermometer tell you when the roast is cooked the way you want it. Place potatoes in an uncovered pan in the oven with the meat for the last 40 to 45 minutes before dinner; increase the time 10 or 15 minutes if potatoes are frozen. Do not thaw frozen potatoes before putting them in the oven. Meanwhile, cook the green beans and arrange an attractive tray with the uncooked vegetables and some of your own homemade bread and butter and mustard pickles.

SERVING SUGGESTIONS

This is a sit-down dinner and carving the roast gets the spotlight. To make carving easier, be sure the meatman separated the backbone from the ribs. Then you can remove the backbone in the kitchen before carrying the platter to the dining table. If the host does not wish to carve the roast at the dining table, he can follow the same directions in the kitchen without spectators. Arrange the slices on the platter, overlapping them.

To carve a standing rib roast the easiest way, place the largest side down. If the roast wobbles, cut a wedge-shaped slice from the large end so the roast will stand firm.

Insert fork below the first rib. Slice from the outside of the roast to the rib side. Cut several slices in this manner. Then cut along the inner side of the rib to release a slice. Slide knife under slice and lift to serving plate. Repeat until everyone is served.

Pass the potatoes, green beans and relishes. Either serve the dessert at dinner's end, or later in the evening.

STANDING RIB ROAST

Place the roast, fat side up, in a shallow roasting pan. The ribs form a natural rack that holds the meat out of the drippings. Season with salt and pepper if you like; salt penetrates the meat no more than ½" at the most.

Insert the meat thermometer into the thickest part of the meat so that it neither touches a bone nor rests in fat. Do not cover, add water or baste meat while cooking.

Roast meat in a slow oven (325°) to the desired stage of doneness—rare, medium or well done. Let the meat thermometer tell you when the beef is cooked the way you want to serve it. Timing by the clock is approximate at best. Since meat carves easier if allowed to stand or "set" 15 to 20 minutes after removed from the oven, take it out when the thermometer registers 5 to 10° lower than the temperature for the desired degree of doneness. It will continue to cook out of the oven and reach the desired temperature.

Guide for Cooking a 6- to 8-lb.
Standing Rib Roast in 325° Oven

Temperature	Total Cooking Time
140° (rare)	2¾ to 3 hours
160° (medium)	3 to 3½ hours
170° (well done)	3¾ to 4 hours

SPECIAL STUFFED BAKED POTATOES

Cumin, a seasoning used since biblical times and an ingredient in chili powder, gives potatoes a subtle new flavor

8 medium baking potatoes	1½ c. milk
2 (1½ oz.) envelopes sour cream sauce mix	¼ c. butter or regular margarine
1 tsp. ground cumin	6 tblsp. grated process American cheese
1 tsp. salt	
Dash of pepper	4 slices bacon

Bake potatoes in hot oven (425°), 50 to 60 minutes until tender.

Meanwhile, combine sauce mix, cumin, salt, pepper and milk. Let stand 10 minutes to blend flavors.

Cut a slice from top of potatoes and discard. Scoop out potatoes, saving shells. Place in large electric mixer bowl and beat, adding the sauce mixture and butter. Beat until light and fluffy, adding more milk if necessary. The amount needed varies with the potatoes.

Fill potato shells with fluffy potatoes, sprinkle with grated cheese and heat in slow oven (325°) 40 to 45 minutes, or until thoroughly heated. Cook bacon until crisp; drain and crumble. Sprinkle over tops of potatoes. Makes 8 servings.

FAVORITE GREEN BEANS

Seasonings from Italian-American kitchens make this special

2 (10 oz.) pkgs. frozen green beans
1 tblsp. salad oil
1 tblsp. wine vinegar
1 tsp. chopped shallots or green onion
¼ tsp. garlic salt
¾ c. croutons
2 to 3 tblsp. grated Parmesan cheese

Cook beans by package directions; drain if necessary.

Combine oil, vinegar, shallots and garlic salt. Pour over beans. Add croutons; heat and stir until well heated. Pour into serving dish and sprinkle with cheese. Makes 6 to 8 servings.

STRAWBERRY/CHEESE PIE

Tastes like elegant cheese cake . . . it's topped with strawberry glaze

1¾ c. graham cracker crumbs
¼ c. sugar
½ c. melted butter or regular margarine
2 (8 oz.) pkgs. cream cheese at room temperature
3 eggs
⅔ c. sugar
⅛ tsp. vanilla
1 (10 oz.) pkg. frozen strawberries, thawed
1 tblsp. cornstarch
Few drops red food color

To make crust, combine crumbs with ¼ c. sugar; stir in melted butter. Press into 10″ pie pan to make shell.

For filling, beat cheese until light and fluffy. Add eggs, one at a time, beating well after each addition. Beat in ⅔ c. sugar and vanilla. Pour into pie shell. Bake in slow oven (325°) 50 minutes. Cool and chill.

For glaze, in small saucepan blend together a little of the strawberry liquid and cornstarch. Add remaining strawberries. Cook over medium heat, stirring constantly until thickened and clear. Remove from heat; stir in red food color. Cool. Spread over pie and chill. Makes 8 servings.

DISTINCTIVE POT ROAST DINNER

California Pot Roast*
Fluffy Rice   Buttered Broccoli
Tossed Green Salad
Fruit Dessert Tree*

Almost every hostess at some time faces a situation when she wants to serve guests a distinctive dinner. Frequently it's the pending arrival of a rather sophisticated guest. Try this menu—it's impressive.

TIMETABLE

Do-Ahead: Build the tree for the fruit a day or a few days ahead. Wash, drain, chill and store salad greens in plastic bags a day ahead. Assemble fruits and cheese for the dessert treat and refrigerate.

On Guest Day: Put the pot roast on to cook about 3½ to 4 hours before dinnertime. Cooked in a tightly covered Dutch oven, it will require little watching, except to check occasionally to see if you need to add a little water. During the last half hour before dinner, cook the rice and frozen broccoli; arrange fruit on tree. Toss salad and make coffee.

SERVING SUGGESTIONS

This is a sit-down dinner with the dessert served in the living room. Carve the meat in the kitchen or at the table. Arrange salad in individual bowls or on plates. If you wish, have it on the table when guests are seated. Served this way, it becomes an appetizer-salad and separate first course. For the main course, pass the bowls of rice and broccoli and the gravy in bowl or gravy boat. Suggest that everyone move to the living room to "pick" fruit from the tree for dessert. Serve coffee.

CALIFORNIA POT ROAST

Tender, brown pot roast carries a delightful oriental flavor

2 tblsp. flour	¼ c. water
1½ tsp. salt	¼ c. honey
⅛ tsp. pepper	¼ c. soy sauce
½ tsp. curry powder	2 tblsp. chopped candied ginger,
1 (3½ to 4 lb.) blade or arm pot	or ¼ tsp. ground ginger
roast	Water
3 tblsp. fat or drippings	¼ c. flour

Combine 2 tblsp. flour, salt, pepper and curry powder. Dredge meat in mixture.

Melt fat in heavy pan or Dutch oven; brown meat well on all sides. Pour off excess fat. Add ¼ c. water, honey, soy sauce and ginger. Cover tightly and cook slowly 3 to 3½ hours, or until meat is tender.

Remove meat from pan. Add enough water to cooking liquid to make 2 cups. Thicken with ¼ c. flour to make gravy. Makes about 8 servings.

FRUIT DESSERT TREE

One perfect way to end a guest dinner is with a fruit and cheese

Place your fruit tree on a low coffee table or buffet where you can see it from the dining table.

To build your tree, assemble trays, cake stands and footed dishes, graduated in size; place the heaviest pieces on the bottom. Roll florist's clay (available from a florist) into long thin strips. Use clay to anchor each dish firmly to the one below it. If your trays and dishes don't match in color and material, cover glass or metal pieces with contact paper and spray with copper or gold paint.

Begin at the bottom to stack fruits and work up (we used five layers). Intersperse fruits with green leaves from your yard—ivy, holly, laurel, or whatever you have or can get.

Supplement your own homegrown fruits with an assortment from the food store. Add color with a few out-of-season strawberries or cherry tomatoes. Quarter fresh pineapple by cutting right through the crown (leaves). Remove the core with a sharp knife, loosen fruit from rind, then cut in bite-size pieces to spear with toothpicks.

Serve at least three cheeses. We recommend pineapple cheese, blue or Roquefort, Liederkranz and an aged Cheddar. Set a basket of interesting crackers nearby. Some of your guests may prefer to eat them instead of fruit with the cheese.

Keep your tree to replenish throughout the holiday season. Refrigerate perishable fruits and most cheeses until just before guests arrive.

GRILLED OR BROILED
POT ROAST DINNER

Grilled or Broiled Pot Roast*
Texas Gumbo Rice*
Country Coleslaw*
Strawberry Ice Cream
Brownies
Coffee   Iced Tea

Your friends will think you're a magician when you serve them broiled or grilled pot roast that's tender like steak and tastes like it. The secret is the marinade in which the beef chills at least 24 hours, but better 48 hours. The pot roast is 2½ to 3″ thick so you need to cook it a little longer than 2″ steaks, or about 1 hour. And to produce a topnotch "steak," baste the meat about every 5 minutes while it broils in the kitchen or over charcoal in the yard.

The host, if he takes over the grilling, will have a real opportunity to demonstrate his expertise. For cooking meat 1 hour, he will want to use a thicker bed of coals than for quick-cooking fish and meats.

As accompaniment, the rice dish, which simmers in a skillet, scores high. With broiled pot roast, it is best to serve a companion dish that cooks on top of the range. Coleslaws vary greatly, but the true country-kitchen type with sour cream dressing surpasses other kinds, we think.

TIMETABLE

Do-Ahead: Make barbecue sauce, pour over beef, cover and chill 2 days, turning meat occasionally.

On Guest Day: Have the coals at the proper stage for grilling a good hour before dinnertime. When the beef starts to cook, fix the rice dish, allowing 30 minutes for it from start to finish. Shred fresh, crisp cabbage with a sharp knife; a blunt or dull-edged knife bruises it. Add the dressing just before serving.

SERVING SUGGESTIONS

Eat indoors or out, whichever is more convenient. Regardless of where you dine, be sure to slice the grilled or broiled meat diagonally across the grain.

GRILLED OR BROILED POT ROAST

Truly delicious cooked over coals or in the range broiling oven

1 (about 4 lb.) boneless round chuck or rump pot roast, cut 2½ to 3" thick	1 tblsp. soy sauce
	½ tsp. crushed rosemary leaves
	6 tblsp. wine vinegar
2 cloves garlic, minced	2 tblsp. ketchup
2 tblsp. salad oil	1 tblsp. Worcestershire sauce
¼ tsp. dry mustard	1 tblsp. bottled steak sauce

Place beef in shallow baking dish.

Sauté garlic in oil until golden. Blend in mustard, soy sauce, rosemary and vinegar. Pour sauce over meat. Cover and refrigerate 24 to 48 hours, turning meat occasionally.

Place roast on cold broiler grid about 4 to 5" from heat.

To the sauce remaining from marinating meat, add ketchup, Worcestershire sauce and bottled steak sauce. Use to baste meat during cooking.

Broil meat on one side about 10 minutes; baste with sauce and turn. Broil on other side about 7 minutes, basting with sauce. Reduce heat (or spread out coals) and continue broiling, turning and basting roast with sauce every 5 minutes for 35 to 45 minutes more, depending on size of roast. Slice meat diagonally to serve. Makes about 8 servings.

TEXAS GUMBO RICE

Rice cooks with tomatoes, green pepper, onion, okra and corn. Bacon and chili powder contribute a taste of Texas

4 slices bacon	1 (16 oz.) can whole kernel corn
1 large onion, minced	(undrained)
6 medium tomatoes, cut up	2 tsp. salt
1 green pepper, chopped	¼ tsp. pepper
1 c. sliced okra	½ tsp. chili powder
	½ c. long grain rice

Cook bacon in large skillet until crisp. Remove from pan and drain.

Measure 3 tblsp. bacon fat into skillet; add onion and sauté until tender. Add remaining ingredients. Cover and simmer 20 minutes, or until rice is tender. Place in serving dish; crumble bacon over top. Makes 6 servings.

COUNTRY COLESLAW

Use cabbage shredded fine, tossed with dressing just before serving

6 c. finely shredded cabbage	¾ tsp. salt
⅓ c. finely chopped onion	½ tsp. dry mustard
¾ c. dairy sour cream	Dash of pepper
6 tblsp. mayonnaise or salad	Paprika
dressing	

Combine cabbage and onion. Place in large salad bowl.

Blend together sour cream, mayonnaise, salt, mustard and pepper. Pour over cabbage. Toss to distribute dressing. Sprinkle lightly with paprika. Makes 8 servings.

COUNTRY STEAK DINNER

Charcoal Grilled or Broiled Beef Steaks*
Grated au Gratin Potatoes*
Buttered Peas with Almonds
Fresh Mushroom Salad* or Tossed Salad with Creamy Dressing*
Orange/Peanut Cake*
Coffee

People acquainted with country steak dinners take an invitation to one enthusiastically. It's a great American feast. If you look in the freezer in farm homes, you'll know the reason why—among the packages of beef, a few are labeled to reserve to share with friends. These are the exceptionally good steaks, cut 2" thick.

Now that Americans appreciate that cooking over coals is an excellent way to handle a fine steak, part of the kitchen occasionally moves outdoors and the chef who takes over there is often the host. The hostess, with the help of the older children, assumes responsibility for the remainder of the dinner.

This menu gives you a choice of cooking steak over charcoal or broiling it in the kitchen. Grilling steaks outdoors divides the work and delivers beef to the table with superb flavors. And it frees the oven in the kitchen for cooking other foods, such as big baked potatoes.

Baked potatoes appeal whenever they appear in the steak dinner, but timing the cooking often creates trouble. These favorites need to reach the table promptly when done. To help avoid a timing problem, this menu suggests grated potatoes teamed with cream and cheese. They wait more successfully if the steak is not ready. And they are out-of-this-world in taste. You can prepare the potatoes for baking and freeze them—a good make-ahead.

A currently popular addition to the meal is the Fresh Mushroom Salad favored especially by young people. Because the mushrooms are not always available in many localities, we suggest a good tossed salad as an alternate. Both salads have a creamy dressing.

The dessert, a generous orange-flavored cake made with a mix is decorated with peanut brittle trim. Men like the crunchy sweet.

TIMETABLE

Do-Ahead: Bake the cake a day ahead. Fix the potatoes and chill them overnight, or freeze them for a few days. Frozen steaks cut 2″ thick are best thawed (or at least partially thawed) before grilling or broiling. Thaw them in the refrigerator for 24 to 36 hours before cooking.

On Guest Day: Frost the cake with whipped cream and decorate with peanut brittle about 3 hours before dinner. Keep it in the refrigerator until time to cut and serve it. Work out your timetable— His Timetable for grilling beef steak over coals or Her Timetable for broiling the steak in the oven. Allow plenty of time to have the steak ready at dinnertime. Put the potatoes in the oven about 1 hour before you want to serve them. Meanwhile, cook the peas by package directions. Make the coffee; then fix the salad during the last few minutes before dinner.

SERVING SUGGESTIONS

Serve the steak on a *warm* platter. Garnish it with a few very thin lemon slices and dot with butter or margarine. Arrange a parsley bouquet on the platter if you wish. Sprinkle buttered, hot peas with toasted slivered almonds just before serving, or heat them briefly in the melted butter before adding them to the peas. Serve the dessert at dinner's end, or postpone its appearance until later in the evening.

CHARCOAL GRILLED OR BROILED BEEF STEAKS

Trim off excess fat from high-quality sirloin, porterhouse or T-bone steaks. Allow about 1 lb. per person for bone-in steaks, ½ to ¾ lb. for boneless.

Brown meat on one side before turning; it should be about half done. Use timetable for a guide even though the timing is approximate. Grilling and broiling are mainly an art rather than a science. Season with salt and pepper after browning. Salt penetrates the meat no more than ½″ at the most and it draws out juices that interfere with browning. To check for doneness, cut into the meat—near the bone if there is one.

Season the cooked meat with salt and pepper and serve at once on a warm platter.

Timetable for Charcoal-Grilling Beef Steaks on One Side

Rare	Medium	Well
12 to 13 minutes	15 to 17 minutes	22 to 25 minutes

Timetable for Broiling 2″ Beef Steaks on One Side

Cut	Rare	Medium
Sirloin	16 to 20 minutes	23 minutes
Porterhouse and T-bone	20 minutes	23 minutes
Club	17 minutes	18 to 23 minutes

To Charcoal-Grill Steaks: Cut remaining fat on edges at 2″ intervals to prevent curling. Be careful not to cut into lean meat. Rub heated grill with suet to grease lightly. Lay steak on grill about 4″ from coals (gray embers) and use the timetable as a guide.

To Broil Steaks: Set oven control at broil (550°), or follow range manufacturer's broiling guide. Cut remaining fat around edges at 1″ intervals to prevent curling. Rub heated broiler rack with suet to grease lightly. Broil meat 3 to 5″ from source of heat. Use timetable as a guide to cooking time.

GRATED AU GRATIN POTATOES

You partially cook the potatoes, shred them, combine with other ingredients and bake. They require no last-minute attention

6 to 8 medium red potatoes	Salt
6 to 8 oz. mild Cheddar cheese or	Pepper
process American cheese	1 c. heavy cream

Cook potatoes in jackets until almost tender; do not cook completely. Cool and remove skins. With coarse grater, grate a layer of potatoes into a buttered 9″ square shallow baking dish. Grate a thin layer of cheese evenly over them. Season with salt and pepper as desired. Repeat until baking dish is full. Pour cream over. Bake, uncovered, in moderate oven (350°) 50 to 55 minutes, until a golden brown. Makes 8 servings.

NOTE: To freeze the potatoes, bake 40 to 45 minutes. Cool, wrap and freeze. To serve, partially thaw and pour over from ¼ to ⅓ c. additional cream. Place in slow oven (325°) 35 to 40 minutes. If a deep casserole is used, increase the baking time a few minutes.

FRESH MUSHROOM SALAD

Mushrooms, a faithful partner to steak, appear in a new way

2 c. water
2 tblsp. lemon juice
1 lb. fresh mushrooms, cut in ⅛"
    slices
½ c. heavy cream

1½ tsp. grated onion
⅛ tsp. white pepper
1 tsp. salt
Lettuce
Chopped fresh chives

Bring water and lemon juice to a boil in saucepan. Add mushrooms, cover pan and reduce heat. Simmer gently 2 to 3 minutes. Remove from heat, drain and pat mushrooms dry with paper towels. In a 2-qt. bowl combine cream, onion, pepper and salt. Add mushrooms and toss lightly in creamy mixture until well coated. Serve on lettuce and garnish with chopped chives. Makes 4 to 6 servings.

TOSSED SALAD WITH CREAMY DRESSING

It's the special dressing that makes this salad taste so good

¾ c. mayonnaise
¼ c. milk
½ tsp. salt
½ tsp. lemon-pepper seasoning

1 large head iceberg lettuce,
    shredded
2 medium tomatoes, peeled and
    quartered
1 medium green pepper, diced

In a small bowl combine mayonnaise, milk, salt and lemon-pepper; mix well. Cover and refrigerate at least 1 hour.

At serving time place lettuce, tomatoes and green pepper in big salad bowl, pour over dressing and toss gently. Serve at once. Makes 8 servings.

ORANGE/PEANUT CAKE

Even steak-and-potatoes men find this cake irresistible

1 (1 lb. 2.5 oz.) pkg. orange
    chiffon cake mix
1½ c. heavy cream

3 tblsp. confectioners sugar
½ tsp. almond extract
½ lb. peanut brittle

Prepare batter and bake cake by package directions. Cool and store as package directs.

About 3 hours before serving cake, whip cream with sugar in a chilled bowl until stiff, adding almond extract during the last minute or two of beating. Spread on top and sides of cake.

Crush peanut brittle with rolling pin and sprinkle over the cake. Place in refrigerator at once. Makes 10 servings.

SUNDOWN BARBECUE

Grilled Flank Steak*
Potato Salad*
Vegetable Salad Tray
Mayonnaise Dip   Creamy Cheese Dip*
Garlic Bread
Lattice Apple Pie with Cream*

You will recognize this menu as a men's special. Not that it does not please women and children, for it does. But, starting with grilled beef and ending with apple pie, it's bound to appeal to the masculine members of the party.

As the timetable shows, you prepare most of the food for the meal on barbecue day. This creates no hardship because you can get all the cooking out of the way before noon. The steak, of course, must be grilled during the last 15 minutes before eating, but this is the host's chore. While he cooks the beef, the hostess and children can take the salad, vegetable tray, bread and the dips to the table and pour the beverages—milk for the youngsters, coffee for the adults.

TIMETABLE

Do-Ahead: Make marinade a day before you want to use it, cover and chill. It's a good idea to pour it over the steak, cover and let it chill overnight, although you can leave this until the following day. Fix the blue cheese dip and chill overnight.

On Guest Day: Bake pies in the morning—two of them for 8 to 12 servings. Make the potato salad and chill several hours. Turn the steak in the marinade several times during the day. Prepare the vegetables for the tray sometime during the afternoon; put celery sticks, cauliflowerets and peeled thick cucumber slices in ice water. Add peeled tomatoes, quartered, or cherry tomatoes when assembling vegetables on tray at serving time. Stir a little lemon juice into mayonnaise and chill for a raw vegetable dip children especially like. Stir it before serving. Let the host take charge of lighting the charcoal and getting the coals to the right stage for cooking the steaks at the proper time. It takes from 8 to 15 minutes for total cooking, depending on degree of doneness desired.

SERVING SUGGESTIONS

Eat indoors or out, whichever you prefer. The weather may make the decision for you. Near the vegetable tray, designed secretly by the menu planner to include uncooked vegetables in the meal, set the bowls containing the dips. Warm the pie in a preheated slow oven (300°) 5 to 8 minutes just before sitting down to eat the main course. Turn the heat off and leave pie in oven until time to cut and serve it. Faintly warm, this apple pie is at its best.

GRILLED FLANK STEAK

Steak is best broiled very rare and cut across grain to serve

2 unscored flank steaks, about 1½ lbs. each
3 c. Special Marinade

At least 2 hours before barbecue time, place the steaks in Special Marinade. (Two hours is the minimum time.) It should cover the steaks. Turn steaks at least two or three times while in the marinade.

Set grill about 6" above hot coals. (Hold your hand, palm down, over the grill near the cooking level. If you can keep it there only about 2 seconds, it is hot enough for the steaks.)

Grease grill lightly, place steaks on grill and cook to desired doneness. For total cooking time, allow about 8 minutes for rare to medium (4 minutes for each side); 10 to 15 minutes for medium to well done (5 to 8 minutes on each side). Turn once during grilling. Serve hot, cut diagonally across the grain. Makes 8 servings.

N O T E : You can cook the steak in the broiling oven. Broil it 2 or 3" from heat, about 5 minutes on each side. When cooked this way it is called London Broil.

SPECIAL MARINADE

Give sauce a share of credit for steak's wonderful flavor

1½ c. salad oil	2 tsp. coarse black pepper
¾ c. soy sauce	½ c. wine vinegar
¼ c. Worcestershire sauce	2 tsp. parsley flakes
2 tblsp. dry mustard	2 cloves garlic, crushed
2 tsp. salt	⅓ c. lemon juice

Combine all ingredients; stir to blend. Make this sauce the day before using if possible. Makes 3 cups.

POTATO SALAD

Add the salad dressing to the warm potatoes for superior flavors

6 to 8 potatoes	¼ c. chopped onion
⅔ c. salad dressing	½ c. diced celery
2 tblsp. vinegar	2 tblsp. chopped green pepper
1½ tsp. salt	2 tblsp. diced sweet pickle
⅛ tsp. ground red pepper (more if you like it)	3 hard-cooked eggs, sliced

Cook potatoes in jackets; let cool 15 to 30 minutes, until you can handle them.

Meanwhile, mix together salad dressing, vinegar, salt and red pepper.

Peel and cube warm potatoes (should have about 6 c.); combine with remaining ingredients. Add salad dressing carefully, stirring in lightly. Let chill in refrigerator 2 to 4 hours before serving. Sprinkle lightly with paprika, if desired. Makes 6 to 8 servings.

N O T E : You can double this recipe for 12 to 16 servings.

CREAMY CHEESE DIP

For a great eating experience, dunk raw vegetables in tangy dip

¼ lb. blue or Roquefort cheese	¼ tsp. coarsely ground black pepper
1 c. mayonnaise	¼ tsp. garlic salt
½ c. dairy sour cream	Salt to taste
2 tblsp. lemon juice	Dash of ground red pepper
2 tblsp. chopped parsley	
1 tsp. grated onion	

Place cheese in bowl and mash with a fork; gradually blend in mayonnaise and sour cream, creaming until smooth.

Add remaining ingredients and mix thoroughly. Chill several hours or overnight. Makes 2 cups.

LATTICE APPLE PIE WITH CREAM

Try the old-time custom of pouring cream on pie, or the new way of spreading on sour cream and sprinkling with brown sugar

Pastry for 2-crust 9″ pie	½ tsp. ground allspice
4 large quick-cooking apples, peeled and cut in eighths	3 tblsp. butter or regular margarine
1 c. sugar	Brown sugar
½ tsp. ground cinnamon	Dairy sour or sweet cream

Arrange apples in pastry-lined pan. Sprinkle with ½ c. sugar mixed with cinnamon.

Sift together remaining ½ c. sugar and allspice. Cut in butter with pastry blender or fork until mixture is crumbly. Sprinkle over apples and top with pastry lattice; flute edges.

Bake in hot oven (425°) 40 minutes. Turn off heat and leave pie in oven another 10 minutes. Serve pie at table and pass a bowl of brown sugar that pours and a bowl of dairy sour cream, or a pitcher of sweet cream to pour over pie.

HAWAIIAN-STYLE DINNER

Teriyaki Steak*
Fluffy Rice   Orange-Glazed Carrots*
Spinach/Sesame Salad*
Bread Sticks
Poppyseed Cake*   Pineapple

You can treat your guests to this Hawaiian-style dinner even though you live far from the islands. Teriyaki Steak has the spotlight in this meal. In the beginning it is a pot roast, but you convert it into tender steak slices. Marinating the beef in a sauce has much to do with the transformation.

This dinner contains colorful foods, such as orange carrots and crisp, dark green leaves of young spinach. Even the Poppyseed Cake looks different. The fluted tube pan takes the responsibility for this change. Fresh pineapple, if available, accompanies the cake, but in case it is unavailable, serve chilled canned pineapple chunks or slices packed in juice with no sugar added.

TIMETABLE

Do-Ahead: Bake cake a day ahead. Put beef in glass or ceramic baking dish or bowl, cover with the marinade and refrigerate 12 to 24 hours, turning several times. Wash and drain spinach; place in a plastic bag and chill. Make salad dressing. If serving fresh pineapple, cut it up, and sugar lightly. Cover and chill.

On Guest Day: Put beef in preheated broiler at least 30 minutes before dinnertime. Meanwhile, cook rice, toast sesame seeds by spreading in small shallow pan and heating in a moderate oven (350°) until light brown. Cook carrots. Toss salad at the last minute.

SERVING SUGGESTIONS

Carve meat in kitchen or at the table, as desired. Serve it on a warm platter. Pass rice and carrots in bowls. Dust the cooled cake with confectioners sugar.

TERIYAKI STEAK

Be sure to carve steak diagonally across grain in thin slices

½ c. soy sauce
⅓ c. water
1 tblsp. brown sugar
½ tsp. ground ginger

1 clove garlic, minced
1 (3 to 4 lb.) boneless bottom round, chuck or rump pot roast, cut 2 to 2½″ thick

Combine soy sauce, water, brown sugar, ginger and garlic. Pour over pot roast in glass or ceramic dish; cover and refrigerate 12 to 24 hours, turning roast occasionally.

Remove meat from marinade, place on broiler rack and broil 5 to 6″ from source of heat about 15 minutes, or until very crusty. Turn and broil on other side until inside is desired doneness (usually rather rare). To serve, cut meat across grain at slanted angle into thin slices. Serve with drippings and, if desired, additional teriyaki sauce, made as for marinade. Makes 8 servings.

ORANGE-GLAZED CARROTS

The orange flavor enhances the taste of orange-colored carrots

10 medium carrots, peeled and sliced	½ tsp. salt
	½ tsp. ground ginger
2 tblsp. sugar	½ c. orange juice
2 tsp. cornstarch	¼ c. butter

Slice carrots crosswise on the bias about ½" thick. Cook, covered, in a little boiling salted water (½ tsp. salt to 1 c. water) until just tender, about 20 minutes. Drain.

Meanwhile, combine sugar, cornstarch, salt and ginger in a small saucepan. Add orange juice; cook, stirring constantly, until mixture thickens and bubbles. Boil 1 minute. Stir in butter. Pour over hot carrots and toss to coat with orange sauce. Makes 8 servings.

SPINACH/SESAME SALAD

Add sesame seeds at the last minute so they'll retain crispness

1 lb. young spinach (2 qts.)	¼ tsp. paprika
½ c. sugar	1 tblsp. finely grated onion
¼ c. vinegar	1 tblsp. Toasted Sesame Seeds
¼ c. salad oil	(see Index)
½ tsp. salt	

Wash spinach; drain, dry, place in plastic bag and chill.

In a small saucepan combine sugar and vinegar; bring to a boil. Remove from heat. Pour into a small jar; add oil, salt, paprika and onion; mix well. Cover and chill.

Tear spinach into bite-size pieces. Add enough of the dressing (shake before using) to coat leaves. Add sesame seeds, toss and serve immediately. Makes 6 servings.

POPPYSEED CAKE

Salad oil gives cake a rich flavor, it's baked in an interesting shape

4 eggs, well beaten	1½ tsp. baking soda
2 c. sugar	⅔ c. evaporated milk
1½ c. salad oil	3 tblsp. poppyseeds
3 c. sifted flour	Confectioners sugar (optional)
½ tsp. salt	

Combine eggs and sugar and beat well; add oil and blend.

Sift together flour, salt and soda; add alternately with milk to beaten mixture. Stir in poppyseeds. Spoon into well-greased and floured 10″ fluted tube pan. Bake in moderate oven (375°) 40 to 45 minutes, or until cake tests done. Cool on rack 10 minutes, then remove from pan. Dust with sifted confectioners sugar, if desired.

FONDUE FOURSOME

CowBelles' Beef Fondue*   Dipping Sauces*

Tossed Green Salad

Sliced Hard Rolls

Fruit

When entertaining a couple at an evening meal, whether dinner or supper, give beef fondue a try. This main dish responds to many names, but in farm and ranch country it's called CowBelles' Beef Fondue. CowBelles, the wives of cattlemen, say a menu featuring cook-your-own steak is an easy-on-the-hostess choice that produces a meal their husbands really like. These people know good beef when they see it. Only the very tender cuts enter their fondue pots.

If you have more than one fondue pot with a metal cooker, or can borrow one, you can increase your guest list. More than four fondue forks dipping into the same pot often tangle. And it's easier to keep the cooking oil at the proper temperature with a foursome participating.

Serve several sauces in bowls. Let everyone spoon his selections for dunking onto his plate, or if you have enough small bowls or Chinese teacups without handles, give everyone his own sauces. We give you recipes for some delicious ones; you may also set out ketchup, chili sauce, prepared mustard, prepared horse-radish and some bottled meat sauces, however. Some men prefer to dunk their beef in these old favorites. And remember to put salt and pepper shakers on the table.

Make the remainder of the meal simple . . . a tossed green salad or lettuce wedges with a choice of bottled dressings. Sliced hard rolls or French bread will be enjoyed. Wind up with fruit, such as a cup of orange and grapefruit sections with sliced bananas, or with some frozen sliced peaches, partially thawed. Keep the coffeepot filled.

TIMETABLE

On Guest Day: Make the sauces and chill. Cut the trimmed beef in bite-size cubes. Wash, drain and chill salad greens in a plastic bag. Make the fruit cup an hour before mealtime and refrigerate, or put the frozen peaches in the refrigerator to partially thaw. Set the table, slice the rolls, make the coffee and toss the salad. Heat the cooking oil in the metal fondue cooker on the kitchen range. Carry it to the table and place over fondue burner. (If using an electric fondue pot, heat the oil on its unit.) Start cooking at once.

SERVING SUGGESTIONS

Provide everyone with a plate, fondue fork, dinner fork and teaspoon. Have plenty of paper napkins handy.

COWBELLES' BEEF FONDUE

Have beef cubes at room temperature when you dip them into hot oil

Salad oil   Dipping Sauces
Salt
1½ lbs. trimmed beef tenderloin,
   rib-eye or sirloin, cut in ¾"
   cubes

Pour oil into metal fondue cooker to the depth of 2". Never fill it to more than half its capacity. Heat on range to 425° on fat thermometer. Add 1 tsp. salt. Carry to the table. (Or follow manufacturer's directions with electric fondue pot.) Start cooking at once. If the oil cools during the cooking, reheat it.

Spear meat with fondue fork and dip it into the hot oil. It cooks quickly, or in 10 to 20 seconds for rare beef, about 50 seconds for well done. Transfer beef to dinner fork and dip it in your choice of sauces. Makes 4 servings.

N O T E : You can cook 1" cubes of raw pork like the beef, but give them 2 to 3 minutes in the hot oil to make sure they are well done. You also can cook ¾" cubes of chicken or turkey meat and lamb, or fully cooked ham, like the beef. It takes 2 to 3 minutes for the chicken and turkey, ¾ to 1 minute for lamb and 1 minute for the ham to cook.

DIPPING SAUCES FOR MEAT AND CHICKEN FONDUES

Garlic Butter: Cream ½ c. butter until fluffy. Stir in 1 small clove garlic, crushed. Cover and let stand at room temperature ½ to 1 hour, in refrigerator for longer storage. Makes about ½ cup.

Countryman's Choice: Combine 6 tblsp. ketchup, 6 tblsp. chili sauce, 2 tblsp. prepared horse-radish, 2 tsp. lemon juice and, if you like, a dash of hot pepper sauce. Makes about 1 cup.

Dill Sauce: Combine 1 c. dairy sour cream, 1 tblsp. chopped chives, 1 tsp. vinegar, ½ tsp. grated onion, ½ tsp. dill weed and salt to season, about ¼ tsp. Mix well. Makes about 1 cup.

Swiss Cheese Sauce: Blend ½ c. mayonnaise and ¼ c. grated Swiss cheese. Makes about ⅔ cup.

Green Goddess Dip: Blend 2 tblsp. milk into 2 (3 oz.) pkgs. cream cheese; beat well. Stir in ½ c. chopped cucumber, 1 tsp. finely chopped onion, ½ tsp. salt and ¼ tsp. ground cumin. Makes about 1⅓ cups.

Wine Sauce: Combine ¾ c. sauterne and ¼ c. ketchup in saucepan. Stir and bring to a boil. Reduce heat and simmer uncovered about 5 minutes. (The wine's alcohol evaporates and leaves the characteristic grape flavor in the sauce.) Meanwhile, make a paste with 4 tsp. cornstarch and 2 tblsp. cold water. Stir into wine mixture. Add 1 tblsp. butter or regular margarine and cook 1 minute. Makes about ¾ cup.

Brown Mushroom Sauce: Melt 2 tblsp. butter or regular margarine in saucepan; blend in 2 tblsp. flour. Remove from heat and stir in ⅔ c. beef broth (canned or homemade). Return to heat and cook and stir until mixture thickens. Remove from heat. Stir in 1 (3 oz.) can chopped mushrooms, drained and chopped more finely, 1 tsp. Worcestershire sauce and ½ c. dairy sour cream. Heat, but do not let come to a boil. Serve hot. (Reheat at serving time if made ahead.) Makes about 1⅓ cups.

Horse-radish Sauce: Whip ½ c. chilled heavy cream; fold in 3 tblsp. prepared horse-radish, well drained. Season with salt, about ½ tsp. Makes about 1 cup.

IOWA CORN DINNER

Broiled Ground Beef*   Potatoes Basque Style*
Corn on the Cob   Sliced Tomato Platter
Onion/Mustard Buns*   Peach Melba Parfait*

Summer is the delightful time when corn feasts bring families together in many communities around the country to enjoy two of America's food gifts to the world, sweet corn and tomatoes. When you puncture a few kernels of sweet corn with your thumbnail and a milky juice squirts out, it's time to have a corn cookout or dinner. Chances are good that at the same time dead-ripe tomatoes will hang red and heavy on the vines.

This menu gives the two garden specialties the spotlight and teams them with complementary foods. Ground beef, seasoned and shaped like a porterhouse steak (as many steaks as you need) broils to perfection. Cook it kindly and it will taste almost as good as a porterhouse—better, hamburger fans say. Serve the Onion/Mustard Buns with it for a happy surprise.

Be generous with tomatoes, provide plenty of potatoes and at the end of the feast bring out Peach Melba Parfait featuring fresh peaches.

TIMETABLE

Do-Ahead: You can bake the rolls a day or several days ahead, cool, wrap and freeze.

On Guest Day: Peel chilled tomatoes, cut in thick slices and place on platter. Drizzle on a little salad oil if you wish and sprinkle with fresh chopped basil leaves.

Make Peach Melba Parfait and put it in refrigerator just before you prepare the potatoes. Put potatoes on to cook about 30 minutes before mealtime. Preheat the broiler so it will be ready for the meat 15 minutes before dinner. Gather, husk and remove silks from corn and put it on to cook in cold unsalted water to cover when you put the meat in the broiler. Bring water to a full rolling boil, lift out the corn with tongs, drain and serve.

SERVING SUGGESTIONS

Since the meat and corn are at their best when piping hot, this is not a meal that waits successfully. Carry these foods to the table last and start the butter dish and salt shaker, so important to corn lovers, on their rounds immediately.

BROILED GROUND BEEF

Some people call this pennywise steak—everyone calls it good

1½ lbs. ground round steak	3 tblsp. grated onion
1 tsp. salt	1 egg
¼ tsp. pepper	⅓ c. milk
2 tsp. Worcestershire sauce	Melted shortening

Combine all ingredients except shortening; mix until blended. Form entire mixture into the shape of a porterhouse steak about ¾" thick. Place on cold broiler grid. Brush with melted shortening.

Broil 4 to 5" from heat about 8 minutes on each side until well browned. Use two spatulas for easy turning. Makes 6 servings.

POTATOES BASQUE STYLE

Potatoes and other vegetables cook quickly in chicken broth

½ c. finely chopped onion	Water
½ c. chopped celery	2 lbs. potatoes, peeled and cut in
½ c. shredded carrot	1" cubes (about 4 c.)
1 clove garlic, minced	½ tsp. salt
2 tblsp. butter	⅛ tsp. pepper
1 (10½ oz.) can chicken broth	Chopped fresh parsley

Sauté onion, celery, carrot and garlic in melted butter in a 10" skillet until tender.

Combine chicken broth with enough water to make 2 cups. Add chicken broth, potatoes, salt and pepper to sautéed vegetables. Cover; simmer for 10 minutes. Remove cover. Simmer, stirring occasionally, 20 minutes or until broth is thickened. Sprinkle with parsley. Makes 4 to 6 servings.

ONION/MUSTARD BUNS

Tired of plain buns? Try these seasoned specials—you'll love them

1 pkg. active dry yeast	2 c. scalded milk
¼ c. warm water (110 to 115°)	6 c. sifted flour
2 tblsp. sugar	1 egg, slightly beaten
1 tblsp. prepared mustard	2 tblsp. instant minced onion
1½ tsp. salt	¼ c. water
½ tsp. pepper	1 egg, beaten
2 tblsp. instant minced onion	2 tblsp. water
2 tblsp. salad oil	

Dissolve yeast in warm water.

Combine sugar, mustard, salt, pepper, 2 tblsp. instant onion and oil in large bowl. Stir in milk. Cool until lukewarm.

Add 2 c. flour to milk mixture, beating until smooth. Add yeast and slightly beaten egg. Stir in enough remaining flour to make a soft dough.

Turn onto floured surface; knead until smooth, about 5 to 8 minutes. Place in greased bowl; invert to grease top. Cover; let rise until doubled, about 1½ hours. Punch down. Divide dough in half. Let rest 10 minutes. Pat each portion of dough into a 9″ square. Cut each square into 9 portions. Tuck corners under to form buns. Flatten with palm of hand. Let rise until doubled, about 30 minutes.

Meanwhile, combine 2 tblsp. minced onion and ¼ c. water; allow to stand 5 minutes.

Combine beaten egg and 2 tblsp. water; brush rolls with mixture. Sprinkle with onion. Bake in moderate oven (375°) 20 minutes, or until golden brown. Makes 18 buns.

PEACH MELBA PARFAIT

New version of Peaches Melba—mold this beauty in glass dishes

1 (3 oz.) pkg. raspberry flavor gelatin	1 (3 oz.) pkg. peach flavor gelatin
2 c. hot water	½ c. cold water
1 (10 oz.) pkg. frozen raspberries (1¼ c.)	1 pt. vanilla ice cream
	1½ c. diced fresh peaches

Dissolve raspberry gelatin in 1 c. hot water in bowl. Add unthawed raspberries. Stir occasionally to separate berries. Let thaw (it will begin to set).

Pour 1 c. hot water over peach gelatin in another bowl; stir to dissolve. Add ½ c. cold water. Add ice cream in eight chunks; stir to melt. Refrigerate until thick enough to mound up.

Spoon slightly thickened raspberry mixture into 8 dessert dishes.

When ice cream mixture has thickened, fold in peaches and spoon over raspberry mixture. Chill at least 30 minutes before serving. Makes 8 servings.

COUNTRY FAMILY DINNER

Meat Balls in Sour Cream*
Fluffy Rice or Mashed Potatoes
Calico Green Salad*
Dill Pickle Slices
Hot Rolls   Crab Apple Jelly
Cherry Torte*

Swedish meat balls go American in this dinner. Corn chips replace the traditional bread crumbs and provide a subtle flavor difference. Because the food appeals to and is suitable for both children and adults, this is an excellent menu to follow when you entertain a family.

While you do all the cooking on the day company comes, getting this dinner is neither time-consuming nor difficult. The meat balls in gravy taste great spooned over rice, but, if little children are present, you may wish to serve mashed potatoes instead. Packaged instant potatoes make quick work out of fixing them. The rolls and jelly also are favorites with youngsters.

TIMETABLE

Do-Ahead: Make sure you have the necessary ingredients on hand, especially those used less frequently, such as corn chips, dairy sour cream, olives for salad and canned cherry pie filling. Wash and drain the salad greens a day ahead. Chill them in plastic bags. Make the salad dressing and put the bottle of olives in the refrigerator.

On Guest Day: Make the Cherry Torte. Brown bread cubes for salad. About 45 minutes before dinnertime, mix, shape and put meat balls in oven to brown. Put rice on to cook; heat and season the canned or frozen green beans. Place all the salad ingredients, except bread cubes and dressing, in the salad bowl. Make sauce and add the meat balls to it.

SERVING SUGGESTIONS

This is a sit-down dinner. It is a good idea to serve the plates in the kitchen to adjust size of servings for people of different ages. Smaller ones, for young children, larger ones for teen-age boys. If you are serving mashed potatoes, arrange mounds of them on plate. Make a depression in each one with the back of a spoon. Fill with melted butter and sprinkle the yellow pools with chopped chives (or parsley for children). Spoon the meat balls alongside.

MEAT BALLS IN SOUR CREAM

Ground beef plays many roles in meals—this is a tasty one

1 c. crushed corn chips	1 c. finely chopped onion
1 c. milk	2 tblsp. flour
1 clove garlic, minced	1 can condensed beef broth
1 tblsp. parsley flakes	½ c. water
1 tsp. salt	1 tsp. Worcestershire sauce
Dash of pepper	1 c. dairy sour cream
2 lbs. lean ground beef	Paprika
3 tblsp. butter or regular margarine	Hot cooked rice

Combine corn chips, milk, garlic, parsley, salt and pepper. Add beef and mix well. Shape in small balls and place in large, shallow pan. Bake in moderate oven (375°) 20 minutes, shaking pan several times to turn balls.

Melt butter in a 3-qt. saucepan; add onion and cook until tender, but do not brown. Blend in flour. Add beef broth, water and Worcestershire sauce all at once. Cook, stirring until mixture comes to a boil. Reduce heat and blend in sour cream. Heat, but do not boil. Add meat balls and stir gently to avoid breaking them. Sprinkle with paprika. Serve over cooked rice, or with mashed potatoes. Makes 8 servings.

CALICO GREEN SALAD

Homemade or other firm-textured bread makes the best cubes

4 slices white bread
¼ c. butter or regular margarine
2 cloves garlic, minced
½ head romaine, torn in bite-size pieces
1 medium head iceberg lettuce, torn in bite-size pieces

¾ c. sliced pimiento-stuffed olives
¾ c. thinly sliced carrots
¼ c. minced green onion
Vinegar/Oil Dressing

Trim crusts from bread; cut bread in ½" cubes.

Melt butter in skillet; add garlic and cook 1 minute without browning, stirring constantly. Add bread cubes and cook, tossing to prevent burning, until golden brown. Drain on paper toweling until cool.

Place romaine, head lettuce, olives, carrots and onion in salad bowl. Just before serving, toss with Vinegar/Oil Dressing (shake well before using). Add bread cubes and toss again. Makes 8 servings.

Vinegar/Oil Dressing: Combine ⅔ c. salad oil, 2 tblsp. red wine vinegar, ½ tsp. salt, ⅛ tsp. orégano leaves, crushed, and a dash of pepper. Chill. Shake before using.

CHERRY TORTE

Big dessert has a crumb crust, cherry filling and meringue on top

Crust:
2 c. sifted flour
½ tsp. salt
¼ c. confectioners sugar
¾ c. butter or regular margarine
1 tsp. grated lemon peel
½ c. finely chopped walnuts
Filling:
1 (1 lb. 8 oz. or 1 lb. 5 oz.) jar cherry pie filling

1½ tsp. cornstarch, dissolved in 1 tblsp. water
1 tblsp. butter or regular margarine
Meringue:
4 egg whites
⅛ tsp. salt
⅛ tsp. cream of tartar
½ tsp. vanilla
8 tblsp. sugar

Sift together dry ingredients for crust; cut in butter to make a mixture the consistency of coarse cornmeal. Toss with lemon peel and nuts. Press into shallow 2-qt. glass baking dish. Bake in moderate oven (375°) 20 minutes, or until lightly browned.

Combine pie filling and cornstarch mixture; cook over medium heat, stirring constantly, until thickened. Remove from heat; stir in butter. Pour hot filling into hot crust; top with meringue.

To make meringue, combine egg whites, salt, cream of tartar and vanilla; beat until foamy. Beat in sugar, 1 tblsp. at a time, beating thoroughly after each addition. Swirl on pie filling. Brown in moderate oven (350°) about 15 minutes. Makes 10 to 12 servings.

FOUR-SEASON DINNER

Glazed Beef Balls*   Indiana Succotash*
Lettuce   Red Clover Salad Dressing*
Hard Rolls
Applesauce Meringue Pie*

This menu is good for any month on the calendar; it's adaptable to seasonal changes. You needn't tinker with the beef, however—it's right for meals the year around.

To make succotash in the good old summertime you can gather green beans fresh from the vines and cut sweet corn from the cob. But when it's snowing, try canned or frozen beans and corn (easier and quicker).

You can fill the baked pie shell with that wonderful tart-sweet applesauce made with early-summer fruit. If you do, you can cut in half the amount of lemon juice and grated peel which point up the flavor of sauce from bland, sweet apples.

Tailoring meals and recipes to fit the season, or to the foods most available and to the weather, is a well-established pattern in farm kitchens. The country woman always has had to be a flexible cook!

TIMETABLE

Do-Ahead: You can make the salad dressing and applesauce a day ahead; refrigerate. You also can bake the pie shell.

On Guest Day: Mix and shape meat balls a couple of hours before you plan to serve them. They need to chill at least an hour. Make the glaze while the meat balls bake. Cut the green beans for the succotash some time while meat balls are chilling. Cook them so they'll be ready to season and heat with the corn. (Cutting beans is somewhat tedious; you *can* use larger pieces, but the fine ones look and taste better.) The recipe is a big one, but appetites are also big when succotash appears.

Bake the pie at any time during the day. Be sure to cool it away from drafts so the meringue will stay tall.

SERVING SUGGESTIONS

This is an excellent dinner to serve buffet style. To serve more than 6 people, you will need to fix 2 recipes of beef balls and make 2 pies. Serve beef balls on a big platter and sprinkle with fresh parsley snipped with scissors.

GLAZED BEEF BALLS

Fine, tasty way to glamorize ground beef for special occasions

½ c. fine bread crumbs
1 tsp. salt
¼ tsp. pepper
1 tblsp. grated onion
½ tsp. prepared horse-radish
1 tblsp. Worcestershire sauce

1 egg, beaten
½ c. tomato juice
2 tblsp. salad oil
1 lb. lean ground beef
Glaze

Blend together all ingredients, except beef and Glaze. Add to beef, mixing well. Chill at least 1 hour.

Shape meat mixture in balls about the size of walnuts. Place in shallow baking pan; bake in extremely hot oven (500°) 10 to 12 minutes, or until browned. Add to Glaze and heat. Makes about 24 balls.

Glaze: Combine in saucepan, ¼ c. brown sugar, firmly packed, 2 tblsp. flour, 1 tsp. dry mustard, ¼ c. chili sauce, ¼ c. dark corn syrup, ½ tsp. salt, dash of Tabasco sauce and ¼ c. orange juice. Cook and stir until slightly thickened.

INDIANA SUCCOTASH

Expert seasonings explain the popularity of this vegetable duo

1½ lbs. green beans
1½ tsp. salt
1½ c. green onions with tops
6 tblsp. butter

2 (1 lb. 1 oz.) cans whole kernel
corn, drained
¾ tsp. paprika
¾ tsp. celery salt
1 tsp. sugar

Cut beans in rounds about the size of the yellow corn kernels; cook with ½ tsp. salt in water to cover about 15 minutes, or just until tender. Drain.

Sauté green onions in butter until transparent (do not brown); add corn, 1 tsp. salt, paprika, celery salt and sugar, then beans.

Simmer, covered, about 10 minutes to blend seasonings and heat thoroughly. Makes 12 servings.

N O T E : Fresh corn, cut from the top, may be used when available instead of canned corn.

RED CLOVER SALAD DRESSING

Men especially like this ketchup-flavored, bright red dressing

1 c. honey	½ c. ketchup
1½ tblsp. salt	½ c. lemon juice
1 tblsp. dry mustard	1 c. vinegar
1½ tblsp. paprika	2 c. salad oil

Mix all ingredients, except salad oil, with electric mixer until well blended.

Gradually add salad oil, beating constantly, to blend well and to obtain the consistency of mayonnaise.

Use to serve with greens or fruits. Makes about 5 cups.

APPLESAUCE MERINGUE PIE

Few apple pies equal this one in beauty, and it's delicious. The makings for it usually are on hand—pie shell in freezer, eggs in refrigerator, applesauce in cupboard. Making pie is an easy and fast assembly job—it bakes only to brown the meringue

Baked 9″ pie shell	1 tblsp. cornstarch
2 c. sweetened applesauce	3 eggs, separated
Juice of 1 lemon	¼ tsp. cream of tartar
2 tsp. grated lemon peel	¼ tsp. salt
¼ tsp. salt	6 tblsp. sugar
¼ tsp. ground cinnamon	½ tsp. vanilla

Combine applesauce, lemon juice, peel, ¼ tsp. salt, cinnamon, cornstarch and slightly beaten egg yolks in saucepan; cook until thick and smooth. Cool slightly. Pour into baked pie shell. Spread filling to level.

Cover warm filling with meringue made of beaten egg whites, cream of tartar, ¼ tsp. salt, sugar and vanilla. Spread to cover entire filling; seal to pastry.

Bake in hot oven (425°) 10 to 12 minutes, until meringue is nicely browned. Makes 8 servings.

COMBINATION
FAMILY-FRIENDS DINNER

Meat Ball Stew*
Green Bean Salad
French Cheese Bread*
Vanilla Ice Cream
Choco/Apple Cupcakes*   Caramel Frosting*

This is the kind of family meal you're proud to share with an unexpected last-minute guest. If your son calls and wants to bring a friend home from school for dinner before they take off for the football game or other athletic event, you can be confident the boys will like what they eat. And if you and your husband, shortly before mealtime, decide to invite a neighboring couple for dinner and the evening, you will feel equally comfortable about the food you prepared.

The main dish, a stew, contains vegetables and ground beef shaped in expertly seasoned balls. Sliced French bread, spread with a cheese mixture and toasted, supplies flavorful crispness. The salad is the one food you may wish to dress up a little. One way to do this is to garnish the individual servings with half of a deviled egg.

Caramel-frosted cupcakes, served with a scoop of ice cream, glasses of cold milk and a hot beverage for the grownups sends people from the table satisfied and ready to enjoy the evening.

TIMETABLE

Do-Ahead: Bake and frost the cupcakes a day (or several days) ahead and freeze them. You also can make the salad a day ahead, cover and chill.

On Guest Day: See Index for Green Bean Salad recipe (included in "Make-Ahead Dinner" menu). Cook bacon for garnishing salad at any time convenient, but add it just before serving. An hour before dinnertime, start preparing meat balls and vegetables. Put them on to cook about 35 minutes before you want to serve them. Meanwhile, slice the French bread, spread with cheese mixture. Toast just before you dish up the stew. If cupcakes are frozen, set them out on the kitchen counter to thaw just before you sit down to eat dinner.

SERVING SUGGESTIONS

Serve the stew in a bowl, the salad on individual plates and the bread in a basket or roll warmer. Pass the food around the table family style, letting everyone help himself. Serve the dessert from the kitchen, a cupcake on each dessert plate accompanied with a scoop of ice cream from the freezer.

MEAT BALL STEW

Three reasons men praise this stew: the meat, potatoes and gravy

1½ lbs. ground beef
1 c. soft bread crumbs
¼ c. finely chopped onion
1 egg, beaten
1 tsp. salt
½ tsp. marjoram leaves
¼ tsp. thyme leaves
2 tblsp. salad oil
1 can condensed tomato soup

1 (10½ oz.) can condensed beef broth
4 medium potatoes, peeled and quartered
4 carrots, scraped and cut in 1″ chunks
8 small white onions, peeled
2 tblsp. chopped fresh parsley

Combine ground beef, bread crumbs, chopped onion, egg, salt, marjoram and thyme. Shape into 24 meat balls. Brown in oil in 4-qt. Dutch oven. Remove meat balls as they brown.

Combine soup and broth in Dutch oven. Add meat balls, potatoes, carrots and white onions. Bring to a boil; cover and simmer 30 minutes, or until vegetables are tender. Add parsley. Makes 6 to 8 servings.

FRENCH CHEESE BREAD

Serve this crunchy cheese-topped French bread hot from the oven

¾ stick butter
¾ stick regular margarine
½ tsp. garlic salt
⅓ c. grated Parmesan cheese

¼ c. grated process American cheese
1 loaf French bread, cut in ¾″ slices

Melt butter and margarine; add garlic salt. Stir in cheeses. With pastry brush, spread butter mixture evenly on one side of bread slices. Broil buttered side until light golden and bubbling hot. Makes about 21 slices.

CHOCO/APPLE CUPCAKES

Next time you bake these cupcakes spread with your favorite fudge frosting instead of caramel. Both are good; so are unfrosted cakes

½ c. shortening	1 tsp. ground cinnamon
1 c. sugar	½ tsp. ground allspice
1 egg	1½ squares unsweetened
1¾ c. sifted flour	chocolate, grated
1 tsp. baking soda	1¼ c. unsweetened applesauce
½ tsp. salt	Caramel Frosting (optional)

Cream shortening and sugar until light and fluffy. Add egg; beat well.

Sift together dry ingredients. Stir in grated chocolate. Add to creamed mixture alternately with applesauce; mix after each addition.

Fill greased muffin-pan cups two thirds full. Bake in moderate oven (375°) 20 minutes. Cool, then frost with Caramel Frosting, if desired. Makes 18.

CARAMEL FROSTING

Press a pecan or walnut half on each frosted cupcake for a quick trim

½ c. butter	¼ tsp. salt
1 c. dark brown sugar, firmly packed	¼ c. milk
	2 c. sifted confectioners sugar

Melt butter in a saucepan over low heat, but do not let it brown. Stir in brown sugar and salt. Bring to a boil over medium heat and boil hard 2 minutes, stirring all the time. Remove from heat.

Add milk and stir vigorously. Return pan to heat and bring mixture to a full boil again. Remove from heat at once and set aside to cool to lukewarm; it will take about 20 minutes.

Stir confectioners sugar into the lukewarm mixture and beat until smooth. If frosting hardens too much to spread, beat in a few drops of milk. Makes enough to frost about 18 cupcakes or two 8 or 9" cake layers.

DIFFERENT COUNTRY DINNER

Tuna-Stuffed Tomatoes*
Crackers   Hot Chicken Broth
Beef/Vegetables Californian*
Hot Steamed Rice*
Buttered Peas   Hot Rolls
Apricot Custard Ice Cream*
Chocolate Cake

For an imaginative, up-to-date country dinner, follow this menu. Your friends who have traveled, young people who have worked or been in military service overseas, and those who like to experiment with international dishes in their own kitchens will like this menu particularly. (Avoid inviting people who are only ardent meat-and-potato fans.)

This dinner is not Chinese although it shows a couple of Far Eastern influences—in the method of cooking rice in which the Chinese excel, for instance, and in the fast-cook beef-vegetable main dish.

The menu begins with an appetizer course featuring farm favorites —cherry tomatoes, tuna and hot chicken broth—served in a distinctive way. Dinner ends with a velvety homemade custard ice cream flavored with tart-sweet dried apricots. Three foods listed in the menu are optional—peas, hot rolls and chocolate cake.

TIMETABLE

Do-Ahead: Bake the cake a day ahead if you like, or use a packaged mix and bake it on party day. You can freeze the ice cream, pack it in freezer containers and put in the freezer a day or several days ahead. If you prefer to serve it after it has ripened in the can of the crank freezer, put the dried apricots in a bowl the night before, add water, cover and let them stand overnight to soften and absorb the liquid. It's permissible to scoop out the tomatoes, invert them on a plate (to drain) and refrigerate.

On Guest Day: If you did not freeze the ice cream the previous day, freeze it at your convenience in the afternoon and let it ripen. Stuff the tomatoes and chill. Assemble ingredients for the main dish and cut meat in thin strips. Put the rice on to cook about 45 minutes before dinner. Heat the chicken broth. Assemble the tomatoes and crackers and place mugs for broth on tray. Ask your husband or the older children to carry them to the living room and serve the guests while you cook the remainder of the dinner. Heat the peas (you can use the frozen peas in butter sauce that require only heating). Put rolls wrapped in heavy-duty foil in moderate oven (350°) 10 to 12 minutes. Then cook the main dish. You'll have it ready to serve in less than 15 minutes.

SERVING SUGGESTIONS

Arrange stuffed tomatoes on a large plate, the crackers on another plate. Pour the heated chicken broth (homemade or canned) into a pitcher for easy pouring into mugs. Serve the plates in the kitchen. Serve the ice cream the traditional farm way in dessert bowls set on individual plates, the cake slices on the same plates.

TUNA-STUFFED TOMATOES

Colorful and satisfying finger food to enjoy as prelude to dinner

24 to 30 cherry tomatoes	2 tblsp. chopped ripe olives
1 (7 oz.) can tuna, drained	¾ tsp. seasoned salt
1 green onion, finely chopped	Parsley

Wash and drain tomatoes. Cut a thin slice off the top of each and scoop out the pulp. Invert to drain.

Combine tuna, onion, olives and salt; mix well. Stuff into tomato shells and top each stuffed tomato with a tiny sprig of parsley. Refrigerate until serving time. Makes 24 to 30 stuffed tomatoes.

NOTE: These also are pretty—and nice—filled with your favorite avocado dip.

BEEF/VEGETABLES CALIFORNIAN

Celery and onions should cook only until they are barely tender

2 tblsp. salad oil
1½ lbs. flank steak, cut in thin
   strips
1 tsp. sugar
2 tblsp. soy sauce
2 c. cut celery (cut diagonally in
   1" pieces)
1 sweet onion, thinly sliced
1 (5 oz.) can water chestnuts,
   drained and chopped
½ (10 oz.) pkg. frozen
   French-style green beans

¼ lb. fresh mushrooms
1 chicken or beef bouillon cube
½ c. hot water
1 tblsp. cornstarch
¼ c. cold water
1 (10 oz.) pkg. frozen, chopped
   spinach, or ½ lb. spinach,
   cleaned and cut-up
Hot Steamed Rice

Heat oil in large skillet. Add meat, sprinkling with sugar and soy sauce. Cook and stir until meat loses red color. Push it to one side of skillet and add celery, onion, water chestnuts, green beans and mushrooms.

Fry, tossing lightly while cooking. Cook only until celery and onions are tender-crisp.

Dissolve bouillon cube in hot water; add to mixture in skillet.

Add cornstarch to cold water. Add to skillet and heat. Add spinach and cook, tossing while heating. Serve at once over Hot Steamed Rice. Makes 4 to 6 servings.

N O T E : For more servings, cook the same ingredients a second time. Do not try to double recipe and cook the double amount.

HOT STEAMED RICE

The Chinese are accomplished rice cooks. This is their method

1⅓ c. regular long grain rice   2⅓ c. cold water

Place rice in sieve and rinse well under running cold water. Drain.

Put rice in a 2-qt. heavy saucepan and add cold water. Bring to the boiling point quickly over high heat (about 5 minutes). Lower heat; cover and simmer (do not let boil) 20 minutes, or until rice is dry. Turn off heat and let stand, tightly covered, 20 minutes longer. Stir with fork to separate grains. Makes 4 cups.

APRICOT CUSTARD ICE CREAM

Rich creamy custard ice cream luscious with the taste of apricots

1 (8 oz.) pkg. dried apricots	1½ c. milk
1½ c. hot water	4 eggs, slightly beaten
1¾ c. sugar	1 qt. heavy cream
¼ c. flour	1 tblsp. vanilla
Dash of salt	

Place apricots in a small bowl, pour on hot water. Cover and let stand overnight. By morning the fruit will be soft and the water will be absorbed. Do not cook. Put apricots through a food mill or whirl in blender to make a purée.

Combine sugar, flour and salt in large saucepan; stir in milk. Cook and stir over medium heat until sauce thickens and bubbles; let it cook 1 minute. Remove from heat. Gradually stir about ¾ c. of hot mixture into eggs; stir constantly. Add eggs to hot milk mixture in saucepan; cook and stir over medium heat about 1 minute. Remove from heat. Pour into a large mixing bowl and cool.

When mixture is cool, stir in cream, vanilla and apricot purée; cover and refrigerate until cold.

Pour cold ice cream mixture into 2-qt. freezer can, filling two thirds to three fourths full. Adjust dasher and cover. Pack crushed ice and rock salt around can, using 6 parts ice to 1 part salt.

Turn dasher slowly until the ice melts enough to make a brine. Add more ice and salt, mixed in the proper proportion to maintain the ice level. Turn the handle fast and steadily until it turns hard. Then remove the ice until the level is below the lid of can; take off lid and remove the dasher.

Plug the hole in lid and cover can with several thicknesses of waxed paper or foil to make a tight fit for the lid. Pack more ice-salt mixture, using 4 parts ice to 1 part salt, around can and filling the freezer. Cover with a blanket, canvas or other heavy cloth, or with newspaper. Let the ice cream ripen 4 hours before serving. Or put it in the home freezer to ripen. Makes about 2 quarts.

DINNER ON FRIDAY

Spicy Grape Juice Frost*
Easy Beef Burgundy* or Traditional Beef Burgundy*
Toasted French Bread
Tossed Green Salad
Chocolate/Almond Cheese Cake*

Follow this blueprint for the first dinner when long-absent friends arrive late Friday afternoon to spend the weekend. There's so much talking when such guests appear that it's difficult for a hostess to keep her mind on food preparations. You can forget about them until the last few minutes before mealtime if you use this plan.

With the beef in the oven and the French bread ready to toast, you can put the main dish out of your thoughts knowing it will turn out beautifully. The simple version of Beef Burgundy listed in the menu skips the browning of the meat and it simmers lazily in the oven without watching. Just in case you prefer to make the more traditional dish, we include the recipe also—take your choice.

A tossed green salad fits perfectly into this meal, which ends with a gorgeous dessert. You will have some of the cheese cake left over to put in a welcome appearance on Sunday. With dinner under control, you can enjoy sipping the grape juice appetizer in the living room and take part in the conversation.

TIMETABLE

Do-Ahead: Make Chocolate/Almond Cheese Cake the day before you serve it. Keep in refrigerator. Wash, drain and chill salad greens in a plastic bag.

On Guest Day: Fix grape juice whenever convenient and chill. Cut the beef in cubes early in the day; refrigerate. Slice bread ready for toasting. Three hours before dinnertime put the main dish in the oven to cook slowly. Frost the cake, decorate and return to refrigerator. All you will have to do just before serving is toss the salad and toast the bread.

SERVING SUGGESTIONS

This is a good meal to serve buffet style; most people enjoy helping themselves. Float thin lemon slices in glasses of grape juice. Serve Easy Beef Burgundy in the casserole, the toast in a bread basket or roll warmer and the salad in a big bowl. At dessert time, cut the cake, place on individual plates and carry from kitchen to the table.

SPICY GRAPE JUICE FROST

If you prefer the juice without spices, add sugar and mix with an equal part of orange juice; omit lemon juice

1 (6 oz.) can frozen grape juice concentrate	1 allspice berry
	2 tblsp. sugar
1 stick cinnamon	Lemon juice
3 whole cloves	

Reconstitute grape juice by label directions. Add cinnamon, cloves, allspice and sugar. Simmer in covered saucepan 5 minutes. Strain and discard spices.

Refrigerate until cool. Add lemon juice to taste. Cover and chill until serving time. Pour in glasses half filled with crushed ice. Makes 6 to 8 servings.

EASY BEEF BURGUNDY

Once you cube the beef this dish is exceptionally quick to fix

3 medium onions, sliced	½ tsp. thyme leaves, crushed
2½ lbs. round steak, cut in 1" cubes	¼ tsp. pepper
	3 tblsp. flour
2 (4 oz.) cans mushrooms (stems and pieces)	2 beef bouillon cubes
	2 c. red Burgundy wine
1½ tsp. garlic salt	Toasted French bread slices
½ tsp. marjoram leaves, crushed	

Arrange onion slices on bottom of 3-qt. casserole; top with meat cubes.

Drain mushrooms, reserving liquid. Place mushroom pieces on top of meat. Sprinkle with garlic salt, marjoram, thyme and pepper.

In saucepan gradually blend reserved mushroom liquid into flour to make a smooth paste. Add bouillon cubes and Burgundy and cook, stirring constantly until mixture comes to a boil. The bouillon cubes should be dissolved. If not, remove saucepan from heat and stir mixture until they are dissolved. Pour over meat mixture in casserole.

Cover and bake in moderate oven (350°) 2½ to 3 hours, or until meat is tender. Serve over slices of toasted French bread. Makes 8 servings.

TRADITIONAL BEEF BURGUNDY

This Americanized version of the French stew uses more ingredients and different seasonings, requires more work in preparation and more watching while cooking than Easy Beef Burgundy . . . try both

6 bacon slices	1 c. beef consommé
2 lbs. boneless chuck beef roast	1 tblsp. beef-seasoned stock base
2 tblsp. flour	or 1 beef bouillon cube
Salt	2 bay leaves
Pepper	Dash of thyme leaves, crushed
2 cloves garlic, crushed	6 whole cloves
1 medium onion, chopped	12 white boiling onions
1 c. red Burgundy wine	½ c. fresh mushrooms

Pan-fry bacon until crisp; remove from skillet and set aside.

Cut beef in bite-size pieces, dredge in flour seasoned with salt and pepper. Brown lightly in skillet. Add garlic and chopped onion and brown slightly. Add wine, consommé, stock base, bay leaves and thyme. Stick cloves into one of the boiling onions and add to skillet. Cover and simmer gently 1½ to 2 hours, or until beef is tender.

Thirty minutes before beef is cooked add boiling onions. Fifteen minutes later add the mushrooms. Remove clove-studded onion and bay leaves. Crumble bacon and sprinkle over top; keep warm in chafing dish on the buffet if you wish. Serve with rice or noodles. Makes 6 servings.

CHOCOLATE/ALMOND CHEESE CAKE

A jackpot of good flavors—chocolate, cheese and almonds—in this dessert

1¼ c. graham cracker crumbs (18 crackers)
¾ c. very finely chopped unblanched almonds (about 3½ oz.)
½ c. melted butter or regular margarine
2 tblsp. sugar
4 eggs

1 c. sugar
3 (8 oz.) pkgs. cream cheese
2 squares unsweetened chocolate
2 tsp. vanilla
1 c. dairy sour cream
1 tblsp. sugar
Glacé fruit mix
Toasted slivered almonds

Combine crumbs, chopped almonds, butter and 2 tblsp. sugar; mix well. Line sides and bottom of 9″ spring-form pan with mixture, pressing firmly against pan with back of spoon.

Beat eggs well; gradually add 1 c. sugar, beating until mixture is lemon-colored. Add cheese in small amounts, beating until smooth after each addition.

Melt chocolate over hot water; blend into beaten mixture along with vanilla.

Pour into crumb-lined pan. Bake in moderate oven (350°) 35 to 40 minutes, or until cake is set in center. Remove from oven and cool thoroughly. Loosen up ring and remove side of pan.

Blend sour cream with 1 tblsp. sugar. Spread over torte, making wreath around the edge and a medallion in the center. Garnish with glacé fruit and slivered almonds. Makes 16 servings.

MAKE-AHEAD DINNER

Chilled Tomato Juice
Beef/Noodle Bake*
Peppermint Tapioca*

Sesame Melba Toast
Green Bean Salad*
Chocolate Sauce

The main-dish casserole is a country hostess favorite because it cooks with little or no attention and is easily served. You usually can get it ready for baking hours ahead and refrigerate. All you have to do when getting dinner is tuck it in the oven. There was a time when casseroles meant a mixture of leftovers, but such tasty combinations as this beef-noodle special are company fare. The recipe, shared by a Tennessee homemaker, makes a hearty treat of superior flavors.

This dinner menu is the ideal choice for the woman who returns home from work or other activities about an hour before guests arrive. It is a meal that permits the hostess to be with her guests instead of in the kitchen. And it's a perfect menu for a cooperative meal. All the foods carry successfully.

TIMETABLE

Do-Ahead: You can get the casserole ready to bake a day ahead and refrigerate. The salad and the tapioca dessert are at their best chilled several hours or overnight. You can slice the bread, and spread on the butter-cheese mixture so it will be ready for baking.

On Guest Day: Put the casserole in the oven an hour before dinner time. Make the toast just before the guests arrive. Slice day-old bread ¼" thick. Spread with equal parts butter or margarine and grated Parmesan cheese creamed together. Sprinkle with sesame seeds; place on baking sheet and bake in slow oven (325°) until lightly browned.

SERVING SUGGESTIONS

Serve the tomato juice and toast in the living room. Pass the toast hot from the oven. If you chill the tapioca in dessert glasses it will be ready to serve. Garnish with a little of the crushed red-and-white peppermint candy; pass the chocolate sauce. Serve the bean salad on crisp lettuce.

BEEF/NOODLE BAKE

You can use sour cream with chives for plain cream and onions

1 lb. ground beef	1 (15 oz.) can tomato sauce
1 (2 oz.) can mushrooms, drained	4 oz. noodles, uncooked
1 clove garlic, crushed	4 green onions, finely chopped
1 tsp. salt	1 (8 oz.) pkg. cream cheese
½ tsp. pepper	1 c. dairy sour cream
2 tsp. sugar	½ c. grated Cheddar cheese

Cook and stir ground beef in 10″ skillet until lightly browned. Add mushrooms, garlic, salt, pepper, sugar and tomato sauce. Cover and simmer 15 minutes.

Cook noodles by package directions and drain.

Combine onions, using some of the green tops, with cream cheese and sour cream. Blend well.

In a greased 2-qt. casserole, evenly spread about a fourth of the noodles; top with a fourth of ground beef mixture. Spread about a fourth of the cream cheese mixture over top. Repeat three times; top with Cheddar cheese. Bake in moderate oven (350°) until bubbling hot in center, about 50 minutes if chilled, 30 to 35 minutes if not chilled. Makes 6 to 8 servings.

GREEN BEAN SALAD

To give salad a touch of bright color add 2 tblsp. chopped pimiento

½ c. vinegar
¼ c. salad oil
1 tsp. salt
¼ tsp. pepper
1 tsp. sugar

4 c. cooked green beans
1 medium onion, finely chopped
Lettuce
3 slices fried bacon, crumbled

Blend together vinegar, oil, salt, pepper and sugar; pour over beans and onion. Chill well. Serve on lettuce; sprinkle on bacon just before serving. Makes 6 to 8 servings.

PEPPERMINT TAPIOCA

New version of the old-time favorite pudding. The blending of peppermint and chocolate flavors makes this a taste delight

1 qt. milk
⅓ c. quick-cooking tapioca
⅓ c. finely crushed peppermint
   stick candy
¼ tsp. salt

2 eggs, separated
3 tblsp. finely crushed peppermint
   stick candy
½ tsp. vanilla
Chocolate sauce

Scald milk in double boiler. Combine tapioca, ⅓ c. peppermint candy and salt. Gradually add to hot milk, stirring constantly to prevent lumping. Heat and stir over water until pudding thickens and tapioca is clear.

Beat egg yolks until lemon-colored. Stir in a little of the hot pudding, then add yolks slowly to pudding in double boiler, stirring constantly. Remove from heat.

Beat egg whites until stiff, but not dry; fold into pudding. Add 3 tblsp. peppermint candy and vanilla. Chill. Serve with your favorite chocolate sauce from the supermarket. Makes 6 to 8 servings.

ROYAL PORK DINNER

Pork Roast Danish Style*
Sweet Potato Bonbons*
Gala Baby Limas*
Cabbage Salad Bowl*
Rosy Peaches à la Mode

Some evening when the winter wind howls, seat guests in the warmth and comfort of your home and serve this dinner. It's a country meal long to be remembered. The pork loin with an irresistible brown crust, pecan-decorated sweet potato nuggets, tiny lima beans, country cabbage salad brightened with red radish slices, thin green pepper rings and shredded carrots, and rosy peaches with creamy ice cream topping—with friends to enjoy the food, who could wish for more?

You may want to invite guests who enjoy an adventure in good eating, for the pork roast is different and distinctive. When you use this menu, you may think it requires more effort and time than a regular roast pork dinner, but it's not difficult.

TIMETABLE

Do-Ahead: Rub seasonings on pork roast and refrigerate overnight. Cook sweet potatoes; mash, season, shape, roll in butter and crumbs, top with pecans and refrigerate. Drain canned peach halves well, place in baking dish, melt red raspberry jelly over low heat and pour over them. Cover and chill.

On Guest Day: About 4 hours before dinner, cut pocket in the pork and stuff with fruits, close and sew to keep opening closed. Put it in the preheated oven 2¾ hours before dinnertime. Make the cabbage salad, cover and chill. About 20 minutes before serving time, fix the lima beans. Take the roast from the oven to stand 15 minutes before carving. Then increase oven heat to 450° and bake the sweet potatoes 8 to 10 minutes if they were not chilled, a few minutes longer if refrigerated. Dessert will need attention only at serving time.

SERVING SUGGESTIONS

Garnish the meat platter with a bouquet of parsley or celery leaves and several cherry tomatoes, but do not crowd the roast on the platter (makes carving easier). Line the salad bowl with reserved green cabbage leaves.

PORK ROAST DANISH STYLE

Succulent fruit-stuffed roast, wrapped in buttery crumbs—a beauty

½ tsp. salt
½ tsp. ground cinnamon
½ tsp. ground allspice
½ tsp. pepper
¼ tsp. ground cloves
¼ tsp. ground mace
3 to 3½ lbs. boned pork loin roast
12 pitted prunes

2 medium apples, peeled, cored and cut in sixths
2 tblsp. raisins
¼ tsp. ground cinnamon
¼ c. brandy or apple juice
1½ tblsp. currant jelly, melted
1 c. fresh bread crumbs
¼ c. melted butter

Mix salt, ½ tsp. cinnamon, allspice, pepper, cloves and mace; rub into surface of pork. Refrigerate overnight.

Combine prunes, apples, raisins, ¼ tsp. cinnamon and brandy. Refrigerate overnight.

Drain fruit, reserving liquid. Cut a long, deep pocket the length of the roast. Stuff with fruit. Sew closed with large needle; tie with kitchen twine. Brush roast with liquid drained from fruit.

Roast on rack in slow oven (325°) 1 hour. Remove from oven, and brush with jelly. Coat with bread crumbs. Baste with butter. Return meat to oven and roast 1½ hours longer. Let stand 15 minutes before carving. Makes 6 servings.

SWEET POTATO BONBONS

Marshmallow centers, buttery corn flake coating make these special

3 lbs. sweet potatoes, peeled and cooked
¼ c. butter
½ c. brown sugar, firmly packed
1 tsp. salt

½ tsp. grated orange peel
6 marshmallows, halved
⅓ c. melted butter
4 c. corn flakes, crushed
12 pecan halves

Mash sweet potatoes until light and fluffy. Beat in ¼ c. butter, brown sugar, salt and orange peel. Let cool.

Divide potatoes into 12 equal portions. Center each portion with a marshmallow half, covering it with potatoes; shape in ovals. Coat each with melted butter; roll in corn flakes and top with a pecan half. Place on lightly greased baking sheet.

Bake in very hot oven (450°) 7 to 8 minutes. Serves 6 to 8.

GALA BABY LIMAS

Sour cream and seasoned stuffing mix give the bean flavor a lift

2 (10 oz.) pkgs. frozen baby lima
   beans
¼ c. butter
1 c. herb-seasoned stuffing mix

2 c. dairy sour cream
2 tsp. onion salt
1 c. grated process American
   cheese

Cook beans by package directions in a heavy 10″ skillet; remove from heat and drain. Cool slightly.

Melt butter over low heat in small saucepan. Add stuffing mix; heat and stir to coat crumbs with butter and brown.

Add sour cream, onion salt and cheese to beans. Cook over low heat, stirring constantly, just long enough to heat, but do not let come to a boil. Turn into a warm 1½-qt. bowl or casserole and sprinkle hot crumbs over top. Serve at once. Makes 6 servings.

CABBAGE SALAD BOWL

Color-bright vegetables make this a favorite with extra appeal

1 medium head cabbage
1 small green pepper, cut in thin
   rings
1 c. diced celery
⅔ c. finely shredded carrots
⅓ c. thin radish slices
2 tblsp. minced onion

1 c. salad dressing or mayonnaise
2 tblsp. milk
2 tsp. sugar
2 tblsp. lemon juice or vinegar
¼ tsp. paprika
¾ tsp. salt

Remove outer cabbage leaves and set aside to line salad bowl (if they are not green and pretty, use lettuce leaves). Shred remaining cabbage. Gently toss with green pepper rings, celery, carrots, radishes and onion.

In a small bowl mix salad dressing, milk, sugar, lemon juice, paprika and salt. Add to vegetables and toss lightly. Line salad bowl with reserved cabbage leaves and spoon in the salad. Cover and refrigerate at least 30 minutes, or for several hours. Makes 8 servings.

FAMILY-STYLE COMPANY DINNER

Baked Pork Chops*   Western Carrots*
Buttered Peas   Red Cabbage Salad Mold*
Hot Rolls   Frozen Pumpkin Pie*

This family-style dinner is a happy selection for the host who dislikes to carve meat at the table (or in the kitchen), and for friends who appreciate food set before them that looks and tastes wonderful.

The menu includes four somewhat different foods—beautifully browned pork chops baked with colorful vegetables and chicken soup, fine red cabbage congealed in a gelatin mold, carrots teamed with light raisins and honey-glazed, and pumpkin pie filling on a butter pecan ice cream base held in a crumb or pastry crust and frozen.

Another good feature of the pork chops, at least for the hostess, is that they require practically no attention while baking. They need no basting, but do lift off the cover during the last 15 minutes.

TIMETABLE

Do-Ahead: Make the pie a day ahead and freeze. You can fix the salad then, or the morning of company day, whichever is more convenient.

On Guest Day: Get the pork chops in the preheated oven an hour before you wish to serve dinner. Meanwhile, cook the carrots and just before mealtime, the frozen peas.

SERVING SUGGESTIONS

Place the meat on a warm platter, the vegetables in serving bowls and pass at the table. Serve the salad on lettuce-lined plates and top each serving with a spoonful of salad dressing. Or, if you have attractive green cabbage leaves, substitute them for the lettuce base. Remove the pie from the freezer a few minutes before serving (while you clear the table and refill coffee cups) to make cutting easier.

BAKED PORK CHOPS

These pork chops are fork tender and moist . . . vegetables add color

6 lean loin or rib pork chops, 1″
  thick
Salt (about ¾ tsp.)
Pepper
6 slices tomato (2 medium)

6 slices green pepper (1 large)
6 tblsp. chopped onion
6 tblsp. condensed cream of
  chicken soup

Brown pork chops on both sides in heavy skillet. Place in 13×9×2″ pan. Sprinkle lightly with salt and pepper. (If skillet has ovenproof handle bake chops in it.) Lay a slice of tomato on top of each chop; arrange a ring of green pepper on top of tomato slice and fill with chopped onion. Top each chop with undiluted cream of chicken soup.

Cover pan tightly with foil and bake in slow oven (325°) 45 minutes. Remove cover and bake 15 minutes longer. Makes 6 servings.

NOTE: It is easy to double the recipe and bake 2 pans or skillets of chops if you are entertaining more people.

WESTERN CARROTS

An extra-delicious companion for ham, pork roasts and chicken

1 lb. carrots
1 c. light raisins
¼ to ½ c. water
1 tsp. salt
3 tblsp. brown sugar

2 tblsp. honey
3 tblsp. butter or regular
  margarine
2 tblsp. lemon juice

Peel carrots and cut diagonally in thin slices. Combine with raisins, water and salt (use smaller amount of water if you can watch while cooking to prevent scorching). Cook until tender, about 20 minutes. Drain if necessary.

Sprinkle with brown sugar; add honey, butter and lemon juice. Heat over low heat, stirring often, to glaze carrots, about 10 minutes. Makes 6 to 8 servings.

RED CABBAGE SALAD MOLD

Pickles and pickle juice flavor this attractive, tasty cabbage salad

2 tblsp. lemon juice
⅔ c. sweet pickle juice
2 envelopes unflavored gelatin
3 c. water
¼ tsp. salt

1 c. finely shredded red cabbage
⅓ c. finely chopped sweet pickles
Lettuce
Salad dressing (optional)

Combine lemon and pickle juices in small bowl; sprinkle on gelatin.

Heat water with salt added to the boiling point. Remove from heat and stir in the gelatin mixture. Stir until gelatin dissolves. Cool; refrigerate until mixture mounds slightly when dropped from a spoon. (It will be the consistency of unbeaten egg whites.)

Fold in cabbage and pickles. Pour into a 1½-qt. mold. Cover and chill until firm. Serve on lettuce with salad dressing, if desired. Makes 8 servings.

FROZEN PUMPKIN PIE

New way with an old favorite . . . substitute whipped topping for cream if you wish. A delicious make-ahead dessert

Baked 9″ Crumb Crust
1 pt. butter pecan ice cream,
   softened
1 c. canned or cooked mashed
   pumpkin
1 c. sugar
½ tsp. salt

½ tsp. ground cinnamon
¼ tsp. ground ginger
¼ tsp. ground nutmeg
½ tsp. vanilla
1½ c. miniature marshmallows
1 c. heavy cream, whipped

Spoon ice cream into cool pie shell; spread in even layer. Freeze.

Mix pumpkin, sugar, salt, spices and vanilla. Fold in marshmallows and whipped cream.

Pour into Crumb Crust on top of ice cream. Cover with foil and freeze several hours or overnight. Let thaw at room temperature 5 minutes before cutting. Makes 6 to 8 servings.

Crumb Crust: Mix 1½ c. graham cracker crumbs, 3 tblsp. sugar and ⅓ c. melted butter or regular margarine. Press mixture firmly and evenly into a 9″ pie pan. Bake in moderate oven (350°) 10 minutes. Cool before filling.

PORK DINNER

Pork/Sauerkraut Skillet*
Boiled Potatoes with Parsley Butter
Mixed Fruit Salad*
Hot Rolls   Grape Jelly
Pumpkin Cake*
Coffee

Do you have a husband who may tell you around noon that he has invited a business guest "for dinner tonight"? This menu will help you with such an occasion. And if the guest doesn't ask for the pork-sauerkraut recipe to take home to his wife, it will be surprising. It's delicious plus—and easy and quick.

The potatoes are man-pleasing and using a little imagination with the ever-popular Waldorf produces a delightful salad. Dessert is unforgettable. This menu will prove you're a great cook!

TIMETABLE

Do-Ahead: There's no time for advance preparations, but you'll probably have the convenience foods on hand to make the cake.

On Guest Day: Bake the cake. It's easier than its appearance and taste lead one to believe. If you don't have the sour cream called for in the main dish, this is one ingredient someone in the family may have to pick up. Start cooking the pork about 45 minutes before dinner; you add the cream just before serving. Cook potatoes and fix the salad. Last of all, make the coffee.

SERVING SUGGESTIONS

This is a sit-down country dinner composed of dishes your husband will be proud to pass. No garnishes other than parsley for the potatoes. If you have no parsley, sprinkle buttered potatoes with a little paprika.

PORK/SAUERKRAUT SKILLET

You can add a few caraway seeds if you like the flavor

2½ lbs. pork shoulder, cut in 1"
   cubes
2 tblsp. salad oil
2 c. chopped onion
2 (1 lb.) cans sauerkraut, drained
   and rinsed

2 tsp. paprika
1 tsp. salt
½ c. water
2 c. dairy sour cream

In a 10" skillet brown pork cubes in hot oil. Remove meat from skillet. Add onion to drippings in skillet and cook until tender, but do not brown. Stir frequently.

Return pork to skillet; add sauerkraut, paprika, salt and water. Cover and bring to a boil; reduce heat to low and simmer 35 to 40 minutes, until pork is tender. Remove from heat and stir in sour cream. Heat, but do not let boil. Makes 8 servings.

MIXED FRUIT SALAD

Add cut-up dates to Waldorf salad and you give it a new taste

1 orange
3 c. diced unpeeled red apples
   (about 3)
⅔ c. cut-up pitted dates
⅔ c. chopped celery

½ c. chopped walnuts (black
   walnuts can be used)
¼ c. salad dressing or mayonnaise
1 tblsp. sugar
¾ c. heavy cream, whipped
Lettuce

Peel orange and divide in sections over bowl to catch juices. Cut sections in halves and save juices.

In a medium bowl combine apples, dates, celery, walnuts and orange pieces.

Blend together salad dressing, sugar and reserved orange juice. Fold in whipped cream. Combine with fruit mixture. Serve in lettuce-lined bowl or on individual salad plates. Makes 8 servings.

PUMPKIN CAKE

Filled and frosted, this spice layer cake looks glamorous

1 pkg. spice cake mix (for 2-layer cake)
1 (1 lb.) can pumpkin
2 tsp. baking soda
2 eggs
⅓ c. water

1 (4½ to 5 oz.) pkg. vanilla pudding and pie filling
2½ c. milk
½ c. chopped pecans
2 envelopes dessert topping mix

In a large bowl combine cake mix, pumpkin, baking soda, eggs and water. Beat according to directions on cake mix package. Pour into two greased and lightly floured 9″ round cake pans. Bake in moderate oven (350°) 25 to 30 minutes. Cool 10 minutes; remove from pans. Cool completely on racks.

Meanwhile, prepare pudding as directed on package, but use only 2½ c. milk. Cool; stir in pecans.

Carefully split each cake layer in half crosswise to make four layers. Put layers together with pudding.

Whip dessert topping by package directions. Spread over top and sides of cake. Garnish with extra pecans, if you like. Makes 10 to 12 servings.

DISTINCTIVE HAM DINNER

Party Pork Rolls*
Oven-Creamed Potatoes*
Three-Row Garden Salad*
Orange Sherbet
Holiday Cranberry Cake*

Use this menu when you entertain a group of varying age levels . . . young and old alike enjoy these dishes.

The pork rolls feature two kinds of ham, fresh and smoked. You wrap the meat around an expertly seasoned stuffing. Then you add an orange-cherry glaze to step up flavors and glamorize the platter specialty.

With this typical country main dish, serve creamed potatoes; they bake in the oven with the pork. The gorgeous salad loaf contributes three vegetables to the dinner—cabbage, beets and carrots. The cake turns any meal into a special occasion. Escorted by orange sherbet, it's a dessert you'll want to serve again and again. Its reception always is that good.

TIMETABLE

Do-Ahead: Bake cake a day or several days ahead and freeze. Make the salad to chill overnight. Also fix salad dressing. Cook, cool and chill potatoes so they'll be ready to cream next day.

On Guest Day: About 1½ hours before dinnertime, prepare stuffing and meat rolls. Put in oven. Meanwhile, prepare potato casserole and bake it the last 30 minutes the meat rolls are in the oven. If cake is frozen, bring it from the freezer. Let it thaw in its wrap.

SERVING SUGGESTIONS

This is an excellent meal to serve buffet style. Slice meat and place on platter. You may want to double the recipe, depending on how many guests you are having. Place bubbling potato casserole beside platter.

The whole salad loaf is attractive, but slices on greens also are picture-pretty. You can arrange the individual servings in the kitchen and put them at place settings. For dessert, spoon the orange sherbet into stemmed dessert glasses and pass the cake.

PARTY PORK ROLLS

Doubly delicious with ham, fresh and smoked. See photo in this book

Ham Stuffing:

2 c. ground cooked smoked ham	1 tsp. poultry seasoning
⅛ tsp. pepper	¼ tsp. pepper
½ c. dry bread or cracker crumbs	1 c. dry bread crumbs
1 egg, slightly beaten	¼ c. hot water

Bread Stuffing:

	3 slices fresh ham steak, ½″ thick
¼ c. finely chopped onion	2 tblsp. butter
⅓ c. butter or regular margarine	½ c. orange marmalade
½ c. finely chopped celery	2 tsp. maraschino cherry juice
2 tsp. salt	

Mix together thoroughly all ingredients for ham stuffing.

To make bread stuffing, cook onion in butter until golden. Add remaining ingredients for bread stuffing and mix.

Bone steaks; pound to flatten. Brown lightly in 2 tblsp. butter.

Spread steaks with ham stuffing. Cover evenly with a layer of bread stuffing. Roll as for jelly roll and tie securely with string.

Bake in covered pan in moderate oven (350°) 30 minutes. Remove from oven.

Combine orange marmalade and cherry juice for glaze; spread over pork rolls. Bake, uncovered, 15 to 20 minutes longer. Remove strings; slice each roll into 2" slices. Makes 6 servings.

N O T E : You can double this recipe to make 12 servings.

OVEN-CREAMED POTATOES

The easiest way to cream potatoes—no pot watching or turning

2 c. chopped onions	2 tsp. salt
⅔ c. chopped green pepper	¼ tsp. pepper
½ c. chopped celery	6 c. cubed cooked potatoes (about
½ c. butter or regular margarine	6 medium)
6 tblsp. flour	1 c. shredded Cheddar cheese
4 c. milk	

Cook onions, green pepper and celery in butter until soft (do not brown). Stir in flour. Add milk and cook, stirring constantly, until mixture comes to a boil and is thickened. Stir in salt and pepper.

Place potatoes in a greased 3-qt. casserole. Pour sauce over. Top with cheese. Bake in moderate oven (350°) about 30 minutes, until hot and bubbly. Makes 10 to 12 servings.

THREE-ROW GARDEN SALAD

Color-bright, refreshing salad resembles striped ribbon when served

Orange Layer:
1 (3 oz.) pkg. orange flavor gelatin
1 c. boiling water
¾ c. pineapple juice
2 tblsp. lemon juice
1½ c. finely shredded carrots

Green Layer:
1 (3 oz.) pkg. lime flavor gelatin
1 c. boiling water
¾ c. pineapple juice
2 tblsp. lemon juice
1½ c. grated cabbage

Red Layer:
2 tsp. unflavored gelatin
½ c. cold water
1 (3 oz.) pkg. lemon flavor gelatin
½ tsp. salt
1 c. boiling water
2 tblsp. beet juice
2 tblsp. vinegar
1 c. finely diced cooked beets, well
   drained
1 tblsp. prepared horse-radish
Cheese/Horse-radish Dressing

Prepare layers separately, allowing about 15 minutes between each so that gelatins set at intervals.

To make orange layer, dissolve orange flavor gelatin in boiling water. Add pineapple and lemon juices; chill until syrupy. Fold in carrots.

To prepare green layer, dissolve lime flavor gelatin in boiling water. Add pineapple and lemon juices; chill until syrupy. Fold in cabbage.

To make red layer, soften unflavored gelatin in cold water. Dissolve lemon flavor gelatin and salt in boiling water; immediately stir in unflavored gelatin mixture. Add beet juice and vinegar; chill until syrupy. Fold in beets and horse-radish.

Layer gelatins—orange, green, then red—in 9×5×3" loaf pan. Allow each layer to set before adding second or third layer. Chill until firm.

To unmold set pan in warm (not hot) water about 5 seconds; loosen around beet layer and turn out on platter. Garnish with green fresh carrot tops, young beet leaves or lettuce. Slice, then serve each person individual salad. Pass Cheese/Horse-radish Dressing. Makes 10 servings.

Cheese/Horse-radish Dressing: Soften 1 (3 oz.) pkg. cream cheese; beat until creamy. Blend in ¼ c. mayonnaise, 2 tblsp. light cream or milk, ½ tsp. celery salt and 2 tsp. horse-radish. Fold in 2 tsp. chopped fresh or dried chives (optional). Makes ¾ cup.

HOLIDAY CRANBERRY CAKE

Serve cake the year around . . . too good to limit to holidays

1 pkg. lemon cake mix (for 2-layer cake)	1¼ c. ground cranberries
	½ c. ground walnuts
1 (3 oz.) pkg. cream cheese, softened	¼ c. sugar
	1 tsp. ground mace (optional)
¾ c. milk	Confectioners sugar (optional)
4 eggs	

Blend cake mix, cream cheese and milk; beat with mixer 2 minutes at medium speed. Add eggs; blend and beat 2 more minutes.

Thoroughly combine cranberries, walnuts, sugar and mace; fold into cake batter. Pour into well-greased and floured 10" tube or fluted tube pan. Bake in moderate oven (350°) 1 hour, or until done. Cool 5 minutes, then remove from pan. Complete cooling on rack. Dust with confectioners sugar, if you wish. Serves 10 to 12.

COUNTRY DINNER SPECIAL

Ham/Vegetable Scallop*	Buttered Broccoli
Tossed Green Bean Salad*	Hot Corn Sticks*
Apple/Peanut Sundae*	Molasses Cookies

Put ham and potatoes in a casserole, add onions, carrot slices, a bit of cheese and mushroom sauce. Bake slowly. You will come up with a homespun, farm-style dish that will win praise. It's a great choice when a family with children comes to dinner. Serve this meal on a day when you'll be at home with time to prepare it. There's little make-ahead food in the menu.

TIMETABLE

Do-Ahead: Put cans of green beans and applesauce in refrigerator a day ahead. If you wish to serve cookies, bake them a day ahead, or several days ahead and freeze. Molasses, raisin or oatmeal cookies are a fine selection.

On Guest Day: The main dish needs to bake at least 1½ hours and to stand 15 to 20 minutes after coming from oven before you serve it. It takes about ½ hour to prepare the ingredients for the casserole so they'll be ready to bake. So start getting dinner about 2¼ hours before you want to serve it. Crush the peanut brittle for the sundae at your convenience. During the last half hour before dinner, cook frozen broccoli by package directions and season with butter or margarine. Assemble salad in bowl ready to toss at the last minute. When you take the casserole from the oven turn heat up to 450°, stir up batter for corn sticks and bake. Pass the corn sticks after casserole, salad and broccoli are served. Fix dessert between courses.

SERVING SUGGESTIONS

Serve this dinner buffet style or as a sit-down meal.

HAM/VEGETABLE SCALLOP

New way to scallop ham and potatoes—a tasty company casserole

1½ lbs. center-cut fresh ham steak
1½ tblsp. flour
2 cans condensed cream of
   mushroom soup
2 c. milk
¾ c. shredded sharp process
   cheese

6 c. thinly sliced peeled potatoes
2 c. thinly sliced carrots
½ c. finely chopped onion
1½ tsp. salt
¼ tsp. pepper

Brown ham lightly on both sides in skillet. Remove and set aside.

Stir flour into drippings in skillet until smooth; add the soup. Slowly stir in milk, mixing well. Heat to a boil, stirring constantly. Remove from heat; add cheese and stir until it is melted.

Cut ham in serving-size pieces. Arrange alternate layers of ham, potatoes, carrots and onion in greased 4-qt. carrerole (or two 2-qt. casseroles). Sprinkle vegetable layers lightly with salt and pepper. Cover with hot soup mixture.

Bake, covered, in slow oven (325°) 1 hour; uncover and bake 30 minutes more, or until potatoes and carrots are tender. Let stand 15 to 20 minutes before serving. Makes 8 servings.

TOSSED GREEN BEAN SALAD

All salad ingredients except greens come from the cupboard shelf

1 qt. bite-size pieces salad greens
1 (1 lb.) can cut green beans,
   chilled
6 tblsp. salad oil
2 tblsp. tarragon vinegar

1 tblsp. cider vinegar
Salt
Pepper
Pimiento

Place lettuce or other salad greens in bowl. Top with drained beans (French-cut beans are a good choice). Sprinkle on oil and toss. Sprinkle on vinegars and toss again. Check for salt and pepper. Serve garnished with strips of pimiento or sliced pimiento-stuffed olives. Makes 6 servings.

N O T E : For serving more than 6, double the recipe.

HOT CORN STICKS

Easy to make—rush them hot from the oven to table or buffet

1½ c. cornmeal	½ tsp. baking soda
⅓ c. flour	¼ c. shortening
3 tsp. baking powder	1½ c. buttermilk
2 tsp. sugar	1 egg
1 tsp. salt	

Preheat oven to very hot (450°). Grease corn stick pans and place in oven to heat.

Meanwhile, stir all ingredients in a bowl and beat just to mix, about 30 seconds. Fill warm corn stick pans two thirds full. Bake about 12 to 15 minutes, until golden brown. Makes 17 or 18 corn sticks.

APPLE/PEANUT SUNDAE

This is a tasty way to add glamor with homemade applesauce

3 pts. vanilla ice cream	¼ lb. peanut brittle, crushed
2 c. chilled, sweetened applesauce	

Scoop ice cream into chilled serving dishes. Spoon applesauce on top; sprinkle with peanut brittle. Makes about 9 servings.

PIG ROAST FOR A CROWD

Whole Pit-Roasted Pig*
Sweet Corn   Roasted Apples
Buttered Buns
Barbecue Sauce
Frozen Pineapple Torte*

Visitors to that paradise of the Pacific, Hawaii, return home wearing leis and treasuring fond memories of the pig roast or luau they enjoyed. And as they give a similar party for the members of their couples club, or any group of friends, they often provide as background music the lilting songs of the islands, recorded.

Farm families have—or can get—what it takes to give a mainland version of a luau—a moonlight summer night, plenty of space in the yard, corn on the cob, corn leaves, rocks from a stream and, some farms can provide the pig.

You don't have to fly across the Pacific Ocean to Hawaii and back to learn how to put on a luau. Our tested directions came from two Illinois farmers and their wives who gave successfully such a party for 80 guests. One of our food editors was present for that pig roast and she learned all the secrets.

We add a few foods to the menu that you do not meet in Hawaiian pig roasts. The buns, for instance, and the barbecue sauce, both gestures to sandwich fans. And we add the delectable frozen pineapple dessert, appropriate for a Hawaiian party.

TIMETABLE

Do-Ahead: Dig the pit of the right size and line with rocks. Measurements depend on the size of the pig. Allow 1 lb. dressed meat per person. Make torte for dessert a day or several days ahead.

On Guest Day: Build fire. When stones are hot, place pig in pit. The time for cooking depends on the size of the pig, but it varies from 2 to 4 hours. (See directions that follow.) About an hour before the pig is done, open the pit, add apples and corn on the cob wrapped in heavy-duty foil, cover and continue cooking until pork is tender.

SERVING SUGGESTIONS

Serve picnic style. Provide barbecue sauce and buns for the sandwich makers. Have pitchers of iced tea and a pot of hot coffee available. You may wish to wait until late in the evening to serve the lovely torte and coffee.

WHOLE PIT-ROASTED PIG

You will need:

Whole young pig, dressed and shaved

Rock-lined pit dug ahead of time

Several rounded rocks from a stream, in 1 to 4 lb. weights (Sun dry them for a week)

3 bushels or more of dry hard wood

Green corn stalks and leaves

Big tongs for handling hot rocks

Chicken wire or fencing—enough to encircle pig

2 baling hooks to carry roasted pig

12 clean burlap sacks

Canvas large enough to cover pit

Dig hole about 2½′ deep at center, with diameter of 5½ to 8′ depending on size of pig. Line with rocks.

Stack wood on rocks, Indian-tepee style. Light fire. Place round rocks in fire where they will get most heat.

While fire burns down, wet the burlap, and prepare pig. Rub inside of pig with salt and pepper, and garlic if desired. Place pig on chicken wire. Under legs, make slits big enough to insert round rocks. When fire has burned down and rocks are very hot, use tongs to fill abdominal cavity and slits in legs with hot rocks. Tie front legs together, then back legs. Wrap pig in wire, fastening well (so it can be lifted).

Completely cover ashes and rocks with corn stalks and leaves. Lower pig right onto leaves. Cover it generously on top and sides with more leaves.

Place wet burlap over leaves (this will hold heat and steam).

Cover with large canvas; shovel gravel over canvas to keep steam in.

Cooking time starts now. For 25 lb. pig, allow about 2 hours; for 50 lb. pig, 2½ hours; anything heavier, figure on at least 4 hours. If in doubt about doneness, leave pig in longer (because of steam, it won't burn).

To uncover, remove gravel, canvas, burlap and covering leaves. Lift and carry wire-wrapped pig with hooks. Remove wire to serve.

In Hawaii, the servers dip their hands frequently in cold water as they pull pork apart for individual servings.

What to Cook with the Pig:

About 1 hour before the pig is cooked, partly uncover pit and add apples, wrapped in foil, and corn on the cob. Either wrap corn ears individually in foil or peel back husks, remove silks, replace husks and soak in cold water about 15 minutes before adding to pit. (In Hawaii, whole sweet potatoes are roasted with the pig.) Cover the pit at once after adding apples and corn.

FROZEN PINEAPPLE TORTE

Refreshing light dessert to make the day before you entertain

3 egg yolks	3 egg whites
⅛ tsp. salt	2 tblsp. sugar
½ c. sugar	1 tsp. grated lemon peel
1 (8½ oz.) can crushed pineapple (save juice)	1 c. heavy cream, whipped
2 tblsp. lemon juice	1 c. vanilla wafer crumbs

Beat egg yolks slightly; add salt and ½ c. sugar and beat a little more. Add pineapple juice (drained from crushed pineapple) and lemon juice. Cook over hot, not boiling, water until custard coats a spoon; stir constantly while cooking. Add pineapple and cool.

Make a meringue with egg whites and 2 tblsp. sugar. Fold in pineapple custard, lemon peel and whipped cream.

Coat sides of a greased 13×9×2″ baking pan with ½ c. vanilla wafer crumbs. Pour custard into pan; sprinkle remaining crumbs over the top. Cover and freeze.

Place dessert in refrigerator about 30 minutes before serving. It then will cut easily. Makes 8 to 10 servings.

FARMHOUSE DINNER

Tomato Juice   Corn Chips
Meat-and-Potato Balls*
Missouri Green Beans
Fresh Cucumber/Onion Relish*
Cloud Biscuits*
Orange Meringue Pie*

The motto of many busy women is: Give your guests the feeling that you just put extra plates on the dinner table for them. These hostesses hold that people like to sense they are welcome and that they made little extra work. As a result of this philosophy, the meal often represents country cooking at its best. The food, although it's free of fancy frills, tastes wonderfully good, there's plenty of it and usually one or two "from scratch" baked foods come to the table. Cloud Biscuits and Orange Meringue Pie, for instance.

Who could miss on Meat-and-Potato Balls made by a recipe from an Iowa farm woman? They really are beef, pork, potatoes and rich gravy combined into one platter specialty. The tomato juice appetizer is optional, but it's refreshing and gives the host and guests something to sip in the living room while the hostess in the kitchen rounds up the remainder of the dinner. Season the juice with a little lemon juice, salt and Worcestershire sauce and serve it hot or cold, depending on the weather.

If you are one of the thousands of farm women who believe frozen green beans lack desirable texture, try them cooked by package directions, drained if necessary and seasoned with cream cheese and celery seeds. Toss the hot beans to melt the cheese so it coats them. You will have performed a cooking miracle. The cucumbers are a cross between the fresh vegetable and pickles. If you serve this dinner when cucumber vines are not bearing, you can substitute dill pickles for them.

TIMETABLE

Do-Ahead: You can shape and brown the Meat-and-Potato Balls a day ahead; cool, place in casserole, cover and refrigerate. And if you like, bake the pie shell.

On Guest Day: When convenient, make pie filling, turn it into the pie shell, top with meringue and brown lightly. You can make, roll and cut biscuits, place them on a baking sheet 1 or 2 hours before time to bake them. Keep them in the refrigerator. Make the Cucumber Relish, cool and chill. Put Meat-and-Potato Balls in the oven 1¼ hours before dinnertime. Meanwhile, fix the green beans.

When you take the Meat-and-Potato Balls from the oven, increase the temperature to 450°. Bake biscuits 10 to 14 minutes. Meanwhile, add sour cream to Meat-and-Potato Balls and carry food to table, the biscuits on the final trip before sitting down to eat.

SERVING SUGGESTIONS

Serve Meat-and-Potato Balls on a warm platter and garnish with finely snipped parsley. Pass one serving of biscuits in a napkin-lined basket or roll warmer. Keep the remainder warm in oven with door open and heat turned off. Assign getting the second serving of biscuits to one of the older children. If you want to add a true country note to the pie, sprinkle the meringue with a little flaked coconut just before putting it in the oven to brown.

MEAT-AND-POTATO BALLS

Mild seasonings and sour cream convert this into a platter treat

2 large potatoes, cooked	2 tsp. salt
1 c. milk	2 eggs, slightly beaten
½ lb. ground beef	½ c. flour
1½ lbs. ground lean pork	3 tblsp. shortening
1 medium onion, finely chopped	½ c. hot water
(about ⅓ c.)	1 c. dairy sour cream

Mash potatoes, adding ¼ c. milk.

Combine beef, pork and onion with potatoes. Mix in salt, eggs and remaining ¾ c. milk. Shape in 2″ balls. Roll in flour.

Brown balls in shortening, half of them at a time. Brown on all sides. Arrange in greased 3-qt. casserole; add hot water. Bake uncovered in moderate oven (350°) about 1 hour. Remove from oven. Let stand a few minutes. Just before serving gently spread sour cream over top with a spoon. Makes about 21 balls.

FRESH CUCUMBER/ONION RELISH

A cross between fresh sliced cucumbers and cucumber pickle slices

2 medium cucumbers	½ c. sugar
3 medium onions	1 tsp. salt
½ c. vinegar	

If cucumbers are homegrown, wash, but do not peel. (They will not have a wax coating.) Score them lengthwise with a fork to make green and white stripes. Cut in medium slices. Peel onions and separate into rings. Add to cucumbers in bowl.

Combine vinegar, sugar and salt and stir over low heat until sugar dissolves. Bring to a boil and pour over cucumbers and onions. Cool, cover and refrigerate. Makes 8 to 10 servings.

CLOUD BISCUITS

They are light as clouds and have golden brown tops—truly delicious. To drop dough instead of rolling, increase milk to ¾ cup

2 c. sifted flour
1 tblsp. sugar
4 tsp. baking powder
½ tsp. salt

½ c. shortening
1 egg, beaten
⅔ c. milk

Sift together dry ingredients. Cut in shortening until mixture forms coarse crumbs. Combine egg and milk and add to flour mixture; stir until dough follows fork around bowl. Turn onto lightly floured board and knead lightly about 20 times.

Roll dough ¾" thick, cut with lightly floured 2" cutter, cutting straight down through the dough. Place on ungreased baking sheet.

Bake in very hot oven (450°) 10 to 14 minutes, or until biscuits are golden brown. Makes 2 dozen.

ORANGE MERINGUE PIE

Add 1 tblsp. grated orange peel to filling for stronger orange flavor

Baked 9" pie shell
3 tblsp. cornstarch
1 c. sugar
⅛ tsp. salt
3 egg yolks, slightly beaten
1 c. orange juice
½ c. water
1 tblsp. lemon juice

3 tblsp. butter
1 tblsp. grated orange peel
(optional)
3 egg whites
¼ tsp. cream of tartar
6 tblsp. sugar
¼ tsp. vanilla

Combine cornstarch, 1 c. sugar and salt in medium saucepan. Gradually blend in egg yolks, orange juice and water. Cook over medium heat, stirring constantly, until mixture thickens and boils. Stir and boil 1 minute. Remove from heat.

Stir in lemon juice and butter (orange peel, too, if you add it). Turn at once into pie shell.

Beat egg whites with cream of tartar until foamy. Beat in 6 tblsp. sugar, 1 tablespoon at a time; continue to beat until stiff and glossy. Beat in vanilla. Heap on hot pie filling and spread over it, carefully sealing meringue to edge of crust.

Bake in moderate oven (350°) 12 to 15 minutes, or until meringue peaks are golden brown. Cool away from drafts.

INDIAN SUMMER DINNER

Cider/Pineapple Special*　　　Crackers　　　Cheese
Baked Ham Slice with Cherry Sauce*
Kentucky Potatoes*　　　Green Beans with Almonds*
Lettuce Wedges with Creamy French Dressing*
Parkerhouse Rolls　　　Pumpkin/Ginger Squares*

Golden Indian summer days promote a social state of mind. This time between autumn and winter comes two to three weeks before Thanksgiving celebrations demand attention. A haze spreads over the hills, a relaxing lull permeates country homes after the hectic rush of the harvest season is over. Friends are ready for an exchange of news and ideas—for visiting. So kick off your fall social season with this sit-down dinner for 8.

This meal features foods at their seasonal best. The cider comes from presses and the dessert features pumpkins, many of which still decorate the front door. This dinner tastes and looks wonderful and it's easy to prepare—the ham and potatoes bake leisurely and require almost no attention.

TIMETABLE

Do-Ahead: Make the dessert and salad dressing a day ahead; refrigerate.

On Guest Day: Get the potatoes in the oven 3 hours before you want to serve them. After they've baked 1½ hours, put the ham slice in the oven. Cut bite-size cubes of sharp Cheddar and Swiss cheese, insert picks in them and refrigerate. Heat the Cider/Pineapple Special shortly before you want to serve it. Put the green beans on to cook about 15 minutes before dinnertime. While they cook, fix the salad.

SERVING SUGGESTIONS

Take the hot cider/pineapple drink and serving glasses or mugs, cheese and crackers to the living room soon after the guests arrive.

(You can serve this fruit drink from a punch bowl or pitcher.) Arrange the cheese cubes on a tray surrounding a small bowl of chili sauce. The sauce adds a spot of color and some guests will enjoy dunking cheese in it. Let your husband assume responsibility for this course, for you will need to return to the kitchen to make last-minute preparations. Cut the dessert just before you serve it.

CIDER/PINEAPPLE SPECIAL

Crackers, cheese and this hot drink make good beginnings for meals

1 qt. sweet apple cider	½ c. crushed mint leaves
2 c. unsweetened pineapple juice	1 qt. ginger ale, unchilled

Pour fruit juices into a 2-qt. saucepan. Add mint and bring to a boil. Strain. Bring to a boil again. Add ginger ale and serve at once. Makes 8 to 10 servings.

NOTE: You may omit the mint. If you do, heat juices only once. The mint does add an interesting flavor note.

BAKED HAM SLICE WITH CHERRY SAUCE

Expertly seasoned and slowly baked, the meat captures the fine flavor associated with old-time farm-cured ham. Cherries add color

1 center slice ham, cut 2½" thick (3 lbs.)	2 tblsp. flour
	¼ tsp. dry mustard
1 (1 lb.) can tart cherries	½ tsp. grated lemon peel
½ c. sugar	2 drops red food color
⅛ tsp. salt	

Score edges of ham. Place in baking pan and bake uncovered in slow oven (300°) long enough to heat, or about 1 hour.

Meanwhile, drain cherries. You should have ¾ c. juice. Heat it in a small saucepan. Mix together sugar, salt, flour and dry mustard; add to cherry juice. Cook and stir over medium heat until thick. Add lemon peel, food color and cherries.

Remove ham from oven and pour on the hot cherry sauce. Bake 30 minutes longer. Serve ham, cut in serving portions, on platter and pour over the cherry sauce from baking pan. Or, if you prefer, pass the cherry sauce. Makes 8 servings.

NOTE: To flame the ham, heat ¼ c. brandy in a little pan, but do not let it come to a boil. Pour over the hot ham as soon as it is baked and while still in the pan. Ignite immediately, spooning brandy up into flame. This adds a fruity flavor; the alcohol burns and disappears. Cut and serve.

KENTUCKY POTATOES

Shredding and slowly cooking spuds in sauce develops fine flavor

¼ c. butter or regular margarine	Pepper to taste (about ¼ tsp.)
¼ c. flour	6 c. shredded potatoes (about 7
4 c. milk	large)
2 tsp. salt	¼ c. finely chopped onion

Melt butter in a large saucepan over low heat; remove from heat and blend in flour. Add a little milk slowly, blending until smooth; then add rest of milk and boil 1 minute, stirring constantly. Add salt, pepper, shredded potatoes and onion.

Pour into greased 15½ × 10½ × 1″ jelly roll pan, or shallow casserole (jelly roll pan fits neatly on oven shelf below ham). Bake in slow oven (300°) about 3 hours. Makes 10 servings.

GREEN BEANS WITH ALMONDS

Ideal vegetable dish with ham—the nuts add crunchy texture

3 (10 oz.) pkgs. quick-frozen	¾ c. sliced almonds
French-style green beans	6 tblsp. butter
3 tblsp. butter	

Cook beans in boiling salted water by package directions. Add 3 tblsp. butter and toss to mix.

Sauté almonds in 6 tblsp. butter until light brown. Toss into beans. Makes 8 servings.

LETTUCE WEDGES WITH CREAMY FRENCH DRESSING

A change of pace in French dressings; try it on other greens

1 tsp. sugar	⅓ c. wine vinegar
1 tblsp. paprika	1 egg, beaten
1 tsp. salt	1 c. salad oil
Dash of ground red pepper	Lettuce

Combine sugar, paprika, salt and red pepper.
Add vinegar to egg and beat well. Beat in ¼ c. salad oil, 1 tsp.

at a time. Gradually add remaining ¾ c. salad oil, beating well after each addition. Add combined dry ingredients. Chill.

Cut heads of iceberg lettuce into as many wedges as needed and of the size desired. With a knife, slash each wedge crosswise in several places, but not completely through. Shake dressing; spoon on lettuce. Dressing makes about 1⅔ cups.

PUMPKIN/GINGER SQUARES

You can use 1 tsp. each of ground cinnamon and ginger and ½ tsp. nutmeg if you do not have pumpkin pie spice. The ice milk, although solid like ice cream, contains less fat, more protein

1 c. sugar	2 c. cooked or canned pumpkin
1 tsp. salt	½ gal. vanilla ice milk, slightly
2½ tsp. pumpkin pie spice	softened
1 c. chopped walnuts	Gingersnaps (about 36)

Mix sugar, salt, spice and walnuts with pumpkin. Mix in the ice milk, using a beater.

Line bottom of 13×9×2″ pan with gingersnaps. Pour on half the pumpkin mixture. Cover with another layer of gingersnaps. Pour on remaining pumpkin mixture. Freeze.

To serve, cut in squares or rectangles, and if you and your guests are not counting calories too seriously, garnish with walnut halves and little puffs of whipped cream. Makes 8 to 10 servings.

AUTUMN OVEN DINNER

Cranberry/Apricot Cooler*
Miniature Ham Loaves*
Butternut Squash and Apples*
Celery
Overnight Sourdough Bread*
Cherry/Cheese Salad*

Autumn's cool evenings encourage home entertaining—visiting leisurely indoors with friends, exchanging vacation and other news. This color-bright, one-course, oven dinner matches Nature's brilliant glow on nearby hills. Cranberry juice, yellow winter squash with rosy apple rings and individual ham loaves provide good eating. The crusty loaves of sourdough bread, speckled with browned cornmeal, suggest that autumn is time for home baking sprees. Country meals, like country people, keep in tune with the seasons.

TIMETABLE

Do-Ahead: Bake the bread several days ahead. (The starter needs to ferment about 16 hours.) Cool, slice, reassemble loaves, wrap in heavy-duty foil and freeze. Make the salad a day ahead.

On Guest Day: Put the ham loaves and squash side by side in the oven to bake about 1 hour. Mix the appetizer juices in a pitcher any time during the day and chill. Heat the foil-wrapped bread in the oven alongside the ham and squash until hot, or about 25 minutes if frozen.

SERVING SUGGESTIONS

Float thin lemon or orange slices in the glasses of the Cranberry/ Apricot Cooler. Serve the dinner plates in the kitchen if you wish. Handle the sliced bread like hot rolls; it should be hot enough to melt butter spread on it. Either pass bread in a napkin-lined basket or a roll warmer. Serve the salad-dessert with the remainder of the meal, but when you pour the last cups of coffee, pass a plate of colorful candy mints.

CRANBERRY/APRICOT COOLER

Pour this appetite sharpener from pitcher in small glasses over ice

2 c. cranberry juice cocktail, chilled

1 c. apricot nectar, chilled

3 tblsp. lemon juice

Blend all ingredients and chill. Makes about 9 servings.

MINIATURE HAM LOAVES

These little loaves seem to say to guests: "made especially for you"

1 lb. ground lean ham
½ lb. ground lean pork
½ c. milk
1 egg, beaten
1 c. bread crumbs

¼ c. vinegar
¼ c. water
¼ c. brown sugar, firmly pack
1 tsp. dry mustard

Combine ham, pork, milk, egg and bread crumbs. Shape into 8 loaves of equal size. Place in a 10×6×1½" baking dish.

Combine vinegar with water, brown sugar and mustard, and heat. Pour over the ham. Bake in moderate oven (350°) 1 hour. Makes 8 loaves.

BUTTERNUT SQUASH AND APPLES

You can use buttercup squash—when available—for the butternut

3 lbs. butternut squash	⅔ c. brown sugar, firmly packed
3 baking apples	1½ tblsp. flour
6 tblsp. butter or regular margarine	1¼ tsp. salt

Cut squash in halves, remove seeds and fiber; peel and cut in slices ½ to ¾" thick. Arrange in 13×9×2" baking pan.

Core apples, but do not peel. Cut in ½ to ¾" slices and lay on top of squash.

Mix butter, brown sugar, flour and salt; sprinkle over top of apples and squash. Cover pan tightly with aluminum foil. Bake in moderate oven (350°) about 1 hour, until squash is tender. Makes about 9 servings.

OVERNIGHT SOURDOUGH BREAD

You use all the starter in one baking. Bread tastes like that our grandmothers made by overnight sponge method, but with cornmeal flavor. It tastes best when warm and is heavenly when toasted

1 pkg. active dry yeast	2 tblsp. salad oil
¼ c. warm water (110 to 115°)	½ c. cornmeal
¾ c. milk	4 to 4½ c. flour
2 tblsp. sugar	1 c. lukewarm water
1½ tsp. salt	Melted butter

Dissolve yeast in ¼ c. water.

Scald milk and pour over sugar, salt and oil in big bowl. Cool until lukewarm. Add cornmeal, 1 c. flour and yeast to lukewarm mixture. Cover and put in a warm place to ferment about 16 hours. This is the starter.

After starter has fermented, stir in 1 c. flour and 1 c. lukewarm water. Cover and let stand in warm place 2 hours.

Add enough remaining flour to make a soft dough that you barely can handle. Knead, adding a little flour as necessary, until smooth and elastic, about 10 minutes.

Divide dough in 6 equal parts; shape each to make a little loaf and place on greased baking sheet about 1" apart. Let rise until almost doubled, about 1 hour.

Bake in moderate oven (375°) 30 to 40 minutes, or until golden. Brush with melted butter and cool on racks. Makes 6 loaves.

CHERRY/CHEESE SALAD

The distinctive feature of this luscious fruit salad is the use of canned cherry pie filling. Topping substitutes for salad dressing. When entertaining women for lunch, serve this salad with hot muffins

1 (3 oz.) pkg. raspberry flavor gelatin	1 (3 oz.) pkg. cream cheese
2 c. boiling water	⅓ c. salad dressing or mayonnaise
1 (1 lb. 5 oz.) can cherry pie filling	1 (8 oz.) can crushed pineapple
	½ c. heavy cream, whipped
1 (3 oz.) pkg. lemon flavor gelatin	1 c. miniature marshmallows
	3 tblsp. chopped pecans

Dissolve raspberry gelatin in 1 c. boiling water; stir in cherry pie filling. Pour into a 9" square pan and chill until partially set.

Dissolve lemon gelatin in 1 c. boiling water.

Beat together cream cheese and salad dressing. Gradually add lemon gelatin. Stir in undrained pineapple. Fold in whipped cream, then marshmallows. Spread evenly over cherry layer; sprinkle top with pecans. Chill. Makes 9 servings.

SUMMER FISH DINNER

Oven-Fried Fish*
New Potatoes with Lemon Butter*
Green Beans with Bacon
Tomato/Cucumber Salad
Farm-Style Peach Ice Cream*
Coconut Cookies

When the family fisherman delivers his catch, dressed and cut in filets, to the kitchen, he sets the stage for a company dinner soon to follow. Suggestions for friends with whom he'd like to share his bounty come easy.

In this menu the fish monopolizes the oven. As with chicken, many farm women prefer to fry fish in the oven instead of in a skillet. This method eliminates turning and careful watching. Smooth, round, new little potatoes are a natural accompaniment. The choice of the second vegetable depends on what the garden offers. Are there tender peas to cook and butter or succulent green beans to toss with butter or bacon drippings and crisp bacon pieces?

With thick slices of juicy, ripe tomatoes and crisp cucumbers available, you can decide on a salad in a few seconds. Serve the vegetable team on lettuce, add a few sliced green onions if you like and use your favorite salad dressing.

Among the worthy dessert candidates for ending this meal are fresh peach ice cream, pie or cobbler, or sugared sliced peaches with a pitcher of light cream. You won't go wrong if you choose coconut cookies to serve with the ice cream or sliced fruit.

TIMETABLE

Do-Ahead: It's to be hoped you have coconut cookies in the freezer. Or you can buy them.

On Guest Day: Using fish the same day it leaves the lake, stream or pond is a farm tradition heeded whenever possible. If home-made ice cream wins the dessert position, freeze it first and let it ripen. About an hour before dinner, get the green beans and potatoes ready to cook and the salad vegetables ready to combine. Start cooking vegetables about a half hour before dinner. At the same time, start heating the oven. Allow the fish 12 to 15 minutes in the very hot oven.

SERVING SUGGESTIONS

Hold the garnishes to the minimum and let the appeal of the top-notch foods tempt appetites. Concentrate on the best temperatures for serving the food—the fish, potatoes and beans piping hot, the salad and dessert frosty cold. Lemon wedges on the fish platter and extra snipped chives on the potatoes are optional, but do let the bacon show in the beans.

OVEN-FRIED FISH

For top results use fresh fish, a very hot oven and avoid overcooking

1½ tblsp. salt	1½ c. dry bread crumbs
¾ c. milk	6 tblsp. melted butter or regular
3 lbs. fish filets	margarine

Add salt to milk and stir to mix. Dip filets, cut in serving-size pieces, into milk and roll in crumbs to coat. Place in well-greased shallow pan or pans. It is important to use enough pan space to spread the fish in a single layer. Pour butter over fish.

Place in an extremely hot oven (500°) on rack slightly above center of oven. Bake, uncovered, until fish flakes easily with fork, 12 to 15 minutes. Serve on hot platter. Makes about 9 servings.

N O T E : If your fisherman has not fileted fish, here's the way to do it. Cut down back from head to tail close to backbone. Cut flesh free from rib bones. Skin fish if you like, starting at the tail end. If the fish has scales, remove them before fileting.

NEW POTATOES WITH LEMON BUTTER

Peel potatoes if you like, cook and pour on melted butter but red skins with white bands are pretty and lemon points up flavors

3 lbs. new potatoes (20 to 24 small)	2 tblsp. lemon juice
	2 tblsp. chopped fresh chives
¼ c. melted butter or regular margarine	1 tsp. salt
	Dash of pepper
½ tsp. grated lemon peel	

Scrub potatoes and leave whole, but peel a narrow strip around center. Place in saucepan containing 1″ salted water (1 tsp. salt to 1 c. water), cover and cook until tender, 20 to 25 minutes. Drain.

Meanwhile, heat remaining ingredients in saucepan to boiling. Turn potatoes into serving dish. Stir hot lemon mixture to mix and pour over potatoes; serve at once. Makes 8 servings.

FARM-STYLE PEACH ICE CREAM

This is a cooked custard ice cream with ripe fresh peaches added

1 c. sugar	4 c. heavy cream, chilled
¼ tsp. salt	⅔ c. sugar
2 c. milk	4 c. mashed fresh peaches (8 to
6 egg yolks, beaten	10)
1½ tblsp. vanilla	

Mix 1 c. sugar, salt, milk and egg yolks in a saucepan. Cook and stir over medium heat to scald, or until bubbles appear around the edges of saucepan. Remove from heat and cool to room temperature. Stir in vanilla and heavy cream.

Mix ⅔ c. sugar with peaches and stir into the cream mixture. Pour into freezer can; fill about three fourths full. Add dasher and cover. Adjust crank in proper position. Pack freezer tub one third full of crushed ice; then add alternate layers of ice and rock salt to cover can, using 6 parts ice to 1 part salt. Turn crank until it turns very hard, drain off water.

Remove ice until level is below lid of can. Take off lid and remove dasher. Pack ice cream down with spoon. Plug hole in lid and cover can with several thicknesses of waxed paper or foil. Pack again with ice and salt using 4 parts ice to 1 part salt. Cover with a blanket, canvas or other heavy cloth and let ice cream ripen several hours. Makes ½ gallon.

WINTER FISH DINNER

Sole/Shrimp Roll-Ups*

Baked Potato Sticks*   Buttered Asparagus

Cherry Tomato Salad*

Open-Face Cranberry Pie*

If you and your husband want to invite another couple to a fish dinner in winter, try this menu. It has three merits that make it acceptable and praiseworthy even to meat-and-potato men. The main dish contains the highly favored shellfish, shrimp. While each serving includes only 5 small or 1 large shrimp, it's enough to boost the appeal. Cheese adds to the seasoning. And the potato sticks will please your male meat-and-potato fans.

While country fish dinners are likely summer specials that feature the family fisherman's catch, cold weather fish dinners are increasingly popular. Today's hostesses are using more imagination in preparing the fish available in their markets.

Cherry tomatoes, available the year around, brighten this dinner and accent flavors. A fruit compote would make a splendid dessert, but the one-crust pie is pretty, delicious and unusual. Or you can end the dinner with chilled grapefruit halves.

TIMETABLE

Do-Ahead: Bake, cool and chill crumb crust a day ahead. Make pie filling and turn into crust. Chill overnight.

On Guest Day: Add tomatoes to dressing and chill 3 hours or longer. Get the potatoes in the oven 45 minutes before dinnertime. Prepare roll-ups and place them in the oven after potatoes have baked 20 minutes. They require the same oven temperature. Remove potatoes from oven just before you place fish under broiler to brown lightly. Spoon the topping on the pie just before you serve it.

SERVING SUGGESTIONS

Serve the tomatoes on crisp lettuce or other greens. You can garnish the fish platter with lemon wedges or slices. Serve the silvery package of potatoes in a basket if you have one. Sprinkle potato tops with chopped parsley.

SOLE/SHRIMP ROLL-UPS

If you use frozen fish filets thaw them enough that they'll roll

20 small or 4 large cooked shrimp	1 c. milk
4 wide filets of sole, lightly salted on both sides	½ c. dry white wine
	½ c. light cream
2 tblsp. chopped onion	½ c. grated Parmesan cheese
3 tblsp. butter or regular margarine	1 tsp. lemon juice
	1 tsp. salt
3 tblsp. flour	Pepper

Roll 5 small or 1 large shrimp in each filet. Fasten with two tooth-picks. Lay in shallow greased baking pan.

Cook onion in butter until golden. Blend in flour, milk and wine. Cook and stir until sauce boils and thickens. Blend in cream and cheese; stir in lemon juice, salt and pepper to taste. Pour over fish roll-ups. Sprinkle lightly with a little additional Parmesan cheese.

Bake in hot oven (425°) about 25 minutes. Place under broiler to brown lightly. Makes 4 servings.

BAKED POTATO STICKS

Potatoes cook to perfection with no attention except turning once

4 medium baking potatoes	½ c. shredded process American
¼ tsp. salt	cheese
1 tblsp. finely chopped parsley	½ c. light cream
3 tblsp. butter or regular margarine	

Peel potatoes and cut in lengthwise strips as for French fries. Place on the center of large sheet of heavy-duty aluminum foil. (Use double thickness of foil if you do not have the heavier kind.) Form foil around potatoes to the shape of a baking dish.

Add salt and parsley to potatoes; dot with butter. Sprinkle with shredded cheese. Pour on cream. Bring foil up over potatoes and seal edges to form a tightly closed package. Do not press package. Carefully lift package to a shallow pan.

Bake in hot oven (425°) 45 minutes, turning once (when you put the Sole/Shrimp Roll-ups in oven). To serve, place foil package in a basket or casserole, or on a platter; fold back foil edges. Makes 4 servings.

CHERRY TOMATO SALAD

The trick is chilling tomatoes in the special salad dressing

¼ c. minced parsley	½ tsp. salt
¼ c. salad oil	Pepper (optional)
3 tblsp. wine vinegar	1 tsp. sugar
½ tsp. basil leaves	1 pt. cherry tomatoes
½ tsp. orégano leaves	Lettuce

To make the dressing, combine all ingredients, except tomatoes and lettuce, in a bowl; mix well.

Wash and remove stems from cherry tomatoes; cut them in halves and add to the dressing in bowl. Cover and chill at least 3 hours, stirring gently a few times.

When ready to serve, lift tomatoes with a slotted spoon onto crisp lettuce liners on individual salad plates. Save leftover dressing for tomorrow's salad. Makes 4 servings.

OPEN-FACE CRANBERRY PIE

Tangy sour cream and cranberry sauce blend deliciously in this pie

Baked 9″ Graham Cracker Crumb Crust
¾ c. sugar
1 envelope unflavored gelatin
½ tsp. salt
1 c. cranberry juice cocktail
1 (1 lb.) can whole cranberry sauce
1 c. dairy sour cream
2 tblsp. confectioners sugar

Blend sugar, gelatin and salt in saucepan. Stir in cranberry juice cocktail and cranberry sauce; cook and stir over medium heat until mixture boils. Remove from heat.

Cool and chill until mixture mounds slightly when you drop a small amount from a spoon. Fold in ½ c. sour cream. Pour into chilled Graham Cracker Crumb Crust and refrigerate overnight.

At serving time, sift confectioners sugar over remaining ½ c. sour cream and fold in; spoon over top of pie. Makes 6 to 8 servings.

Graham Cracker Crumb Crust: Mix together 1¼ c. fine graham cracker crumbs, ¼ c. sugar and 6 tblsp. butter until crumbly. Press firmly into a 9″ pie pan. Bake in moderate oven (375°) 6 to 8 minutes, until edges brown. Cool and chill before adding pie filling.

CHAPTER 5

Afternoon and Evening Refreshments

DESSERT PARTIES . . .
SNACKS . . . OPEN HOUSES

Any time of day is a good time to serve the refreshments in this chapter. The Golden Wedding Reception menu is equally correct for afternoon or evening. The homemade, pretty Flower Wedding Cake and Golden Punch will taste delicious either time. After-skating-party refreshments may be for day or evening. The plump Glazed Potato Doughnuts, Popcorn/Peanut Clusters and Tri-Fruit Cooler *always* taste good. The White Cap Punch is an open-house refresher day or evening, and guests enjoy picking "dippers" from the snack tree at any open house during the holidays. (Just give them the chance!)

Even the Moonlight Hayride Supper menu can be adjusted to other events and times, as can the Men's Winter Evening Sandwich Lunch or the Simple Afternoon Tea. The menus that feature coffee or tea and an accompaniment make delightful refreshments for a women's afternoon club meeting, but are just as appropriate for couples to enjoy during a social evening.

This chapter is a treasury of foods that refresh when friends get together. Late Evening Snacks perk up spirits and promote friendly talk and laughter. Strawberry Pink delights women at afternoon bridge parties, but their husbands will welcome the same dessert tastes after evening couples' bridge. Frozen Buttermint Squares, luscious Black Bottom Cupcakes and rich Black-and-White Date Pie always receive compliments. Most everyone delights in dunking bite-size pieces of cake in Caramel Frosting Fondue.

Recipes for all dishes starred (*) are in this cookbook.

REFRESHMENTS TO KEEP ON HAND

Frozen Fruit Salad/Dessert*
Coffee

With this luscious fruit salad or dessert in the freezer, you're always ready for drop-in guests. Especially is it a good idea to keep a supply on hand during the holidays when drop-in visiting reaches the year's peak in country homes.

You can make the fruit salad/dessert right after Thanksgiving Day and have it ready before the Christmas rush gets hectic. If you wish, you can vary the salad from year to year (make it once and you'll make it a tradition) by substituting 1½ c. ground raw cranberries or 3 (1 lb.) pkgs. frozen whole strawberries for the maraschino cherries. If you use the berries, thaw them, drain and save the juice. Use it for part of the orange or pineapple juice called for in the recipe.

TIMETABLE

Do-Ahead: Make the salad a month or a few days ahead and freeze. Quart containers for it are a good size to use.

On Guest Day: A quart of the frozen fruit mixture thaws enough to slice while you make and serve the coffee.

SERVING SUGGESTIONS

For a salad serve slices of the frozen treat on crackling-crisp lettuce or other greens. For a dessert, place slices on individual small plates and, if desired, crown with small puffs of whipped cream, or topping.

FROZEN FRUIT SALAD/DESSERT

Recipe makes a big quantity of this special with a dual role

4 (1 lb. 4 oz.) cans crushed
  pineapple
2 (1 lb.) cans sliced peaches
2 c. fresh white seedless grapes,
  halved, or 2 (1 lb. 4 oz.) cans
1½ c. maraschino cherries, cut in
  eighths
½ lb. marshmallows, quartered
  (30)
2 tsp. crystallized ginger, finely
  chopped
1 envelope unflavored gelatin
¼ c. cold water

1 c. orange juice
¼ c. lemon juice
2½ c. sugar
½ tsp. salt
2 c. coarsely chopped pecans
2 qts. heavy cream, whipped, or
  10 envelopes dessert topping
  mix, whipped, or 1 qt. heavy
  cream and 5 envelopes dessert
  topping mix, whipped
3 c. mayonnaise
Lettuce
Maraschino cherries (for garnish)

Drain fruit; save 1½ c. pineapple syrup. Cut peaches in ½″ cubes. Combine fruit, marshmallows and ginger.

Soften gelatin in cold water.

Heat pineapple syrup to boiling. Add gelatin; stir to dissolve. Add orange and lemon juices, sugar and salt; stir to dissolve. Chill.

When mixture starts to thicken, add fruit mixture and nuts. Fold in whipped cream and mayonnaise.

Spoon into 1-qt. cylinder cartons (paper, plastic or metal). Cover and freeze. Makes 9 quarts.

To serve, remove from freezer and thaw enough to slip out of carton. Cut in 1″ slices. Serve salad on lettuce; garnish with cherries. For dessert, top with whipped cream. Each quart serves 6 to 8.

MAKE-AHEAD
AFTERNOON REFRESHMENTS

Frozen Buttermint Squares*
Chocolate Cookies
Salted Nuts
Hot Tea

Most every hostess delights in introducing her friends to a luscious, new dessert. Frozen Buttermint Squares are so unusual that they'll dominate the conversation. The distinctive delicacy carries the blended flavors of butter mints and strawberries in the gelatin, complemented by the chocolate cookies and tea.

TIMETABLE

Do-Ahead: Bake the cookies at least a day ahead and freeze. Start making the dessert the night before you wish to serve it.

On Guest Day: Complete making the dessert and freeze it at least 2 to 3 hours before serving. Let the cookies thaw at room temperature at least 10 minutes in their foil wrap.

SERVING SUGGESTIONS

If you have fresh mint, you can top the dessert servings with tiny sprigs of it. Arrange a tray of tea accompaniments, such as sugar, milk and/or cream and thin lemon slices.

FROZEN BUTTERMINT SQUARES

You do not dissolve the colorful strawberry flavor gelatin in water

1 (13¼ oz.) can crushed pineapple

1 (3 oz.) pkg. strawberry flavor gelatin

1 (10½ oz.) pkg. miniature marshmallows

1 c. heavy cream

4 oz. soft butter mints, crushed

Combine undrained pineapple, dry gelatin powder and marshmallows; mix well. Cover and chill overnight.

Whip cream; add butter mints and combine with chilled pineapple mixture. Pour into a 9″ square pan. Freeze 2 to 3 hours. Makes 9 servings.

WOMEN'S ONE O'CLOCK DESSERT

Strawberry Pink*
Coffee

What to serve for dessert to women friends is often a real problem. "Six out of eight members of my afternoon bridge club," an Oklahoma farm homemaker reports, "are avid calorie counters. Our custom is for the hostess to serve dessert when guests arrive at 1 P.M. At the end of the afternoon, we always are in a hurry to get home before the children arrive from school. We ban all rich desserts including those containing or garnished with the country favorite, whipped cream. And we constantly search for something different, distinctive and delicious to serve."

Our nomination for an ideal dessert for such occasions is Strawberry Pink. It's a lovely pink color, as its name implies, and tastes like strawberries fresh from the patch even though long icicles may hang from the roof.

TIMETABLE

Make-Ahead: Fix the dessert a day ahead and freeze.

On Guest Day: About 20 minutes before serving time, bring the dessert from freezer and place in refrigerator. Make the coffee. When time to serve the dessert, cut it in individual servings.

SERVING SUGGESTIONS

If available, top each serving with a fresh mint leaf and a whole strawberry.

STRAWBERRY PINK

Also perfect to serve at bridal and baby showers and parties

½ c. regular margarine	1 (10 oz.) pkg. frozen strawber-
½ c. chopped walnuts	ries, thawed
¼ c. brown sugar, firmly packed	1 tblsp. lemon juice
1 c. flour	1 tsp. vanilla
¼ tsp. vanilla	1 c. sugar
2 egg whites	

Put margarine in large baking pan; place in medium oven (350°) until melted. Stir in walnuts, brown sugar, flour and ¼ tsp. vanilla. Return to oven and heat for 8 minutes, stirring frequently, until mixture is lightly browned. Remove from oven and stir; then remove crumbs from pan to cool.

Beat egg whites in large bowl until soft peaks form. Add thawed strawberries, lemon juice and 1 tsp. vanilla. While beating, gradually add the sugar (this should take 20 minutes).

Sprinkle half the cool crumb mixture in bottom of a 13×9×2″

pan. Lightly spread strawberry mixture evenly over the top. Sprinkle remaining half of crumbs over top. Freeze overnight. Makes 9 to 12 servings, depending on size desired.

DESSERT BRIDGE PARTY

Rancho Lemon Custard*   Coffee

The country hostess frequently improvises in preparing food, to "make do" with what she has on hand. And when her experiment is successful, she feels the recipe bears her own trademark. This smooth custard with a rich, unusual lemon-caramel flavor is a good example. An Arizona ranch woman originated this and served it at a dessert bridge party; her neighbor guest was so enthusiastic about the custard that she asked to copy the recipe. She learned that her hostess had baked the dessert in an expensive, imported flan pan, but, undaunted, she decided to try a layer cake pan. It worked. She passed her recipe on to a FARM JOURNAL food editor. We recommend it!

TIMETABLE

Do-Ahead: Bake the custard a day ahead and chill.

On Guest Day: Before guests arrive, invert custard on a large plate. You'll find the top and sides coated with a deep amber caramel.

SERVING SUGGESTIONS

Sprinkle custard, just before serving, with toasted slivered or chopped almonds for delightful flavor and texture contrast. Or flame the dessert at serving time. Heat a little rum (about ¼ c.) in a small pan almost to simmering, but do not let boil. Ignite and slowly pour over top of custard. (The alcohol burns, the rum flavor remains.) Cut like pie and serve at once.

RANCHO LEMON CUSTARD

Velvety, tender custard is quite firm—a treat you'll serve often

1 c. sugar	1 tsp. vanilla
6 eggs	1½ c. light cream
½ tsp. salt	½ c. toasted chopped almonds
1 tblsp. grated lemon peel	(optional)

Place ½ c. sugar in 8" round layer cake pan. Stir constantly over medium heat until sugar liquefies and turns a *light* golden brown. Remove from heat; protect hands with pot holders and roll pan around to coat sides and bottom with melted sugar. Set aside to cool.

Beat eggs with remaining ½ c. sugar until light and lemon-colored. Beat in salt, lemon peel, vanilla and cream. Pour into cake pan (it will be full).

Set pan of custard in pan containing hot water that reaches almost to top of custard pan. Bake in moderate oven (350°) 40 to 50 minutes, until knife inserted in center of custard comes out clean. Remove from oven, place plastic wrap directly on top of custard to cover and chill overnight.

To serve, turn upside down; sprinkle with nuts and cut in wedges like pie. Makes 8 servings.

SIMPLE AFTERNOON TEA

Company Cinnamon Toast*   Tea

Tea for two, or for several friends who stop by without notice, creates no problem for the country hostess. Staples in her kitchen almost always include, besides tea, the makings for this special cinnamon toast—bread, cream, sugar and cinnamon. Serve this teatime treat hot and fragrant from the oven. Be sure the tea is hot and well made. You'll find that most of your guests will give your homespun refreshments extravagant praise.

TIMETABLE

On Guest Day: With little warning friends were coming, you make the preparations after they arrive. If you do not wish to miss out on conversation, invite guests to the kitchen . . . a country custom. You can listen and talk while you fix the toast. Once it's in the oven, assemble the cups, teapot, sugar bowl, plates or trays and place them on a large tray. When the toast is almost golden, make the tea.

SERVING SUGGESTIONS

If you have a lemon, cut it in thin slices for guests who like to add it to their tea. Carry the tea tray to the most inviting spot in your home. This might be by a window with a view of hazy hills in the distance, or by the fireplace in winter. Pour the tea and serve it and the toast on individual plates; pass the sugar and/or lemon slices. A happy, friendly way to spend an hour or two.

COMPANY CINNAMON TOAST

Cream is the ingredient that makes this baked French Toast special. Add a dusting of confectioners sugar just before serving

6 slices bread, 1″ thick	⅔ c. heavy cream
6 tblsp. sugar	¼ c. melted butter or regular
2 tblsp. ground cinnamon	margarine

Cut off crusts and cut each bread slice in 3 strips.

Mix sugar and cinnamon together in a shallow dish. Pour the cream into another shallow dish.

Dip bread strips in cream to coat both sides. Brush strip tops with butter; sprinkle all sides with the sugar-cinnamon mixture to make a thick covering.

Place bread strips on rack in a shallow baking pan. Bake in hot oven (400°) 20 minutes. Serve hot. Makes 18 strips.

COUNTRY EVENING REFRESHMENTS

Black Bottom Cupcakes*   Coffee

Once in a blue moon, as our grandmothers used to describe something exceptionally rare, a recipe comes along that yields such superlative results everyone wants to get a copy of it to use when entertaining. These luscious cupcakes deserve such a reception. We predict that your friends, once they sample them, will ask for the recipe. Be a thoughtful hostess and bake enough cupcakes for seconds.

TIMETABLE

Do-Ahead: You can bake the cupcakes a day or several days ahead and freeze them. (It's easy to bake them the day you entertain.)

On Guest Day: If you froze the cupcakes, sometime in the afternoon transfer them from freezer to refrigerator. Unwrap, but cover loosely with waxed paper. Or thaw them at room temperature in their wrap. This will take about 2 hours.

SERVING SUGGESTIONS

The cakes are so tasty that they need no garnish. Everyone will hope there are more cakes and coffee waiting in the kitchen.

BLACK BOTTOM CUPCAKES

Don't be alarmed by the rather thin cake batter—that's its nature

1 (8 oz.) pkg. cream cheese
1 egg
⅓ c. sugar
⅛ tsp. salt
1 (6 oz.) pkg. semisweet chocolate pieces
1½ c. flour
1 c. sugar
¼ c. cocoa

1 tsp. baking soda
½ tsp. salt
1 c. water
⅓ c. salad oil
1 tblsp. vinegar
1 tsp. vanilla
Sugar for sprinkling on top
½ c. chopped almonds

Combine cheese, egg, ⅓ c. sugar and ⅛ tsp. salt in mixing bowl; beat well. Stir in chocolate pieces, and set aside.

Sift together flour, 1 c. sugar, cocoa, soda and ½ tsp. salt. Add water, oil, vinegar and vanilla. Beat to mix well.

Line muffin-pan cups with paper baking cups; fill one third full with the cocoa batter. Top each with 1 heaping teaspoon reserved cream cheese mixture; sprinkle with sugar and almonds.

Bake in moderate oven (350°) 35 minutes. Makes 20 to 24 cupcakes.

CHOCOLATE EVENING DESSERT

Chocolate Fondue*
Dippers

Give chocolate fondue a chance to be the center of attention. It makes a luscious dessert after an extremely light meal, but for evening refreshments, served with at least three dip candidates and coffee, it takes the prize. There are many recipes for this rich, American dessert. This fondue made with milk chocolate certainly rates as one of the best, and to many people it's *the* best.

Choose the dippers from angel food, pound or sponge cake, maraschino cherries, bananas and marshmallows.

TIMETABLE

Do-Ahead: Bake or buy the cake a day ahead.

On Guest Day: Cut cake in bite-size pieces, place in bowls and cover with napkins to prevent drying. Drain the cherries. Make the fondue just before serving time, and ask the host or a guest to cut the bananas in bite-size chunks. Meanwhile, make the coffee.

SERVING SUGGESTIONS

Provide each guest with a plate, fondue fork and dinner fork. Serve the dippers in bowls within easy reach of everyone. You can use bamboo kabob sticks instead of fondue forks.

CHOCOLATE FONDUE

Chocolate fans of all ages like this dessert. It's a teen-age favorite

1 (12 oz.) milk chocolate bar, cut
  in pieces
6 tblsp. light cream

1 tsp. instant coffee
Dippers

Heat chocolate and light cream in metal fondue cooker over low heat, stirring frequently until chocolate is melted. Stir in the coffee powder. Place fondue on heating unit; keep warm over low heat while dipping bite-size pieces of angel food or pound cake, maraschino cherries, bite-size chunks of bananas and/or large marshmallows. Spear dippers on fondue forks, dip in chocolate fondue, transfer to dinner forks and eat. Makes 6 to 8 servings.

CAKE-AND-COFFEE EVENING

Pound or Angel Food Cake
Caramel Frosting Fondue*
Coffee

There is more than one good way to frost cake. With do-it-yourself parties popular, the hostess need not hesitate to ask her guests of the evening to frost their own pieces of cake. Most of them will think it's fun.

The first step is to select cake that does not break easily. Angel food or pound cake, for instance. Then make Caramel Frosting Fondue and let everyone dunk cubes of cake in it.

If you'd like to use this menu for refreshments during the Halloween season, you can easily expand it. Chilled cider makes a good choice for sipping on autumn evenings. And bite-size chunks of unpeeled red apples dipped in the dessert fondue, taste as good as those memorable caramel apples your mother used to make for children's parties.

TIMETABLE

Do-Ahead: Bake or buy pound or angel food cake a day ahead. Store it tightly covered in a cool place.

On Guest Day: Cut the cake in bite-size pieces, allowing 8 to 12 of them for each person. That provides extras for second helpings. You can make the fondue the last minute before serving, or before guests arrive, reheating it to 230° before pouring it into the fondue pot and placing over low heat on the fondue burner to keep warm. Ask your husband, son or a friend to cut the apples in bite-size pieces *just* before serving so they won't have time to discolor. Or if you wish to cut them ahead, sprinkle them with lemon juice mixed with a little water.

SERVING SUGGESTIONS

At every place on the table, set a serving plate with about 6 pieces of cake on it. Place apple pieces in a bowl to pass. Provide everyone with a fondue and a dinner fork, or use sturdy bamboo sticks, the kind that serve as skewers in cooking, instead of forks. This is one time you'll think a fork is more helpful than a knife in frosting cake!

CARAMEL FROSTING FONDUE

Rich caramel flavor is easy to attain with a candy thermometer. It helps you avoid scorching and development of an unpleasant taste. If sauce gets too thick, stir in a little water. Be sure to use fondue warm, but not hot. Try dipping pretzels and popcorn in it

2 c. brown sugar, firmly packed	1 (15¾ oz.) can sweetened
1 c. light corn syrup	condensed milk (1⅓ c.)
2 tblsp. water	1 tsp. vanilla
½ c. melted butter	

Stir brown sugar, corn syrup and water into saucepan containing melted butter. Bring to a boil over medium heat. Stir in condensed milk and stir and simmer until candy thermometer registers 230°. Remove from heat and add vanilla.

Pour into fondue pot and set over fondue burner on low heat to keep warm. Or cook, and reheat to 230° at serving time. Makes about 3 cups.

NOTE: You may prefer this fondue to the Caramel Fondue with Boys' Burger Supper (see Index).

EVENING'S END REFRESHMENTS

Walnut Whirl*   Small Grape Clusters
Coffee

Country coffee cakes are breads that lead a triple life—they star at morning affairs, such as at breakfast or lunch and coffee parties; in after-dark activities for refreshments following an evening of cards or visiting; sometimes they even assume a dessert role in suppers and dinners, often accompanying a fruit compote. On all occasions coffee, as the name indicates, is the favorite escort.

Some coffee cakes are yeast leavened. Walnut Whirl is an example. It looks good and it tastes even better, especially if it's warm.

TIMETABLE

Do-Ahead: Bake the coffee cake a day or several days ahead, wrap in foil and freeze. Or bake it the day you plan to serve it.

On Guest Day: If the cake is frozen, put it, in foil wrapper, in a moderate oven (350°) 25 to 30 minutes; 12 to 15 minutes if not frozen.

SERVING SUGGESTIONS

A bowl holding small clusters of grapes, whatever kind is available, makes a good accompaniment if you're serving the cake for late evening. The dining room or kitchen table provides a friendly, comfortable setting—gather your family and guests around it.

WALNUT WHIRL

Yeast dough winds around a luscious filling like a jelly roll and then is coiled on baking sheet to rise until doubled and bake slowly to a golden brown. It's work, but well worth the time

¼ c. sugar	1 pkg. active dry yeast
1 tsp. salt	¼ c. warm water (110 to 115°)
¼ c. soft butter or regular margarine	1 egg
¾ c. milk, scalded	3¼ to 3¾ c. flour
	Walnut Filling

Add sugar, salt and butter to milk and cool to lukewarm.

Dissolve yeast in water.

Stir egg and half the flour into milk mixture; stir in yeast and beat until smooth. Work in enough remaining flour to make a dough that is easy to handle.

Turn onto floured surface; knead until smooth. Press ball of dough in greased bowl, turn greased side up. Cover with damp cloth. Let rise in warm place until doubled, about 1½ hours.

Punch down dough; let rise again until almost doubled, about 30 minutes.

Cover worktable with several thicknesses of newspaper, then with large dish towel taped down to hold taut.

Roll out dough on floured towel to approximately 30×20″ rectangle; it will be very thin. With rubber spatula, gently spread Walnut Filling over dough—right to the edges. Starting at wide side, lift cloth and let dough roll up like a jelly roll. Pinch edges to seal.

Coil roll loosely on greased baking sheet; cover and let rise until nearly doubled, about 45 minutes.

Bake in slow oven (325°) 40 to 45 minutes. Remove from baking sheet to rack to cool. Makes about 18 servings.

Walnut Filling: Mix ⅓ c. soft butter or regular margarine, ¾ c. brown sugar, firmly packed, and 1 egg. Stir in ⅓ c. milk, 1 tsp. vanilla, 1 tsp. ground cinnamon and 3 c. walnuts, coarsely ground.

Variation

Short-Cut Walnut Whirl: Make coffee cake with hot roll mix (use 13¾ oz. pkg.). Let dough rise, then roll it out as above.

NEW YEAR'S EVE DESSERT PARTY

Snow-on-the-Mountain*   Coffee

Ring out the old and ring in the new year with delicious Snow-on-the-Mountain, a dessert which delights the guests. Brace yourself for compliments, promises the Iowa woman who serves the dessert at her New Year's Eve watch party.

TIMETABLE

Do-Ahead: Make the dessert a day ahead and place in the refrigerator. The chilling blends flavors and firms the snow mountain for cutting.

On Guest Day: All you have to do is make plenty of coffee and take it and the dessert to the buffet.

SERVING SUGGESTIONS

Let your guests see the spectacular, snowy mountain. Cut and serve it from the buffet or table with everyone gathered around to admire and to anticipate the tempting dessert.

SNOW-ON-THE-MOUNTAIN

Showy, delicious, make-ahead dessert—a real company special

Part 1 (Cake):
4 eggs
1 c. sugar
½ c. sifted flour
1 tsp. baking powder
½ tsp. salt
2 tsp. vanilla
1 c. chopped dates

1 c. chopped nuts
Part 2 (Fruit):
5 oranges
3 bananas
3 tblsp. sugar
Part 3 (Snow):
2 c. heavy cream, whipped
½ c. flaked coconut

To make cake, beat eggs until light; gradually add sugar, beating until it dissolves.

Sift together flour, baking powder and salt; add to egg mixture. Fold in vanilla, dates and nuts. Pour into two greased and floured 8″ round layer cake pans.

Bake in moderate oven (350°) about 30 minutes. Cool about 10 minutes in pans, then turn out and complete cooling on racks.

Meanwhile, prepare fruit. Peel oranges, discard seeds if not using navel oranges, and cut sections in small pieces. (You will have about 3 cups.) Peel bananas and slice. (There will be about 3 cups banana slices.) Toss fruit together to coat bananas with juice from the orange pieces to retard discoloration. Stir in sugar to mix well. Let stand while the cake bakes and cools.

To make mountain, break cooled cake in small pieces. Arrange some of the pieces in a layer about 12″ long and 10″ wide on a large platter, tray or plate. This is the base of the mountain. Put a layer of fruit, then a layer of cake pieces, and repeat, shaping the mountain. It should come to a peak. Frost with whipped cream, and sprinkle with coconut. Chill in refrigerator overnight. Cut and lift to dessert plates with cake server. Makes 20 to 24 servings.

WASHINGTON'S BIRTHDAY DESSERT

Lemon/Cheese Torte*   Tea or Coffee

While this handsome cheese cake with its gleaming red top is ideal for the hostess to feature when entertaining in February, it's equally appropriate and appealing the year round. Cottage and cream cheeses and packaged lemon pudding and pie filling unite in this unusual torte. The dessert is so well liked by the three sons of junior and senior high school age in a Wisconsin farm family that they ask their mother to make it for their birthdays instead of cake. You will find that people of all ages give the torte top rating.

TIMETABLE

Do-Ahead: Bake the cake, glaze and chill in refrigerator overnight.

On Guest Day: Cut the torte at serving time in 8 or 10 wedges.

SERVING SUGGESTIONS

The torte is so attractive and tempting that you may wish to cut and serve it at the table or buffet with your guests watching.

LEMON/CHEESE TORTE

Cheerful red cherry glaze makes this a fine February party dessert

¾ c. finely ground graham cracker crumbs	1 c. light cream
1 tblsp. sugar	2 c. creamed cottage cheese
2 tblsp. melted butter	1 (8 oz.) pkg. cream cheese
1 (3½ oz.) pkg. lemon pudding and pie filling mix	4 egg yolks
⅔ c. sugar	¼ tsp. salt
	4 egg whites, beaten to soft peaks
	Cherry Glaze

Combine crumbs, 1 tblsp. sugar and butter; mix well. (This amount may be doubled for a thicker crust.) Press mixture firmly into bottom of a 9″ spring-form pan (or a 3-qt. casserole, but it's easier to remove in good shape from a spring-form pan).

Combine pudding mix, ⅔ c. sugar and light cream in saucepan. Cook and stir until mixture comes to a full boil and is thickened, about 5 minutes. Mixture may curdle while cooking, but it will be smooth when it boils. Remove from heat.

Combine cottage and cream cheeses (both should be at room temperature). Mix well; add egg yolks, one at a time, mixing well after each addition. Add salt and cooked pudding; blend well. Fold in beaten egg whites and pour over crumb mixture in pan.

Bake in slow oven (300°) 1 hour. Cool to room temperature.

Chill thoroughly. Spread on Cherry Glaze. The cake is best when chilled overnight. Makes 8 to 10 servings.

CHERRY GLAZE

½ (3 oz.) pkg. strawberry flavor gelatin (4 tblsp.)
½ c. boiling water
¼ c. sugar

½ c. juice drained from cherries
1 (16 to 17 oz.) can pitted tart cherries (water pack)

Dissolve gelatin in boiling water; stir in sugar. Add juice drained from cherries. Chill until slightly thickened.

Spread well-drained cherries over top of chilled Lemon/Cheese Torte. Pour gelatin mixture over cherries. Chill until ready to serve.

FEBRUARY DESSERT PARTY

Elegant Chocolate Log*   Coffee

Treat your friends to a log cutting! What could be more appropriate for Lincoln's birthday than this delicate one made with chocolate cake? The Utah homemaker/home economist who shares this recipe makes the cake for very special occasions. When entertaining quite a few guests, she bakes two cakes, fills and rolls them; then she puts them together to make one long log and spreads on the frosting. She serves it on a long antique fish platter and her friends say it makes a stunning dessert. (You can use a tray if your platters are not long enough.)

TIMETABLE

Do-Ahead: A week or several days ahead, bake the cake, roll, fill and frost. Place on baking sheet and freeze. When frozen firm, wrap and return to freezer with seam side of roll down. (Some women prefer to frost the log after freezing and thawing.)

On Guest Day: Take the frozen roll from the freezer, remove wrap, cover loosely and let thaw in refrigerator for several hours. You can bake, roll, fill and frost the roll on guest day. Keep it in refrigerator until serving time. One log makes 8 servings.

SERVING SUGGESTIONS

Set the dessert on buffet or table and slice and serve it with admiring guests watching. They'll have runaway appetites. Ask a co-operative guest to pour the coffee.

ELEGANT CHOCOLATE LOG

A beautiful way to serve chocolate cake—perfect for entertaining

1¼ c. sifted confectioners sugar	1 c. heavy cream, whipped
¼ c. plus 1 tblsp. sifted flour	Sugar (about 2 tblsp.)
½ tsp. salt	8 to 12 marshmallows, cut up
5 tblsp. cocoa	1 square unsweetened chocolate
6 eggs, separated	2 c. confectioners sugar
¼ tsp. cream of tartar	Light cream
1¼ tsp. vanilla	¼ c. finely chopped pecans
1 tblsp. water	

Sift together 1¼ c. confectioners sugar, flour, salt and cocoa three times.

Beat egg whites with cream of tartar until stiff.

Beat egg yolks until thick and lemon-colored; beat in vanilla and water. Add sifted dry ingredients and beat into egg yolks until well blended. Fold in beaten egg whites.

Spread in greased, paper-lined 15½ × 10½ × 1" jelly roll pan. Bake in moderate oven (375°) 15 to 20 minutes. Lightly dust clean dish towel with confectioners sugar; loosen cake around edges with spatula. Invert on towel. Lift off pan and carefully peel off paper. With a sharp knife, cut off cake's crisp edges. Roll up cake gently, from narrow end, by folding edge of cake over and then tucking it in; continue rolling cake, lifting towel higher with one hand as you guide the rolling with the other hand, rolling the towel in the cake (to prevent cake sticking). Let cool on rack (wrap tightly in towel to hold it in shape).

Unroll cake on towel; spread with whipped cream, sweetened to taste with granulated sugar (about 2 tblsp.) and with marshmallows added. Roll like jelly roll.

For frosting, melt chocolate; add 2 c. confectioners sugar with enough light cream to make it spreadable. Spread over cake and immediately sprinkle with chopped nuts. Makes 8 to 10 servings.

ST. PATRICK'S DAY DESSERT PARTY

Lime/Chocolate Fascination*   Hot Tea

If you plan to entertain on St. Patrick's Day, consider serving this make-ahead dessert. It wears its green with distinction and the lime and chocolate flavors blend to perfection. The recipe comes from a Minnesota woman who served it to her afternoon bridge club. Her children nicknamed the dessert "the Green Cake." Their mother calls it Lime/Chocolate Fascination because it never fails to fascinate her friends and family. Call it what you wish, the name will not affect the dessert's beauty or tastiness. Serve it with tea to carry out the Irish menu.

TIMETABLE

Do-Ahead: Put the can of evaporated milk in the refrigerator a day or two before you wish to whip it. Make the dessert a day ahead and refrigerate.

On Guest Day: Chill the dessert plates if refrigerator space permits.

SERVING SUGGESTIONS

To add a touch of glamor to the refreshment, serve a green and a chocolate-coated candy mint on each plate with the dessert. Some women keep candy mints of different colors and flavors in their freezers. It is surprising how frequently they add the right color and sweet note to refreshments. Be sure to wrap the packages of candy in moisture-proof wrap when freezing them. The boxes themselves often are not adequate protection for freezer storage. Let the mints thaw in their wrap at room temperature 4 to 8 hours before you serve them.

LIME/CHOCOLATE FASCINATION

A March special, but good every month—guests of all ages like this

1 (14½ oz.) can evaporated milk
1 (3 oz.) pkg. lime flavor gelatin
2 c. hot water
1 c. sugar
¼ c. lime juice

2 tsp. lemon juice
About 4 drops green food color
2 c. chocolate wafer crumbs (8½ oz.)
½ c. melted butter

Chill milk at least 1 day in refrigerator.

Dissolve gelatin in hot water. Chill until mixture is partly congealed (consistency of unbeaten egg whites). Then whip until fluffy. Stir in sugar, lime and lemon juices and food color to tint a delicate green.

Whip milk until light and fluffy; fold into gelatin mixture.

Combine cookie crumbs and melted butter. Reserve ½ c. crumbs for top. Press remaining crumbs into bottom of a 9″ square pan. Add whipped gelatin-milk mixture. Sprinkle reserved ½ c. crumbs on top. Chill overnight or until firm. Makes 9 servings.

BLACK-AND-WHITE WINTER DESSERT

Black-and-White Date Pie*   Coffee

Take a cold, clear winter night, congenial friends gathered in a comfortable home, a hospitable host and hostess and this date pie and coffee for refreshment. You have the right ingredients for a joyful evening. The dessert is rich in calories, but equally rich in luscious flavors. It gives guests a well-fed feeling and sends them home in a happy frame of mind.

TIMETABLE

Do-Ahead: You can line the pie pan with pastry, bake the pie shell, slip it into a plastic bag and put in a cool place overnight, or freeze it for several days.

On Guest Day: Make the pie. At serving time, whip the cream and spread on pie while your husband or a friend makes the coffee.

SERVING SUGGESTIONS

The Iowa farm woman who contributed this recipe says it is a winter favorite of the bridge club to which she and her husband belong. She serves the dessert from a small table, covered with a black cloth which she embroidered with delicate white snowflake designs. Her dessert plates are white and she uses either black or white napkins. The guests, who have been seated around bridge tables during the evening, enjoy going to the buffet for their own servings.

BLACK-AND-WHITE DATE PIE

Pie is rich enough for 8 servings—just right for two tables of bridge

Baked 9″ pie shell

Bottom Layer:
1 c. chopped fresh dates (8 oz. pkg.)
½ c. water
⅛ tsp. salt
½ c. sugar
1 tsp. cornstarch
1 tsp. butter
1 tblsp. lemon juice

Top Layer:
¾ c. sugar
¼ c. flour
2 tblsp. cornstarch
¼ tsp. salt
2 c. milk
3 egg yolks, beaten
½ tsp. lemon juice
½ tsp. vanilla
¾ c. heavy cream, whipped

To make bottom layer, cook dates with water and salt until they are very soft. Combine sugar and cornstarch; add to dates. Simmer 1 minute. Add butter and lemon juice. Cool; then spread in baked pie shell.

For top layer, combine sugar, flour, cornstarch and salt. Scald milk; gradually add to dry mixture, stirring constantly. Cook over boiling water until mixture thickens. Cool.

Add egg yolks, beaten until foamy. Cook over boiling water 3 minutes. Remove from heat; add lemon juice and vanilla. Partially cool. Spread on top of date mixture in pie shell. Cool thoroughly.

Serve topped with whipped cream. Makes 8 servings.

COLD WEATHER DESSERT BUFFET

Tart Bar with Tart Shells* and Tart Fillings*
Garnishes   Coffee

Sharing the work, as well as the joys of entertaining, is a firmly established custom in the country. Potlucks have long been a popular way. Progressive dinners or suppers are another. This Dessert Buffet made its debut when a Minnesota couple was asked to serve the last course of a progressive dinner for members of a neighborhood club. Now it has become a tradition in the neighborhood.

The Tart Bar, as its creator calls it, has many merits. It capitalizes on the great American liking for pies. Also you can prepare the food ahead. The Tart Bar with its choice of tempting fillings usually intrigues guests into offering to take a turn at filling the crisp pastry shells. Men especially relish the opportunity to indicate their preferences. And sampling more than one kind does not mark anyone as being greedy; it compliments the hostess who prepared the food.

Four different fillings are adequate. We give recipes for Lemon, Pumpkin and Chocolate Cream; other suggestions are canned cherry, blueberry or other canned fruit pie filling and sugared strawberries with whipped cream or dessert topping mix.

TIMETABLE

Do-Ahead: Bake tart shells and make the pastes for the cream fillings several days ahead and freeze, or a day ahead and refrigerate.

On Guest Day: If you have the basic pastes in the freezer, thaw at room temperature as many portions as you will need. Each portion yields enough filling for six 3″ tart shells. To them, add the whipped dessert topping and mix to make a light filling that you can spoon easily into the tart shells; refrigerate fillings several hours. At serving time make the coffee.

SERVING SUGGESTIONS

Arrange rows of empty tart shells on a tray and place on a serving cart on a side table. Around them set bowls of fillings and toppings, such as chopped nuts, flaked coconut, sliced strawberries and whipped cream, to garnish the tarts. Invite guests to come to the "bar" and name the kind of filling they prefer for their tarts. Also give them a choice of toppings. Spoon the filling into the tart shell, add the topping, place the dessert on an individual plate and hand it to the guest. Invite a friend to pour the coffee. Warning: Guests often return for seconds!

TART SHELLS

You can fill tart shells with ice cream and top with dessert sauce

2 c. sifted flour	¾ c. shortening, or ⅔ c. lard
1 tsp. salt	4 or 5 tblsp. cold water

Combine flour and salt in mixing bowl. Cut in shortening with pastry blender or with two knives until mixture is the consistency of coarse cornmeal.

Sprinkle on cold water, 1 tblsp. at a time, tossing mixture lightly and stirring with fork. Add water each time to the driest part of mixture. The dough should be just moist enough to hold together when pressed gently with a fork. It should not be sticky.

Divide pastry into 6 parts. Shape into smooth balls and roll out each ball to make 4½ to 5" circles.

Fit pastry circles over backs of inverted 3½" muffin-pan cups. Make pleats so pastry will fit snugly. Prick entire surface with 4-tined fork. Or fit pastry over inverted custard cups, prick well and set on baking sheet. Refrigerate 30 minutes before baking.

Preheat oven to very hot (450°). Bake tart shells 10 to 12 minutes, or until golden. Cool on racks. Then carefully remove from pans, or custard cups. Fill as desired. Makes about 6 (3") tarts, depending on how thin the pastry was rolled.

N O T E : Regardless of the size of your muffin-pan cups, you can bake tart shells on them. With a string, measure one of the inverted cups up one side, across the bottom and down on the other side. Cut the string this length. Find a bowl, saucer or small plate in the kitchen that has the same diameter as the string. Or cut a cardboard this size. Use for a pattern to cut the rolled pastry in circles. Fit pastry rounds on alternate muffin cups—6 on a pan with 12 cups. Pleat pastry to fit snugly.

CHOCOLATE CREAM TART FILLING

Strong chocolate flavor—delightful with a snowy drift of coconut

½ c. Cocoa Paste
1 envelope dessert topping mix

Thaw Cocoa Paste.

Prepare topping mix according to package directions. Add Cocoa Paste; continue beating until creamy and smooth. Chill in refrigerator several hours before serving. Makes filling for 6 (3") tarts.

COCOA PASTE

1⅓ c. cocoa
1 c. sugar
2 c. boiling water

Combine cocoa and sugar in heavy saucepan. Add water slowly, stirring to make a smooth mixture.

Cook and stir over high heat until mixture boils. Reduce heat to low and continue cooking for 15 minutes, stirring occasionally.

Pour into bowl; cool. Package in ½ c. portions; freeze, or store in refrigerator. (May be stored up to 4 weeks in refrigerator or freezer.) Makes 2 cups.

PUMPKIN CREAM TART FILLING

True pumpkin flavor—spicy! Garnish filled tarts with toasted pecans

1⅓ c. Pumpkin Paste
1 envelope dessert topping mix

Thaw Pumpkin Paste.

Prepare topping mix according to package directions. Add Pumpkin Paste; continue beating until creamy and smooth. Chill in refrigerator for several hours before serving. Makes filling for 6 (3") tarts.

PUMPKIN PASTE

1 c. sugar
½ c. brown sugar, firmly packed
⅓ c. sifted flour
1½ tsp. ground cinnamon

1½ tsp. ground nutmeg
¾ tsp. salt
3 c. canned pumpkin
¾ c. water

Combine sugars, flour, spices and salt. Add to pumpkin in heavy saucepan; mix thoroughly. Add water.

Cook 15 minutes over low heat, stirring occasionally.

Pour into bowl; cool. Package in 1⅓ c. portions; freeze. (May be stored up to 4 weeks in freezer.) Makes 4 cups.

LEMON CREAM TART FILLING

Light and lemony—and so good when topped with sliced strawberries

½ c. Lemon Paste
1 envelope dessert topping mix

Thaw Lemon Paste; keep cold.

Prepare topping mix according to package directions. Add Lemon Paste; continue beating until creamy and smooth. Add more milk for thinner mixture, if desired. Add food color to give lemon color.

Chill in refrigerator several hours before serving. Makes filling for 6 (3″) tarts.

LEMON PASTE

½ c. butter	1 c. boiling water
⅓ c. sifted flour	½ c. lemon juice
1 c. sugar	1 tblsp. grated lemon peel

Melt butter in heavy saucepan. Add flour and stir to make smooth paste. Mix in ¼ c. sugar. Add water slowly, stirring to make a smooth mixture. Add remaining sugar, lemon juice and peel.

Cook and stir over high heat until mixture boils. Reduce heat to low and continue cooking for 15 minutes, stirring occasionally.

Pour into bowl; cool. Package in ½ c. portions; freeze, or store in refrigerator. (May be stored up to 4 weeks in refrigerator or freezer.) Makes 2 cups.

PARTNERSHIP REFRESHMENTS

Snack Cookies*
Golden Pitcher Punch*

Whenever girls and boys get together, something to sip and snack on is in order. Members of some 4-H Clubs, after a busy summer with work projects, welcome winter meetings with their social moments. Homemade cookies and punch are the favorite refreshments. The girls bake the cookies, and while the boys do not "preside" over punch bowls, they take responsibility for the beverage and often help make it or pour it from pitchers.

This menu suggests Golden Pitcher Punch, a pretty fruit juice punch with ginger ale added for sparkle, but the beverage you serve can be as simple as lemonade with attention-getting ice cubes. To make the ice cubes, mix 1 (12 oz.) can red Hawaiian punch and 2 c. cold water. Pour into ice cube trays and freeze 24 hours or until firm. Apple coolers also win friends. To make a good one, pour 1 qt. apple juice over cracked ice in a pitcher. Add 1 (7 oz.) bottle ginger ale.

The oatmeal drop cookies never fail to awaken enthusiasm, especially when decorated with candy- and chocolate-coated peanuts. The candy coating is in different colors that brighten the cookie plate or tray.

TIMETABLE

Do-Ahead: Bake the cookies a day ahead, or if easier, several days ahead and freeze.

On Guest Day: Both cookies and punch may need to travel to a meeting or gathering. If you tote the cookies, leave them in their wrap. They will thaw on the way to the party. Pour the punch over ice cubes in vacuum container; add ginger ale at serving time.

SERVING SUGGESTIONS

Garnishes of very thin orange slices add interest to the pitcher of punch. Display the colorful cookies on a large tray or plate.

SNACK COOKIES

Crisp oatmeal cookies go glamorous with bright confection trim

½ c. shortening	1 c. flour
½ c. sugar	½ tsp. baking soda
½ c. brown sugar, firmly packed	½ tsp. salt
½ tsp. vanilla	1 c. quick-cooking rolled oats
1 egg	Candy- and chocolate-coated
1 tblsp. water	peanuts

Cream together shortening, sugars and vanilla to make a fluffy mixture. Beat in egg and water.

Sift together flour, baking soda and salt. Add to creamed mixture and blend well. Stir in rolled oats.

Drop by rounded teaspoonfuls about 2″ apart onto greased baking sheet. Press candy- and chocolate-coated peanut in center of each.

Bake in moderate oven (375°) 8 to 10 minutes. Makes 3 dozen.

GOLDEN PITCHER PUNCH

Cheerful as sunshine—three fruit juices bubbling with ginger ale

4 c. cold water	1 c. pineapple juice
1½ c. sugar	1 c. orange juice
½ c. lemon juice	1 (28 oz.) bottle ginger ale

Heat water and sugar until sugar is dissolved, about 5 minutes. Add fruit juices and chill. Pour into large pitcher and add ginger ale at serving time. Pour over ice cubes in glasses. Makes 8 servings.

SOCIAL EVENING REFRESHMENTS

Wisconsin Trio-Cheese Ball*		Assorted Crackers
Celery	Mulled Cider*	Coffee

You can depend on a Wisconsin hostess to recognize a superior cheese blend when she tastes it. One of them shares a favorite. She serves it as an appetizer in the living room before a meal, but more frequently after an evening of visiting or cards. She molds the three-cheese mixture into different shapes, such as a ball, loaf or cylinder. Guests slice and spread it on crackers. She also shapes the cheese mixture into tiny balls, but less often because it's more work and they soften so quickly at room temperature.

TIMETABLE

Do-Ahead: Make cheese ball a day or several days ahead, wrap in foil and refrigerate.

On Guest Day: Roll the ball in chopped parsley and pecans. Return to refrigerator. Make Mulled Cider when convenient. Reheat at serving time.

SERVING SUGGESTIONS

Place cheese on large plate, platter or tray and surround with crackers. Or cut unpeeled, cored red apples in wedges, sprinkle with lemon juice to prevent discoloration and arrange around cheese; serve crackers on a separate plate. The apples taste wonderful spread with the cheese and they add a pleasing touch of color. Serve the cider in mugs or cups and float a thin orange slice, stuck with a whole clove, in each. You may wish to offer guests this refreshing drink early in the evening, and serve the cheese and coffee later.

WISCONSIN TRIO-CHEESE BALL

Provide knives for spreading; cheese softens at room temperature

1 (8 oz.) pkg. cream cheese	1 tblsp. Worcestershire sauce
¼ lb. blue cheese, crumbled	½ tsp. salt
1 c. shredded sharp Cheddar cheese (¼ lb.)	½ c. finely chopped pecans
3 tblsp. minced onion	¼ c. finely chopped parsley (about)

Put all ingredients, except pecans and parsley, in bowl. Beat with electric mixer at medium speed until mixture is fluffy. Stir in 3 tblsp. pecans; cover and refrigerate 3 to 4 hours.

Remove cheese from bowl, place on aluminum foil and shape with hands into a large ball (or small 1″ balls). Wrap tightly in foil and return to refrigerator. Cheese is soft unless thoroughly chilled. About 30 minutes before serving, unwrap cheese (reshape in ball if necessary); roll in remaining pecans and parsley. Place on serving plate or tray and keep in refrigerator until serving time. Makes 1 (3″) ball or about 50 (1″) balls. You can also mold into a loaf or other shapes.

MULLED CIDER

Also serve this spicy favorite with doughnuts for Halloween

½ c. brown sugar, firmly packed	¾ tsp. whole allspice
⅛ tsp. salt	½ tsp. whole cloves
2 qts. apple cider	3″ stick cinnamon

Combine brown sugar, salt and cider. Tie spices in clean, thin white cloth and add to cider. Bring slowly to a boil; cover and simmer 20 minutes. Remove spices. Serve hot. Makes 10 servings.

LATE EVENING SNACKS

Crab/Cheese Spread*   Dilled Sour Cream Dip*
Texas Meat Balls* with Red Hot Barbecue Sauce*
Carrot, Cucumber and Zucchini Strips
Hard Tack Cookies*
Coffee

When you go to the basketball game, show, concert or other event with friends, invite the party to stop at your house on the way home. It's an easy way to entertain.

This help-yourself menu can satisfy appetites of varying degrees—and take care of additional guests. The food requires only finishing touches. Make the coffee just before serving time. Let the host help by carrying the snacks to the buffet or table in the living or family room.

A crabmeat spread, meat balls with barbecue sauce and a sour cream dip with plenty of uncooked vegetable dippers plus crackers and, if you like, potato or corn chips offer guests an ample choice. If you wish to end with a sweet touch, bring out a plate of Hard Tack Cookies—they are unusual and always bring compliments.

TIMETABLE

Do-Ahead: You can bake Hard Tack Cookies several days ahead and store them in a covered container.

On Guest Day: Mix and shape meat balls early in the day and refrigerate. Make barbecue sauce. Peel and cut carrots in strips; place them in a jar, add a little water, cover and chill. Before you leave home place the cream cheese on a platter or plate, top with crabmeat and refrigerate. Add the seafood cocktail sauce just before serving. Mix the sour cream dip, cover and chill. After you return home, broil the meat balls and make the coffee; peel the chilled cucumber and cut it and the unpeeled small zucchini in strips.

SERVING SUGGESTIONS

Serve crab spread with a knife for cutting and spreading. Keep meat balls warm in chafing dish or electric skillet, or serve them on a warm platter with the bowl of barbecue sauce near them. Place vegetable dippers on tray alongside sour cream dip. Arrange an assortment of crackers, including shredded wheats, on tray or large plate.

CRAB/CHEESE SPREAD

Open a can of crabmeat, a bottle of seafood cocktail sauce and a package of cream cheese to make this delicious spread—quick

1 (8 oz.) pkg. cream cheese
1 (7½ oz.) can crabmeat, drained and flaked
¾ c. bottled seafood cocktail sauce

Place cream cheese on serving plate or platter and flatten until ½″ in height. Top with crabmeat, then with bottled seafood cocktail sauce. Serve with crackers. Makes about 25 servings.

DILLED SOUR CREAM DIP

Brings out the best flavors of uncooked vegetable dippers

1 c. dairy sour cream
½ c. mayonnaise or salad dressing
1 tblsp. finely chopped green onion
2 tsp. parsley flakes, crushed
1 tsp. dill weed, crushed
1 tsp. bottled salad seasoning

Combine all ingredients. Cover and chill several hours to blend flavors. Serve with carrot, cucumber and zucchini slices. Makes about 1½ cups.

TEXAS MEAT BALLS

Provide plenty of strong picks to spear meat balls for dunking

1 lb. lean ground beef
1 (6 oz.) can evaporated milk
3 tblsp. onion soup mix
2 tsp. Worcestershire sauce
Red Hot Barbecue Sauce

Combine ground beef, milk, soup mix and Worcestershire sauce. Shape into balls, using 1 level tblsp. meat mixture for each ball. Place on rack and broil without turning about 10 to 12 minutes, or until as done as desired. Serve warm with Red Hot Barbecue Sauce. Use picks to dunk meat balls into sauce. Makes about 30 balls.

RED HOT BARBECUE SAUCE

This lively sauce lives up to its name . . . it's really hot

½ c. finely chopped onion	2 tblsp. brown sugar
¼ c. finely chopped green pepper	2½ tblsp. cider vinegar
2 tblsp. butter or regular margarine	1 tblsp. Worcestershire sauce
1½ c. bottled barbecue sauce	⅛ tsp. hot pepper sauce

Cook onion and green pepper in butter over low heat until onion is tender (do not let it brown). Mix in remaining ingredients. Simmer about 15 minutes, until sauce is heated and seasonings are blended. Serve in a bowl. Makes about 2 cups.

HARD TACK COOKIES

Cookies may get too hard several days after baking. Add a slice of bread to cookie jar; in 24 hours they will soften just right

2 eggs	1 c. flaked coconut
1 c. sugar	1 c. chopped dates or raisins
1 c. sifted flour	1 tblsp. confectioners sugar
½ tsp. baking powder	(optional)

Beat eggs until frothy; add sugar and mix.

Sift together flour and baking powder; add to egg mixture. Fold in coconut and dates.

Spread dough in 11×7×1½" pan; bake in slow oven (325°) 30 to 35 minutes. Cut in bars of desired size while hot. Sprinkle with confectioners sugar. Makes about 20 bars.

OPEN-HOUSE REFRESHMENTS

Party Punch*

Chicken Nuggets*   Wiener/Cheese Appetizers*

Upside-Down Cheese Biscuits*

Potato Chips   Crackers

Smoky Cottage Cheese Dip*

Popcorn Snack*

If in doubt about how to entertain when former neighbors, whom your friends wish to see, are your house guests, have a punch party.

Set aside an evening for this open house. You'll find people of all ages enjoy nibbling on snacks, sipping punch and visiting with friends. Nice and informal, encouraging conversation and circulating.

You can serve cold snacks only, but warm ones are especially appetizing. It's a good idea to get them ready ahead for fast last-minute broiling or baking. Perhaps you are fortunate and have a daughter or special friend who will take over part of the quick cooking for you.

In this menu the hot appetizers are miniatures of popular foods everybody likes—fried chicken, hot biscuits and wieners and cheese. The chilled cheese dip with crisp vegetable dippers appeals to everyone. And so does the crunchy Popcorn Snack. It's so good your supply may run out too soon unless you make two batches.

TIMETABLE

Do-Ahead: Make the Popcorn Snack several days ahead (before your house guests arrive). Store it in an airtight container and place in a cool spot. Get the Chicken Nuggets and Wiener/Cheese Appetizers ready to heat just before serving. Cover them and store in refrigerator.

On Guest Day: Make the dip at your convenience, place in bowl and refrigerate. Get carrot and celery sticks and cauliflowerets ready, place in ice water until crisp; then chill them in plastic bags. Make punch just before time to serve it. Sometime during the evening, slip out to the kitchen and bake a pan of the tiny biscuits and carry them to friends while piping hot. What a surprise!

SERVING SUGGESTIONS

Serve punch in a big pitcher or a punch bowl, whichever you prefer. Set pitcher or bowl on tray or large plate and place on table or buffet. Arrange the appetizers around it. Since they are finger food, you need not provide silverware or plates, but do have plenty of picks and paper napkins.

PARTY PUNCH

So easy to make, so pretty to look at and so refreshing to sip

2 (6 oz.) cans frozen pink lemonade concentrate
1 (6 oz.) can frozen grapefruit juice concentrate

2 c. cold water
1 qt. ginger ale, chilled
1 qt. club soda, chilled

Combine concentrates and water in punch bowl; stir until they melt. Add 2 trays of ice cubes and stir. Just before serving, carefully pour ginger ale and club soda down side of bowl. Makes about 25 servings.

CHICKEN NUGGETS

Serve warm or cold—they're tasty both ways, the hit of any party

4 whole chicken breasts (broiler-fryers)
½ c. unseasoned fine dry bread crumbs
¼ c. grated Parmesan cheese

½ tsp. salt
1 tsp. thyme leaves
1 tsp. basil leaves
½ c. melted butter or regular margarine

Bone chicken breasts; remove skin. Cut each breast half into nuggets, about 1¼ to 1½" square.

Combine bread crumbs, cheese, salt, thyme and basil. Dip chicken pieces in melted butter and then in crumb mixture. Place in a single layer on foil-lined baking sheet. Bake in hot oven (400°) until golden, about 10 minutes. Serve with picks. Makes 56 to 60 nuggets.

WIENER/CHEESE APPETIZERS

Watch the youngsters gather round the platter for this tasty snack

2 (5½ oz.) pkgs. fully cooked little wieners
¼ lb. process American cheese (about)

Cut wieners lengthwise in halves but not quite through (about three fourths of the way). Slice cheese in thin 1" slivers. Place a sliver in each wiener. Cover and refrigerate.

At serving time, lay wieners on rack in broiler pan and broil until cheese starts to bubble. Serve at once. Makes about 30 appetizers.

UPSIDE-DOWN CHEESE BISCUITS

Serve these piping hot—they'll be popular so make plenty!

1 (5 oz.) jar pasteurized process cheese spread
1 tblsp. butter or regular margarine

1 can refrigerated biscuits (10)
Chopped fresh parsley (optional)

In a 9" pie pan put cheese spread and butter; place in very hot oven (450°) until butter melts.

Meanwhile, quarter biscuits with kitchen scissors. Stir cheese-butter mixture to combine (mixture will not completely blend). Cover with biscuits, arranging pieces very close together.

Bake in very hot oven (450°) 10 to 12 minutes, until golden brown. Loosen biscuits with spatula and invert at once onto serving plate. Garnish with chopped parsley, if desired. Makes 40 bite-size biscuits.

SMOKY COTTAGE CHEESE DIP

Serve this with carrot, celery and cucumber sticks and cauliflowerets

1 c. cottage cheese	½ tsp. liquid smoke
1 (3 oz.) pkg. cream cheese	¼ tsp. garlic salt
2 tblsp. light cream or milk	½ c. ripe olives, minced
1 tsp. minced onion	

Beat together cottage cheese, cream cheese and cream. Blend in remaining ingredients. Cover and refrigerate. Makes 1⅔ cups.

POPCORN SNACK

Play safe—use candy thermometer. This is too good to risk failure

2 qts. popped corn	1 c. dark corn syrup
2 c. bite-size shredded wheat	¼ tsp. salt
1 (4 oz.) can blanched whole almonds, toasted	½ c. butter or regular margarine
1½ c. sugar	1 tsp. vanilla

Combine popcorn, shredded wheat and almonds in a greased kettle; place in very slow oven (250°) 20 minutes. Keep warm.

Heat sugar, corn syrup, salt and butter in medium saucepan until boiling, stirring constantly. Wipe down sides of saucepan with pastry brush dipped in water and well drained to remove any sugar crystals. Insert candy thermometer and continue cooking without stirring until mixture reaches 290° on thermometer, or until a small amount of mixture dropped in cold water separates into thin hard, but not brittle threads. Remove from heat; add vanilla at once.

Spread corn mixture on two large greased baking sheets. Pour hot syrup over, a little at a time, stirring constantly to coat mixture. Spread quickly on baking sheets. When cool, break in pieces. Store in airtight container. Makes about 2 pounds.

Toasted Almonds: Spread almonds in a single layer in 15½ ×10½ ×1″ jelly roll pan. Bake in moderate oven (375°) about 10 minutes, until a light brown. Remove from pan.

HOLIDAY OPEN HOUSE

White Cap Punch*
Christmas Snack Tree*
Party Cheese Dip*   Quick Mustard Sauce*
Corn Chips   Crackers
Cashew Drop Cookies*   Holiday Gumdrop Cookies*
Caramel Popcorn Balls*   Peanut Brittle
Coffee

When holly wreaths hang on doors and bright lights twinkle on Christmas trees, a friendly spirit permeates the countryside. Take advantage of the season to extend hospitality to neighbors and friends. Treat them to a few evening hours in your home. Invite them to drop by between designated hours that are right for your family and for them.

A snack tree gets the center of attention in this menu. It is both decorative and functional for it holds snacks to dunk in the dips served in bowls at its base. Notice the diversion in beverages—from frigid fruit juice punch to steaming hot coffee—refreshments for people of all ages.

Young people quickly spy the peanut brittle (or other homemade candy of your choice) and the popcorn balls. We give you recipes for two special cookies. The candy gumdrops in one of them are particularly festive in color, and the unusual cashew cookies may be a new eating experience to some of your guests.

TIMETABLE

Do-Ahead: Make the snack tree base several days ahead so it will be ready to trim with food on open-house day. Also make ahead peanut brittle and popcorn balls. Bake cookies and freeze. You can make the dips the day before you'll serve them if it's easier than making them on party day. Refrigerate.

On Guest Day: Make snack tree dippers; refrigerate meat and cheese dippers. Place vegetable dippers in ice water. Make Tomato Roses last of all and chill. When it's almost time for the first car to turn in the drive, make the coffee and punch.

SERVING SUGGESTIONS

Give the snack tree the place of honor on the buffet or table. Arrange the other foods around it. Heap popcorn balls in a market basket for a country look.

WHITE CAP PUNCH

You can increase the number of servings by increasing all ingredients except sherbet—use your judgment on this

2 (6 oz.) cans frozen lemonade concentrate	2 c. water
	1 qt. pineapple sherbet
1 (6 oz.) can frozen orange juice concentrate	1 qt. ginger ale, chilled
	1 qt. club soda, chilled

Combine frozen concentrates and water in punch bowl; stir until concentrates melt. Add 1 pt. sherbet and let stand about 10 minutes. Stir. Just before serving, spoon in remaining sherbet. Carefully pour ginger ale and club soda down the side of punch bowl. Makes 20 to 30 servings.

CHRISTMAS SNACK TREE

Tree shows off colorful snacks for dipping—vary them as you like

Select a Styrofoam cone, 12" to 18" high, at a variety store or florist shop. Give it a firm base by forcing the center part of an 8 or 10" angel food cake pan two inches into the bottom of cone. Anchor pan base to a heavy plate with florist's clay so the tree is secure.

Cover the cone and the base with green foil. Stick toothpicks into appetizers and "trim the tree." Snacks are easier to remove for eating if you make holes in the covered tree with ice pick or skewer, then insert toothpicks. Use Tomato Roses (instructions follow) and evergreens to decorate the base.

How to make Snack Tree dippers

Meat and cheese dippers: Cut 3×1½" rectangles of thinly sliced, cooked ham; roll lengthwise and fasten with toothpicks. Use small cookie cutters to make salami and bologna cutouts. Cut small cubes of semihard cheeses; insert toothpicks carefully.

Vegetable dippers: Wash and separate cauliflower into small flowerets; chill in ice water. For celery fans, cut celery into 1½" lengths. Slit parallel strips one half the length of each piece; chill in ice water until curled. To make carrot daisies, cut peeled carrot crosswise into three pieces. Cut five or six lengthwise notches around the carrot; slice into ½" rounds. Place green pepper square atop carrot slice and insert toothpick. For radish accordions, wash radishes; cut out root ends. Make crosswise parallel notches the length of the radish; crisp in cold water.

TOMATO ROSES

Red roses to make at Christmastime to decorate base of snack tree

Select a large, bright red tomato. Rose is made from outer shell of tomato. With stem end up, insert knife ¾" from stem and cut a crosswise slice only two thirds of the way through (slice serves as base of rose). From this cut, continue peeling tomato in an unbroken spiral, ¾" wide and ⅛" thick.

To form rose, place stem end on plate, skin side down. Starting at free end, roll up spiral toward stem. Secure with a toothpick.

PARTY CHEESE DIP

Three kinds of cheese contribute flavor to this well-seasoned party dip. One taste and its popularity zooms

¼ c. milk	½ small clove garlic
8 oz. cottage cheese	¼ tsp. salt
3 (1") cubes blue cheese	½ tsp. paprika
2 (3 oz.) pkgs. cream cheese, cut in 1" cubes	2 tsp. Worcestershire sauce

Pour milk into the electric blender container. Add cottage cheese; cover and blend on "low" about 20 seconds, or until smooth.

Add blue cheese, cream cheese, garlic, salt, paprika and Worcestershire sauce. Cover and blend on "high" until smooth, about 20 seconds. Refrigerate until serving time. Makes about 1 pint.

N O T E : You can use the electric mixer to make this dip if you don't have a blender.

QUICK MUSTARD SAUCE

Just right for vegetable and meat dippers—and it's so easy to fix

1 pt. dairy sour cream	½ c. prepared mustard
3 tblsp. prepared horse-radish	

Combine ingredients. Serve cold, or heat until mixture simmers and serve warm. Makes 2½ cups.

CASHEW DROP COOKIES

You can omit frosting but it brings out the cookies' wonderful flavor

½ c. butter or regular margarine	½ tsp. ground cinnamon
1 c. brown sugar, firmly packed	⅛ tsp. ground nutmeg
1 egg	¼ tsp. salt
½ tsp. vanilla	⅓ c. dairy sour cream
2 c. sifted flour	1 c. broken cashew nuts
¾ tsp. baking powder	Brown Butter Frosting
¾ tsp. baking soda	

Cream butter and brown sugar until fluffy. Add egg and vanilla; beat well.

Sift together flour, baking powder, baking soda, cinnamon, nutmeg and salt; add to creamed mixture alternately with sour cream. Stir in cashews.

Drop by teaspoonfuls 2" apart onto greased baking sheet. Bake in hot oven (400°) 8 to 10 minutes, until lightly browned. Remove from baking sheet at once and cool on racks. Frost with Brown Butter Frosting. Makes 4 dozen.

Brown Butter Frosting: Cook and stir 3 tblsp. butter or regular margarine until browned (use care not to scorch). Gradually beat in 2 c. sifted confectioners sugar, 2 tblsp. milk and ¾ tsp. vanilla to make a smooth frosting of spreading consistency. Spread on cooled cookies.

HOLIDAY GUMDROP COOKIES

Bright colored candy in cookies adds gaiety to holiday buffets

1 c. shortening	¼ tsp. ground cinnamon
1 c. sugar	1⅓ c. quick-cooking rolled oats
1 c. brown sugar, firmly packed	1 c. chopped nuts
1 tsp. vanilla	1 c. shredded coconut
2 eggs	1 c. chopped gumdrops (do not
2 c. sifted flour	use black licorice-flavored
1 tsp. baking soda	candies)
½ tsp. salt	

Cream together shortening and sugars until fluffy. Stir in vanilla; then add eggs, one at a time, beating well after each addition.

Sift together flour, soda, salt and cinnamon. Add to creamed mixture. Stir in remaining ingredients. (Use scissors to cut gumdrops easily.)

Drop by teaspoonfuls about 2″ apart onto well-greased baking sheet. Bake in moderate oven (350°) 10 to 12 minutes. Cool on racks. Makes about 7 dozen.

CARAMEL POPCORN BALLS

Let the children help make these all-time country holiday favorites

2 qts. popped corn	½ c. water
¾ c. sugar	1 tsp. white vinegar
¾ c. brown sugar, firmly packed	1 tsp. salt
½ c. light corn syrup	¾ c. butter or regular margarine

Put popcorn in large bowl and keep warm in slow oven (300°).

Combine sugars, corn syrup, water, vinegar and salt in a 2-qt. saucepan. Bring to a boil over medium heat, stirring frequently. Cook, stirring constantly, to the hard ball stage, 260° on candy thermometer.

Reduce heat to low and stir in butter. When melted, slowly pour hot syrup in thin stream over popcorn, stirring to coat all kernels. Cool briefly. Butter hands and shape mixture in balls of desired size. Cool on waxed paper. Makes about 16 (3″) popcorn balls.

SKATING PARTY REFRESHMENTS

Glazed Potato Doughnuts*
Popcorn/Peanut Clusters*
Bowl of Apples
Tri-Fruit Cooler*

Youngsters like to return home after skating, a few friends "in tow," to find tempting refreshments waiting in the kitchen. You can make ahead all the foods in this menu; perhaps your daughter can do it, or at least help in the preparations. The rewards for your efforts will be rich even if all you do is watch the excited youngsters when they see a fresh batch of glazed doughnuts displayed on cooling racks.

TIMETABLE

Do-Ahead: Make Popcorn/Peanut Clusters a day ahead, cool and store in airtight containers. Polish the apples until they shine.

On Guest Day: How about making the doughnuts while the skating party is in progress? You will need to be at home for at least 2 hours to make the doughnut dough, let it rise, roll, cut and let rise again. Count on about an hour longer to fry the hot cakes, glaze and let them cool. In the meantime, combine the fruit juices and chill.

SERVING SUGGESTIONS

Pour the fruit juice blend into tall glasses over cracked ice; add a scoop of colorful sherbet. Set out the remainder of the refreshments in generous bowls either in the kitchen or family room. Stay in the background while the youngsters "pitch in."

GLAZED POTATO DOUGHNUTS

Fresh from the fry kettle and glazed, they're an unsurpassed treat

1 pkg. active dry yeast	2 eggs, beaten
¼ c. warm water (110 to 115°)	5 to 6 c. sifted flour
1 c. milk, scalded	1 lb. confectioners sugar
¼ c. shortening	6 tblsp. water
¼ c. sugar	1 tblsp. vanilla
1 tsp. salt	
¾ c. mashed potatoes (instant may be used)	

Dissolve yeast in warm water.

Combine milk, shortening, sugar and salt. Cool until lukewarm. Stir in yeast, potatoes and eggs. Gradually add enough flour to make a soft dough. Turn onto floured surface; knead until smooth and satiny. Place in lightly greased bowl; turn over to grease top. Cover. Let rise in warm place until doubled, 1 to 1½ hours.

Roll to ½" thickness; cut with 3" doughnut cutter. Cover; let rise until doubled, about 30 minutes.

Meanwhile, stir confectioners sugar, water and vanilla together. (Glaze will look like very thick cream.)

Fry doughnuts in deep hot fat (375°). Drain on absorbent paper. Drop hot doughnuts into glaze. Place on cooling rack until glaze is set. Makes about 3½ dozen.

POPCORN/PEANUT CLUSTERS

A country confection for people of all ages; it never goes begging

2½ qts. popped corn	½ c. butter or regular margarine
2¼ c. light brown sugar (1 lb.)	2 tsp. salt
½ c. light corn syrup	1 c. salted peanuts
½ c. water	2 tsp. vanilla

Put popcorn in baking pan and keep warm in slow oven (300°).

Combine brown sugar, corn syrup, water, butter and salt in a large saucepan. Cook over moderate heat, stirring occasionally, until mixture reaches 290° on candy thermometer (soft crack stage).

Meanwhile, put popcorn and peanuts in a large buttered bowl; toss to mix well.

Add vanilla to hot syrup. Pour syrup in a thin stream over the popcorn mixture, tossing to mix well and coat corn and peanuts completely with boiling hot syrup. Work fast.

Spread in a thin layer on buttered baking sheets or platters. Using two buttered spoons, immediately separate into small (bite-size) clusters. Makes about 3 quarts.

TRI-FRUIT COOLER

Fruit juice blend tastes good, is pretty and quickly quenches thirst

1 (6 oz.) can frozen orange juice concentrate, thawed
1 qt. apple juice, chilled

1 pt. strawberry or raspberry sherbet

Combine thawed concentrate and apple juice in a large bowl. Beat until well blended. Pour into tall glasses over cracked ice. Top each serving with a small scoop of sherbet. Makes 6 to 8 servings.

MOONLIGHT HAYRIDE SUPPER

Frankfurters   Coney Buns
Home Baked Beans*
Crisp Lettuce Relish*
Ketchup   Mustard   Cucumber Pickles
Sundae Bar

Consult the calendar to find out when the moon will be full. Then invite friends to supper and a moonlight hayride. Instead of hitching old Dobbin and his partner to the flatbed, today's rides are courtesy of a tractor.

Keep the food simple and serve it picnic style at a table in the yard or on the porch. This can be before or after the ride—or better still, serve the main course when guests arrive, the dessert at the end of the evening.

Frankfurters are important in this meal; allow a minimum of two for each person. (Better have extras if there are boys in the crowd.) You can cook them in the house. Just drop franks in a kettle of boiling water and simmer until hot, 5 to 10 minutes, depending on their size. Or you can grill them outdoors over medium coals for 12 to 15 minutes, or until they are heated through, turning often.

The relish is a vegetable salad cut fine. Home baked beans are a highlight of the meal. A hand-cranked ice cream freezer filled with vanilla ice cream is something to return to at the end of the ride. Especially if you set up a make-your-own-sundae bar.

TIMETABLE

Do-Ahead: Bake the beans several days ahead (at least one day) and freeze before the hayride. They freeze successfully and it's easy to reheat them.

On Guest Day: Make the ice cream and let it ripen in the freezer can a few hours. Or make it several days ahead and put in the freezer. (Use your favorite recipe, if you like, but we give a recipe for Homemade Vanilla Ice Cream in the menu "Chicken Barbecue Dinner"—see Index.) Fix vegetables for relish an hour or two ahead, cover and chill, but toss with dressing shortly before serving so the lettuce will stay crisp.

SERVING SUGGESTIONS

Serve frankfurters on a spacious platter wth ketchup and prepared mustard on one side, a basket of split coney buns (long) on the other side handy for people who want to pop franks in them. Serve the beans in a bean pot if you have one, or in a casserole.

At dessert time, bring out a tray holding an array of sundae toppings, such as chocolate and butterscotch sauces or syrups, maple syrup, sliced or crushed fresh strawberries or sliced peaches (sprinkled with 2 tsp. ascorbic acid powder dissolved in about 3 tblsp. water to 1 qt. fruit to prevent darkening). If fresh berries and peaches are not in season, serve strawberry or peach preserves instead (both are good on ice cream). Relax and watch the enjoyment a help-yourself sundae bar provides.

HOME BAKED BEANS

If you live in New England fix Boston baked beans instead of this midwestern and western kind. Both types have ardent champions

2 lbs. navy or pea beans
1 lb. salt pork, or bacon
1 lb. brown sugar
1 (1 lb. 12 oz.) can tomatoes
2 medium onions, chopped (about ¾ c.)

2 tblsp. prepared mustard
½ tsp. salt
½ tsp. pepper

Wash and pick over beans; cover generously with water and soak overnight. Next morning, simmer beans in salted water until they test done. (An easy test is to bite into a bean to find out if it's tender.) Drain beans and save liquid.

Put salt pork or bacon through food chopper, or chop. (If you use bacon, pour boiling water over and let stand 3 to 5 minutes; drain and grind.) Place it in the bottom of a large bean pot or deep casserole. Alternately layer cooked beans with a mixture of brown sugar, tomatoes, onions, mustard, salt and pepper on top of salt pork. Pour on the water in which beans cooked and add enough hot water to cover beans. Adjust the lid, or cover with aluminum foil.

Bake in slow oven (300°) 6 to 8 hours, stirring occasionally and adding more hot water if necessary.

This recipe makes 15 to 25 generous servings. Put the leftover beans in a freezer container and store in the freezer to reheat for the next barbecue.

CRISP LETTUCE RELISH

Quick, easy way to give familiar mixed vegetable salad a new look

1½ qts. shredded head lettuce (iceberg)
2 medium cucumbers, peeled and finely diced
1⅓ c. diced radishes

¾ c. thinly sliced green onions
1 c. vinegar/oil salad dressing (equal parts oil and vinegar with salt and pepper to season)

Cut head lettuce on board, using a French chef's knife, into ½" slices; then cut crisscross to make of relish consistency (not too fine). Add prepared cucumbers, radishes and onions; chill until ready to serve. At the last minute, toss lightly with salad dressing (you can use bottled French dressing, or see Index for the Vinegar/Oil Dressing recipe used with Calico Green Salad). Makes 8 servings.

MEN'S WINTER EVENING SANDWICH LUNCH

Hot Cheese/Tomato Sandwiches*   Dill Pickles
Buttered Pumpernickel Toast   Tossed Green Salad
Ranch House Raisin Cookies*   Cherry/Chocolate Cookies*
Coffee

This menu features food most men like. It is a top favorite of a Colorado man and three of his neighbors with whom he shared the late lunch one cold night when they met at his mountain ranch home to discuss mutual business interests. The host's wife made the advance preparations. He took over at serving time. It's so easy and so pleasing to everyone who tastes it. If you wish to convert the menu into the main evening meal, add a vegetable such as peas with mushrooms or corn with green pepper or pimiento, and substitute apple pie for the cookies. And double the sandwich recipe.

TIMETABLE

Do-Ahead: Bake the cookies unless you have a supply in the freezer.

On Guest Day: Wash salad greens, drain well and chill in a plastic bag. You can get the open-face sandwiches ready to broil several hours before serving them; put them in the refrigerator. When time for lunch, put sandwiches under broiler to heat, but watch them, for it's easy to overdo the cooking. Toss the salad; make coffee.

SERVING SUGGESTIONS

Set toaster, sliced pumpernickel and butter on table so everyone can make additional toast. Serve the plates in the kitchen. On them place sandwiches and dill pickles. Serve the salad in individual bowls, or on individual plates. Pour the coffee.

HOT CHEESE/TOMATO SANDWICHES

Tomato slices and cheese sauce on pumpernickel toast—really good

4 c. shredded sharp Cheddar
cheese (1 lb.)
3 tblsp. flour
½ tsp. dry mustard
¾ c. beer or milk
2 tsp. Worcestershire sauce

1 tblsp. butter or regular
margarine
1 egg
4 slices pumpernickel toast
Chopped chives (optional)
8 thick tomato slices

Combine cheese, flour and mustard; toss with fork to coat cheese with flour. Place in 2-qt. saucepan; add beer, Worcestershire sauce and butter. Heat over medium heat, stirring constantly until cheese melts and sauce is smooth.

Beat egg slightly and add a little hot cheese sauce; stir to mix. Add to cheese sauce and stir until blended. Remove from heat.

Place pumpernickel toast on an ovenproof platter or baking dish. Pour on all but ½ c. cheese sauce; sprinkle with chives. Then top each piece of toast with 2 tomato slices. Spoon remaining sauce over tomatoes. (You can cover with foil and refrigerate several hours and broil just before serving.) Run under broiler until hot, lightly browned and bubbly. Serve with extra buttered pumpernickel toast, if desired. Makes 4 servings.

RANCH HOUSE RAISIN COOKIES

You cook the raisins before you stir them into the cookie mixture

½ c. raisins
1 c. water
1 c. brown sugar, firmly packed
½ c. shortening
1 egg
½ tsp. vanilla

1¾ c. sifted flour
½ tsp. salt
½ tsp. baking powder
½ tsp. baking soda
½ c. chopped nuts

Bring raisins to a boil with water. Cool thoroughly.

Cream sugar and shortening until fluffy. Add egg and vanilla. Beat to mix.

Sift together flour, salt, baking powder and soda. Alternately add to creamed mixture with cooled raisins (there should be ½ c. liquid with raisins; if not, add water to make ½ c.). Stir in nuts.

Drop dough by teaspoonfuls at least 2″ apart onto greased baking sheets.

Bake in moderate oven (350°) 10 to 12 minutes. Remove cookies and cool on racks. Makes 4 dozen.

CHERRY/CHOCOLATE COOKIES

Cherry-chocolate blend tastes good; try making them wth nuts, too

½ c. butter or regular margarine	½ tsp. baking soda
1 c. sugar	½ tsp. salt
1 egg	2 c. cut-up maraschino cherries,
2 squares unsweetened chocolate,	drained, or cut-up candied
melted and cooled	cherries
⅓ c. buttermilk	Chocolate Frosting
1 tsp. vanilla	Maraschino cherry halves, well
1¾ c. sifted flour	drained (for garnish)

Thoroughly mix butter, sugar, egg, chocolate, buttermilk and vanilla.

Sift together flour, soda and salt; stir into chocolate mixture. Add cherries and mix to distribute in dough. Cover and chill an hour or longer. (Dough is soft.)

Drop dough 2″ apart onto ungreased baking sheet. Bake in hot oven (400°) 8 to 10 minutes, or until almost no imprint shows when touched with finger. Remove from baking sheet at once; cool on racks. Frost tops with Chocolate Frosting and garnish each cookie with a maraschino cherry half, rounded side up. Makes about 54 cookies.

Chocolate Frosting: Melt 2 squares unsweetened chocolate and 2 tblsp. butter over medium heat. Remove from heat and blend in 2 to 3 tblsp. light cream. Stir in about 2 c. sifted confectioners sugar, or enough to make a frosting of spreading consistency.

NOTE: 1 c. chopped pecans may be substituted for 2 c. cut-up cherries. Decorate frosted cookies with nuts.

GOLDEN WEDDING RECEPTION

Flower Wedding Cake*
Golden Punch*
Yellow and White Candy Mints   Salted Nuts
Coffee

Golden wedding receptions can be as simple as punch and cake, as delicious and beautiful as Golden Punch and Flower Wedding Cake.

You make the lovely cake with a recipe developed by home economists in our Countryside Kitchens. It is the answer to many requests for a wedding cake that tastes as good as it looks.

You make the cake from scratch, baking it in a 1" deep jelly roll pan and an 8" square pan 2" deep. Use of deeper pans destroys top results. The secret to success in making the cake is to organize the production steps. Follow the timetable.

The pastel yellow flowers that decorate the wedding cake are plastic, but you dip them in a glaze for a glossy coating. The pretty punch is refreshing—do have coffee also for guests who prefer it.

TIMETABLE

Do-Ahead: A week before the reception dip the flowers in Dipping Frosting. Lay them in a waxed paper-lined box and store in a dry place. Bake the cake a week ahead, cool and freeze. Or bake it a day ahead, cool and wrap in waxed paper to prevent drying. Build the cake a day before the reception, spreading it with your choice of fillings. Spread surfaces first with Sealing Frosting to avoid crumbing. Decide where to place the flowers so you can arrange them quickly the next day. Chill cans of apricot nectar and pineapple juice and the bottles of carbonated beverage for the punch.

On Guest Day: Frost the cake and place the flowers on it. Fill the punch bowl with a large plastic bag holding ice cubes to chill it. It is easy to lift out the bag at the last minute and to add the punch.

SERVING SUGGESTIONS

Set the cake on a large plate or tray and encircle it and the punch bowl with delicate ferns, or with ivy. Float a few thin orange slices in the punch. Lift off the top tier of the cake and save it for the honored couple. Cut the middle tier in 14 pieces, the bottom tier in 36 pieces. You will have 50 servings of wedding cake that really taste good.

FLOWER WEDDING CAKE

You'll need to make two recipes of this cake to make the 3-tier beauty. Cake serves 50

3⅓ c. sifted cake flour	½ c. shortening
4 tsp. baking powder	1¾ c. sugar
1½ tsp. salt	1 egg yolk
7 egg whites	2 tsp. vanilla
½ c. sugar	1 tsp. almond extract
½ c. butter	1⅓ c. milk

Pans are important. This cake *must* bake in shallow layers. Do not try to bake deeper cakes. Line a 15½ × 10½ × 1″ jelly roll pan and an 8″ square baking pan with plain brown paper. (*Do not* grease and flour pans, since this makes a crust that's too heavy.)

Sift cake flour, baking powder and salt together 3 times.

Beat egg whites until foamy. Add ½ c. sugar gradually; continue beating only until meringue will hold *soft* peaks. Set aside.

Cream butter and shortening together until well blended and smooth. Gradually add 1¾ c. sugar; beat until light and fluffy. Add the egg yolk and beat until well blended.

Add extracts to milk. Add milk alternately with dry ingredients to the creamed mixture, a small amount at a time; beat after each addition until smooth.

Add meringue and beat thoroughly into batter.

Spread batter in the two pans, about ½″ deep in each pan. Spread batter out to corners, leaving a slight depression in center. Tap pans sharply on counter top several times to remove large air bubbles.

Bake in moderate oven (350°) 25 to 30 minutes.

Cool on racks 10 minutes. Remove from pans and finish cooling on racks. To keep from drying, wrap as soon as cool.

ALMOND CREAM FILLING AND SEALING FROSTING

Take your pick of this or Orange/Raisin Filling—both luscious

4 egg yolks, slightly beaten	2 tsp. vanilla
1⅓ c. evaporated milk	2 c. finely chopped toasted
1⅓ c. sugar	almonds
½ c. butter or regular margarine	

Blend yolks and milk in saucepan; stir in sugar and butter. Cook over medium heat, stirring constantly, until thick and bubbling. Add vanilla.

Remove 1½ c. of this cooked mixture and add almonds to it. Cool; stir occasionally until of spreading consistency.

Sealing Frosting: Cool remainder of filling. Add 1½ to 2 c. sifted confectioners sugar and beat until of thin spreading consistency.

ORANGE/RAISIN FILLING

Golden raisins and orange candy teamed deliciously with almonds

½ c. sugar
2 tblsp. flour
2 c. light raisins, ground
1 c. water

1 c. finely cut orange gumdrops
1 c. finely chopped toasted almonds

Combine sugar and flour. Add to raisins in saucepan. Add water and stir to dissolve. Cook, stirring constantly, until thick.

Add gumdrops and cook 3 minutes.

Add almonds and cool thoroughly before using.

Sealing Frosting: Blend 2 slightly beaten egg yolks with ⅔ c. evaporated milk in saucepan. Stir in ⅔ c. sugar and ¼ c. butter or regular margarine. Cook over medium heat, stirring constantly, until thick and bubbling.

Remove from heat; add 1 tsp. vanilla and cool.

Stir in 1½ to 2 c. sifted confectioners sugar and beat to thin spreading consistency.

Bottom Tier: Trim crusts from the two 15½ × 10½ × 1″ cakes to make smooth straight sides.

Cut 9½″ square and 4″ square from each cake. Reserve the 4″ squares for top tier. (You'll have some scraps.)

Cut 9½″ square of cardboard and cover with foil. Place 9½″ square of cake on cardboard. Spread desired filling evenly over cake top. Place other 9½″ cake square on filling and press firmly.

Spread thin layer of Sealing Frosting over sides and top of this tier. Pull spatula over surface to make smooth straight sides.

Middle Tier: Trim crusts from the two 8″ square cakes to make 6½″ squares.

Cut 6½″ square of cardboard and cover with foil. Place 6½″

square of cake on cardboard. Spread with desired filling. Top with other 6½″ square of cake. Center 6½″ tier on bottom tier. Cover top and sides with Sealing Frosting.

Top Tier: Repeat procedure (using cardboard and foil) for two 4″ squares. Center this on middle tier. Seal top and sides with frosting.

FLUFFY WHITE FROSTING

Looks like a white satin cloud

2 egg whites	¼ tsp. cream of tartar
1½ c. sugar	1 tsp. vanilla
⅓ c. water	

Combine all ingredients, except vanilla, in top of double boiler. Beat 1 minute on high speed with electric mixer.

Place over boiling water. Cook 7 minutes, beating all the time on high speed with electric mixer.

Remove from hot water. Turn frosting into bowl. Add vanilla; beat until of spreading consistency.

TO DECORATE CAKE

Let Sealing Frosting set before you apply Fluffy White Frosting.

Decide on placement of flowers before you apply final frosting.

Apply Fluffy White Frosting, starting with sides of bottom tier. Hold spatula perpendicular to tray and pull along carefully to make smooth sides and square corners. Apply to ledge of tier, building a ridge along outer edge. Repeat for each tier.

When frosting just begins to set, arrange flower design.

To Make Decorations

Select plastic flowers in pastel colors such as yellow or pink. For an orderly and attractive design, use no more than three varieties of flowers. Flowers that have definite form and petals that outline sharply show off best when dipped.

Wash plastic flowers in warm suds and rinse in clear water; dry. Cut individual flowers from stalk with a wire cutter, leaving a stem to hold when you dip it.

Dip plastic flowers in Dipping Frosting (recipe follows). Twirl in hand to distribute frosting evenly. Hold in hand a few minutes until frosting begins to set. Place on rack to dry. For thicker coating, you will probably want to dip again after first coating dries. When final coating is dry, snip off remaining stems.

Work out your desired arrangement for flowers before applying Fluffy White Frosting. Then when this final frosting is applied and just beginning to set, place flowers in desired spots.

DIPPING FROSTING

2 c. sugar
1 c. water
⅛ tsp. cream of tartar

1 to 1½ c. sifted confectioners sugar

Combine 2 c. sugar, water and cream of tartar in saucepan. Cook to a thin syrup (226° on candy thermometer). Remove from heat and cool to lukewarm (112°).

Add confectioners sugar gradually, stirring until smooth. Mixture should be of pouring consistency.

Place over warm water to keep frosting at right consistency for dipping. If too hot, plastic flowers will soften.

A little experimenting will determine the best consistency for coating. If you don't like appearance of flowers on first dipping, wash off frosting, pat dry with dish towel and redip.

GOLDEN PUNCH

This punch is on the tart side. It's refreshing, colorful, easy to fix

1 (6 oz.) can frozen orange juice concentrate
1 (6 oz.) can frozen lemonade concentrate
1 (12 oz.) can apricot nectar

2 c. pineapple juice
½ c. lemon juice
1 qt. lemon-lime carbonated beverage, or 1 qt. ginger ale
Sherbet

Reconstitute orange juice and lemonade as directed on cans. Combine in punch bowl with apricot nectar, pineapple juice and lemon juice.

Pour bottled carbonated beverage or ginger ale slowly down side of bowl. Drop scoops of pineapple, orange, lime or raspberry sherbet into punch. (Sherbet is not necessary, but it is decorative and delicious.) Makes about 3½ quarts without sherbet. With sherbet, punch makes about 30 servings. (You may want to double recipe.)

INDEX